The **Rough Guide** to

Hawaii

written and researched by

Greg Ward

ROUGH GUIDES

NEW YORK · LONDON · DELHI

www.roughguides.com

Contents

Blue Hawaii color section following p.216

Hiking in Hawaii color section following p.408

WITHDRAWN

◀◀ Ala Moana Beach Park, Oahu ◀ Secret Beach, Kauai

Kauai

NA PALI COAST

Princeville

Hanalei

Kapa'a

Līhu'e

Waimea

Po'ipū

Pu'uwai

Niihau

Hale'iwa

Oahu

Kāne'ohe

Kailua

Pearl Harbor

Honolulu

Waikīkī

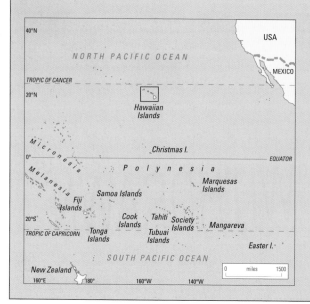

40°N

USA

NORTH PACIFIC OCEAN

MEXICO

TROPIC OF CANCER

20°N

Hawaiian
Islands

Micronesia

Christmas I.

EQUATOR

0°

Polynesia

Melanesia

Marquesas
Islands

Fiji
Islands

Samoa Islands

20°S

Cook
Islands

Tahiti

Society
Islands

Mangareva

TROPIC OF CAPRICORN

Tonga
Islands

Tubuai
Islands

Easter I.

SOUTH PACIFIC OCEAN

New Zealand

0   miles   1500

160°E   180°   160°W   140°W

Feet
13000
9800
6500
3300
1600
700
330
0

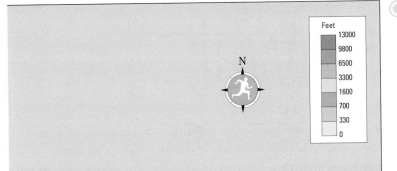

N

Molokai

Kaluako'i
*Kalaupapa
Peninsula*
Halāwa Valley
Maunaloa
Kaunakakai

Kapalua
Kā'anapali
Kahului
Maui

Lana'i City
Lahaina
Wailuku
Wailua

Lanai
*Manēle
Bay*
Kīhei
Wailea
Mākena
Hāna

*HALEAKALĀ
NATIONAL
PARK*

Kahoolawe

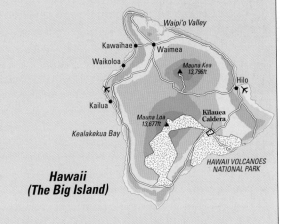

Waipi'o Valley

Kawaihae
Waimea

Waikoloa

*Mauna Kea
13,796ft*

Hilo

Kailua

*Mauna Loa
13,677ft*
**Kīlauea
Caldera**

Kealakekua Bay

*HAWAII VOLCANOES
NATIONAL PARK*

*Hawaii
(The Big Island)*

0   miles   40

Introduction to

Hawaii

The islands of Hawaii poke from the Pacific more than two thousand miles off the west coast of America. In total, there are well over a hundred of them, the weather-beaten summits of a chain of submarine volcanoes that stretches almost to Japan. Most, however, are no more than tiny atolls. Only the seven largest, lying south of the Tropic of Cancer at the southeast end of the archipelago, are inhabited, and only six welcome visitors. Those are Oahu (the site of the state capital Honolulu and its resort annex of Waikīkī), Hawaii itself (more commonly known as the Big Island in a vain attempt to avoid confusion), Maui, Lanai, Molokai, and Kauai.

All the islands share a similar topography, having been formed in the same way and exposed to the same winds and rains. Each is much wetter on its north and east – **windward** – coasts, which are characterized by stupendous sea cliffs, verdant stream-cut valleys, and dense tropical vegetation. The south and west – **leeward** or "Kona" – coasts are much drier, often virtually barren, and make ideal locations for big resorts.

With its majestic volcanoes and palm-fringed beaches, Hawaii holds some of the most superb scenery on earth. Firmly established among the world's greatest vacation playgrounds, it combines top-quality hotels and restaurants with almost unlimited opportunities not only for sheer self-indulgence, but also for activities such as surfing, diving, golf, and hiking. Visiting Hawaii does not, however, have to be expensive; budget facilities on all the islands are listed throughout this book, together with advice on making the most of your money.

Despite the crowds, the islands have not been ruined by tourism. Resort development is concentrated into surprisingly small regions – Waikīkī is the classic example, holding half the state's hotel rooms in just two square miles – and it's always possible to venture off into pristine wilderness or to camp on the seashore or mountainside.

'Akaka Falls, Big Island

• Hawaii's **first human settlers**, Polynesian voyagers, arrived less than two thousand years ago. The first European sailor known to have reached the islands was England's **Captain Cook**, in 1778. Hawaii remained an independent kingdom until 1898, when it became a territory of the United States. It was admitted as the fiftieth US state in 1959.

• The combined **land area** of all the Hawaiian islands is 6470 square miles; the Big Island alone accounts for 4028 square miles. The state's **population** is 1.29 million people, of whom 910,000 live on Oahu. The Big Island holds 171,000, Maui 141,000, and Kauai almost 63,000. Molokai has around 7000, and Lanai just 3000, while Niihau is home to a mere 250 citizens.

• More than twenty percent of Hawaiians regard themselves as combining two or more races, as opposed to 1.5 percent in the US as a whole.

• 7.5 million tourists visit Hawaii each year, of whom five million come from the US, and around 1.5 million from Japan. By far the **most popular island** remains Oahu, with 4.7 million visitors a year. Maui comes second, welcoming 2.3 million, while 1.5 million spend time on the Big Island, and 1.1 million on Kauai. Fewer than 100,000 visit either Molokai or Lanai, and Niihau is barred to outsiders altogether.

• Mauna Kea on the Big Island is the **highest mountain** in the Pacific, at 13,796 feet. Mount Wai'ale'ale on Kauai is the **wettest place** on earth, receiving an average of 451 inches per year.

Where to go

The key decision in any Hawaiian itinerary is whether to go to **Oahu**, and specifically **Waikīkī**, which holds virtually all its accommodation. If you enjoy cities, and prefer nightlife and crowds to deserted beaches – or simply if you don't want to drive – then it's worth staying for three or four days in Waikīkī. Otherwise, unless you're a **surfer** heading for the legendary North Shore, you may end up wishing you'd allowed for more time elsewhere.

Each of the other islands – referred to as the **Neighbor Islands** – has its own strengths and weaknesses. Maui, Kauai, and the Big Island all offer accommodation for every budget, and all cost the same to reach from Oahu, as well as being accessible by direct

Flora and fauna

While Hawaii does face serious environmental problems, as detailed on p.549, that it remains so staggeringly beautiful is thanks in large part to the diversity of its flora and fauna.

When the islands first emerged from the Pacific, as outcrops of barren lava, a new species – perhaps a windblown bird or a floating seed or insect – managed to find them but once every 100,000 years. Each evolved at breakneck speed, to produce such unique variations as the spectacular silversword plant (see p.354) or the fifty distinct honey-creepers, ranging from the scarlet *'i'iwi* to the tiny yellow *'anianiau*, that were descended from a single finch. Then came the first Polynesian voyagers, carrying coconut palms and bananas, pigs and dogs. The Europeans in turn brought horses and cattle, as well as pests like the mosquito and the mongoose, and the process is continuing to this day, as "stowaway" species arrive clinging to tourist jets.

flights from the US West Coast. The best for **beaches** is probably Maui, followed by Kauai and then the Big Island; for **scenery**, and also **hiking**, Kauai beats the Big Island, with Maui well behind. The Big Island boasts the awesome spectacle of the world's most active **volcano** – Kīlauea, which has been erupting ever since 1983 – although slumbering Haleakalā on Maui is also impressive.

Among more specialized interests, Maui offers the best conditions for **windsurfing** and **whale watching**; Maui and the Big Island are equally well equipped for **diving**, **snorkeling**, and **golf**; and the Big Island has great deep-sea **fishing**, as well as being the best suited for a **touring** vacation. The appeal of the lesser islands rests largely on their sense of seclusion; Molokai

> **The Big Island boasts the awesome spectacle of the world's most active volcano – Kīlauea**

is a down-home, inexpensive, and very traditional Hawaiian island, while **Lanai** has become a haven for the mega-rich.

Visitors in search of the **ancient Hawaii** may be disappointed by the few vestiges that remain. The Hawaiians themselves destroyed many of their *heiaus* (temples) following the collapse of the traditional religion, and traces of the pre-contact way of life tend to survive only in out-of-the-way places (notably on the Big Island and Molokai). Otherwise, what is presented as "historic" usually post-dates the missionary impact. The former plantation villages often have an appealing air of the nineteenth-century West about them, with their false-front stores

and wooden boardwalks, but of the larger towns only Honolulu on Oahu, Lahaina on Maui, and Kailua on the Big Island offer much sense of history.

If you have **one week** or less, it makes sense to concentrate on just one island. Five days on either Kauai or the Big Island, combined with two days in Waikīkī, makes a good introduction to the state, while if you fly direct to Maui you can explore that island in depth and still have time to cross over to Molokai or Lanai. With **two weeks**, you could spend four or five days each on three of the major islands – though it would be easy to fill a week or more on the Big Island – and it's worth considering a couple of days on Molokai as well. Any more than two weeks, and you can consider seeing all the major islands.

> With its majestic volcanoes and palm-fringed beaches, Hawaii holds some of the most superb scenery on earth

When to go

▼ Bishop Museum, Honolulu

Although Hawaii's **high season** for tourism is mid-December to March, when typical room rates for mid-range hotels rise by perhaps $30 per night, its climate remains pretty constant year-round.

Specific information for each island appears in the chapter

9

Kailua Beach, Oahu

introductions throughout this book. In general, despite the power of the tropical sun, Hawaii is not prone to extremes. **Temperatures** in all the major coastal resorts vary between a daily maximum of around 80°F (27°C) from January to March up to perhaps 87°F (30°C) from July to October. Average minimum temperatures remain in the region of 68°F (20°C) at sea level year-round, though you should

> **Hawaii's climate remains pretty constant year-round.**

bring warm clothing if you plan to visit the summits of the volcanoes on Maui or the Big Island. **Rainfall** is heaviest from December to March, and anecdotally seems to have become heavier in recent winters. Even so, while the mountaintops are among the wettest places on earth, you'd have to be unlucky to get enough rain in any of the resort areas to spoil your vacation.

The main seasonal variation to affect tourists is in the state of the ocean. Along protected stretches of the shoreline, you can expect to be able to swim all year round in beautiful

Hawaiian language

Almost everyone in Hawaii speaks English, and as a rule the Hawaiian language is only encountered in the few words – such as *aloha* or "love," the all-purpose island greeting, and *mahalo*, meaning "thank you" – that have passed into general local usage. A glossary of Hawaiian words appears on p.582.

The **Hawaiian alphabet** consists of just twelve letters, together with two punctuation marks, the macron and the glottal stop. Strictly speaking, the word Hawaii should be written **Hawai'i**, with the glottal stop to show that the two "i"s are pronounced separately; the correct forms for the other islands are O'ahu, *Lāna'i*, Moloka'i, Kaua'i, Ni'ihau, and Maui. Convention has it, however, that words in common English usage are written without their Hawaiian punctuation. Thus, although this book uses Hawaiian place names wherever possible, all the island names appear in their familiar English form.

▲ Waimanu Valley, Big Island

Hawaiian food and ritual

Eating was a serious business in ancient Hawaii, attended by many rituals and taboos. Only men were allowed to cook or prepare food. Women were forbidden to eat pork, bananas, or coconuts, as well as several kinds of fish, or to use the same utensils or even eat at the same table as the men.

These days, although Hawaii boasts many fabulous restaurants, there's no such thing as an authentic "Hawaiian" restaurant. The closest you can come to eating traditional foods is at a **lū'au**, a "feast" staged for tourists where you should be able to sample *poi*, a purple-gray paste made from the root of the taro plant (which is still being cultivated in the traditional painstaking way in such time-hallowed spots as Molokai's Hālawa Valley and Kauai's Hanalei Valley); *kālua* pork, an entire pig wrapped in leaves and baked in an underground oven; *poke*, marinated raw fish, shellfish, or octopus; and *lomi-lomi*, made with raw salmon. You're unlikely, however, to be given another historically authentic specialty: boiled hairless dogs. For more on eating and drinking, see p.37.

seas where the water temperature stays between 75°F and 82°F (24–28°C). From October to April, however, high surf can render unsheltered beaches dangerous in the extreme, and some beaches even lose their sand altogether. Conditions on specific beaches are indicated throughout this book; see also the section on ocean safety on p.41.

For most of the year, the trade winds blow in from the northeast, though they're occasionally replaced by humid "Kona winds" from the south. Hurricanes are very rare, though tsunamis (often erroneously called tidal waves) do hit from time to time, generally as a result of earthquakes or landslides caused by volcanic eruptions.

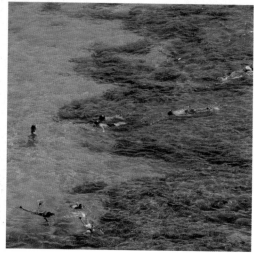

Hanauma Bay, snorkel spot, Oahu

12

34

things not to miss

It's not possible to see everything that Hawaii has to offer in one trip – and we don't suggest you try. What follows is a selective taste of the highlights on the islands: unique tropical wonders, fabulous beaches, exhilarating outdoor activities, and fashionable resorts. They're arranged in five color-coded categories, which you can browse through to find the very best things to see, do, and experience. All highlights have a page reference to take you straight into the guide, where you can find out more.

| ACTIVITIES | CONSUME | EVENTS | NATURE | SIGHTS |

01 Helicopter trips Page **439** • Taking a helicopter tour of Kauai is the perfect, albeit expensive, way to get a bird's-eye view of the island's spectacular scenery – its hidden waterfalls, tall sea cliffs, and lush valleys.

03 Oahu's Circle-Island Drive
Page **134** • To get away from the bustle on Oahu, drive the full length of the gorgeous windward shore, pausing at the many remote beaches along the way.

02 The Kīlauea eruption
Page **264** • Kīlauea volcano on the Big Island, whose name means "much spewing," has been in a constant state of eruption since 1983; see it from a helicopter or, when conditions are right, on foot.

04 Chinatown
Page **95** • Honolulu's most atmospheric quarter makes a welcome change from Waikīkī, join the locals in exploring the open-air markets, shopping for herbs and other delicacies, or simply hanging out and "talking story."

05 **Hawaiian monarchy** Page **89** • Discover the pride and the passion that still surrounds the tragic saga of Hawaii's royal family, as witnessed by the statues and museums of Honolulu, and especially 'Iolani Palace.

06 **Swimming with dolphins** Page **198** • The Disneyesque *Hilton Waikoloa Village* hotel, on the Big Island, is wildly popular with families – and especially with those who get to swim with its resident dolphins.

07 **Merrie Monarch festival** Page **227** • *Hula* shows and festivals take place on all the islands throughout the year, but this Big Island event is the highlight of the annual calendar.

08 **Wai'ānapanapa State Park** Page **364** • Not far from the time-forgotten village of Hāna, this ravishing black-sand beach offers the best camping along the Maui coast.

09 **Nu'uanu Pali** Page **107** • Just minutes from central Honolulu, this state park provides visitors with their first heart-stopping glimpse of the stunning scenery of windward Oahu.

10 **Kalalau Trail** Page **489** & *Hiking in Hawaii* **color section** • Perhaps the most exhilarating and demanding trail in all the islands, this coastal hike traces Kauai's North Shore for eleven stupendous miles.

11 **Lāna'i City** Page **382** ● Lanai's only town, all but unchanged despite the passing of the plantation era, has a friendly village atmosphere that just invites you to while away a lazy day.

13 **Unique wildlife** Page **549** ● From silversword plants to the rarest 'ō'ō 'ā'ā honey-creeper, you'll never cease to be awed by the islands' tropical flora and fauna.

12 **Kona coffee** Page **183** ● Be sure not to leave the Big Island without sampling some strong, flavorful Kona coffee, a gourmet specialty grown on the slopes above Kealakekua Bay.

17

14 **Hālawa Valley** Page **440** ● This lush valley at Molokai's eastern tip, home to some of Hawaii's first-ever settlers, can be explored on superbly informative guided hikes.

15 Hanauma Bay Page **129** • Just a short bus ride out from Waikīkī, lagoon-like Hanauma Bay formed when a crater wall collapsed, to create Oahu's best-loved snorkeling destination.

16 Night-time in Waikīkī Page **122** • Though it might sound cheesy or kitsch, few can resist the romance of an evening spent listening to Hawaiian music of Oahu's premier resort, rounded off with a moonlit stroll.

17 Garden of the Gods Page **393** • These eerie rock formations, located down a dirt road in central Lanai, make a superb spot to catch a radiant sunset.

18 Haleakalā Crater Page **346** • Every day, legions of visitors drive through the darkness to catch the unforgettable moment when the sun's first rays strike the multi-colored crater of Haleakalā, at the core of eastern Maui.

19 Big Beach Page **336** • Beyond its resorts and high-rise hotels, Maui still holds ravishing unspoiled beaches, where you may well find the sands undisturbed by a single footprint.

20 **Kehena Beach** Page **249** • A pristine, palm-fringed, black-sand beach created by lava from nearby Kīlauea, Kehena is a favorite with the back-to-nature inhabitants of the Big Island's "alternative" Puna district.

21 **Pāpōhaku Beach** Page **429** • Molokai's windswept western shore is seldom safe for swimming, but it's great for long solitary strolls – and sunset views all the way to Waikīkī.

22 **Mānele Bay Hotel** Page **388** • Even if you can't afford the room rates on the former pineapple island of Lanai, you can always pamper yourself with poolside cocktails at this lavish beachfront hotel.

23 **Hiking in Hawaii Volcanoes National Park** Page **250** & *Hiking in Hawaii* color section • As you venture along the well-marked trails of the Big Island's most visited tourist attraction, a single step can take you from dense rainforest to a stark volcanic moonscape.

24 Princeville Page **474** • Kauai's stunning Nā Pali cliffs can be experienced along grueling hiking trails or simply admired from afar as you enjoy a cocktail in the exclusive Princeville resort.

25 Surfing Page **428** & *Blue Hawaii* **color section** • This traditional Polynesian sport may have spread all over the globe, but for locals and tourists alike, Hawaii's thunderous waves still represent the ultimate challenge.

26 Punchbowl Crater Page **101** • This natural volcanic amphitheater, towering above downtown Honolulu, makes an appropriate setting for the National Memorial Cemetery of the Pacific.

27 **Mauna Kea** Page **243** • Even Hawaii sees a little snow sometimes – at least if you drive to the summit of the Pacific's highest mountain, on the Big Island. It's a surreal landscape, where powerful astronomical telescopes stand juxtaposed with traditional Hawaiian shrines.

28 **Secret Beach** Page **471** • Hidden away on Kauai's North Shore, Secret Beach may be the finest – and most enticingly named – strand on an island that's bursting with delightful sands.

29 **Kalaupapa Peninsula**
Page **418** • Pilgrims flock to take the legendary Molokai Mule Ride down to Father Damien's celebrated leper colony, located on an all-but-inaccessible promontory at the foot of the world's tallest sea cliffs.

30 **Whale migrations** Page **299** & *Blue Hawaii* **color section** • Cavorting humpback whales, who spend each winter calving in the warm Hawaiian waters, are frequently visible off the beaches of West Maui.

31 **'Akaka Falls** Page **234** • Mighty 'Akaka Falls is simply the largest of countless waterfalls that cascade down the richly vegetated flanks of the Big Island's Hāmākua Coast.

32 **Molokini Crater** Page **325** • Though the ocean has all but submerged this long-extinct crater off the Maui coast, a slender crescent wall survives to shelter the boat-loads of snorkelers and divers who come to ogle its colorful fish population.

33 **Kōke'e State Park** Page **514** • Perched above the dazzling rainbow-hued gorge of Waimea Canyon, this lushly vegetated state park offers breathtaking views of the remote valleys along Kauai's North Shore.

34 **Lahaina** Page **290** • Maui's laid-back Lahaina has lost none of its charm in making the transition from whaling port to vacation resort.

Basics

Basics

Getting there

You'll almost certainly have to fly to get to the Hawaiian islands. Honolulu receives by far the most flights, but there are direct services to Maui, the Big Island and Kauai as well, so there's no need to pass through Honolulu if you don't plan to spend any time in Oahu. Though the winter is peak season in Hawaii, fares are typically highest from around June to August, and again around Christmas and New Year. As a rule, flying on weekdays costs less than weekends.

Flights from North America

Most **flights** to Hawaii from the US mainland and Canada land at the state capital, **Honolulu**, on the island of Oahu. Virtually every large US airline flies to Honolulu, with United being the major carrier; Hawaiian Airlines also runs its own services to and from the western states. The only other airports that receive nonstop flights from the continental US are Kahului on **Maui** (from Burbank, Dallas, LA, Oakland, Orange County, Portland, Sacramento, Salt Lake City, San Diego, San Francisco, San Jose, and Seattle); Kona/Keahole on the **Big Island** (from Denver, Los Angeles, Oakland, Orange County, and San Francisco); and Līhu'e on **Kauai** (from Los Angeles and San Francisco only).

So long as you arrive in Honolulu by about 7pm, you should be able to connect with an onward flight to any of the other islands. In most cases it will be with one of the two main inter-island carriers – Aloha Airlines and Hawaiian Airlines. For more details, see "Inter-island travel" on p.31.

As for the **journey time**, crossing the Pacific from the West Coast to Honolulu takes roughly five hours. For details on time differences, see p.50.

Flights from the US West Coast

The best rate you're likely to find for a round-trip fare **from the West Coast to Honolulu** will probably be between US$300 and US$500. **Los Angeles** is generally the cheapest departure point and is served by six carriers: Hawaiian, United, American, Continental, Northwest, and Delta.

Hawaiian Airlines flies from ten mainland US cities to Honolulu. Three or four flights leave daily from **Los Angeles**; two from **Seattle**; and one each from **Las Vegas**, **Oakland**, **Orange County**, **Phoenix**, **Portland**, **Sacramento**, **San Diego**, and **San Francisco**. United sends four daily flights to Honolulu from **San Francisco**, three from **Los Angeles**, one from **San Diego**, and one from **Seattle**.

Of the **other operators** who fly to Honolulu from the West Coast, American has four daily flights from Los Angeles, and one from San Francisco; Delta offers two daily flights from Los Angeles and one from San Francisco; Northwest has daily services from Los Angeles, Portland, San Francisco, and Seattle; Aloha flies once daily from Oakland and Orange County; and Continental flies once from Los Angeles.

Finally, Midwest-based charter airline ATA Airlines offers two daily flights to Honolulu from Oakland and Los Angeles, one daily from Las Vegas and Ontario, California.

To the Neighbor Islands

Most nonstop flights to Kahului airport on **Maui** arrive from **Los Angeles**; United and American fly the route twice daily, and Delta once. United runs three flights daily from **San Francisco**, while Hawaiian has daily service from San Diego, Portland and Seattle. Aloha flies nonstop to Kahului once daily from Oakland, Orange, Sacramento and San Diego, and American twice from Los Angeles. ATA operates daily flights to Kahului from Las Vegas, Los Angeles, Oakland, and Phoenix.

In addition, United operates two daily services from Los Angeles and three from San

Francisco to Kona on the **Big Island**, and flies twice daily from both San Francisco and Los Angeles to Līhu'e on **Kauai**. American offer direct daily flights from Los Angeles to both Kona and Līhu'e. ATA flies daily to Kona from Oakland, as does Delta from Seattle; Aloha also flies to Kona daily from Orange County.

Flights from the rest of the US

Most visitors traveling from the **Midwest and East Coast** to Hawaii fly via California. However, there are some nonstop flights. American flies daily to Honolulu from both **Chicago** and **Dallas** (twice); Continental flies twice from **Houston** and once from **Newark**; Delta twice from **Atlanta**, and once each from **Cincinnati** and **Salt Lake City**; Northwest once from **Minneapolis**; and United once daily from **Chicago** and **Denver**.

In addition, American flies daily from **Dallas** to Kahului on Maui; Delta flies once daily from **Salt Lake City** to Kahului; and United once daily from **Denver** to Kona on the Big Island. All flights take 8–10 hours. The best available deals on round-trip fares from the Midwest and East Coast tend to range upwards from US$550.

Flights from Canada

Vancouver is the only Canadian city from which you can fly nonstop to Hawaii. Air Canada offers two flights daily to Honolulu, while United flies once, and WestJet flies to both Honolulu and Maui in winter only; typical return fares range upwards from Can$550. Getting to Hawaii from anywhere else in Canada will require you to change planes either in Vancouver, or on the US mainland, which gives you more flexibility. Thus if you're flying from Toronto or Montréal, the routing permutations are almost endless – Air Canada via Vancouver; American Airlines via Chicago or Dallas; Delta via Cincinnati or Atlanta; Northwest via Minneapolis; United via Los Angeles or San Francisco; and so on. Expect to pay upwards of Can$800.

Travel agents

Air Brokers International ☏1-800/883-3273, ⊛www.airbrokers.com. Consolidator and specialist in Round the World and Circle Pacific tickets.

Airtech ☏212/219-7000, ⊛www.airtech.com. Flight broker; also deals in consolidator fares.
Flightcentre ☏1-866/967-5351, ⊛www .flightcentre.us, ⊛www.flightcentre.ca. Rock-bottom fares worldwide.
STA Travel US ☏1-800/781-4040, Canada ☏1-888/427-5639, ⊛www.statravel.com. Worldwide specialists in independent travel.
Travel Cuts US ☏1-800/592-2887, Canada ☏1-888/246-9762, ⊛www.travelcuts.com. Long-established student-travel organization.
Worldtek Travel ☏1-800/243-1723, ⊛www .worldtek.com. Discount travel agency for worldwide travel.

Tour operators

American Airlines Vacations ☏1-800/321-2121, ⊛www.aavacations.com. Independent package tours to Hawaii, taking care of your flight, accommodation, and car rental.
Backroads ☏510/527-1555 or 1-800/462-2848, ⊛www.backroads.com. Biking tours of the Big Island, with stays in top-quality accommodation, priced from $2900 for five nights, not including airfares.
Continental Airlines Vacations ☏1-800/301-3800, ⊛www.covacations.com. Individually tailored Hawaiian vacations, including flights, hotel, and car rental.
Delta Vacations ☏1-800/654-6559, ⊛www .deltavacations.com. Good-value Hawaiian package vacations with all combinations of flights, hotel, and car rental. A five-night stay in Waikīkī from New York starts at under $1000.
Globus and Cosmos ☏1-800/221-0090, ⊛www.globusandcosmos.com. Independent and escorted tours in multi-island combinations; eight days on Oahu and Maui, or thirteen days on Oahu, Maui, Kauai, and the Big Island. Land-only rates start around $1000, but they can also arrange airfare and such for you.
New England Hiking Holidays ☏603/356-9696 or 1-800/869-0949, ⊛www.nehikingholidays.com. Guided seven-day springtime hiking tours of the Big Island, for $1965, excluding airfare.
Pleasant Hawaiian Holidays ☏1-800/742-9244, ⊛www.pleasantholidays.com. The leading supplier of independent packages, combining flights, car rental, accommodation, etc, on any island. Eight days on Maui, Oahu or both from LA can cost under $800.
Sierra Club ☏415/977-5522, ⊛www.sierraclub .org. Guided wilderness tours, geared towards families; a ten-day trip to Hawaii Volcanoes National Park on the Big Island costs around $1500.

Tauck Tours ☎ 203/226-6911 or 1-800/788-7885, ⊕ www.tauck.com. Fully escorted tours, staying at the very top hotels. Eleven nights on Oahu, Kauai, Maui and the Big Island cost $3990; excluding airfare.
United Vacations ☎ 1-800/328-6877, ⊕ www.unitedvacations.com. Custom-made individual vacations, combining islands and hotels to your specifications. Four-night trips from the West Coast start at around $700.
Windsurfari ☎ 808/871-7766 or 1-800/736-6284, ⊕ www.windsurfari.com. Windsurfing and custom vacation packages on Maui, including condo, car, and equipment rental – but not flights – from $500 per week.

Flights from Britain and Ireland

Unless you're visiting Hawaii as part of a round-the-world trip, the only cost-effective way to reach the islands from **Britain** or **Ireland** is to fly via the mainland United States or Canada. Your options, therefore, are more or less the same as they are for North Americans; fly to one of the mainland US cities mentioned on p.27 and change there for your onward trip.

With a ten-hour flight across the Atlantic to the West Coast, and a five-hour flight over the Pacific, that makes for a very long journey. However, it is possible to get to any of the four major islands – Oahu, Maui, Kauai and the Big Island – on the same day that you set off from London, thanks to the ten- or eleven-hour time difference (see p.50) and the great number of flights that leave the West Coast airports each afternoon. In any case, it's the journey home that's the really exhausting leg – if you fly direct, you're likely to arrive home on the second morning after you leave, having "lost" two nights' sleep.

Connections **from Ireland** are more problematic. If you fly direct to the US mainland, you'll have to spend a night before catching an onward flight to Hawaii, though it is possible to catch an early-morning plane to London to pick up a flight from there.

A typical return ticket from London to Hawaii through the operators and specialists listed on the night costs around £450 from January to March, and up to as much as £800 in July and August.

Travel agents and tour operators

American Holidays Northern Ireland ☎ 028/9031 0000, Republic of Ireland ☎ 01/673 3840 ⊕ www.american-holidays.com.
Bon Voyage UK ☎ 0800/316 3012, ⊕ www.bon-voyage.co.uk.
British Airways Holidays UK ☎ 0870/850 9850, ⊕ www.baholidays.co.uk.
Hawaiian Holidays ☎ 020/7001 9130, ⊕ www.hawaiian-holidays.co.uk.
North America Travel Service UK ☎ 020/7499 7299, ⊕ www.northamericatravelservice.co.uk.
North South Travel UK ☎ 01245/608291, ⊕ www.northsouthtravel.co.uk.
Page & Moy UK ☎ 0870/833 4012, ⊕ www.pageandmoy.com.
STA Travel UK ☎ 0870/163 0026, ⊕ www.statravel.com.
Titan HiTours UK ☎ 0845/375 0245, ⊕ www.titantravel.co.uk.
Trailfinders UK ☎ 0845/058 5858, ⊕ www.trailfinders.com.
United Vacations ☎ 0870/111 0110, ⊕ www.unitedvacations.co.uk.

From Australia and New Zealand

There's no shortage of flights from Australia and New Zealand to **Honolulu**, and very little price difference between airlines. Several airlines operate daily services, with journey times of around nine hours.

From Australia, most flights to Honolulu are out of **Sydney**. Both Air Canada, code sharing with United, and Qantas, code sharing with American Airlines, offer daily nonstop service, from around Aus$850 in low season up to more like Aus$1500 in high season. For around the same price, United flies via Auckland.

From New Zealand, the best deals to Honolulu are the direct flights out of Auckland offered by Air New Zealand, which can cost as little as NZ$1400 return in low season, and by Air Canada, which tend to be a little more expensive. For similarly low fares, Qantas can also take you from Auckland to Honolulu via either Sydney or Western Samoa.

Travel agents and tour operators

Creative Tours ⊕ www.creativeholidays.com.au.
STA Travel Australia ☎ 1300/733 035, New Zealand ☎ 0508/782 872, ⊕ www.statravel.com.

Fly less – stay longer! Travel and climate change

Climate change is a serious threat to the ecosystems that humans rely upon, and air travel is among the fastest-growing contributors to the problem. Rough Guides regard travel, overall, as a global benefit, and feel strongly that the advantages to developing economies are important, as is the opportunity of greater contact and awareness among peoples. But we all have a responsibility to limit our personal impact on global warming, and that means giving thought to how often we fly, and what we can do to redress the harm that our trips create.

Flying and climate change

Pretty much every form of motorized travel generates CO_2 – the main cause of human-induced climate change – but planes also generate climate-warming contrails and cirrus clouds and emit oxides of nitrogen, which create ozone (another greenhouse gas) at flight levels. Furthermore, flying simply allows us to travel much further than we otherwise would do. The figures are frightening: one person taking a return flight between Europe and California produces the equivalent impact of 2.5 tons of CO_2 – similar to the yearly output of the average UK car.

Fuel-cell and other less harmful types of plane may emerge eventually. But until then, there are really just two options for concerned travelers: to reduce the amount we travel by air (take fewer trips – stay for longer!), and to make the trips we do take "climate neutral" via a carbon-offset scheme.

Carbon-offset schemes

Offset schemes run by ⓦwww.climatecare.org, ⓦwww.carbonneutral.com and others allow you to make up for some or all of the greenhouse gases that you are responsible for releasing. To do this, they provide "carbon calculators" for working out the global-warming contribution of a specific flight (or even your entire existence), and then let you contribute an appropriate amount of money to fund offsetting measures. These include rainforest reforestation and initiatives to reduce future energy demand – often run in conjunction with sustainable development schemes.

Rough Guides, together with Lonely Planet and other concerned partners in the travel industry, are supporting a **carbon-offset scheme** run by climatecare.org. Please take the time to view our website and see how you can help to make your trip climate neutral.

ⓦwww.roughguides.com/climatechange

Sydney Travel Australia ☏02/9220 9230, ⓦwww.sydneytravel.com.
Trailfinders Australia ☏1300/780 212, ⓦwww.trailfinders.com.
travel.co.nz New Zealand ☏0800/468 332, ⓦwww.travel.co.nz.
travel.com.au Australia ☏1300/130 482, ⓦwww.travel.com.au.

Airlines and booking flights online

Good deals can often be found through discount or auction sites, as well as through the websites of the airlines themselves. These online services avoid the costs of agents and middlemen, but be warned that the bargain prices are usually for non-refundable, non-changeable deals.

Online booking

ⓦwww.expedia.co.uk (in UK), ⓦwww.expedia.com (in US), ⓦwww.expedia.ca (in Canada), ⓦwww.lastminute.com (in UK), ⓦwww.opodo.co.uk (in UK), ⓦwww.orbitz.com (in US), ⓦwww.travelocity.co.uk (in UK), ⓦwww.travelocity.com (in US), ⓦwww.travelocity.ca (in Canada), ⓦwww.zuji.com.au (in Australia), ⓦwww.zuji.co.nz (in New Zealand).

Airlines

Aer Lingus US and Canada ☏1-800/IRISH-AIR, UK ☏0870/876 5000, Republic of Ireland ☏0818/365 000, ⓦwww.aerlingus.com.
Air Canada US and Canada ☏1-888/247-2262, UK ☏0871/220 1111, Republic of Ireland

ⓣ01/679 3958, Australia ⓣ1300/655 767, New Zealand ⓣ0508/747 767, ⓦwww.aircanada.com.
Air New Zealand Australia ⓣ13 24 76, New Zealand ⓣ0800/737 000, ⓦwww.airnz.co.nz.
Aloha Airlines ⓣ1-800/367-5250, ⓦwww.alohaair.com.
American Airlines ⓣ1-800/433-7300, UK ⓣ0845/778 9789, Republic of Ireland ⓣ01/602 0550, Australia ⓣ1300/650 747, New Zealand ⓣ0800/887 997, ⓦwww.aa.com.
ATA Airlines ⓣ1-800/435-9282, ⓦwww.ata.com.
British Airways US and Canada ⓣ1-800/ AIRWAYS, UK ⓣ0870/850 9850, Republic of Ireland ⓣ1890/626 747, Australia ⓣ1300/767 177, New Zealand ⓣ09/966 9777, ⓦwww.ba.com.
Continental Airlines US and Canada ⓣ1-800/523-3273, UK ⓣ0845/607 6760, Republic of Ireland ⓣ1890/925 252, Australia ⓣ02/9244 2242, New Zealand ⓣ09/308 3350, International ⓣ1800/231 0856, ⓦwww.continental.com.
Delta US and Canada ⓣ1-800/221-1212, UK ⓣ0845/600 0950, Republic of Ireland ⓣ1850/882 031 or 01/407 3165, Australia ⓣ1300/302 849, New Zealand ⓣ09/379 3370, ⓦwww.delta.com.
Hawaiian Airlines US and Canada ⓣ1-800/367-5320, Australia ⓣ02/9244 2377, ⓦwww.hawaiianair.com.
Northwest/KLM US ⓣ1-800/225-2525, UK ⓣ0870/507 4074, Australia ⓣ1-300-767-310, ⓦwww.nwa.com.
Qantas Airways US and Canada ⓣ1-800/227-4500, UK ⓣ0845/774 7767, Republic of Ireland ⓣ01/407 3278, Australia ⓣ13 13 13, New Zealand ⓣ0800/808 767 or 09/357 8900, SA ⓣ11/441 8550, ⓦwww.qantas.com.
United Airlines US ⓣ1-800/UNITED-1, UK ⓣ0845/844 4777, Australia ⓣ13 17 77, ⓦwww.united.com.
US Airways US and Canada ⓣ1-800/428-4322, UK ⓣ0845/600 3300, Ireland ⓣ1890/925 065, ⓦwww.usair.com.
Virgin Atlantic US ⓣ1-800/821-5438, UK ⓣ0870/380 2007, Australia ⓣ1300/727 340, SA ⓣ11/340 3400, ⓦwww.virgin-atlantic.com.
WestJet US and Canada ⓣ1-888/WEST-JET, UK and Ireland 0800/5381 5696, ⓦwww.westjet.com.

Inter-island travel

Virtually all travel between the Hawaiian islands has long been done by air, although the new Superferry service may change that. The air route between Honolulu and Kahului on Maui ranks as the busiest domestic route in the entire United States, with more than three million passengers each year. Honolulu is the main hub; apart from very short hops, it's unusual to be able to fly between two of the outer islands without a stop on Oahu.

Flights and fares

Two airlines, **Hawaiian** and **Aloha**, have long dominated inter-island travel. Each connects Honolulu at least ten times daily with the airports at Kona and Hilo on the Big Island, Kahului on Maui, and Līhu'e on Kauai. In addition, Aloha operates two flights daily between Kahului and Kona, Hilo and Līhu'e, while Hawaiian has one flight on each of those routes. **Island Air**, which operates in close affiliation with Aloha, offers around five flights each day to Kapalua on Maui, and the islands of Molokai and Lanai, from Honolulu,

and two between Molokai and Kahului on Maui. Hawaiian also provides one or two daily services to Lanai.

Every now and then, a usurper triggers a price-cutting war that hugely benefits travelers for a time, before fares drop so low that the newcomer goes bankrupt. The latest to try, **Go!**, was at the time this book went to press, offering nonstop flights from Honolulu to Kona, Hilo, Kahului, and Līhu'e for a standard fare of just $29 one-way. Hawaiian, Aloha and Island had all felt obliged to match, quite a shake-up considering their fares had previously crept up to more like $100.

A number of small–scale airlines also operate in Hawaii. **Pacific Wings** offers connections between all the islands, and also serves less-used airports such as Kalaupapa on Molokai, Hāna and Kapalua on Maui, and Waimea on the Big Island. Other players include **Paragon Air**; for full details, see p.400.

Don't expect to be able to fly late in the evening; the last scheduled flights on all the airlines usually depart at around 7pm from Honolulu, and 8pm from the Neighbor Islands.

Inter-island carriers

Aloha US & Canada ☎1-800/367-5250, Oahu ☎808/484-1111, Neighbor Islands ☎1-800/367-5250, ⊛www.alohaair.com.

Go! US & Canada ☎1-888/435-9462, Oahu and Neighbor Islands ☎1-888/435-9462, ⊛www.iflygo.com.

Hawaiian US & Canada ☎1-800/367-5320, Oahu and Neighbor Islands ☎1-800/882-8811, ⊛www.hawaiianair.com.

Island US & Canada ☎1-800/323-3345, Oahu ☎808/484-2222, Neighbor Islands ☎1-800/652-6541, ⊛www.islandair.com.

Pacific Wings US & Canada ☎808/873-0877, Oahu and Neighbor Islands ☎1-888/575-4546, ⊛www.pacificwings.com.

Ferries and cruises

Under Hawaii's long-awaited **Superferry** system, which as this book went to press was expected to commence operations in the summer of 2007, huge catamarans capable of carrying cars and trucks will connect Honolulu with both Maui and Kauai in around three hours for one-way fares starting at $42 per passenger, plus $55 per vehicle. Sailings to the Big Island were promised for 2009 ($52/$65). For the latest news, check ⊛www.hawaiisuperferry.com.

In addition, two scheduled ferry services depart from Lahaina on Maui. **Expeditions** (☎808/661-3756 or 1-800/695-2624, ⊛www.go-lanai.com) runs five boats each day to Manele Bay on Lanai, while the **Molokai Princess** (☎808/662-3535 or 1-877/500-6284, ⊛www.mauiprincess.com) makes two daily round-trips between Lahaina and Kaunakakai on Molokai. For details of both, see p.293.

The main operator of **cruises** between the islands is Norwegian Cruise Lines (☎1-866/234-0392, ⊛www.ncl.com). They offer weekly, week-long cruises out of Honolulu that visit Kauai, Maui, and the Big Island, with fares starting as low as $500 per person.

Getting around

The only way to explore the Hawaiian islands thoroughly is to drive. Those planning a completely Waikīkī-centered vacation will find that Oahu has a reasonable public transport system; everywhere else, if you're not on a package tour, you'll be floundering from the moment you touch down at the airport.

Renting a car

The demand for **rental cars** in Hawaii is great – in addition to the millions of tourists, there are all the locals who can't take their cars with them when they travel from island to island.

That said, there's such a plentiful supply that competition among the rental companies is fierce, and the average Honolulu rate of $45 per day ranks as the lowest of all the hundred largest cities in the US.

The **national rental chains** are represented on all the major islands, and every airport in the state has at least one outlet. Call their toll-free numbers for reservations (see below), as most individual offices cannot even advise on rates or availability. With so much competition, and so many short-lived special offers, it's hard to quote specific prices, but a target rate for the cheapest economy car with unlimited mileage should be something around $35 per day or $175 per week. Avis and Hertz allow drivers to pay the weekly rate even when driving different cars on different islands; all the rest charge separately for each vehicle. To rent a car, drivers must be over 21, and those between ages 21 and 24 often have to supply additional guarantees or simply pay extra.

Before you commit yourself to a rate, check whether your airline – or your hotel, B&B, or hostel – can offer a discount on car rental. Some hotels even supply free cars for guests who stay for a week or longer.

When you rent, you'll probably be pressured to pay as much as $20 extra per day for **Collision Damage Waiver** (CDW), a form of insurance that absolves you of liability for any damage to your vehicle. Controversially, Hawaii is a "no-fault state," meaning that drivers are always held responsible for whatever befalls their own vehicle, so CDW cover is more important here than elsewhere. American car owners should call their insurance companies to check if they're covered by policies they already hold; some credit card companies also provide card holders with car-rental insurance coverage. Whether or not you choose to buy CDW is a purely personal decision. Some people regard it as little short of extortion; others feel it gives them peace of mind.

Car rental companies

Alamo US ☎ 1-800/462-5266, ⊛ www.alamo.com.
Avis US ☎ 1-800/230-4898, Canada ☎ 1-800-272-5871, UK ☎ 0870/606 0100, Republic of Ireland ☎ 021/428 1111, Australia ☎ 13 63 33 or 02/9353 9000, New Zealand ☎ 09/526 2847 or 0800/655 111, ⊛ www.avis.com.
Budget US ☎ 1-800/527-0700, Canada ☎ 1-800-268-8900, UK ☎ 0870/156 5656, Australia ☎ 1300/362 848, New Zealand ☎ 0800/283 438, ⊛ www.budget.com.
Dollar US ☎ 1-800/800-3665, ⊛ www.dollar.com.
Enterprise Rent-a-Car US ☎ 1-800/261-7331, ⊛ www.enterprise.com.
Hertz US & Canada ☎ 1-800/654-3131, UK ☎ 020/7026 0077, Republic of Ireland ☎ 01/870 5777, New Zealand ☎ 0800/654 321, ⊛ www.hertz.com.
National US ☎ 1-800/CAR-RENT, UK ☎ 0870/400 4581, Australia ☎ 0870/600 6666, New Zealand ☎ 03/366 5574, ⊛ www.nationalcar.com.
Thrifty US and Canada ☎ 1-800/847-4389, UK ☎ 01494/751 540, Republic of Ireland ☎ 01/844 1950, Australia ☎ 1300/367 227, New Zealand ☎ 09/256 1405, ⊛ www.thrifty.com.

Driving in Hawaii

On the whole, **driving** in Hawaii is both easy and enjoyable. Most of the islands effectively have just one main road, so there's little risk of getting lost, and with such small distances to cover no one seems to be in too much of a hurry.

However, there are a few provisos. **Honolulu** is a large and confusing city, with major rush-hour traffic congestion and a shortage of parking spaces. Since the city has a good bus system, there's no real need to drive while you're there, and renting a car at the airport after a tiring flight can be a recipe for disaster. Elsewhere, the **coastal highways** can be slow and tortuous, and often narrow to a single lane to cross tiny bridges. Bear in mind, too, that it's dark by 7pm, and stretches of road between towns are not lit, so driving at night can be difficult.

Apart from the fact that in Hawaii, as in the rest of the US, you drive on the right, the one rule of the road that can trouble foreign visitors is that, unless specifically prohibited, drivers are allowed, after a careful pause, **to turn right on a red light**.

Typical **gas prices** are around thirty percent above the US average, so you can easily pay $2.40–3.25 per gallon. Keep a closer eye on your fuel gauge than usual; sightseeing expeditions can carry you 25 miles into the wilderness on dead-end roads, which makes for a fifty-mile round-trip before you see another gas station.

Cycling

As detailed throughout the Guide, **bikes** are available for rent on all the Hawaiian islands,

Flight-seeing tours

Helicopter **flight-seeing tours** have long been established as a must-do activity for any visitor to Hawaii. On most of the islands, you can circle the entire island in a relatively short flight and feel that you've glimpsed wonders you would otherwise never have seen.

However, the industry ran into difficulty in the 1990s, with fifteen accidental deaths in three years. Most of those involved plunges over the enormous Nā Pali cliffs of Kauai, while on the Big Island there was a much-publicized incident in which a camera crew crash-landed as they filmed Kīlauea and were trapped for two days in the erupting crater. As a result, restrictions were hastily imposed, requiring all single-engine aircraft, including helicopters, to maintain a minimum altitude of at least 500 feet. Two further fatal crashes on Kauai in March 2007 may result in still stricter new regulations. Helicopter rides these days are now more sedate affairs, not the roller-coaster rides they used to be, and they no longer swoop down to hover over single spots. However, fixed-wing, twin-engine aircraft can still fly low; as they're cheaper than helicopters, they make a good-value alternative to a chopper flight. Operators on each island are listed in the relevant chapter introductions.

usually for in-town use rather than long-distance explorations. There's also a craze for "**downhill cycling adventures**," in which groups of tourists are taken by van to some appropriately lofty spot and then allowed to freewheel back to base. The most famous of these is the daily dawn descent from the top of Haleakalā on Maui, from which you can ride forty miles without pedalling once (see p.347). Cycles are not allowed, however, on hiking trails in national or state parks.

Some of the companies listed on p.28 organize guided **cycle-touring** vacations, but few visitors bring their own bikes and tour the islands themselves. There's no great reason why not; the Big Island in particular would make an excellent destination for a camping trip by bike, while over the last decade Maui has added cycle lanes to all its main highways.

"Getting around" sections for each island, with full details of public transport and island tours, appear in the introductions to each chapter.

Public transport

While Oahu can boast an excellent bus network – detailed on p.61 – **public transport** on the other islands is minimal in the extreme. Maui, Kauai, and the Big Island both have very limited bus systems, Lanai has a very localized shuttle service, and Molokai has nothing at all. To get to or from the airport, you can always call a taxi or minivan service, but that's no way to go sightseeing.

The only **railroads** still operating in Hawaii are the "Sugar Cane Train," which offers daily musical excursions between Lahaina and Kā'anapali on Maui (see p.293), and a short stretch in southwest Oahu, where the Hawaii Railway Society runs Sunday afternoon jaunts (see p.156).

Accommodation

Prospective visitors who think of Hawaii as an expensive destination will be alarmed to hear that the average cost of a single night's accommodation is around $175. That figure, however, is boosted by the three- or four-hundred-dollar rates for the lavish resorts at the top end of the spectrum. On all the islands, you can reasonably expect to find a good standard of hotel, condo, or B&B for around $100 per night: Molokai is the cheapest, followed in ascending order by Oahu, the Big Island, Kauai, Maui, and Lanai. Overall occupancy rates seem to hover around seventy percent or lower, so at most times of the year it should be possible to book a room at short notice.

All these prices are based on the hotel's own **rack rates** – the rate you'll be offered if you simply walk through the door and ask for a room for the night. While there's little room for bargaining in the smaller inns or B&Bs, in the larger hotels it's very possible to find significantly cheaper rates online, or to cut costs by buying a **package deal** through one of the operators or airlines listed in the "Getting there" section.

Detailed advice on where to stay on each individual island, with specific recommendations, appears at the start of the relevant chapter. With the exception of the Big Island, it's relatively easy to explore each island from a single base. Few people tour from place to place on any one island, staying in a different town each night, and in any case hotels much prefer guests to make reservations well in advance.

Resorts

These gigantic, sprawling enclaves, each holding hundreds or even thousands of rooms, and frequently run by a major chain such as *Hyatt Regency* or *Sheraton*, are more than just hotels. Often located far from any town, they are equipped with their own restaurants, stores, swimming pools, beaches, golf courses, tennis courts, walking trails, and anything else you can think of, all designed to ensure that guests never feel the need to leave the property. Such luxury doesn't come cheap – typical ocean-view rooms are likely to cost over $300 a night, and suites can go for $2000 or more – and since the resorts are located purely for sun rather than culture or even scenery, they often hold little to remind you that you're in Hawaii at all.

Accommodation price codes

Throughout this book, **accommodation prices** have been graded with the symbols below, according to the least expensive double room for most of the year, not including state taxes of 11.25 percent.

Both hostels and budget hotels usually keep the same rates throughout the year, but in more expensive properties, rooms normally priced above $100 tend to rise by an average of $20–40 in the peak seasons – from Christmas to Easter and June to August. However, it's possible to obtain much better rates for top-range accommodation by booking your room as part of an all-inclusive package.

❶ up to $40	❹ $100–150	❼ $250–300
❷ $40–70	❺ $150–200	❽ $300–400
❸ $70–100	❻ $200–250	❾ over $400

This kind of development was pioneered on Maui and the Big Island during the 1960s, when entrepreneurs realized that the islands' bleak and inhospitable leeward coasts were dry and hot enough to make it worth constructing brand-new oases from scratch. Where beaches didn't exist they were sculpted into the coastline; coconut palms were flown in and replanted; and turf was laid on top of the lava to build championship-quality golf courses.

Hawaii's prime **resort concentrations** can be found in Waikoloa, Mauna Lani, and Mauna Kea on the Big Island; Po'ipū on Kauai; and Kā'anapali, Kapalua, and Wailea on Maui. Additional individual resorts scattered around the islands include the *Ihilani Resort* and *Turtle Bay Resort* on Oahu, the *Lodge at Kō'ele* and *Manele Bay Hotel* on Lanai, and the *Princeville Hotel* on Kauai.

Hotels, motels, and condos

In addition to the paramount example of Waikīkī on Oahu, large clusters of conventional **hotels** have grown up in areas such as Kīhei on Maui, Kailua on the Big Island, and Wailua on Kauai. While these may look far less opulent and distinctive than the resorts described above – and barely distinguishable from each other – the standard of the rooms is dependably high. You can expect an en-suite bathroom and a balcony of some description as well (which is universally known as a *lānai*). Room rates vary from perhaps $275 per night at the top of the spectrum down to a little below $100. Virtually every hotel has at least one **restaurant**, where charges can be billed to your room account.

The distinction between a hotel room and a **condominium** apartment is not always clear, as the same building may hold some private condo apartments and others rented by the night to short-term guests. The difference lies in the types of facilities each offers. An individual condo unit is likely to be more comfortable and better equipped than a typical hotel room, often with a kitchenette, but on the other hand, a condominium building may not have a lobby area, daily housekeeping service, restaurants, or other hotel amenities.

Incidentally, it's worth mentioning that, paradoxically enough, many of Hawaii's oldest hotels rank among its very best. That's because regulations dictating how close to the ocean it's possible to build have become much stricter in recent years, so delightful beachfront accommodations like the *Hanalei Colony Resort* on Kauai, and the *Mauian* and its neighbors on Maui's Napili Bay, could never be constructed these days.

Motels on the usual American model are very rare, and representatives of the major national motel chains all but nonexistent. Certain older towns do, however, retain basic hotels that were originally built to accommodate migrant agricultural laborers. In most cases these are minimally equipped flophouses, which may charge as little as $30 per night, though those that haven't shut down altogether have tended to upgrade over time.

Bed and breakfasts

The definition of **bed and breakfast** accommodation stretches from a simple room or two in a private home, through self-contained, self-catering cottages, to luxurious fifteen-room inns; surprisingly, not all include breakfast. In principle, however, the standards are very high. The cheapest rooms, perhaps sharing a bathroom with one other guest room, start around $75 per night, while for $125 per night you can expect your own well-furnished apartment, with all facilities. The owners are often friendly and full of advice on making the most of your vacation.

Most small-scale B&Bs are located away from the busier tourist areas, in the more scenic, but slightly wetter or cooler parts of the islands where people actually choose to live. Thus there are particular concentrations in the upcountry meadowlands of Maui and the Big Island, across the mountains from Honolulu on Oahu's windward coast, and a couple of miles back from the ocean on the east coast of Kauai. If you plan to spend a night or two at Hawaii Volcanoes National Park on the Big Island, there's little alternative to the wide assortment of B&Bs in the nearby village of Volcano.

For a reliable selection of top-quality B&Bs on all the islands, it's well worth contacting

Hostels

Each of the four largest islands has at least one budget hostel, where you can get a bed in a dormitory for under $20 per night or a very basic private double room for $30–45. Few of these are affiliated to international hosteling organizations, and some only admit non-US citizens. As a rule, they're strongly geared towards young surfers.

Big Island

Arnott's Lodge, Hilo	p.222	*Pineapple Park*, Kealakekua	p.191
Hilo Bay Hostel, Hilo	p.222	*Pineapple Park*, Hilo	p.222
Holo Holo Inn, Volcano	p.268	*Pineapple Park*, Volcano	p.268

Kauai

Kauai International Hostel, Kapa'a   p.462

Maui

Banana Bungalow, Wailuku	p.318	*Northshore Hostel*, Wailuku	p.318

Oahu

Backpacker's Vacation Inn,		Pacific Ohana, Waikīkī	p.68
Pūpūkea	p.153	Polynesian Hostel Beach Club,	
Hale Aloha Hostel, Waikīkī	p.69	Waikīkī	p.69
Hosteling International		Waikīkī Beachside Hotel &	
Honolulu, Honolulu	p.76	Hostel, Waikīkī	p.68

locally based agencies like **Hawaii's Best Bed & Breakfasts** (☎808/985-7488 or 1-800/262-9912, ⊛www.bestbnb.com) or **Bed & Breakfast Hawaii** (☎808/822-7771 or 1-800/733-1632, ⊛www.bandb-hawaii.com).

Eating and drinking

Gone are the days when the Hawaiian islands were self-sufficient Gardens of Eden; the state now produces less than twenty percent of the food it consumes, and in many ways eating in Hawaii can be much like eating anywhere else in the US. Polynesian cuisine can mean little more than putting a pineapple ring on top of a burger, and amazingly enough, more than half of all the Spam eaten in the United States is consumed in Hawaii.

That said, visitors hoping for memorable culinary experiences can sample from an array of cuisines, brought to the islands by immigrants from all over the world. In addition, the presence of thousands of **tourists**, many prepared to pay top rates for good food, means that the islands have some truly superb fine dining restaurants, run by internationally renowned chefs.

Bear in mind that all restaurants and bars in Hawaii are now obliged by law to forbid **smoking**.

Local restaurants

While the national fast-food chains are well represented in Hawaii, locally owned budget restaurants, diners, and takeout stands throughout the state serve a hybrid cuisine that draws on the traditions of Japan, China, Korea, and the Philippines as well as the US mainland. The resultant mixture has a slight but definite Hawaiian twist. In fact, the term "**local**" food has a distinct meaning in Hawaii, and specifically applies to this multicultural mélange.

Breakfast tends to be the standard combination of eggs, meat, pancakes, muffins, or toast. At midday, the most popular option is the **plate lunch**, a tray holding meat and rice as well as potato or macaroni salad and costing between $6 and $9. **Bento** is the Japanese version, with mixed meats and rice; in Filipino diners, you'll be offered **adobo**, which is pork or chicken stewed with garlic and vinegar and served in a similar way. Korean barbecue, **kal bi** – prepared with sesame – is especially tasty, with the word "barbecue" indicating that the meat or fish has been marinated rather than necessarily cooked on an open grill. One simple but filling recipe – thought to be of Chinese origin – is **saimin** (pronounced *sy-min* not *say-min*), a bowl of clear soup filled with noodles and other mixed ingredients that has become something of a Hawaiian state dish. The carbohydrate-packed **loco moco** is a fried egg served on a hamburger with gravy and rice, while the favorite local dessert is **shave ice**, slushy scrapings of ice flavored with rainbow-colored syrups. Finally, a **malasada** is a sweet Portuguese donut, best eaten hot and fresh.

Food in general is often referred to as *kaukau*, and the general term for snacks is **pūpūs** (pronounced *poo-poos*) – the kind of finger food that is given away at early evening Happy Hours.

Fine dining

Some of the world's most lavish and inventive **restaurants** can be found at the

Hawaiian fish

Although the ancient Hawaiians were expert offshore fishermen, as well as being highly sophisticated fish farmers who maintained intricate networks of inshore fishponds, the great majority of the fish eaten in Hawaii nowadays is imported. Local fishing is not done on a large enough scale to meet the demand, and in any case many of the species that tourists expect to find on menus thrive in much cooler waters. Thus salmon and crab come from Alaska, mussels from New Zealand, and so on, although Maine lobsters are farmed in the cold waters of the deep ocean off Honokōhau on the Big Island, and aquafarms on several islands are raising freshwater species.

Some of the Pacific species caught nearby are listed below by their common Hawaiian names. Of these it's worth trying *opah*, which is chewy and salty like swordfish; the chunky *'ōpakapaka*, which because of its red color (associated with happiness) is often served on special occasions; the succulent white *ono* (which means "delicious" in Hawaiian); the beautifully tender *moi*, often steamed or fried whole in Chinese restaurants; and the dark *'ahi*, the most popular choice for sashimi.

'ahi	yellow-fin tuna	*mano*	shark
aku	skipjack tuna	*moi*	thread fish
a'u	swordfish or marlin	*onaga*	red snapper
'ehu	red snapper	*ono*	mackerel/tuna-like fish
hāpu'upu'u	sea bass	*'ōpae*	shrimp
hebi	spear fish	*opah*	moonfish
kākū	barracuda	*'ōpakapaka*	pink snapper
kalekale	pink snapper	*pāpio*	pompano
kāmano	salmon	*uhu*	parrotfish
kūmū	red goat fish	*uku*	gray snapper
lehi	yellow snapper	*ulua*	jack fish
mahimahi	dorado or dolphin fish	*weke*	goat fish

more exclusive resort regions of Hawaii. These are the places where something approaching a distinctive Hawaiian cuisine is being created, known variously as **Pacific Rim**, **Euro-Asian**, or **Hawaii Regional**. In its ideal form it combines foods and techniques from all the countries and ethnic groups that have figured in Hawaiian history, using the freshest ingredients possible. The top chefs – such as Roy Yamaguchi, who runs **Roy's** restaurants on all four major islands, and Sam Choy, who owns restaurants on Oahu and the Big Island – seek to preserve natural flavors by such methods as flash-frying meat and fish like the Chinese, baking it whole like the Hawaiians, or even serving it raw like the Japanese. The effect is enhanced by the delicate addition of Thai herbs and spices, and by the sheer inventiveness that it shares with modern Californian cooking.

Throughout the islands, you'll also find plenty of conventional **American** shrimp and steak specialists, as well as high-class **Italian**, **Thai**, and **Chinese** places. Many restaurants offer all-you-can-eat **buffets** one or more nights of the week; they all sacrifice quality for quantity, so you might as well go for the cheaper ones. Lastly, to cater for that much-prized customer, the Japanese big spender, many of the larger hotels have authentic and very good **Japanese** restaurants, which tend to specialize in discreet sushi and sashimi dining rather than the flamboyant *teppanyaki* style, where knife-juggling chefs cook at your table.

Local ingredients

As well as the many kinds of fish listed in the box opposite, widely used local ingredients include **ginger** and **macadamia nuts** (large, creamy, and somewhat bland white nuts

said to contain a hundred calories per nut, even when they aren't coated with chocolate). Bright red **'ohelo berries**, which taste like cranberries, and are served up in gourmet restaurants, but they were once sacred to the volcano goddess Pele, and to eat one was punishable by death. **Avocados** are widely grown and are even richer than you may be used to, as are fruits such as **guava** (an imported pest that's a staple for hikers, as it grows wild along most wilderness trails), **papaya**, and **mango**. Watch out also for the small yellow **apple bananas**, with their distinct savory tang and, of course, the ever-present **coconut**.

Drink

The usual range of **wines** (mostly Californian, though both Maui and the Big Island have their own tiny wineries) and **beers** (mainly imported either from the mainland or Mexico) are sold at Hawaiian restaurants and bars, but at some point every visitor seems to insist on getting wiped out by a tropical **cocktail** or two. Among the most popular are the **Mai Tai**, which should contain at least two kinds of rum, together with orange Curaçao and lemon juice; the **Blue Hawaii**, in which vodka is colored with blue Curaçao; and the **Planter's Punch**, made with light rum, grenadine, bitters, and lemon juice.

Tap **water** in Hawaii is safe to drink, though it's a scarce enough resource in places that some restaurants will only bring it to your table on request.

Deliciously rich local coffees are available in small cafés and espresso bars throughout the state, although Hawaii's most famous gourmet product, **Kona coffee**, refers only to coffees grown on the southwestern slopes of the Big Island. For more details, see p.183.

Entertainment and festivals

If you consider wild nightlife essential to the success of your Hawaiian vacation, head straight for the bright lights and glitter of Waikīkī. Everywhere else on the islands, with the possible exception of Lahaina on Maui, any attempt to do some serious clubbing is likely to prove a severe disappointment. That's not to say there's nothing going on at all, but Hawaii is a rural state, and away from Honolulu there's nothing larger than a small country town. On Maui they call 10pm "Maui midnight" because everyone has gone to bed; Kauai and the Big Island are even sleepier.

Full entertainment listings for Honolulu and Waikīkī appear on pp.122–127. Otherwise most of the nightlife in Hawaii is arranged by the major **hotels** – almost all put on some form of entertainment for their guests, and many feature live musicians every night. The music as often as not consists of medleys of Hawaiian hits from the 1950s, but the setting is usually romantic enough to make the experience enjoyable. **Restaurants** and **cafés** also use live music to attract diners, whether in the form of full-fledged bands or simple acoustic strummers.

Unless you coincide with one of the major annual festivals, you're unlikely to see an authentic *hula* performance, though all the main islands have several commercial *lūʻaus*, a sort of mocked-up version of the open-air, ocean-front Hawaiian feasts that are traditionally held to celebrate a baby's first birthday. These can be great fun if you're in the right mood, but they seldom bring you into contact with locals. Big-name touring musicians tend to perform in Honolulu, and with luck on Maui as well, while the other islands have to settle for regular concert appearances by the stars of the Hawaiian music scene. For more about *hula* and Hawaiian music, see p.562.

Public holidays are listed on p.49.

Annual festivals and events

Jan Maui Pro Surf Meet; surfing competition, Honolua Bay and Hoʻokipa Beach (Maui)
late Jan Ka Molokai Makahiki; traditional sports and *hula*, Kaunakakai (Molokai)
early Feb Whale Fest Week; whale-related events, Lahaina and Kāʻanapali (Maui)

Feb Mardi Gras, Hilo (Big Island)
March 17 St Patrick's Day Parade, Waikīkī (Oahu)
March Run to the Sun; foot race, Pāʻia to Haleakalā (Maui)
March 26 Prince Kūhīo Day; statewide celebrations
week after Easter Merrie Monarch Festival, Hilo (Big Island)
May 1 Lei Day; statewide celebrations
3rd Sat in May Molokai Ka Hula Piko; hula festival, Pāpōhaku Beach Park (Molokai)
late May International Festival of Canoes, Lahaina (Maui)
late May Bankoh Hoʻomanaʻo; outrigger canoe race, Kāʻanapali (Maui) to Waikīkī (Oahu)
June 11 Kamehameha Day; statewide celebrations
mid-June Maui Film Festival, Wailea (Maui)
late June Kihoʻalu, slack-key guitar festival, Maui Arts and Cultural Center (Maui)
July 4 Parker Ranch Rodeo, Waimea (Big Island)
July 4 Makawao Rodeo, Makawao (Maui)
early July Quicksilver Cup; windsurfing competition, Kanahā Beach Park (Maui)
mid-July Big Island Hawaiian Music and Slack Key Festival, Hilo (Big Island)
mid-July Hawaii International Jazz Festival, Honolulu (Oahu)
mid-Aug Hawaiian International Billfish Tournament, Kailua (Big Island)
early Sept Queen Liliʻuokalani Long-Distance Canoe Races, Kailua (Big Island)
Sept/Oct Aloha Festival; consecutive week-long festivals on each island
early Oct Ironman Triathlon World Championship, Kailua (Big Island)
Oct 31 Halloween parade, Lahaina (Maui) and Waikīkī (Oahu)
late Oct/early Nov Aloha Classic; windsurfing competition, Hoʻokipa (Maui)
early Nov World Invitational Hula Festival, Honolulu (Oahu)

first 2 wks Nov Hawaii International Film Festival, Honolulu (Oahu)

mid-Nov Triple Crown of Surfing, Hawaiian Pro, Ali'i Beach Park, Hale'iwa (Oahu)

late Nov PGA Grand Slam; golf tournament, Po'ipū (Kauai)

late Nov/early Dec Triple Crown of Surfing, World Cup, Sunset Beach (Oahu)

early Dec Triple Crown of Surfing, Pipe Masters, Banzai Pipeline (Oahu)

2nd Sun in Dec Honolulu Marathon (Oahu)

Dec 25 Hawaii Bowl, Aloha Stadium, Honolulu (Oahu).

Note that the exact dates of surfing contests, and in some cases the venues as well, depend on the state of the waves. A more detailed selection of festivals and events on each island appears in the relevant chapter introduction.

Ocean sports and beach safety

Hawaii's vast tourism industry is rooted in the picture-book appeal of its endless palm-fringed sandy beaches and crystal-clear turquoise ocean. The opportunities for sea sports in the islands are almost infinite, ranging from snorkeling and scuba diving to fishing and whale watching, as well as Hawaii's greatest gift to the world, the art of surfing. It's all too easy, however, to forget that Hawaiian beaches can be deadly as well as beautiful, and you need to know exactly what you're doing before you enter the water.

No one owns any stretch of beach in Hawaii. Every beach in the state – defined as the area below the vegetation line – is regarded as **public property**. That doesn't mean that you're entitled to stroll across any intervening land between the ocean and the nearest highway; always use the clearly signposted "public right of way" footpaths. Whatever impression the large oceanfront hotels may attempt to convey, they can't stop you from using the beaches out front; they can only restrict, but not refuse to supply, parking places for non-guests.

What constitutes the **best beach** in Hawaii is a matter of personal taste, but there are candidates on each of the major islands. For sheer looks, head for **Mākena Beach** on Maui, **Sunset Beach** on Oahu, **Kē'ē Beach** on Kauai, **Kehena Beach** on the Big Island, or **Pāpōhaku Beach** on Molokai. If you want to swim in safety as well, then try **Hāpuna Beach** on the Big Island, **'Anini** on Kauai, **Kailua** on Oahu, or the **Kama'ole** beaches on Maui. And for glamour, of course, there's no beating **Waikīkī**.

See the color section *Blue Hawaii* for more details on the state's beaches, along with surfing and whale watching.

Ocean sports

With average water temperatures of between 75°F and 82°F (24–28°C), the sea in Hawaii is ideal for a wide range of ocean sports.

Snorkeling

Probably the easiest activity for beginners is **snorkeling**. Equipped with mask, snorkel, and fins, you can while away hours and days having face-to-face encounters with the rainbow-colored populations of Hawaii's reefs and lava pools. Well-known sites include **Hanauma Bay** in southeast Oahu, **Kealakekua Bay** on the Big Island, and the islet of **Molokini** off Maui.

You can **rent** snorkel equipment on all the islands, at rates ranging upwards from $5 per day/$10 per week. One reliable source on every island is Snorkel Bob's (ⓦwww.snorkelbob.com).

Scuba diving

With endless networks of submarine lava tubes to explore, and the chance to get close to some amazing marine life forms, Hawaii makes a great **scuba diving** destination. The Big Island and Maui are the most popular of the islands, but experts rate Lanai even higher, and Kauai is also acquiring a reputation; you'll find a detailed overview, plus lists of diving-boat operators, in the introduction to each chapter. The typical cost for a two-tank boat diving trip for a certified diver is around $110; beginners pay around $20 more than that, and every operator offers short courses leading to certification. Note that for medical reasons you shouldn't dive within 24 hours of flying or even ascending significantly above sea level, for example towards the summits of Haleakalā on Maui or Mauna Kea on the Big Island.

Surfing

The place that invented **surfing** – long before the foreigners came – remains its greatest arena. A recurring theme in ancient legends has young men frittering away endless days in the waves rather than facing up to their duties; now young people from all over the world flock to Hawaii to do just that. The sport was popularized early in the twentieth century by champion Olympic swimmer **Duke Kahanamoku**, the original Waikīkī Beach Boy. He toured the world with his sixteen-foot board, demonstrating his skills to admiring crowds, and was responsible for introducing surfing to Australia.

Waikīkī lost its best surf breaks when it was relandscaped at the start of the tourist boom, but with advances in techniques and technology, surfing has never been more popular. Oahu's fabled **North Shore** is a haven for surf-bums, who ride the waves around Waimea Bay and hang out in the coffee bars of Hale'iwa. Favored spots elsewhere include **Hanalei Bay** on Kauai and **Honolua Bay** on Maui, but surfing at such legendary sites is for experts only. However much you've surfed at home, you need to be very sure you're up to it before you have a go in Hawaii; start by sampling the conditions at the lesser surf-spots to be found on all the islands. Be warned that surfing is forbidden at some of Hawaii's most popular beaches, to prevent collisions with ordinary bathers.

Surfing lessons for beginners are on offer in most tourist areas, costing anything from $25 per hour and coming with a guarantee that you'll ride a wave on your own before it's over. They're great fun, and they really work. An equally exhilarating way to get a taste for the surf is to use a smaller **boogie board**, which you lie on.

Windsurfing

Since Robby Naish of Kailua won the first world championships in the 1970s, at the age of 13, Hawaii has been recognized as the spiritual home of **windsurfing**. Maui is the prime goal for enthusiasts from around the world, and many of them find that Hawaiian waters present challenges on a vastly different scale to what they're used to at home. If you find an oceanfront parking lot on Maui filled with shiny rental cars and bursting with tanned tourists sporting Lycra clothing and expensive equipment, the chances are you're at a beginners' beach. Salt-caked local rustbuckets and cut-off denims are the markers of demanding beaches like **Ho'okipa Beach Park**, the venue for windsurfing's World Cup.

Fishing

Big-game **fishing**, for marlin especially, is a major attraction for many visitors to Hawaii. On the Kona coast of the **Big Island**, Kailua plays host each August to the prestigious Hawaiian International Billfish Tournament, while fishing charter vessels are available year-round at Honokōhau Harbor, a few miles north. A smaller selection of boats leave from Lahaina and Mā'alaea harbors on **Maui**.

Details on fishing regulations, and licenses for freshwater fishing ($5–20), can be obtained in person or online from the Division of Aquatic Resources in Honolulu (☎808/587-0109, ⊛www.hawaii.gov/dlnr).

Whale watching

A large proportion of the North Pacific's three thousand **humpback whales** winter in Hawaiian waters, between late November and early April. They're especially fond of the shallow channels between Maui, Molokai, and Lanai, and are often clearly visible from the coastal highways. In season, **whale-watching** boats set off from all the major islands, and most operators are confident enough to guarantee sightings.

Ocean safety

Hawaii is the remotest archipelago on earth, which means that **waves** have two thousand miles of the Pacific Ocean to build up their strength before they come crashing into the islands. Anyone born in Hawaii is brought up with a healthy respect for the sea, and learns to watch out for all sorts of signs before they swim. You'll be told to throw sticks into the waves to see how they move, or to look for disturbances in the surf that indicate powerful currents. Unless you have local expertise, however, you're better off sticking to the official beach parks and most popular spots, especially those that are shielded by offshore reefs. Not all beaches have lifeguards and warning flags, and unattended beaches are not necessarily safe. Look for other bathers, but whatever your experience elsewhere, don't assume you'll be able to cope with the same conditions as the local kids. Always ask for advice and above all follow the cardinal rule – **never turn your back on the water**.

The beaches that have the most accidents and **drownings** are those where waves of four feet or more break directly onto the

Emergency numbers

Police, fire brigade and ambulance
☎911
Ocean Search and Rescue
☎1-800/552-6458

shore. This varies according to the season, so beaches that are idyllic in summer can be storm-tossed death traps between October and April. If you get caught in a rip current or undertow and find yourself being dragged out to sea, stay calm and remember that the vast majority of such currents disappear within a hundred yards of the shore. Never exhaust yourself by trying to swim against them, but simply allow yourself to be carried out until the force weakens, and then swim first to one side and then back to the shore.

Sea creatures to avoid include *wana* (black spiky **sea urchins**), Portuguese man-of-war **jellyfish**, and **coral** in general, which can give painful, infected cuts. **Shark attacks** are much rarer than popular imagination suggests; in 2006, 62 occurred worldwide, of which four were fatal and only three of which, all non-fatal, occurred in Hawaii. Those that do happen are usually due to "misunderstandings," such as surfers idling on their boards who look a bit too much like turtles from below. That probably occurred in the notorious case of 13-year-old Kauai surfer Bethany Hamilton, who lost her left arm while surfing at Tunnels Beach in 2003.

Sun safety

Only expose yourself to the harsh **tropical sun** in moderation; a mere fifteen to thirty minutes is the safe recommendation for the first day. The sun is strongest between 10am and 3pm, and even on overcast days human skin still absorbs harmful UV rays. Use plenty of **sunscreen** – doctors recommend Sun Protection Factor (SPF) 30 for Hawaii – and reapply after swimming. Note, however, that some marine life sanctuaries forbid the use of sunscreen by bathers, which should be enough to discourage you from swimming altogether. Drink lots of (nonalcoholic) liquids as well, to stave off dehydration.

Hiking and camping

Hawaii is one of the most exciting hiking destinations imaginable. Well-maintained trails guide walkers through scenery that ranges from dense tropical rainforest to remote deserts and active volcanoes. At times, you may even find yourself in some pretty uncompromising wilderness.

However, **camping** in Hawaii need not be a battle with the elements. All the islands hold lovely oceanfront campgrounds where you don't have to do anything more than drive in and pitch your tent; some offer cabins for rent so you needn't even do that.

For more information – including top hikes and photos – see the *Hiking in Hawaii* color section.

Camping

Advice on the best **campgrounds** on each island, and how to obtain permits to stay at them, is given in the introduction to each chapter of the Guide. The majority of campgrounds are in the public **parks** scattered across each island. There's a complicated hierarchy of county, state, and national parks, each with different authorities, so it's not always obvious whom to contact for permission to camp in a particular spot. However, one thing you cannot do is just set up your tent on some unoccupied piece of land; only camp at designated sites.

On a camping (as opposed to backpacking) vacation, your best bet is to spend most of your time at the **County Beach Parks** ranged along the shoreline of each island. The most appealing of these are on the **Big Island** – where Spencer Beach Park and Punalu'u are especially attractive – and along the north shore of **Kauai**, but Maui and Oahu also have their moments.

County authorities are engaged in a constant struggle to discourage semi-permanent encampments of homeless local people from developing at certain sites, so precise regulations on maximum lengths of stay, and even whether a particular park is open at all, tend to change at a moment's notice. On Oahu, for example, all public campgrounds are closed on Wednesday and Thursday nights.

Many of the campgrounds in Hawaii's **state** and **national** parks are in remote spots that can only be reached on foot, but they tend to be set amid utterly sublime scenery. Among the best are the backcountry sites along the **Kalalau Trail** on Kauai's Nā Pali coast, and the national park campgrounds in **Hawaii Volcanoes** park on the Big Island and atop **Haleakalā** on Maui, both of which also offer rudimentary cabins for rent.

For a full list of state parks and their facilities, contact the Department of Land and Natural Resources in Honolulu (℡808/587-0300, Ⓦwww.hawaii.gov/dlnr).

Hiking

All the best **hiking trails** in Hawaii are described in detail in the relevant chapters. Every island has at least one inspiring trail, but the two best destinations for hikers have to be Kauai and the Big Island.

Kauai has the dual attractions of the spectacular Nā Pali coast, where the **Kalalau Trail** clings to the cliffs through eleven miles of magnificent unspoiled valleys, and Kōke'e State Park high above, where the **Alaka'i Swamp Trail** and the **Awa'awapuhi Trail** trek through the rainforest for amazing overviews of similar rugged scenery.

On the Big Island, it would be easy to spend a week day-hiking trails such as the **Halemaumau** and **Kīlauea Iki** trails in Volcanoes National Park, without the thrill wearing off, and there's potential for countless longer backpacking expeditions.

Maui offers the **Sliding Sands Trail** through the heart of Haleakalā, and mountain hikes like the **Waihe'e Ridge Trail**, while on Molokai, with local guides, you can clamber through the verdant **Hālawa Valley** to reach a pair of superb waterfalls. Even Honolulu

National parks admissions

Hawaii has two fully-fledged national parks, **Haleakalā** on Maui (p.346) and **Hawaii Volcanoes** on the Big Island (p.250), while the Big Island also holds a national monument, the **Puʻuhonua O Hōnaunau** (p.187).

All charge for admission, but also sell the park system's national passes. The $50 **National Parks** pass, which provides admission to all national parks and monuments, will suffice for visitors to Hawaii. Both the **Golden Access** passport, free to US citizens or residents with disabilities, and the **Golden Age** passport, available to US citizens or residents aged over 62 for a $10 one-time fee, offer unlimited admission for life to all national parks in the US.

itself has the lovely rainforest trails through **Makiki** and **Mānoa** valleys.

As a rule, all trails remain passable all year, but you can expect conditions to be much muddier between November and April.

Equipment and safety

Hiking trails in Hawaii tend to fall into two basic types. There are the beautiful scenic ones, to waterfalls or through lush valleys, which tend to be very wet and muddy; and then there are the harsh exposed ones across rugged volcanic terrain, where the bare lava rock is capable of slashing any footwear to ribbons. Either way, a sturdy pair of **hiking boots** is essential. Other equipment should include rain gear, a flashlight, insect repellent, sunscreen and sunglasses, some attention-seeking device such as a whistle or a piece of brightly colored clothing, and a basic first aid kit. If you're backpacking, of course, you'll need a waterproof tent and sleeping bag as well. Take things slowly if you're heading up the volcanoes on Maui or the Big Island, as there's a real risk of altitude sickness; if you feel symptoms such as a heavy pulse, shortness of breath, headache, and nausea, come back down again. Warm clothing is also essential, especially with night temperatures low enough to cause hypothermia.

While hiking, be wary of following even dry streambeds and never wade across streams that are more than waist-high; and allow plenty of time to finish any trail by sunset, which is never later than 7pm and usually much earlier. On typical Hawaiian trails you shouldn't reckon on walking more than 1.5 miles per hour. Most hiking deaths occur when hikers are stranded on cliffs or ledges and then panic; certain trails, as indicated throughout this book, but especially on Kauai, have some really hair-raising spots that you should avoid if you're prone to vertigo.

Carry plenty of **water** when you hike, and drink it as you need it – don't try to conserve water supplies as it takes more water to recover from dehydration than it does to prevent it. Never drink untreated water; **leptospirosis**, a bacterial disease carried by rats and mice in particular, can be contracted through drinking stream water (filtering alone will not purify it) or even from wading through fresh water if you have any cuts or abrasions. Symptoms range from diarrhea, fever, and chills through to kidney or heart failure, and appear in anything from two to twenty days. In case of infection, seek treatment immediately; for more information, call the Hawaii Department of Health on Oahu (☎808/586-4586, ⓦwww.state.hi.us/health).

Shopping

Honolulu is very much the shopping capital of Hawaii, and any stories you may have heard about Japanese tourists coming to Hawaii specifically to shop apply almost exclusively to Honolulu, where malls like the Ala Moana Center hold outlets of all the big names in world fashion. Residents of the other islands, too, tend to think nothing of flying over to Oahu for a day's shopping, and if you don't spend much time on the island you may come home from your vacation with fewer gifts and souvenirs than you expected. The prints, posters and T-shirts piled high along the sidewalks of Waikīkī and other tourist areas are all well and good if you think that a gecko on a surfboard is real neat, but stores and galleries selling high-quality indigenous arts and crafts are few and far between. For more on shops and malls in Honolulu and Waikīkī, see p.127.

Hawaiian crafts and produce

Some of the most attractive products of Hawaii are just too ephemeral to take home. That goes for virtually all the orchids and tropical flowers on sale everywhere, and unfortunately it's also true of *leis*.

Leis (pronounced *lays*) are flamboyant decorative garlands, usually composed of flowers such as the fragrant *melia* (the plumeria or frangipani) or the bright-red *lehua* blossom (from the *'ō'hia* tree), but sometimes also made from feathers, shells, seeds, or nuts. They're worn by both men and women, above all on celebrations or gala occasions – election-winning politicians are absolutely deluged in them, as are the statues of Kamehameha the Great and Queen Lili'uokalani in Honolulu on state holidays. Sadly, not every arriving tourist is festooned

with a *lei* these days, but you'll probably be way-*leied* at a *lū'au* or some such occasion, while if you're around for Lei Day (May 1), everyone's at it. If you want to buy one, most towns have a store or two with a supply of flower *leis* kept in refrigerated cabinets, but Chinatown in Honolulu is the acknowledged center of the art.

Colorful Hawaiian **clothing**, such as aloha shirts and the cover-all "Mother-Hubbard"-style *mu'umu'u* dress, is sold everywhere, though classic designs are surprisingly rare, and you tend to see the same stylized prints over and over again. Otherwise, the main local crafts to look out for are *lau hala* **weaving**, in which mats, hats, baskets, and the like are created by plaiting the large leaves (*lau*) of the spindly legged pandanus (*hala*) tree, and **wood turning**, with fine bowls made from native dark woods such as *koa*.

Travel essentials

Costs

Although it's possible to have an inexpensive vacation in Hawaii, there's no getting away from the fact that prices on the islands are consistently higher – on the scale of around forty percent – than in the rest of the United States. Locals call it the "Paradise Tax" – the price you pay for living in paradise.

How much you spend each day is, of course, up to you, but it's hard to get any sort of breakfast for under $8, a cheap lunch can easily come to $15, and an evening meal in a restaurant, with drinks, is likely to cost $30 or more per person, even if you're trying to economize. All the major islands have at least one hostel, charging around $20 for a dorm bed, but otherwise even the cheapest hotels tend to charge over $80 a night for a double room, and a rental car with gas won't cost less than $30 a day. It's easy to spend $100 per person per day before you've done anything: pay for a snorkel cruise or a *lū'au*, and you've cleared $150.

Throughout the Guide, you'll find detailed price information for lodging and eating on all the islands. Unless otherwise indicated, hotel price symbols (explained on p.35) refer to the price of a double room for most of the year, while restaurant prices are for food only and don't include drinks or service.

A state **sales tax** of 4.166 percent is currently imposed on all transactions, and is almost never included in the prices displayed in stores or on menus. Hotels impose an additional 7.25 percent tax, adding a total of 11.42 percent to accommodation bills.

Electricity

Hawaii's electricity supply, like that on the US mainland, uses 100 volts AC. Plugs are standard American two-pins.

Entry requirements for foreign travelers

Under the **visa waiver scheme**, passport-holders from Britain, Ireland, Australia, New Zealand, and most European countries do not require visas for trips to the United States, including Hawaii, so long as they stay less than ninety days in the US, and have an onward or return ticket. Instead you simply fill in the visa waiver form handed out on incoming planes. Immigration control takes place at your point of arrival on US soil.

For you to be eligible for the visa waiver scheme, your passport must be **machine-readable**, with a barcode-style number. All children need to have their own individual passports. Holders of older, unreadable passports should therefore either obtain new ones or apply for visas prior to travel. For full details, visit ⓦhttp://travel.state.gov.

Gay and lesbian travelers

The greatest concentration of gay and lesbian activism in Hawaii is in Honolulu, though the state as a whole is liberal on social issues. During the 1990s, Hawaii was at the forefront of the national movement towards the legalization of same-sex marriages, and a 1997 state law granted equal rights to same-gender couples and their families in most areas of the law. "Gay marriage" as such, however, is not yet on the statute book, and the activist baton has in recent years passed to other states.

Full listings for Honolulu's gay and lesbian scene appear on p.126. Gay-friendly **accommodation** can be found on all the islands, including the *Waikīkī Beachside Hotel & Hostel* (see p.69) and *Cabana at Waikīkī* (see p.70) in Waikīkī; the *Sunseeker Resort* (see p.328) on Maui; *Mahina Kai* (see p.468) on Kauai and *Hale Ohia* (see p.268) on the Big Island.

Pacific Ocean Holidays (PO Box 88245, Honolulu HI 96830-8245; ☏808/944-4700 or 1-800/735-6600, ⓦhttp://gayhawaii vacations.com) organizes all-inclusive **package vacations** in Hawaii for gay and lesbian travelers, and maintains the useful ⓦwww.gayhawaii.com website.

The best-known gay **beaches** are Queen's Surf and Diamond Head on Oahu, Donkey Beach on Kauai, Honokōhau Beach on the Big Island, and the Little Beach at Mākena on Maui.

Inoculations

No inoculations or vaccinations are required by law in order to enter Hawaii, though some authorities suggest a polio vaccination.

Insurance

In view of the high cost of medical care in the US, all travelers visiting the US from overseas should be sure to buy some form of **travel insurance**. American and Canadian citizens should check that you're not already covered – some homeowners' or renters' policies are valid on vacation, and credit cards such as American Express often include some medical or other insurance, while most Canadians are covered for medical mishaps overseas by their provincial health plans. If you only need trip cancellation/interruption coverage (to supplement your existing plan), this is generally available at about $6 per $100.

Rough Guides has teamed up with Columbus Direct to offer you **travel insurance** that can be tailored to suit your needs. Products include a low-cost **backpacker** option for long stays; a **short break** option for city getaways; a typical **holiday package** option; and others. There are also annual **multi-trip** policies for those who travel regularly. Different sports and activities (trekking, diving, etc) can usually be covered if required.

See our website (®www.roughguides insurance.com) for eligibility and purchasing options. Alternatively, UK residents should call ☎0870/033 9988; Australians should call ☎1300/669 999; and New Zealanders should call ☎0800/55 9911. All other nationalities should call ☎+44 870/890 2843.

Internet access

Internet access is fairly widely available in Hawaii. Most public and university libraries offer free access; hostels tend to have a computer or two where guests can check email; and both copier outlets and Internet cafés allow customers to go online.

If you're carrying a laptop and want to get connected, browse ®www.kropla.com for details of how to plug in your laptop on the road. **Wireless access** is widespread.

Mail

There are **post offices** in all the main towns, generally open between 8.30am and 4pm on weekdays and for an hour or two on Saturday mornings. Mail service is extremely slow as all mail between Hawaii and the rest of the world, and even between Hawaiian islands other than Oahu, is routed via Honolulu. From anywhere except Honolulu, allow a week for your letter to reach destinations in the US and as much as two weeks or more for the rest of the world. From Honolulu itself, reckon on four days to the mainland US and eight days to anywhere else.

Maps

The best general-purpose **maps** of the individual islands – there's one each for Oahu, the Big Island, Maui, and Kauai, while Molokai and Lanai are combined on a single sheet – are published by the University of Hawaii, at $3.95, and are widely available at island bookstores.

Plenty of free maps are also distributed on the islands themselves – you'll almost certainly get a booklet of maps from your rental car agency. These can be useful for pinpointing specific hotels and restaurants, but only the University of Hawaii maps are at all reliable for minor roads.

If you need detailed **hiking maps**, call in at the state parks office in Honolulu or on each specific island, as detailed in the relevant chapters; their free map of Kauai, for example, is excellent. You could also buy the **topographic maps** produced by the United States Geological Survey (®www.usgs.gov), which are widely sold at specialist bookstores in Hawaii.

Money

Most visitors find that there's no reason to carry large amounts of cash or travelers' checks to Hawaii. Automatic teller machines (**ATMs**), which accept most cards issued by domestic and foreign banks, can be found almost everywhere; call your own bank if you're in any doubt. The two major banks are the Bank of Hawaii, which belongs to the Plus network of ATMs, and the First Hawaiian Bank, which belongs to the Plus and Cirrus networks. Even the smallest town tends to hold a branch of one or the other.

If you do want to take **travelers' checks** – which offer the great security of knowing that lost or stolen checks will be replaced – be sure to get them issued in US dollars. Foreign currency, whether cash or travelers' checks, can be hard to exchange, so foreign travelers should change some of their money into dollars at home.

For most services, it's taken for granted that you'll be paying with a **credit card**. Hotels and car rental companies routinely require an imprint of your card whether or not you intend to use it to pay.

Phones

The **telephone area code** for the entire state of Hawaii is ☎808. Calls within any one island count as local; you don't need to dial the area code and it costs a flat-rate 50¢ on pay phones. To call another island, put ☎1-808 before the phone number; charges vary according to the time of day and distance involved.

Calling home from Hawaii

Hotels impose huge surcharges, so it's best to use a **phone card** for long-distance calls. In preference to the ones issued by the major phone companies, you'll find it simpler and cheaper to choose from the various pre-paid cards sold in almost all supermarkets and general stores.

To place a call **from Hawaii** to the rest of the world, dial ☎011 then the relevant country code as follows:

Australia	61
Britain	44
Canada	1
Ireland	353
New Zealand	64

To make an international call **to Hawaii**, dial your country's international access code, then 1 for the US, then 808 for Hawaii.

Mobile phones

If you want to use your **mobile** phone in Hawaii, you'll need to check with your phone provider whether it will work there, and what the call charges are. Unless you have a tri-band phone, it is unlikely that a mobile bought for use outside the US will work inside the States, while many US phones only work within their local area code.

Public holidays

As well as observing the national public holidays, Hawaii also has a number of its own:

Jan 1 New Year's Day
3rd Mon in Jan Dr Martin Luther King Jr's Birthday
3rd Mon in Feb Presidents' Day
March 26 Prince Kūhiō Day
Easter Monday
May 1 Lei Day
Last Mon in May Memorial Day
June 11 Kamehameha Day
July 4 Independence Day
3rd Fri in Aug Admission Day
1st Mon in Sept Labor Day
2nd Mon in Oct Columbus Day
Nov 11 Veterans' Day
4th Thurs in Nov Thanksgiving
Dec 25 Christmas Day

Quarantine

Very stringent restrictions apply to the importation of all plants and animals into Hawaii, mainly as a protection for the state's many endangered indigenous species. Cats and dogs have to stay in **quarantine** for 120 days, though by meeting certain very specific conditions that period can be reduced to thirty or even five days. If you were hoping to bring an alligator or a hamster, forget it. Full regulations on animals and plants are detailed online at ⓦ www.hawaiiag.org.

Restrooms

Doors in some public restrooms are labeled in Hawaiian: *Kāne* for Men, *Wahine* for Women.

Senior travelers

Hawaii is a popular destination for senior travelers; most attractions offer reduced rates for seniors and many hotels have special deals on rooms in quiet periods. For discounts on accommodation and vehicle rental, US residents aged 50 or over should consider joining the American Association of Retired Persons (℡1-800/424-3410; ⊛www.aarp.org). The Golden Age passport, which entitles holders to free admission to US National Parks, is detailed on p.45.

The University of Hawaii at Hilo on the Big Island runs Elderhostel programs each summer on all the Hawaiian islands (℡808/974-7555, ⊛http://conference.uhh .hawaii.edu/elderhostel.html). Participating senior citizens take courses in various aspects of Hawaiian culture and history, with fees covering board, lodging, and tuition. Elderhostel's national website is ⊛www .elderhostel.org.

Smoking

Smoking is now banned in all restaurants and bars in Hawaii.

Time

Unlike most of the United States, Hawaii does not observe Daylight Saving Time. Therefore, from 2am on the second Sunday in March until 2am on the first Sunday in November, the time difference between Hawaii and the US West Coast is three hours, not the usual two; the time difference between Hawaii and the mountain region is four hours, not three; and the islands are six hours earlier than the East Coast, not five. Hawaiian time is from ten to eleven hours behind the UK. In fact it's behind just about everywhere else; although New Zealand and Australia might seem to be two and four hours respectively behind Honolulu time, they're on the other side of the International Date Line, so are actually almost a full day ahead.

Tipping

Wait staff in restaurants expect tips of at least fifteen percent, in bars a little less. Hotel porters and bellhops should receive at least $2 per piece of luggage, and housekeeping staff at least $2 per night.

Tourist information

The Hawaii Visitors and Convention Bureau (HVCB) has offices (known as chapters) on every island. Its official website, ⊛www .gohawaii.com, also holds links to businesses and operators on all the islands, though bear in mind that they pay to have their activities publicized.

Racks of leaflets, brochures, and magazines – a good source of free offers and discount coupons – are prominently displayed in all the major hotels, malls, and airports. In heavily touristed areas, such as Waikīkī, Kihei, and Lahaina on Maui, Kapa‘a on Kauai, and Kailua on the Big Island, you'll also find plenty of **activities centers**. Masquerading as information kiosks, these are primarily concerned with persuading you to buy tickets for some specific activity such as a cruise, horse ride, island tour, or whatever; the worst are often fronts for time-share companies as well.

Hawaii Visitors Bureau offices

Main Office Waikīkī Business Plaza, Suite 801, 2270 Kalākaua Ave, Honolulu, HI 96815 ℡808/923-1811 or 1-800/464-2924, ⊛www .gohawaii.com.
Big Island Visitors Bureau 250 Keawe St, Hilo, HI 96720 ℡808/961-5797 or 1-800/648-2441; and 250 Waikoloa Beach Drive, Suite B-15, Waikoloa HI 96748 ℡808/886-1655, ⊛www .bigisland.org.
Destination Lanai PO Box 700, Lāna‘i City, HI 96763 ℡808/565-7600 or 1-800/947-4774, ⊛www.visitlanai.net.
Kauai Visitors Bureau 4334 Rice St, Suite 101, Līhu‘e, HI 96766 ℡808/245-3971 or 1-800/262-1400, ⊛www.kauaidiscovery.com.
Maui Visitors Bureau 1727 Wili Pā Loop, Wailuku, HI 96793 ℡808/244-3530 or 1-800/525-6284, ⊛www.visitmaui.com.
Molokai Visitors Association PO Box 960, Kaunakakai, HI 96748 ℡808/553-3876 or 1-800/800-6367 (US & Canada), ⊛www .molokai-hawaii.com.
Oahu Visitors Bureau 733 Bishop St, Suite 1872, Honolulu, HI 96813 ℡808/524-0722 or 1-877/525-6248, ⊛www.visit-oahu.com.

Useful websites

Web addresses for hotels, activity operators, and other businesses are listed throughout the Guide. You can also find copious links and listings on sites such as Aloha from Hawaii (⊛www.aloha-hawaii.com); ⊛www.bigisland .com; ⊛www.e-hawaii.com; ⊛www.maui.net;

and ⓦwww.kauai.com. The most useful sites for current news and listings are run by the two daily Honolulu newspapers, the *Star Bulletin* (ⓦwww.starbulletin.com) and the *Advertiser* (ⓦwww.honoluluadvertiser.com), and also the weekly papers on each island such as *Honolulu Weekly* (ⓦwww.honolulu weekly.com), Maui's *Haleakala Times* (ⓦwww .haleakalatimes.com), and the *Hawaii Island Journal* (ⓦhttp://hawaiiislandjournal.com).

Travelers with disabilities

When it comes to meeting the needs of travelers with disabilities, Hawaii is among the best-equipped vacation destinations in the world. Oahu has been ranked as the most accessible place in the United States by the Society for the Advancement of Travel for the Handicapped (ⓦwww.sath .org), a nonprofit travel industry group that includes tour operators, travel agents, managers of hotels, and airlines as well as people with disabilities. Given time, the organization will pass on all queries to the relevant members.

The **State of Hawaii Disability and Communication Access Board** produces a wide range of reports on facilities for disabled travelers on each of the islands; you can download these from their website (☎808/586-8121, ⓦwww.state.hi.us/health /dcab/). In addition, Access–Able (ⓦwww .access–able.com) carries detailed reports on the accessibility of hotels and other facilities throughout Hawaii.

Rental cars with hand controls are available from Avis and Hertz outlets; arrangements should be made at least a month in advance. On Oahu, transportation for travelers with disabilities, including sightseeing tours and trips to special events, is available through Handi-Cabs of the Pacific (☎808/524-3866, ⓦwww.handicabs.com), while CR Newton (☎808/949-8389 or 1-800/545-2078, ⓦwww.crnewton.com), rents wheelchairs, scooters, and crutches. Most TheBus vehicles are adapted to suit passengers with physical disabilities.

Guide dogs for the blind are exempt from Hawaii's otherwise strict **quarantine** regulations; full details can be obtained from the Animal Quarantine Facility (☎808/483-7171, ⓦwww.hawaii.gov).

Weddings

To get **married** in Hawaii, you must have a valid state license, available from the Department of Health, Marriage License Office, 1250 Punchbowl St, Honolulu HI 96813 (☎808/586-4545; ⓦwww.hawaii.gov/doh), or agents on the other islands (hotels have details). Licenses cost $60 and are valid for thirty days; there's no waiting period. Weddings are very big business here; most major resorts offer their own marriage planners, and the Hawaii Visitors Bureau keeps full lists of organizers.

Guide

Guide

Oahu

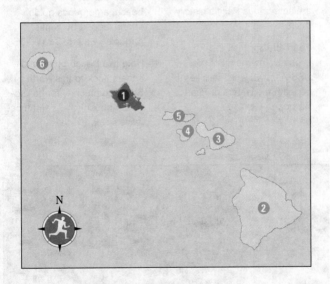

CHAPTER 1 # Highlights

* **Waikīkī Beach** Learn to surf, or just sip a cocktail, on Hawaii's most famous beach. See p.77

* **Nu'uanu Pali State Park** Site of an ancient battle and now a breathtaking viewpoint overlooking windward Oahu. See p.107

* **Bishop Museum** The world's finest collection of Polynesian artifacts brings Pacific history to life. See p.108

* **Pearl Harbor** Visit the evocative memorial of the USS *Arizona*, which still lies beneath the waters of Pearl Harbor. See p.110

* **Auntie Genoa Keawe** Every Thursday, this amazing octogenarian falsetto singer offers Waikīkī's finest weekly musical treat. See p.123

* **Ala Moana Center** Every visitor to Honolulu spends at least half a day in this vast, cosmopolitan shopping mall. See p.127

* **Kailua Beach** Oahu's loveliest beach, a gorgeous golden strand lapped by gentle turquoise waters. See p.136

* **Hale'iwa** Beach bums and surfers flock to this North Shore community for its laid-back atmosphere... and those waves. See p.148

△ Waīkīki from the ocean

Oahu

A round three quarters of the population of Hawaii – just over 900,000 people – live on the island of **Oahu**. Around half of them are packed into the city of **Honolulu**, which remains the financial and political power-house of the whole archipelago. While it's a genuinely vibrant city in its own right, the fact that ninety percent of visitors to Hawaii spend at least one night on Oahu inevitably means that tourism dominates the local economy.

The vast majority of hotel rooms on the island are squeezed into the tower-block enclave of **Waikīkī**, just east of downtown Honolulu. Although that's a blessing for local residents, it makes it hard for visitors to create their own personal, individual travel experiences on Oahu. Surfers flock to the fabled **North Shore** on the island's opposite end just over an hour's drive away, but almost everyone else ends up in Waikīkī, where even the most determined hedonist can find the hectic resort lifestyle palls after a few days.

Honolulu itself is a remarkably attractive city, ringed by eroded volcanoes and reaching back into a succession of gorgeous valleys, and as a major world crossroads it has a broad ethnic mix, plus strong cultural traditions and lively nightlife. There are great beaches scattered all over the island – not just in Waikīkī – while plantation towns, ancient ruins, and luscious scenery await more adventurous explorers.

Tourist organizations like to claim that Oahu means "the gathering place." Both the translation, and the common suggestion that in order to see Hawaii, you must first see Oahu, are spurious. Don't feel that Oahu is a place to be avoided at all costs, but if you spend more than a few days in Waikīkī at the start of your Hawaiian vacation, you may end up wishing that you'd moved on to the other islands a little faster.

A brief history of Oahu

Before the coming of the foreigners, Oahu was probably the least significant of the four major Hawaiian islands. Nonetheless, it was among the very first places in the state to attract Polynesian settlers. Traces of occupation dating back to around 200 AD have been found at Kahana Valley and Bellows Field. The windward valleys of the east coast are thought to have held sizeable agricultural populations, while the sheltered coastline of Pearl Harbor supported an intricate network of fishponds. Not until the eighteenth century, however, did any individual chief become powerful enough to subdue the whole island, and by that time the rulers of both Maui and the Big Island were capable of launching successful invasions.

Captain Cook never set foot on Oahu. However, shortly after he was killed at Kealakekua Bay during his second visit to the Hawaiian islands in 1779, his two

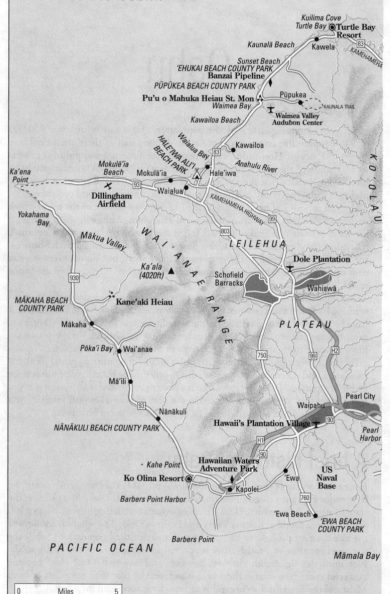

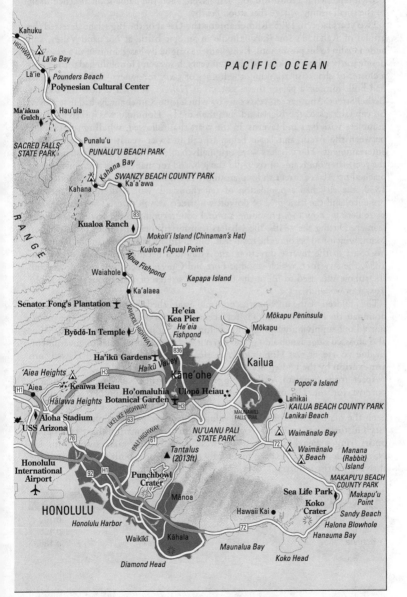

N

PACIFIC OCEAN

Kahuku
Lāʻie Bay
Lāʻie
Pounders Beach
Polynesian Cultural Center

Maʻakua Gulch   Hauʻula

SACRED FALLS STATE PARK

Punaluʻu
PUNALUʻU BEACH PARK

Kahana Bay
SWANZY BEACH COUNTY PARK
Kahana   Kaʻaʻawa

83

Kualoa Ranch

Mokoliʻi Island (Chinaman's Hat)
Kualoa (ʻĀpua) Point

ʻĀpua Fishpond

Waiahole
Kapapa Island
Kaʻalaea

Senator Fong's Plantation

KAHEKILI HIGHWAY

Heʻeia Kea Pier
Heʻeia Fishpond

Mōkapu Peninsula

Byōdō-In Temple

Mōkapu

Haʻikū Gardens
Haikū Valley
836

Kāneʻohe

Kailua

ʻAiea Heights
H3
Keaiwa Heiau
Hoʻomaluhia Botanical Garden

Ulopō Heiau

Popoiʻa Island

Hālawa Heights
LIKELIKE HIGHWAY
63
H3

Lanikai
KAILUA BEACH COUNTY PARK
Lanikai Beach

H1
ʻAiea
Aloha Stadium
USS Arizona

78

MAUNAWILI FALLS TRAIL

NUʻUANU PALI STATE PARK
PALI HIGHWAY
61

72
Waimānalo Bay
Waimānalo Beach

Honolulu International Airport

92
H1

Tantalus (2013ft)

Manana (Rabbit) Island

Punchbowl Crater

Mānoa

Sea Life Park
Koko Crater

MAKAPUʻU BEACH COUNTY PARK
Makapuʻu Point

HONOLULU

Hawaii Kai
72
Sandy Beach
Halona Blowhole
Hanauma Bay

Honolulu Harbor

Kāhala

Waikīkī

Maunalua Bay

Koko Head

Diamond Head

ships put in at Waimea Bay on Oahu's North Shore. By the time Captain Vancouver (who had been midshipman on the *Discovery*) returned in 1792, the island had been conquered by Chief Kahekili of Maui. In 1793, Captain William Brown, a British fur trader, noted the existence of a safe anchorage near the spot where the Nu'uanu Stream had created a gap in the coral reef fringing southeastern Oahu. The Hawaiians knew this as *He Awa Kou*, "the harbor of Kou," but Brown renamed it **Honolulu**, or "fair haven," and the name soon attached itself to the small fishing village that stood nearby.

Two years later, in 1795, **Kamehameha the Great** of the Big Island defeated the armies of Kahekili's son Kalanikūpule in an epic battle at Nu'uanu Valley, and added Oahu to his possessions. Kamehameha originally based himself in a grass hut beside the beach at **Waikīkī**. Within ten years, however, Honolulu had turned into a cluster of shacks surrounding the homes of sixty foreigners, and Kamehameha had built himself a palace there, known as *Halehui*, at what is now the foot of Bethel Street. Another ten years on – by which time Kamehameha had first moved his capital back to the Big Island, and then died – Honolulu was a thriving port, complete with bars and taverns. In the years that followed, **whaling** ships sailing between the Arctic and Japan began to call in twice-yearly for provisions and entertainment. The whalers were originally hauled in by Hawaiians standing on the reef; later on, teams of oxen did the job, and for many years an immense rope reached up Alakea Street to loop around a capstan at the foot of Punchbowl. By 1830, the city had a population of ten thousand, with a dominant American presence, and the basic grid of downtown streets was in place. The **missionaries** were here by now too, providing a moral counterpoint to the lawlessness of the seamen. During the 1840s, the whalers transferred their affections to Lahaina on Maui, which had become the royal seat, but in time King Kamehameha III moved his court in the reverse direction, and Honolulu became capital once again. In 1857, the city **fort**, which stood at Fort and Queen streets, was torn down, and the rubble was used to fill in the fifteen-acre stretch of waterfront where Aloha Tower now stands.

The children of the missionaries not only established the businesses that were to dominate the Hawaiian economy for a century – four of the "Big Five" (see p.537) started out supplying whaling ships, before moving into the sugar industry – but also amassed huge landholdings, and gravitated into leading roles in government. In due course, it was Honolulu's American elite that maneuvered Hawaii into **annexation** by the United States.

Apart from **tourism**, Oahu's biggest business these days is as an offshore outpost for the **US military**; on any given day, the numbers of military personnel and tourists on the island are roughly the same. These two forces have been the main influences in the development of modern Honolulu. While the city's historic core remains recognizable, great transformations have taken place on its fringes. **Pearl Harbor**, to the west, is completely taken over by the US Navy, while Waikīkī has been repeatedly reshaped and rebuilt as the focus of the thriving tourist industry.

Oahu overview

Very roughly speaking, Oahu is shaped like a butterfly, with its wings formed by the volcanoes of the **Wai'anae Range** in the west and the wetter, mostly higher **Ko'olau Range** in the east. In between lies the narrow, flat Leilehua Plateau, with the triple lagoon of **Pearl Harbor** at its southern end. The symmetrical outline is only spoiled by the more recent eruptions that elongated its southeast coastline, producing craters such as Punchbowl, Diamond Head, and Koko Head.

With all its suburbs and satellite communities, **Honolulu** stretches along a substantial proportion of the southern coast, squeezed between the mountains and the sea. The golden beaches of **Waikīkī** are what draw in the tourists, but the city can also boast of having world-class museums, a historic downtown area, and some surprisingly rural hiking trails.

Just across the Ko'olaus, the green cliffs of the **east** or **windward coast** are magnificent, lined with relatively calm and secluded beaches and indented with time-forgotten valleys. Towns such as **Kailua**, **Kāne'ohe**, and **Lā'ie** may be far from exciting, but you're unlikely to tire of the sheer beauty of the shoreline drive – so long as you time your forays to miss the peak-hour traffic jams.

Mere mortals can only marvel at the winter waves that make the **North Shore** the world's premier surfing destination; for anyone other than experts, entering the water at that time is almost suicidal. However, **Waimea**, **Sunset**, and **'Ehukai** beaches are compelling spectacles, little **Hale'iwa** makes a refreshing contrast to Waikīkī, and in summer you may manage to find a safe spot somewhere along the North Shore for a swim.

Although the **west** or **leeward coast** of Oahu also holds some fine beaches – including the prime surf spot of **Mākaha** – it remains very much off the beaten track. There's just one route in and out of this side of the island, and the locals are happy to keep it that way.

Getting around Oahu

Oahu is blessed with an exemplary network of public **buses**, officially named **TheBus** (☎ 808/848-5555 or ⓦ www.thebus.org for route information). Radiating out from downtown Honolulu and the Ala Moana Center, the system covers the whole of Oahu. All journeys cost $2 (ages 6–17 $1), with free transfers

Oahu favorites: beaches			
Swimming beaches			
Kailua Beach Park	p.136	Waikīkī Beach	p.77
Mālaekahana Bay	p.143	Waimānolo Beach	p.133
Sandy Beach	p.132		
Snorkel spots			
Hanauma Bay	p.129	Shark's Cove	p.152
Sans Souci Beach	p.82	Waimea Bay Beach Park	p.151
Surf sites			
'Ehukai Beach Park	p.154	Pūpūkea Beach Park	p.152
Mākaha Beach	p.158	Sunset Beach	p.153

to any connecting route if you ask as you board. One of the best sightseeing routes is TheBus #52 or #55, which circles the whole of the Koʻolau Range, including the North Shore and the windward coast, still for just $2. The only disadvantage is that passengers are not allowed to carry large bags or bulky items including surfboards, which rules out using TheBus to get to or from the airport.

For full details of transportation between Waikīkī and the airport, see p.65. Services in Honolulu and Waikīkī are summarized on p.67, together with companies offering **island tours**. If you want to explore Oahu at your own pace, you'd do best to rent a **car** through one of the agencies listed on p.33. However, with parking expensive and traffic heavy, a car is a liability in Waikīkī itself, so think carefully before renting one for your entire stay.

Where to stay

The overwhelming majority of Oahu visitors stay in **Waikīkī**, a couple of miles east of central Honolulu. The city itself holds a handful of hotels, but there are very few alternatives in the rest of the island; the only hotels are the *Turtle Bay Resort* and *Ihilani* resorts, at the far northeast and southwest corners respectively, while the bargain *Backpackers Vacation Inn*, on the North Shore, caters to the surf crowd. Other than a few tiny B&Bs at Kailua and Kāneʻohe on the windward coast, that's about it.

According to official figures, the average room in Waikīkī costs around $150. There's a heavy premium for oceanfront accommodation, however, and away from the beach – bearing in mind that nowhere in Waikīkī is more than a few minutes' walk from the sea – it's easy enough to find something for half that. The sheer quantity of rooms ensures that you're unlikely to find yourself stranded if you arrive without a reservation, and there are several hostels available for budget travelers.

You can **camp** in county parks on Oahu for free, and in state parks for $5 per night, with a permit from the relevant office. However, few sites are worth recommending, and none of those is especially convenient to Honolulu. Furthermore, all county and state campgrounds are closed on both Wednesday and Thursday nights, and you can't stay at any one site for more than five days in one month. The best options among the **state parks** are those at Keaīwa Heiau (see p.146), Mālaekahana Bay (p.143), Waimānolo Bay (p.133), and Kahana Valley (p.142); appealing **county parks** include Bellows Field Beach (p.133), Kaiaka Bay Beach Park, a mile out of Haleʻiwa near the mouth of Kaiaka Bay (p.150), and Keaʻau Beach Park on the Leeward Shore (p.158). The **state parks office** accepts postal applications seven to thirty days in advance; it's located in Room 310, 1151 Punchbowl St, Honolulu HI 96813 (Mon–Fri 8.30am–3.30pm; ☎808/587-0300, ⓦwww.hawaii.gov/dlnr/dsp). **County** permits can be obtained, in person only, from 650 S King St (Mon–Fri 7.45am–4pm; ☎808/523-4525, ⓦwww.co .honolulu.hi.us/parks) or from the subsidiary "City Hall" in the Ala Moana Center (Mon–Fri 9am–4pm, Sat 8am–4pm; ☎808/973-2600).

When to go

Of all major US cities, Honolulu is said to have both the *lowest* average annual maximum temperature and the *highest* minimum, at 85°F and 60°F respectively. Neither fluctuates more than a few degrees between summer and winter. Waikīkī remains a balmy tropical year-round resort, and the only seasonal variation likely to make much difference to travelers is the state of the **surf** on the North Shore.

For surfers, the time to come is from October to April, when mighty winter waves scour the sand off many beaches and come curling in at heights of twenty feet or more. In summer, the surf-bums head home, and some North Shore beaches are even safe for family swimming.

As for **room rates**, peak season in Waikīkī runs from December to March, and many mid-range hotels lower their prices by twenty or thirty dollars during the rest of the year. Waikīkī is pretty crowded all year, though, and coming in summer will not yield significant savings.

Oahu festivals and events

early Jan	International Bodyboarding Association World Tour, Banzai Pipeline
mid-Jan	Pacific Island Arts Festival, Thomas Square, facing Honolulu Academy of Arts
late Jan	Pipeline Pro surfing competition, 'Ehukai Beach Park
Jan/Feb	Narcissus Festival and Chinese New Year, Chinatown
early Feb	NFL Pro Bowl, Aloha Stadium, Honolulu
Feb	Buffalo's Big Board Surfing Classic, Mākaha Beach
3rd Mon in Feb	Presidents' Day; Great Aloha Run, from Aloha Tower to Aloha Stadium
early March	Honolulu festival, downtown Honolulu
mid-March	Hawaii Music Awards Week, Waikīkī
March 17	St Patrick's Day Parade, Waikīkī
March 26	Honolulu celebrations mark Prince Kūhīo Day, state holiday
Easter Sunday	Easter Sunrise Service at dawn, Punchbowl, Honolulu
May 1	*Lei* Day; public holiday, statewide celebrations
May 2	*Lei* ceremony at Royal Mausoleum, Honolulu
late May	Molokai–Oahu kayak race ends at Hawaii Kai
late May	Maui–Oahu Bankoh Ho'omana'o canoe race ends at Waikīkī Beach
June 11	Kamehameha Day; public holiday, statewide celebrations, Honolulu to Waikīkī parade
late June	King Kamehameha *Hula* Festival, Blaisdell Center, Honolulu
late June	Taste of Honolulu food festival, Civic Center Grounds, Honolulu
mid-July	Hawaii International Jazz Festival, Honolulu
3rd Sat in July	Prince Lot *Hula* Festival, Moanalua Gardens, Honolulu
early Aug	State Farm Fair, Aloha Stadium, Honolulu
mid-Sept	Aloha Festival, island-wide
late Sept	Molokai–Oahu women's outrigger canoe race ends at Waikīkī
early Oct	Molokai–Oahu men's outrigger canoe race ends at Waikīkī
Oct 31	Halloween parade, Waikīkī
First 2 wks Nov	Hawaii International Film Festival, Honolulu
mid-Nov	World Invitational *Hula* Festival, Honolulu
mid-Nov	Triple Crown of Surfing; Hawaiian Pro, Ali'i Beach Park, Hale'iwa
late Nov/early Dec	Triple Crown of Surfing; World Cup, Sunset Beach
early Dec	Triple Crown of Surfing; Pipe Masters, Banzai Pipeline
2nd Sun in Dec	Honolulu Marathon
Dec 25	Christmas Day; Hawaii Bowl, Aloha Stadium, Honolulu

Note that the exact dates of surfing contests, and in some cases the venues as well, depend on the state of the waves.

Honolulu and Waikīkī

Stretching for around a dozen miles along the southern coast of Oahu, and home to 400,000 people, **HONOLULU** is by far Hawaii's largest city. As the site of the islands' major **airport** and of the legendary beaches and skyscrapers of **WAIKĪKĪ**, it also provides most visitors with their first taste of Hawaii. Many, unfortunately, leave without ever realizing quite how out of keeping it is with the rest of the state.

△ Canoe and surfboards, Waikīki Beach

Honolulu only came into being after the arrival of the foreigners; from the early days of sandalwood and whaling, through the rise of King Sugar and the development of Pearl Harbor, to its modern incarnation as a tourist playground, the fortunes of the city have depended on the ever-increasing integration of Hawaii into the global economy. Benefits of this process include an exhilarating energy and dynamism, and the cosmopolitan air that comes from being a major world crossroads. The drawback has been the rampant overdevelopment of Waikīkī.

The **setting** is beautiful, right on the Pacific Ocean and backed by the dramatic *pali* (cliffs) of the Koʻolau mountains. **Downtown Honolulu**, centered on a group of administrative buildings that date from the final days of the Hawaiian monarchy, nestles at the foot of the extinct **Punchbowl** volcano, now a military cemetery. It's a manageable size, and a lot quieter than its glamourous image might suggest. Immediately to the west is livelier **Chinatown**, while the **airport** lies four or five miles further west again, just before the sheltered inlet of **Pearl Harbor**.

The distinct district of **Waikīkī** is about three miles east of downtown, conspicuous not only for its towering hotels but also for the furrowed brow of another extinct volcano, **Diamond Head**. Although Waikīkī is a small suburb, and one that many Honolulu residents avoid visiting, for package tourists it's the tail that wags the dog. They spend their days on Waikīkī's beaches, and their nights in its hotels, restaurants, and bars; apart from the odd expedition to the nearby **Ala Moana** shopping mall, the rest of Honolulu might just as well not exist.

The sun-and-fun appeal of Waikīkī may wear off after a few days, but it can still make an excellent base for a longer stay on Oahu. Downtown Honolulu is easily accessible, and has top-quality museums like the **Bishop Museum** and the **Academy of Arts**, as well as some superb rainforest hikes, especially in the **Makiki** and **Mānoa** valleys, just a mile or so up from the city center. You can also get a bus to just about anywhere on the island, while the North Shore beaches are less than two hours' drive away by rented car.

Arrival and information

For details of **flights** to and from Honolulu's **International Airport**, see pp.27–31 (long-distance), and pp.31–32 (inter-island). Roughly five miles west of the downtown area, its runways extend out to sea on a coral reef. The main **Overseas Terminal** is flanked by smaller **Inter-Island** and **Commuter** terminals, and connected to them by the free Wikiwiki shuttle service. All are located on a loop road, which is constantly circled by a wide array of hotel and rental-car pickup vans, taxis, and minibuses.

Virtually every arriving tourist heads straight to Waikīkī; if you don't have a **hotel or hostel reservation** use the courtesy phones in the baggage claim area, where you'll also find boards advertising room rates. Several competing **shuttle buses**, such as Airport Waikīkī Express (☎808/954-8652 or 1-866/898-2519, ⓦ www.robertshawaii.com; $9 one-way, $15 round-trip), Island Express (☎808/944-1879, ⓦ www.islandexpresstransport.com; $10 one-way, $19 round-trip), and Reliable Shuttle (☎808/924-9292, ⓦ www.reliableshuttle.com; $11 one-way, $19 round-trip), pick up regularly outside the terminals and will carry passengers to any Waikīkī hotel. A **taxi** from the airport to Waikīkī costs $25–30, depending on traffic.

In addition, **TheBus** #19 and #20 run to Waikīkī from the airport, leaving from outside the Departures lounge of the Overseas Terminal. The ride costs $2 one

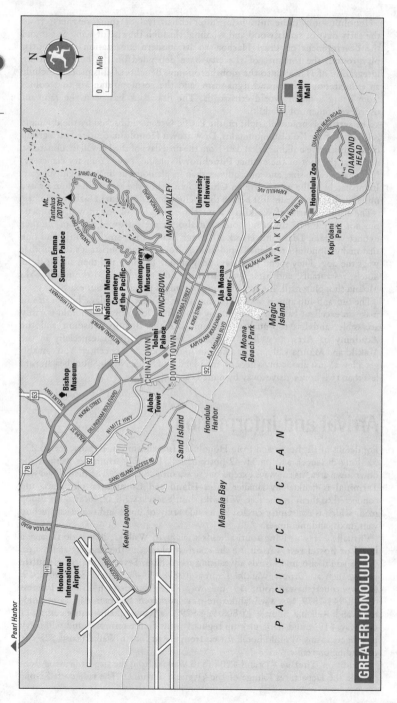

N

0 ——— 1 Mile

Pearl Harbor

Honolulu International Airport

PU'ULOA ROAD

H1

Keehi Lagoon

LAGOON DRIVE

SAND ISLAND ACCESS RD

Sand Island

Mãmala Bay

P A C I F I C   O C E A N

78

92

76

NIMITZ HWY

DILLINGHAM BOULEVARD

KALIHI ST

N KING STREET

MOANALUA FWY

63

MOANALUA FWY

Bishop Museum

H1

Aloha Tower

Honolulu Harbor

CHINATOWN

DOWNTOWN

'Iolani Palace

92

BERETANIA STREET

S. KING STREET

KAPIOLANI BOULEVARD

ALA MOANA BLVD

Ala Moana Center

Ala Moana Beach Park

Magic Island

PALI HIGHWAY

61

NUUANU AVENUE

National Memorial Cemetery of the Pacific

PUNCHBOWL

Contemporary Museum

Queen Emma Summer Palace

ROUND TOP DRIVE

TANTALUS DRIVE

Mt. Tantalus (2013ft)

MÃNOA VALLEY

ROUND TOP DRIVE

University of Hawaii

WAIKIKI

KALÃKAUA AVE.

ALA WAI BLVD

Kapi'olani Park

Honolulu Zoo

KAPAHULU AVE.

Kãhala Mall

H1

DIAMOND HEAD ROAD

DIAMOND HEAD

GREATER HONOLULU

way, but you have to be traveling light: TheBus won't carry large bags, cases, or backpacks.

Car rental outlets abound; see p.68 for advice on driving in Honolulu. The nine-mile – not at all scenic – **drive** from the airport to Waikīkī can take anything from 25 to 75 minutes. The quickest route is to follow H-1 as far as possible, running inland of downtown Honolulu, and then watch out for the Waikīkī exit.

Information

There are no visitor **information** centers worth visiting in Waikīkī or Honolulu. The best place to pick up printed material is the Arrivals hall at the airport, but almost every hotel runs its own information desk with further racks of brochures, and kiosks around Kalākaua Avenue offer greatly discounted rates for island tours, helicopter rides, dinner cruises, surfing lessons, and so on. To get information in advance, access the websites of the **Hawaii Visitors Bureau** (☏ 808/923-1811 or 1-800/464-2924, ⓦ www.gohawaii.com) or the Island of Oahu (ⓦ www.visit-oahu.com).

Honolulu's main **post office**, facing the inter-island terminal at the airport at 3600 Aolele St, Honolulu, HI 96820 (Mon–Fri 7.30am–8.30pm, Sat 8am–4.30pm), is the only one in the city that accepts **general delivery** (poste restante) mail. There are other post offices at 330 Saratoga Rd in Waikīkī (Mon, Tues, Thurs & Fri 8am–4.30pm, Wed 8am–6pm, Sat 9am–noon); at the Ala Moana Center (Mon–Fri 8.30am–5pm, Sat 8.30am–4.15pm); and downtown in the Old Federal Building at 335 Merchant St (Mon, Tues, Thurs & Fri 8am–4.30pm, Wed 8am–6pm).

Getting around

While renting a car enables you to explore Oahu in much greater depth, **driving** in Honolulu is not a pleasant experience. The **traffic** on major roads, such as H-1 along the northern flanks of the city, and Likelike Highway and the Pali Highway across the mountains, can be horrendous, and **parking** is always a problem. You may find it easier to travel by **bus**, thanks to the exemplary TheBus network.

Buses

A network of over sixty **bus** routes, officially named TheBus and centered on downtown Honolulu and the Ala Moana Center, covers the whole of Oahu (☏ 808/848-5555, ⓦ www.thebus.org). All journeys cost $2 (ages 6–17 $1), with free transfers on to any connecting route if you ask as you board. The **4-Day Pass**, available from ABC stores in Waikīkī, offers four days' unlimited travel on TheBus for $20; $40 **monthly passes** are also available. The most **popular routes** with Waikīkī-based tourists are #2 to downtown, #8 and #58 to Ala Moana, #19 and #20 to the airport, #20 and #42 to Pearl Harbor, #22 to Hanauma Bay, #57 to Kailua and Kāne'ohe, and the bargain "**Circle Island**" buses that take four hours to tour Oahu, still for just $2: #52 (clockwise) and #55 (counterclockwise).

For tourists, the main alternative to TheBus is the ridiculously expensive **Waikīkī Trolley** (ⓦ www.waikikitrolley.com; 1-day pass adults $25, ages 4–11 $12; 4-day pass adults $45, ages 4–11 $18), which runs open-sided trolleys on three separate lines. The **Red Line** tours from Waikīkī to Ala Moana, the water-front, downtown Honolulu, Chinatown, and the Bishop Museum (every 45min; first departure *Hilton Hawaiian Village* 10am, terminates *Hawaii Prince* 6.26pm); the **Blue Line** connects Waikīkī with Sea Life Park by way of Diamond Head and Kahala Mall, but does not drop passengers at Hanauma Bay (hourly; first departure

DFS Galleria 9am, terminates *Ohana Waikīkī West* 6.15pm); and the **Pink Line** simply shuttles between Waikīkī and the Ala Moana Center (every 8min; first departure DFS Galleria 9.30am, terminates *Hilton Hawaiian Village* 8.04pm).

Car and bike rental

All the major **car rental** chains have outlets at the airport, and many have offices in Waikīkī as well. Reservations can be made using the national toll-free numbers listed on p.33, but check first to see if you can get a better room-and-car deal through your hotel. Bear in mind that Waikīkī hotels charge anything from $8 to $30 per night for **parking**, although there are meters on the backstreets of Waikīkī, near the Ala Wai Canal. Downtown, the largest metered parking lot is on the edge of Chinatown at Smith and Beretania streets.

Several companies in and near Waikīkī rent out **bicycles**, **mopeds** and **motorbikes**, including Adventure On Two Wheels, which adjoins the *Island Hostel* at 1946 Ala Moana Blvd (☎808/944-3131), and has another outlet at 2552 Lemon Rd (☎808/921-8111); Big Kahuna Rentals, 407 Seaside Ave (☎808/924-2736 or 1-888/451-5544, ⓦwww.bigkahunarentals.com); and the good-value Mopeds Direct, 750 Kapahulu Ave (☎808/732-3366). Typical rates for bikes are $15 per day (8am–6pm) or $20 for 24 hours; mopeds around $40 per day, or from $130 per week; and a Harley-Davidson motorbike will set you back perhaps $150 for a day, $750 for a week. Bear in mind that, given the steep mountains and busy highways that separate Honolulu from the rest of the island, a bicycle is only really practicable for getting between downtown Honolulu and Waikīkī.

Taxis

Honolulu **taxi** firms include Charley's (☎808/531-1333, ⓦwww.charleystaxi .com), and TheCab (☎808/422-2222, ⓦwww.thecabhawaii.com). An average ride from Waikīkī to downtown Honolulu costs $12–15. Handicabs of the Pacific (☎808/524-3866, ⓦwww.handicabs.com) provides transportation and tours for **disabled visitors**.

Bus tours

Countless operators in Waikīkī, such as Polynesian Adventure Tours (☎808/833-3000 or 1-800/622-3011, ⓦwww.polyad.com), E Noa Tours (☎808/591-2561 or 1-800/824-8804, ⓦwww.enoa.com), and Roberts (☎808/954-8652 or 1-866/898-2519, ⓦwww.robertshawaii.com), advertise bus tours of Honolulu and Oahu. Typical choices range from $22 for an excursion to Pearl Harbor, or $30 for a half-day tour of Pearl Harbor and downtown Honolulu, upto $60 for a full-day island tour, or up to $90 if you want to stop at destinations like the Polynesian Cultural Center or Waimea Valley.

Walking tours

Perhaps because both Waikīkī and downtown Honolulu are so easy to explore on your own, few organized **walking tours** are available. As well as the tours of Chinatown detailed on p.95, however, it's also possible, on the first Friday of each month, to join free tours of either the central downtown area, or the Royal Mausoleum neighborhood near the Pali Highway (see p.106), which rendezvous at the Damien Statue outside the State Capitol at 1pm (☎808/948-3299).

For more energetic **hiking** in different areas all over the island, the Hawaii chapter of the Sierra Club sponsors treks and similar activities on weekends (☎808/538-6616, ⓦwww.hi.sierraclub.org), while the Hawaii Nature Center arranges hikes most weekends (☎808/955-0100, ⊛www.hawaiinaturecenter .org). Likehike (☎808/455-8193, ⊛www.gayhawaii.com/likehike) is a gay hiking club that runs group hikes on alternate Sundays. On the first Saturday and Sunday of each month, the Clean Air Team (☎808/948-3299) organizes two free hikes, one up Diamond Head and one to Diamond Head Lighthouse; both meet at 1pm in front of Honolulu Zoo.

Accommodation

Practically all the **accommodation** available in the city of Honolulu is confined to **Waikīkī**, which holds an extraordinary concentration of hotels in all price ranges. Unless you're happy to spend hundreds of dollars per night for world-class luxury, however, Waikīkī rooms are far from exciting. Most are in anonymous tower blocks, charging at least $120 for a standard en-suite double room, with another $60 for an ocean view, and $60 more again if they're right on the seafront. Few have any sort of personal touch, and there are no local B&Bs. Assuming that you're committed to staying in Waikīkī in the first place – and you shouldn't feel that you *have* to come to Waikīkī just because you're coming to Hawaii – think carefully about what you plan to do, and how much you want to spend. The very cheapest accommodation option is a dorm bed in a hostel, but as long as you don't mind missing out on a sea view, or having to walk a few minutes to the beach, you can find adequate rooms for around $75 a night. To get your first-choice hotel in peak season, always **reserve** well in advance. However, with so many rooms available it's usually possible to find something at short notice.

Except for the top-of-the-line properties, there's little point choosing a hotel with a **swimming pool** – most are squeezed onto rooftop terraces, overlooked by thousands of rooms in the surrounding high-rises and attracting all the dirt and fumes of the city. There are no **campgrounds** in Waikīkī, and camping at Honolulu's only site, Sand Island State Park (see p.100), is not recommended.

Note that although Waikīkī is part of Honolulu, any hotel said to be in "Honolulu" in this chapter is outside Waikīkī.

Waikīkī hostels

Hale Aloha Hostel (Hostelling International Waikīkī) 2417 Prince Edward St ☎808/926-8313, ⊛www.hostelsaloha.com. This informal, AYH-affiliated youth hostel in the heart of Waikīkī is housed in a turquoise four-story building a couple of minutes from the beach. Dorm beds in four-person rooms are $20 ($23 for nonmembers), while the five double studio rooms cost $48 or $54; guests share a kitchen and patio. Office open 7–3am; no curfew; seven-day max stay. Reservations recommended, especially for double rooms. ❶–❷
Pacific Ohana 2552 Lemon Rd ☎808/921-8111. The least appealing of the Lemon Road hostels offers four-bed dorms that share bathrooms for $20 per person, and two-bed studios with bath and kitchen for $75. ❶–❸
Polynesian Hostel Beach Club 2584 Lemon Rd ☎808/922-1340, ⊛www .hawaiihostels.com. Former motel converted into a

clean, safe, and efficient private hostel, a block from the sea at the Diamond Head end of Waikīkī. All the air-conditioned dorm rooms have en-suite bathrooms; some hold four bunk beds ($25 per person), some six ($23 per person), and some ten ($20). You can also get a "semi-private" room, sharing a bathroom, for $45 single, $54 double, or a studio for $67. Van tours of the island offered. Free use of snorkel gear and boogie boards, plus cheap bike and moped rentals, and Internet access. ❶–❷
Waikīkī Beachside Hotel & Hostel 2556 Lemon Rd ☎808/923-9566, ⊛www.waikikibeachside hostel.com. By far the liveliest of the hostels along Lemon Road, near the park in eastern Waikīkī, and thus despite the name not actually "beachside." Beds in eight-person dorms cost $23, in four-person dorms $32; they also have "semi-private" double rooms, sharing bathroom and kitchen, for $67. It looks a lot smarter from the outside than it does once you go in, but amenities include

free continental breakfasts, a big-screen TV, Internet access, and snorkel and surf equipment rental. ①–②

Waikīkī hotels: budget

Aloha Punawai 305 Saratoga Rd ☎808/923-5211 or 1-866/713-9694, ⓦwww.alternative-hawaii .com/alohapunawai. Miniature hotel, opposite the post office, whose 19 well-priced studios and apartments – all air-conditioned – are furnished in a crisp Japanese style. All units have kitchens, bathrooms, balconies, and TV, but no phones; only the slightly pricier "deluxe" options will sleep three guests. Small discounts for weekly stays. ④

Aqua Continental 2426 Kūhio Ave ☎808/922-2232 or 1-866/406-2782, ⓦaquaresorts.com. Plain but very presentable refurbished rooms, in a 27-story high-rise in the heart of Waikīkī, two blocks back from the beach; no balconies, and very few ocean views. ③

The Breakers 250 Beach Walk ☎808/923-3181 or 1-800/426-0494, ⓦwww.breakers-hawaii.com. Intimate hotel on the western edge of central Waikīkī, close to the beach. All its two-person studio apartments and four-person garden suites have kitchenettes, phones, TV, and a/c, there's a bar and grill beside the flower-surrounded pool, and there's even a Japanese tea-house. Limited free parking. ④

Hawaiian King 417 Nohonani St ☎808/922-3894 or 1-800/247-1903, ⓦwww.hawaiianking-hotel .com. Each room in this venerable low-rise condo hotel, three blocks back from the beach in central Waikīkī, is privately owned, so they differ considerably, and they're not especially fancy, but all have kitchen, a/c, and balcony. Discounted weekly and monthly rates. ④

🏃 **Hawaiiana Hotel** 260 Beach Walk ☎808/923-3811 or 1-800/367-5122, ⓦwww.hawaiianahotelatwaikiki.com. Abounding with tiki statues and the like, this pleasant low-rise family hotel, close to the beach and central Waikīkī, is the most appealing of the budget options in the immediate area. All the rooms, arranged around two pools, have kitchenettes, some have *lānais*, and they're equipped to varying degrees of luxury. ④–⑥

Kai Aloha 235 Saratoga Rd ☎808/923-6723, ⓦkaialoha.magicktravel.com. Tiny, very central hotel, with *lānai* studios plus apartments that sleep up to four, all with kitchenettes, bathrooms, TV, and a/c. ③

Ohana East 150 Ka'iulani Ave ☎808/922-5353 or 1-800/462-6262, ⓦwww.ohanahotels.com. While the rooms – and the bathrooms – are on the small side, the staff and services are as good as you'd expect of the Ohana chain, and the convenient location, a block back from the beach and very close to several good restaurants, makes it a very dependable option, especially for budget-conscious families. ④

Royal Grove 151 Uluniu Ave ☎808/923-7691, ⓦwww.royalgrovehotel.com. Small-scale, family-run hotel with a homey feel in central Waikīkī. The facilities improve the more you're prepared to pay, but even the most basic rooms, which lack a/c, are of a reliable standard, albeit undeniably faded, and hold two beds. There's also a courtyard pool – making the *Royal Grove* one of Waikīkī's best bets for budget travelers – a piano for guest use, and all sorts of retro bric-a-brac scattered around the shared spaces. Special weekly rates apply April–Nov only. ②

Waikīkī Prince 2431 Prince Edward St ☎808/922-1544, ⓦwww.waikikiprince.com. Slightly drab but perfectly adequate and very central budget hotel (not be confused with the upscale *Hawaii Prince Hotel Waikīkī*; see p.74). All rooms have a/c, en-suite baths, and basic cooking facilities, but no phones; the "very small" and "small" categories are even cheaper than "economy" units, while "standard" is top of the range. Office open 9am–6pm only; seventh night free April–Nov. ②

Waikīkī hotels: mid-range

Aqua Bamboo & Spa 2425 Kūhio Ave ☎808/922-7777 or 1-866/406-2782, ⓦaquaresorts.com. Very central and stylish "boutique hotel," two blocks back from the beach, with less than a hundred rooms spread across its 12 stories. All units have appealing furnishings and live plants, with at least one *lānai*, plus free high-speed Internet and a large-screen LCD TV. ④

Aqua Island Colony 445 Seaside Ave ☎808/923-2345 or 1-866/406-2782, ⓦaquaresorts.com. Anonymous-looking 44-story high-rise at the quieter inland side of Waikīkī, still around five minutes' walk of the beach. The hotel holds conventional rooms as well as more luxurious suites; all are furnished to a high standard and have their own balconies, though many of the bathrooms are small. ④

Cabana at Waikīkī 2551 Cartwright Rd ☎808/926-5555 or 1-877/902-2121, ⓦwww .cabana-waikiki.com. Boutique hotel, charging over the odds because it's geared towards gay men. All its 19 nice but not exquisite mini-suites hold kitchenettes and extra daybeds, and guests get free breakfasts, plus free cocktails some nights. There's a small, clothes-optional outdoor hot tub. ④

Ilima Hotel 445 Nohonani St ☎808/923-1877, 1-800/801-9366 (HI) or 1-800/367-5172 (US & Canada), ⓦwww.ilima.com. Good-value small hotel, near the canal on the *mauka* side of central Waikīkī and catering to a mainly local clientele. The spacious condo units each offer two double beds, a kitchen, additional sofabeds, and free local calls, and there's limited free parking. ❺

Imperial of Waikīkī 205 Lewers St ☎808/923-1827 or 1-800/347-2582, ⓦwww.imperialofwaikiki.com. Studio rooms and one- or two-bedroom balcony suites in a tower block set slightly back from the beach, just south of Kalākaua Avenue. A bit hemmed in by the oceanfront giants, but not bad for

groups traveling together; check online for bargain rates. The best views are from the terrace around the 27th floor pool. ❹

🏃 **New Otani Kaimana Beach Hotel** 2863 Kalākaua Ave ☎808/923-1555 or 1-800/356-8264, ⓦwww.kaimana.com. Intimate Japanese-toned hotel, stylish and airy, on quiet and secluded Sans Souci Beach (see p.82). Half a mile east of the bustle of central Waikīkī, it boasts the lovely backdrop of Diamond Head. Its *Hau Tree Lanai* restaurant is reviewed on p.118. Valet parking only. ❺

Outrigger and Ohana hotels

The family-oriented **Outrigger** chain currently runs eleven hotels in Waikīkī, divided into two categories to convey their differences. Five of the most luxurious carry the Outrigger brand name, while the rest are **Ohana** (which means "family" in Hawaiian) hotels.

Outrigger has been moving consistently upmarket in recent years, most obviously by spearheading the redevelopment of the Beachwalk area. Several of its older properties have closed, while new additions include the *Regency on Beachwalk* and the *Luana Waikīkī*. Nonetheless, by Waikīkī standards, all the Outrigger and Ohana properties remain competitively priced. Even the oceanfront *Outrigger Waikīkī On The Beach* is less opulent than places like the *Royal Hawaiian* or the *Hilton Hawaiian Village*, and costs significantly less per night. You can expect to find Internet rates for all the Ohana properties at well under $150 per night, and for that you'll get a clean, well-maintained room with standard but smart hotel furnishings.

A high proportion of Outrigger and Ohana guests are on all-inclusive vacation packages. If you contact either chain directly, or access their websites, look for special offers, and especially their plethora of room-and-car deals. Standard room rates, however, remain constant year-round; where the price codes below indicate ranges, these refer to the best available online rates for a standard double room without and with ocean views. Most properties hold more expensive suites.

Outrigger hotels

Luana Waikīkī, 2045 Kalākaua Ave	❻–❽	(see p.74)
Reef, 2169 Kālia Rd	❻–❽	
Regency on Beachwalk, 255 Beachwalk	❻–❽	
Waikīkī On The Beach, 2335 Kalākaua Ave	❼–❽	(see p.75)
Waikīkī Shore, 2161 Kālia Rd	❼–❾	

Outrigger reservations	ⓦwww.outrigger.com
US & Canada	☎1-800/688-7444
Worldwide	☎303/369-7777

Ohana hotels

East, 150 Ka'iulani Ave	❹	(see p.70)
Islander Waikīkī, 270 Lewers St	❹	
Maile Sky Court, 2058 Kūhīo Ave	❸	
Waikīkī Beachcomber, 2300 Kalākaua Ave	❹	
Waikīkī Malia, 2211 Kūhīo Ave	❹	
Waikīkī West, 2330 Kūhīo Ave	❹	

Ohana reservations	ⓦwww.ohanahotels.com
US & Canada	☎1-800/462-6262
Worldwide	☎303/369-7777

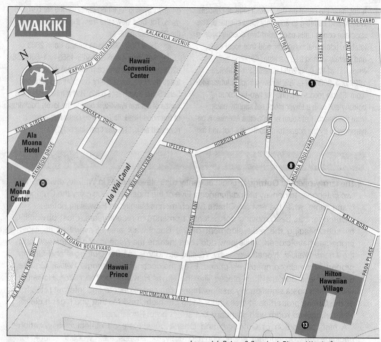

WAIKĪKĪ

Hawaii Convention Center

Ala Moana Hotel

Ala Moana Center

Hawaii Prince

Hilton Hawaiian Village

Kalakaua Avenue

Kapiolani Boulevard

Kahakai Drive

Kona Street

Atkinson Drive

Ala Moana Park Drive

Ala Moana Boulevard

Holomoana Street

Ala Wai Canal

Ala Wai Boulevard

McCully Street

Nui Street

Pau Lane

Dudoit La

Ena Road

Hobron Lane

Makaloa Lane

Lipeepee St

Kaiulu Road

Ala Moana Boulevard

Kalia Road

Paoa Place

① ⑧ ⑬

Leonardo's Bakery & Samchoy's Diamond Head ▲

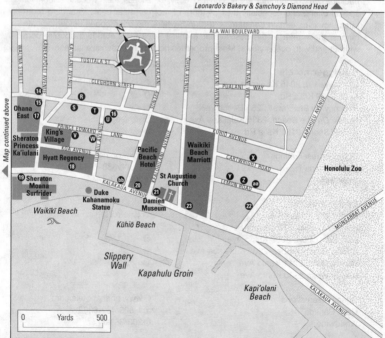

Map continued above ◀

Ala Wai Boulevard

Tusitala St

Cleghorn Street

Walina Street

Kanekapolei Avenue

Kaiulani Avenue

Lili'uokalani Avenue

Ohua Avenue

Paoakalani Avenue

Kealohilani Avenue

Pualani Way

Walina Way

Kapahulu Avenue

Prince Edward Lane

Koa Avenue

Kalakaua Avenue

Kūhiō Avenue

Cartwright Road

Lemon Road

Monsarrat Avenue

Kalakaua Avenue

Ohana East

Sheraton Princess Ka'iulani

King's Village

Hyatt Regency

Sheraton Moana Surfrider

Pacific Beach Hotel

St Augustine Church

Damien Museum

Waikīkī Beach Marriott

Honolulu Zoo

● Duke Kahanamoku Statue

Waikīkī Beach

Kūhiō Beach

Slippery Wall

Kapahulu Groin

Kapi'olani Beach

⑭ ⑮ ⑰ ⑲ ⑱ ⑳ ㉑ ㉓ ㉒
R S T U ⑯ V W bb X Y Z aa

0   Yards   500

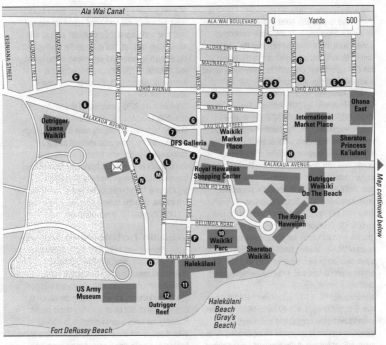

Map continued below

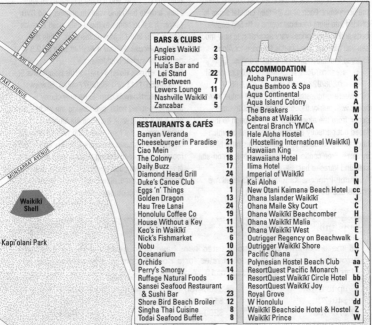

BARS & CLUBS

Angles Waikīkī	2
Fusion	3
Hula's Bar and Lei Stand	22
In-Between	7
Lewers Lounge	11
Nashville Waikīkī	4
Zanzabar	5

RESTAURANTS & CAFÉS

Banyan Veranda	19
Cheeseburger in Paradise	21
Ciao Mein	18
The Colony	18
Daily Buzz	17
Diamond Head Grill	24
Duke's Canoe Club	9
Eggs 'n' Things	1
Golden Dragon	13
Hau Tree Lanai	24
Honolulu Coffee Co	19
House Without a Key	11
Keo's in Waikīkī	15
Nick's Fishmarket	6
Nobu	10
Oceanarium	20
Orchids	11
Perry's Smorgy	14
Ruffage Natural Foods	16
Sansei Seafood Restaurant & Sushi Bar	23
Shore Bird Beach Broiler	12
Singha Thai Cuisine	8
Todai Seafood Buffet	8

ACCOMMODATION

Aloha Punawai	K
Aqua Bamboo & Spa	R
Aqua Continental	S
Aqua Island Colony	A
The Breakers	M
Cabana at Waikīkī	X
Central Branch YMCA	O
Hale Aloha Hostel (Hostelling International Waikīkī)	V
Hawaiian King	B
Hawaiiana Hotel	I
Ilima Hotel	D
Imperial of Waikīkī	P
Kai Aloha	N
New Otani Kaimana Beach Hotel	cc
Ohana Islander Waikīkī	J
Ohana Maile Sky Court	C
Ohana Waikīkī Beachcomber	H
Ohana Waikīkī Malia	F
Ohana Waikīkī West	E
Outrigger Regency on Beachwalk	L
Outrigger Waikīkī Shore	Q
Pacific Ohana	aa
Polynesian Hostel Beach Club	T
ResortQuest Pacific Monarch	bb
ResortQuest Waikīkī Circle Hotel	G
ResortQuest Waikīkī Joy	U
Royal Grove	dd
W Honolulu	Z
Waikīkī Beachside Hotel & Hostel	W
Waikīkī Prince	

Outrigger Luana Waikīkī 2045 Kalākaua Ave ℡ 808/955-6000 or 1-800/445-8811, Ⓦ www.outrigger.com. Smart, totally remodeled condo block, back from the beach at the western end of Waikīkī, that's become one of the jewels in the Outrigger chain. Characterful, individually styled kitchenette studios and hotel rooms, with an upscale Hawaiian flavor. ⑤–⑧

Pacific Beach Hotel 2490 Kalākaua Ave ℡ 808/922-1233 or 1-800/367-6060, Ⓦ www .pacificbeachhotel.com. The *Pacific Beach* has 830 rooms in two separate towers, at the Diamond Head end of Kalākaua Avenue, and also offers a pool, ocean-view spa, and tennis facilities. The high central tower contains the Oceanarium – a three-story fish tank that's the focus for diners in the *Oceanarium* restaurant (see p.117). Best rates online. ⑤

ResortQuest Pacific Monarch 2427 Kūhiō Ave ℡ 808/923-9805 or 1-866/774-2924, Ⓦ www .pacific-monarch.com. Tall condo building in the heart of Waikīkī holding small studios with kitchenettes, plus larger four-person suites with full kitchens and *lānais*, and a rooftop swimming pool. Best rates online. ⑤–⑥

ResortQuest Waikīkī Circle Hotel 2464 Kalākaua Ave ℡ 808/923-1571 or 1-877/997-6667, Ⓦ www .resortquesthawaii.com. Bright and cheery turquoise-and-white octagonal tower, dwarfed by its surroundings but one of the cheapest options along the oceanfront. Each of its thirteen circular floors is divided into eight identical rooms with two double beds and a *lānai*; prices vary according to how much sea you can see. The hotel is the base for Aloha Express Tours; see p.80. Best rates online. ④

ResortQuest Waikīkī Joy 320 Lewers St ℡ 808/923-2300 or 1-877/997-6667, Ⓦ www.resortquesthawaii.com. Good-value little hotel, with quirky though dated pastel-trimmed decor, from the airy garden lobby through to the faded but perfectly adequate rooms, all of which have whirlpool baths and incongruous retro hi-fi systems. Free continental breakfast, plus an on-site café and karaoke bar. ④

Sheraton Princess Ka'iulani 120 Ka'iulani Ave ℡ 808/922-5811 or 1-866/500-8313, Ⓦ www.princess-kaiulani.com. Ugly tower-block hotel, with drab, old-fashioned public spaces and well over a thousand rooms, usually packed with vacationing families. Not quite on the seafront but big enough to command wide views of the ocean and mountains. The tiny street-level pool is somewhat marred by traffic noise. City view ④, ocean view ⑤

Waikīkī Parc 2233 Helumoa Rd ℡ 808/921-7272 or 1-800/422-0450, Ⓦ www.waikikiparc.com. Modern high-rise set slightly back from the beach, operated by the same management as the *Halekūlani* opposite, and offering a taste of the same luxury at somewhat more affordable prices, though recent renovations have increased rates significantly. Very tastefully decorated top-of-the-line rooms, plus the superb *Nobu* restaurant (see p.118). City view ⑤, ocean view ⑥

Waikīkī hotels: expensive

Halekūlani 2199 Kālia Rd ℡ 808/923-2311 or 1-800/367-2343, Ⓦ www .halekulani.com. Stunning oceanfront hotel, arranged around an exquisite courtyard and pool, in a prime location for views along the beach to Diamond Head, but aloof from the resort bustle. Probably the most luxurious option in Waikīkī – even if you're not staying in the opulent Vera Wang honeymoon suite, you'll have a huge room with *lānai*, a deep bath and walk-in shower, and DVD player. It's also home to the highly rated *Orchids* (see p.118) and *La Mer* restaurants, while the open-air *House Without a Key* bar (see p.123) is perfect for sunset cocktails. ⑨

Hawaii Prince Hotel Waikīkī 100 Holomoana St ℡ 808/956-1111 or 1-888/977-4623, Ⓦ www .princeresortshawaii.com. Extremely classy Japanese-styled hotel, overlooking the yacht harbor and just a short walk from the Ala Moana Center (which makes it a long walk from Waikīkī proper). Its twin towers have spacious and very comfortable rooms with floor-to-ceiling ocean views (though not *lānais*), plus two good restaurants, and it even has its own golf course, albeit half an hour's drive away. Look for good deals online. ⑥–⑨

Accommodation price codes

All the accommodation options listed here have been graded with the symbols below, which refer to the quoted rates for a double room in high season (Dec to March), not including state taxes of 10.17 percent. For a full explanation, see p.35.

① up to $40	④ $100–150	⑦ $250–300
② $40–70	⑤ $150–200	⑧ $300–400
③ $70–100	⑥ $200–250	⑨ over $400

Hilton Hawaiian Village 2005 Kālia Rd ☎808/949-4321 or 1-800/445-8667, ⓦwww .hawaiianvillage.hilton.com. With 3400 rooms and counting, the *Hilton* is the largest hotel in Hawaii and the largest non-casino hotel in the US (the second largest in the world). It's a scaled-down version of all Waikīkī, holding a hundred of the exact same stores and restaurants you'd find out on the streets. The center of Waikīkī is a 15min walk away, and since there's a good pool, a great stretch of beach (see p.79), and even a lagoon populated by penguins and flamingos, there's little incentive to leave the hotel precincts – which is, of course, the point. Even self-parking costs $20 per night. Garden view ❻, ocean view ❼, ocean front ❽

Hyatt Regency Waikīkī Resort And Spā 2424 Kalākaua Ave ☎808/923-1234 or 1-866/333-8881, ⓦwaikiki.hyatt.com. Very lavish, very central property, across the road from the heart of Waikīkī Beach, and consisting of two enormous towers engulfing a central atrium equipped with cascading waterfalls and tropical vegetation. Also holds an upmarket shopping mall, an open-air pool, 1230 "oversized" rooms, a spa, and nine restaurants, of which two, *Ciao Mein* and *The Colony*, are reviewed on p.118. ❼–❾

Outrigger Waikīkī On The Beach 2335 Kalākaua Ave ☎808/923-0711 or 1-800/688-7444, ⓦwww .outrigger.com. Flagship Outrigger hotel, in prime position close to the center of Waikīkī Beach, with good restaurants and entertainment. The rooms closest to the ocean offer great views and facilities, including huge whirlpool baths; those further back are less special, but the rates are very reasonable for such a choice location. ❼–❽

The Royal Hawaiian 2259 Kalākaua Ave ☎808/923-7311 or 1-866/716-8109, ⓦwww.royal-hawaiian.com. The 1920s "Pink Palace" (see p.83), now owned by Sheraton, remains one of Waikīkī's best-loved landmarks. The atmospheric original building, which seeps vintage glamor, still commands a great expanse of beach and looks over a lawn to the sea; pink through and through, it remains a lovely place to hang out, with elegant rooms and peaceful gardens at the back. Sadly, though, it's now flanked by a less atmos-pheric tower block holding additional suites. Includes a full-service spa. On Monday, a *lū'au* is held on the ocean-facing lawn (see p.125). ❽

Sheraton Moana Surfrider 2365 Kalākaua Ave ☎808/922-3111 or 1-866/716-8109, ⓦwww .moana-surfrider.com. Waikīkī's oldest hotel, built at the end of the nineteenth century (see p.83). Despite extensive restoration, the "Colonial" archi-tectural style of the original building – now the focus of the Banyan wing – remains intact, though

these days it's flanked by two huge towers. The main lobby, with its tongue-and-groove walls, memorabilia cabinets, soothing sea breezes and old-time atmosphere, is a delight – prepare yourself to pick through countless Japanese wedding parties – and the beachfront setting, with its broad veranda and colossal banyan tree, is unsurpassed. Many of the actual rooms, however, are surprisingly faded and worn. City view ❼, ocean view ❽

W Honolulu 2885 Kalākaua Ave ☎808/922-1700 or 1-877/945-8357, ⓦwww.whotels.com. Very chic – some might say pretentious – hotel, part of an exclusive international chain, that's set a few yards back from the ocean just over half a mile east of Waikīkī (a condo tower blocks views from the lower stories). All 48 rooms have balconies (though some face Diamond Head rather than the ocean), CD players, and cordless phones, and the *Diamond Head Grill* restaurant (see p.118) is on the second floor. ❾

Waikīkī Beach Marriott Resort & Spa 2552 Kalākaua Ave ☎808/922-6611 or 1-800/367-5370, ⓦwww.marriottwaikiki.com. This huge, totally renovated property consists of two giant towers facing the eastern end of Waikīkī Beach; while not historic, it has a stylish, contemporary Hawaiian feel, and offers Waikīkī's best value at.the top end of the spectrum. As well as a state-of-the-art spa, it holds several excellent restaurants, including the wonderful *Sansei* (see p.118), while the *Moana Terrace* hosts superb Hawaiian musicians (see p.123). City view ❼, ocean view ❽

Honolulu YMCAs and hostels

Central Branch YMCA 401 Atkinson Drive ☎808/941-3344, ⓦwww.ymcahonolulu.org. Set in attractive grounds opposite the Ala Moana Center, just outside Waikīkī, with an on-site swimming pool and a beach nearby. Accommodations include plain rooms with shared bath for men only ($35 single/$46 double), plus some nicer en-suite doubles available to women too ($43 single/$59 double). All guests must reserve at least two weeks in advance, and have a definite check-out date; no walk-ins accepted. ❶–❷

Fernhurst YWCA 1566 Wilder Ave ☎808/941-2231, ⓦwww.ywca.org. Women-only lodging, not far west of the University of Hawaii and quite a way from the ocean, that's intended primarily for locals in need. Double rooms share a bathroom with one other room, and cost $38 per person; some can be rented by single travelers for $48. Rates include simple buffet breakfasts and dinners; a $35 membership is compulsory. ❶–❷

Hosteling International Honolulu 2323-A Seaview Ave ☎808/946-0591, ⓦhostelsaloha.com. Youth hostel in a college residence in Mānoa, a couple of miles north of Waikīkī. There's no direct bus from the airport: change at Ala Moana Center to TheBus #6 or #18; get off at Metcalfe Street/University Avenue, one block south of the hostel. Office hours 8am–noon and 4pm–midnight; no curfew. Beds in the single-sex dorms (two are male, three female) cost $16 for AYH/IYHA members, $19 for nonmembers, while the private double room costs $42 and $48 respectively, with a three-night maximum stay for nonmembers. ①–②

Honolulu hotels and B&Bs

Ala Moana Hotel 410 Atkinson Drive ☎808/955-4811, 1-800/446-8990 (HI) or 1-800/367-6025 (US & Canada), ⓦwww.alamoanahotel.com. Thousand-room tower block right alongside the Ala Moana Center, just down the road from the Convention Center, and five minutes' walk from Waikīkī. Managed by Outrigger, it consists of individually-owned condo units, which vary but are generally of a high standard. Though it's targeted primarily at business visitors and shopaholics, it offers the lively *Rumours* nightclub and some good restaurants, and there's an excellent beach close at hand (see p.100). Look for special rates online. Rooms ④–⑥, suites ⑦–⑨

Best Western Plaza 3253 N Nimitz Highway ☎808/836-3636 or 1-800/800-4683, ⓦwww.bestwesternhonolulu.com. Large hotel fronting the highway, half a mile by free shuttle bus from the airport; like the nearby *Honolulu Airport Hotel*, it's

perfectly adequate for an exhausted layover between flights but convenient neither for the city nor the beach. ④

Honolulu Airport Hotel 3401 N Nimitz Highway ☎808/836-0661 or 1-800/462-6262, ⓦwww.honoluluairporthotel.com. Three-hundred-room chain hotel, operated by Outrigger, close to the airport by a noisy freeway, and served by free 24-hour shuttles; the rooms are acceptable, but it's not a place you'd spend more than one night. ④

Mānoa Valley Inn 2001 Vancouver Drive ☎808/947-6019, ⓦwww.manoavalleyinn.com. One of Honolulu's most relaxing options: a plush, antique-filled B&B inn, near the University of Hawaii in lush Mānoa Valley, with seven suites and one self-contained cottage. Waikīkī feels a lot farther away than the mile it really is. Sit in one of the wicker chairs on the back porch and linger over breakfast. ④–⑤

Pagoda Hotel 1525 Rycroft St ☎808/941-6611 or 1-800/367-6060, ⓦwww.pagodahotel.com. This tower block, located within easy walking distance of the Ala Moana Center, roughly halfway between downtown Honolulu and Waikīkī, is very much a budget rather than a fancy option. Conventional, if undeniably ageing, hotel rooms and one- and two-bedroom suites, plus two pools and a "floating restaurant." ④

ResortQuest at the Executive Center Hotel 1088 Bishop St ☎808/539-3000 or 1-877/997-6667, ⓦwww.resortquesthawaii.com. All-suite downtown hotel, enjoying great harbor views from the top of a forty-story skyscraper. Geared to business travelers, but with prices that compare well with similar standard Waikīkī hotels. ⑥

Waikīkī

On any one day, half of all the tourists in the state of Hawaii are crammed into the tiny, surreal enclave of **WAIKĪKĪ**, three miles east of downtown Honolulu. Effectively, it's an island in its own right, a two-mile-long, quarter-mile-wide strip sealed off from the rest of the city by the Ala Wai Canal and almost completely surrounded by water. Its incredible profusion of skyscrapers, jostling for position along the shoreline, hold enough hotel rooms to accommodate more than 100,000 guests, restaurants by the hundred, and stores providing anything the visitor could possibly want.

Long before Kamehameha the Great built a thatched hut here at the start of the nineteenth century, Waikīkī – the name means "spouting water" – was a favored residence of the chiefs of Oahu. They coveted not only its waterfront coconut groves and well-stocked fishponds, but also the then mosquito-free swamps and wetlands that lay immediately behind them – prime taro-growing land at a time when such land was a rare and valuable resource. By the end of that century, however, with Hawaii annexed by the United States, it was considered all but useless. Waikīkī's value lay instead in its being the best beach within easy reach of Honolulu. When the *Moana* hotel went up in 1901, signaling the start of the tourist boom, a handful of inns were already dotted among the luxurious homes of elite missionary and merchant families.

However, Waikīkī only began to regain a significant population during the 1920s, when a vast program of land reclamation was initiated. The Ala Wai Canal was dug to divert the mountain streams into flowing around the edge of Waikīkī, and the central area was filled in with chunks of coral sawn from the reef that then ran the full length of the shoreline. Since then, Waikīkī has mushroomed beyond belief. Looking beyond the tower blocks, to Diamond Head or the mysterious valleys that recede into the mountains, will remind you that you're on a Pacific island, but there's precious little of the real Hawaii left in Waikīkī.

As long as you're prepared to enter into the spirit of rampant commercialism, it's possible to have a great time in Waikīkī. You could, just about, survive with little money, buying snacks from the omnipresent ABC convenience stores, but there would be no point – there's very little to see, and the only alternative to surfing and sunbathing is to shop until you drop.

Waikīkī Beach

Viewed objectively, **Waikīkī Beach** would rank pretty low down any list of Hawaii's best beaches. Even on Oahu, it's not hard to find a stretch of deserted, palm-fringed shoreline, whereas at Waikīkī you can hardly see the sand for the sunbathers, and the traffic on Kalākaua Avenue outroars the surf. Somehow, however, that barely seems to matter. Waikīkī Beach may be crowded, but it's crowded with enthusiastic holiday-makers, wringing every last minute's pleasure they can from being on one of the most famous beaches in the world. Incidentally, whatever it may look like, no hotel ever owns the beach adjacent to it; public access is guaranteed on every single beach in Hawaii. One consequence of that is that hotels are never allowed to set up beach chairs and umbrellas, meaning shade on the beach is in short supply.

Simply glance towards the ocean, and you'll be caught up in the ever-changing action. At the edge of the water, family groups splash while oblivious honeymoon couples gaze hand-in-hand at the horizon; beyond them, circling surfers await the next wave, now and then parting abruptly to allow outrigger canoes to glide through; further still, pleasure yachts and parasailers race back and forth; and, out in the deep-water channel, cruise liners, merchant ships, aircraft carriers, and oil tankers make their stately way towards the docks of Honolulu and Pearl Harbor.

Meanwhile, the beach itself plays host to a constant parade of characters; undiscovered starlets in impenetrable sunshades sashay around in the latest swimsuits; local beach boys busy themselves making new friends and renting out the occasional surfboard; overexcited children dart between the sedate seniors with their fancy deckchairs and bulging coolers; and determined European backpackers pick their way through the throng on their dogged search for the perfect plot of sand. On the sidewalk behind, jet-lagged new arrivals wonder how they'll ever get through the crush to dabble their toes in the Pacific for the first time.

Waikīkī's natural setting is just as beguiling as its melee of activity. Off to the east, the sharp profile of **Diamond Head** rises up from the ocean, while straight back inland the lush green Koʻolau Mountains soar between the skyscrapers. In the early evening especially, as the orange sun sinks far out to sea and the silhouettes of the palm trees grow ever starker, the overall effect is magical.

△ Surfers at Waikīkī Beach

Few visitors, however, realize that Waikīkī Beach is almost entirely **artificial**. The landscaping that created Waikīkī changed the ocean currents so that its natural beaches were swept away; ever since, the hotels have had a considerable stake in importing sand. So much was shipped in – much of it from Pāpōhaku Beach, on Molokai (see p.429) – that the contours of the sea bottom have been permanently altered. As a result, the **surfing** conditions at what is generally acknowledged to be the birthplace of the modern sport are no longer all that spectacular – which is why the experts head straight up to Oahu's North Shore.

Waikīkī Beach applies to the full length of the Waikīkī shoreline, from the Ala Wai Harbor in the west to within a couple of hundred yards of Diamond Head, but within this stretch are many distinct sections, each with its own name.

Central Waikīkī Beach

The **center** of the beach – the segment that everyone tends to call Waikīkī Beach – is the point near Duke Kahanamoku's statue (see p.83) where the buildings on the ocean side of Kalākaua Avenue come to a halt, and the sidewalk turns into a beachfront promenade. Swimmers here enjoy the best conditions of the entire seafront, with softly shelving sands, and waters that are generally calm.

With so many visitors eager to sample Hawaii's signature **watersports**, this is also the prime spot for commercial activity operators. Several concession stands rent out **surfboards**, typically for $10 per hour, and offer **surfing lessons** for beginners at around $40 per hour, with prices ranging upwards if you want a solo lesson. You can also take a $10 ride in a colorful, traditional **outrigger canoe**, paddled by experts – it's a similarly exhilarating experience to surfing, but requires far less effort. The main operator is Aloha Beach Services (℡808/922-3111, ext 2341). Note however that, thanks to all that sand, **snorkeling** conditions throughout Waikīkī are poor; as described on p.129, keen snorkelers should head instead for Hanauma Bay, eight miles east.

Royal-Moana Beach

To the **west**, central Waikīkī Beach merges into **Royal-Moana Beach**, fronting the *Royal Hawaiian* and *Sheraton Moana* hotels. It can sometimes be a struggle to walk along this narrow, busy strip because of the crowds it draws, but the swimming here is, again, excellent. It's also ideal for **novice surfers**: head slightly to the right as you enter the water to reach the easy break known as Canoes' Surf (so called because these gentle waves were all the heavy old *koa* canoes could ride). The waves are slightly stronger further left, at the Queen's Surf break.

Halekūlani Beach

West of the *Royal Hawaiian*, a raised walkway curves in front of the *Sheraton Waikīkī*, where the sea comes right over the sand. After a tiny little "pocket beach," where the swimming is fine but to find any shade you have to crouch beneath some very low branches, a long arrow-straight walkway squeezes between the waves and the opulent *Halekūlani Hotel*. At the far end comes a slightly larger stretch of beach, extending a hundred yards or so from the *Halekūlani* as far as the *Outrigger Reef* resort. This is generally known as **Halekūlani Beach**, or, in memory of a small inn that previously stood here, **Gray's Beach**, but to the ancient Hawaiians it was renowned as Kawehewehe, a place where the waters were said to have special healing properties. It too is a popular swimming spot, though erosion in recent years has scoured away much of the sand on the seabed, so reef shoes are advisable. If you're coming from Kālia Road, look out for the inconspicuous footpaths that squeeze through to the beach on either side of the *Halekūlani*.

Fort DeRussy and Kahanamoku beaches

Beyond Gray's Beach, the sands grow broader as you pass in front of the military base and the *Hale Koa* hotel, which although it's reserved for military personnel has a beachfront bar that's open to all customers. The walking can be a bit slow on the thick sand of **Fort DeRussy Beach** itself, but it's backed by some pleasant lawns and an open pavilion naturally sheltered by interlaced trees. Concessions stands here rent out surf and boogie boards, along with huge, garish pedalos. Few people swim at this point, however, as the ocean floor is sharp and rocky.

The westernmost section of the Waikīkī shorefront, **Kahanamoku Beach**, flanks the *Hilton Hawaiian Village*. Duke Kahanamoku's grandfather was granted most of the twenty-acre plot on which the hotel now stands in the Great Mahele of 1848. Thanks to its carefully sculpted shelf of sand, the beach where the Duke

The listings below provide a selection of **water-based activities** on Oahu, all readily accessible to visitors based in Waikīkī. **Activities desks** in the hotels, and **"activity centers"** elsewhere, sell tickets for waterborne pursuits of all kinds. If you're prepared to shop around, you'll find rates much lower than those quoted by the operators; look for discount coupons in free magazines, and flyers distributed on street corners. Activity centers also offer **discounts** on airport shuttles, land-based tours (see p.63), excursions to the *lū'aus* (p.125), and on air tickets and packages to the other Hawaiian islands.

Activity centers

Aloha Express *Waikīkī Circle Hotel*, 2464 Kalākaua Ave ☏ 808/924-4030.

Hawaii Tour & Travels 339 Saratoga Rd ☏ 808/922-4884, ⓦ www .hawaiitourandtravels.com.

Magnum Tickets & Tours 2134 Kalākaua Ave ☏ 808/923-7825.

Tours 4 Less 159 Ka'iulani Ave ☏ 808/923-2211.

Dinner and sightseeing cruises

Ali'i Kai Catamaran ☏ 808/954-8652 or 1-888/898-2519, ⓦ www.robertshawaii.com. This giant catamaran offers kitsch sunset dinner cruises along Waikīkī Beach, leaving from Pier 5, near Honolulu's Aloha Tower, at 5.30pm daily. $61, ages 3–11 $33.

Navatek I ☏ 808/973-1311, ⓦ www.atlantisadventures.com. Giant, very smooth-sailing catamaran, based at Pier 6 in Honolulu, which provides evening dinner cruises, complete with bland entertainment (poor-quality buffet $68, ages 2–12 $45; slightly better formal dining $95, ages 2–12 $60), and also a lunch buffet cruise, which include whale-watching in winter ($52, ages 2–12 $26).

Outrigger Catamaran ☏ 808/922-2210. Regular departures from Halekūlani Beach, immediately in front of Waikīkī's *Outrigger Reef* hotel, including ninety-minute sunset and sail-powered trips for $35, and longer snorkel cruises for $45, plus whale watching in winter.

Star of Honolulu ☏ 808/983-7827 or 1-800/334-6191, ⓦ www.starofhonolulu.com. The cost of a dinner cruise on this enormous ship, which leaves from pier 8 beside Aloha Tower, depends on which of its four decks you opt for. The seven-course French dinner with jazz on the top deck is $170, with no child reductions; all other passengers get to see the same Polynesian revue, with a steak-and-lobster dinner on decks 2 and 3 costing $99 for adults, $71 for kids, and dinner on the bottom deck

was raised is ideal for family bathing, but it lacks the concentrated glamor or excitement of central Waikīkī.

Kūhīo Beach

Large segments of the long beach that runs **east** of central Waikīkī did not exist until well after World War II. Previously, the shoreline at what's now broad **Kūhīo Beach** held only sporadic patches of sand, and several structures stood *makai* (on the ocean side) of Kalākaua Avenue as recently as 1970. Now, however, Kūhīo Beach is one of Waikīkī's busiest areas. The protective walls and breakwaters that jut out into the ocean here shelter two separate lagoons in which swimming is both safe and comfortable. The easternmost of these walls, the **Kapahulu Groin**, projects from the end of Kapahulu Avenue, following the line of the vanished Ku'ekaunahi Stream. Standing well above the waterline, it makes a good vantage point for photos of the Waikīkī panorama. On the other hand, the long, seaweed-covered **Slippery Wall**, parallel to the beach roughly fifty yards out, is washed

costing $70 (kids $42) or $48 ($29) depending on whether you want crab or chicken with your steak. Daytime cruises are cheaper, with 2hr whale-watching trips at $25 per person in winter.

Diving

A typical rate for a two-tank scuba-diving boat trip on Oahu is $100. The best sites near Waikīkī are the wrecks visited by Atlantis Submarines, as described below; otherwise Wai'anae in the west offers good conditions, Hanauma Bay makes a good shore dive, and there are various fine sites on the North Shore that can only be dived in summer. Operators include the **Aloha Dive Shop** at Koko Marina, not far from Hanauma Bay (☏808/395-5922, ⊛www.alohadiveshop.com); **Surf'n'Sea** in Hale'iwa (☏808/637-3337 or 1-800/899-7873, ⊛www.surfnsea.com); and **Ocean Concepts** in Wai'anae (☏808/677-7975 or 1-800/808-3483, ⊛www.oceanconcepts.com). An unusual variation is offered by **Bob's Hawaii Adventure** at Koko Marina (☏808/943-8628); no diving experience is required to take a half-hour ride along the ocean floor on an **underwater moped**, for $120.

Submarines

Atlantis Submarines ☏808/973-9811 or 1-800/548-6262, ⊛www.atlantisadventures.com. On these memorable one-of-a-kind trips, passengers are ferried to a spot from a quay at the *Hilton Hawaiian Village*, about a mile off Waikīkī, to rendezvous with two separate submarines. The 64-seater (adults $102, under-12s, who must be at least three feet tall, $51) is a bit more comfortable than the 48-seater ($81/$41), but the 45min cruise on either is substantially the same, descending a hundred feet beneath the waves to pass a sunken airplane and an artificial reef before circling a full-size shipwreck, with a certainty of seeing colorful fish and a likelihood of spotting sharks and turtles. Prices tend to drop each day from lunchtime onwards.

Other watersports

Surfboard rental, **surfing lessons**, and **outrigger canoe** rides in Waikīkī are detailed on p.79; for details of Surf 'n' Sea, the North Shore's major operator, see p.150. The best place on Oahu to rent a **kayak** is Kailua Bay on the Windward Coast; for details of operators, see p.136. You can **parasail** off Waikīkī, although the boats set off from Kewalo Basin to the west, with Aloha Parasail (☏808/521-2446) or Hawaiian Parasail (☏808/591-1280), or in Koko Marina with Hawaii Watersports Center, with whom you can also **waterski** (☏808/395-3773, ⊛www.hawaiiwatersportscenter.com).

over by every wave. Daredevil locals boogie-board just outside the wall, but the currents are so strong that you should only join them if you really know what you're doing. Similarly, don't try to swim to the east of the Groin; it's all too easy to blunder into deep spots created by underwater drifts.

At 6pm each night, a conch shell blows to signal the start of a free **hula show** on the lawns beside Kūhīo Beach. With island musicians and dancers performing by the light of flaming torches, it's a perfect way to relax at sunset, at the end of another hard day.

Kapi'olani Park Beach

East of the Kapahulu Groin, at the end of the built-up section of Waikīkī, comes a gap in the beach where the sand all but disappears and the waters are not suitable for bathing. Not far beyond, however, to either side of the Waikīkī Aquarium (described on p.86), **Kapi'olani Park Beach** is a favorite with local families and fitness freaks, and is also known for having a strong gay presence. Banyans and coconut palms offer plenty of free shade and its lawns make a perfect picnic spot. Waikīkī's only substantial stretch of reasonably unspoiled coral reef runs a short distance offshore, shielding a pleasant, gentle swimming area. The most used segment of the beach, nearest to Waikīkī, is **Queen's Surf Beach Park** – confusingly named after a long-gone restaurant that was itself named after the Queen's Surf surf break, back to the west off central Waikīkī.

A short way past the Aquarium stands the solemn concrete facade of the decaying **War Memorial Natatorium**. This curious combination of World War I memorial and swimming pool, with seating for 2500 spectators, was opened with a 100-meter swim by Duke Kahanamoku (see p.83) in 1927. During its inaugural championships, Johnny "Tarzan" Weissmuller set world records in the 100-, 400- and 800-meter races. Ironically, the Natatorium never really recovered from being used for training by the US Navy during World War II, and for many years it has remained in a very sorry state indeed, despite constant proposals for its restoration.

Sans Souci and Kaluahole beaches

East of the Natatorium, palm-fringed **Sans Souci Beach** commemorates one of Waikīkī's earliest guesthouses, built in 1884 and twice stayed in by Robert Louis Stevenson. In addition to being sheltered enough for young children, the beach also offers decent snorkeling. That's unusual for Waikīkī, where most of the reef has been suffocated by dumped sand. The *New Otani Kaimana Beach* hotel (see p.71), now occupying the site of the *Sans Souci*, marks the return of buildings to the shoreline and is as far as most visitors would think to stroll along Waikīkī Beach. However, beyond it lies the **Outrigger Canoe Club Beach**, which was leased in 1908 by the club on the condition that its waters be set aside for surfing, canoeing, and ocean sports. The club headquarters was later replaced by the first of the *Outrigger* chain of hotels, but the ocean remains the preserve of surfers and snorkelers.

As Kalākaua Avenue heads out of Waikīkī beyond the Outrigger Canoe Club Beach, curving away from the shoreline to join Diamond Head Road and skirt the base of the volcano, it passes a little scrap of sandy beach known as **Kaluahole Beach** or **Diamond Head Beach**. Though too small for anyone to want to spend much time on the beach itself, it does offer some quite good swimming, and makes a good launching-point for windsurfers.

Diamond Head Beach Park and beyond

The coast immediately to the east of Kaluahole Beach, officially **Diamond Head Beach Park**, is much too rocky and exposed for ordinary swimmers. It is, however, noteworthy as the site of the 55-foot **Diamond Head Lighthouse**, built in 1899 and still in use. The area also has a reputation as a nudist hangout, especially popular with gay men.

A short distance further on, the highway, by now raised well above sea level, rounds the point of Diamond Head; the island of Molokai to the east is visible across the water on clear days. Little scraps of sand cling here and there to the shoreline, but those who pick their way down to the ocean from the three roadside lookouts that constitute **Kuilei Cliffs Beach Park** tend to be keen surfers.

Opposite the intersection where Diamond Head Road loops back inland and Kāhala Avenue continues beside the ocean, **Kaʻalāwai Beach**, at the end of short Kulumanu Place, is a narrow patch of white sand favored by snorkelers and surfers. It is brought to a halt by Black Point, where lava flowing from Diamond Head into the sea created Oahu's southernmost point.

Inland Waikīkī

Away from the beaches, any walking you do in Waikīkī is likely to be from necessity rather than from choice; there's little in the way of conventional sightseeing. The inland roads may once have been picturesque lanes that meandered between the coconut groves and taro fields, but they're now lined by dull concrete malls and hotels built over the last twenty years. In addition, the daytime **heat** can make walking more than a few blocks uncomfortable.

However, vestiges of the old Waikīkī are still scattered here and there, as pointed out by the helpful surfboard-shaped placards of the waterfront **Waikīkī Historical Trail**. There are also a couple of museums illustrating aspects of Hawaiian history, and the lawns of Kapiʻolani Park to the east make a welcome break from the bustle of the resort area. It may come as a surprise that for some people Waikīkī still counts as home; you'll probably see groups of seniors strumming their ʻukuleles or playing chess in the oceanfront pavilions.

West from the Duke Kahanamoku statue

The logical place to start a walking tour is in the middle of Waikīkī Beach, on seafront **Kalākaua Avenue**, where a statue of **Duke Kahanamoku** (1890–1968) is always wreathed in *leis*. The archetypal "Beach Boy," Duke represented the US in three Olympics, winning swimming golds in both 1912 and 1920. His subsequent exhibition tours popularized the Hawaiian art of surfing all over the world, and as Sheriff of Honolulu he continued to welcome celebrity visitors to Hawaii until his death in 1968. Sadly, the statue stands with its back to the ocean, a pose Duke seldom adopted in life; otherwise he'd be gazing at the spot where in 1917 he rode a single 35-foot wave a record total of one and a quarter miles.

Slightly west of the statue, alongside a small police station in a railed enclosure, are four large boulders known as the **sacred stones** of either Ulukou (which is the name of this spot) or Kapaemāhū (the name of a Tahitian magician-priest). These are said to embody the healing and spiritual powers of Kapaemāhū and three of his brother wizards, who set them in place before returning to their home island of Raiatea in the fourteenth century.

A little further west, the wedge of the **Sheraton Moana Surfrider** forces Kalākaua Avenue away from the ocean. Though not Waikīkī's first hotel, the *Moana* is the oldest left standing, and has been transformed back to a close approximation of its original 1901 appearance. Like all Waikīkī hotels, the *Moana* is happy to allow nonguests in for a peek, indeed it even offers free guided tours (Mon, Wed & Fri 11am & 5pm). At any time, the luxurious settees of its long Beaux Arts lobby make an ideal spot to catch up with the newspapers.

Follow Kalākaua Avenue west from here, and you'll come to the **Royal Hawaiian Shopping Center**, Waikīkī's most upmarket mall (though not a patch on Honolulu's Ala Moana Center; see p.127), and across from that the funkier open-air **International Marketplace**, which has a bargain food court (see p.127). Once the site of an ancient *heiau*, and later of the ten-thousand-strong royal Helumoa coconut grove – of which a few palms still survive – the beachfront here is today dominated by the **Royal Hawaiian Hotel**, also known as the "Pink Palace." Its Spanish-Moorish architecture was all the rage when it opened in 1927, with a room rate of $14 per night, but its grandeur is now somewhat swamped by a towering new wing.

The area to the west of the *Royal Hawaiian* has been the focus over the last few years of a huge redevelopment project, spearheaded by the Outrigger group of hotels, under the overall name of **Waikīkī Beach Walk**. So far, it amounts to little more than the turning of what was previously a rather run-down couple of blocks along Lewers Street, stretching towards the sea, into a sort of glitzy annex of the upscale end of Kalākaua Avenue. As this book went to press, a couple of high-end new hotels

△ Lei-garlanded statue of Duke Kahanamoku

were about to open, as well as restaurants including a branch of *Roy's*, but no big-name retailers had yet announced plans to open stores here. Major changes are more likely to follow the opening of the much-trumpeted **Trump International Hotel**, a 350-foot hotel and condo development currently scheduled to open in 2009. Even before ground was broken on that project in 2006, every condo in the building was sold – a total of $700 millon in sales – on the first day of availability.

Fort DeRussy

On maps, the military base of **Fort DeRussy** looks like a welcome expanse of green at the western edge of the main built-up area of Waikīkī. In fact, it's largely taken up by parking lots and tennis courts, and is not a place to stroll for pleasure. At its oceanfront side, however, the **US Army Museum** (Tues–Sun 10am–4.15pm; free) is located in a low concrete structure which, as Battery Randolph, housed massive artillery pieces that were directed by observers stationed atop Diamond Head during World War II. Displays here trace the history of warfare in Hawaii back to the time of Kamehameha the Great, with the bulk of the collection consisting of the various guns and cannons that have been used to defend Honolulu since the US Army first arrived, four days after annexation in 1898. One photo shows a young, giggling Shirley Temple perched astride a gun barrel during the 1930s, but the mood swiftly changes with a detailed chronicling of the state's pivotal role during the Pacific campaign against Japan.

East from the Duke Kahanamoku statue

The first thing you come to as you head **east** from the Duke Kahanamoku statue is a magnificent, well-groomed Indian Banyan tree, supported by two "trunks" that on close inspection turn out to be tangled masses of aerial roots. This area has been attractively landscaped in the last few years, and kitted out with appealing little lagoons and waterfalls as well as shaded pavilions and open-air benches. Across the street, the central atrium of the *Hyatt Regency Waikīkī* hotel holds a much larger waterfall, surrounded by palm trees. Display cases scattered around the first and second floors of the hotel contain a mish-mash of artifacts, from antique Chinese shoes to 1950s' *hula* dolls.

Father Damien, the nineteenth-century Belgian priest who ranks with Hawaii's greatest heroes, is commemorated in the simple **Damien Museum** at 130 Ohua Ave (Mon–Fri 9am–3pm; free; ☏808/923-2690), one block east of the *Pacific Beach Hotel*. This unobtrusive shrine sits beneath a schoolroom behind the angular modern Catholic church of **St Augustine**. Damien's life and work is evoked by an assortment of mundane items, such as receipts for cases of soda and barrels of flour, and

Street names of Waikīkī

Waikīkī's unfamiliar **street names** may be easier to remember if you know the stories that lie behind them:

Helumoa Road Literally, "chicken scratch"; the road crosses the site of a *heiau* used for human sacrifices, which was frequented by chickens that scratched for maggots amid the corpses.

Ka'iulani Avenue The young Princess Victoria Ka'iulani (1875–99) was immortalized in a poem by Robert Louis Stevenson.

Kālaimoku Street Kamehameha the Great's prime minister, Kālaimoku, who died in 1827, also called himself "William Pitt" in honor of his British equivalent.

Kalākaua Avenue Originally named Waikīkī Road, it was renamed in honor of the "Merrie Monarch" (1836–91; see p.538) in 1905.

Kūhīo Avenue Prince Jonah Kūhīo Kalaniana'ole (1871–1922), or "Prince Cupid," bequeathed much of the eastern end of Waikīkī to the city upon his death.

Lili'uokalani Avenue Queen Lili'uokalani was the last monarch to rule over Hawaii (1838–1917; see p.539).

Nāhua Street Chiefess Nāhua once owned an oceanfront estate in Waikīkī.

'Olohana Street The captured English sailor, John Young (1745–1835; see p.301), was known as Olohana to the Hawaiians after his naval cry of "All hands on deck."

Tusitala Street Named after author Robert Louis Stevenson, whose Hawaiian name was taken from the Samoan word for "story-teller."

Uluniu Avenue Literally, "coconut grove," it marks the site of a cottage owned by King David Kalākaua.

his prayer books and vestments. Although he established churches all over Hawaii, Damien's fame derives principally from his final sojourn in the leper colony at **Kalaupapa** on Molokai. He eventually succumbed to the disease himself on April 15, 1889, at the age of 49; harrowing deathbed photos show the ravages it inflicted upon him. For a full account of Father Damien's life, see box, pp.420–421.

Kapi'olani Park

Beyond the eastern limit of central Waikīkī, as defined by Kapuhulu Avenue, lies Hawaii's first-ever public park, **Kapi'olani Park**. This much-needed breathing space was established in 1877 by King David Kalākaua, and named for his queen. It originally held a number of ponds, until the completion of the Ala Wai Canal in 1928 cut off its supply of fresh water. Now locals flock to its open green lawns, with joggers pounding the footpaths, and practitioners of t'ai chi exercising in slow-motion beneath the banyans. The park was long the home of the kitsch **Kodak Hula Show**, but sadly that tradition has ended. However, the adjoining **Waikīkī Shell** hosts large concerts, especially in summer, while the Royal Hawaiian Band performs on the park's **bandstand** on Sundays at 2pm.

Honolulu Zoo

Honolulu Zoo occupies a verdant wedge on the fringes of Kapi'olani Park (daily 9am–5.30pm, last admission 4.30pm; adults $8, ages 6–12 $1; ☎808/971-7171, Ⓦwww.honoluluzoo.org), with its main entrance barely a minute's walk from the bustle of Waikīkī. Sadly, it's all a bit too dilapidated and unkempt to merit a thorough recommendation, and it's surprisingly hard to spot many of its animals in their ageing enclosures. On the positive side, the tropical undergrowth and blossoming trees can look pretty against the backdrop of Diamond Head, and kids may enjoy the chance to see species that range from wallowing hippos and gray kangaroos to unfortunate monkeys trapped on tiny islands in a crocodile-infested lagoon. The zoo's pride and joy, the African Savanna exhibit – a world of reddish mud where the "black" rhinos end up pretty much the color of their surroundings – is reasonably successful in recreating the swamps and grasslands of Africa.

Waikīkī Aquarium

A few minutes' walk further east along the Kapi'olani Park waterfront stands the disappointingly small **Waikīkī Aquarium** (daily 9am–5pm; adults $9, seniors and students $6, ages 13–17 $4, ages 5–12 $2; Ⓦwww.waikikiaquarium.com). Windows in its indoor galleries offer views into the turquoise world of Hawaiian reef fish, among them the lurid red frogfish – an ugly brute that squats splay-footed on the rock waiting to eat unwary passersby – and a teeming mass of small sharks. The highlight has to be the "leafy seadragon," a truly bizarre Australian relative of the relatively normal seahorse; there's also a whole tank devoted to sea life from Hanauma Bay. Outside, the mocked-up "edge of the reef," complete with artificial tide pools, feels a bit pointless with the real thing just a few feet away. Nearby is a long tank of Hawaiian monk seals, dog-like not only in appearance but also in their willingness to perform tawdry tricks for snacks. As well as a description of traditional fish farming, there's a display of the modern equivalent, in which mahimahi fish grow from transparent eggs to glistening six-footers in what resemble lava lamps.

Diamond Head

The craggy 762-foot pinnacle of **Diamond Head**, immediately southeast along the coast from Waikīkī, is Honolulu's most famous landmark. It's among the youngest of the chain of volcanic cones – others include Punchbowl and Koko Head – that stretch across southeast Oahu. All were created by brief, spectacular blasts of the Ko'olau vent, which reawakened a few hundred thousand years ago after slumbering for more than two million years. The most recent of the series date back less than ten-thousand years, so geologists consider further eruptions possible. Diamond Head itself was formed in a matter of a few days or even hours: the reason its southwestern side is so much higher than the others is that the trade winds were blowing from the northeast at the time.

△ Diamond Head above Queen's Surf Beach

Ancient Hawaiians knew Diamond Head as either Leiʻahi ("wreath of fire," a reference to beacons lit on the summit to guide canoes) or Laeʻahi ("brow of the yellow-fin tuna"). They built several *heiaus* in and around it, slid down its walls to Waikīkī on *hōlua* land-sleds as sport, and threw convicted criminals from the rim. Its modern name derives from the mistake of a party of English sailors early in the nineteenth century, who stumbled across what they thought were diamonds on its slopes and rushed back to town with their pockets bulging with glittering but worthless calcite crystals. For most of the twentieth century, the interior was sealed off by the US armed forces, who based long-range artillery here during World War I, and after Pearl Harbor used the bunkers to triangulate and aim the guns of Waikīkī's Fort DeRussy. Only in the 1960s was it reopened as the **Diamond Head State Monument** public park.

Access to the crater is via a short road tunnel that drills through the surrounding walls from the peak's *mauka* side. The entrance is around two miles by road from Waikīkī; it's not a particularly pleasant walk, so most people either drive or take the bus. Buses #22 and #58 from Waikīkī climb up Monsarrat Avenue past the zoo to join Diamond Head Road, and stop not far from the tunnel; if you're driving, you can also follow the shoreline highway below the mountain and climb the same road from the bottom.

Because the floor of the crater stands well above sea level – it's gradually filling in as the walls erode – Diamond Head is not quite so dramatic from the inside. In fact, the lawns of the crater interior are oddly bland, almost suburban. Often parched, but a vivid green after rain, they're still dotted with little-used military installations, some of which remain restricted. There have been suggestions that these should be replaced by tennis and golf facilities, but the prevailing wisdom is to allow the place to return to nature in due course.

The climb to the rim

The only reason anyone comes to Diamond Head is to hike the hot half-hour trail up to the rim for a grand **panorama** of the whole southern coast of Oahu. So many walkers hit the trail each day, plenty of whom treat the undertaking as a joyless endurance test, that this is very far from a wilderness experience, and serious hikers looking for great natural splendors are advised to head elsewhere. Not that this is an easy climb; it's surprisingly steep, with several long concrete staircases, and it's exposed to the morning sun, so unprepared tourists often end up in considerable distress. Be sure to bring water, and wear suitable footwear and a hat.

Rangers stationed alongside the parking lot collect $5 per vehicle, or $1 from each walk-in hiker; the paved trail is open daily from 6am until 6pm. Having first climbed slowly away from the crater floor, it meanders up the inside walls. Many of the holes visible but out of reach on the hillside are ancient burial caves. Before long, you're obliged to enter the vast network of ugly military bunkers and passageways that riddle the crater. After passing through the first long, dark and cramped tunnel – watch out for the bolts poking from the ceiling – take time to catch your breath before tackling the very tall, narrow flight of yellow-painted concrete steps that leads up between two high walls to the right.

At the top of the steps, you come to another tunnel, then climb a dark spiral staircase through four or so cramped tiers of fortifications, equipped with eye-slit windows and camouflaged from above. Beyond that, a final outdoor staircase leads to the summit, where you get your first sweeping views of Waikīkī and Honolulu. In theory an official geodetic plate marks the highest point, but no matter how often it's replaced it soon gets stolen again. On days when a *kona* (southwest) wind is blowing, planes landing at Honolulu Airport approach from the east, passing low enough over Diamond Head for you to see the passengers inside.

Weary hikers who can't face the walk back to Waikīkī can catch the waiting taxis in the parking lot back on the crater floor.

Downtown Honolulu

Downtown Honolulu, the administrative heart of first the kingdom, and now the state, of Hawaii, stands a few blocks west of the original city center. Most of the compact grid of streets where the port grew up is now taken up by Chinatown, while downtown is generally considered to focus on the cluster of buildings that surround **'Iolani Palace**, home to Hawaii's last monarchs. This is certainly an attractive district, with several well-preserved historic buildings, but it's not a very lively one. At lunchtime on weekdays office workers scurry through the streets, but the rest of the time the contrast with the frenzy of Waikīkī is striking. With few shops, bars, or restaurants to lure outsiders, the whole place is usually empty by 8pm.

'Iolani Palace

The stately, four-square **'Iolani Palace**, dominating downtown from the center of its spacious gardens, was the official home of the last two monarchs of Hawaii. It was built for **King David Kalākaua** in 1882, near the site of a previous palace that had been destroyed by termites, and he lived here until his death in 1891. For his sister and successor, **Queen Lili'uokalani**, it was first a palace, and then, after her overthrow in 1895 (see p.539), a prison. Until 1968, by which time the termites had pretty much eaten up this palace too, it was the Hawaiian state capitol building. Following the completion of the new Capitol in 1969, it was turned into a museum.

Visitors can choose between three different ways to see the palace. The first-floor **state apartments**, reached via grand exterior staircases, and the royal family's **private quarters** on the second floor can be seen on **guided tours** in the morning (Tues–Sat 9–11.15am, every 20min; adults $20, ages 5–12 $5, under-5s not admitted; reservations advised on ☎808/522-0832; ⓦwww.iolanipalace.org), or on self-guided **audio tours** later on (Tues–Sat 11.45am–3pm; adults $12, ages 5–12 $5, under-5s not admitted). The self-guided **basement galleries** are open to visitors on either kind of tour, or you can also pay to access only those galleries (Tues–Sat 9am–4.30pm; adults $6, ages 5–12 $3, under-5s admitted free).

Although the palace has become a symbol for the sovereignty movement, and is occasionally the scene of large pro-independence demonstrations, the tours are firmly apolitical. Guides revel in the lost romance of the Hawaiian monarchy without quite acknowledging that it was illegally overthrown by the United States. The fact that visitors have to shuffle around in cotton bootees to protect the hardwood floors adds to the air of unreality. Apart from the *koa*-wood floors and staircase, however, the palace contains little that is distinctively Hawaiian. In the large **Throne Room**, Kalākaua held formal balls to celebrate his coronation and fiftieth birthday, and Lili'uokalani was tried for treason for allegedly supporting moves for her own restoration. The *kapu* stick separating the thrones of Kalākaua and his wife Kapi'olani was made from a narwhal tusk given to Kalākaua by a sea captain. Other reception rooms lead off from the grand central hall, with all available wall space taken up by portraits of Hawaiian and other monarchs. Though the plush upstairs **bedrooms** feel similarly impersonal, there's one touching exhibit – a quilt made by Queen Lili'uokalani during her eight months under house arrest.

Prize items in the basement display cases include two wooden calabashes presented to King Kalākaua on his fiftieth birthday in 1886. One, the tall, slender *ipu* of

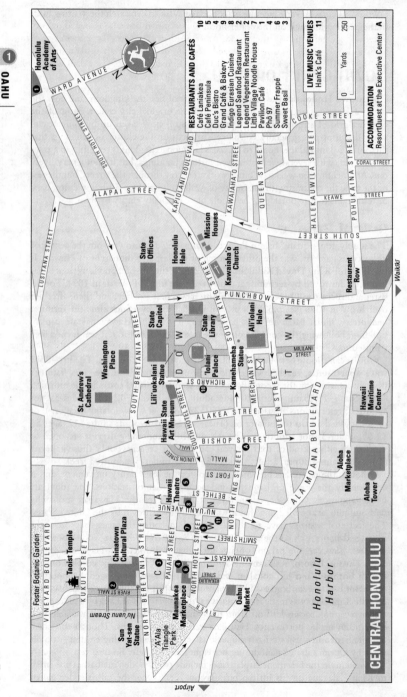

CENTRAL HONOLULU

RESTAURANTS AND CAFÉS	
Café Laniakea	10
Café Peninsula	5
Duc's Bistro	4
Grand Café & Bakery	9
Indigo Eurasian Cuisine	8
Legend Seafood Restaurant	2
Legend Vegetarian Restaurant	2
Little Village Noodle House	7
Pavilion Café	1
Phò 97	6
Summer Frappé	4
Sweet Basil	3

LIVE MUSIC VENUES	
Hank's Café	11

ACCOMMODATION	
ResortQuest at the Executive Center	A

0   250
Yards

▶ Waikīkī

▶ Airport

Lono'ikimakahiki I, was then claimed to be five hundred years old. Retrieved from the royal burial ground at Ka'awaloa on the Big Island, it was said in legend to have once held all the winds of the world. Among other extraordinary treasures are a feather cloak that Kamehameha I seized from his defeated rival Kīwala'o in 1782 (see p.533); Kalākaua's own crown; and a brooch that Queen Lili'uokalani wore to Queen Victoria's Golden Jubilee celebrations in 1887.

A grass-covered mound in the palace garden marks the original resting place of King Kamehameha II and Queen Kamamalu. Their remains, brought here by George Byron (the cousin of the poet) after they died of measles in England in 1824, were later moved to the royal mausoleum in Nu'uanu (see p.106).

The palace's **ticket office** is housed in the castellated 'Iolani Barracks on the west side of the grounds, an odd structure that pre-dates the palace by about fifteen years, and also holds a gift store. Anyone **driving** to the palace will find plenty of metered visitor parking within the palace grounds.

Queen Lili'uokalani Statue, the State Capitol, and Honolulu Hale

On the northern side of 'Iolani Palace, beyond the impressive banyan tree at the foot of the palace steps, a walkway separates the grounds from the State Capitol to the north. At its center, a statue of **Queen Lili'uokalani** looks haughtily towards the state's present-day legislators. Festooned with *leis* and plumeria blossoms, she's depicted holding copies of her mournful song *Aloha 'Oe*, the Hawaiian creation chant known as the *Kumulipo*, and her draft Constitution of 1893, which precipitated the coup d'état against her.

Hawaii's **State Capitol** is a bizarre edifice, propped up on pillars, and with each of its two legislative chambers shaped like a volcano. It took little more than twenty years from its opening in 1969 for flaws in its design to force its closure for extensive and very expensive rebuilding. In front of the main entrance, there's a peculiar cubic statue of Father Damien (see box, pp.420–421) created by Marisol Escobar in 1968. Well-tended memorials to Hawaiians who died in Korea and Vietnam stand in the grounds to the west.

The seat of Honolulu's city government – **Honolulu Hale**, opposite the eastern end of the walkway – is a more successful architectural experiment. An airy 1920s melding of Italianate and Spanish-Mission styles, with whitewashed walls, ornate patterned ceilings, and red-tiled roofs, it boasts a grand central atrium that's packed with colorful murals and sculptural flourishes.

Washington Place and St Andrews Cathedral

Though Punchbowl Crater looms large as you look north from the Capitol, and you may be able to spot visitors on the rim, it's a long way away by road. Much closer at hand, across Beretania Street, is the white-columned, Colonial-style mansion known as **Washington Place**. During the 1860s, Queen Lili'uokalani resided here as plain Mrs Dominis, wife to the governor of Hawaii under King Kamehameha V. After her dethronement she returned to live here as a private citizen once more, and died at the mansion in 1917. It became the official residence of the governor of Hawaii five years later, although the present governor lives in a separate house in the grounds. Free tours for groups of up to 12 are available by appointment (Mon–Fri only; reservations must be made at least 48 hours in advance on ☎808/586-0248).

Behind Washington Place, and a short distance to the east, rises the central tower of **St Andrews Cathedral**. Work began on this Gothic-influenced

Episcopal church in 1867, in realization of plans formed ten years previously by King Kamehameha IV, who wanted to encourage Anglican missionaries to come to Hawaii to counterbalance the prevailing Puritanism of their American counterparts. Construction work only ended in 1958, with the completion of the Great West Window, a stained-glass rendition of the story of Hawaiian Christianity.

The Kamehameha Statue and Ali'iolani Hale

The flower-bedecked, gilt figure of **Kamehameha the Great** (1758–1819), the first man to rule all the islands of Hawaii, stares northwards across King Street towards 'Iolani Palace from outside Ali'iolani Hale. Kamehameha is depicted wearing the *'ahu'ula* (royal cloak), *malo* (loincloth), *ka'ei* (sash), and *mahiole* (feather helmet), and clutching a spear. The work of Thomas R. Gould, an American sculptor based in Florence, the statue was commissioned by the Hawaiian legislature in 1878 to celebrate the centenary of the arrival of Captain Cook. On its way to Hawaii, however, it was lost in a shipwreck, so a second copy was cast and dispatched. That arrived in 1880 and was unveiled by King Kalākaua at his coronation in 1883; surplus insurance money from the lost statue paid for the sequence of four panels depicting scenes from Kamehameha's life around its base. Meanwhile, the original statue, which was found floating off the Falkland Islands, was purchased by a whaling captain in Port Stanley, and also turned up in Hawaii. It was packed off to Kamehameha's birthplace on the Big Island. Ceremonies are held at the Honolulu statue on June 11 each year to mark Kamehameha Day, a state holiday.

Erected in 1874, **Ali'iolani Hale** – "House of the Heavenly King" in Hawaiian – was Hawaii's first library and national museum; it was also the first building taken over by the conspirators who overthrew the monarchy in 1893. Throughout its history, however, its main function has been as the home of the state's Supreme Court. The first floor houses the fascinating **Judiciary History Center** (Mon–Fri 9am–4pm; free; ⓦwww.judiciaryhistorycenter.org). This outlines the story of Hawaiian law from the days of the ancient *kapu* onwards and chronicles the Supreme Court's role in replacing the tradition of collective land ownership with the concept of private ownership. There's also a scale model of Honolulu in 1850, watched over by the now-vanished fort and with thatched huts still dotted among its Victorian mansions.

Hawaii State Art Museum

Immediately west of 'Iolani Palace, across Richards Street from the palace ticket office but entered via South Hotel Street, the excellent **Hawaii State Art Museum** (Tues–Sat 10am–4pm; free; ⓣ808/586-0900; ⓦwww.hawaii.gov/sfca) fills the second floor of an impressive 1920s Spanish-Mission building with displays of the state's collection of contemporary art. Broadly speaking, the 'Ewa galleries to the west hold small-scale works in different media that explore Hawaii's natural and urban environment, including Mark Hamasaki's hard-hitting photos of the devastation caused by the H-3 freeway project. Look out too for the most popular painting, taken from Masami Teraoka's hilarious Hanauma Bay Series, in which local snorkelers are deliberately styled after Japan's *ukiyo-e* tradition of brightly colored woodblock prints. Under the title of "Precious Resources: The Land and the Sea," the Diamond Head galleries to the east feature displays on Pacific voyaging, including a model of the *Hōkūle'a* canoe, some fine *koa*-wood carved bowls, and large, lyrical paintings of Hawaiian landscapes.

Kawaiaha'o Church

Although **Kawaiaha'o Church** (Mon–Fri 8am–4pm, Sunday service 9am; free), just east of 'Iolani Palace near the junction of Punchbowl and King streets, was erected in 1842, less than twenty years after the first Christian missionaries came to Hawaii, it was the fifth church to stand on this site. According to its Protestant minister, Rev. Hiram Bingham, each of the four predecessors was a thatched "cage in a haymow." This one, by contrast, was built with thousand-pound chunks of living coral, hacked from the reef. It's not especially huge, but the columned portico is grand enough, topped by a square clock-tower. Inside, broad balconies run down both sides of the nave, lined with royal portraits. Below, plaques on the walls honor early figures of Hawaiian Christianity, such as Henry 'Opukaha'ia (see p.534). The plushest pews – at the back of the church, upholstered in velvet and marked off by *kahili* standards – were reserved for royalty.

In the **gardens** on the *mauka* side of the church, a fountain commemorates the site of a spring formerly known as *Ka wai a Ha'o*, "the water of Ha'o." A rare treasure in this barren region, it was reserved for *ali'i nui*, or high chiefs, such as chiefess Ha'o. The small mausoleum in the grounds fronting the church holds the remains of **King Lunalilo**, who ruled for less than two years after his election in 1872. Feeling slighted that his mother's body had not been removed from the churchyard to the royal mausoleum, he chose to be buried here instead. The rest of the graves in the **cemetery** around the back serve as a brief introduction to Hawaii's nineteenth-century missionary elite, with an abundance of Castles and Cookes, Alexanders and Baldwins, and the only president of the Republic, Sanford B. Dole.

The Mission Houses

The lives of Hawaii's first Christian missionaries are recalled in the restored **Mission Houses** behind Kawaiaha'o Church. Standing cheek by jowl at 553 S King St, these three nineteenth-century buildings commemorate the pioneers of the Sandwich Islands Mission, who arrived from Boston in 1820. The only way to see inside the actual buildings is on a guided tour (Tues, Wed, Fri & Sat 11am & 2.45pm, Thurs 2pm; adults $10, under-19s $6; ☏808/531-0481, ⓦwww .missionhouses.org), but displays in the separate visitor center (Tues–Sat 10am–4pm; $5, or $13 combination with tour) provide a sense of the missionary impact from a native Hawaiian perspective, and include models of the mission station as it stood in the 1820s and 1850s.

The oldest edifice, the two-story **Frame House**, was shipped in whole from New England in 1821. Reluctant to let outsiders build permanent structures, the king only allowed it to go up with the words "when you go away, take everything with you." Local fears that its cellar held weapons for a planned takeover of the islands were allayed when Kamehameha's principal adviser, Kalanimoku, built a house with a larger cellar across the street. The house, whose tiny windows were entirely unsuited to the heat of Honolulu, was home to four missionary families. A kitchen had to be added because cooking outdoors attracted too much attention from the islanders, as it was *kapu* (taboo) for women to prepare food.

One of the missionaries' first acts, in 1823, was to set up the **Print House**, which produced the first Hawaiian-language Bible – *Ka Palapala Hemolele*. The current building – not the original, but its 1841 replacement – holds a replica of its imported Ramage printing press, whose limitations were among the reasons why to this day the Hawaiian alphabet only has twelve letters.

The largest of the three buildings, the **Chamberlain House**, started life in 1831 as the mission storehouse. As the missionary families became increasingly embroiled in the economy of the islands, that role turned it into the commercial headquarters of Castle & Cooke, one of the original "Big Five" (see p.537).

Honolulu Academy of Arts

Honolulu residents take great pride in the stunning fine art on display at the **Academy of Arts**, 900 S Beretania St (Tues–Sat 10am–4.30pm, Sun 1–5pm; tours Tues–Sat 10.15am, 11.30am & 1.30pm, Sun 1.15pm; open 11am–5pm, with free admission, on third Sun of month; otherwise $7, seniors and students $4, under-13s free; ⓣ808/532-8700, ⓦwww.honoluluacademy.org). Few tourists find their way here – half a mile east of the Capitol – but two or three hours wandering the galleries of this elegant former private home, with its Eastern-influenced architecture, open courtyards and fountains, is time well spent.

The bulk of the Academy's superb collection of **paintings** adorns the galleries surrounding the **Mediterranean Court**. Highlights include Van Gogh's *Wheat Field*, Gauguin's *Two Nudes on a Tahitian Beach*, and one of Monet's *Water Lilies*. Other pieces date from the Italian Renaissance, with two separate *Apostles* by Carlo Crivelli, as well as engravings by Rembrandt and Dürer; more recent canvases include lesser works by Picasso, Léger, Braque, Matisse, and Tanguy. Under the theme of "East meets West," the final parts of this section explore cross-cultural contacts between Europe, India, and China. An entire room on Captain Cook and the Pacific is papered with gloriously romantic French wallpaper from around 1804, depicting an idyllic South Seas landscape in which Cook's death is a minor unfortunate detail.

An even larger area on the first floor is devoted to **Asian** art and artifacts, with a succession of galleries displaying Korean, Japanese, "pan-Asian Buddhist," and, especially, **Chinese** works. Among the latter are beautiful Neolithic-era ceramics, four-thousand-year-old jade blades, and columns from a four-thousand-year-old Han tomb that resemble Easter Island statues. There then follows a cornucopia of masterpieces: Buddhist and Shinto deities, plus *netsuke* (toggles) and samurai armor from Japan; Tibetan *thangkas* (religious images); Indian carvings ranging from Rajasthani sandstone screens to a stone Chola statue of Krishna; Mayan effigies and Indonesian stick figures; Melanesian masks incorporating such elements as boars' tusks and cobwebs; and pottery from the pueblos of Arizona and New Mexico. One last street-level gallery holds the Academy's **Modern and Contemporary** collection, which ranges from a Francis Bacon triptych to a Nam June Paik video installation.

Upstairs on the second floor of the newer Luce Pavilion, most of the works in **The Arts of Hawaii** are of mainly historic interest. Although you can find larger and more absorbing collections of ancient Hawaiian artifacts at the Bishop Museum (see p.108) or 'Iolani Palace (see p.89), the early depictions of Hawaii here by Western artists are well worth seeing. These include an 1816 painting of Kailua on the Big Island by the Russian Louis Choris – whose well-known portrait *Kamehameha in Red Vest* is here only as a reproduction – and several dramatic renditions of the changing face of the volcano at Kīlauea. A few key works by Georgia O'Keeffe, who was enamored of the islands' verdant cliffs and waterfalls, demonstrate her distinctively surreal, sexually charged landscapes of Maui's 'Iao Valley and Hāna coast.

The Academy's appealing and inexpensive **courtyard café** makes a highly recommended lunchtime stop (see p.120).

Chinatown

Barely five minutes' walk west of 'Iolani Palace, a pair of matching stone dragons flank either side of Hotel Street, marking the transition between downtown Honolulu and the oldest part of the city, **Chinatown**. For well over a century, this was renowned as the city's red-light district. Though almost all the pool halls, massage parlors, and tawdry bars that formerly lined the narrow streets are gone, its fading green clapboard storefronts and bustling market ambience still make Chinatown seem like another world. Cosmopolitan, atmospheric, and historic in equal proportions, it's the one local neighborhood that's genuinely fun to explore on your own, though you can join an organized **walking tour** of Chinatown with the Hawaii Heritage Center, 1168 Smith St (Tues & Fri 9.30am; $10; ☏808/521-2749) or the Chinatown Museum (min group of 4; Mon–Sat 10.30am; $10; ☏808/595-3358).

While Chinatown retains its traditional Asian flavor, it's also attracted a considerable influx in recent years of hip, creative types, who are most evident in its lively **art scene**. The regular **First Friday** event, in which galleries stay open 5–8pm on the first Friday of each month, enabling visitors to take early-evening strolls from gallery to gallery before adjourning to local bars and restaurants, has been so successful that it has spawned the self-explanatory Second Saturday and Third Thursday programs.

Exploring Chinatown

Of the district's two main axes, N Hotel and Maunakea streets, **Hotel Street** best lives up to the old lowlife reputation, with neon signs advertising long-gone fleshpots – *Club Hubba Hubba Topless-Bottomless* to name but one – and drunken sailors lurching to and from assorted sawdust-floored bars. At the intersection with Maunakea Street stands the ornate hundred-year-old facade of **Wo Fat's Chop Sui** restaurant, now occupied by a Chinese supermarket. Its main rival as the leading local landmark is the Art Deco **Hawaii Theatre**, further east at 1130 Bethel St, which has been painstakingly restored. Guided tours of the theater ($5) take place every Tuesday at 11am, but a better way to appreciate the gorgeous interior is by attending one of its varied program of (mostly one-off or short-run) performances; contact ☏808/528-0506 or ⊛www.hawaiitheatre.com for current schedules.

Many of Chinatown's old walled courtyards have been converted into open malls, but the businesses within remain much the same. Apothecaries and herbalists weigh out dried leaves in front of endless arrays of bottles, shelves, and wooden cabinets, while groups of deft-fingered women gather around tables to thread *leis*. Every hole-in-the-wall store holds a fridge bursting with colorful blooms, and appetizing food smells waft from backstreet bakeries. If you get hungry, browse through the Oriental food specialties at **Oahu Market**, on N King and Kekaulike. One of the fastest-selling items is *ahi* (yellow-fin tuna), used for making *sashimi* or *poke*, but this is also the place to go if you're looking for pig snouts or salmon heads. However, for the best selection of fast food in Chinatown visit the **Maunakea Marketplace**, a couple of blocks north and entered from either Hotel or Maunakea streets. Another tempting food market, piled high with shiny eggplants, great mountains of gnarled ginger roots, and twitchy live crabs, it also has a good little food court, inside the main building. The temperature is likely to be sweltering, but the choice of cuisines – Filipino, Vietnamese, Korean, Thai, Malaysian, Hong Kong – is good, and at the lowest prices in Honolulu.

Chinatown is bordered to the west by **Nu'uanu Stream**, which flows down to Honolulu Harbor. **River Street**, running alongside, becomes a restaurant-filled pedestrian mall between Beretania and Kukui streets. At the port end stands a *lei*-swaddled statue of **Sun Yat-sen**, while over Kukui Street at the opposite end is the tiny, ornate-roofed Lum Hai So Tong **Taoist temple**, erected by a "friendly society" in 1899 and now perched above a couple of little stores. Most of the interior of the block next to the mall is occupied by the **Chinatown Cultural Plaza**, filled with slightly tacky souvenir stores and conventional businesses that cater to the Chinese community.

The Chinese in Hawaii

Strangely enough, there was a Hawaiian in China before there were any **Chinese** in Hawaii – Kai'ana, a chief from Kauai, was briefly abandoned in Canton in 1787 by a British fur-trader he had thought was taking him to Europe. Within three years, however, Chinese seamen were starting to jump ship to seek their fortunes in the land they knew as Tan Hueng Shan, the Sandalwood Mountains. Trading vessels regularly crossed the Pacific between China and Hawaii, and Cantonese merchants and entrepreneurs became a familiar sight in Honolulu. Even the granite that paved the streets of what became Chinatown was brought over from China as ballast in ships.

Some of Hawaii's earliest Chinese settlers were **sugar boilers**, and the islands' first sugar mill was set up by a Chinese immigrant on Lanai in 1802. American capital proved itself more than a match for any individual Chinese endeavor, however, and the Chinese only began to arrive in Hawaii in sizeable numbers when the sugar plantations started importing laborers in 1852. Workers were usually indentured for five years, so by 1857 Chinese laborers were leaving the plantations and using their small savings to finance their own businesses. At first, the majority were on Kauai, where they began to turn neglected Hawaiian farmlands in places such as Hanalei Valley (see p.480) into rice paddies, even using water buffalo shipped over from China.

In time, however, the Chinese settled increasingly in Honolulu, where "friendly societies" would help new arrivals find their feet. Inevitably, many of these were renegades and outlaws, ranging from gang members to political dissidents. **Sun Yat-sen**, for example, who became the first President of the Republic of China when the Manchu Dynasty was overthrown in 1911, was educated at 'Iolani School. By the 1860s there were more Chinese than white residents in Hawaii. With the native Hawaiian population shrinking, the pro-American establishment in Honolulu felt threatened. In response, they maneuvered to ensure that white residents could vote for the national legislature while Asians could not. They also induced the plantations to switch their recruiting policies and focus on other parts of the globe.

At the end of the nineteenth century, Chinatown was at its zenith. Its crowded lanes held more than seven thousand people, including Japanese and Hawaiians as well as Chinese. When bubonic plague was detected in December 1899, however, city authorities decided to prevent its spread by systematic burning. The first few controlled burns were effective, but on January 20, 1900, a small fire started at Beretania and Nu'uanu rapidly turned into a major conflagration. The flames destroyed Kaumakapili Church as well as a 38-acre swathe that reached to within a few yards of the waterfront. White-owned newspapers were soon rhapsodizing about the opportunity to expand downtown Honolulu, convincing the Chinese community, which never received adequate compensation, that the destruction was at the very least welcome and at worst deliberate.

Nonetheless, Chinatown was rebuilt, and the fact that almost all its surviving structures date from that rebuilding gives it an appealing architectural harmony. Chinatown has since 1974 been declared a **preservation district**, and it still remains Honolulu's liveliest, most characterful quarter, albeit much more commercial than it is residential. Most local Chinese, like the rest of the city's inhabitants, live in outlying suburbs.

Foster Botanical Garden

At the top end of River Street, and entered via a short driveway that leads off N Vineyard Boulevard beside the Kuan Yin Buddhist temple, is the 14-acre **Foster Botanical Garden** (daily 9am–4.30pm, last admission 4pm; adults $5, under-13s $1; guided tours, no extra charge, Mon–Sat 1pm). Established in the mid-nineteenth century as a sanctuary for Hawaiian plants and a testing ground for foreign species, it has become one of Honolulu's best-loved city parks. Thanks to the H-1 freeway racing along its northern flank, it's not exactly the quietest of places, but it's usually filled with birds nonetheless. Different sections cover spices and herbs, flowering orchids, and tropical trees from around the world. As well as sausage trees from Mozambique, the latter collection includes a spectacular "cannonball tree", a giant *quipo*, and a *bo* (or *peepal*) tree supposedly descended from the *bo* tree at Bodh Gaya in north India where the Buddha achieved enlightenment.

Waterfront Honolulu

It's all too easy to lose sight of the fact that central Honolulu stands just a few yards up from the turquoise waters of the Pacific, clean enough here to support conspicuous populations of bright tropical fish. Unfortunately, pedestrians exploring Chinatown or downtown have to brave the fearsome traffic of the **Nimitz Highway** in order to reach the ocean. That effort is rewarded by a short but enjoyable stroll along the segment of the waterfront that stretches for a couple of hundred yards east of the venerable **Aloha Tower**. Until 1857, this area was covered by the waves; then the city fort, which had previously stood at Fort and Queen streets, was torn down, and the rubble used to fill in a 15-acre expanse of the sea floor. Now, in addition to watching the comings and goings of **Honolulu Harbor**, you can join a sunset dinner cruise or similar expedition from the piers nearby or learn something of the port's history in the **Hawaii Maritime Center**.

Long and surprisingly quiet **beaches** fringe the shoreline a little further to the east, especially in the vicinity of the **Ala Moana** district, which is home to the city's largest beach park as well as a huge shopping mall.

Aloha Tower

The **Aloha Tower**, on Pier 9 of Honolulu Harbor, was built in 1926 to serve as a control center for the port's traffic and a landmark for arriving cruise passengers. At 184ft high, it was then the tallest building in Honolulu; with its four giant clock-faces, each surmounted by the word "ALOHA," it was also the most photographed. Seventy years of skyscraper construction made it seem progressively smaller and smaller, but the tower returned to prominence in the late 1990s as the centerpiece of the **Aloha Tower Marketplace** shopping mall.

With far fewer parking spaces available here than at the major malls, the stores at Aloha Tower are heavily dependent on day-trippers from Waikīkī. After-work downtowners keep the mall's restaurants and music venues busy in the evenings, especially at weekends, but during the day it can seem somewhat forlorn. However, with the mall walkways ending right at the dockside, and several of the restaurants and bars offering large open-air terraces, it still makes an appealing place to get a sense of the ongoing life of the port. Cargo vessels from all over the world tie up alongside, and there's always something going on out in the water.

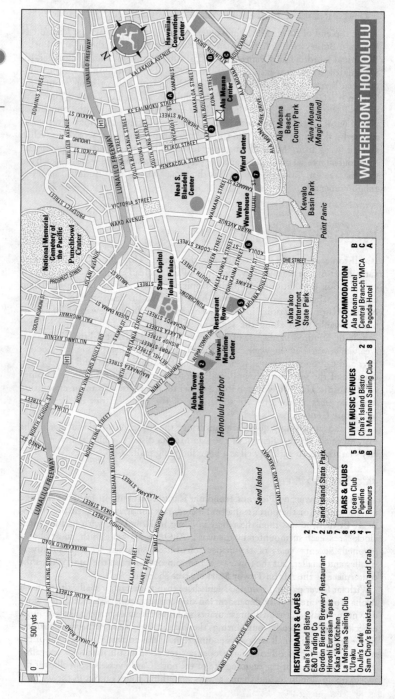

WATERFRONT HONOLULU

0   500 yds

RESTAURANTS & CAFÉS

Chai's Island Bistro	2
E&O Trading Co	7
Gordon Biersch Brewery Restaurant	2
Hiroshi Eurasian Tapas	5
Kaka'ako Kitchen	7
La Mariana Sailing Club	8
L'Uraku	3
OnJin's Café	4
Sam Choy's Breakfast, Lunch and Crab	1

BARS & CLUBS

Ocean Club	5
Pipeline	6
Rumours	B

LIVE MUSIC VENUES

Chai's Island Bistro	2
La Mariana Sailing Club	8

ACCOMMODATION

Ala Moana Hotel	B
Central Branch YMCA	C
Pagoda Hotel	A

Taking a free trip up to the tenth-floor **Observation Deck** of the now rather shabby Aloha Tower itself is also worthwhile (daily 9am–5pm). Balconies on each of its four sides, originally used as lookouts by harbor pilots, offer views that are just short of ugly – freeways, airport runways, and grimy harbor installations – but provide an excellent orientation to the city. As you look towards Diamond Head, which may well be obscured by haze, the twin pink-trimmed "stereo speakers" of the Waterfront Towers condominiums loom above the black glass of Restaurant Row; meanwhile, Pearl Harbor sprawls to the west, and the green mountains soar inland.

Hawaii Maritime Center

A short walk east of the Aloha Marketplace, the **Hawaii Maritime Center**, at Pier 7 (daily 8.30am–5pm; adults $7.50, under-18s $4.50; ☎808/536-6373, ⓦwww .bishopmuseum.org), illustrates Hawaii's seafaring past in riveting detail. You may prefer to explore the museum at your own pace, rather than following the audio-cassette tour, but start in any case on the second floor, as displays follow a roughly chronological order. Exhibits here trace the voyages of **Captain Cook**, who sailed the world in small flat-bottomed boats originally designed for trips along the English coast. Items on display include a crude copper plaque left by an English ship at the site of Cook's death, and a cannonball found nearby.

The next section delves into the **whaling** industry with exhibits such as intricate scrimshaw carved by nineteenth-century seamen on ivory smoothed with sharkskin "sandpaper," and a walk-through reconstruction of a whaling ship. In the center of the gallery hangs the skeleton of a humpback whale beached on Kahoolawe in 1986. The rest of the floor is given over to posters, timetables, menus, and reconstructed interiors covering the growth of **tourism** and the heyday of cruise ships and passenger ferries – Hawaii's last inter-island steamer, the *Humu'ula*, ceased regular runs in 1952. Having examined plans and photos showing the development of Honolulu Harbor, you can see the whole thing yourself by climbing the 81 steps up the museum's observation tower.

Downstairs, the focus turns to **Polynesian** seafaring. A full-sized, double-hulled canoe cut in half and framed in cross section behind clear plastic shows the equipment and cargo carried by the first voyagers. There's also a section on Polynesian tattoos and ancient medicines, along with photos of Waikīkī's first surfing clubs, prominently featuring Olympic champion Duke Kahanamoku, who popularized the sport during the early 1900s.

For many visitors, however, the chief attractions are the two distinguished vessels moored on the adjacent dock. The **Falls of Clyde**, floating to the right of the entrance, is the only four-masted, full-rigged sailing ship left in the world. Built of wrought iron in Glasgow in 1878, it's also the world's only sail-powered oil tanker; after years of ferrying sugar and passengers between California and Hawaii, it was converted to carry petroleum in 1907. Visiting the partially restored ship is an eerie experience, its musty old captain's quarters, rusting storage trunks and discarded ephemera giving it a ghostly feel.

When it's not sailing to Tahiti, New Zealand, or the far reaches of the South Pacific, the replica Polynesian canoe **Hōkūle'a** is moored at the end of the pier. Its voyages have inspired a huge revival of interest in traditional methods of navigation (for a full account, see p.546), and parties of eager schoolchildren flock here for close-up inspections. You can only go on board on a guided tour, which normally take place on weekdays only. During its frequent absences, visitors have to content themselves with "navigating" an enjoyable computer simulation of the *Hōkūle'a*.

The western waterfront: Sand Island

Honolulu Harbor, which is inaccessible to casual viewing west of the Aloha Tower, is a relatively narrow deep-water channel shielded from the open ocean by the bulk of **Sand Island**. The seaward side of the island is a state park, where the plentiful supply of restrooms, showers, and pavilions does little to alleviate the impression that you're trapped in an industrial wasteland. There's a certain amount of sandy beach, and locals come to hang out and fish, but it's hard to see why any tourist would drive five miles to get here. If you insist on doing so, follow Nimitz Highway almost as far as the airport, and then loop back along Sand Island Access Road.

East to Waikīkī: Ala Moana

East of Aloha Tower and the Maritime Center, **Ala Moana Boulevard** runs along the shoreline towards Waikīkī, passing a few more of Honolulu's main **shopping malls** – the Ward Warehouse, the Ward Centre, and the pick of the bunch, the **Ala Moana Center**. The stores here seem to increase both in quality and quantity each year, and for an ever-greater proportion of visitors to Waikīkī, the Ala Moana district is their only foray into Honolulu proper. For details on Honolulu shopping, see p.127.

The first spot where you can enter the ocean in this stretch is Point Panic in **Kaka'ako Waterfront State Park**. Serious board- and body-surfers swear by its powerful waves, but a lack of sand, an abundance of sharks, and the fact that the surf hammers straight into a stone wall combine to ensure that few visitors are tempted to join them. Even though there's no beach, the park itself is nice enough, with its grassy hills, paved pathways, and pavilions. Next up, across from the Ward Warehouse, **Kewalo Basin Park** occupies the thin oceanfront groin that shelters the Kewalo Basin Harbor, used by several small-boat operators. Though the setting is attractive enough, the park's role as a hangout for local transients makes it a bit of a no-go area for outsiders.

Though tourists tend not to realize it, the long green lawns across Ala Moana Boulevard from the malls flank a superb **beach** – the long white-sand strand preserved as the **Ala Moana Beach County Park**. This is where Honolulu city-dwellers come to enjoy excellent facilities and, especially during working hours, a relative absence of crowds. Like most of the beaches in Waikīkī, it's artificial, having been constructed during the 1930s on the site of a garbage dump. Inshore swimming is generally safe and good, and there's some potential for snorkeling around the reef; just watch out for the steep drop-off, only a few yards out at low tide.

At its eastern end, Ala Moana Beach curves out and around a long promontory. Known as **Magic Island** or **'Aina Moana**, this too is artificial. It was one of the most ambitious elements of the state's plans to expand tourism in the early 1960s, the idea being to reclaim an "island" of shallow coral reef, connect it to the mainland, and build luxury hotels on it. The hotels never materialized, so the vast sums of money involved have instead resulted in the creation of a tranquil park with roomy lawns, a gently sloping beach, and a lovely little crescent lagoon at its tip. It's worth wearing reef shoes if you go in the water, however; the sea floor remains rocky.

Tantalus and Makiki Heights

If constant glimpses of the mountains that soar inland of downtown Honolulu entice you into exploring, there's no better choice of route than **Tantalus** and

Round Top drives. They're actually a single eight-mile road that climbs up one flanking ridge of **Makiki Valley** and then wriggles back down the other, changing its name from Tantalus Drive in the west to Round Top Drive in the east. Along the way you'll get plenty of views of Honolulu and Waikīkī, but the real attraction is the dense rainforest that cloaks the hillside, its greenery often meeting overhead to form a tunnel. It's a slow drive, which in places narrows to just a single lane of traffic, but a spellbinding one.

To join Tantalus Drive from downtown, follow signs for the Punchbowl cemetery until you reach the right turn onto Pūowaina Drive, and head straight on instead. Coming from Waikīkī, take Makiki Street up from Wilder Avenue, which runs parallel to and just north of H-1 west of the university. It's also possible to skip the bulk of the circuit by taking **Makiki Heights Drive**, which holds the stimulating **Contemporary Museum** as well as trailheads for some superb mountain **hikes**.

Punchbowl: National Memorial Cemetery

The extinct volcanic caldera known as Punchbowl, perched above downtown Honolulu, makes an evocative setting for the **National Memorial Cemetery of the Pacific** (March–Sept daily 8am–6.30pm, Oct–Feb daily 8am–5.30pm). To ancient Hawaiians, this was Pūowaina, the hill of human sacrifices; somewhere within its high encircling walls stood a sacrificial temple. It's now possible to drive right into the crater – having first spiralled around the base of the cone to meet up with Pūowaina Drive from the back – and park in one of the many small bays dotted around the perimeter road.

Beneath the lawns that carpet the bowl-shaped interior, well over 25,000 dead of US Pacific wars, and also Vietnam, now lie buried. Famous names here also include the Hawaiian astronaut Ellison Onizuka, killed when the *Challenger* shuttle exploded, but no graves are singled out for special attention. Instead, each gravestone, marked perhaps with a bouquet of ginger and heliconia, is recessed into the grass, with space left for their families or still-living veterans to join those laid to rest. At the opposite end to the entrance rises the imposing marble staircase of the **Honolulu Memorial**, where ten "Courts of the Missing" commemorate a further 28,778 service personnel listed as missing in action. It culminates in a thirty-foot marble relief of the prow of a naval ship, bearing an extract from the letter sent by President Lincoln to Mrs Bixby, whose five sons were believed to have been killed in the Civil War: "The solemn pride that must be yours to have laid so costly a sacrifice upon the altar of freedom."

Only when you climb the footpath to the top of the crater rim and find yourself looking straight down Punchbowl Street to the Capitol do you appreciate how close this all is to downtown Honolulu. During World War II, before the creation of the cemetery, this ridge held heavy artillery trained out to sea.

Contemporary Museum

At 2411 Makiki Heights Drive, a short distance east of that road's intersection with Mott-Smith Drive, a grand 1920s country estate houses the lovely **Contemporary Museum** (Tues–Sat 10am–4pm, Sun noon–4pm; $5, free on the third Thurs of every month, under-13s free; ☏808/526-1322, ⓦwww.tcmhi.org). The grounds are tastefully landscaped with ornamental Oriental gardens that offer a superb overview of Honolulu and are packed with playful sculptures, while the venue itself is really more of an art gallery than a museum, and hosts changing exhibitions of up-to-the-minute fine art. Few last more than eight weeks, but each is installed with lavish attention to detail. A separate pavilion houses a permanent display of the sets created by David Hockney for the Metropolitan Opera's production of Ravel's *L'Enfant et les Sortilèges*, accompanied by a recording of the work playing constantly. Excellent lunches, with daily specials priced at $10–12, are available at the on-site *Contemporary Café* (Tues–Sat 11.30am–2.30pm, Sun noon–2.30pm; ☎808/523-3362), and there's also a very good gift store.

Makiki Forest Recreation Area

Honolulu's finest **hiking trails** wind their way across and around the slopes of **Makiki Valley**. The network is most easily accessed via a short spur road that leads inland from a hairpin bend in Makiki Heights Drive, roughly half a mile east of the Contemporary Museum, or half a mile west of the intersection with Makiki Street. Follow the dead-end road to park in a large lot on its left side, just beyond a sign that announces you've entered the **Makiki Forest Recreation Area**.

Walking a little further on from here will bring you to the ramshackle green trailers of the **Hawaii Nature Center**, a volunteer educational group that works mainly with schoolchildren and organizes guided hikes, open to all, on weekends (information on ☎808/955-0100 or ⓦwww.hawaiinaturecenter.org). If you haven't already picked up trail maps from the state office downtown (see p.62), you might find some at the center.

Makiki Valley trails

To take the best loop trip within Makiki Valley, you don't need to go as far as the Hawaii Nature Center. Set off instead across the Kanealole Stream, which flows parallel to the road on its right-hand side, on the clearly signed **Maunalaha Trail**. A short way up, you'll come to a T-junction, with the Kanealole Trail arrowed to the left and the Maunalaha to the right. Follow the Maunalaha, and you swiftly switchback onto the ridge for a long straight climb, often stepping from one exposed tree root to the next. Despite being in the shade most of the way, it's a grueling haul. Looking back through the deep green woods, you'll glimpse the towers of downtown Honolulu and then of Waikīkī. At first you can see the valleys to either side of the ridge, but before long only Mānoa Valley to the east is visible. After roughly three-quarters of a mile, you come to a **four-way intersection** at the top of the hill.

This is the point to decide just how far you want to walk. The shortest route back to the trailhead is simply to return the way you came, while turning **left** onto the **Makiki Valley Trail** lets you complete a highly recommended loop hike of 2.5 miles. The first stretch of the Makiki Valley Trail is the most gorgeous of the lot. A gentle descent angled along the steep valley wall, it heads inland to cross Moleka Stream at Herring Springs, amid a profusion of tiny bright flowers. Climbing away again you're treated to further ravishing views of the high valley, bursting with bright gingers and fruit trees. Birds are audible all around, and dangling lianas festoon the path. Take **Kanealole Trail**, which cuts away to the left shortly before this trail meets Tantalus Drive, and you'll drop back down through endless guava trees to your starting point near the Nature Center.

Alternatively, you can head **right** at the four-way intersection to take the **'Ualaka'a Trail**, adding an enjoyable if muddy half-mile to the loop trip. Plunging into the forest, the level path soon passes some extraordinary banyans, perched on the steep slopes with their many trunks, which have engulfed older trees. Having rounded the ridge, where a magnificent avenue of Cook pines marches along the crest in parallel rows, an arm-span apart, you curve back to cross Round Top Drive twice. In between the two crossings, take the short spur trail that leads left and up to the highest point on the hike. A clearing here perfectly

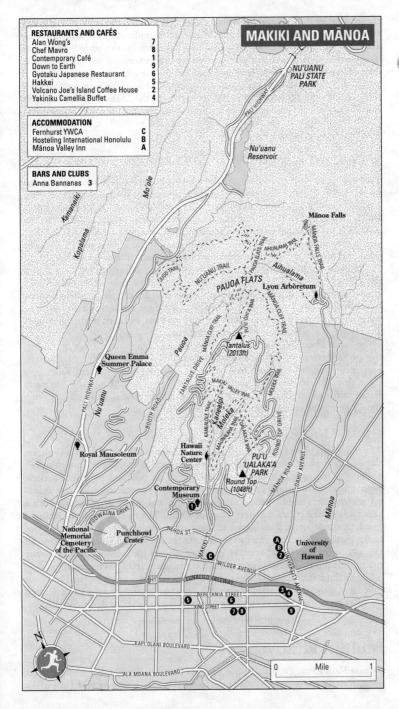

MAKIKI AND MĀNOA

RESTAURANTS AND CAFÉS

Alan Wong's	7
Chef Mavro	8
Contemporary Café	1
Down to Earth	9
Gyotaku Japanese Restaurant	6
Hakkei	5
Volcano Joe's Island Coffee House	2
Yakiniku Camellia Buffet	4

ACCOMMODATION

Fernhurst YWCA	C
Hosteling International Honolulu	B
Mānoa Valley Inn	A

BARS AND CLUBS

Anna Bannanas	3

NU'UANU PALI STATE PARK

Nu'uanu Reservoir

Mānoa Falls

AIHUALAMA TRAIL
MANOA FALLS TRAIL
Aihualama

JUDD TRAIL
NU'UANU TRAIL
PAUOA FLATS TRAIL

PAUOA FLATS

Lyon Arborètum

MANOA CLIFF TRAIL
PU'U OHIA TRAIL

Queen Emma Summer Palace

Tantalus (2013ft)

TANTALUS DRIVE
MANOA CLIFF TRAIL
MOLEKA TRAIL

Pauoa

MAKIKI VALLEY TRAIL

KANEALOLE TRAIL
Kanealp̄i
Moléka

ROUND TOP DRIVE
'UALAKA'A TRAIL

Royal Mausoleum

Nu'uanu

Kamanaiki

Kopalama

Mo'ole

PALI HIGHWAY

BOOTH ROAD

Hawaii Nature Center

MAUNALAHA TRAIL

PU'U 'UALAKA'A PARK

Round Top (1048ft)

Mānoa

MANOA ROAD

OAHU AVENUE

Contemporary Museum
1

POWAINA DRIVE

National Memorial Cemetery of the Pacific

Punchbowl Crater

NEHOA ST

MAKIKI ST

A **B**
2

University of Hawaii

C
WILDER AVENUE

UNIVERSITY AVENUE

H1 LUNALILO FREEWAY

3 **4**
BERETANIA STREET

5 **6** KING STREET

7 **8** **9**

KAPI'OLANI BOULEVARD

N

ALA MOANA BOULEVARD

0   Mile   1

frames Diamond Head against the ocean, with Waikīkī to the right of Diamond Head and the gleaming silver dome of the sports stadium at the University of Hawaii straight below. Once you rejoin the main trail on the far side of Round Top Drive – it starts fifty yards to the right – a brief woodland walk, down to the left, returns you to the four-way junction.

Finally, it's also possible to continue **straight ahead** from the four-way intersection. As first the **Moleka Trail**, and subsequently the **Mānoa Cliff Trail**, this route brings you in roughly three miles to the Nu'uanu Pali Lookout, described on p.107. You're now almost four miles from your car, so you're faced with a total hike of around eight miles.

Tantalus trails

Tantalus Drive is at its highest just below the 2013-foot pinnacle of **Tantalus** itself, near the point where the road changes its name to Round Top Drive. Two roadside parking lots here stand close to the trailhead for the three-quarter-mile **Pu'u 'Ōhi'a Trail**. The initial climb up through the eucalyptus trees to the summit is steep enough to require the aid of a wooden staircase, which comes out after a few hundred yards onto a little-used paved track. Follow this to the right until you reach a fenced-off electrical substation, then cut down the footpath to the left, which leads through a dense grove of bamboo before veering right to join the **Mānoa Cliff Trail**. By now you'll have seen the vastness of Nu'uanu Valley extending away to your left; heading left brings you, in a couple of hundred yards, to the **Pauoa Flats Trail**. As that in turn heads for three quarters of a mile into the valley, it's met first by the Nu'uanu Trail from the west, and then by the Aihualama Trail from Mānoa Falls (see p.105) from the east.

The Pauoa Flats Trail ends at a vantage point poised high above Nu'uanu Valley, though for even more dramatic views you can double back slightly and climb the knife-edge ridge to your left, from where it's obvious how Nu'uanu Valley cuts right through the heart of Oahu. Down below the lookout, the **Nu'uanu Reservoir** is an artificial lake that's kept stocked with crayfish and catfish; fishing is only permitted on three weekends in the year.

Pu'u 'Ualaka'a Park

The single best view along Round Top Drive comes at **Pu'u 'Ualaka'a Park**, on the western flank of Mānoa Valley. There's not much of a park here, though there's a sheltered hilltop picnic pavilion at the first of its two parking lots. Continue beyond that to the second lot, however, where a paved walkway leads to a railed-off viewing area right at the end of the ridge, and you'll be rewarded with a panorama of the entire southern coast of Oahu. The twin craters of Diamond Head to the left and Punchbowl to the right most readily draw the eye, but looking away to the west you can see beyond the airport and Pearl Harbor and all the way to Barber's Point. Pools of glittering glass in the parking lot attest to the many break-ins up here, so don't spend too long away from your vehicle.

The small summit that separates the two lots is Round Top itself. The Hawaiians called it 'Ualaka'a ("rolling sweet potato"), because Kamehameha the Great decreed the planting of sweet potatoes here, which when dug up rolled down the hillside.

Mānoa Valley

Mānoa Valley may lie just a couple of miles north of Waikīkī, but it's light-years away from the commercial hustle of the city. Behind the **University of Hawaii** – a magnet for students from around the Pacific, but of no great appeal for casual visitors – lies a quiet residential suburb that peters out as it narrows into the mountains, culminating in a spectacular tropical **waterfall**.

University of Hawaii

The main campus of the **University of Hawaii** sprawls along University Avenue in Mānoa, bounded on its southern side by H-1, Honolulu's major east–west freeway. Courses at the university focus largely on its specialties of geology, marine studies, astronomy, and other Pacific-related fields. As only a tiny proportion of students live on campus, there are fewer stores, restaurants, and clubs in the vicinity than you might expect. The **Campus Center**, set a little way back from University Avenue, is the place to head for general information and orientation. **Hemenway Hall** alongside holds the inexpensive, weekday-only *Mānoa Garden* café, as well as a movie theater.

Lyon Arboretum

To drive to the uppermost reaches of Mānoa Valley, continue along University Avenue beyond the campus, cross E Mānoa Road onto Oahu Avenue, and then turn right onto Mānoa Road itself. Immediately you'll see the silver stream of Mānoa Falls amid the trees at the head of the valley. Mānoa Road comes to a halt just beyond the **Lyon Arboretum**, which belongs to the university and preserves Hawaiian and imported trees in a reasonable approximation of their native environment (Mon–Fri 9am–4pm; free; T 808/988-0456, W www.hawaii.edu /lyonarboretum). Several short trails crisscross beneath the canopy.

Mānoa Falls

At three quarters of a mile each way, the hike to **Mānoa Falls**, towering 160 feet high at the head of Mānoa Valley, is the most rewarding short trail on Oahu. Considering how close it is to the heart of Honolulu, it offers an amazing sense of delving deep into a gorgeous tropical rainforest. Expect to spend around an hour and a half away from your vehicle, and don't wait to get bitten before you cover yourself with mosquito repellent. Signs posted at the end of the road, beyond the Lyon Arboretum, warn drivers not to park illegally. The area is notorious for **break-ins**, so it's unwise to leave valuables in your car. The one place you clearly *can* park is in the large lot of the defunct Paradise Park, where there's usually an attendant to collect the $5 fee.

The trail to the falls follows straight on ahead. Having passed over a footbridge and through a soggy meadow, it soon starts to climb beside one of the two main tributaries of Mānoa Stream. After scrambling from root to protruding root, over intertwined banyans and bamboos, you come out at the soaring high falls, where the flat, mossy cliff face is at enough of an angle that the water flows rather than falls into the small pool at its base. Sadly, thanks to recent landslides, access to the foot of the falls is strictly forbidden.

Many hikers combine the trek to the falls with tackling the much more demanding **Aihualama Trail**, switchbacking steeply up to the west from an inconspicuous intersection just short of the falls. After something over a mile, it comes out on top of the ridge, amid a thick cluster of bamboo, to connect with the Makiki network of trails half a mile short of the Nu'uanu Pali Lookout (see p.107).

Pali Highway

Of the three roads that negotiate the Ko'olau Mountains to connect Honolulu with windward Oahu, only the **Pali Highway** and **Likelike Highway** hold much potential for sightseeing. Both can get hideously congested at peak times, but the Pali Highway in particular is an exhilarating drive, whether you head straight for the clifftop **Nu'uanu Pali Lookout**, or call in at the various **royal sites** on the way up. (The Hawaiian word *pali* simply means "cliff.")

The third route, the **H-3** freeway, opened in 1997, having taken 37 long years to complete thanks to disputes over its environmental and archeological impact. H-3 was originally intended for military use as a direct link between Pearl Harbor and the Marine Corps base at Kāne'ohe, but with windward communities now housing an ever-higher proportion of Honolulu's workforce, the newest highway has considerably eased the strain for commuters.

Royal Mausoleum

The Gothic-influenced **Royal Mausoleum** is located very near the top of Nu'uanu Avenue, shortly before it joins the Pali Highway. It's very easy to miss – there's no sign, so watch out on the right as soon as you've passed the Japanese cemetery – and frankly it's not worth losing any sleep over if you do. The drab, gray mausoleum, built in 1865 to replace the overcrowded Kamehameha family tomb at 'Iolani Palace, stands at the end of a short oval driveway ringed with lumpy palm trees (Mon–Fri 8am–4pm; free). It's now simply a chapel, as the bodies it held for its first forty years or so were later moved to various sarcophagi dotted around the lawns. Kamehameha the Great was buried in secret on the Big Island (see p.175), but most of his closest family, as Christians, now lie here. His widow Ka'ahumanu, along with Kamehamehas II to V, are in the pink granite tomb to the left, while members of the separate Kalākaua dynasty were reinterred in the gilded vault beneath the central black column. Incidentally, this spot is said to be the precise site where the Nu'uanu Valley battle began in 1795 (see box below).

The Battle of Nu'uanu Valley

For early foreign visitors, the ride to the top of Nu'uanu Pali was an essential part of a Hawaiian itinerary. As their horses struggled up, native guides would recount tales of the epic **Battle of Nu'uanu Valley** in 1795, in which Kamehameha the Great (from the Big Island) defeated Kalanikūpule and conquered the island of Oahu. No two versions completely agree, but according to James Macrae, who accompanied Lord Byron to Hawaii in 1825 (soon enough after the battle to meet some of the survivors), Kamehameha's army landed at Honolulu to find Kalanikūpule waiting for them in Nu'uanu Valley. Kamehameha sent men along the tops of the ridges to either side, and advanced towards Kalanikūpule in the center himself. By this time, Kamehameha's entourage included Europeans and, crucially, a few European guns. Isaac Davis, who five years previously had been the sole survivor of a Hawaiian raid on a small boat at Kawaihae on the Big Island, positioned himself at the front of the attack.

Before the usual ritual of challenges and counter-challenges could even begin, Davis killed Kalanikūpule's leading general with a single lucky shot. The soldiers of Oahu turned and ran, pursued all the way to the head of the valley. When they reached the top, where the thousand-foot Nu'uanu Pali precipice drops away on the far side, they had no choice. Almost to a man, the remaining warriors hurtled to their deaths. Kalanikūpule managed to hide out in Oahu's mountains for several months, before he was captured and sacrificed to Kamehameha's personal war god.

Queen Emma Summer Palace

A couple of miles up the Pali Highway, just over half a mile after its intersection with Nu'uanu Avenue, a former royal retreat stands on the brow of a small hill to the right of the road. The **Queen Emma Summer Palace** made a welcome escape from the heat of Honolulu for the former Emma Rooke, who married King Kamehameha IV in 1856, was queen consort until 1863, and lived here until her death in 1885. It's now run as a somewhat cloying shrine to Emma by the Daughters of Hawaii, a group composed of descendants of missionary families (daily 9am–4pm; adults $6, under-12s $1; ⊤808/595-3167, Ⓦwww.daughtersofhawaii.org).

Behind its entrance stairway and six Doric pillars, the single-story white frame house is surprisingly small. Guided tours proceed at a snail's pace through rooms lined with royal souvenirs; only the splendidly grumpy Princess Ruth relieves the monotony of the official portraits. Among touching memorabilia of the young Prince Albert Edward – Queen Emma's only child, who died at the age of four – are his beautiful *koa*-wood crib, carved to resemble a canoe rocked by the waves, and a fireman's outfit he once wore in a parade. Gifts from Queen Victoria, after whose husband the boy was named, make up a large proportion of the items on display. Both Victoria and Emma were widowed – Emma was only 27 when her husband died a year after their son – and the two women continued to exchange presents for the rest of their lives.

Nu'uanu Pali State Park

Half a mile up the Pali Highway beyond Queen Emma's palace, an inconspicuous right turn leads onto **Nu'uanu Pali Drive**. Other than having to drive slower, you lose nothing by taking this detour, which curves back to meet the highway two miles up. There are no specific stops en route, but the dense tropical canopy, lit with flashes of color, makes for an appealing drive.

Back on the highway, it's now just a mile until the next right turn – confusingly, it too is Nu'uanu Pali Drive – which leads in a few hundred yards to **Nu'uanu Pali State Park** (daily 4am–8pm; free). Miss this, and you'll bypass a staggering overview of the cliffs of windward Oahu; the highway goes into a tunnel at this point, and emerges much lower down the hillside. At the edge of a small parking lot – which is the most notorious spot in the state for **car break-ins**, so leave no valuables in your vehicle – the railed viewing area of the **Nu'uanu Pali Lookout** turns out to be perched near the top of a magnificent curtain of green velvet, plunging more than a thousand feet. Straight ahead lie the sprawling coastal communities of **Kailua** and **Kāne'ohe**, separated by the Mōkapu Peninsula, but your eye is likely to be drawn to the north, where the mighty *pali* seems to stretch away forever, with a waterfall in every fold.

It was over this fearsome drop that the defeated warriors of Oahu were driven in 1795 (see box opposite); placards at the overlook explain the course of the battle and point out assorted landmarks. Notches higher up the ridge are said to have been cut to provide fortified positions for the defenders, an estimated four hundred of whose skulls were found down below when the Pali Highway was built a century later. The stairs that head down to the right lead to the highway's original route as it edges its way above the precipice. It's blocked off about a mile along, but walking to the end makes a good, if windy, mountain hike.

If you're heading across the island, you have to drive back down to rejoin the highway where you left it. To the right, Nu'uanu Pali Drive crosses over the tunnel and meets the highway's other carriageway on the far side, to drop back into Honolulu.

Likelike Highway

You're most likely to use the Pali Highway (see p.105) to get to windward Oahu from Honolulu, but the **Likelike Highway** is a less spectacular alternative. Pronounced *leek-e-leek-e*, the road is named after the younger sister of Queen Lili'uokalani. Starting roughly two miles to the west of the Pali Highway, it runs through residential Kalihi Valley and then passes through its own tunnel to emerge just above Kāne'ohe. There's no great reason to cross the island this way – the traffic is unlikely to be any easier – but you'll have to drive a short stretch of Likelike Highway to visit Honolulu's best museum, the Bishop Museum.

Bishop Museum

The best museum of Hawaiian history, anthropology, and natural history – and the world's finest collection of the arts of the Pacific – is located in the largely residential Kahili neighborhood, two miles northwest of downtown Honolulu. To reach the **Bishop Museum**, at 1525 Bernice St, catch TheBus #2 from Waikīkī or drive to the foot of Likelike Highway and follow the signs from the first exit on the right (daily 9am–5pm; adults $15, ages 4–12 and seniors $12; prices include the planetarium; ☏808/847-3511, ⓦwww.bishopmuseum.org).

The Bishop Museum was founded in 1889 by Charles Reed Bishop to preserve the heirlooms left by his wife, Princess Bernice Pauahi, the last direct descendant of Kamehameha the Great. Spread across four large buildings on a 12-acre hillside estate, it sets out to present authentic Polynesian culture, as opposed to the ersatz kind so often found in Waikīkī.

The first section you come to, beyond the ticket hall, is Hawaii's only **planetarium**. Master navigator Nainoa Thompson of the *Hōkūle'a* studied the virtual sky here during the 1970s to reinvent traditional Polynesian navigational techniques, as used in the voyages described on pp.546–548. Shows take place daily at 11am and 2pm, plus Friday and Saturday at 7pm; admission to those alone costs $4.50. An attendant stationed in the adjoining **observatory** helps visitors to make their own observations.

The museum's huge main building houses the bulk of its historic displays. The grand **Hawaiian Hall**, its original core, was closed for extensive renovations at the time of writing, and was not expected to reopen before the middle of 2008 at the earliest. Besides a much-needed face-lift, the aim of the redesign is more accurately to reflect traditional Hawaiian belief systems, and provide a more systematic account of the islands' way of life before the Europeans arrived. The hall will, however, continue to hold many of the same exhibits as before, including a scale model of the Big Island's Waha'ula *heiau*, which was overrun by lava from Kīlauea during the 1990s; a sharkskin drum that was once used to announce human sacrifices in a similar *luakini* temple on the seaward slopes of Diamond Head – the only such drum known to have survived the overthrow of the *kapu* system; and a full-sized *hale*, or traditional hut, brought here from Hā'ena on Kauai. Some of the museum's most treasured artifacts remain on display in a small ante-room while the Hawaiian Hall is being worked on, including Kamehameha the Great's personal wooden effigy of the war god Kūkā'ilimoku, found in a cave in Kona on the Big Island, and a crested feather helmet that probably belonged to Kalaniopu'u of the Big Island.

The other half of the main building, not affected by the renovations, is the **Polynesian Hall**, which emphasizes the full diversity of Polynesia. After the breaking of the *kapu* (see p.545), the Hawaiians themselves set about destroying the relics of their ancient religion; most other Polynesian cultures have preserved

△ Bishop Museum

far more of their heritage. Stunning exhibits here include woven-grass masks and dance costumes from Vanikoro, modeled skulls and figures from Vanuato, stark white and red sorcery charms from Papua New Guinea, and stick charts used by Micronesian navigators. The Maoris of New Zealand are represented by the facade of a storehouse, carved in high relief with human figures and inlaid with abalone-shell eyes.

Next door, the **Castle Building** hosts top-quality temporary exhibitions, while across the lawn the new **Science Adventure Center** holds high-tech displays on earth and life sciences, aimed largely at local schoolchildren. Its centerpiece is an enormous artificial volcano, which constantly "erupts" fountains of glowing orange liquid; kids can twiddle various knobs to mimic the natural forces responsible for different kinds of eruption. Down in the basement, another less spectacular volcano pumps out black wax that piles up in much the same way as the Hawaiian islands themselves.

The Bishop Museum holds an excellent bookstore as well as a snack bar. On the first Sunday of every month, known as **Family Sunday**, Hawaii residents are allowed in free, and the lawns play host to food stalls, *hula* performances, and other activities.

Pearl Harbor

Ancient Hawaiians knew the vast inlet of **Pearl Harbor**, reaching deep into the heart of Oahu, as *Wai Momi*, "water of pearl", on account of its pearl-bearing oysters. Their canoes had no need of deep-water anchorages, but Westerners came to realize that by dredging its entrance they could create the finest harbor in the Pacific. Such was its strategic potential that the desire to control Pearl Harbor played a large and explicit role in the eventual annexation of Hawaii by the United States. The US first received permission to develop installations here in 1887, in return for granting Hawaiian sugar duty-free access to US markets, and construction of the naval base commenced in 1908.

To this day, the 12,600-acre Pearl Harbor Naval Complex is the headquarters from which the US Pacific Fleet patrols just over a hundred million square miles of ocean. The entire fleet consists of approximately two hundred ships, two thousand aircraft and 239,000 personnel, while Pearl Harbor itself is the home port for around twelve surface vessels and sixteen nuclear submarines. Even though there's a small city's worth of operations, only the **Arizona Memorial**, commemorating the surprise Japanese attack with which Pearl Harbor remains synonymous, along with two lesser attractions, are open to civilians, meaning a half-day is plenty of time to see everything.

Arizona Memorial

Almost half the victims of the December 1941 Japanese attack on Pearl Harbor (see p.112), were aboard the battleship **USS Arizona**. Hit by an armor-piercing shell that detonated its magazine and lifted its bow twenty feet out of the water, it sank within nine minutes. Of its crew of 1514 – who had earned the right to sleep in late that Sunday morning by coming second in a military band competition – 1177 were killed. The *Arizona* still lies submerged where it came to rest, out in the waters of the harbor along "Battleship Row," next to Ford Island. Its wreck is spanned (though not touched) by the curving white **Arizona Memorial**, maintained by the National Park Service in honor of all the victims of the attack; small boats ferry a stream of visitors out from the mainland.

The **visitor center** for the memorial is located six miles west of Honolulu, just over a mile after Kamehameha Highway cuts off to the left of H-1 (center open daily 7.30am–5pm; tours 8am–3pm; closed New Year, Thanksgiving & Christmas Day; free; ☎808/422-0561, ⓦwww.nps.gov/usar). It takes up to an hour to drive across town from Waikīkī; the large warning signs that you'll see as you approach, restricting admission to the naval base, don't apply to memorial visitors. TheBus

△ The submerged remains of the USS Arizona

#20 runs direct from Waikīkī, as do overpriced commercial tours (typically around $25 per person, with the operators listed on p.68). No reservations are accepted, so each individual has to pick up his or her own numbered ticket for the free memorial tour on arrival. The average wait is around ninety minutes, while in peak season it can easily be two or three hours before you're called to board the ferry. Many people try to beat the crowds by arriving early, but if anything your

The attack on Pearl Harbor

As the winter of **1941** approached, with German soldiers occupying most of Europe and moving into Soviet Russia, and Japanese forces advancing through Southeast Asia, the United States remained outside the global conflict. However, negotiations to halt Japanese progress had stalled, and on November 27 the US government sent secret "war warnings" to its military units throughout the world. The version received by the commanding general in Hawaii read: "Japanese future action unpredictable but **hostile action** possible at any moment. If hostilities cannot, repeat cannot, be avoided the United States desires that Japan commit the first overt act."

A few days earlier, a Japanese attack fleet, with six aircraft carriers among its 33 vessels, had sailed from northern Japan. By maintaining strict radio silence, it dodged American surveillance. The conventional wisdom was that it must be heading towards the Philippines, site of the furthest-flung US base in the Pacific, and a detachment of B-17 "Flying Fortress" aircraft was sent from Hawaii to bolster the islands' defenses. In fact, however, Hawaii itself, where **Pearl Harbor** had since the previous spring been the headquarters of the US Pacific Fleet, was the target. The Japanese fleet sailed there along an icy, rarely used northerly course, keeping well clear of usual shipping lanes. The Japanese did not expect to achieve complete surprise and were prepared to engage the US fleet in battle if they met on the open sea; but reconnaissance flights from Pearl Harbor only covered the likeliest angle of attack, from the southwest, and the Japanese approach was not detected. By the early morning of December 7, the fleet was in position 230 miles northwest of Oahu.

The first wave of the attack, consisting of 183 aircraft, was launched at 6am. As the planes passed over the western Wai'anae mountains, they were picked up by radar screens at a nearby tracking station. When the operators called Honolulu with the news that a large group of aircraft had been spotted, they were told "Well, don't worry about it," in the belief that these were replacement B-17s arriving from the mainland. Meanwhile, the cloud cover had lifted to give the attackers a perfect view of Pearl Harbor, where seven of the US fleet's nine battleships lay at anchor along "Battleship Row." At 7.53am, Commander Mitsuo Fuchida sent the codeword "*Tora! Tora! Tora!*" (Tiger! Tiger! Tiger!) to his flagship, the *Akagai*, signaling that a surprise attack was under way.

Within two hours the US Navy lost eighteen warships: eight battleships, three light cruisers, three destroyers and four auxiliary craft. In addition to 87 Navy planes, simultaneous attacks on other bases on Oahu destroyed 77 Air Force planes and damaged 128 more. Following recent warnings, the planes were parked wingtip-to-wingtip on the airfields. This was supposed to make them easier to protect against sabotage by possible Japanese agents among the *nisei* (Hawaiian residents of Japanese ancestry); instead it left them utterly exposed to aerial attack. During the onslaught, the expected squadron of B-17s arrived from California; unarmed, several were shot down.

In total, 2403 US military personnel were killed, and 1178 wounded. The Japanese lost 29 aircraft, plus five midget submarines that had sneaked into Pearl Harbor during the previous night in the hope of torpedoing damaged ships. Ten hours later, Japanese aircraft did indeed attack Clark Airfield in the Philippines, and there too they destroyed large numbers of aircraft on the ground. The next day, declaring the

chances of a short wait may be better in the afternoon. As a result of heightened security measures since the terrorist attacks of 2001, no bags of any kind are permitted on the ferry.

Perhaps because so many of the 1.5 million annual visitors are Japanese, the displays in the visitor center are surprisingly even-handed, calling the attack "a daring gamble" by Admiral Yamamoto to knock out the US fleet and give the

United States to be at war with Japan, **President Franklin D. Roosevelt** condemned the "dastardly" Pearl Harbor attack as "a date which will live in infamy."

The official postwar **inquiry** into "the greatest military and naval disaster in our nation's history" set out to explain why the attack was possible, let alone successful. Considering why the fleet was based in Hawaii in the first place, instead of the relative safety of the US West Coast, it was told that, despite its weakness at the time, that would have signaled a lack of US will to resist Japanese expansion in the Pacific. As to whether the fleet's vulnerability had invited the attack, Japanese plans were drawn up expecting a much larger fleet at Pearl Harbor, and they were disappointed to find that both US aircraft carriers were out of port. The fact that the Japanese withdrew from Hawaii almost immediately, instead of following up their initial success by destroying port installations such as the vast oil tanks, and thereby crippling US Navy operations for years – or even by invading the islands – suggests that if anything they overestimated US defenses.

No hard evidence has been produced to support revisionist assertions that Roosevelt knew the attack was coming, but allowed it to happen because he wanted an excuse to join the war, or that the British knew, and they deliberately failed to warn the Americans for the same reason. It makes no sense, if Roosevelt did know, that he didn't at least alert US defenses a few hours in advance, when an unprovoked Japanese attack was demonstrably imminent.

Mistakes were certainly made. Among the most glaring was the fact that Navy authorities were never told of intercepted messages from Tokyo in which the Japanese consulate in Honolulu was asked to divide the moorings in Pearl Harbor into five separate areas and specify which ships were anchored in each section. The best explanation can probably be found in a pair of statements by the two leading protagonists. The overall Japanese commander, reporting to his superiors a fortnight later, wrote that "good luck, together with negligence on the part of the arrogant enemy, enabled us to launch a successful surprise attack." Admiral Husband E. Kimmel, in charge of the US Pacific Fleet, was asked informally why he had left the ships exposed in Pearl Harbor, and replied, "I never thought those little yellow sons-of-bitches could pull off such an attack, so far from Japan." Although Kimmel was stripped of his rank in the immediate aftermath, he was posthumously promoted back to admiral by both Senate and Congress in 1999.

In the long run, the Japanese decision to provoke the US into all-out **war in the Pacific** was to prove suicidal. What's more, most of the vessels damaged and even sunk at Pearl Harbor eventually returned to active service. Only the *Arizona* and the *Utah* could not be salvaged, while the *Oklahoma* sank once again, 500 miles off the Big Island. By contrast, just two of the Japanese ships that were involved in the attack survived the war; four of the anti-aircraft carriers were sunk during the Battle of Midway. In 1945, the *West Virginia*, risen from the waters of Pearl Harbor, was in Tokyo Bay to witness the Japanese surrender.

In a little-known footnote, the *Phoenix*, which was unscathed by the 1941 onslaught, was sold to Argentina ten years later. Renamed the *General Belgrano*, the last surviving warship from the attack on Pearl Harbor was sunk by the British during the Falklands War in 1982.

Japanese time to conquer Southeast Asia. The center has long been scheduled to hold a new **museum**, designed to trace the events leading up to the attack, the bombing itself, and the course of the war in the Pacific. Only a few exhibits are currently in place, however, including models of both the *Arizona* and the Japanese flagship, the *IMS Akagi* ("Red Castle"); a Japanese aerial torpedo used in the attack; and some personal items salvaged from the wreck.

Until the museum is completed, the best place to get a sense of what happened is in the waterfront **garden** outside. From here, you see the low and undramatic mountain ridges that ring Pearl Harbor, together with the gap down the center of the island through which the first planes arrived. Captioned photographs clearly illustrate the disposition of the ships moored along "Battleship Row" on the fateful morning, as well as their eventual fate. Survivors of the attack are often on hand to tell their stories.

When your number finally comes up, you're first shown a twenty-minute film that pays tribute to "one of the most brilliantly planned and executed attacks in naval history." Crisp-uniformed Navy personnel then usher you onto open-sided boats, which they steer for ten minutes across a tiny fraction of the naval base. You disembark at the memorial, whose white marble walls are inscribed with the names of the dead. The outline of the *Arizona* is still discernible in the clear blue waters, and still seeping oil, while here and there rusty metal spurs poke from the water. All those who died when the *Arizona* went down remain entombed in the wreckage, occasionally joined by veteran survivors who choose to be buried here. You're free to stay for as long as you choose, although almost everyone simply returns on the next boat, which usually arrives in around fifteen minutes.

USS Bowfin Submarine Museum and Park

Located alongside the *Arizona* visitor center, but entirely separate to the park-service memorial, the privately owned **USS Bowfin Submarine Museum and Park** serves as an alternative distraction if you have a couple of hours to wait before your ferry (daily 8am–5pm; sub and museum, adults $10, under-13s $4; museum only, adults $5, under-13s $3; combined with *Missouri* admission adults $21, ages 4–12 $11, tickets sold until 2.30pm; ☏ 808/423-1341, ⓦ www.bowfin .org). Its main focus, the claustrophobic *Bowfin* itself, is a still-floating, 83-man submarine that survived World War II unscathed, having sunk 44 enemy vessels. Once you've explored it on a self-guided audio tour – complete with a first-person account of one of the *Bowfin*'s most hair-raising missions, narrated by the captain in charge – you can learn more about the whole story of twentieth-century submarines in the adjoining museum.

The park outside, to which access is free, holds various missiles and torpedoes, including a Polaris A-1 ballistic missile, and the Japanese naval equivalent of a *kamikaze* airplane, a *kaiten*. Such manned, single-seater torpedoes were designed for suicide attacks on larger ships; only one, piloted by its inventor, ever succeeded in sinking a US Navy ship. A memorial garden alongside commemorates 52 US submarines lost during the war in the Pacific, listing over 3500 crew "On Eternal Patrol."

USS Missouri

Since 1998, the decommissioned battleship **USS Missouri**, also known as the "Mighty Mo", has been permanently moored close to the Arizona Memorial. The last battleship to be constructed by the United States, she was christened in January 1944. After service in the Pacific and Korean wars, she was decommissioned in 1955 and remained mothballed until being refitted in 1986. Operation Desert Storm saw the *Missouri* firing Tomahawk missiles into Iraq, but she was finally retired once more in 1992, as the last operational battleship in the world. Should the need arise, she's still capable of being recommissioned in 45–90 days.

Several different US locations competed for the honor of providing a final berth for the *Missouri*. Pearl Harbor won, on the basis that the place where World War II began for the United States should also hold the spot where it ended; the Japanese surrender of September 2, 1945, was signed on the deck of the *Missouri*, then moored in Tokyo Bay. In addition to being a monument in her own right, part of the battleship's new role is as a recruiting tool for the US Navy; it's even possible to arrange kids' sleep-over parties on board.

Since the battleship is located alongside Ford Island, which is officially part of the naval base, visitors can only reach it by shuttle bus. These depart from the USS Bowfin visitor center, which is also where you purchase tickets (daily 8.30am–5pm, tickets sold 8am–3.45pm; adults $16, ages 4–12 $8; Chief's Guided Tours $23/$15; Explorer's Tour $40/$20; T 808/973-2494 or 1-877/644-4489, W www .ussmissouri.org).

Having crossed the harbor on a retracting bridge, you're deposited at the entrance gate. Depending on whether you've paid extra to join one of the regular hour-long "Chief's Guided Tours" – which you might as well, given that you're interested enough to have made it this far – you're then shepherded either towards your personal guide or simply left to climb up to the deck. The overwhelming first impression is the *Missouri*'s sheer size; at 887 feet long, she's the length of three football fields and armed with colossal twin gun turrets. By contrast, once you go below decks, the crew's quarters are cramped in the extreme, bringing home the full claustrophobic reality of her long and dangerous missions. The principal highlights are the dimly lit Combat Engagement Center, set up as it was during the Gulf War but now looking very antiquated; the surrender site, on the deck nearby; and the spot where a *kamikaze* fighter careered into the side of the ship, as captured in a dramatic photo. Only visitors on the $40 Explorer's Tour get to see the fire and engine rooms, three levels below the main deck.

Restaurants

With most of its 100,000 daily visitors eating out at least once a day, **Waikīkī** supports an incredible number and variety of **restaurants**. In the rest of **Honolulu**, you'll find somewhere to eat pretty much anywhere you go – the shopping malls are packed with places, albeit bland – but only the restaurants of **Chinatown** merit a special trip from Waikīkī.

Waikīkī

Almost all of Waikīkī's hotels have an on-site American restaurant, and usually one or two other more specialized options as well. As you'd expect, the standards in the major hotels are very high, but out on the streets the emphasis is on keeping the price low, rather than the quality high. Many of the better restaurants don't bother to open for lunch, but takeouts, fast-food chains. and snack bars are everywhere you turn; the largest concentrations are along **Kūhīo Avenue** and, with more Japanese options, on **Kalākaua Avenue** immediately west of Lewers Street. The easiest **fast-food** option is the food court in the International Marketplace on Kalākaua, where takeout counters include the likes of *Joe's Hamburger Grill*, *Yummy Korean B-B-Q*, and *Bautista's Filipino Kitchen*.

Inexpensive

Daily Buzz *Ohana East*, 150 Kai'ulani Ave T 808/922-2223. Tucked away off the main lobby of the *Ohana East* hotel, this convenient, slightly faded coffee corner offers good espresso drinks, cooked breakfasts, sandwiches and bagels, plus Internet access. The quirky attempts at tiki styling don't add much atmosphere, but it's a friendly spot. Daily 6am–2pm.

Eggs 'n' Things 1911B Kalākaua Ave T 808/949-0820. All-night diner and local institution, drawing a big breakfast crowd – surfers, night workers, bright-eyed tourists – for its bargain omelets, waffles, and crepes. The Early Riser (5–9am) and Late Riser (1–2pm & 1–2am) specials give you three pancakes and two eggs for just $4.25. No reservations, so expect a wait. Daily 11pm–2pm.

Honolulu Coffee Co *Sheraton Moana Surfrider*, 2365 Kalākaua Ave ☎808/533-1500. This soothing, airy coffeehouse in the lovely old *Moana Surfrider* shares the hotel's understated decor, with huge open windows, paneling, and simple darkwood furniture. The exquisite patisserie makes a great accompaniment for expertly made espresso drinks and freshly ground Kona coffee. Daily 6am–10pm.

Leonard's Bakery 933 Kapahulu Ave ☎808/737-5591. Long-standing Portuguese bakery on the northeastern fringes of Waikīkī, renowned for its delicious, inexpensive desserts and the wildly popular sugary and donut-like malassadas. Sun–Thurs 6am–9pm, Fri & Sat 6am–10pm.

Perry's Smorgy 2380 Kūhio Ave ☎808/926-0184. All-you-can-eat buffet, served indoors or in a Japanese-style garden. The food neither looks edible nor tastes of anything much but the place is always crowded with bargain-hunters. Choose from the $7 breakfast (ham, beef hash, sausages, pancakes, pastries, juices), the $8 lunch (mahimahi, Southern fried chicken, garlic bread, rice, baked macaroni, desserts), the $11 dinner (beef, shrimp, ribs, turkey, teriyaki chicken), or the $11 Sun brunch. Daily 7–11am, 11.30am–2.30pm & 5–9pm; Sun brunch 11.30am–2.30pm.

Ruffage Natural Foods 2443 Kūhio Ave ☎808/922-2042. Tiny wholefood grocery with a takeout counter and limited patio seating.

The selection is great, with granola breakfasts and delicious real-fruit and honey smoothies; avocado and bean-sprout sandwiches and vegan burritos; and salads, pasta and tofu dishes. Most items cost less than $7. From 6pm to midnight the front section transforms into an inexpensive sushi bar. Mon–Sat 9am–midnight.

Shore Bird Beach Broiler *Outrigger Reef*, 2169 Kalia Rd ☎808/922-2887. Perennially popular, cheap-and-cheerful open-air hotel restaurant, right on the beach, where the sumptuous views – if you're lucky enough to get an oceanfront table – make up for the less than inspiring food. The breakfast buffet costs $12, while dinner with an open salad bar is $18–23, depending on your choice of entree. Guests can cook their own meat or fish at a communal grill; kids adore it. Daily 7–11am & 4.30–10pm.

Moderate

Arancino 255 Beach Walk ☎808/923-5557. Authentic Italian trattoria – albeit decorated a lurid orange – in central Waikīkī. Alongside the basic dinner menu of pasta dishes and pizza ($9–18) are tasty specials such as a steamed clams appetizer ($9.50), and spaghetti alla pescatore ($18), with all kinds of fish swimming in olive oil and garlic. There's another branch at the *Waikīkī Beach Marriott* (☎808/931-6273), open the same hours. Daily 11.30am–2.30pm & 5–10.30pm.

Cheeseburger in Paradise 2500 Kalākaua Ave ☎808/923-3731. The Waikīkī outlet of this successful Maui burger joint occupies a prime position, across the street from the ocean, with airy open windows and retro 1950s tiki/beachcomber

Honolulu and Waikīkī: favorite restaurants

Buffet	*Todai Seafood Buffet*	Waikīkī	p.117
Chinese	*Indigo*	Honolulu	p.122
Fast food	International Marketplace	Waikīkī	p.115
	Maunakea Marketplace	Honolulu	p.95
Gourmet	*Alan Wong's*	Honolulu	p.121
Greek	*Olive Tree Café*	Honolulu	p.121
Italian	*Arancino*	Waikīkī	p.116
Japanese	*L'Uraku*	Honolulu	p.122
Korean	*Yakiniku Camellia Buffet*	Honolulu	p.121
Local	*Kaka'ako Kitchen*	Honolulu	p.119
Oceanfront	*Orchids*	Waikīkī	p.118
Pacific Rim	*Sam Choy's Diamond Head*	Waikīkī	p.118
Pūpūs	*Duke's Canoe Club*	Waikīkī	p.117
Seafood	*Sansei*	Waikīkī	p.118
Steak	*The Colony*	Waikīkī	p.118
Thai	*Sweet Basil*	Honolulu	p.120
Vietnamese	*Phô 97*	Honolulu	p.120

style. The food, however, is nothing to write home about – best go for the cheeseburgers ($10–12) over the salads. Daily 7am–midnight.

Duke's Canoe Club *Outrigger Waikīkī*, 2335 Kalākaua Ave ☎808/922-2268, ⓦwww.dukeswaikiki.com. Right on the beach, with an open-air *lānai*, this crowded chain restaurant offers great views along with a feast of retro tiki and surf styling, with vintage photos and memorabilia dotted around the jungle hut decor. The buffet breakfasts (until 10.30am) are not bad value at $15, but for lunch it's best to ignore the buffet ($13) in favor of the *pūpū* menu, which includes large plates of tasty crab-and-macadamia nut wontons ($9). At night, the large, unimaginative dinner menu is lined with chicken, steak, and fish entrees at around $20. Big-name Hawaiian musicians play Fri–Sun 4–6pm. Daily 6.30am–midnight.

Golden Dragon Hilton Hawaiian Village, 2005 Kālia Rd ☎808/946-5336. The classiest Chinese restaurant in Waikīkī, with garden seating overlooking a lagoon, and a tasteful indoor dining room. The food is good, and prices not as high as you might expect, with entrees such as crispy lemon chicken, roast duck, and noodles with fish or chicken starting at around $17. Seafood dishes – seared ocean scallops, opakapaka in black bean sauce – cost a little more, while a tempting range of set menus cost $34–55 per person. Daily except Mon 6–9.30pm.

House Without a Key *Halekūlani*, 2199 Kālia Rd ☎808/923-2311. Waikīkī Beach's loveliest venue for an open-air sunset cocktail – complete with top-quality live Hawaiian music (see p.123) – has a far less frenetic atmosphere than the other oceanfront places, and gorgeous views from every table. The food is tasty and relatively simple, and especially good value in the evening. At lunch saimin goes for $13, while a chicken and sage-roasted apple salad is $17; the dinner menu features lots of *pūpūs*, including a combination platter of coconut shrimp, lemongrass beef skewers and seafood spring roll for $16.50. Daily 7am–9pm.

Keo's in Waikīkī 2028 Kūhiō Ave ☎808/951-9355, ⓦwww.keosthaicuisine.com. Keo's has long proclaimed itself to be Hawaii's best Thai restaurant, and its walls are festooned with photos of celebrities enticed by trademark dishes such as the "Evil Jungle Prince" curry. There's no disputing that the food tastes good, and with all entrees except the very fanciest seafood options costing under $16, prices are reasonable. Breakfast is both American and Asian; lunch and dinner are entirely Thai. There's another branch, *Keoni by Keo's* at

2375 Kūhiō Ave. Sun–Thurs 7am–2pm & 5–10.30pm, Fri & Sat 7am–2pm & 5–11pm.

Oceanarium *Pacific Beach Hotel*, 2490 Kalākaua Ave ☎808/922-6111. Functionally furnished restaurant with one big gimmick – one wall of the dining room is a three-story aquarium, so as you eat your meal you can watch 400 live fish, plus the occasional scuba diver. The food itself is much less enthralling than the view; the day starts with a continental breakfast (6–11am) for $11 or a $16 buffet. Lunchtime noodles, burgers, salads, or sandwiches all cost around $12, while for dinner you can either go for a $32 prime rib and seafood buffet, or order individual meat or fish entrees averaging $20. Daily 6am–10pm.

Singha Thai Cuisine 1910 Ala Moana Blvd ☎808/941-2898, ⓦwww.singhathai.com. Bright, elegant, dinner-only spot serving delicious Thai food with a definite Hawaiian tinge, including fresh fish and scallop dishes ($20 and up), plus curries and pad Thai (both around $16), and hot-and-sour soups ($6). Signature entrees, including spicy Siamese fighting fish, cost $20–32. Thai dancers perform nightly 7–9pm. Daily 4–10pm.

Todai Seafood Buffet 1910 Ala Moana Blvd ☎808/947-1000, ⓦwww.todai.com. Large, bustling outlet of a superb Japanese chain, in western Waikīkī. Lunch costs $15 (Mon–Fri) or $17 (Sat & Sun), while dinner is $28 (Mon–Thurs) or $29 (Fri–Sun), and the range and quality of the food makes it a real bargain. Delicious seafood dishes at the 160-foot buffet bar include hand-made sushi rolls, ahi poke, sashimi, shrimp, oysters, and scallops on the half-shell; cooked noodle dishes; and chicken teriyaki and pork for diehard carnivores. Even the desserts are good. Mon–Thurs 11.30am–2pm & 5.30–9.30pm, Fri 11.30am–2pm & 5–10pm, Sat 11.30am–2.30pm & 5–10pm, Sun 11am–2.30pm & 5–10pm.

Expensive

Banyan Veranda *Sheraton Moana Surfrider*, 2365 Kalākaua Ave ☎808/921-4600. Fancy restaurant in one of Waikīkī's most atmospheric old hotels. Full "sunrise" ($29) or Japanese-style ($31) breakfasts are available, along with à la carte choices, daily except Sun, when the lavish brunch costs $45. Instead of lunch, an elaborate afternoon tea is served, which has become quite a Waikīkī tradition: $30 buys a plate of finger sandwiches and pastries and a pot of tea to be enjoyed as you listen to a Hawaiian guitarist, while for $35 you get a couple of glasses of fizz too. A four-course prix-fixe dinner (5.30–9pm) costs $58 (you can also go à la carte, with entrees like onaga for around $35); your meal is accompanied by live Hawaiian music and, occasionally, the shrieks of noisy revelers in the beachfront bar. Mon–Sat 7–11am, 1–4pm & 5.30–9pm; Sun 9am–1pm, 3–4pm & 5.30–9pm.

Ciao Mein *Hyatt Regency Waikīkī*, 2424 Kalākaua Ave ☎ 808/923-2426. Huge restaurant serving an odd but successful mixture of Chinese and Italian cuisine. Not all dishes actually combine the two, though "Collision Cuisine" specials at around $24 include "Hot Bean Salmon alla Siciliana" and seafood funn lasagne. There's a tasty focaccia appetizer for $9, and most pasta entrees cost $19. Chinese entrees include sizzling Mongolian beef and honey walnut shrimp (both $26), and there are vegetarian options, too. Daily 6–10pm.

The Colony *Hyatt Regency Waikīkī*, 2424 Kalākaua Ave ☎ 808/923-1234. Appetizers at the most traditional of the Hyatt's restaurants include a three-onion soup for $8. Steaks ($35 and up) are the specialty here, grilled over kiawe wood and available in all sorts of combinations (steak with lobster is $72); you can also get a delicious fresh catch for $28, or a "Hukilau" of steamed seafood for two or more at $32 per person. Most diners set the ball rolling with one of the restaurant's fine martinis, and then save space for the Chocolate in Paradise dessert – sixteen layers of chocolate cake bliss. Daily 5–10pm.

Diamond Head Grill *W Honolulu*, 2885 Kalākaua Ave ☎ 808/922-3734, ⊛ www.w-dhg.com. Over-designed hotel restaurant, kitted out with lots of gleaming metal and specializing in Pacific Rim cuisine. The French-influenced food is quite good, however, with appetizers like ginger and *ahi* tartar ($13) or foie gras ($19), and entrees such as rack of New Zealand lamb ($40) or roasted walu ($34). Despite the name, the only views you get at dinnertime are of the long curving bar. Breakfast is rather more ordinary hotel food. Daily 7–10.30am & 6–10pm.

Hau Tree Lanai *New Otani Kaimana Beach Hotel*, 2863 Kalākaua Ave ☎ 808/921-7066. Open-air restaurant, set beneath the shade of two magnificent spreading hau trees beside Sans Souci Beach. Well away from the fray of Waikīkī Beach, it's a peaceful spot, perfect for romantic sunsets. Cuisine is mostly continental/American, but with added Pacific Rim touches: choose from top-quality breakfasts (go for the sweetbread French toast with coco-macadamia nut), lunches ranging from sandwiches to crab-cake burgers or seared garlic *ahi* (around $15), or dinner entrees like duck confit or seafood mixed grill ($25–35). Daily 7–11am, Mon–Sat 11.30am–2pm & 5.30–9pm; Sun 10am–2pm & 5.30–9pm.

Nobu *Waikīkī Parc*, 2233 Helumoa Rd ☎ 808/921-7272, ⊛ www.nobumatsuhisa.com. This book went to press just before the eagerly awaited opening of the first Hawaiian outpost of Japanese-Peruvian chef Nobu Matsuhisa's empire, spreading outdoors from the *Parc's* ultra-smart lobby. Expect exquisite, and expensive, sushi, sashimi, and "special cold dishes," with set dinners starting at around $30 for a sashimi platter with appetizers, soup and rice, or $80 and up for the chef's tasting menu.

Nick's Fishmarket *Waikīkī Gateway Hotel*, 2070 Kalākaua Ave ☎ 808/955-6333, ⊛ www.nicksfishmarket.com. Fancy fish restaurant, with dark leatherette seating, glittering glass and mirrors, and a formal, romantic atmosphere. The cooking is not especially innovative, but the preparation is meticulous and the range of choices amazing. Appetizers ($12–18) include coconut shrimp and oysters Rockefeller. A typical main dish like Hawaiian swordfish costs around $30, a mixed seafood grill $42, and lobsters up to $75. Simpler *pūpūs* are served until midnight in the less formal adjoining lounge, which also has live music. Mon–Thurs & Sun 5.30–10pm, Fri & Sat 5.30–11pm.

🏃 **Orchids** *Halekūlani* 2199 Kālia Rd ☎ 808/923-2311. Open to the ocean and affording divine views of Diamond Head, this minimal space afroth with orchids in the classiest hotel on Waikīkī Beach is well worth splashing out for. The food, fusing Asian and island cooking, is outstanding, if pricey – you can get a Madras seafood curry at lunch for $21, but it's most romantic at night, when entrees like *ahi*-seared sashimi with spices, *moi* with hearts of palm, and steamed *onaga* start at $30.The elaborate Sun brunch is a local favorite for special occasions. Mon–Sat 7.30–11am, 11.30am–2pm & 6–10pm, Sun 9.30am–2.30pm & 6–10pm.

Sam Choy's Diamond Head 449 Kapahulu Ave ☎ 808/732-8645, ⊛ www.samchoy.com. Usually buzzing with dressed-up locals, this "New Hawaiian" restaurant – basically Pacific Rim, with a Hawaiian emphasis – showcases the cuisine of TV chef Sam Choy. Though the location, a mile or so northeast of Waikīkī, is unprepossessing, the dining room itself is comfortable, lined with local art and with a bustling open kitchen. The food is splendid, with $25–33 entrees, such as seafood *laulau* (steamed in ti leaves) and wasabi-crusted ono, flavored with local herbs and spices; to start, don't miss Choy's trademark fried *poke* ($11). The $25 Sun brunch buffet includes *poke* done five ways, macadamia nut-crusted chicken and *kalua* pig. Mon–Thurs 5.30–10pm, Fri & Sat 5–11pm, Sun 9.30am–2pm & 5.30–10pm.

🏃 **Sansei Seafood Restaurant & Sushi Bar** *Waikīkī Beach Marriott Resort*, 2552 Kalākaua Ave ☎ 808/931-6286, ⊛ www.sanseihawaii.com. The food at this local favorite is outstanding and well priced, whether you go for the Pacific Rim menu or stick to the sushi bar. À la carte sushi starts at $5 (try the Sansei Special, with spicy crab, cilantro, cucumber and avocado, dusted with *furikake*). Entrees like grilled *opah* over fresh *nalo* greens, roasted Japanese jerk chicken, or duck breast in a foie gras demi-glaze, range

$18–40. Best of all, the $68 "Omakase" tasting menu for two is an amazing bargain, giving a balanced feast of seafood, sushi and sashimi. The adjoining karaoke bar gets going when the restaurant closes, with a limited half-price appetizer and sushi menu. Daily 5.30–10pm; late-night sushi Fri & Sat until 2am.

Honolulu

No single district of **Honolulu** can quite match Waikīkī for its sheer concentration and variety of eating options. Although **downtown** is all but deserted at night, nearby **Chinatown** abounds in inexpensive Chinese and Vietnamese places, with the Maunakea Marketplace a total delight for fans of Asian-style fast-food, while the malls along the **waterfront** – especially Aloha Tower Marketplace, Restaurant Row, and the Ward Center – hold plenty of alternatives. Many of Honolulu's finest restaurants are also tucked away in tourist-free zones around the university or in more upscale residential areas. If you're out sight-seeing bear in mind that both the Honolulu Academy of Arts (see p.94) and the Contemporary Museum (see p.101) have good cafés.

Inexpensive

Cafe Laniakea YWCA, 1040 Richards St ☎808/524-8789. Lunch-only downtown cafeteria, very close to 'Iolani Palace, promising "local first, organic whenever possible, with Aloha always." Lots of inexpensive vegetarian dishes, with salads at $8–10, along with sandwiches ($9–10) and daily specials such as a half chicken or grilled salmon ($11–13). Mon–Fri 11am–2pm.

Café Peninsula 1147 Bethel St ☎808/566-6979. Friendly and appealingly eccentric Chinatown coffee shop near the Hawaii Theater. Overstuffed with sprawling rattan armchairs and sofas, offering a quirky selection of books to read and a Chinese pop music soundtrack, it attracts a quiet local crowd of students and business people. Simple plate lunches such as spam with rice and egg ($5), and saimin ($4.25), are served, along with sandwiches, bagels, espresso drinks and iced herbal teas. Mon–Fri 9am–5pm.

Down to Earth 2525 S King St ☎808/947-7678. Long-standing natural food store near the university. The inexpensive deli counter offers a full vegetarian menu including curries, baked pies and pastas – some with tofu, some with cheese – plus sandwiches, salads and wraps, fresh fruit smoothies and juices. Daily 7.30am–9pm.

Grand Café & Bakery 31 N Pauahi St ☎808/531-0001. Airy Chinatown restaurant, established in the 1920s, where the appealingly old-fashioned feel extends to the menu. Choose from comfort food – pot roast, meat loaf – or more modern choices like grilled asparagus and poached egg salad and tasty pastries and desserts. Breakfasts are particularly

fine, based on tempting dishes like Banana Foster French toast. Tues–Fri 7am–1.30pm, Sat & Sun 8am–1pm, first Fri of month also 5.15–7.45pm.

Gyotaku Japanese Restaurant 1824 S King St ☎808/949-4584. During the day, this is a hotspot for locals grabbing bento boxes – butterfish, teriyaki beef, tempura– for around $7. The dining room offers more bento, as well as a fine range of sushi and tempting noodles, wa-zen and kamameshi, from $12. The *poke* don teishoku ($15) is particularly tasty, with the fresh *poke* served over rice. No reservations. Bento take out daily 9.30am–2.30pm; restaurant Sun–Thurs 11am–9pm, Fri & Sat 11am–10pm.

Kaka'ako Kitchen Ward Center, 1200 Ala Moana Blvd ☎808/596-7488. Cheery mall restaurant that dishes up home-cooking, Hawaiian-style. The presentation is no-frills – after ordering at the counter, you eat with plastic cutlery from styrofoam boxes – but the food is healthy and excellent. Everything from the tempura catfish to the island-style chicken linguine costs $7–10, with daily specials for carnivores (meat loaf, pot roast, curry) and veggies (stir-fry tofu, eggplant parmesan) alike. Breakfast options include mahi mahi with eggs for $7.25. Mon–Thurs 7–10am & 10.30am–9pm, Fri 7–10am & 10.30am–10pm, Sat 7–11am & 11.30am–10pm, Sun 7–11am & 11.30am–5pm.

Legend Seafood Restaurant 100 N Beretania St ☎808/532-1868. Chinatown seafood specialist in a modern building whose big plate-glass windows look out over the Nu'uanu Stream. The lunchtime dim sum trolleys are piled with individual portions at $3–5; full Chinese meals, with entrees including whole lobster or crab at $10–20, are served at both lunch and dinner. Mon–Fri 10.30am–2pm & 5.30–9pm, Sat & Sun 8am–2pm & 5.30–9pm.

Legend Vegetarian Restaurant 100 N Beretania St ☏ 808/532-8218. Bright Chinese vegetarian restaurant in the heart of Chinatown open for lunch only. The menu features beef balls, cuttlefish, pork ribs, and tenderloin, but all the dishes are actually tofu or other vegetarian ingredients shaped and flavored to resemble meats and fishes. There's also a wide selection of vegetarian dim sum, plus conventional vegetable dishes. Entrees are priced well under $10. No alcohol. Daily except Wed 10.30am–2pm.

Mei Sum 65 N Pauahi St at Smith ☏ 808/531-3268. No-frills, high-quality dim sum restaurant, where the trolleys are heaving all day long with a wide assortment of tasty snacks priced between $2 and $3.15 each. Tasty options include seafood or mushroom chicken dumplings, turnip cake, deep fried scallops in taro leaves, and char siu buns. Noodle, rice, and wonton entrees, featuring chicken, prawns, scallops, or calamari, are also available for $7–10 per plate. A full dinner for four is just $36. Daily 7am–8.45pm.

Pavilion Café Honolulu Academy of Arts, 900 S Beretania St ☏ 808/532-8734. With its zestful Mediterranean sandwiches and salads, this appealing little lunch-only courtyard bistro makes the perfect midday stop while exploring downtown. Tues–Sat 11.30am–2pm, plus third Sun of each month 11.30am–2pm.

Phô 97 176 Maunakea Marketplace, Maunakea St ☏ 808/538-0708. This large Chinatown restaurant, technically in the Maunakea Marketplace but entered direct from Maunakea Street, is the best place to sample Vietnamese phô (noodle soup). There are also lots of Cambodian, Thai, and Vietnamese noodle and rice dishes, as well as barbecued pork, simmered catfish, and crab meat soup. The portions are huge, and almost nothing costs more than $7. Mon–Sat 8am–9pm, Sun 8am–7pm.

Summer Frappé 1120 Maunakea St, store 192 ☏ 808/722-9291. Hole-in-the-wall juice and snack bar in the courtyard behind Chinatown's Maunakea Marketplace food hall. With shaded outdoor seating, it's a great place to restore yourself with a delicious fresh smoothie, made with exotic fruits, or a fruity bubble tea studded with tapioca pearls. Daily 7.30am–6pm.

Sweet Basil 1152A Maunakea St ☏ 808/545-5800. Small and spotless, this lovely Thai restaurant – a rarity in Chinatown – is an absolute winner for its tasty, and healthy home cooking (with no MSG). The astonishingly good-value lunch buffet ($9) includes four hot curries,

with a different special every day, plus four zingy Thai salads, two soups and fruit for dessert. À la carte options ($5–15) include simple curries and veggie choices through noodle dishes to sizzling seafood entrees. Mon–Thurs 10.30am–2pm, Fri & Sat 10.30am–2pm & 5–9pm.

Volcano Joe's Island Coffee House 1810 University Ave ☏ 808/941-8449, ☒ www.volcanojoes .com. Across the street from the university campus, and handy to the Hosteling International Honolulu (see p.76), this casual café is a convenient stop-off on the way to or from Manoa Falls. Breakfast includes waffles and pastries, while lunch and dinner ($5–8) revolves around wraps, pizza, salads and vegan specials. Local bands play on Mon evenings. Coffeehouse Mon–Fri 6am–8pm, Sat & Sun 7am–8pm; bistro daily 11am–10pm.

Moderate

E&O Trading Co 1200 Ala Moana Blvd, Ward Center, Bldg 4 ☏ 808/591-9555. This elegant pan-Asian restaurant, part of a Californian/Hawaiian chain, makes a soothing stop in the Ward Center. Strewn with Indonesian textiles and temple art, it serves similarly eclectic cuisine, with satay (around $7) and Indonesian corn fritters ($7) sitting next to char-siu smoked black cod ($23) and tandoori chicken ($17). Lunch and dinner menus are broadly similar, with a few lunch specials for $13 – firecracker chicken stir-fried with asparagus, for example. Sun–Thurs 11.30am–10.30pm, Fri & Sat 11.30am–11.30pm.

Gordon Biersch Brewery Aloha Tower Marketplace, 101 Ala Moana Blvd ☏ 808/599-4877. This chain brewpub offers one of Aloha Tower's more stylish options, with seating either outdoors on a large dockside terrace, or indoors near a long bar brimming with beers from around the globe. For lunch ($9–16) try a pizza, a goat cheese and hummus salad, or the cashew chicken stir-fry. The dinner menu offers the same pizzas and salads, Hawaiian regional dishes such as sesame seared *ahi* ($22.50), plus Japanese and Thai-tinged choices. Live music Wed–Sat evenings. Mon–Thurs & Sun 10am–10pm, Fri & Sat 10am–11pm; bar open until midnight Mon–Thurs & Sun, 1am Fri & Sat.

Hakkei 1436 Young St ☏ 808/944-6688, ☒ www .hakkei-honolulu.com. Specializing in *washoku* cuisine, with unfussy dishes like *oden* (a flavorful hotpot cooked with anything from turnips and pumpkin to tofu and Japanese fish cake), crispy rice, home-made pickled vegetables and fresh veggies. The daily lunch specials – deep-fried butterfish, mushroom and soybean hotpot, scallop *kamameshi* – represent the best value. Daily except Tues 11.30am–2pm & 5.30–11pm.

Little Village Noodle House 1113 Smith St ⊤ 808/545-3008. Smart and friendly restaurant in the heart of Chinatown, offering a perfectly prepared range of delicious Chinese dishes from Singapore noodles ($8) through salt and pepper pork ($9.50) to clams in black bean sauce ($13.50). The special Hong Kong menu has congees and noodle soups from $5. Sun–Thurs 10.30am–10.30pm, Fri & Sat 10.30am–midnight.

La Mariana Sailing Club 50 Sand Island Access Rd ⊤ 808/848-2800. An atmospheric old-time restaurant on an obscure stretch of Honolulu's industrial waterfront. The decor, original 1950s cocktail lounge styling mixed with South Seas thrift store kitsch, is the real thing, and the ambience – created by a crowd of eccentric locals and in-the-know tourists – slightly surreal. Hearty fish appetizers like *taco poke* (marinated octopus) cost between $6 and $13, while full dinners such as seafood brochette or *ahi* Cajun go for under $20. The main draw, however, is the impromptu live Hawaiian music on Fri evenings, from 6pm until 9pm; for more details, see p.123. Daily 11am–3pm & 5–9pm.

Olive Tree Café 4614 Kīlauea Ave ⊤ 808/737-0303. Simple, understated Greek deli, adjoining but not technically within Kāhala Mall, with some outdoor seating. The value is unbeatable, and the food is great, ranging from refreshing tomato and feta cheese salads to a lovely ceviche of New Zealand mussels ($7), to *souvlaki* skewers of chicken or fish ($9–11). No credit cards. Daily 5–10pm.

OnJin's Café 401 Kamake'e St ⊤ 808/589-1666. Bright little café, one block inland from the Ward Center, offering quality cooking at very reasonable prices. At lunchtime, when orders are taken at the counter, pretty much everything costs $7.50–10 – and that includes the crispy snapper in lemon beurre blanc ($8.25), and the daily specials like Thursday's roast leg of lamb, as well as wraps, burgers, and sandwiches. The service is more formal in the evening, and the prices are significantly higher, with entrees such as half a duck in Grand Marnier for $18.50, and bouillabaisse for $24. Mon–Sat 11am–10pm, Sun 11am–9pm.

Yakiniku Camellia Buffet 2494 S Beretania St ⊤ 808/946-7955. Authentic, cheap and cheerful Korean buffet restaurant about a mile north of Waikīkī, just south of the university. The few non-Korean speakers who venture in have to fend for themselves, joining families and hungry locals heaping their plates again and again. Whether at lunch ($12) or dinner ($19), the food is a treat; you select slices of marinated beef, chicken, or pork from refrigerated cabinets and grill them yourself at the gas-fired burners set into each table. There are also lots of vegetables, as well as a wide

assortment of super-fresh salads, including octopus, seaweed, *ahi poke*, pickles, and delicious tiny dried fish. Daily 10.30am–10pm.

Expensive

Alan Wong's 1857 S King St ⊤ 808/949-2526, ⓦ www.alanwongs.com. Though expensive and hard to find – it's tucked away on the third floor in a nondescript area southwest of the university – *Alan Wong's* is one of Honolulu's most fashionable gourmet rendezvous, thanks to its fantastic contemporary Hawaiian cuisine. Besides changing daily specials, appetizers always include the signature "da bag," a giant foil bag holding clams steamed with *kalua* pig, *shiitake* mushrooms, and spinach ($11.50), and "poki-pines", crispy *ahi poke* wontons with avocado and wasabi ($15). Typical entrees ($26–52) include ginger-crusted *onaga* (snapper) and oil-poached lamb rib-eye with three sauces. The nightly tasting menus cost $75 (five courses) and $95 (seven courses). Valet parking only. Daily 5–10pm.

Chai's Island Bistro Aloha Tower Marketplace, 101 Ala Moana Blvd ⊤ 808/585-0011, ⓦ www.chaisislandbistro.com. Beautifully decorated pan-Asian restaurant, half indoors and half out, at the inland side of the Aloha Tower Marketplace. Though it's owned by the same chef as Waikīkī's *Singha Thai* (see p.117), the food can be a bit hit or miss and is not the main reason to visit: Chai's books the absolute crème de la crème of Hawaiian musicians to perform live, as detailed on p.123. Miss the show, scheduled for 7–8.30pm, and you'll be paying well over the norm for entrees like *sake* steamed *moi* ($40) or grilled Mongolian lamb chops ($38). Lunches are signifcantly cheaper. Mon, Sat & Sun 4–10pm; Tues–Fri 11am–10pm.

Chef Mavro 1969 S King St ⊤ 808/944-4714, ⓦ www.chefmavro.com. Despite his restaurant's unfashionable Mānoa location, Greek-born chef George Mavrothalassitis stands out in Honolulu's gourmet dining scene for his seasonally changing prix fixe menus (three courses $65, $98 with a different wine for each course; four courses $71/$115; six courses $102/$150), and his eleven-course "dégustation" menu for four ($150/$212). The menu sounds fussy – roasted loin of kurobuta pork with sansho jus, apple quinoa and savoy cabbage gribiche, say, or kobe-style roasted bavette and braised short rib with pancetta Brussels sprouts, truffle-accented celery root purée and Pinot Noir sauce – but the food itself, a fusion of nouvelle contemporary Hawaiian, is delicate and delightful. Daily except Mon 6–9.30pm.

Duc's Bistro 1188 Maunakea St ⊤ 808/531-6325. Sophisticated Asian-influenced French restaurant in

Chinatown, which hosts live jazz nightly except Thurs. Dinner appetizers ($8–12) include gravadlax, escargots and, unusually in Hawaii, oysters on the half shell; a basic lemongrass chicken entree costs $14, fancier options like duck breast in Grand Marnier or flambéed steak are $22–30. Portions and prices are significantly smaller at lunchtime. Mon–Sat 11.30am–2pm & 5–10pm.

Hiroshi Eurasian Tapas Restaurant Row, 500 Ala Moana Blvd ☏ 808/533-4476, ⓦ www .dkrestaurants.com. Anyone familiar with Spanish tapas shouldn't expect the same experience here; though they profess to offer small plates, these are more like largish appetizers, and prices ($7–16) mean that costs easily mount up. As expected from the folks behind the superlative *Sansei* restaurants, the food, combining Mediterranean and pan-Asian cuisines – foie gras sushi, truffled crab cake, miso butterfish, Portuguese sausage potfillers – is across the board delicious, and the atmosphere contemporary and vibrant. Larger plates – onaga with cauliflower purée, wilted tatsoi and fresh basil, for example – cost $20–28. Daily 5.30–9.30pm.

🏃 **Indigo** 21 Nu'uanu Ave ☏ 808/521-2900, ⓦ www.indigo-hawaii.com. Chinatown's classiest option, a lovely space with indoor and outdoor seating, serves delicious nouvelle "Eurasian" crossover food. In addition to the good-value $17 lunch buffet, you can select from a broad range of dim sum ($7–12), including "thousand loved crab cakes", and entrees like wokked "Buddhist" vegetables ($16). Dinner entrees ($19–30) include Shanghai duck with soft bao buns, ginger ham shanks, and *moi* roasted in a banana leaf. The adjoining late-night *Green Room Lounge* has live music and dancing Tues–Sat. Tues–Thurs

11.30am–2pm & 6–9.30pm, Fri 11.30am–2pm & 6–10pm, Sat 6–10pm.

🏃 **L'Uraku** 1341 Kapi'olani Blvd ☏ 808/955-0552, ⓦ www.luraku.com. Quirky, hip Japanese restaurant on a busy street a block inland from the Ala Moana Center. The interior is festooned with crudely hand-painted umbrellas that trace the saga of a lost Somalian cat. Most of the menu is solidly Japanese, but there's a strong Italian flavor as well, including a daily pasta special. Delicious appetizers, ranging from a single baked oyster ($2.50) up to a bento box filled with goodies ($13), are matched by entrees ($16–28) that include steamed fish and garlic steak. A dinner "tasting" menu is $34 ($47 with wine), while at lunchtime on weekends they offer a bargain $16 set meal. Daily 11am–2pm & 5.30–10pm.

Sam Choy's Breakfast, Lunch and Crab 580 N Nimitz Hwy ☏ 808/545-7979, ⓦ www.samchoy .com. A mile or two west of downtown, tightly sandwiched between the west- and east-bound sides of the Nimitz Highway, this garish Hawaiian diner looks unenticing from the outside. Inside you'll find a full-sized sampan fishing boat, the gleaming *Big Aloha* microbrewery, and crowds of diners eager to gorge on celebrity chef Choy's trademark local cuisine. Crab is a feature, of course, along with hefty breakfasts (from $6) – go for the Hawaiian specialties, like kalua pork loco moco – and plate lunches ($9–15) that come very big indeed – the fried *poke* ($12) is a must. Evening entrees ($18–30) include fresh fish, paella, crabs' legs, and roasted or steamed whole crabs and lobsters. Restaurant Mon–Thurs 7am–3pm & 5–9.30pm, Fri & Sat 7am–4pm & 5–10pm, Sun 7am–4pm & 5–9.30pm; brewery daily 10.30am until late.

Entertainment and nightlife

Tourists staying in Waikīkī will find plenty of resort **entertainment** on offer, with (often free) **Hawaiian music** performances combined with theatrical spectaculars and live gigs in other genres. In addition, Waikīkī also has plenty of **nightclubs**, geared more towards younger tastes in music. Nightlife in the rest of Honolulu is more diverse, ranging from some very upscale clubs frequented by wealthy urban professionals to a grungier scene for surfers and students who wouldn't be seen dead in Waikīkī. Various magazines and papers will keep you abreast of what's going on; the best are the free *Honolulu Weekly* newspaper (ⓦ www.honoluluweekly.com), and the *TGIF* section of Friday's *Honolulu Advertiser* (ⓦ www.honoluluadvertiser .com). See p.63 for a list of annual festivals and events on Oahu.

Hawaiian entertainment

It's not hard to find **Hawaiian entertainment** in Waikīkī, with many of the grander hotels featuring accomplished Hawaiian musicians most evenings.

Although some are very good indeed – and Auntie Genoa Keawe at the *Waikīkī Beach Marriott* is absolutely unmissable (see below) – it's well worth looking out for events that are arranged for Hawaiian, rather than tourist, audiences, such as the frequent one-off performances and benefit concerts at downtown's beautiful Hawaii Theater (see p.95).

Away from the hotels, the best regular **free shows** of Hawaiian music are given by the **Royal Hawaiian Band** (Ⓦ www.royalhawaiianband.com), which, throughout the year except August, gives hour-long performances on Fridays at noon on the lawns of 'Iolani Palace downtown, and Sundays at 2pm in Waikīkī's Kapiolani Park.

For more on *hula* and Hawaiian music, and recommendations on specific musicians to watch out for, see p.562.

Banyan Veranda *Sheraton Moana Surfrider*, 2365 Kalākaua Ave, Waikīkī ☎ 808/922-3111. Open-air beach bar that was home to the nationally syndicated Hawaii Calls radio show from the 1930s to the 1970s. Steel guitar and *hula* dancers nightly 5.30–7.30pm, followed by small Hawaiian ensembles 7.30–10.30pm. No cover but a one-drink minimum.

🏃 **Chai's Island Bistro** Aloha Tower Marketplace, 101 Ala Moana Blvd ☎ 808/585-0011. This very expensive Thai restaurant (see p.121) books the finest Hawaiian musicians to perform for diners nightly 7–8.30pm. The precise schedule varies, but currently includes long-term residencies by Sista Robi Kahakalau (Sun), Robert Cazimero (Tues), the Brothers Cazimero (Wed), and regular appearances by one or both members of Hapa.

Duke's Canoe Club *Outrigger Waikīkī*, 2335 Kalākaua Ave, Waikīkī ☎ 808/922-2268. Smooth Hawaiian sounds wash over this oceanfront cocktail bar nightly from 4–6pm and 10pm–midnight. On weekends, the afternoon show is usually a big-name "Concert on the Beach." No cover charge.

🏃 **Honey's at Ko'olau** *Ko'olau Golf Club* 45-550 Kionaole Rd, Kāne'ohe ☎ 808/236-4653. You'll need a car and a good map to find this unlikely windward hangout. Cross the mountains on the Pali Hwy, turn left onto Kamehameha Hwy, and then left again immediately north of H-3; *Honey's* is downstairs in the clubhouse (and the "Honey" in question is Don Ho's mother). The reason to make the effort? Genial 'ukulele wizard Eddie Kamae, founding member of the Sons of Hawaii, presides over a hugely enjoyable afternoon jam session on Sun 3.30–6pm. Arrive early to get a good seat; full food menu available. No cover.

🏃 **House Without a Key** *Halekūlani*, 2199 Kālia Rd, Waikīkī ☎ 808/923-2311. This very romantic, very spacious beach bar was named after

a Charlie Chan mystery that was written by Earl Derr Biggers after a stay at the hotel. In keeping with its name, the *House Without a Key* barely has walls, let alone a door, which affords it the most wonderful vistas and spectacular ocean sunsets. The evening cocktail hour (5–9pm) is an unmissable bargain, with very gentle, old-time Hawaiian classics performed under an ancient *kiawe* tree and *hula* dancing by a former Miss Hawaii (two of whom alternate). You're led to your seats, which avoids the scrum for an oceanfront spot at other beach bars. Drinks prices are very reasonable and service is friendly and courteous. No cover.

La Mariana Sailing Club 50 Sand Island Access Rd ☎ 808/848-2800. An extremely quirky waterfront restaurant – the food is reviewed on p.121 – with an authentic 1950s ambience, hidden away amid the docks of Honolulu. The week's high point is Fri eve, from 8.30pm onwards, when pianist Ron Miyashiro and a group of semi-professional singers work their way through a nostalgic set of classic Hawaiian songs, but there's also live piano music nightly except Mon 5–9pm. Not to be missed, as it's practically the last of a dying breed. No cover.

🏃 **Moana Terrace** *Waikīkī Beach Marriott*, 2552 Kalākaua Ave, Waikīkī ☎ 808/922-6611. A consistently good roster of Hawaiian musicians perform at this lively, open-air, third-story cocktail bar, across the road from the beach (Mon–Wed, Fri & Sat from 7pm, and Sun from 8pm). The biggest treat of all comes on Thurs, when local legend Auntie Genoa Keawe, a magnificent falsetto singer now approaching her ninetieth birthday, leads an informal jam session 6–8.30pm. No cover.

Paradise Lounge *Hilton Hawaiian Village*, 2005 Kālia Rd, Waikīkī ☎ 808/949-4321. Live *hula* and Hawaiian music, headlined by popular local group Olomana, Fri & Sat 8pm–midnight. No cover.

Bars, live music, and dancing

There's rarely a clear distinction between **bars**, **live music venues**, and **nightclubs** in Honolulu – for that matter, many restaurants get in on the act as well.

△ Auntie Genoa Keawe

While there's plenty of live music around, the overall standard tends to be disappointing. In addition, few Waikīkī clubs get to build a regular clientele, so the atmosphere is unpredictable. The biggest touring acts tend to appear at Pearl Harbor's Aloha Stadium (℡808/483-2500; ⓦwww.alohastadium.hawaii.gov) or downtown's Blaisdell Center (℡808/527-5400; ⓦwww.blaisdellcenter.com); watch for announcements in the local press. The venues listed below all have a cover charge, unless otherwise noted.

Anna Bannanas 2440 S Beretania St, Honolulu ℡808/946-5190. University district bar with reasonable prices, live R&B and reggae most nights, and a hectic weekend atmosphere. Daily 9pm–2am.

Hank's Cafe 1038 Nuʻuanu Ave, Honolulu ℡808/526-1410, ⓦwww.hankscafehonolulu.com. Small art gallery–cum–bar in Chinatown, with an appealing retro feel, staging regular live music

Lū'aus

If you insist on going to a **lū'au** – a commercialized approximation of a traditional Hawaiian feast – while you're in Waikīkī, the most convenient option is at the *Royal Hawaiian Hotel* on Monday at 6pm (℡ 808/931-8383). Their *lū'au* is expensive at $100 adults, $55 ages 5–12, but the Waikīkī Beach setting is romantic, and the price includes a reasonable spread of food and a somewhat cramped but enthusiastic show of Hawaiian music and dance on the oceanfront stage. The two biggest *lū'aus* on Oahu, advertised everywhere, are *Germaine's* (nightly, 6pm; adults $65, ages 14–20 $55, ages 6–13 $45; ℡ 808/949-6626 or 1-800/367-5655, ⓦ www.germainesluau .com) and *Paradise Cove* (nightly 6pm; adults $73, ages 13–18 $63, ages 4–12 $53; ℡ 808/842-5911 or 1-800/775-2683, ⓦ www.paradisecove.com). What their ads may not make clear is that both take place thirty miles from Waikīkī, in the far southwestern corner of the island. The price – you may well be offered cheaper rates by an activity center – includes an hour-long bus trip each way (singalongs compulsory), and your reward at the end is the chance to spend hours looking at tacky souvenirs, eating bland food, drinking weak cocktails, and watching third-rate entertainment.

Finally, as detailed on p.144, there's also a *lū'au* at the Polynesian Cultural Center in Lā'ie, near Oahu's northeastern tip (Mon–Sat 5.15–6.30pm; ℡ 808/293-3333 or 1-800/367-7060, ⓦ www.polynesia.com). That potentially offers a more "educational" experience than the rest, as you can only attend as part of a longer visit to the center, but it's still basically a stage show accompanied by an unremarkable buffet dinner. The cheapest admission price for *lū'au* visitors is $80 for adults, $56 ages 3–11, plus a minimum of $19 per person for transportation from Waikīkī.

jams, some Hawaiian, some not. On the second floor, in what was once a tattoo parlor – hence the impressive mural – you'll find *The Dragon Upstairs*, which puts on live jazz Thurs–Sun. Mon 3–10pm, Tues–Sun 3pm–2am.

Lewers Lounge *Halekūlani*, 2199 Kālia Rd, Waikīkī ℡ 808/923-2311. Sophisticated nightspot that looks more like an English drawing room than a Waikīkī bar. Live jazz nightly 8.30pm–12.30am, at its best Tues–Fri, when bass player Bruce Hamada performs.

Nashville Waikīkī 2330 Kūhīo Ave, Waikīkī ℡ 808/926-7911, ⓦ www.nashvillewaikiki.com. If you're hankering to hoedown in Hawaii, this country music club below the *Ohana West* has plenty of room to show off your rhinestones. Check ahead, though; it also hosts hip-hop and DJ nights. There are pool tables and darts, too. Daily 4pm–4am.

Ocean Club Restaurant Row, 500 Ala Moana Blvd ℡ 808/531-8444, ⓦ www.oceanclubonline.com. Big, loud, and glitzy bar/nightclub that's a major hangout for downtown's after-work crowd. No T-shirts or those 23 years old allowed (except Thurs, when ages 21 & 22 are also welcome). The short menu of seafood snacks is half-price before 8pm;

after that, there's a $5 cover charge, and the dancing continues late into the night. Tues–Fri 4.30pm–4am, Sat 7pm–4am.

Pipeline 805 Pohukaina St, Honolulu ℡ 808/589-1999, ⓦ www.pipelinecafe.net. Just behind the Ala Moana Center, this is a favorite with the surf set, who come for DJ music most nights, and perhaps one rock or reggae gig per week (the only time there's a cover charge). Door policy varies nightly between over-20s and over-17s; call to check. Mon–Thurs 9pm–4am, Fri & Sat 10pm–4am.

Rumours *Ala Moana Hotel*, 410 Atkinson Drive, Honolulu ℡ 808/955-4811. Mainstream, old-style disco in a business hotel behind the Ala Moana Center. Extremely popular with the after-work local crowd. Friday's '70s night is a fixture on many calendars. Thurs 5pm–2am, Fri 5pm–4am, Sat 9pm–4am.

Zanzabar Waikīkī Trade Center, 2255 Kūhīo Ave, Waikīkī ℡ 808/924-3939, ⓦ www.zanzabarhawaii .com. Extremely opulent nightclub, bursting with Egyptian motifs, and pumping out dance music to the well-heeled youth of Honolulu. Nightly except Mon 8pm–4am.

Shows

The last few years have seen a slight return to the days when Waikīkī's hotels felt honor bound to stage their own Las Vegas–style, big-budget shows. There's

Gay Honolulu

While Honolulu's gay scene is focused on **Kūhīo Avenue** in central Waikīkī, the legendary *Hula's Bar and Lei Stand* has found a permanent new home; see below. For gay travelers, an evening at *Hula's* is the obvious first step. Step two would be to join the weekly **catamaran cruise** organized by *Angles* (see below) on Sundays at 1pm ($25). For general information, contact the Center, 614 South St, Honolulu (☎808/951-7000, ⒲thecenterhawaii.org). *Pacific Ocean Holidays* (PO Box 88245, Honolulu HI 96830-8245; ☎808/944-4700 or 1-800/735-6600, ⒲gayhawaiivacations.com) organizes all-inclusive **package vacations** in Hawaii for gay and lesbian travelers, and maintains the useful ⒲www.gayhawaii.com **website**. Taking the Plunge (☎808/922-2600, ⒲www.takemediving.com) is a highly recommended gay-friendly **scuba diving** company, while a gay **hiking** club, Likehike (☎808/455-8193, ⒲www.gayhawaii.com /likehike), organizes different group hikes on alternate Sundays.

Gay bars and clubs

Angles Waikīkī 2256 Kūhīo Ave, Waikīkī ☎808/926-9766 or 923-1130, ⒲www .angleswaikiki.com. Dance club with lively bar and street-view patio, plus bar games including pool and darts. Daily 10am–2am.

Fusion 2260 Kūhīo Ave, Waikīkī ☎808/924-2422, ⒲www.gayhawaii.com/fusion. Wild, split-level nightclub, with male strippers, drag acts, free karaoke Mon & Tues, and special drink discounts. Mon–Thurs 9pm–4am, Fri & Sat 8pm–4am, Sun 10pm–4am.

Hula's Bar and Lei Stand *Waikīkī Grand Hotel*, 134 Kapahulu Ave, Waikīkī ☎808/923-0669, ⒲www.hulas.com. Waikīkī's most popular and long-standing gay club occupies a suite of ocean-view rooms on the second floor of the *Waikīkī Grand*, across from the Honolulu Zoo. In addition to a state-of-the-art dance bar equipped with giant video screens, there's a more casual lounge area. Daily 10am–2am.

In-Between 2155 Lau'ula St, Waikīkī ☎808/926-7060, ⒲www.inbetweenonline.com. Local gay karaoke bar in the heart of Waikīkī, open Mon–Sat 4pm–2am, Sun 2pm–2am.

---

nothing very exceptional on offer, and with tour groups as the main clientele it's all firmly middle-of-the-road, but if you're looking for family fun you could do a lot worse. For most of the shows below, specific prices are not listed because you can get much better deals by buying **reduced-price tickets** through "activity centers" (see p.80). Expect to pay around $30 if it's possible to book for the show alone (and bear in mind you'll be expected to drink once you're there), or more like $60 if you eat as well.

Blue Hawaii *Waikīkī Beachcomber Hotel*, 2300 Kalākaua Ave, Waikīkī ☎808/923-1245. Jonathan von Brana, along with a perky troupe of dancing girls, evokes the spirit of Elvis in a musical tribute that takes him from the beaches of Hawaii to the stage of the *Las Vegas Hilton*. Some of his moves might seem a little incongruous – jumping jacks? Elvis? really? – but he doles out enough logo-emblazoned scarves and teddy bears to keep the fans happy. High-energy support is provided by the Love Notes, a doo-wop group who've been around the block a few times. Nightly, except Tues, 6.15pm.
Creation – A Polynesian Odyssey Ainahau Showroom, *Sheraton Princess Ka'iulani*, 120

Ka'iulani Ave, Waikīkī HI 96815 ☎808/931-4660. Lavish Polynesian revue, complete with fire-dancing, *hula*, and a buffet dinner. Tues & Thurs–Sun 6pm.
Magic of Polynesia *Waikīkī Beachcomber Hotel*, 2300 Kalākaua Ave, Waikīkī ☎808/971-4321, ⒲www.magicofpolynesia.com. Spectacular, enjoyable magic show, starring illusionists John Hirakawa (Tues–Sat) or Michael Villoria (Sun & Mon), featuring all the disappearing lovelies and severed heads you could ask for, along with tattooed Polynesian warriors, maidens in coconut bras, and Samoan fire dancers. Two shows nightly at 5pm & 8pm.

Society of Seven Outrigger Main Show Room, 2335 Kalākaua Ave, Waikīkī ☎808/922-6408, ⓦwww.outriggerentertainment.com. Very long-standing song-and-dance ensemble, which performs Broadway musical routines and pop hits with amazing energy. Nightly, except Mon, 8.30pm.

Shopping

Virtually all the shops in both Honolulu and Waikīkī are in purpose-built **malls**, so shopping in the city is easy, if not all that exciting. For many years, Honolulu's **Ala Moana Center** held undisputed sway as the city's premier mall for serious shoppers, but it has been so successful in attracting big spenders that new rivals now seem to be springing up all the time. Even Waikīkī has made a definite move away from its traditional emphasis on souvenirs and beach accessories.

Waikīkī shopping

If you want to buy a T-shirt, a beach mat, or a monkey carved out of a coconut, Waikīkī is definitely the place for you. Kalākaua and Kūhio avenues especially are lined with cut-price souvenir stores; there are 37 shops in the ABC chain alone, all open daily from 7am to midnight and selling basic groceries along with postcards, sun lotions, and other tourist essentials.

Waikīkī's largest malls, the monolithic **Royal Hawaiian Shopping Center** and the **DFS Galeria**, across the street at 330 Royal Hawaiian Ave, are aseptic, upmarket enclaves, packed with designer-clothing shops, jewelry stores and sunglasses emporiums. The trend these days is for the major hotels to build their own upscale shopping malls; the two largest, the *Hyatt Regency* and, especially, the *Hilton Hawaiian Village*, now hold conglomerations of stores to rival any in Honolulu. For the moment, the venerable 1950s-style open-air **International Marketplace**, 2330 Kalākaua Ave (daily 10am–10.30pm), survives, though encroaching development may soon force its closure. With its simple wooden stalls scattered among the trees, it has a lot more atmosphere than the malls, though the "crafts" on sale tend to be made in Taiwan, while the "psychic readers" are as a rule devoid of paranormal powers.

The only bookstore in central Waikīkī is a **Borders Express** on the third floor of the otherwise tacky and unappealing Waikīkī Marketplace mall, at 2250 Kalākaua Ave (☎808/922-4154; daily 9.30am–9.30pm). While modern imitations and reproductions are available everywhere you look, it's harder than you'd expect to find that quintessential emblem of old Hawaii, the authentic **aloha shirt**. Whether you're prepared to spend thousands of dollars for an original, or happy to settle for a well-priced replica, head to Bailey's, 517 Kapahulu Ave (☎808/734-7628, ⓦalohashirts.com).

Honolulu shopping

The **Ala Moana Center** (Mon–Thurs 9.30am–9pm, Fri 9.30am–10pm, Sat 8am–10pm, Sun 10am–7pm; ☎808/955-9517, ⓦwww.alamoana.com), a mile west of Waikīkī, has since 1959 been Hawaii's main shopping destination; neighbor-island residents fly to Honolulu specifically in order to shop here. One of the largest open-air malls in the world, and still growing year on year, it holds several major department stores, including Sears, Macy's, and Neiman Marcus. Couture designers are represented by the likes of Armani, Burberry, Gucci, Vuitton and Jimmy Choo; upscale street-style by DKNY, Diesel and Shanghai Tang; and Hilo Hattie's adds a cheerful, inexpensive Hawaiian flavor. Be sure to explore the Japanese Shirokiya, which has a fabulous upstairs food hall, piled high with sushi and *poi*, and also stocks a great array of bargain electronics.

The various **Ward** malls – the Center, Warehouse, Farmers Market, Gateway Center and Village Shops – spread themselves across four blocks along and behind Ala Moana Boulevard, starting a couple of blocks west of the Ala Moana Center. Accessible, like the Ala Moana Center, on both TheBus and the Waikīkī Trolley pink line ($2), this complex, in particular the Ward Center, has become a serious rival to its bigger neighbor, with a more intimate atmosphere and some distinctive locally owned stores. Highlights include the large Borders book and music store in the Ward Center (Mon–Thurs 9am–11pm, Fri & Sat 9am–midnight, Sun 9am–10pm; ☏808/591-8995); the excellent Native Books/Na Mea Hawaii in the Ward Warehouse (Mon–Thurs 10am–9pm, Fri & Sat 10am–10pm, Sun 10am–7pm; ☏808/596-8885, ⓦnativebookshawaii.com), which stocks a great range of local craft products, along with Hawaiian books and CDs; and the very feminine jewelry, home furnishings, and gifts in Cottage by the Sea, again in the Ward Warehouse (Mon–Sat 10am–9pm, Sun 10am–5pm; ☏808/591-9811, ⓦwww.cottagehawaii.com).

Downtown's **Aloha Tower Marketplace** (Mon–Sat 9am–9pm, Sun 9am–6pm; ☏808/566-2337, ⓦwww.alohatower.com; see p.97) has failed to lure significant numbers of tourists away from Ala Moana, and is looking a little tired, verging on the downmarket, but the dockside setting makes it a fun place to wander around. Most of the seventy or so stores are one-of-a-kind rather than chain outlets, and souvenir possibilities range from the grunting "Mr Bacon" pigs at Mag-Neat-O to the wooden salad bowls, turtles and cannibal forks at Hawaiian Pacific Arts and Crafts. You can also buy beautifully crafted instruments at the Hawaiian Ukulele Company (☏808/536-3228, ⓦwww.thehawaiianukulelecompany.com), or quirky cowboy-cum-aloha shirts at Out of the West (☏808/521-5552).

Only a couple of miles from Waikīkī, *mauka* of Diamond Head, the **Kāhala Mall**, 4211 Waialae Ave (Mon–Sat 10am–9pm, Sun 10am–5pm; ⓦwww.kahalamallcenter.com), is almost as chic as – though smaller and far less frenzied than – Ala Moana. As well as Macy's, Longs Drugs, Banana Republic, Reyn's aloha wear, Compleat Kitchen, an eight-screen movie theater, and an assortment of restaurants, it holds an excellent Barnes & Noble bookstore.

It's also well worth strolling the streets and markets of **Chinatown**, which hold all sorts of unexpected and one-of-a-kind stalls and stores. Among them is the funky fashion boutique *Bad Sushi*, 935 River St (daily noon–8pm; ☏808/548-7874, ⓦwww.badsushihawaii.com), and *Xin Xin's Fashion*, 1011C Maunakea St (Mon–Sat 9.30am–5pm, Sun 9.30am–3pm; ☏808/531-8885), where you'll find a fine selection of satin cheong sams, pretty parasols and exquisite little paper ornaments.

Finally, for distinctive Hawaiian gifts, it's also worth heading to the stores at both the Honolulu Academy of Arts (see p.94) and the Contemporary Museum (see p.101).

Southeast Oahu

The high mountain crest of the Koʻolau Range curves away to the east beyond Honolulu, providing Oahu with its elongated **southeastern promontory**. The built-up coastal strip is squeezed ever more tightly between the hills and the ocean, but not until you reach **Koko Head**, eight miles out from Waikīkī and eleven from downtown, do you really feel you've left the city behind. Thereafter, however, the shoreline is so magnificent – punctuated by towering volcanoes, sheltered lagoons, and great beaches – that there have been serious proposals to designate the entire area as a state park devoted to ecotourism, under the Hawaiian name of Ka Iwi (which literally means "the bone," and is also the name of the 25-mile ocean channel that separates southeast Oahu from the island of Molokai).

Kāhala and Hawaii Kai

H-1 ends at the Kāhala Mall, just beyond Diamond Head, to become Hwy-72, or **Kalanianaʻole Highway**. Both **Kāhala** itself, and **Hawaii Kai** further along, are upmarket residential communities that have little to attract visitors, and no desire to encourage them. Hawaii Kai spreads back inland to either side of the large Kuapa Pond, an ancient fishpond that has been remodeled to create the Koko Marina. The main reason to stop is to eat at the dinner-only gourmet restaurant *Roy's* (6600 Kalanianaʻole Highway; ℡808/396-7697), the first incarnation of the well-known island chain, though the adjoining mall also holds a number of water-sports operators. None of the beaches along this stretch merits even a pause.

Hanauma Bay and around

Beautiful **Hanauma Bay** is barely half a mile beyond Hawaii Kai, just across the volcanic ridge of Koko Head. So curved as to be almost round, the bay was created when part of yet another volcano – southeast Oahu is one long chain of minor volcanic cones – collapsed to let in the sea. This spellbinding spot, where a thin strip of palms and sand nestles beneath a green cliff, has long been famous as Oahu's best place to **snorkel**. As a result, it receives almost a million visitors per year, which in turn poses a constant threat to the fragile underwater environment. In fact, overuse has killed off much of the coral reef near the shore, and since the 1960s, Hanauma Bay has been a Marine Life Conservation District where organized tour parties are banned. While the reef itself is far from spectacular, it is slowly recovering, and the sea holds enough brightly colored fish to satisfy visitors. Beyond Hanauma to the northeast, the coastal Kalanianaʻole Highway holds further worthwhile stops, including **Sandy Beach** with its notoriously rough surf.

Visiting Hanauma Bay

Hanauma Bay is open daily except Tuesday between 6am and 7pm in summer, 6am and 6pm in winter; it stays open until 10pm on the second and fourth Saturday of each month in summer, and the second Saturday only in winter (for

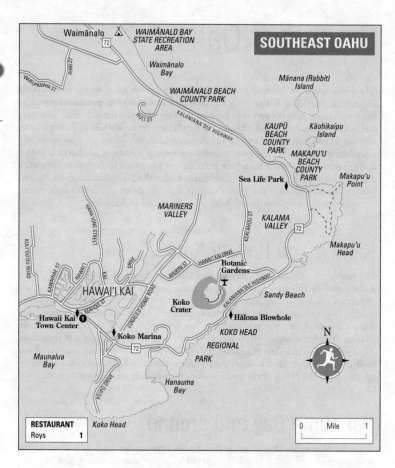

recorded details, call ☎808/396-4229). Admission is $5 for adults, free for under-13s, with parking an additional $1. If driving, you won't be allowed in if the parking lot is full; to be absolutely sure of a place, arrive by 9am.

A large **visitor center** is built into the hilltop rocks overlooking the bay, next to the parking lot just off the highway, and alongside the stop used by TheBus #22, the regular "Beach Bus" from Waikīkī. On arrival, all first-time visitors are required to watch a video about Hanauma and marine conservation in general; it's full of banal songs about "drifting through a turquoise dream," and "don't step on me, here in the sea." An average of twelve swimmers drown at Hanauma each year, though, so it's worth paying attention to the safety tips.

The beach is five minutes' walk from the visitor center, down a gently winding road used only by a regular open-sided trolley (50¢ down, $1 up). As you walk down, the ridge that is the sole remaining vestige of the crater rim rises like a rich green curtain ahead of you, but the vegetation on the more exposed northeast side of the bay, off to your left, is generally dry and faded. From up here you can see patches of reef in the turquoise water, standing out against the sandy seabed, and swarms of fish are clearly visible. On the beach you'll find showers and drinking fountains but no food or water – the only snack bar is up near the visitor center. A pavilion here rents out **snorkel equipment**, at around $6 per day (you'll be asked to leave some form of deposit; rental car keys, but not hotel keys, are acceptable); use of a locker to store your valuables costs $5.

Snorkeling at Hanauma feels a bit like snorkeling in an aquarium. You'll see a lot of fish, but it can all feel rather tame and predictable. The shallowness of the water near the shore makes it hard to stay off the reef, but it's essential that you try – walking on a coral reef not only kills the reef, but can easily cause cuts that take weeks to heal. Reasonably skilled swimmers who want to see living coral, and bigger fish, can swim out to the deeper waters beyond the inner reef. The largest gap in the reef, at the parking lot end of the bay, is known as the **Backdoor Channel**, but the current through it can be very strong, and it's safer to use the one known as **Telephone Cables**, closer to the middle of the beach. Another fearsome current sweeps across the mouth of the bay; dubbed the "Molokai Express", it's capable of carrying you all the way to Oahu's easterly neighbor.

Whether or not you go in the water, it's worth spending a few hours at Hanauma Bay no matter how crowded it is. The crisp green lawns along the foot of the *pali*, dotted with banyan trees, are ideal for picnics. Due to landslides, however, you cannot walk along the rocky ledge at either end of the beach, just above sea level. That means you can no longer reach the indelicately named **Toilet Bowl** – a natural hole in the lava at the far northeastern limit of the bay, which repeatedly fills with gushing sea water and then gurgles dry – or the similar **Witch's Brew** to the west.

Koko Crater

Koko Head Regional Park, which covers Koko Head and Hanauma Bay, extends another couple of miles northeast to take in **Koko Crater**. The youngest – and thus the largest and most completely formed – of southeastern Oahu's volcanic cones, this is considerably higher than Koko Head and makes a very impressive spectacle. Like its neighbor, it is topped by a double crater. The road up its far side – reached direct from Hawaii Kai, or by doubling back further along the coastal highway – comes to a dead end at Koko Crater Stables. Alongside this you'll find the barely developed **Botanic Garden** (daily 9am–4pm; free), where a twenty-minute stroll is rewarded by a grove of sweet-smelling, heavy-blossomed plumeria trees. It's no longer possible to walk up to or around the crater rim, however.

Hālona Blowhole

A couple of miles beyond Hanauma Bay, where Kalaniana'ole Highway squeezes its way between Koko Crater and the ocean, a roadside parking lot enables

Hiking up Koko Head

A dirt road leads away immediately right after the highway turnoff for Hanauma Bay – before the parking lot – to climb straight along the bare ridge above the beach. While the road is closed to drivers, whether it's open to hikers seems to vary. Take it if you can – there are great views from the 642-foot summit of **Koko Head**, roughly fifteen minutes' walk away. From there you can see back to the similar peak of Diamond Head above Waikīkī, and also walk down a footpath around the lesser of its two craters to peek into the southern end of Hanauma Bay.

round-island drivers – and a *lot* of tour buses – to stop off for a look at the **Hālona Blowhole**. The coastline around here consists of layer upon layer of flat lava, each sheet set slightly back from the one below to form a stairway that climbs up from the sea. At the Hālona Blowhole, the waves have carved out a cave below the visible top layer, and as each new wave rushes in, it's forced out through a small hole to create a waterspout that can reach up to fifty feet high. The blowhole itself does not go straight down, but is stepped; if you fall in – and people do – it's almost impossible to get out.

Little **Hālona Cove**, to the right of the blowhole overlook and sheltered by tall stratified cliffs, holds enough sand to make a welcome private beach, if you're lucky enough to have it to yourself. Only swimming within the cove itself is at all safe, and even then only in summer.

Sandy Beach

Avoiding the crowds is not at all the point at **Sandy Beach**, half a mile further on as the shoreline flattens out between Koko Crater and Makapu'u Head. Kids from all over Oahu meet up here most weekends for what's said to be the best **body-surfing** and **boogie-boarding** in Hawaii. This is also one of the few places on the island where the waves remain high enough in summer to tempt pro surfers. Tourists who try to join in soon find that riding surf of this size takes a lot of skill and experience; the beach itself is notorious for serious injuries. If you just want to watch, settle down in the broad sands that lie southwest of the central lava spit. There are normally several kite flyers around as well. Swimming is never safe at Sandy Beach, but beyond the spit it's all but suicidal.

Makapu'u Point

The rising bulk of Oahu's easternmost point, **Makapu'u Head**, pushes Hwy-72 away from the coastline as it swings round to run back up the island's windward flank. Shortly before it finishes climbing up the last low incline of the Ko'olau Ridge, there's just about room to park beside the road at **Makapu'u State Wayside**. A dirt road here snakes off to the right, soon curving south towards the hillock of Pu'u O Kipahulu. An hour-long hike (there and back) wends around the hill and back north along the line of the coastal cliffs to **Makapu'u Point**. From the railed-off viewing platform at the end, you can look straight down the cliffs to the Makapu'u lighthouse down below, out to Molokai on the horizon, back to Koko Head, and up along the spine of eastern Oahu.

Rounding Makapu'u Point on the highway – especially if you manage to stop at the small official **lookout** at the top – is an equally memorable experience. The coastal *pali* suddenly soars away to your left, while straight out to sea a couple of tiny islands stand out in misty silhouette. The larger of the two, Manana – also known as **Rabbit Island** – was named for its population of wild rabbits, who share their home only with seabirds. Legendary Hawaiian musician Gabby Pahinui recorded an album called *Rabbit Island Music Festival*, but the title is an in-joke; both Manana and its neighbor, Kaohikaipu, or Turtle Island, are bird sanctuaries, and off-limits to humans.

Makapu'u Beach County Park

Few drivers who skip the lookout can resist stopping to drink in the views as they descend from Makapu'u Point. The first proper parking lot, however, is down below, at **Makapuʻu Beach County Park**. In summer, this is a broad and attractive strip of sand; in winter, pounded by heavy surf, it's a rocky stretch. Swimming is rarely safe even at the best of times – ask the lifeguards if you're in doubt. Like Sandy Beach (see opposite), however, it's a much loved **body-surfing** and **boogie-boarding** site, and with the same propensity to lure unwary tourists into the water, it boasts a similarly dismal record of fatalities.

Sea Life Park

Immediately opposite the Makapuʻu Beach parking lot is the entrance to the expensive **Sea Life Park**, which tends to hold greater appeal for children than for their parents (daily 9.30am–5pm; adults $29, ages 4–12 $19; ☎808/259-7933 or 1-866/365-7466, ⓦwww.sealifeparkhawaii.com). Along with the predictable dolphin and porpoise shows, it holds a giant Reef Tank, a penguin enclosure, and a hospital for injured monk seals. You can also have your own close-up encounter with the dolphins, for a fee that ranges $100–200 for adults, $70–200 for kids, depending on how much contact you have. In addition, the park raises rare green sea turtles for release into the ocean and has even bred a **wholphin** – half-whale, half-dolphin. A couple of snack bars, where live entertainment is provided by costumed characters, plus a bar run by the *Gordon Biersch Brewery*, make it all too possible to find yourself spending an entire day here.

Waimānalo

WAIMĀNALO, four miles on from Makapuʻu, holds one of the highest proportions of native Hawaiians of any town on Oahu, and has become a stronghold of supporters of the movement for Hawaiian sovereignty, thanks in part to its role as the home of the late singing superstar Israel Kamakawiwoʻole (see box, p.567). The main drag, lined with fast-food joints, is far from picturesque, but as long as you take care not to intrude, you can get a real glimpse of old-time Hawaii by exploring the backroads. The small family-run farms and nurseries along Waikupanaha Street, which runs inland along the base of the *pali*, are particularly rural and verdant.

The most compelling reason to come to Waimānalo, however, is its **beach**. At over three miles long, it's the longest stretch of sand on Oahu, and the setting, with high promontories at both ends and a green cradle of cliffs behind, is superb. The most accessible place to park, and also the safest swimming spot, is **Waimānalo Beach County Park** at its southern end, but wherever you start you're likely to feel tempted to stroll a long way over the seemingly endless sands.

About a mile further north, where the fir trees backing the beach grow thicker again beyond a residential district, you come to the **Waimānalo Bay State Recreation Area**. The waves here are a little rougher than those at the county park, but it feels even more secluded, and you can **camp** for up to five days with a permit from the state parks office in Honolulu ($5; closed Wed & Thurs; see p.62).

Further on still, and reached by a separate road off the highway, lies **Bellows Field Beach Park**. Access to this pristine spot, ideal for lazy swimmers and novice body-surfers, is controlled by the adjoining Air Force base; the public is only allowed in between noon on Friday and 8am on Monday. The county parks office (see p.62) runs the **campground**, which is also open on weekends only.

Windward Oahu

Less than ten miles separate downtown Honolulu from Oahu's spectacular **windward coast**. Climb inland along either the **Pali Highway** (see p.105) or **Likelike Highway** (see p.108), and at the knife-edge crest of the Ko'olau Mountains you're confronted by amazing views of the serrated *pali* that sweeps from northwest to southeast. As often as not, the abrupt transition from west to east is marked by the arrival of **rain** – it has, after all, been raining on this side of the island for several million years, cutting away at the cliffs to create a long, sheer wall.

The mountain highways drop down to the twin residential communities of **Kailua** and **Kāne'ohe**. Both are large towns by Hawaiian standards, and neither holds much to appeal to visitors. However, the adjacent **beaches** here are quite superb – **Kailua Beach County Park** in particular is a sun-kissed, sparkling-watered strand that's idyllic for swimming. If quality beach time is your major vacation priority, it's well worth coming to Kailua for the whole day, or even basing yourself in one of the handful of local B&Bs rather than in Waikīkī.

If, on the other hand, you're trying to see as much of Oahu as possible on a single day's driving tour, you'd probably do better to avoid Kailua and Kāne'ohe altogether, and head straight off north on **Hwy-83**. This clings to the coastline all the way up to Oahu's northernmost tip, which is sandwiched between a tempting fringe of golden sand and a ravishing belt of well-watered farmland and tree-covered slopes. On most Hawaiian islands, the windward shore is too exposed to be safe for swimming, but here a protective coral reef makes bathing possible at a succession of narrow, little-used **beaches**. All are open to the public, but use proper paths to reach them. Oahu is also exceptional among the Hawaiian islands in having a chain of picturesque little **islets** just offshore; you're unlikely to set foot on any of them, but they provide a lovely backdrop.

Though driving through such luscious scenery is a real joy, there are few specific reasons to stop. The **Byōdō-In Temple**, testament to the importance of the Japanese presence in Hawaii, is a tranquil stop, while further north the very different **Polynesian Cultural Center** attracts a million visitors each year. Otherwise you might want to spend an hour or two hiking in the backcountry, in places like **Kahana Valley** or **Hau'ula**.

Kailua

The shorefront town of **KAILUA** stretches along Kailua Bay roughly four miles down from the Nu'uanu Pali Lookout (see p.107), and four miles north from Waimānolo. Now little more than an exclusive suburb of Honolulu, it was once a favorite dwelling place for the chiefs of Oahu, surrounded by wetlands and rich soil ideal for growing *taro*. Exploring the little side streets that lead off Kalaheo Avenue as it follows the bay may fuel your fantasies of relocating to Hawaii, but inquiring about real estate prices will bring you back to reality, and any time you have here is best spent on the stunning beach.

Almost the only remaining vestige of Kailua's past is **Ulupō Heiau**, an ancient temple whose construction was attributed to the legendary *menehune* and which later became a *luakini*, dedicated to human sacrifice. This long, low platform of rounded

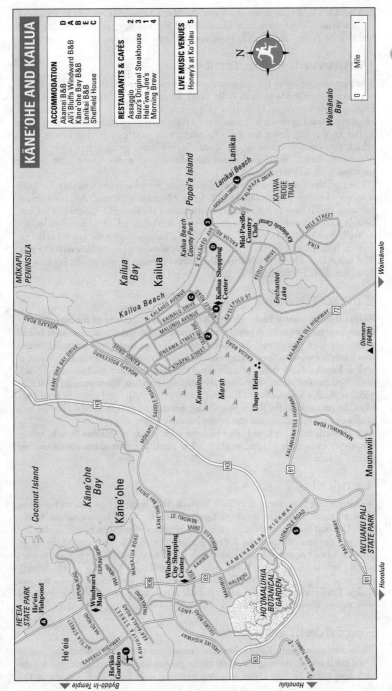

KĀNE'OHE AND KAILUA

ACCOMMODATION
Akamai B&B   D
Ali'i Bluffs Windward B&B   A
Kāne'ohe Bay B&B   B
Lanikai B&B   E
Sheffield House   C

RESTAURANTS & CAFÉS
Assaggio   2
Buzz's Original Steakhouse   3
Hale'iwa Joe's   1
Morning Brew   4

LIVE MUSIC VENUES
Honey's at Ko'olau   5

N

0   Mile   1

lava boulders looks out across the Kawainui Marsh from a hillock just to the left of Kailua Road. To get there, take Uluo'a Road, the first left turn after Kailua Road breaks away from Kalaniana'ole Highway, and then turn right.

Maunawili Falls Trail

The best way to enjoy the spectacular rainforest around Kailua is to take a half-day hike along the **Maunawili Falls Trail**. To reach the trailhead, follow the Pali Highway down from Honolulu. Opposite the point where Kamehameha Highway branches to the left, you'll see a right turn onto Auloa Road; don't take it, but keep going down the Pali Highway to the *next* intersection on the right, which confusingly is also Auloa Road. Follow that, forking left soon to join Maunawili Road. You'll find the trailhead just over a mile along, close to the junction with Kelewina Road.

The trail itself starts on an unpaved road, but soon becomes a muddy footpath through the lush vegetation that lines the Maunawili Stream. After about ten minutes, you'll have to ford the broad stream for the first of four times; you may be able to use stepping stones each time, but don't depend on it. It's a lovely hike in itself, with plentiful views of the wild hills all around, with the reward at the far end, an hour or so from the road, of the low, wide and pretty **Maunawili Falls**. The water beneath the pools is usually shallow enough to wade right beneath the flow, but don't try to climb the slippery stream bed to the top.

Kailua Beach

Kailua Beach County Park, which fills the colossal main curve of the bay, is utterly gorgeous – it's the prettiest beach on the whole island – and makes an ideal family swimming spot year-round. The soft wide sands slope down into turquoise waters much used by **windsurfers**; it's normally possible to rent windsurfing equipment, as well as **kayaks**, from vans and stalls along the park approach road or on the beach itself. You can also arrange kayak rental by calling Hawaiian Watersports (☏ 808/255-4352) or Kailua Sailboards and Kayaks (☏ 808/262-2555). Just be sure to keep away from the area around the Ka'elepulu Canal, which is often turned into a lagoon by a sandbar across its mouth, and can be unpleasantly polluted.

Head north from here, and once past the park you're on **Kailua Beach**, where the waves hit a little harder, so there's less sand, but swimming conditions are generally safe.

Lanikai

Walking south from the county park beyond Alāla Point brings you within a few hundred yards to the less crowded **Lanikai Beach**, which is very similar to the park. **Lanikai** itself consists of just a few short streets of priceless homes, all but cut off from the rest of Kailua by Ka'iwa Ridge. The coastal road beyond the beach park becomes a one-way loop immediately south of the ridge, forcing you to turn slightly inland on A'alapapa Road. Take the second right here (Ka'elepulu Street), park near the gate of the Mid-Pacific Country Club, and you'll see the **Ka'iwa Ridge Trail** leading away to the left. Just a few minutes' steep climbing is rewarded with superb views up and down the coast and out to the tiny islands in the bay.

Practicalities

There are no hotels in Kailua, but with advance planning you should be able to find a **B&B room**. Among the nicest of the private homes offering lodging are the very hospitable *Sheffield House*, just two minutes' walk from Kailua Beach at 131

Ku'ulei Rd (☎808/262-0721, Ⓦwww.hawaiisheffieldhouse.com; ❸–❹); *Lanikai B&B*, across from Lanikai Beach at 1277 Mokulua Drive (☎808/261-1059 or 1-800/258-7895, Ⓦwww.lanikaibb.com; ❹), which has a studio room facing the mountains and a larger seaview apartment; and *Akamai B&B*, 172 Ku'umele Place (☎808/261-2227 or 1-800/642-5366, Ⓔakamai@aloha.net; ❸), with two small, well-equipped en-suite units. Agencies such as Lanikai Beach Rentals (☎808/261-7895 or 1-800/258-7895, Ⓦwww.lanikaibeachrentals.com) also offer a wide selection of properties in the area.

The most atmospheric places to **eat** in Kailua are by the beach, and though the food at *Buzz's Original Steakhouse*, 413 Kawailoa Rd (daily 11am–3pm & 5–10pm; ☎808/261-4661), is nothing amazing – wood-grilled steaks, fresh fish, salad bar and cocktails – its location, set among the palms across from Kailua Bay, with a wraparound *lānai*, is irresistible. Around the intersection of Kailua and Ku'ulei roads, a few hundred yards inland from the beach park, Kailua has the feel of a genuine little community, holding assorted neighborhood stores as well as the **Kailua Shopping Center** mall at 572 Kailua Road. *Morning Brew* here (daily 6am–8pm; ☎808/262-7770) is a friendly local coffee house, serving healthy sandwiches and salads, that's bravely clinging on despite the presence of *Starbucks* opposite. *Assaggio*, tucked away on a quiet side street a block north, at 354 Uluniu Ave, is a popular upmarket Italian restaurant (Mon–Thurs 11.30am–2.30pm & 5–9.30pm, Fri & Sat 11.30am–2.30pm & 5–10pm, Sun 5–9.30pm; ☎808/261-2772).

The Mōkapu Peninsula

Kailua's northern limit is defined by Oneawa Ridge, stretching towards the ocean and culminating in the **Mōkapu Peninsula**. More of an island than a peninsula, joined to the rest of Oahu by two slender causeways, Mōkapu is entirely taken up by a Marine base, and no public access is permitted. The newest trans-Ko'olau highway, H-3, was originally commissioned to connect the base with Pearl Harbor. Incidentally, archeologists have found the extensive sand dunes along Mōkapu's northern shore to be the richest ancient burial site in all Hawaii.

Kāne'ohe

Slightly smaller than Kailua, and boasting a far less robust economy, as well as considerably fewer visitor amenities, **KĀNE'OHE** is seldom seen as an exciting destination in its own right. That's largely because none of its silty beaches are suitable for swimming. However, seven-mile **Kāne'ohe Bay**, reaching northwards from the Mōkapu Peninsula, is the largest bay in Hawaii and, once you're outside the main built-up strip, one of the most beautiful. If you want to join the local pleasure-boaters out on the calm waters of the bay, take a one-hour **cruise** from He'eia Kea Pier on the glass-bottomed *Coral Queen* (Mon–Sat 10am, 11am, noon & 1.30pm; adults $15, under-13s $7; ☎808/292-8470).

He'eia State Park, on the headland immediately before the pier, is a landscaped area set aside largely for its views of the adjoining **He'eia Fishpond**. Ancient Hawaiians built the low curving stone walls that enclose this saltwater lagoon, which is once again being used to raise mullet. What little you see from the park probably won't hold your attention long, however. Tiny **Coconut Island**, out to sea, is used for marine research by the University of Hawaii, but is still better known to many thanks to the credits sequence of *Gilligan's Island*.

Inland, Kāne'ohe holds several attractive public **gardens**. One of the quietest and most relaxing of these is the **Ho'omaluhia Botanical Garden** (daily 9am–4pm; free), at the top of Luluku Road, which loops back into the hills off Kamehameha Highway between Pali and Likelike highways. Take any of the pleasant short trails away from the visitor center, and you'll soon be out in the wilderness. If you'd prefer a more commercial display of flowers, fruits, and orchids, head instead for **Senator Fong's Plantation**, near Kahalu'u in northern Kāne'ohe (daily 10am–2pm; adults $14.50, under-13s $9; ℡808/239-6775, ⓦwww.fonggarden.com), where trams whisk visitors along the paved walkways. The smaller, free **Ha'ikū Gardens**, just off Hwy-83 at the entrance to glorious Ha'ikū Valley, is an attractive little lily pond that serves mainly to lure diners into the on-site *Hale'iwa Joe's* restaurant (Mon–Thurs 5.30–9.30pm, Fri & Sat 5.30–10.30pm; ℡808/247-6671; for a review of the branch in Hale'iwa, see p.150).

Byōdō-In Temple

A clearly marked side road *mauka* of Hwy-83 (Kahekili Highway) just beyond central Kāne'ohe leads to the interdenominational cemetery known as the **Valley of the Temples** (daily 8.30am–4.30pm; free, except for Byōdō-In Temple, adults $2, under-12s $1). Several religions have chapels and monuments here, but the one that draws in casual visitors is the Japanese Buddhist **Byōdō-In Temple**, built in the 1960s to celebrate a hundred years of Japanese immigration to Hawaii. This unexpected replica of a 900-year-old temple at Uji in Japan looks absolutely stunning, its red roofs standing out from the trees at the base of the awesome *pali*.

Having parked outside the temple gates, you cross an arching footbridge to stroll through the peaceful gardens. A fishpond here is so full of orange, gold, and mottled carp that they squeeze each other out of the water in their frenzy for fish food. Before reaching the main pavilion, you're encouraged to ring a three-ton brass bell. Once inside (with your shoes left at the threshold), you're confronted by a nine-foot meditating Buddha made of gilded, lacquered wood. Japanese visitors pay quiet tribute, while excited tourist groups take quick photos of themselves

△ Byōdō-In Temple

with the Buddha before dashing back to the bus; it's worth sitting for a while before you leave, allowing the tranquility of the place truly to touch you.

Practicalities

Like Kailua, Kāne'ohe has a number of small-scale private **B&Bs**. Both the *Kāne'ohe Bay B&B*, 45-302 Pu'uloko Place (reserve through Hawaii's Best B&Bs; ☎808/235-4214 or 1-800/262-9912, ⓦwww.bestbnb.com; ❺) and *Ali'i Bluffs Windward B&B*, 46-125 Ikiiki St (☎808/235-1124 or 1-800/235-1151, ⓦwww.hawaiiscene.com /aliibluffs; ❸) offer two guest rooms overlooking Kāne'ohe Bay, with en-suite facilities and swimming pools. The setting of the *Kāne'ohe Bay* in particular is superb, and the hosts are experts on all things local. None of the main-road **eating** options is especially appetizing. *Chao Phya Thai*, in the Windward City mall where Likelike and Kamehameha highways meet (Mon–Sat 11am–2pm & 5–9pm, Sun 5–9pm; ☎808/253-3355), sells tasty Thai food at bargain prices. Otherwise take your pick from burgers, *saimin*, or Korean fast food as you head north.

Kualoa Point and Mokoli'i

At **Ka'alaea**, a mile north of the Byōdō-In Temple, Kahekili Highway joins Kamehameha Highway on its way up from He'eia State Park, and the two then run on together as Kamehameha Highway. The tumbling waterfalls at the heads of the Waihe'e and Waiahole valleys, visible as you look inland, are superb, but the next point worthy of a halt is at the northern tip of Kāne'ohe Bay, five miles up from the highway intersection.

From the verdant lawns of **Kualoa Point**, out on the headland, you can look through a straggle of windswept coconut palms to conical **Mokoli'i Island**. To ancient Hawaiians, this picturesque little outcrop was the tail of a dragon killed by Pele's sister Hi'iaka as she made her way to Kauai (see p.487); its more banal modern nickname is "Chinaman's Hat." At low tide, you can wade out to it along the reef – the water should never rise more than waist high, and reef shoes are an absolute must – to find a tiny hidden beach on its northern side. Otherwise, content yourself with a swim back at the point from the thin shelf of sand at Kualoa Park.

Kualoa Ranch

Roughly 200 yards north of Kualoa Park, a driveway *mauka* of the highway (left if you're heading north) leads into the expansive grounds of **Kualoa Ranch**. Until recently a conventional cattle ranch, this now plays host to flocks of Japanese tour groups. Individual travelers are welcome to sign up for any of the wide range of activities on offer, which include horse riding, kayaking, a gun range, and all-terrain vehicle excursions. For full details, including rates and schedules for specific activities, contact ☎808/237-7321 or ⓦwww.kualoa.com. An hour on a horse or all-terrain vehicle costs $57, two hours $91, or you can come for a whole day and join four activities for $140.

Ka'a'awa

Several more good beaches lie immediately north of Kāne'ohe Bay, in the area broadly known as **KA'A'AWA**. There's no danger of failing to spot them; in places the highway runs within a dozen feet of the ocean. So long as the surf isn't obviously high, it's generally safe to park by the road at any of the consecutive

Kanenelu, **Kalaeʻōʻio**, and **Kaʻaʻawa** beaches, and head straight into the water. Only **Swanzy Beach County Park**, a little further along, really demands caution on account of its unpredictable currents. It became a beach park thanks to a rich Kailua resident of the 1920s, who donated this land to the state on condition that they didn't create any other public parks nearer her home.

Kahana Valley

The whole of the deeply indented **Kahana Valley**, tucked in behind a high serrated *pali* immediately around the corner from the rock formation known as the Crouching Lion, is officially known as **Ahupuaʻa O Kahana State Park**. In ancient Hawaii, the fundamental economic and geographical unit was the *ahupuaʻa*, a wedge of land reaching from the high mountains down to a stretch of coastline; Kahana is now the only *ahupuaʻa* to be entirely owned by the state. Still farmed by native Hawaiian families, it aims to be a "living park," though what that means isn't all that clear. In theory, the residents educate visitors in Hawaiian traditions, but while they still grow traditional crops, they don't dress up or pretend to *be* ancient Hawaiians. Even when the small **visitor center** (officially Mon–Fri 7.30am–4pm; ☏808/237-7766), just back from the highway as it curves around Kahana Bay, is closed, as it often seems to be, you should be able to pick up brochures outside that detail the valley's **hiking trails**. Be sure to bring waterproof clothing if you plan to do any hiking; upper Kahana Valley receives 300 inches of rain per year.

Kahana trails

The easiest of Kahana Valley's attractive trails, the **Kapaʻeleʻele Koʻa Trail**, ascends the northern flank of the bay for great ocean views. Taking around half an hour to complete, it starts by following the dirt road that heads to the right in front of the visitor center. After passing a few houses, the trail leads into a lush meadow scattered with fruit trees, and then veers left at a far-from-obvious junction to climb into the woods. It soon reaches a clearing where you can gaze across the valley to the high walls on the far side, and watch as it recedes away inland. Not far beyond, a few weather-worn stones mark the site of the **Kapaʻeleʻele Koʻa** itself, an ancient fishing shrine. As usual at such places, signs warn you not to "move, remove, or wrap rocks" – a reference to the common but largely bogus practice of tying a small stone in a *ti* leaf as an offering. A steep climb then leads up to **Keaniani Kilo**, a *kilo* being a vantage point from which keen-eyed Hawaiians would watch for schools of fish (usually *akule*, or big-eyed scad), and signal canoes waiting below to set off in pursuit. There's nothing here now, and young trees have partially obscured the beach, but it's a lovely spot. The trail then drops down to the highway, and you can make your way back along the beach.

To take the **Nakoa Trail**, which heads for the back of the valley, drive for roughly half a mile inland from the visitor center, then park at the stop sign at the edge of the small residential area. Assuming that it hasn't been raining (in which case the valley streams will be too high to cross; check at the visitor center), you can then keep walking along the main valley road for another fifteen minutes, before the trail sets off to ramble its way up and around the valley walls. It runs for roughly four miles, with some great views and plenty of mosquitoes to keep you company. For a shorter adventure, simply head left at the trails's start and you'll soon come to an idyllic little swimming hole in **Kahana Stream**.

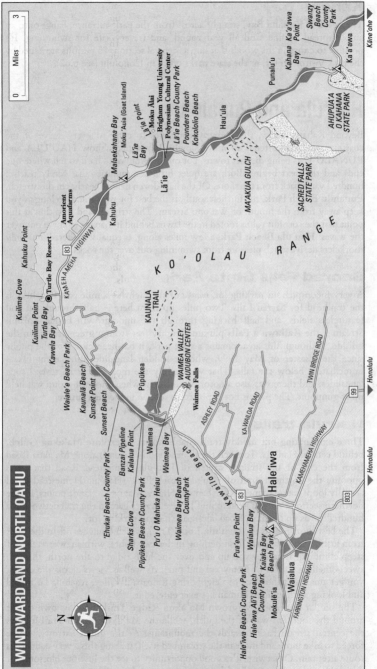

WINDWARD AND NORTH OAHU

0 — Miles — 3

N

▶ Ka'ena Point
▶ Kāne'ohe
▶ Honolulu
▶ Honolulu

KO'OLAU RANGE

Kahuku Point
Kuilima Point
Kuilima Cove
Turtle Bay
Kawela Bay
Kawela Beach Park
'Ehukai Beach County Park
Waiale'e Beach
Kaunalā Beach
Sunset Beach
Sunset Point
Banzai Pipeline
Kalalua Point
Sharks Cove
Pūpūkea Beach County Park
Pūpūkea
Waimea
Waimea Bay
Pu'u O Mahuka Heiau
Waimea Bay Beach County Park
Waimea Falls
WAIMEA VALLEY AUDUBON CENTER
KAUNALA TRAIL

Turtle Bay Resort
Amorient Aquafarms
Kahuku
Malaekahana Bay
Moku 'Auia (Goat Island)
Lā'ie Bay
Lā'ie Point
Moku 'Alai
Lā'ie
Brigham Young University
Polynesian Cultural Center
Lā'ie Beach County Park
Pounders Beach
Kokololio Beach
Hau'ula
MA'AKUA GULCH
SACRED FALLS STATE PARK
Punalu'u
Kahana Bay
AHUPUA'A O KAHANA STATE PARK
Ka'a'awa
Ka'a'awa Point
Swanzy Beach County Park

KAMEHAMEHA HIGHWAY

Hale'iwa Beach County Park
Hale'iwa Ali'i Beach County Park
Mokulē'ia
Pua'ena Point
Waialua Bay
Kaiaka Bay Beach Park
Waialua
FARRINGTON HIGHWAY
Hale'iwa
KAMEHAMEHA HIGHWAY
ASHLEY ROAD
KA'WAILOA ROAD
TWIN BRIDGE ROAD

Kawailoa Beach

99
83
803

Kahana Bay

The beach at **Kahana Bay**, straight across from the park entrance, hangs onto an ample spread of fine sand all year round, and is very safe for swimming. It's possible to **camp** in the woods that line its central section; $5 permits are issued by the park visitor center, or the state parks office in Honolulu (see p.62).

Hau'ula and Punalu'u

Beyond Kahana Valley, the highway continues to cling to every curve of the coastline, and traffic tends to move slowly. Island maps show **HAU'ULA** and **PUNALU'U** as being distinct towns, but on the ground it's hard to tell where one ends and the next begins. Both are quiet little communities that barely reach a hundred yards back from the shore. Of the half-dozen named beaches in this stretch, **Punalu'u Beach Park**, the furthest south, is the best for swimming, so long as you keep away from the mouth of Wai'ono Stream. The strip of sand is so thin at this point that the coconut palms rooted in the lawns behind it manage to curve out over the waves. **Hau'ula Beach Park**, a few miles along, is equally sheltered, but only snorkelers derive much pleasure from swimming out over the rocks.

Sacred Falls State Park

A very inconspicuous parking lot, *mauka* of the highway a mile past Punalu'u, is the trailhead for Sacred Falls. Two miles up from here – half through flat and featureless fields, and half hacking through the undergrowth beside Kalanui Stream – the **Kaliuwa'a Falls** plummet eighty feet from a green crevice in the hillside. Although this area remains a state park, it has been closed to the public since the disaster of May 1999, when a sudden landslide killed eight hikers immediately below the falls. That was merely the most recent of several such landslides, and there was also a notorious incident when a tourist group was held up at gunpoint. The park is not expected to reopen in the near future.

Hau'ula trails

Three exhilarating but muddy trails enable hikers to explore **Ma'akua Gulch**, behind central Hau'ula. To reach them, head *mauka* (inland) along Ma'akua Road from the end of the straight stretch of Hau'ula Homestead Road that starts opposite the northern limit of Hau'ula Beach Park. (Hau'ula Homestead Road actually loops round to meet Kamehameha Highway at two separate points; it's the northern section that you need to find.) The entrance gate to the trail network is a hundred yards up Ma'akua Road, alongside a small parking lot.

The best short hike is the **Hau'ula Loop Trail**, which branches off to the right from just beyond the gate. In something under two hours, with a few stretches of steep climbing, it carries you up and over the high ridge to the north, through sweet-smelling forests of ironwood and pine. As well as views across the ocean, you get amazing panoramas of neighboring Kaipapa'u Valley, reaching far inland and looking as though no human has ever entered it.

The similar but more overgrown **Ma'akua Ridge Trail** twists its own circuit around the southern wall of the gulch, while the **Ma'akua Gulch Trail** follows the central stream back towards the mountains. As the gulch narrows, you're forced to hike more and more in the streambed itself, making this a very dangerous route after rain. Otherwise, it's a good opportunity to see the luscious blossoms for which Hau'ula – meaning "red *hau* trees" – is named.

Lā'ie

The neat, even prim air of the town of **LĀ'IE**, three miles on from Hau'ula, is understandable once you learn that it was founded by Mormons in 1864, and remains dominated by the Latter-Day Saints to this day. This was the second major Mormon settlement in Hawaii; the first, on Lanai, was abandoned when church elders discovered that its president, William Gibson, had registered all its lands in his own name. Gibson went on to be Prime Minister of Hawaii, while his congregation moved to Oahu. Lā'ie now holds an imposing **Mormon Temple**, built in 1919 as the first such temple outside the continental United States (a visitor center, not the temple itself, is open daily 9am–9pm), and a branch of the Mormon-run **Brigham Young University**, but is best known to visitors for a less obviously Mormon enterprise, the **Polynesian Cultural Center**.

Mormon colleges tend not to spawn lively alternative scenes, and Lā'ie is no exception. Local students do at least get to body-surf the heavy waves at **Pounders Beach** at the south end of town, but if you lack their know-how don't be tempted to join in. **Kokololio Beach** just south of that is an attractive curve of sand where swimming is only safe in summer, while **Lā'ie Beach** in the center of town is prone to strong currents. The two-part **Mālaekahana Bay State Recreation Area** further north provides the best local recreational swimming, and also makes an excellent place to camp (pick up a free state permit in Honolulu; see p.62). At low tide, it's possible to wade out from here to **Goat Island**, a bird sanctuary where the Mormons once kept their goats, which has a beautiful protected beach on its north shore.

The Polynesian Cultural Center

An incredible one million paying customers each year head to Lā'ie for the **Polynesian Cultural Center**. Billed as a "cultural theme park," it's a large, landscaped compound where, in a haphazard mixture of the real and the bogus, each of seven separate "villages" is dedicated to a different island group. Each village includes a few typical structures, with indoor and outdoor space for demonstrations of traditional crafts and activities, ranging from food production or wood carving to music, dances, fire-walking and games. In addition to Hawaii, Tahiti, and the Marquesas, the further-flung cultures of Fiji, Tonga, Samoa, and New Zealand are represented. As an introduction to the enormous diversity of the Pacific, it's not at all bad, though the emphasis is very much on entertainment, and kids are likely to enjoy it more than adults.

To see anything of note, you'll need to time each individual village tour to coincide with the intricate daily schedule of presentations, so be prepared to spend at least half a day here in total. As well stopping by each village, you can ride up and down the central lagoon in a large canoe, or take a tram trip into neighboring Lā'ie. The compound also holds an IMAX cinema, free to all visitors, and countless souvenir and gift stores, snack bars and restaurants. These all remain open into the evening, but the main reason visitors stay after the villages close around 5.30pm are for the **lū'au**, a seated buffet dinner accompanied by Hawaiian music and dance that runs from 5.15pm to 6.30pm, and **Horizons**, a spectacularly staged song-and-dance extravaganza that starts at 7.30pm and ends at 9pm.

The center is largely staffed by students from the adjoining university, who don't necessarily come from the relevant parts of the Pacific. The information presented is laced with Mormon theology, and can thus be wildly divergent from conventional cultural and academic beliefs. Thus the Polynesians are said not to have migrated east to west across the Pacific from Southeast Asia, but to be descended

Visiting the Polynesian Cultural Center

Simply put, there's no cheap way to visit the **Polynesian Cultural Center** (Mon–Sat noon–9pm; ☏808/293-3333 or 1-800/367-7060, ⊛www.polynesia.com). Each of its various "packages" entitles you to explore the villages, take a canoe ride and tram tour, and see an *Imax* movie. The **Admission/Show Package** (adult $55, ages 3–11 $40) also offers seating at the *Horizons* show; with the **Ali'i Lū'au Package** ($80/$56) you get a flower *lei*, a ticket for the *lū'au*, and better seating at the show; the **Ambassador Package** ($115/$80) gives you a guided tour, a fancier *lei*, an "Ambassador Buffet" dinner instead of the *lū'au*, even better seating at the show, and various other fripperies; the **Ambassador Lū'au Package** ($115/$80) is the same but you go to the *lū'au* instead of the buffet; and the **Super Ambassador Package** ($205/$155) buys "fine dining" rather than the *lū'au*, plus loads of extra behind-the-scenes tours. With each of those packages, you can return to the center within the next three days to explore any villages you've missed, but the only show you're entitled to see is the IMAX film. In addition, each package offers a **Twilight** version, in which you can arrive at the center at 4pm or later and pay a reduced rate of around $10–20 below the usual fee, this time with no re-admission privileges. Finally, the center also offers round-trip **transportation** from Waikīkī, at $19 per person (no reductions) for a seat in a motor-coach, or $28 for a mini-bus. It costs $5 to park your own vehicle at the center.

from one of the lost tribes of Israel, and to have arrived from Central America under the leadership of a certain Hagoth.

Practicalities

A rather decrepid **motel** – anonymous and well away from the ocean, but reasonably inexpensive – is located less than a hundred yards north of the Polynesian Cultural Center. Each room at the *Laie Inn*, 55-109 Laniloa St (☏808/293-9282 or 1-800/526-4562, ⊛www.laieinn.com; ❸), has its own *lānai* overlooking the swimming pool. The motel shares its driveway with the oddest *McDonald's* you ever saw, converted from a leftover section of the Polynesian Cultural Center and still featuring an entrance carved to resemble a South Seas longhouse. There are several predictable **fast-food** places in and around the Lā'ie Shopping Center, a little further north, but none quite as distinctive.

Kahuku

KAHUKU, a couple of miles on from Lā'ie, may look run-down by comparison, but is considerably more atmospheric. Though the plantation it served went out of business in 1971, the rusting hulk of the **Kahuku Sugar Mill** still overshadows this small town. Assorted outbuildings now house a half-hearted shopping mall, but it's all in a sorry state. Unidentified lumps of machinery are dotted around the courtyard, painted in peeling pastel blues and yellows. Most of the old mill workings remain in place, though, with some parts color-coded according to their former function. The *Country Kitchen* (Mon–Sat 9am–5pm; ☏808/293-2110) here serves up shrimp and barbecue, and you can also pick up freshly cooked shrimp from a couple of white trucks stationed permanently beside the highway; of the two, *Giovanni's*, serves the spicier food. Behind the sugar mill are a few dirt lanes holding tin-roofed plantation homes. The long **beach** beyond is not suitable for swimming, but stretches a full five miles up to Turtle Bay if you fancy a solitary, bracing hike.

Beyond Kahuku, the highway veers away from the shore to run alongside the **Amorient Aquafarms**. Fresh shrimp from this series of ponds can be bought from additional trucks stationed along the highway nearby. The Walsh Farms complex of small, brightly painted shacks and funky vans at the far end sells fresh fruit, shrimp, and an entertaining mixture of antiques and junk.

Turtle Bay

Just before Kamehameha Highway rejoins the ocean on the North Shore, an obvious spur road leads *makai* past some expensive condos and private homes to end at **Turtle Bay**. Photogenic beaches lie to either side of **Kuilima Point** here – long, wave-raked Turtle Bay to the west, and the sheltered artificial lagoon of Kuilima Cove to the east – but apart from surfers the only visitors likely to head this way are those staying at the luxury hotel on the point itself.

The thousand-acre **Turtle Bay Resort**, 57-091 Kamehameha Hwy (☎808/293-6000 or 1-800/203-3650, ⓦ www.turtlebayresort.com; ❻–❾), holds almost five hundred ocean-view rooms, as well as three swimming pools, a luxury spa, horse-riding facilities, two golf courses, ten tennis courts, a surf school, and three restaurants. Priced far beyond the pockets of most of the surfing crowd, its presence is not very welcome with North Shore residents, who are forever campaigning to prevent its further expansion. If you can afford it, though, it offers a truly fabulous resort experience, and makes a great escape from Waikīkī. The resort's signature **restaurant**, *21 Degrees North* (Tues–Sat 6–10pm), is reached via a kitschy enclosed walkway of artificial waterfalls. Both its indoor and outdoor seating offer great views of the foaming white North Shore surf, spotlit at night, while the pricey but flavorful New Hawaiian menu features appetizers like pan-seared scallops and shrimp satay ($13) and entrees ($28–40) such as pan-seared *moi* wrapped in nori or mac-nut rack of lamb.

Run by separate management, and open to the warm ocean breezes on the sands of Kuilima Cove, the effortlessly stylish *Ola* is the perfect island restaurant (Mon–Thurs & Sun 11am–3pm & 5.30–9.30pm, Fri & Sat 11am–3pm & 5.30–10pm; ☎808/293-0801). Its contemporary Hawaiian cuisine is exceptional, based on fresh ingredients and regional specialties – among entrees priced at around $30, try the slow-poached *togarashi* smoked salmon with sweet potato and edamame succotash – while the laid-back atmosphere makes it hard to leave.

If you're travelling by **bus**, the *Turtle Bay Resort* marks the spot where TheBus #55 from the south becomes #52 as it heads west, and vice versa.

Central Oahu

Thanks to the island's slender central "waist," much the quickest route from Honolulu to the North Shore lies across the flat agricultural heartland of **central Oahu**. Cradled between the mountains, the **Leilehua Plateau** was created when lava flowing from the Koʻolau eruptions lapped against the older Waiʻanae Range.

Sugar cane and pineapples raised in its rich volcanic soil were the foundation of the Hawaiian economy until less than fifty years ago. As commercial farming has dwindled, however, the area has acquired a dejected atmosphere. More people than ever live in towns such as **Waipahu** and **Wahiawā** – many of them personnel from the military bases tucked into the hillsides – but there's very little here to interest tourists. If you plan to drive around Oahu in a single day, you'd do better to press straight on to Hale'iwa (see p.148).

'Aiea and Pearl City

Whichever road you follow, you have to drive a long way **west of Honolulu** before you reach open countryside. H-1, the main "interstate," curves past the airport and Pearl Harbor, while Hwy-78 sticks closer to the Ko'olau foothills, but they eventually crisscross each other to run through the nondescript communities of **'AIEA** and **PEARL CITY**. Restaurants where commuters can grab a quick meal appear on all sides, but neither town has a center worth stopping for.

Keaīwa Heiau State Park

Only **Keaīwa Heiau State Park**, on a hilltop above 'Aiea proper, merits a detour from the highway, and even then appeals more to local residents than to outsiders. 'Aiea Heights Drive, the road that leads up to it, heads right from the second stoplight after the Aloha Stadium turnoff on Hwy-78, and then twists for almost three miles through a sleepy residential area.

Keaīwa Heiau, whose ruined walls are on the left as soon as you enter the park, was a center where healers known as *kahuna lapa'au* once practiced herbal medicine, using plants cultivated in the surrounding gardens. The most famous of those healers was Keaīwa – "the mysterious" – himself. Lots of *ti* plants, together with a few larger *kukui* trees, still grow within the otherwise well-maintained precinct, which also holds a little shrine and a central ring of stones that encloses a small lawn. This layout is largely conjectural, however, as the *heiau* was severely damaged during the sugar plantation era.

There are no views from the *heiau*, but a mile-long **loop road** circles the ridge that lies beyond, where the ironwood forest is punctuated with meadows and picnic areas looking out over Pearl Harbor. Halfway around, you'll come to the trailhead for the **'Aiea Loop Trail**, a five-mile circuit through the woods with views of the interior valleys as well as Honolulu. The highlight is the wreckage of a World War II cargo plane that crashed into a remote gully.

Should you plan to stay, **camping** at the park's cool, secluded campground (closed Wed and Thurs) costs $5, with a state permit (see p.62).

Waipahu

Just beyond Pearl City, both H-2 and Kamehameha Highway (Hwy-99) branch away to head north across the central plateau. Only a mile or so west, however, the small town of **WAIPAHU** holds one of Hawaii's best historical **museums**, an evocative memorial to the early days of immigration. It's also home to the unexpectedly upmarket **Waikele Center** shopping mall, with its Borders bookstore and lots of discount "factory outlets."

Hawaii's Plantation Village

A mile south of H-1 on Waipahu Street in Waipahu, just below the sugar mill to which it owes its existence, stands **Hawaii's Plantation Village** (Mon–Fri 9am–3pm, Sat 10am–3pm; hourly guided tours Mon–Sat 10am–2pm; adults $13, seniors $10, under-12s $5; ℡808/677-0110, ⓦwww.hawaiiplantationvillage .org). It's a loving, nonprofit re-creation of the living conditions of the almost 400,000 agricultural laborers who migrated to Hawaii between 1852 and 1946, and were largely responsible for spawning the ethnic blend of the modern state.

Enthusiastic local guides lead visitors around a small museum and then through a "time tunnel" onto the former plantation estate. Simple houses – some have always stood on this site, others were brought in from elsewhere – contain personal possessions, illustrating both how much the migrants brought with them, and how much the different groups shared with each other in creating a common Hawaiian identity. Cumulatively, the minor domestic details – pots, pans, buckets, family photographs, even the tiny boxing gloves used to train Filipino fighting cocks – make you feel the occupants have merely stepped out for a minute. The most moving artifacts in the museum are the *bangos*, the numbered metal badges that helped the *lunas* (whip-cracking Caucasian plantation supervisors) to distinguish each worker from the next. Goods could be obtained in the company store by showing your *bango*, the cost of which was deducted from your next pay packet.

Wahiawā

All routes across central Oahu – whether you take H-2 or Kamehameha Highway from Pearl City, or the more scenic **Kunia Road** (Hwy-750) that leads up through the fields from Waipahu – have to pass through the large town of **WAHIAWĀ** in the heart of the island. The main drag holds the dismal array of bars, fast-food outlets, and gun stores that you'd expect to find this close to the **Schofield Barracks**, Oahu's largest military base (which by all accounts is actually very pretty, if you can get through the gates).

A couple of mildly diverting sites lie just outside the town. The **Wahiawā Botanical Gardens** (daily 9am–4pm; free), a mile east, is a reasonably attractive enclave of tropical trees and flowers that's welcome if you live here but nothing special by Hawaiian standards. To the north, on Whitmore Avenue off Kamehameha Highway, faintly marked reddish-brown lava boulders beneath a cluster of palm trees in a pineapple field constitute an archeological site known as **Kukaniloko**, or more colloquially as the **Birthing Stones**. Tradition had it that any chief hoping to rule Oahu had to be born here; the equivalent site on Kauai is described on p.458.

Dole Plantation

The single-story modern building of the **Dole Plantation** stands to the east of Kamehameha Highway roughly a mile north of Wahiawā (daily 9am–5.30pm; free, but includes several paying attractions; ⓦwww.dole-plantation.com). Though the large number of cars and tour buses parked outside might lead you to expect something more interesting, the plantation is basically a large covered mall-cum-marketplace that sells an assortment of tacky pineapple-related souvenirs and craft items, as well as fresh pineapples and pineapple products such as juices and frozen "whips." You can also, should you so wish, take uproarious photographs of yourself with your head poking through a cardboard cutout of a pineapple playing a ʻukulele.

Behind the mall, extensive gardens of pineapples and more authentic Hawaiian plants can be explored either on foot ($3.75, under-13s $3) or on half-hourly excursions on the Pineapple Express motorized "train" ($7.50, under-13s $5.50). A separate section holds what the *Guinness Book of Records* considers to be the world's largest **maze** ($5, under-13s $3), again composed of Hawaiian plants. The aim here is not to reach the center, let alone escape; instead you're expected to traipse around in the hot sun to find six separate color-coded "stations."

The North Shore

Although the surfing beaches of Oahu's **North Shore** are famous the world over, the area as a whole is barely equipped for tourists. **Waimea**, **Sunset**, and **'Ehukai** beach parks are all laid-back roadside stretches of sand, where you can usually find a quiet spot to yourself. In summer, the tame waves may leave you wondering what all the fuss is about; see them at full tilt in the winter, between October and April, and you'll have no doubts. If you plan to do some surfing – and this is no place for casual amateurs – then you'd do best to base yourself in **Pūpūkea** (see p.152). Otherwise, you can see all there is to see in an easy day-trip from Waikīkī, with a pause to shop and snack in **Hale'iwa**.

Hale'iwa

The main town on the North Shore stands at the point where Kamehameha Highway reaches the ocean, 24 miles north of Honolulu. For most visitors, **HALE'IWA** (pronounced "*ha-lay-eve-a*") comes as a pleasant surprise. It's one of the very few communities on Oahu whose roots have not been obscured by a century of rebuilding and development, despite the fact that tourists have been coming here ever since the opening of a direct train line from Honolulu in 1899.

Since the 1960s, the town has become a gathering place for **surfers** from all over the world. Many of the first arrivals, lured here from California by the cult movie *Endless Summer*, seem to have remained not only in Hawaii, but also in the 1960s. The town these days is still bursting with businesses like surf shops, tie-dye stores, wholefood restaurants, and galleries of ethnic knickknacks. Add those to a scattering of upfront tourist traps, and local stores and diners, and you've got an intriguing, energetic blend that entices many travelers to stay for months.

That said, there's precious little to see in Hale'iwa. Its main street, **Kamehameha Avenue**, runs for a mile from the Paukauila Stream to the Anahulu River, well back from the ocean, passing a cluster of gas stations and then a succession of funky, low-rise malls. In the largest of these, the North Shore Marketplace, a storefront proclaiming itself a **Surf Museum** (open "most afternoons"; free) traces the history of Hawaiian surfboards from the hollow wooden boards of the 1930s through early fiberglass models from the 1950s, and holds shrines to Duke Kahanamoku in particular, and the 1960s in general. Only as you approach the river do you finally come to the heart of Hale'iwa, a short stretch of old-fashioned boardwalk lined with false-front wooden buildings. One of these houses is

HALE'IWA

▲ Waimea

83

PACIFIC

OCEAN

Waialua Bay

Hale'iwa
Beach Park

Jamesons
by the Sea

Hale'iwa Ali'i
Beach Park

Surf'n'Sea

Hale'iwa
Joe's

Anahulu River

Rainbow
Bridge

BYPASS ROAD

Hale'iwa Eats

Matsumoto's

Kaiaka Bay
Beach Park

Hale'iwa
Shopping
Plaza

Coffee
Gallery

Kaiaka
Bay

KAMEHAMEHA AVE

Cholo's Homestyle
Mexican

HALE'IWA

North
Shore
Market-
place

Celestial
Natural
Foods

HALE'IWA ROAD

PA'ALA'A ROAD

Kiki'i Stream

Shell

Paukauila Stream

Texaco

WAIALUA BEACH ROAD

KAMEHAMEHA HIGHWAY

99

KAUKONAHUA ROAD

Honolulu ▶

N

0   Yards   500

930

Matsumoto's, a Japanese grocery store that has become so renowned for its **shave ice** – the Hawaiian equivalent of a sno-cone, a mush of ice saturated with sickly sweet syrup – that it's now an all-but-obligatory stop on round-island tours.

Beyond that, the narrow Rainbow Bridge crosses Anahulu River, affording great views upstream towards the green slopes of the Anahulu Valley. The small bay at the rivermouth is **Waialua Bay**, with Hale'iwa Harbor sheltered by a breakwater on its southwestern side. Southwest of the harbor, **Hale'iwa Ali'i Beach Park** is a favorite place for local kids to learn to surf – there are even **free surfing lessons** on weekend mornings in winter – but inexperienced outsiders who have a go are taking their lives in their hands. That was the pretext for making this the fictional location of TV's *Baywatch Hawaii*, a short-lived, state-subsidized experiment in relocating the Californian show to Hawaii that cost Hawaiian taxpayers dear.

Hale'iwa watersports equipment and bike rental

The best-known **surf outfitter** in Hale'iwa is Surf 'n' Sea; look for the brightly painted van to the left of the highway immediately across Rainbow Bridge (62-595 Kamehameha Hwy; daily 9am–7pm; ℡808/637-9887 or 1-800/899-7873, ⓦwww .surfnsea.com). As well as renting surfboards ($6 per hour, $30 per day), body-boards ($5/$20), windsurfing boards ($13/$50), and snorkel equipment ($7 half-day, $10 all day), they organize quality dive trips (shore dives one tank $75, two tanks $100; two-tank boat dives $110), provide lessons in surfing and windsurfing ($75 for two hours, $160 half-day), and sell new and used boards and souvenirs. Barnfield's Raging Isle, in the North Shore Marketplace (℡808/637-7700, ⓦwww.ragingisle.com), also sells surfboards and rents **mountain bikes** (from $40 for 24hr).

Just to reach the waves at Hale'iwa Ali'i, you have to pick your way across a tricky shallow coral reef; once you're out there you're at the mercy of strong crosscurrents. You're better off swimming at **Hale'iwa Beach Park**, on the northeast shore of the bay, where it's much safer.

Practicalities

There's nowhere to stay in Hale'iwa itself. Visiting surfers either put up at the *Backpacker's Vacation Inn* in Pūpūkea (see p.153), or find themselves a room or a home to rent as close to the beaches as they can. Bulletin boards listing short-term rentals can be found in and around local surf shops and coffee bars; a typical one-room apartment costs around $1000 per month. It is, however, possible to **camp** under the ironwoods of **Kaiaka Bay Beach Park** provided you have a free county permit (see p.62). A mile out of town along a loop drive off Hale'iwa Road, the beach itself is too near the murky mouth of Kaiaka Bay to be of much use for swimmers.

Places to eat, by contrast, line Kamehameha Avenue, including plenty of vegetarian options. In the North Shore Marketplace, *Cholo's Homestyle Mexican* (daily 8am–9pm; ℡808/637-3059) is a festive, very lively Mexican joint with some outdoor seating. The long menu offers the usual favorites – and a few more local choices, including *ahi* quesadillas – for around $8–12, plus a good range of icy mojitos. Also in the marketplace, *Coffee Gallery* (℡808/637-0085) has a cool dark-wood gallery where you can sit and drink espresso drinks, fruity smoothies and fresh juices; they also serve a small selection of wraps and burritos. Further west, the friendly *Paradise Found Café* consists of a few colorful booths at the back of the Celestial Natural Foods store, 66-443 Kamehameha Hwy (Mon–Sat 9am–5pm, Sun 9am–4pm; ℡808/637-4540), where you can pick up delicious veggie breakfasts from $6, humungous lunches for $7–10, and thirst-quenching smoothies from $4. *Hale'iwa Eats*, closer to the ocean at 66-079 Kamehameha Hwy (Tues–Sun noon–8pm; ℡808/637-4247), is a glass-fronted diner that serves good, simple Thai curries and noodle dishes for under $10.

Several more conventional steak houses and tourist haunts are located nearer the harbor. The pick of the bunch is *Hale'iwa Joe's*, at the mouth of the Anahulu River (Mon–Thurs & Sun 11.30am–9.30pm, Fri & Sat 11.30am–10.30pm; ℡808/637-8005), which has an outdoor terrace at the back. At lunchtime, sandwiches or salads cost around $10, and most of the items on the dinner menu are also available; in the evening, sushi or *poke* appetizers cost around $8 and steamed fish more like $20, while a New York steak is $25. Just across the river, the similarly priced *Jamesons by the Sea*, 62-540 Kamehameha Hwy (daily 11am–9pm; ℡808/637-4336), is famous for its sunset views.

Kawailoa

Despite appearances, Hale'iwa was not so much a plantation town as a fishing and farming community. Around the turn of the century, indentured plantation laborers gravitated to the shoreline as their contracts with the Waialua Sugar Company expired. So long as they worked for the plantation, however, they lived in the hilltop settlement of **KAWAILOA**, a mile east of Hale'iwa. Frozen in time by the decline in the sugar industry, Kawailoa is still up there, a few red-dirt streets of simple timber-frame homes surrounded by ever-encroaching tropical gardens.

Waimea Bay

Long **Kawailoa Beach** stretches for almost five miles northeast of Hale'iwa, interrupted repeatedly by rocky reefs and swept by fierce currents. Driving along the highway, however, virtually the first glimpse you get of the ocean is as you crest a small promontory to look down on **Waimea Bay**. This is perhaps the most famous **surfing** spot in the world, thanks to what are generally believed to be the biggest rideable waves on the planet. During the summer, it's often calm as a lake, but in winter the break off its craggy headlands can remain over twenty feet high for days at a time. Anywhere else, even the waves right on the beach would count as monsters, and lethal rip currents tear along the shoreline. While entering the ocean at Waimea in winter is extremely dangerous for anyone other than expert surfers, the beautiful sands of **Waimea Bay Beach County Park** are usually crowded with swimmers, snorkelers, and boogie-boarders in summer.

Until a huge flood in 1894, Waimea River flowed freely into the sea, and the valley behind was densely populated. Most of its farms and homes were destroyed, however, and the mouth of the river is now blocked by a sandbar that forms part of the beach park.

Waimea Valley Audubon Center

Inland of the highway bridge that crosses Waimea River lies one of Oahu's most beautiful valleys, which is now run as the **Waimea Valley Audubon Center** (daily 9.30am–5pm; adults $8, ages 4–12 $5; parking $2; ☎808/638-9199, ⓦwww.audubon.org). Until a few years ago it was an "Adventure Park" that uneasily combined cultivating rare Hawaiian plant species with entertaining busloads of tourists with all-terrain vehicle rides and cliff-diving shows. That enterprise went bankrupt amid accusations that the plants were being neglected, and the valley is now primarily a botanical center showcasing carefully maintained, scrupulously labeled **gardens** planted with Polynesian flowers and trees.

The valley also holds a number of **archeological sites**, the most prominent of which is the restored *Hale O Lono* or "House of Lono," an ancient *heiau* whose three stone terraces rise next to the main gate; in fact you can take a look without paying to enter. Once inside the center proper, you can wander for roughly a mile along stream-side walkways that pass the fenced-off ruins of further *heiaus* and ancient burial sites, as well as a mock-up of a Hawaiian village. Just be sure you wear repellent to deter the ever-present mosquitoes. Following the path to the far end, a lovely walk even if you have no great interest in learning about plants, brings you to the double, sixty-foot **Waimea Falls** at the head of the valley. Visitors are permitted to swim in the pool below.

Death in Waimea Valley

In 1779, shortly after Captain Cook's death at Kealakekua Bay on the Big Island (see p.186), one of his ships, the *Resolution*, put in at Waimea to collect water for the long voyage north. **Waimea Bay**, the first spot on Oahu to be visited by foreigners, was described by the new captain, Charles Clerke, as "by far the most beautifull Country we have yet seen among the Isles . . . bounteously cloath'd with Verdure, on which were situate many large Villages and extensive plantations."

Thirteen years later, on May 12, 1792, one of Clerke's crew returned to Waimea. **Lieutenant Richard Hergest**, in command of the *Daedalus*, had become separated from the rest of an expedition led by Captain George Vancouver. By this time, Kamehameha the Great's access to European weapons was enabling him to defeat all his rivals. However, when locals eager to barter for arms came aboard the *Daedalus*, Hergest refused to trade and threw their leader overboard, leaving him to swim ashore ignominiously. Hergest then took a party ashore, landing in Waimea Bay just west of the river mouth. As his men filled their casks, he set off to explore inland. Accompanying him were a young astronomer, **William Gooch** – who just a week earlier had stayed as an overnight guest in Kamehameha's hut in Kealakekua – and a Portuguese sailor named Manuel. A mile or so up the valley the unarmed men were alarmed to see a group of Hawaiians rushing down the slopes towards them from the Pu'u O Mahuka *Heiau* (see opposite). Each was a fearsome **pahupu** or "cut-in-two" warrior, having tattooed half his body – either top to bottom, or his entire head – completely black. Hergest, Gooch, and Manuel were swiftly killed, and their corpses taken as sacrificial offerings to another *heiau* at Mokulē'ia, to be baked and stripped of their flesh.

Waimea was then under the control of warrior priests who lived at the Pu'u O Mahuka *Heiau*. Their leader, **Koi**, had been stationed here by Chief Kahekili of Maui to guard the traditionally rebellious north coast of Oahu; he was probably the man whom Hergest pushed into the ocean, and it was probably he who took his revenge. Nonetheless, when Vancouver called into Waikīkī the next year and demanded that the culprits be handed over for trial, he was presented with three men picked virtually at random. Although no one seriously believed they were guilty, they were summarily executed as an example of British justice. In 1799, the tattooed Koi was pointed out to another visiting captain at Waikīkī, who shot and wounded him in his canoe, and then hanged him.

This story is told in full in *The Death of William Gooch*; see Books, p.572.

The *Waimea Falls Grill*, a café close to the main entrance, serves good inexpensive snacks, such as *ahi* tuna and avocado sandwiches, and you don't have to pay the admission fee to reach it.

Pūpūkea

Immediately beyond Waimea Bay, Kamehameha Highway starts to cruise beside a succession of magnificent surfing beaches. Driving here demands patience; at the best of times, vehicles pull off without warning, while during major competitions traffic slows to a virtual standstill. **Pūpūkea Beach County Park**, which, like Hanauma Bay (see p.129), is a Marine Life Conservation District, stretches for well over a mile from the mouth of Waimea Bay. At its western end, the Three Tables surf break is named after three flat-topped chunks of reef, where plenty of unwary swimmers have come to grief, while **Shark's Cove** to the east, riddled with submarine caves, is a popular site for snorkelers and scuba divers in summer.

PŪPŪKEA itself is a low-key community, with a few stores and no restaurants. While real-estate prices here have been rising for years, steadily pushing out its large population of international surf-bums, political campaigns have so far kept it free of large-scale development. Pūpūkea holds by far the best **accommodation** along the North Shore. ♣ The *Backpacker's Vacation Inn*, 59-788 Kamehameha Hwy (☏ 808/638-7838, Ⓦ www.backpackers-hawaii.com; ❶–❹), was founded by Mark Foo, a daredevil Hawaiian surfer who died surfing in California in 1994. Its rambling main building, *mauka* of the highway, has dorm beds for $25 per night in high season, and simple private double rooms sharing kitchen and bath for $65. Across the street, in low oceanfront buildings, good-value studio apartments with great views start at $125. The *Plantation Village*, a hundred yards down the road, across from the sea and run by the same management, consists of nine restored plantation cabins, with more dorm beds, plus private rooms and larger cabins at slightly higher rates. All rates are discounted for stays of a week or longer, and drop by ten percent between April and November. Communal buffet dinners on Tuesday, Wednesday, Friday, and Sunday cost $7, and there's a free daily bus to Honolulu Airport. They also provide free snorkeling equipment and boogie boards, rent out bicycles at $5 per day, offer Internet access at $8 per hour, and arrange island tours, plus whale watching in winter and scuba diving in summer.

Pu'u O Mahuka Heiau State Monument

For a superb view of Waimea Valley and the bay, head up to the **Pu'u O Mahuka Heiau**, perched on the eastern bluff above the mouth of the river. As Oahu's largest temple of human sacrifice, this was once home to a terrifying brotherhood of *pahupu* warrior-priests (see opposite). To reach it, turn off the coastal highway at the Foodland supermarket, a few hundred yards beyond the bay. Having climbed the hill on twisting Pūpūkea Road, turn right onto a narrow paved track that skirts the cliff edge for just under a mile.

The parking lot at the end of the track is alongside the higher of the temple's two tiers. The meadow that appears to lie just beyond the *heiau* is in fact on the far side of the deep cleft of Waimea Valley. **Trails** lead around and partly through the old stone walls, within which it's easy to make out the outlines of several subsidiary structures; most were originally paved with water-worn stones carried up from Waimea Bay. The main "altar" at the *mauka* end, which is usually covered with offerings of flower *leis*, pineapples, vodka and water, probably bears little resemblance to its original configuration. From the little loop path around the java plum trees nearby, you can see right along the North Shore to Ka'ena Point in the western distance; the *heiau* was positioned here partly so that beacon fires could signal to Wailua on Kauai.

Kaunala Trail

Beyond the *heiau* turnoff, Pūpūkea Road heads inland for another two miles, to end at the gates of a Boy Scout Camp. From here, the five-mile **Kaunala Trail**, open to the public on weekends only, runs along the thickly wooded crest of a high mountain ridge. As well as views of the deep and inaccessible gorges to either side, if the clouds clear you'll eventually see Oahu's highest peak, **Mount Ka'ala** (4020ft), far across the central plains.

Sunset Beach

With its wide shelf of yellow sand, lined by palm trees, **Sunset Beach**, to the northeast of Pūpūkea, is perhaps the most picture-perfect beach on Oahu. Only occasional gaps between the oceanfront homes allow access, but once you get there you're free to wander for two blissful miles of paradise-island coastline. Unless you come on a calm and current-free summer's day (ask the lifeguards), it's essential to stay well away from the water; the "Sunset Rip" has been known to drag even beachcombers out to sea.

In winter, when the waves are stupendous, Sunset Beach fills with photographers in search of the definitive surfing shot, while reckless pro surfers perform magazine-cover stunts out on the water. Each of the breaks here has its own name, the most famous being the **Banzai Pipeline**, where the goal is to let yourself be fired like a bullet through the tubular break and yet manage to avoid being slammed down onto the shallow, razor-sharp reef at the end. To watch the action, walk a few hundred yards west (left) from **'Ehukai Beach County Park**, to where a small patch of lawn separates the beach from the road.

Sunset Beach proper, a mile past 'Ehukai, was where North Shore surfing first took off, following advances in surfboard technology in the early 1950s, and remains the venue for many contests. The break known as **Backyards** is renowned for being especially lethal, though it's a popular playground for windsurfers. **Kaunala Beach** beyond that, the home of the **Velzyland** break, is the last major surf spot before the highway curves away towards Turtle Bay (see p.145) and the windward coast. Velzyland offers reliable rather than colossal waves, but riding them with any degree of safety requires immense precision.

Practicalities

No formal overnight accommodation is available beyond the *Backpacker's Vacation Inn* in Pūpūkea (see p.153). As for **eating**, short-lived fruit stands, shrimp shacks and snack bars come and go along the *mauka* side of Kamehameha Highway from Pūpūkea onwards, especially in the little cluster of buildings and tents alongside the giant totem pole dedicated to Maui Pōhaku Loa, six miles north of Hale'iwa between Sunset and 'Ehukai beaches.

West from Hale'iwa

The coast of northern Oahu to the **west of Hale'iwa** lacks suitable surfing beaches, and is so rarely visited that most people don't really count it as part of the North Shore at all. The area's principal landmark is the **Waialua Sugar Mill**, slowly rusting away at the foot of the Wai'anae Mountains since the closure of the local sugar company in 1996. A moderately interesting driving tour leads down the backroads of the village of **Waialua** and along oceanfront Crozier Drive to even smaller **Mokulē'ia**, but while that gives you attractive views of Hale'iwa in the distance, you might as well go straight to Hale'iwa itself.

Ka'ena Point

The westernmost promontory of Oahu, **Ka'ena Point**, is only accessible on foot or mountain bike; it's not possible to drive all the way around from the North Shore to the Leeward Shore. As Farrington Highway runs west of Waialua and Mokulē'ia, the landscape grows progressively drier, and the road eventually grinds to a halt a couple of miles beyond **Dillingham Airfield**, where Honolulu Soaring offers **glider flights** (from $60 per person; daily 10am–5.30pm; ☎808/637-0207, ⓦwww.honolulusoaring.com).

On the far side of the gate where the road finally ends, you can follow either a bumpy, dusty dirt road beside the steadily dwindling Wai'anae Ridge, or a sandy track that straggles up and down across the coastal rocks. The only sign of life is likely to be the odd local fisherman, perched on the spits of black lava reaching into the foaming ocean.

After roughly an hour of hot hiking, the ridge vanishes altogether, and you squeeze between boulders to enter the **Ka'ena Point Natural Area Reserve**. This largely flat and extremely windswept expanse of gentle sand dunes, knitted together with creeping ivy-like *naupaka*, is used as a nesting site in winter by Laysan **albatrosses**. At the very tip, down below a rudimentary lighthouse – a slender white pole topped by flashing beacons – tiny little beaches cut into the headland. Winter waves here can reach more than fifty feet high, the highest recorded anywhere in the world, and way beyond the abilities of any surfer, though humpback whales often come in close to the shore.

From Ka'ena Point, you can see the mountains curving away down the leeward coast, as well as the white "golfball" of a military early-warning system up on the hills. Just out to sea is a rock known as **Pōhaku O Kaua'i** ("the rock of Kauai"); in Hawaiian legend, this is a piece of Kauai, which became stuck to Oahu when the demi-god Maui attempted to haul all the islands together.

If you'd prefer to try the slightly longer hike to Ka'ena Point from the end of the road on the western coast, see p.158.

The leeward coast

The **west** or **leeward coast** of Oahu, cut off from the rest of the island behind the Wai'anae Mountains, is only accessible via **Farrington Highway** (Hwy-93), which skirts the southern end of the ridge. Customarily dismissed as "arid," the region may not be covered by tropical vegetation, but the scenery is still spectacular. As elsewhere on Oahu, the mountains are pierced by high green valleys – almost all of them inaccessible to casual visitors – while fine beaches such as Mākaha Beach Park line the shore.

However, the traditionally minded inhabitants of towns such as **Nānākuli** are not disposed to welcome the encroachment of hotels and golf courses, and visitors tend to be treated with a degree of suspicion. The further north you go, the stronger the military presence becomes, with soldiers in camouflage lurking in the hillsides, and helicopters flying overhead. Farrington Highway once ran all the way around Ka'ena Point, at the northwest corner of the island – which explains why the road has the same name on both coasts – but it's no longer possible to drive right up to the point.

The southwest corner

The strip development that characterizes both sides of Hwy-1 from Honolulu to Waipahu finally comes to an end as you enter the southwest corner of Oahu.

Long-cherished plans by the state authorities to turn this region into a major tourism and residential center seem finally to be approaching fruition, however, as the former plantation settlement of 'Ewa becomes ever more overshadowed by the burgeoning modern community of Kapolei.

'Ewa

A couple of miles south of Farrington Highway along Fort Weaver Road, 'EWA is a picturesque hamlet of wooden sugar-plantation homes arranged around a well-kept village green. Other than snapping a few photos along the back lanes, the only reason to come here is to take a train excursion with the Hawaii Railway Society, based just west of town along Renton Road. Their souvenir store and museum is open all week (Mon–Sat 9am–3pm, Sun 10am–3pm; free), but only on Sunday afternoons does the restored *Waialua* #6 locomotive set out on its ninety-minute round-trip journey westwards to Kahe Point (1pm and 3pm; adults $10, seniors and under-13s $7; ☎808/681-5461, Ⓦwww.hawaiianrailway.com). On the second Sunday of each month, at the same times but by reservation only, you can have a private narrated tour in the comfort of a restored luxury parlor car ($15).

'Ewa Beach Park, three miles south of the village, is an attractive oceanfront park popular with sailors from the nearby base. It has plenty of sand, and views across to Diamond Head, but the water tends to be too murky for swimming, and there's an awful lot of seaweed around.

Kapolei

Until recently, the name KAPOLEI did not appear on even the most detailed maps of Oahu. Now, however, it's the island's fastest-growing town, stretching alongside H-1 as the road approaches its end in the southwest corner of the island. Homes, movie theatres, and shopping malls have sprung up at an astonishing rate, but the new town has so far made only one bid to attract tourists, in the shape of the Hawaiian Waters Adventure Park, at 400 Farrington Hwy just off exit 1 from Hwy-1 (adults $35, ages 4–11 $25; ☎808/674-9283, Ⓦwww.hawaiian waters.com). Hawaii's first water park follows the model of its predecessors in California, Florida, and elsewhere, with lots of swirling plastic tubes for visitors to raft or simply slide down, children's play areas, and an exhilarating wave pool. It's all great fun, though with so many wonderful beaches on the island to compete with, it hasn't yet succeeded in attracting great numbers of visitors. In principle, it's open daily from 10.30am until dusk, but it often seems to shut its gates as early as 4pm, and it's closed altogether some days in winter; call ahead before you make the drive.

Ko Olina Resort

A great deal of money was poured during the 1980s into landscaping the Ko Olina Resort, just north of Barbers Point at the southwest tip of the island. Four successive artificial lagoons were blasted into the coastline, each a perfect semicircle and equipped with its own crescent of white sand. Work also began on creating a marina for luxury yachts at the Barbers Point Harbor. However, apart from the *Ihilani Resort*, very few of the other projected developments, which were supposed to include residential estates, condo buildings, shopping centers, and more hotels, have so far materialized. Its chief neighbors, the relentlessly tacky *lū'au* sites belonging to *Paradise Cove* and *Germaine's* (see p.125), are something of a poor relation.

The Marriott Ihilani Resort and Spa, 92-1001 Olani St, Kapolei HI 96707-2203 (☎808/679-0079 or 1-800/626-4446, Ⓦwww.ihilani.com; ❽–❾) is a largely successful attempt to mimic the resort hotels of the outer islands. It's an absolute idyll if you can afford it; its fifteen stories of state-of-the-art rooms are equipped with every high-tech device imaginable, from computerized lighting and air-conditioning systems to CD players and giant-screen TVs. The adjoining spa boasts thalassotherapy and sauna facilities, plus rooftop tennis courts and a top-quality golf course. The in-house restaurants are excellent – a meal at the least expensive, the poolside *Naupaka Terrace*, will set you back at least $50, though its delicate Pacific Rim fish dishes are well worth trying. Alternatives include the formal *Azul* grill, and a nearby branch of *Roy's*, the upscale Pacific-Rim chain, overlooking the golf course at 92-1220 Aliinui Drive (Mon–Thurs & Sun 11am–9.30pm, Fri & Sat 11am–10pm; ☏808/676-7697).

Nānākuli

Farrington Highway reaches the Wai'anae coast at **Kahe Point Beach Park**, near the section known as "Tracks" because of the adjacent railroad tracks. As well as being a small but pretty strip of sand, this is Oahu's most popular year-round **surfing** site. The waves offshore remain high (but not overpoweringly so) even in summer, and break much closer to the shore than usual. Since the bay itself is relatively sheltered, swimming usually only becomes dangerous in the depths of winter.

A couple of miles further on, **NĀNĀKULI** is the southernmost of a string of small coastal towns. According to local legends, its name means either "look at knee" or "pretend to be deaf" – neither of which seems to make much sense. The population is largely Hawaiian, and there's little attempt to cater to outsiders. **Nānākuli Beach Park**, which runs alongside the highway all through town, is another good summer swimming beach, while **Zablan Beach** at its southern end is much used by scuba divers. The beach immediately north of Nānākuli is called **Ulehawa** or "filthy penis," after a particularly unsavory ancient chief.

Wai'anae

WAI'ANAE, five miles up the coast, centers on curving **Poka'i Bay**. Thanks to the breakwaters constructed to protect the boat harbor at its northern end, the main sandy beach here is the only one on the leeward coast where swimming can be guaranteed safe all year round. An irresistible backdrop is provided by the high-walled valley behind.

Beyond a flourishing coconut grove at the tip of the flat spit of land that marks the southern end of Poka'i Bay stand the ruined walls of **Kū'īlioloa Heiau**. Unusual in being virtually surrounded by water, this three-tiered structure is said to mark the place where the first coconut tree to be brought from Tahiti was planted in Hawaiian soil. Kamehameha offered sacrifices here before launching his first invasion attempt against Kauai (see p.436).

Mākaha

MAKAHA, or "savage," the last of the leeward towns, was once the hideout of a dreaded band of outlaws. Now famous for the savagery of its **waves**, it began to attract surfers in the early 1950s. Before World War II, virtually all Oahu surfing was concentrated in Waikīkī. When changes in the ocean conditions there, and the development of new techniques and equipment led surfers to start looking elsewhere, Mākaha was the first place they hit on. The waves at its northern end are said to be the largest consistently reliable surf in Hawaii, and several major surfing contests are still held at **Mākaha Beach Park** each year. In summer, when sand piles up in mighty drifts, it's often possible to swim here in safety, and Mākaha retains enough sand to remain a beautiful crescent beach even in winter.

You'll probably notice what look like hotels along the oceanfront near Mākaha Beach, but they're all long-term rental condos intended for local families. With a county permit, however (see p.62), it's possible to **camp** at **Kea'au Beach Park**, in an attractive but somewhat exposed location another couple of miles up the coast, in view of Ka'ena Point. Swimming in the rocky sea here, with its pounding surf, is not recommended, but the numbered campsites are pleasant enough.

A couple of miles back from the ocean in Mākaha Valley – follow Mākaha Valley Road inland beyond the defunct *Sheraton Mākaha Resort*, and the astonishingly ugly Mākaha Towers apartment blocks – the private driveway of the Mauna Olu Estates leads to **Kāne'āki Heiau**. The most thoroughly restored ancient temple in Hawaii, it was excavated by Bishop Museum archeologists in 1970 and can now be visited with permission from the security guards at the gate (Tues–Sun 10am–2pm; free); you'll have to leave a driver's license or passport as surety. Its principal platform of weathered, lichen-covered stones is topped once more by authentic thatched structures such as the *anu'u* ("oracle tower"), as well as carved images of the gods. The *heiau* originated as an agricultural temple to the god Lono in the fifteenth century. Two hundred years later, around the time of Kamehameha the Great, it was converted into a *luakini*, where human sacrifices were dedicated to the god Ku – a typical progression indicating that the valley had come to support a large enough population to have its own paramount chief.

The road to Ka'ena Point

Beyond Mākaha, the highway traces a long, slow curve up the coast to Yokohama Bay. Barely populated, and splendidly bleak, this region attracts very few visitors other than a handful of daredevil surfers prepared to risk its sharks, currents, and mighty waves. Inland, the rolling green slopes of **Mākua Valley** also conceal dangerous secrets. Used by the Air Force for bombing practice during and after World War II, the valley is still barred to the public owing to unexploded ordnance. Gaping **Kāneana Cave** to the south is too vandalized to be worth investigating.

Not even the sturdiest 4WD vehicle could negotiate the dirt road that continues from the end of the highway. In any case, the dunes beyond were designated as the **Ka'ena Point Natural Area Reserve** to help repair damage done by military jeeps and motorbikes. However, an exposed one-hour **hike** along the route of the old railroad tracks will bring you to the very tip of the island. The walk is substantially similar to the corresponding trail along the North Shore, described on p.155.

2

The Big Island

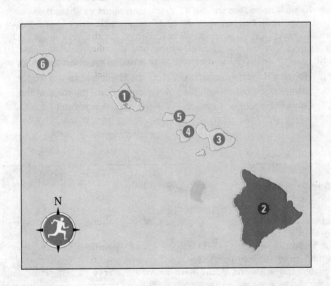

CHAPTER 2 # Highlights

* **The Coffee Shack** Simple roadside café, serving up fresh Kona coffee to go with its stupendous ocean views. See p.184

* **Pu'uhonua O Hōnaunau** Atmospheric "place of refuge" that conjures up vivid images of life in ancient Hawaii. See p.187

* **Kona Village Resort** The oldest of the Big Island's luxury resorts remains the most idyllic. See p.195

* **Hāpuna Beach** A magnificent palm-fringed beach with the calmest turquoise waters imaginable. See p.203

* **Hwy-250** The drive along the pastoral flanks of Kohala Mountain is among the most beautiful in all Hawaii. See p.213

* **Mauna Kea** Join the locals in gathering snowballs from the Pacific's highest peak to take to the beach. See p.243

* **Kehena Beach** Wild parrots and naturists share the pleasures of this little-known black-sand beach. See p.249

* **Kīlauea eruption** Watch as the Big Island grows bigger day by day, courtesy of the lava gushing from Kīlauea. See p.250

△ Hāpuna Beach

The Big Island

All the Hawaiian islands were formed by volcanic action, but only on the island officially named **Hawaii** are those volcanoes still active – which is why it's larger than all the other neighboring islands put together, and is universally known as the **Big Island**. Visitors flock here to watch the fiery eruptions that continue to shape the youngest land on earth. Such sheer rawness might make the island seem an unlikely tourist destination, but it also offers everything you could want from a tropical vacation – dependable sunshine, sandy beaches, warm turquoise fish-filled waters, swaying coconut palms, and pristine rainforest.

Though tourism is crucial to its economy, the Big Island lags well behind Oahu and Maui in terms of annual visitors. It has nothing to match the Waikīkī skyscrapers or the large-scale strip development of the west Maui shoreline. In the 1960s the island was expected to emerge as the first serious rival to Oahu. Large sums were spent on building a highway system to cope with the anticipated influx, and luxury resorts shot up on bare lava, while more reasonably priced hotels appeared in the Kailua area. As things turned out, however, it was Maui that mushroomed, to become plagued by traffic problems and overcrowding. Save for the immediate vicinity of Kailua, the Big Island remains relatively stress-free.

The Big Island is not the cheapest destination in Hawaii – though it does have a few budget inns and hostels – and it can't compete with Honolulu for frenzied shopping or wild nightlife. The entire island has the population of a medium-sized town, with 171,000 people spread across its four thousand square miles; it has its fair share of restaurants, bars, and so on, but basically it's a rural community. There's plenty of opportunity to be active – hiking in the state and national parks, deep-sea fishing off the Kona coast, golfing in the Kohala resorts, or snorkeling in Kealakekua Bay – but most visitors are content to while away their days meandering between beach and brunch.

As befits the birthplace of King Kamehameha, the first man to rule all the Hawaiian islands, the Big Island maintains strong links with its Polynesian past. Little more than two centuries have passed since the isolation of its original inhabitants came to an end, and their *heiaus*, petroglyphs, and abandoned villages are scattered throughout the island. Otherwise, though many of its smaller towns have an appealing air of the nineteenth-century West about them, with their false-front stores and wooden boardwalks, few historical attractions are likely to lure you away from the beaches. Any time you can spare to go sightseeing is better spent exploring the waterfalls, valleys, and especially the volcanoes that were so entwined with the lives of the ancient Hawaiians.

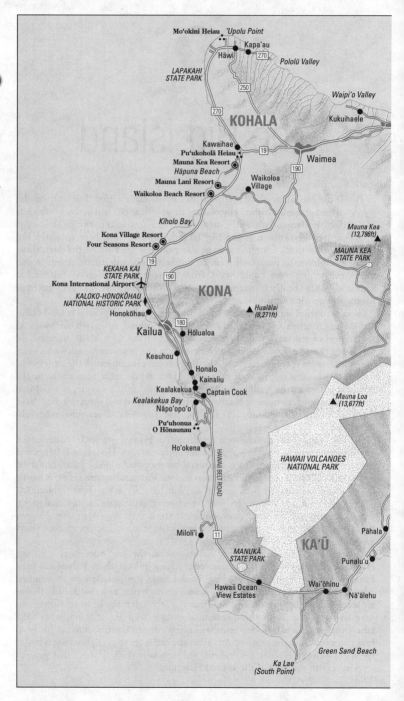

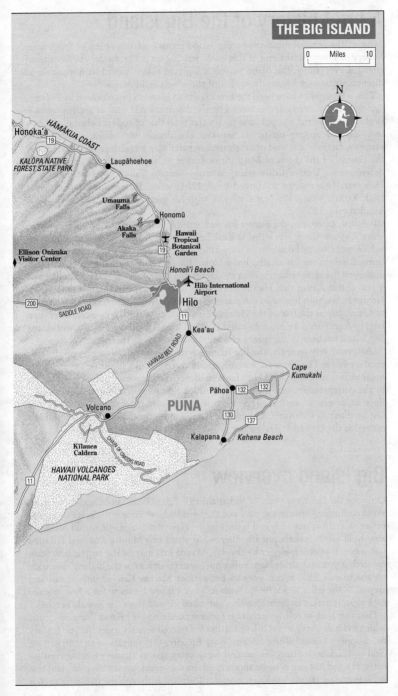

THE BIG ISLAND

0   Miles   10

N

Honoka'a
19
HĀMĀKUA COAST
KALŌPA NATIVE
FOREST STATE PARK
Laupāhoehoe

Umauma
Falls
Honomū
Akaka
Falls
Hawaii
Tropical
Botanical
Garden
19
Honoli'i Beach

Ellison Onizuka
Visitor Center

Hilo International
Airport
Hilo

200
SADDLE ROAD
11
Kea'au

HAWAII BELT ROAD

Cape
Kumukahi

Pāhoa   132   132
PUNA
130
137
Volcano
Kalapana   Kehena Beach

Kīlauea
Caldera
CHAIN OF CRATERS ROAD

HAWAII VOLCANOES
NATIONAL PARK
11

A brief history of the Big Island

Most of the seminal moments of Big Island history are recounted in the general history of Hawaii at the end of this book, starting on p.529; before the Europeans changed everything, the island was so significant that it would be impossible to disentangle its own history from that of the whole archipelago.

This is thought to have been the first Hawaiian island to be colonized by Polynesian voyagers, as early as the second or third century AD, and in ancient times it probably supported a population far greater than that of today. Politically, it was long divided among up to six separate chiefdoms, with major potential for intrigue, faction, and warfare; the north in particular was also prone to fall under the control of the chiefs of Maui. At one stage – the precise date is impossible to determine – **'Umi-a-Liloa** emerged from Waipi'o Valley to unite the island. However, factionalism continued until 1791, when **Kamehameha the Great** from Kohala won a ten-year civil war with his great rival Keōua from Ka'ū, as detailed on p.533.

By then, of course, the Europeans had arrived. Kamehameha had been present when Captain Cook was killed at Kealakekua Bay (see p.186), and with European aid he went on to become the only ruler ever to conquer all the other islands. Immediately after his death, his widow, Ka'ahumanu, and his son, Liholiho, destroyed the ancient *kapu* system by celebrating a banquet together at Kailua, and it was also at Kailua that Hawaii's first Christian missionaries reached the islands. However, within a few years the seat of power had passed irreversibly to the island of Oahu. Just as the fate of the Hawaiian islands has for the last two centuries been largely determined by economic and political events in the rest of the world, the Big Island has been at the mercy of events and changes in Honolulu.

Until relatively recently, the Big Island's economy depended largely on the rich produce of the Hāmākua plantations, traded through Hilo. Now, however, all the sugar mills have closed, and Hilo finds itself regarded as something of a backwater by the entrepreneurs who have flooded into the sunny spots along the Kona coast. Even so, despite a frantic rush of investment, tourism has yet to replace all the jobs lost by plantation closures. Otherwise, the island occupies a couple of specialized niches, as the United States' largest producer of both **ginger** and **coffee**.

Big Island overview

Only for the last sixty years or so has the title "Big Island" been widely used, to avoid confusion between the state and the island whose name it took. It's an appropriate nickname: not only is this the biggest Hawaiian island – it would comfortably hold all the others put together – but thanks to **Mauna Loa** and **Kīlauea** volcanoes, it's getting bigger by the day. Mauna Loa may be the largest mountain on earth if you include its huge bulk under water, but it's not the highest mountain on the island. That honor goes to the extinct **Mauna Kea**, slightly north and around 100ft taller at 13,796ft. With its peak capped by snow for a few months each year, it makes an incongruous sight when viewed from the Kohala beaches.

The great bulk of tourist activity is concentrated along the **Kona** (leeward) coast, which extends north and south of **Kailua** for around seventy miles. As you first fly in, dropping toward Kona International Airport, this appears as an unrelenting field of black lava. However, around forty years ago its virtues of being consistently dry and hot began to be appreciated. Resort development took off, and this became one of Hawaii's prime tourist destinations. Although the five-mile stretch from Kailua south to Keauhou has acquired an unbroken succession of hotels and condos, Kailua itself remains recognizable as the sleepy little town where Kamehameha the Great had his palace. To the **south**, reached by a gorgeous road through lush coffee groves, lies **Kealakekua Bay**, where Captain Cook met his end, with the nearby **Puʻuhonua O Hōnaunau**, or "Place of Refuge," bearing witness to a vanished Hawaiian way of life and death.

The **northernmost** spur of the Big Island is its oldest segment, named after the first of its five volcanoes to appear above the ocean – the long-extinct **Kohala Mountain**. The Big Island's largest **coral reefs** – albeit small by most standards – lie just offshore, and its only sizeable **white-sand beaches** have been washed into nearby sheltered coves. Although the landscape gets more dramatic the further north you go, facilities for tourists are almost entirely restricted to **South Kohala**. This region, too, consists of barren lava flats, but lavish resorts such as the Disney-esque *Hilton Waikoloa Village* are now tucked into inlets all along the coastline.

Continuing around the island, beyond the upland cattle country of **Waimea** – home to the Parker Ranch and generations of lasso-toting *paniolo* cowboys – you reach the magnificent **Hāmākua Coast**, to be confronted by archetypal South Seas scenery. Even before the emergence of commercial agriculture, these rain-drenched slopes formed the fertile heartland of Hawaii: broad, green **Waipiʻo Valley** was capable of feeding the entire island. After a century of growing sugar, however, the small towns here are reeling from the closure of the plantations. So is the Big Island's only city, its capital **Hilo**, where attempts to attract tourists have always been thwarted by the rainfall. Nonetheless it's an attractively low-key community, renowned for spectacular flowers and orchids.

Finally, the **south** of the island is dominated by the exhilarating wilderness of **Hawaii Volcanoes National Park**. Apart from the steaming craters and cinder cones of Mauna Loa and Kīlauea, its terrain ranges from arctic tundra and sulphurous desert to lowland rainforest and remote Pacific beaches. This is one of the world's most exciting hiking destinations, with scores of trails running through still-active craters. Here and there along the shore the volcanoes have deposited beaches of jet-black sand, while near **South Point** – the southernmost point of the United States – you can hike to a remote beach composed of green(ish) sand. Otherwise, the southern coastline is now sparsely populated, and few visitors bother to leave the highway in the time-forgotten regions of **Puna** and **Kaʻū**.

Getting to the Big Island

Although the much-vaunted Hawaii Superferry (see p.32) is scheduled to start **boat services** to the Big Island from Honolulu in 2009, for the moment the only

Big Island favorites: beaches			
Green Sand Beach	p.273	Punaluʻu Beach	p.271
Hāpuna Beach	p.203	Spencer Beach Park	p.205
Kekaha Kai State Park	p.194		
Snorkel and dive spots			
Kahaluʻu Beach	p.178	Puʻuhonua O Hōnaunau	p.187
Kaunaʻoa Beach	p.204	Wai Ōpae Tide Pools	p.249
Kealakekua Bay	p.184		

Big island favorites: hikes			
Green Sand Beach	p.273	Kīlauea Iki	p.261
Halemaʻumaʻu Trail	p.260	Pololū Valley	p.217
Kealakekua Bay	p.184	Puʻu Huluhulu	p.263
Kīlauea eruption	p.264	Waipiʻo Valley	p.237

way to get there is to **fly**. The island has two main airports. **Kona International Airport** is on the west coast, seven miles north of Kailua (see p.171); **Hilo International Airport** is on the outskirts of Hilo (see p.221), on the east coast. Most tourists arrive at Kona, but Hilo is kept busy with local travelers, and the two airports receive similar numbers of flights each day. The vast majority of each day's arrivals come from Honolulu. As detailed on p.28, the only **nonstop flights** to the Big Island from the US mainland are to Kona; United, American, Delta, Aloha, and ATA currently offer services. It's also possible to fly direct to **Waimea** from Honolulu and Maui on tiny Pacific Wings (☏808/887-2104 or 1-888/575-4546, ⓦwww.pacificwings.com).

Getting around the Big Island

The only practicable way to explore the Big Island is to **drive**. All the major automobile rental chains are represented at both main airports; the relevant phone numbers are listed on p.33.

In a sense, there's just one main road, the **Hawaii Belt Road**, which circles the entire island. Other than in central Kailua, traffic problems are all but nonexistent, and if you have to, you can get from anywhere on the island to anywhere else pretty quickly. It's possible to sleep in Kailua and catch a plane out from Hilo the next day, while a nightly exodus of cars drive the hundred-plus miles from the volcanoes back to Kona. Unlike all the other islands, however, the Big Island is too big to make it worth attempting a complete one-day circuit, and visiting the volcanoes as a day-trip from Kona won't give you enough time at the park.

You should also keep a close eye on your fuel gauge. **Gas stations** are common around Kailua and Hilo, but in several regions, including the National Park, you can drive up to fifty miles without seeing one.

Some of the national chains forbid drivers to take ordinary vehicles onto lesser roads such as **South Point Road** (see p.272) or the high-altitude Saddle Road (see p.242). If you're determined to explore those areas, you could always rent a **4WD vehicle** from Harper Car & Truck Rentals (☏1-800/852-9993 or 808/969-1478, ⓦwww.harpershawaii.com), whose rates start from $80 per day. This also enables you to drive to the summit of Mauna Kea, but you still can't go off-road along the dirt track to Green Sand Beach (see p.273), or down the surfaced but incredibly steep road into Waipiʻo Valley (see p.240).

As for **public transport**, the Hele On Bus Company (☏808/961-8744) runs **buses** between Hilo and Kailua (Mon–Sat, 1 daily; full timetable on p.221), and between Hilo and the volcanoes (Mon–Fri, 1 daily; see p.254).

Details on seeing the island by **air** are listed opposite; for **boat tours** see p.188 and p.193; and for getting around by **motorbike** or **bicycle**, see p.172. Otherwise, the only alternatives to driving are the **minibus tours** run by companies such as Roberts Hawaii (☏808/329-1688 or 1-866/898-2519, ⓦwww.robertshawaii.com), who do a volcano tour from Hilo for $55 and a circle-island tour from Kailua for $64.

Big Island flight-seeing

Unlike the other Hawaiian islands, the Big Island is too large to see in a single air tour, but it has the incomparable attraction of the unpredictable Kīlauea eruption. If it's the volcano you want to see, opt for a flight from Hilo or Volcano; many of the cheaper ones on the Kona side go up the Kohala coast and miss Kīlauea, while if you do want to reach the volcano from Kona you'll find yourself paying for a *long* flight.

Prices generally start at around $150 for a 45-minute flight, and can reach up to $400 for a full circle-island flight with a good long stare at the eruption. Shop online for the best rates. If you're traveling in a group of four or more, it makes sense to charter a helicopter by the hour, which costs from around $780, and devise your own flight path.

For more about flight-seeing tours in general, see p.34.

Helicopters

	Number	Web (ⓌWWW.)	Departs
Blue Hawaiian	☏808/961-5600	bluehawaiian.com	Hilo, Waikoloa
Paradise	☏808/969-7392	paradisecopters.com	Hilo, Kona
Safari	☏808/969-1259	safarihelicopters.com	Hilo
Sunshine	☏808/871-0722	sunshinehelicopters.com	Hilo, Hāpuna
Tropical	☏808/961-6810	tropicalhelicopters.com	Hilo, Kona

Fixed-wing

	Number	Web (ⓌWWW.)	Departs
Big Island Air	☏808/329-4868	bigislandair.com	Kona
Island Hoppers	☏808/329-0018	fly-hawaii.com	Hilo, Kona

The most active and adventurous tours available on the Big Island are those offered by Hawaii Forest & Trail (☏808/331-8505 or 1-800/464-1993, Ⓦwww.hawaii-forest.com). From their base near Kona International Airport, they take half- and full-day van tours to all corners of the island, including hiking trips to places like Volcanoes National Park and Pololū Valley, and a tour to the top of Mauna Kea. Prices range from $100 to $170 per person.

Where to stay

Where you **stay** depends on what sort of vacation you're planning. If most of your time will be spent on the beach, consider the prime beach areas of the **Kona** and **Kohala coasts**, which are filled with upscale hotels, condos, and self-contained resorts. Many of the cheapest options on this side of the island are in **Kailua**, though that town too has its share of luxury properties. Elsewhere, **Hilo** offers large hotels as well as smaller, more characterful inns, while both the **National Park** area and **Waimea** have some medium-scale lodges and an abundance of **B&Bs** in private homes.

Official statistics put the **average cost** of Big Island accommodation at over $200 per night. That alarming figure, however, is boosted by the rates at the mega-resorts of Kohala; the average cost for the Kailua area is a more reasonable $130 per night, and Hilo's average is considerably less. At most times of the year it's possible to book a room at short notice.

Bear in mind when you book that it's barely possible to see the entire island from a single base. Even if you plan to concentrate on the Kona or Kohala coasts, reckon

②

Big Island favorites: accommodation

Arnott's Lodge, Hilo (①–③) p.222
Manago Hotel, Captain Cook (①–③) p.191
Kona Tiki Hotel, Kailua (②–③) p.173
Kohala Village Inn, Hāwī (②–④) p.216
Dolphin Bay Hotel, Hilo (③–④) p.222

Hale Ohia, Volcano (③–⑤) p.268
Shipman House B&B Inn, Hilo (⑥) p.223
Hilton Waikoloa Village (⑥–⑦) p.198
Hāpuna Beach Prince (⑧–⑨) p.204
Kona Village Resort (⑨) p.195

on spending at least a night or two in the National Park area, or possibly in Hilo. It may even be worth simply not using a pre-paid Kona-side room for one night, to give yourself time at the volcanoes.

When to go

Throughout the year, sea-level thermometers rarely drop below the low seventies Fahrenheit (around 22°C) in the daytime, or reach above the low eighties (around 28°C); at night the temperature seldom falls below the low sixties. Average daily temperatures in Hilo range from 71°F in February to 76°F in August, while Kailua fluctuates between 72°F and 77°F. Waimea has similar daily maximums, but drops to the low fifties (around 11°C) at night. Volcano Village too can get cold at night, while temperatures at the summit of Mauna Kea, which receives snow in winter, range from 31°F up to 43°F.

In principle the rainiest months are from December to February, but where you are on the island makes far more difference than what time of year it is. Hilo is the wettest city in the US, with an annual rainfall of 128 inches, and Volcano Village is even wetter, but the Kona coast, and especially the Kohala resort area, receive very little rain at any time. Kawaihae in Kohala gets a mere ten inches each year.

As in the rest of Hawaii, the state of the **ocean** varies with the seasons. It's possible to swim all year round in more sheltered areas, but the high surf between October and April makes certain beaches (identified throughout this chapter) extremely dangerous.

Big Island favorites: camping

Halapē, Volcanoes National Park	p.266
Hāpuna Beach, Kohala	p.204
Kalōpā State Park, Hāmākua	p.236
Kulanaokuaiki, Volcanoes National Park	p.262
Nāmakani Paio, Volcanoes National Park	p.257
Punaluʻu County Beach Park, Kaʻū	p.271
Spencer County Beach Park, Kohala	p.205
Waipiʻo Valley, Hāmākua	p.242

For state park camping permits, contact the Division of State Parks, 75 Aupuni St, Hilo HI 96720 (rates vary; ☎808/974-6200). County park permits, at $5 per day, are administered by the Department of Parks and Recreation, 25 Aupuni St, Hilo HI 96720 (Mon–Fri 7.45am–4.30pm; ☎808/961-8311, ⓦwww.hawaii-county.com), which has subsidiary offices at Hale Hālawai on Aliʻi Drive in Kailua (same hours), Yano Hall in Captain Cook (Mon–Fri noon–2pm), and Waimea Community Center in Waimea (Mon–Fri 8.30–10.30am).

Big Island festivals and events

By far the most important of the Big Island's annual festivals is Hilo's **Merrie Monarch Festival**, a *hula* showcase for which tickets sell out almost immediately. For more details, see p.227.

Feb	Mardi Gras, Hilo
Feb	Waimea Cherry Blossom Festival, Waimea
March	Kona Brewers Festival, Kailua
March 26	Prince Kūhiō Day (public holiday)
April	Merrie Monarch Festival, Hilo
May 1	Lei Day (public holiday)
May	Jazz Getaway, Honoka'a
June 11	Kamehameha Day (public holiday); Floral Parade in Kailua, also ceremonies at Kapa'au
mid-June	Great Waikoloa Food, Wine & Music Festival, Waikoloa
late June	Pu'uhonua O Hōnaunau Cultural Festival
late June	Kona Marathon, Kailua
July 4	Parker Ranch Rodeo, Waimea
mid-July	Kīlauea Cultural Festival, Volcano
mid-July	Big Island Hawaiian Music and Slack Key Festival, Hilo
late July	Kīlauea Volcano Wilderness Runs, Volcano
Aug–Oct	International Festival of the Pacific, Hilo
mid-Aug	Hawaiian International Billfish Tournament, Kailua
3rd Fri in Aug	Admissions Day (public holiday)
early Sept	Queen Lili'uokalani Long-Distance Canoe Races, Kailua
early Sept	Parker Ranch Round-up Rodeo, Waimea
Sept	Aloha Week Festival, island-wide
early Oct	Ironman Triathlon World Championship, Kailua
early Oct	Tahiti Fête of Hilo
Oct	Hāmākua Music Festival, Honoka'a
early Nov	Kona Coffee Cultural Festival, South Kona
Nov	Taro Festival, Honoka'a
Nov	Hawaii International Film Festival, island-wide
mid-Nov	King Kalākaua Hula Festival, Kona
Dec	Christmas Parade, Waimea

Mention should also be made of a unique Big Island phenomenon. While the summits of Mauna Loa and Mauna Kea are renowned for having the clearest air on earth, down below, when the tradewinds drop, the island is prone to a choking haze of sulphurous volcanic emissions known as "**vog**". The pollution on such days hits levels worse than those in Los Angeles or London; the only spot on the island that is consistently downwind of Kīlauea, the Ka'ū Desert, is a lifeless wasteland.

Nightlife and entertainment

Most of what limited **nightlife** the Big Island has to offer is arranged by the major hotels, and many feature live musicians every night. In a typical week, the biggest

Big Island favorites: eating

These restaurants are in ascending order of price, not quality.

The Coffee Shack, Captain Cook p.184
Ocean Sushi Deli, Hilo p.230
Hilo Bay Café, Hilo p.229
Bamboo Restaurant and Bar, Hāwī p.215
Cassandra's Greek Taverna, Kailua p.179
Restaurant Kaikodo, Hilo p.229

Merrimans, Waimea p.212
Roy's, Waikoloa p.200
Brown's Beach House, Fairmont Orchid
p.202
Coast Grille, Hapuna Beach Prince p.204

events are the various *lū'aus* listed on p.180, but visiting artists from the other islands or the mainland also make regular concert appearances. Most such activity happens in the prime tourist areas of Kona and Kohala, but Hawaiian performers with strong local followings also schedule appearances in Hilo.

Kailua

The largest town on the Kona side of the Big Island, **KAILUA** is also the oldest Western-style community on the island. Hawaii's first Christian missionaries arrived here from New England in 1820, while before that it was a favorite home of Kamehameha I. However, it didn't expand significantly beyond its picturesque harbor, which centers on a palace and church built in the 1830s, until a boom in tourism during the 1980s suddenly made this the island's busiest holiday area. Since then, its original core has been increasingly swamped by new development, with a ribbon of high-rise hotels and sprawling condos stretching away south along the coast for several miles, and ugly modern shopping malls climbing ever further up the hillside. Locals decry its apparently unstoppable transformation into "Kona-fornia," and the loss of almost all its Hawaiian identity. In fact, although construction continues, Kailua's heyday as a resort seems to be over; the great majority of new tourism investment is now taking place further up the coast, while Kailua is seen increasingly as a downmarket destination.

That said, Kailua is still a very long way from the overkill of Waikīkī. When Mark Twain called it "the sleepiest, quietest, Sundayest looking place you can imagine" he meant to be pejorative, but if you've come to relax you'll probably find its low-key pleasures appealing. At least one of the local beaches is bound to suit you, and there are plenty of alternative activities. In particular, sitting on the *lānai* of one of the many waterfront cafés and bars, for a blast of Kona coffee in the morning or for a cocktail at sunset, is enough to make anyone feel that all's well with the world.

Many new arrivals assume that Kailua, not Hilo, is the island's capital. Infuriated residents of Hilo console themselves with the thought that hardly anyone seems to get the name of their rival right. Officially, the town is called Kailua, hyphenated by the post office to "Kailua-Kona" to distinguish it from the Kailuas on Oahu and Maui. Most tourists, however, have only heard of Kona and not of Kailua. Compound that with the fact that most of the businesses and other facilities that people generally refer to as being "in Kona" are in fact in Kailua, and you have a recipe for confusion.

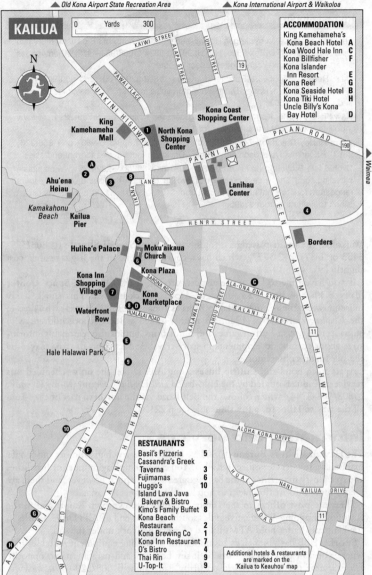

KAILUA

0   Yards   300

N

ACCOMMODATION

King Kamehameha's Kona Beach Hotel	A
Koa Wood Hale Inn	C
Kona Billfisher	F
Kona Islander Inn Resort	E
Kona Reef	G
Kona Seaside Hotel	B
Kona Tiki Hotel	H
Uncle Billy's Kona Bay Hotel	D

KAIWI STREET

ALAPA STREET

LUNIA STREET

PAWAI PLACE

KUAKINI HIGHWAY

19

King Kamehameha Mall

❶ North Kona Shopping Center

Kona Coast Shopping Center

PALANI ROAD

PALANI ROAD

190

▶ Waimea

Ahu'ena Heiau

A

❷

❸ B

LANE

ILIAHI

Lanihau Center

QUEEN KA'AHUMANU

Kamakahonu Beach

Kailua Pier

HENRY STREET

❹

Hulihe'e Palace

❺ **Moku'aikaua Church**
❻

Borders

Kona Plaza

SARONA ROAD

KAILUA STREET

ALA-ONA ONA STREET

G

Kona Inn Shopping Village

❼

Kona Marketplace

ALAROU STREET

KALANI STREET

❽ D

HUALALAI ROAD

Waterfront Row

E

11

Hale Halawai Park

❾

HIGHWAY

KUAKINI

❿

ALOHA KONA DRIVE

ALI'I DRIVE

F

HUALALAI ROAD

NANI KAILUA DRIVE

11

RESTAURANTS

Basil's Pizzeria	5
Cassandra's Greek Taverna	3
Fujimamas	6
Huggo's	10
Island Lava Java Bakery & Bistro	9
Kimo's Family Buffet	8
Kona Beach Restaurant	2
Kona Brewing Co	1
Kona Inn Restaurant	7
O's Bistro	4
Thai Rin	9
U-Top-It	9

G

WALUA RD

KUAKINI HIGHWAY

ALI'I DRIVE

H

Additional hotels & restaurants are marked on the 'Kailua to Keauhou' map

Hōlualoa ▼

Arrival and information

Kona International Airport, the Big Island's laid-back but still busiest airport, sprawls across the lava seven miles north of Kailua. Most arriving passengers rent a car immediately from the usual outlets (listed on p.33) or arrange to be picked up by their hotels. Taxis from the airport rank charge around $25 to Kailua, $45 to

Bike and motorbike rental and tours

For general advice on **cycling** in Hawaii, see p.33. The nonprofit Big Island Mountain Bike Association (PO Box 6819, Hilo HI 96720-8934 ⑦808/961-4452, ⓦhomepages .interpac.net/~mtbike) can suggest specific routes.

DJ's Rentals 75-5663A Palani Rd, Kailua ⑦808/329-1700 or 1-800/993-4647, ⓦwww.harleys.com. Harley-Davidson motorcycles from $150 per day, plus scooters and mopeds at $50.

Hawaiian Pedals Kona Inn Shopping Village, Kailua ⑦808/329-2294, ⓦwww .hpbikeworks.com. Mountain bikes for $20 per day or $70 per week.

Kona Harley-Davidson 74-5615 E Luhia St, Kailua ⑦808/326-9887 or 1-866/326-9887, ⓦkonaharleydavidson.com. Harley-Davidson motorcycles for rent and sale.

Orchid Isle Bicycling Kailua ⑦808/327-0087 or 1-800/219-2324, ⓦwww.orchidisle bicycling.com. The widest program of cycling tours on the island; one-day tours range from four to eight hours and cost from $125, or you can take a multi-day circle-island tour starting from $1895.

Waikoloa; the multi-passenger shuttle vans run by **Speedi Shuttle** (⑦808/329-5433 or 1-877/242-5777), which has a courtesy phone in the baggage area, cost slightly less.

If you have time to kill at the airport, drop in at the **Onizuka Space Center** (daily 8.30am–4.30pm; $3), next to Aloha's check-in area. This small, lively museum was built as a memorial to Kona astronaut Ellison Onizuka, who died in the *Challenger* disaster of 1986. It's mainly aimed at local schoolchildren, who enjoy its many push-button games and simulations, but it's also reasonably informative about current developments in space travel, and explains the role played by the Big Island's observatories.

Apart from hotel-run **shuttle buses** along Ali'i Drive, the only scheduled **bus** service in Kailua is offered by the Hilo-based *Hele On Bus Company* (Mon–Sat only; ⑦808/961-8744), which follows the Belt Road via the northern part of the island all the way to Hilo; for a full timetable see p.221.

Information and services

The **Hawaii Visitors Bureau** (⑦808/961-5797, ⓦwww.bigisland.org) no longer maintains a full-service office in Kailua. You can pick up any number of brochures and free glossy magazines in the baggage area at the airport, however, and there are plenty more information racks in hotels and restaurants in town.

There are **post offices** in the Lanihau Center in downtown Kailua and in the Keauhou Shopping Village, five miles south at the far end of Ali'i Drive. **Banks** in the Lanihau Center hold ATMs linked to every network under the sun.

Snorkel Bob has a branch of his inimitable snorkeling equipment rental service, where you can pick up all sorts of jokey booklets and paraphernalia, opposite *Huggo's*, near the *Royal Kona Resort* (daily 8am–5pm; ⑦808/329-0770, ⓦwww .snorkelbob.com), and another just south of the airport, behind *Home Depot*, at 73-4976 Kamanu St (same hours and website; ⑦808/329-0770).

Accommodation

Well over half of all the Big Island's **hotel** and **condo rooms** are concentrated in or near Kailua, the vast majority of them along the roughly five-mile oceanfront stretch of Ali'i Drive. Although, in terms of quality, the area is falling way behind the resorts to the north, there are still some attractive and good-value places to be found, and if you prefer to spend your vacation in a real town rather than a self-contained resort, Kailua is still the island's best option.

Ali'i Drive also holds a handful of **B&Bs**, though visitors in search of a traditional B&B experience tend to prefer to drive the three miles up from the ocean to the idyllic seclusion of the "coffee town" of Hōlualoa. B&Bs there, along with a wide range of inexpensive, small-scale alternatives to Kailua's hotels, are listed under "South Kona Accommodation" on p.190.

If you plan to spend your entire vacation in Kailua, remember that you can get far better rates by booking an all-inclusive package before you leave home.

King Kamehameha's Kona Beach Hotel 75-5660 Palani Rd ☏ 808/329-2911 or 1-800/367-2111, ⊛ www.konabeachhotel.com. Long-established family-oriented hotel, definitely showing its age but still worth considering for its central location and general Hawaiian "feel." Focusing on picturesque Kamakahonu Beach (see p.178), it also has a pool, a small shopping mall, and an unexceptional restaurant. Kayaks, pedaloes, and other watersports equipment are available for rent. The lobby hosts Hawaiian music performances and crafts displays, while the gardens make an attractive setting for *lū'aus* (Tues–Thurs & Sun 5pm; $68). Check online for special deals, and details of the "Paradise on Wheels" package, including car rental, parking and breakfast. ❹.

Koa Wood Hale Inn 75-184 Ala-Ona Ona St ☏ 808/329-9633, ⊛ www.alternative-hawaii.com /affordable/kona.htm. This budget hostel, a few hundred yards from the town center – reached by taking Kalani Street up from Kuakini Highway at *McDonald's*, and then the second turn on the left – is a cleaner reincarnation of the unlamented *Patey's Place*, which used to be four doors up the street. Popular with backpackers and surfers, it offers dorm beds for $25, or basic private doubles for $65, with mountain bikes for rent, and Internet access. ❶–❷

Kona Billfisher 75-5841 Ali'i Drive ☏ 808/329-3333 or 1-800/244-4752, ⊛ www.konahawaii .com. Well-maintained, good-value condos in a complex of three-story units that sprawls up the hillside, a short walk south of central Kailua. Each unit has a kitchen and balcony, and even the one-bedroom options have a living room that can be used as another bedroom. Extra fees are charged for cleaning and even air-conditioning, so the rates aren't quite as cheap as they may appear. ❹

Kona Islander Inn Resort 75-5776 Kuakini Hwy ☏ 808/329-3333 or 1-800/244-4752, ⊛ www .konahawaii.com. These centrally located 1960s condos, just behind the Coconut Grove Marketplace, may not seem the height of style from the outside, but they're perfectly adequate and offer some of the

coast's best rates. Kitchen facilities are minimal. Prices rise significantly from mid-Dec through March. The front desk is also a reservations office for several other local condo resorts. ❸

Kona Reef 75-5888 Ali'i Drive ☏ 808/329-6438 or through SunQuest Vacations 1-800/367-5168 (US) or 1-800/800-5662 (Canada), ⊛ www.sunquest -hawaii.com. Attractive modern condo development, on the southern edge of Kailua, with several levels of very comfortable, one-, two- and three-bed units dropping down to the ocean. No on-site beach, but there's a good pool. ❺

Kona Seaside Hotel 75-5646 Palani Rd ☏ 808/329-2455 or 1-800/560-5558, ⊛ www.sand -seaside.com. The 225-room property sprawls across central Kailua, just up from Ali'i Drive. Several three-story wings of small, far from fancy but good-value air-conditioned rooms cluster around a central pool, while a newer six-floor building overlooks another, smaller, pool. Look for discount rates online, and you can usually get a good rate using the courtesy phone at the airport. ❸

Kona Tiki Hotel 75-5968 Ali'i Drive ☏ 808/329-1425, ⊛ www.konatiki.com. This three-story, 15-room, motel-style property, inches from the ocean a mile south of central Kailua, is an absolute gem for budget travelers. The winter season is often completely booked up two years in advance. All the clean, comfortable rooms have private oceanfront balconies or patios, some also have kitchenettes, and rates even include breakfast beside the small pool. No TVs or phones, and credit cards aren't accepted; three-night minimum stay. Standard ❷, kitchenette ❸

Outrigger Keauhou Beach Resort 78-6740 Ali'i Drive ☏ 808/322-3441 or 1-800/688-7444, ⊛ www.outrigger.com. Seven-story hotel jutting into the sea on a black-lava promontory at the southern end of Kahalu'u Beach Park, five miles south of central Kailua. As part of recently upgrading to the chain's *Outrigger* status, all rooms have been renovated to a high standard of comfort. Facilities include tennis courts and a pool; trails around the grounds lead past ruined temples and petroglyphs. There's a nice open-air restaurant, the *Kamaaina Terrace*, while the adjoining *Verandah Lounge* offers live Hawaiian music. ⑤

Outrigger Royal Sea Cliff Resort 75-6040 Ali'i Drive ☎808/329-8021 or 1-800/688-7444, ⓦwww .outrigger.com. White, multilevel complex of luxurious studios and one- and two-bedroom suites, dropping down to the coast a mile south of central Kailua, and laid out around a lush courtyard garden. You can't swim in the sea here, but it has fresh- and saltwater pools, plus a sauna and hot tub. ⑤

Sheraton Keauhou Bay Resort 78-128 Ehukai St ☎808/930-4900 or 1-866/716-8109, ⓦwww .sheratonkeauhou.com. The former *Kona Surf Resort*, five miles south of central Kailua, reopened in 2005, making the most of a spectacular oceanfront location to become the most upscale resort along Kailua's coastal strip. It's heavily geared towards families, with a pool complex and waterslide to compensate for the lack of a beach, but the actual rooms are enormous and luxurious. ⑤

Uncle Billy's Kona Bay Hotel 75-5739 Ali'i Drive ☎808/329-6488 or 1-800/367-5102, ⓦwww .unclebilly.com. Friendly, central budget hotel, run by the same family as the *Hilo Bay Hostel* (see p.222). Not at all fancy, occasionally noisy, but reasonably comfortable rooms, all with a/c and private bath, are arranged around a small pool and *Kimo's* restaurant (see p.179). The best rates are online. ④

The Town

Central Kailua still retains something of the feel of a seaside village. Every visitor should set aside an hour or two to take a leisurely oceanfront stroll along the old Seawall, whose scenic route runs for a few hundred yards around the bay from the **Ahu'ena Heiau**, jutting into the ocean in front of the *King Kamehameha* hotel, to the **Hulihe'e Palace** and **Moku'aikaua Church**.

At its heart is the jetty of **Kailua Pier**, a small expanse of asphalt popular with anglers, courting couples, and surf-bums alike. Until as recently as the 1960s there were still cattle pens here, but these days most commercial boats leave from the marina at Honokōhau Harbor, three miles north (see p.192), and aside from those times when it's teeming with cruise-ship passengers, ferried here from the behemoths anchored offshore, the mood tends to be slightly aimless. At least the time-honored tradition of fishermen displaying their catches in the early evening persists, with the biggest fish of all weighing in during August's International Billfish Tournament. More gleaming flesh is on show in mid-October each year, when the pier is the starting-point of the 2.4-mile swimming leg of the **Ironman Triathlon**, which also requires its participants to cycle 112 miles and run a marathon on the same day.

The resort area stretches away to the south, while up from the seafront ever-increasing numbers of **shopping malls** seem to appear each year, catering more to the needs of local residents, and less to those of tourists, the higher you climb from the shoreline. For everyday shopping and services, locals tend to head for Costco or Kmart, on the northeastern edge of town, or the **Lanihau Center** near the main stoplights on the highway.

Ahu'ena Heiau

The **Ahu'ena Heiau** guards the mouth of Kailua Bay in a too-good-to-be-true setting beside a sandy little beach, in front of the *King Kamehameha* hotel. Kamehameha the Great held sway from this ancient temple, dedicated to Lono, between his return from Honolulu in 1812 and his death here on May 8, 1819. Soon afterwards, his son Liholiho, spurred on by Kamehameha's principal queen, Ka'ahumanu, broke the ancient *kapu* system by hosting a banquet here, and thereby inadvertently cleared the way for the missionaries.

Thanks to detailed drawings made in 1816, archeologists have been able to restore the *heiau* to its original appearance, but because it still possesses great spiritual significance, all access to the platform is forbidden. You can get a close-up view by walking to the end of the King Kamehameha beach – officially Kamakahonu Beach (see p.178) – or by swimming out a short way. The *heiau* itself is small, but follows the conventional Hawaiian template, consisting as it does of three distinct structures set on a *paepae* (platform) of black volcanic rock. The largest hut is the *hale mana* ("house of spiritual power"), a place of prayer and council. The smaller *hale pahu* ("house of the drum") alongside is thatched with *hala* leaves, while the ramshackle, tapering structure nearby is the *anu'u*, or "oracle tower," used by the priests to intercede with the gods. In addition, half a dozen *ki'i akua*, carved wooden images symbolizing different gods, stand on the platform. The tallest, a god of healing known as Koleamoku, has a golden plover on his head, in honor of the migratory bird that's credited with having guided Polynesian voyagers to Hawaii in the first place.

After his death, Kamehameha's bones were prepared for burial on a similar rock platform adjacent to the *heiau*, then interred in a location that remains a secret to this day. The platform still exists, though the *hale pohaku* that stood upon it, in which the ceremonies took place, has long since disappeared.

Hulihe'e Palace

Though the four-square, two-story **Hulihe'e Palace** (Mon–Sat 9am–4pm, Sun 10am–4pm; ℗808/329-1877, Ⓦwww.daughtersofhawaii.com), facing out to sea from the center of Kailua, was built in 1838 for Governor John Adams Kuakini, it soon passed into the hands of the Hawaiian royal family. Feeling more like a quaint Victorian private residence than a palace, it was constructed using lava rock, coral, and native hardwoods, but you wouldn't know that from a glance at its coffee-colored modern exterior. As the palace sustained heavy damage in the earthquake of October 2006, it was not open for full tours as this book went to press. Instead, it was only possible to enter the central lobby, which remained intact, and peer into the rooms to either side, where the walls were seriously cracked. The palace contents, including massive *koa*-wood furniture, photos, and ancient Hawaiian artifacts, have been put in storage, and visitors are invited to pay $4 to watch a video of its former glories. Check the website for updates on repair work, and to see whether the $6 tours have resumed.

Pleasant *lānais* run the full length of the ocean side of both the first and second floors. Visitors are free to wander into the well-maintained gardens, which play host to free *hula* performances on the fourth Sunday of each month (except June & Dec).

Moku'aikaua Church

The original **Moku'aikaua Church**, directly opposite the palace, was the first church to be built on the Hawaiian islands. It was constructed in 1820 for the use of Reverend Asa Thurston, one of the first two Christian missionaries dispatched to Hawaii from New England (see p.534), who had arrived in Kailua Bay on April 4 of that year. At that time it closely resembled a *heiau*, being just a thatched hut perched on a stone platform. The current building was erected immediately before Hulihe'e Palace by the same craftsmen, and incorporates large chunks of lava into a design clearly related to the clapboard churches of New England. Open daily from dawn to dusk, it's free to visitors, and particularly welcomes worshippers to its Congregational services (Sun 8am & 10.30am).

The church itself is not of great interest, though a section has been set aside as a museum of the early days of Hawaiian Christianity. Displays include a large model of the ship *Thaddeus*, Hawaii's equivalent of the *Mayflower*, and an exhibition on traditional Polynesian navigational techniques featuring, among other things, a fascinating Micronesian "stick chart," in which an intricate latticework of pandanus (*hala*) twigs and cowrie shells depicts ocean currents, swells, and islands. Such charts were committed to memory rather than carried on board, and served to guide canoes across thousands of miles on the open Pacific.

A bizarre "sausage tree" grows in the grounds of the church. A native of Mozambique, it is named after the pendulous, elongated, and foul-smelling fruit that dangles on long cords from its branches. One of only two on Hawaii, it was planted here on a whim in the 1920s.

South along Ali'i Drive

Heading south from both the church and palace, **Ali'i Drive** is at first fringed with modern malls housing T-shirt stores, boutiques, and restaurants. Beyond Kailua proper, it stretches five miles along a rugged coastline scattered with tiny lava beaches and lined all the way with hotels and condos. The only thing you could call a "sight" along here is the tiny, blue, and highly photogenic **St Peter's Church**, built in 1880. It takes perhaps a minute to admire its waterfront setting, on a tiny patch of lawn at the north end of Kahalu'u Bay, and to glance in through the open door at the etched glass window above the altar. The one weekly Mass said here is at 7.30pm on Saturday. A bare platform of lava boulders alongside is all that remains of the Kue'manu Heiau (see p.178). Ali'i Drive comes to an end in what's nominally the distinct community of **Keauhou**, which isn't a "town" in any sense of the word. Apart from the **Keauhou Shopping Village**, set a long way up from the ocean, it simply consists of a succession of seafront hotels.

Kailua's beaches

Considering its reputation as a resort, central Kailua is surprisingly short of **beaches**. There are enough patches of sand along Ali'i Drive to satisfy those who

△ St Peter's Church

like the convenience of being able to walk to and from their hotels, but most visitors tend to drive north when they fancy a swim. The Big Island's best beaches – such as the Kekaha Kai State Park (p.194), Hāpuna Beach (p.203), and Spencer Beach Park (p.205) – start ten miles or more up the coast, but a good nearby alternative is the Old Kona Airport park, just a few minutes from town.

Camping is not permitted on any of the beaches covered in this section.

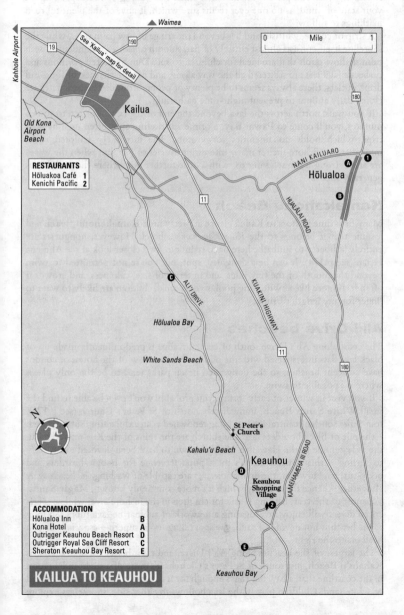

KAILUA TO KEAUHOU

RESTAURANTS
Hōluakoa Café 1
Kenichi Pacific 2

ACCOMMODATION
Hōluakoa Inn   B
Kona Hotel   A
Outrigger Keauhou Beach Resort   D
Outrigger Royal Sea Cliff Resort   C
Sheraton Keauhou Bay Resort   E

Old Kona Airport State Recreation Area

When Kona International Airport opened in 1970, it replaced a small airport on the northern outskirts of Kailua whose site was then set aside for public use as the **Old Kona Airport State Recreation Area**. Though it's not all that attractive, it's now Kailua's most extensive and popular beach. Driving in along the long former runways, which run parallel to the sea, is either hair-raising or fun depending on your state of mind, as no one ever seems sure which, if any, of the plentiful road markings to follow.

A strip of coarse, whitish sand lies beyond the fringe of low palm trees, while the shoreline itself consists almost entirely of flat, smooth *pāhoehoe* lava, indented with calm shallow pools that are ideal for children to splash in. Sheltered pavilions and barbecue facilities are scattered all the way along, and despite the lack of food and drink outlets, there always seems to be plenty of people around. The park gates are closed daily at 8pm to prevent night-time gatherings.

If you walk north across the lava beyond the end of the beach for ten to fifteen minutes, you'll come to **Pawai Bay**, a prime **snorkeling** spot often used by boat trips, which holds no amenities for visitors. The intricately sculpted rocks immediately offshore shelter many interesting species of fish, but when the waves are at all strong it's much safer to swim a little further out, where the visibility is generally superb.

Kamakahonu Beach

Many first-time visitors to Kailua glance at pretty little **Kamakahonu Beach** and assume that it belongs to the *King Kamehameha* hotel. However, nonguests are entirely at liberty to sunbathe here or to swim out for a closer look at the Ahu'ena Heiau (see p.174). It can be a delightful spot, but you're not permitted to swim beyond the mouth of the tiny inlet, and in terms of size, calmness, and crowds it often feels more like a swimming pool, so only small children are likely to want to linger for any length of time.

Ali'i Drive beaches

The coast along Ali'i Drive south of central Kailua is predominantly made up of black lava flats interspersed with the odd sandy cove. Few of the hotels or condos have adjacent beaches, so the designated beach parks tend to be the only places where it's possible to swim.

If you visit in winter or early spring, you probably won't even be able to find the small **White Sands Beach**, immediately north of St Peter's Church (see p.176), four miles south of central Kailua. Long renowned as an exhilarating surfing beach – the pile of black boulders near the church are the ruins of the Kue'manu Heiau, the only temple in the Hawaiian islands known to have been devoted exclusively to surfing – this remains Kona's most popular venue for boogie-boarders and body-surfers. However, the dramatic waves are capable of washing the beach away altogether – hence the name by which it's more commonly known, **Magic Sands**. For most of the year, bathing is safe for children in the inshore area, while experienced divers will enjoy investigating a network of submarine lava tubes. So long as the beach is not devoid of sand, the snorkeling too is superb – especially if you head off to the right.

The largest of the beaches along Ali'i Drive, and even better for snorkeling, is **Kahalu'u Beach**, just south of St Peter's Church. It's more of a slight indentation in the coastline than a bay, but that's enough for it to hang on to a fair-sized spread of white sand. Children play in the lava hollows to either side, snorkelers explore deeper but still sheltered pools, and strong swimmers and scuba divers use the shelving sand to reach the open waters of the bay. Large segments remain of a long breakwater, which originally protected the whole area and was supposedly constructed to aid fish-farming by early Hawaiians – the *menehune* who, according to legend, were here long before the main Polynesian migration of the twelfth and thirteenth centuries.

Generally this is a safe spot, but high surf conditions can create a devastating rip current. Don't venture into the water if you're in any doubt; if you get caught by the current, your best strategy, as ever, is to allow yourself to be swept out beyond its reach rather than exhaust yourself trying to fight it.

Restaurants

Though Kailua is filled with **places to eat**, there's little that could be considered fine dining. Each of its many malls has at least a couple of restaurants, while those that stand more than a block or so up from the ocean, such as the Lanihau Center, also house outlets of every imaginable fast-food chain. Asian cuisines, especially Thai, are also strongly represented. Most of the restaurants along Ali'i Drive tend to be pricier, but offer views of the bay and serve slightly better food. Even along the waterfront, however, there are still some determinedly old-fashioned, inexpensive diners. Bear in mind that lots of great places, ideal for lunch in particular, can be found along Hwy-11 in South Kona, including the *Nasturtium Café* (see p.184) and the *Coffee Shack* (see p.184).

Inexpensive

Island Lava Java Bakery & Bistro Ali'i Sunset Plaza, 75-5799 Ali'i Drive ☎808/327-2161. Seafront mall café/bakery, with several open-air tables, and offering delicious Kona coffee, plus exotic juices, fresh breads, coconut croissants, waffles, cookies, sandwiches, and cakes. The perfect place for a light ocean-view breakfast or an after-dinner coffee, it also offers Internet access. Daily 6am–10pm.

Kimo's Family Buffet *Uncle Billy's Kona Bay Hotel*, 75-5739 Ali'i Drive ☎808/329-1393. The palm-fringed and vaguely Polynesian open-air terrace beside the hotel pool hosts very plain but good-value all-you-can-eat buffets, costing $8 for breakfast and $11 or $12 for dinner. Daily 7–10.30am & 5.30–9pm.

Kona Brewing Co 75-5629 Kuakini Hwy ☎808/334-2739. Large brewpub in an unexciting mall behind the *King Kamehameha* hotel, with lots of indoor and outdoor seating but no views. As well as home-brewed beers like Longboard Lager and even a Kona Coffee Stout, they sell inventive salads and sandwiches in both half and full sizes ($7–12), and tasty, inexpensive pizzas made to your specifications. Food service stops an hour before closing time. Sun–Thurs 11am–10pm, Fri & Sat 11am–11pm.

U-Top-It Ali'i Sunset Plaza, 75-5799 Ali'i Drive ☎808/329-0092. What do you top? A "taro

pancrepe," as in a purple pancake made with taro flour. Top them with whatever you fancy, from egg, spam or sausage to banana, whipped cream and mac nuts (that one's called a Hula Girl). All of them cost under $10 and taste pretty good, plus burgers and other fast-food snacks are offered. Daily except Mon 7.30am–2pm.

Moderate

Basil's Pizzeria 75-5707 Ali'i Drive ☎808/326-7836. Unadventurous Italian eatery, immediately north of Moku'aikaua Church. Seated near the door you can enjoy sea views; further back there's little to do but dig into either the individual pizzas ($12–14), a variety of pasta entrees, or tasty Italian daily specials. Daily 11am–9.30pm.

Cassandra's Greek Taverna Kona Square, 75-5669 Ali'i Drive ☎808/334-1066. A friendly European taverna with a large open-air, ocean-view deck across from the *King Kamehameha* hotel. At lunchtime a Greek salad costs $9, or $12 with shrimp, while in the evening appetizers such as *taramasalata* or *dolmades* run to $6–10, a substantial *moussaka* is $18, and sensational *uvetsi* dishes, of shrimps or scallops baked with feta cheese, are $20. Daily 11am–10pm.

Fujimamas 75-5719 Ali'i Drive ☎808/327-2125. Appealing upscale Asian restaurant just south of Moku'aikaua Church in central Kailua,

179

Big Island lūʻaus

There are currently six regular **lūʻaus** on the Big Island, all based at major Kona-side hotels. The *Kona Village Resort*'s *lūʻau* wins hands down for atmosphere, due in part to its remote location.

Island Breeze *King Kamehameha's Kona Beach Hotel* ☏808/326-8111, Ⓦwww.islandbreezeluau.com; Tues–Thurs & Sun 5pm; $68.

Kamahaʻo Lūʻau *Sheraton Keauhou Beach Resort* ☏808/930-4900, Ⓦwww.sheratonkeauhou.com/kamahao.htm; Mon & Fri 5pm; $80.

Kona Village Lūʻau *Kona Village Resort* ☏808/325-4214; Fri 5pm; $85.

Lava Legends and Legacies *Royal Kona Resort* ☏808/329-3111; Mon, Wed & Fri 5pm; $72.

Legends of the Pacific *Hilton Waikoloa Village* ☏808/885-1234; Tues & Fri 5.30pm; $82.

Royal Lūʻau *Waikoloa Beach Marriott* ☏808/886-6789; Wed & Sun 5.30pm; $75.

with a classy indoor dining room as well as lots of outdoor seating beneath giant parasols. Originally based in Tokyo, it serves food from all over Southeast Asia, at very reasonable prices – almost nothing costs over $25, and lunch is a real bargain, with $10 specials including soup, salad and entree. Dinner entrees include satay leg of lamb for $23 or corn crusted opakapaka for $21. Daily, except Mon, 11.30am–2.30pm & 5–10pm.

Kona Inn Restaurant Kona Inn Shopping Village, 75-5744 Aliʻi Drive ☏808/329-4455. This conventional waterfront fish place, on an open-air *lānai* facing the ocean across tranquil lawns, is arbitrarily divided into two sections. The *Café Grill* sells bar snacks, salads, and sandwiches, while on the more formal restaurant menu clam chowder and sashimi feature among the dinner appetizers, and

entrees – mostly seafood, but including steaks – cost $20–30. *Café Grill* daily 11.30am–9.30pm, dinner daily 5–9pm.

Thai Rin Aliʻi Sunset Plaza, 75-5799 Aliʻi Drive ☏808/329-2929. Smart, somewhat minimalist Thai restaurant, facing the sea in front of a modern mall, south of central Kailua toward *Huggo's*. Weekday lunch specials go for $8–9; for dinner, try *satay* or *poocha* (crab and pork patties) to start, for $8–9, followed by either tom yum soup or one of the many Thai curries ($10–17). Daily 11am–9.30pm.

Expensive

Huggo's 75-5828 Kahakai St ☏808/329-1493. Large oceanfront *lānai*, where lunch includes salads, burgers, and sandwiches, for $9–23. The

Shopping

Generally speaking there's little difference among Kailua's various malls, though as a rule those closer to the sea tend to be more firmly geared toward tourists, with the predictable array of T-shirts, sun hats, postcards, and sundry souvenirs on sale, and the odd ABC convenience store thrown in. For everyday shopping and services, locals tend to head for Costco or Kmart, on the northeastern edge of town, or the **Lanihau Center** near the main stoplights on the highway. The **Crossroads Center**, well above town on the main Kuakini Highway, boasts a large Borders bookstore and an even bigger Safeway.

The two-part **Kona Marketplace**, just south of Mokuʻaikaua Church, holds assorted galleries, trinket shops, and jewelry stores, while the **Kona Inn Shopping Village** across Aliʻi Drive, the largest and most tourist-oriented seafront mall, has several clothing stores and activity operators. Perched above the sea at the far southern end of Aliʻi Drive, the modern **Keauhou Shopping Village** centers on KTA and Longs Drug superstores. It also houses a multi-screen movie theater, a post office, a couple of coffee bars, the recommended *Kenichi Pacific* restaurant (see opposite), and a few unexciting fast-food places.

dinner menu features a range of Pacific Rim dishes, including fish stuffed with prawns, typically priced at $25–39. Prices owe as much to the lovely location as to the food, so come while there's light to enjoy the views. For breakfast, the nominally distinct *Java on the Rocks* espresso bar takes over the location. There's often live evening entertainment, usually with Hawaiian music 6–8pm and a local easy-listening band later on. Daily 6.30–11am & 11.30am–10pm, bar open until midnight.

Kenichi Pacific Keauhou Shopping Village ☎ 808/322-6400. Smart sushi/Pacific Rim place in an upscale but anonymous mall, well up from the ocean. It's five miles south of central Kailua, so it's most likely to appeal to hotel guests staying in Keauhou, but the food is unquestionably good, with appetizers like fried squid priced at $8, fish and meat entrees at $21–32, and sushi rolls at $5–10. Mon, Sat & Sun 5–9.30pm, Tues–Fri 11.30am–1.30pm & 5–9.30pm.

Kona Beach Restaurant *King Kamehameha's Kona Beach Hotel*, 75-5660 Palani Rd ☎ 808/329-2911. Completely enclosed, not very atmospheric dining room, with a $15 breakfast buffet every morning. Most full dinners, such as steaks or prime rib, cost around $20, though there's also a $25 Hawaiian buffet on Monday nights; a $29 crab and tempura one on Tues and Thurs; and a $32 seafood and rib buffet on Fri and Sat nights. Sunday's champagne brunch buffet ($32), served 9am–1pm, is the best meal of the week. Mon–Sat 6–10.30am & 5.30–9pm, Sun 6am–1pm & 5.30–9pm.

O's Bistro Crossroads Shopping Center, 75-1027 Henry St ☎ 808/327-6565. Popular, classy all-day bistro, making the most of a dull mall setting adjoining Safeway, just off Hwy-19 a mile up from the ocean. Formerly known as *Oodles of Noodles*, it now claims to serve "world-class cuisine from around the globe," the main difference seeming to be it now serves tacos, burritos and French toast for breakfast. It's a little pricey for lunch, when entrees range $13–23 – dinner entrees reach up towards $30 – but the food is excellent, combining Asian and Italian flavors. A wok-seared *ahi* (tuna) casserole, with shiitake cream, costs $19 all day. Daily 10am–9pm.

South Kona

South of Kailua and Keauhou, the Belt Road, as **Hwy-11**, sets off on its loop around the island by rising away from the sea through attractive verdant uplands. Trees laden with avocados, mangos, oranges, and guavas stand out from the general greenery, and the route is characterized by the blossom of coffee bushes and the occasional aroma of the mills.

Kealakekua Bay, along the south Kona coast, is where Captain Cook chose to anchor in 1779, as it was then both the best harbor and the main population center on the island. Within a century, however, the seafront slopes were largely abandoned, and these days even the area higher up tends to be inhabited only by assorted farmers and New Age newcomers. Most tourists scurry through, put off perhaps by the lack of beaches and the dilapidated look of the small towns that sprawl along the highway. However, many of these hold one or two welcoming local cafés or intriguing stores, and it's certainly worth dropping down to visit the restored **Pu'uhonua O Hōnaunau**, or "Place of Refuge."

Hōlualoa

HŌLUALOA, the first and nicest of the coffee-growing towns, is the only one that's not located on Hwy-11, the main Belt Road circling the island. Instead, you'll only see it if you choose to detour inland and upwards from Kailua. Though located barely three miles from central Kailua, it's a sleepy little village that feels a

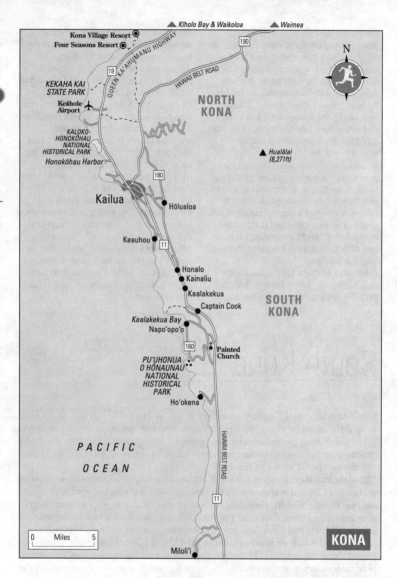

long way removed from the hurly-burly below. It consists of a single quiet road (Hwy-180) that meanders across the flanks of Hualālai, 1400ft up from the ocean, and is lined on either side with small galleries and workshops, as well as orchards brimming with tropical blooms.

Although Hōlualoa has built a reputation for itself as an **artistic community**, the ongoing real-estate boom has served to price many artists and galleries out of the market. Sadly, there isn't nearly as much locally produced art on show here as there once was, and few of the galleries that remain are particularly distinctive.

Kona coffee

Succulent, strong-smelling **Kona coffee** has been grown on the Kona coast since the first seedlings arrived from Brazil in 1828. Strictly speaking, the Kona name only applies to beans grown between 800ft and 2000ft up the western slopes of Hualālai and Mauna Loa. This narrow strip, extending from Hōlualoa to Hōnaunau, offers perfect greenhouse conditions: bright sunny mornings, humid rainy afternoons, and consistently mild nights.

Though Kona boasts an enviable reputation, and demand always outstrips supply, the work of planting and tending the coffee bushes and harvesting the ripe red "cherry" from the tangled branches is too labor-intensive to appeal to large corporations, and the business remains in the hands of around 750 small-scale family concerns. Around four thousand acres are currently under cultivation in Kona, with the long-standing Japanese farmers having been joined by an influx of back-to-the-land *haoles*.

Independent farmers have long campaigned to restrict the label "Kona" to coffee consisting of one hundred percent pure Kona beans. Hawaiian state law, however, which allows any coffee containing at least ten percent Kona-grown beans to be sold as Kona coffee, has had the unfortunate effect of encouraging Californian bulk buyers to use a smattering of Kona beans to improve lesser coffees and then to sell them at inflated prices. In a locally notorious case, the Berkeley-based owner of the Kona Kai brand was convicted in the late 1990s of a multimillion-dollar fraud that involved passing off Costa Rican coffee as true Kona.

Coffee **prices** in the area range from around $20 per pound for the lowest ("prime") grade up to as much as $50 for a pound of the gourmets' favorite, Peaberry. Roadside outlets serve fresh Kona coffee in whatever form you desire. On Nāpoʻopoʻo Road, a mile or so up from the ocean, the **Coffee Roasting Company**, run by the Japanese coffee giant UCC, is a small store that gives out free sample coffees and also has a paying espresso bar (Mon–Sat 9am–5pm, Sun 10am–5pm). The huge, rusty old roasting mill alongside – a former pineapple cannery – belongs to the **Kona Pacific Farmers Cooperative**, and it's both more informative and cheaper to walk around the back of the building to reach their friendly and inexpensive store, where you can buy freshly grown coffee and macadamia nuts and learn more about farming and roasting in general (daily 8am–4pm; ☎808/328-2411, ⓦwww.kpfc.com).

Visitors are welcome at working coffee farms such as the **Bay View Farm**, on Painted Church Road half a mile north of the Painted Church, (daily 9am–5pm; free; ☎808/328-9658 or 1-800/662-5880, ⓦwww.bayviewfarmcoffees.com), and **Greenwell Farms**, just off the highway in Kealakekua (Mon–Sat 8am–4pm; free; ☎808/323-2275 or 1-888/592-5662, ⓦwww.greenwellfarms.com). In addition, the **Kona Historical Society** offers regular tours of the old Uchida coffee farm, restored to illustrate agricultural life during the 1920s and 1930s (1hr tour Mon–Fri 9am–1pm $10; ☎808/323-3222, ⓦwww.konahistorical.org).

The friendly German-owned *Hōluakoa Café* (Mon–Sat 6.30am–3pm; ☎808/322-2233), at the north end of the village, serves **coffees and snacks** in a pleasant garden. On Thursday evenings it also opens from 7pm until 10pm for live music. **Accommodation** in Hōlualoa is reviewed on pp.190–191.

Along Hwy-11: the coffee towns

Technically, there are four separate towns within the first four miles south of the junction of Hwy-180 and Hwy-11, though where one ends and the next begins is far from obvious. Any points of interest can be easily spotted as you drive through, be they wayside coffee stalls, antiquated general stores, local diners, or simply junkyards.

If you want to sample the atmosphere, the best stop comes just south of tiny Honalo, in the shape of **KAINALIU**'s friendly *Aloha Angel Café* (daily 7.30am–8pm; ℗808/322-3383). Housed in the lobby and *lānai* of the 1930s Aloha Theater – still an active theater, with performances by local groups and visiting musicians, along with the occasional movie – this local gathering spot serves coffees, salads, sandwiches, cooked breakfasts and pastries, plus a dinner menu that includes fish tacos ($15), tofu curry ($18), and steak and seafood (up to $23).

A little further on, the funky *Nasturtium Café* is housed in a converted gas station at 79-7491 Mamalahoa Hwy (Tues–Fri 11am–4pm, Sat 10.30am–2.30pm; ℗808/322-5083), though there's much more wood and open space than that might sound – not to mention art on the walls. It offers wholesome, tangy salads and sandwiches, like a grilled eggplant and hummus wrap and even a seared ostrich sandwich, for $10–15.

In **KEALAKEKUA**, a couple of miles south of Kainaliu, the **Kona Historical Society Museum** is set back from the highway in a former general store known as the Greenwell Home (Mon–Fri 9am–3pm; $2; ℗808/323-3222). The low-key collection of photographs and heirlooms documents Kona's history from the perspective of its immigrant farmers, and also offers walking tours of a restored old coffee farm (see p.183). Nearby, just south of mile marker 116, the *Keei Café* (Tues–Sat 5.15–9pm; ℗808/322-9992) is a high-quality local café that has been so successful that it's repeatedly relocated along the highway, each time closer to Kailua and in smarter premises. Now perched above a hot-tub store, it serves an Asian-tinged dinner menu with entrees, including pan-seared fresh catch or rib-eye steak, all priced under $20, and there's an emphasis on home-grown produce.

Immediately beyond Kealakekua, a minor road branches off the highway to lead down to Nāpo'opo'o Beach (see opposite), at the southern end of Kealakekua Bay. Stay on the main road, however, and you soon find yourself in the small community of **CAPTAIN COOK**, which is most noteworthy as the site of the venerable *Manago* hotel and restaurant, reviewed on p.191.

South of Captain Cook's minimal "downtown," *makai* of the highway just north of mile marker 108, the ⚑ *Coffee Shack* (daily 7.30am–3pm; ℗808/328-9555) is the quintessential South Kona café, serving wonderfully fresh coffee on a terrace perched above gorgeous gardens and enjoying staggering views all the way down to Kealakekua Bay. Their smoothies are sensational too, as are the cooked breakfasts and the colossal $8–10 sandwiches using fresh-baked breads like the "Greek Isle," made with olives, feta, and yoghurt.

Kealakekua Bay

KEALAKEKUA BAY may be familiar because of Captain Cook's fatal encounter with the rulers of old Hawaii – as well as the *Little Grass Shack* of the song – but it's a surprisingly inaccessible spot. Very few visitors make it as far as the actual site of Cook's death, on the north shore of the bay, and most of those who see the obelisk to the navigator's memory do so from the south side, across a mile of sea. **Nāpo'opo'o Beach** is the only point that can be reached by car; to see the bay otherwise, you either have to undertake a strenuous hike or come by boat.

The name Kealakekua, which means "pathway of the god," refers to the five-hundred-foot cliff that backs the sheltered crescent bay. It was said that this *pali*, which slopes down from north to south, was used as a slide by the god Lono when

Kealakekua snorkel cruises

The whole of Kealakekua Bay is an **underwater state park**. Much of it is very deep, as the sheer *pali* drops straight down beneath the surface of the ocean. The shallowest and most sheltered spot is in the immediate area of Captain Cook's monument, where the reef provides perfect conditions for snorkelers. Swarms of yellow butterfly fish and tangs, plus parrotfish, triggerfish, and hundreds of other species can always be found circling near the edge.

Snorkel cruises are extremely popular, so the number of vessels allowed into the bay each day is strictly limited. If possible, choose a boat that starts from Keauhou, as this gives you more time at Kealakekua. Bear in mind that passengers are forbidden to set foot ashore, so snorkeling has to be your priority. The following operators are recommended:

Captain Zodiac (☎808/329-3199, ⊛www.captainzodiac.com). Two daily departures from Honokōhau – which is a long way from Kealakekua – in a rubber raft, at 8.15am and 1pm; both last four hours and cost $90 (ages 4–12 $75).

Fair Wind (☎808/345-0268, ⊛www.fair-wind.com). All trips depart from Keauhou Pier. Schedules vary, but as a rule, the large *Fair Wind II* catamaran sails on 4hr 30min trips at 9am daily ($115, ages 4–12 $70) plus 2pm around three days per week ($105/65), while the *Hula Kai* hydrofoil – which only carries passengers aged 8 and over, and also offers scuba diving, operates a 5hr morning cruise daily at 9.30am ($150), plus shorter afternoon snorkeling ($125) or whale-watching trips ($70).

Sea Paradise (☎808/322-2500, ⊛www.seaparadise.com). This spacious sailing catamaran leaves Keauhou daily except Sun at 8.30am ($95, ages 4–12 $60; 4hr).

Sea Quest (☎808/329-7238, ⊛www.seaquesthawaii.com). Bouncy six-person Zodiac rafts without any shade leave from Keauhou at 8am ($85, ages 6–12 $72; 4hr) and 1pm ($64/$54; 3hr).

he needed to leave his mountain home in a hurry. The cliff was created by a massive landslide around 120,000 years ago, which in turn generated an enormous tsunami that washed clean over the island of Kahoʻolawe and reached three thousand feet up the more distant island of Lanai. When Cook was here, around 80,000 Hawaiians are thought to have lived on the coastal lava plain that extends to the north and south. Though the mummified bodies of their chiefs, and possibly that of Cook as well, remain entombed in lava-tunnel "caves" high on the cliff face, all that remains below are overgrown walls and ruined *heiaus*.

Although Kealakekua Bay is officially a "State Historical Park," plans to restore the area around Cook's monument, and build a visitor center atop the cliffs, have yet to come to fruition. The waters of the bay itself are more formally protected as a Marine Life Conservation District, and offer some of the best snorkeling on the island.

Walking to the bay

Walking down to the site where Cook was killed – or, more accurately, walking back up again – is a serious undertaking, though well worth it for keen hikers. With no facilities at the bottom, not even water, you have to carry everything you need; allow a total walking time of at least four hours for the round-trip.

The unmarked trail starts a hundred yards down Nāpoʻopoʻo Road, which leaves Hwy-11 a quarter-mile before Captain Cook. Park where you can here, then start hiking down a dirt road that drops to the right, and keep going straight when that road veers off to the right within a couple of hundred yards. A rutted track, fringed with bright purple and red flowers, continues down for about a mile through open pastureland and avocado orchards. Eventually the vegetation thins

The death of Captain Cook

When **Captain James Cook** sailed into Kealakekua Bay on January 17, 1779, he was on his second visit to the Hawaiian islands, on his way home after a year spent searching in vain for the fabled Northwest Passage. His ship, the *Resolution*, had circled the Big Island for seven weeks, trading with canoes that came alongside but not allowing anyone ashore. Finally Cook anchored in this sheltered bay, where a vast crowd of Hawaiians had gathered to greet him. For three weeks, he was feasted by Chief Kalaniopu'u and his priests, attending temple ceremonies and replenishing his supplies.

The departure of the *Resolution*, amid declarations of friendship, might have been the end of things, had it not been forced to return just a week later, following a violent storm. This time the islanders were not so hospitable and were far from keen to part with further scarce resources. On February 14, Cook led a landing party of nine men in a bid to kidnap Kalaniopu'u and force the islanders to return a stolen small boat. In an undignified scuffle, surrounded by thousands of warriors, including the future Kamehameha the Great, Cook was **stabbed** and died at the water's edge. His body was treated as befits a dead chief: the skull and leg bones were kept, and the rest cremated (though supposedly his heart was eaten by children who mistook it for a dog's).

The **interpretation** of Cook's death has always been surrounded by controversy. It became widely believed by Europeans that the Hawaiians had taken Cook to be the great god Lono. The legend goes that, by chance, Cook had arrived at the temple of Lono at the height of the Makahiki festival, a major annual celebration in honor of Lono. The billowing sails of the *Resolution* were taken to be Lono's emblems, while the ship itself was believed to be the floating island of tall trees on which he was expected to voyage around Hawaii.

Some argue, however, that this story is based in part on a European view of Cook and of primitive people in general, rather than on Polynesian perceptions of the man. The European mentality of the time assumed that a noble figure of the Enlightenment such as Cook must appear god-like to the superstitious "natives." His voyage was

out, and you find yourself on very exposed black lava fields, picking your way over jagged rocks. Avoid climbing this stretch in the midday sun.

From this high vantage point you can discern the worn path of the old King's Trail that once encircled the entire island, paved with river-rounded boulders. The trail then drops abruptly down to the foot of the hill, before pushing its way into a tangle of scrubby undergrowth at the bottom. Soon you can make out the ruined black walls of the long-vanished Hawaiian village of **KA'AWALOA**, half submerged by twisted pandanus trees. Somewhere here stood the house of the high chief Kalaniopu'u, whose attempted kidnapping by Captain Cook precipitated the final drama of Cook's life (see pp.186–187).

The trail reaches the sea at the precise spot where Cook died; a bronze **plaque** lies in a rocky pool under a couple of inches of water. Fifty yards away to the left, on what is legally a small patch of England, stands a white marble **obelisk**, 27 feet high, that was raised to Cook's memory in 1884. Regulations have recently been introduced forbidding anyone from standing on the monument. Visiting ships traditionally set their own small plaques in the cement at its base – a tradition that continues to this day. An equally well-established tradition is for such plaques to be prised away by souvenir hunters, so the most interesting ones, together with all earlier memorials, have long since disappeared.

Snorkelers from visiting cruise boats (see box, p.188) will ensure that you don't have the place to yourself, although they're not allowed to leave the water. There's

perceived by the British as bringing civilization and order to heathen lands, while Cook saw himself as a stern father forever having to chastise the islanders who were his "insolent" children. His last recorded words are "I am afraid that these people will oblige me to use some violent measures; for they must not be left to imagine that they have gained an advantage over us." Cook would have been shocked had he realized that the Hawaiians surmised that "Brittanee" must be suffering from a severe famine, judging by the hunger of its sailors.

Cook may have wanted to be seen as the representative of a superior civilization and creed, but to Pacific islanders his superiority was largely a matter of **firepower**. A common theme in European contacts with the peoples of Polynesia is the attempt to draw well-armed foreigners into local military conflicts. Ironically, in 1777 Cook had sailed away from Tonga, having named it one of "the Friendly Islands," without ever knowing that he had narrowly avoided a plot to kill him and seize his ships. It's impossible now to say whether the elaborate ceremonies at Hikiau Heiau in Kealakekua Bay (see below), during which Cook was obliged to prostrate himself before an image of the god Kū, were designed to recognize him as Lono, or simply an attempt to incorporate him into the *kapu* system (see p.545) as a man of equal ranking with the high chiefs.

The major anomaly in the Cook-as-Lono legend is quite why the Hawaiians would have killed this "god." Some say it was a ritual sacrifice, while others argue that the man who struck the final blow had only just arrived from upcountry, and didn't know that Cook was a "god." The usual explanation, that it was simply an accident, serves both to perpetuate the idea of Hawaiians as "innocent" savages, and to absolve Cook himself of any responsibility for his fate. Though the British version of the dismantling of Hikiau Heiau has the priests eager to cooperate in return for iron trinkets, other sources, including Hawaiian tradition, have Cook's peremptory behavior seen as outrageous, sacrilegious enough to merit his death. That suggests that while the chiefs may well have seen Cook as a valuable potential ally, the priests and commoners viewed him as a blasphemer, and when he antagonized the chiefs by seizing Kalaniopu'u, deference gave way to defiance.

no beach here, so if you want to swim out and join them, you just have to scramble in the best you can.

Napo'opo'o Beach County Park

To drive to the south shore of Kealakekua Bay, follow Nāpo'opo'o Road down from just before Captain Cook as it twists for four miles around the great *pali*. It reaches sea level at the small, usually crowded, parking lot of **Napo'opo'o Beach County Park**, and then continues a few yards north to dead-end at the "beach" itself. Not that there's much of one; Nāpo'opo'o used to be a reasonably pleasant beach, but all its sand has progressively been whipped away – a process completed by Hurricane Iniki in 1992 – and it now consists of a jumble of black lava boulders.

The **snorkeling** at Nāpo'opo'o remains as good as ever, however – once you've eased across the rocks at the water's edge. Fish congregate in greater numbers on the far side, near the conspicuous obelisk, but you may be swimming with the sharks for a mile to get there. Many visitors make the crossing by **kayak** instead. There aren't any rental outlets down here, but there are plenty in Kailua and on the upper highway around Kealakekua town. It's only legal to launch kayaks into the water from the ramp beside the jetty at the parking lot.

For centuries, the waters here have been a favorite haunt of **"spinner" porpoises**. Marine biologists have yet to explain why, but the porpoises gather in schools of up to a hundred individuals to while away the afternoons arching in and out of the water. Mark Twain described them as "like so many well-submerged wheels," but they do vary their routines by spinning vertically and even flipping the occasional somersault. At the end of the day, they head out once more to the open sea, to feed on the deep-water fish that come to the surface at night.

Stone steps beside the end of the road climb the stout black-lava tiers of **Hikiau Heiau**, the temple where Captain Cook was formally received in January 1779. During a baffling ceremony that lasted several hours, he was fed putrefied pig, had his face smeared with chewed coconut, and was draped with red *tapa* cloth. Shortly afterwards, it was also the site of the first Christian service on the islands – the funeral of William Whatman, an elderly member of Cook's crew who died of a stroke. Nothing remains of the structures that once stood on the temple platform – indeed, Cook may well have precipitated his death by dismantling the wooden palings that surrounded it for use as firewood. Visitors are not allowed onto the platform, but it is possible to clamber your way around the perimeter, to get a sense of its scale and atmosphere.

Puʻuhonua O Hōnaunau

A featureless one-lane road runs south from Nāpoʻopoʻo for four miles, across the scrubby coastal flatlands, before meeting another road down from the main highway. The two converge at the entrance to the single most evocative historical site in all the Hawaiian islands, **PUʻUHONUA O HŌNAUNAU NATIONAL HISTORICAL PARK** (daily 7.30am–5.30pm; $5 per vehicle; ☎808/328-2288, ⓦwww.nps.gov/puho; US National Park passes are sold here and valid).

This small peninsula of jagged black lava, jutting out into the Pacific, holds the preserved and restored remains of a royal palace, complete with fishpond, beach, and private canoe landing, plus three *heiaus*, guarded by carved effigies of gods. However, it is most famous for the **puʻuhonua** sanctuary that lies firmly protected behind the mortarless masonry of its sixteenth-century Great Wall.

Visiting the park

Visits to Puʻuhonua O Hōnaunau start at the small information desk at the far end of the parking lot. A schedule of daily talks by rangers is posted here, while immediately to the right is a sequence of large 3-D tiled murals, illustrating themes explained by brief taped messages.

Next you descend along paved walkways through the black lava field, into a grove of rustling giant palms. A couple of typical structures have been erected here on individual lava platforms – a small tent-like shelter for storage, and a larger house, as used by the *aliʻi* (chiefs). To one side is a small but perfect sandy **beach** that once served as the royal canoe landing. Picnicking, sunbathing, and smoking are all forbidden here, but swimming and snorkeling are permitted. Away to the left is the King's Fishpond, as placid as a hotel swimming pool. Various lava boulders nearby were hollowed out by early Hawaiians to serve as bowls or salt pans; one was leveled to create a playing surface for *kōnane*, a game in which black and white pebbles were used as counters.

A simple A-frame thatched structure serves as a carving shed, and usually holds one or two idols on which work is still in progress. Master craftsmen also fashion outrigger **canoes** here, from mighty trunks of beautiful dark *koa* wood.

Beyond the royal area, the L-shaped **Great Wall** – 10ft high and up to 17ft wide – runs across the tip of the promontory, sealing off the sanctuary itself. Its

△ Pu'uhonua O Hōnaunau

northern end is guarded by the **Hale O Keawe Heiau**, once used to house the bones of powerful chiefs, possibly including those of Captain Cook. When dismantled and stripped by Lord George Byron in July 1825, this was the last *heiau* in the islands to remain in perfect condition. Now, like the houses, it has been reconstructed. All the fearsome wooden *ki'i* idols that surround it are modern reproductions, but they're still eerie in their original setting.

Cities of Refuge

Pu'uhonuas used to be promoted to tourists under the name of **"Cities of Refuge"** because of their alleged parallels with the cities mentioned in the Bible. That term is now discouraged, as these were not cities but sacred precincts, and unlike the Jewish model, they served not to protect the innocent but to absolve the guilty. The idea was that any condemned criminal who succeeded in reaching a *pu'uhonua* would undergo a ritual lasting a few hours – at the very most, overnight – and then be free to leave. As *pu'uhonuas* always stood near strongly guarded royal enclaves, however, the condemned had first to run a gauntlet of armed warriors by land, or dodge canoeists and sharks by sea.

The survival of the fittest was a fundamental principle of ancient Hawaiian law, in which might was generally considered to be right. The laws were determined by gods, not men, and concerned not with acts such as theft and murder but with infractions of the intricate system of *kapu* – for which the penalty was always death. *Pu'uhonuas* provided a sort of safety valve to spare prime citizens from summary execution. They served other purposes as well. In times of war, noncombatants, loaded with provisions, could go to the nearest one to sit out the conflict, while defeated armies might flee to a *pu'uhonua* to avoid death on the battlefield. Each island had at least one, and the Big Island is thought to have had six. Other sites included Waipi'o Valley and Coconut Island in Hilo. In addition, certain high chiefs, such as Kamehameha's wife Queen Ka'ahumanu, were considered to be living, breathing *pu'uhonuas*.

Few buildings now stand beyond the wall. Apart from a couple of bare *heiau* platforms, there's just a scattering of trees on the rippling *pāhoehoe* lava that runs into the ocean. One large gray stone, supposedly the favorite spot of the chief Keōua, is surrounded by six holes that may have held the wooden poles of a canopy. Black crabs scuttle across the waterfront rocks, and countless pools are alive with tiny, multicolored fish.

You can't linger on the beach in the main part of the park, but stretches of **public beach** lie both north and south. The northern section, within sight of the sanctuary, is a renowned snorkeling spot, while a short walk or drive south from the parking lot brings you to the more attractive southern section. Even here there's very little sand along the shoreline, which consists of a broad expanse of black lava, but the shady grove beneath the coconut palms makes a great place for a picnic. Visitors who come for the beach alone are not obliged to pay the *pu'uhonua* admission fee.

In ancient times, the coastal flatlands to the south were densely populated, and traces remain everywhere of house-sites and other structures. Much of this area now belongs to the park, which intends at some point to lay out trails through the most rewarding archeological areas.

St Benedict's Painted Church

When you visit the *pu'uhonua*, be sure also to make the slight detour north from Hwy-160, the spur road to Hwy-11, to see **St Benedict's Painted Church**. This small wooden church, an intriguing hybrid of medieval Europe and Hawaii, was decorated between 1899 and 1904 by a Belgian priest, Father John Velge, with brightly colored Biblical and allegorical scenes. Columns with Hawaiian texts erupt into palm leaves on a vaulted ceiling depicting a tropical sky, and the walls behind the altar are painted with a *trompe l'oeil* Gothic cathedral modeled on that of Burgos, Spain. Orchids and *leis* festoon the altar and statuary within, while purple bougainvilleas fill the lush tropical gardens outside. The spectacular views down the hillside at sunset look out over the flat expanse of trees that line the coast between Hōnaunau and Nāpo'opo'o.

South Kona accommodation

Low-key **accommodation** options are scattered throughout the various "coffee towns," ranging from simple village hotels to luxurious B&Bs. Not all are conspicuous from the main road; several of the most distinctive properties are hidden away from view on the lush South Kona slopes.

B&Bs

Aloha Guest House 84-4780 Māmalahoa Hwy, Captain Cook ☎808/328-8955 or 1-800/897-3188 (US & Canada), ⓦwww.alohaguesthouse.com. Comfortable, spacious guest rooms, all en suite, on a German-owned farm a mile up from the highway. There are tremendous views, and rates include fresh fruits and coffee. ⑤–⑦

Dragonfly Ranch: Healing Arts Retreat 84-5146 Keala O Keawe Rd, Captain Cook ☎808/328-2159, ⓦwww.dragonflyranch.com. Tropical retreat, just below the Painted Church, geared to New Age

travelers. While its somewhat basic facilities may be a bit too "back to nature" for some tastes, it offers "vibrational healing modalities" such as lomilomi massage, aromatherapy, and the like. One of the two rooms in the main house has a bathroom, the other just a shower, and there are three separate suites with stereos, TVs, and outdoor showers. Rooms ④, suites ⑤

Hōlualoa Inn B&B 76-5932 Māmalahoa Hwy, Hōlualoa ☎808/324-1121 or 1-800/392-1812, ⓦwww.holualoainn.com. Exquisite B&B, just below the main road through Hōlualoa, three miles and

1400ft up the hill from Kailua. The six tasteful en-suite guest rooms are arranged around a Japanese-style open-plan living room, plus there's a pool, hot tub, and home-grown coffee. A crow's-nest seating area on top of the small central wooden tower looks down on the rest of Kona, enjoying incredible views. Reservations are essential, and there's a two-night minimum stay. No children under 13. **❼**

Rainbow Plantation 81-6327B Māmalahoa Hwy, Captain Cook ☎808/323-2393 or 1-800/494-2829, Ⓦwww.rainbowplantation.com. Appealing en-suite B&B accommodation on a working coffee plantation, off Hwy-11, a quarter of a mile north of the top of Nāpo'opo'o Road. There are two guest rooms, a separate cottage, and even a converted fishing boat. **❸**

Hotels and hostels

Kona Hotel 76-5908 Māmalahoa Hwy, Hōlualoa ☎808/324-1155. Extremely basic, very old-fashioned (and very pink) family-run hotel in the attractive village of Hōlualoa, three miles up-slope from Kailua. The plainest of double rooms go for $30 a night. **❶**

🏃 **Manago Hotel** PO Box 145, Captain Cook ☎808/323-2642, Ⓦwww.managohotel .com. Century-old wooden hotel in the center of Captain Cook, offering some of the best-value and most characterful "local" lodging on the island. Cheaper rooms, in the main building, share bathrooms and have minimal facilities, but those in the newer three-story wing, where the rates rise floor by floor, enjoy magnificent ocean views. Each of the faintly musty conventional suites has a small *lānai*, a strong hot shower, and a period-piece radio, but no phone; there's also one deluxe Japanese room, costing $75 per night. The *Manago's* paneled dining room (daily except Mon 7–9am, 11am–2pm & 5–7.30pm), cooled by whirring fans and ocean breezes, serves full break-fasts for $6, while later in the day a couple of lightly breaded pork chops go for $9.50. **❶–❸**

Pineapple Park 81-6363 Māmalahoa Hwy, Kealakekua ☎808/323-2224 or 1-877/800-3800, Ⓦwww.pineapple-park.com. Clean, appealing hostel-cum-hotel, attached to a kayak rental place on Hwy-11, halfway between mileposts 110 and 111. A bunk in one of the downstairs dorms costs just $25, while en-suite rooms start at $65 per night. The nicest private rooms enjoy far-reaching views, as does the upstairs *lānai*. The same owners run other budget hotel/hostels in Hilo, and near Hawaii Volcanoes National Park; see p.222 and p.268. Dorms **❶**, rooms **❷–❸**

Ho'okena Beach County Park

Continue south along Hwy-11, for just under three miles from the Hwy-160 turnoff, and another small road leads to the sea at **Ho'okena Beach County Park**. The vegetation thins out as you drop the two miles down the hillside, but the park itself is pleasant enough. It consists of a genuine, if grayish, sandy beach, pressed against a small *pali*, and shaded with coconut palms and other trees. Getting in and out of the water across the sharp lava can be a bit grueling, but the **snorkeling** is excellent.

This sheltered, south-facing bay was once a regular port of call for inter-island steamers, but it now houses very few buildings. It does have toilets and a picnic area, and also allows camping; permission must be obtained from the Department of Parks and Recreation in Hilo (☎808/961-8311) at a cost of $5 per day. *Neoki's Corner*, at the foot of the road, sells soft drinks and has public showers.

Miloli'i

The last point in South Kona from which access to the sea is practical is another twelve miles beyond Ho'okena, where a very tortuous five-mile single-lane road winds down the steep, exposed ridge of Mauna Loa. Having reached the sea at **Ho'opuloa** – no more than a few houses on bare rock – the road follows the coastline south, to drop to the small bay of **MILOLI'I**. The tiny stretches of beach here are mere indentations in the black lava along the shore, filled with a scattering of white coral and black lava pebbles, and backed by groves of coconut palms. The thick tongue of the most recent lava flow (dating from 1926) can be seen spilling over the sparse slopes above; it obliterated Ho'opuloa, and disputes over the allocation of land to rehouse the victims lasted for well over fifty years thereafter.

At the south end of the cove there's another county beach park, with a thatched picnic shelter and a rest room, near an especially sheltered pond that's a favorite with children. Camping is once again permitted, but this is too public a spot for that to hold much appeal, and most visitors content themselves with snorkeling around the rocks. A short way back from the sea, the Miloli'i Grocery Store sells snacks and sodas. The road ends next to the pastel-yellow, red-roofed Hau'oli Kamana'o Church.

North Kona

Until the 1970s, it was barely possible to travel overland along the coast **north of Kailua** – and few people had any reason to do so. Then Queen Ka'ahumanu Highway, Hwy-19, was laid across the lava, serving the new airport and granting access to previously remote beaches. Many of these were swiftly engulfed by plush resorts – especially in the South Kohala district – but, with the road running on average a mile in from the ocean, the beaches remain occasional, distant bursts of greenery in an otherwise desolate landscape.

Despite the huge sums spent on all this construction, Big Island tourism is only now starting to approach the scale that was originally envisaged. While Kailua itself is prone to serious congestion, once you get north of the airport you'll notice that the highway system remains more than adequate to handle the volume of traffic.

Honokōhau Harbor

A couple of miles north of Kailua, a short avenue leads down to narrow **Honokōhau Harbor**, which provides safe moorings for the town's pleasure boats and thereby leaves the jetty in Kailua free from congestion. The only reason for coming here is to take one of the many boat trips that leave from the far end of the quay, and the most appealing spot to sit and watch the proceedings is the open-air deck of the *Harbor House* (Mon–Sat 11am–7pm, Sun 11am–5.30pm; ☎808/326-4166), a bar in the central Kona Marina complex that also offers a menu of reasonably priced snacks and sandwiches. To its left is a line of fishing charter vessels, together with an information kiosk on what they offer, the Charter Desk (☎808/329-5735 or 1-888/566-2487, ⓦwww.charterdesk.com).

If you have an hour or two to kill before or after an excursion, you can hike south for ten minutes across the lava to small, secluded and sandy '**Alula Beach**, which is ideal for snorkeling, or take a five-minute walk around to the north of the harbor, which will bring you to the southern access of the Kaloko-Honokōhau National Historical Park.

Boat trips on the Kona and Kohala coasts

Most Kona and Kohala coast boat trips depart from Honokōhau Harbor, though some also leave from the pier in the center of Kailua. Precise timings vary from day to day; contact the companies below for details. Activities desks in Kailua can usually offer discounted rates.

Dive boats

One-dive cruises tend to cost $65–85, two-dive trips more like $95–125, with a $20–30 surcharge for unqualified divers, and equipment rental costing $5 per item. Most operators offer certification courses for upwards of $500. Kailua offers a particular treat in the form of **night dives** to see the massive manta rays attracted by artificial lights around the *Sheraton Keauhou Bay Resort*; prices are similar to those for day dives.

The following is a selective list of recommended operators.

Big Island Divers	☎808/329-6068	ⓦwww.bigislanddivers.com
Aloha Dive Company	☎808/325-5560	ⓦwww.alohadive.com
Jack's Diving Locker	☎808/329-7585	ⓦwww.jacksdivinglocker.com
Kohala Divers	☎808/882-7774	ⓦwww.kohaladivers.com
Kona Honu Divers	☎808/324-4668	ⓦwww.konahonudivers.com
Pacific Rim Divers	☎808/334-1750	ⓦwww.pacificrimdivers.com

Snorkel cruises

Typical morning or afternoon snorkel cruises cost $60–95. The prime destination is Kealakekua Bay; for more details, see p.188.

Body Glove	☎1-800/551-8911	ⓦwww.bodyglovehawaii.com
Captain Zodiac	☎808/329-3199	ⓦwww.captainzodiac.com
Dolphin Discoveries	☎808/322-8000	ⓦwww.dolphindiscoveries.com
Fair Wind	☎808/345-0268	ⓦwww.fair-wind.com
Kamanu	☎808/329-2021	ⓦwww.kamanu.com
Sea Paradise	☎808/322-2500	ⓦwww.seaparadise.com
Sea Quest	☎808/329-7238	ⓦwww.seaquesthawaii.com

Sightseeing cruises

Atlantis Submarines (☎1-800/548-6262, ⓦwww.atlantisadventures.com; $80, under-13s $40). Cramped but fascinating hour-long ocean-floor cruises, with foolhardy divers trying to entice sharks alongside. Daily at 10am, 11.30am, & 1pm from Kailua Pier.

Captain Dan McSweeney's Whale Watch (☎808/322-0028, ⓦwww.ilovewhales .com; $70, children under ninety pounds $60). Between Christmas and March, when there's an excellent chance of sneaking up on some humpback whales, three-hour tours departs 7.30am & 11.30am daily from Honokōhau. In April, and from July to Christmas, the only tours are Tues, Thurs, Sat at 7.30am.

Lilikoi Dawn (☎808/936-1470, ⓦwww.dolphinshawaii.com; $65, under-13s $40). Seasonal whale-watching half-day trips from Honokōhau Harbor.

Deep-sea fishing

Fishing trips cost from $80 per person for a half-day to $500-plus for the entire boat for a full day. For a broad selection of charter vessels, contact the Charter Desk (☎808/329-5735 or 1-888/566-2487, ⓦwww.charterdesk.com).

Kaloko-Honokōhau National Historical Park

The **Kaloko-Honokōhau National Historical Park**, north of the harbor and south of the airport (daily 8am–5pm; free; ℡808/329-6681, Ⓦwww.nps.gov /kaho), was established in 1978 to preserve one of the state's last surviving natural wetlands. It's administered by the National Park Service, which is slowly attempting to achieve the contradictory objectives of restoring the area to its pre-contact appearance, making it accessible to visitors, and keeping it unchanged to protect endangered Hawaiian waterbirds.

As described above, it's possible to walk directly into the oceanfront portion of the park, which most visitors see as its most appealing part, from Honokōhau Harbor. The park service has, however, built a new (and so far not very informative) **visitor center** just off the main highway, half a mile north of the harbor turn-off and immediately south of milepost 97. Although the lava landscape that lies towards the ocean looks forbidding, the trail that drops from the opposite side of the parking lot is surprisingly shady, and offers a pleasant ten-minute stroll through assorted native vegetation.

Once you reach the sea, the obvious direction to head is left, towards the pleasant **'Ai'opio Beach**, where an ancient *heiau*, the Hale O Mono, stands guard over a succession of tiny little sandy coves. (This is also where you'll arrive if you walk in from Honokōhau Harbor.) In the water immediately in front of the *heiau*, shallow walls across the lava form the boundaries of the small 'Ai'opio Fishtrap, in which fish would be deposited at high tide. Walking north along the shore brings you to more sophisticated relics of ancient Polynesian aquaculture, in the form of large artificial **fishponds** used to raise species such as mullet. The first, the 'Aimakapa Fishpond, is now largely the preserve of waterbirds like the *ae'o* (Hawaiian black-necked stilt) and the *alae ke'oke'o* (Hawaiian coot). Beyond that, the massive dry masonry wall of the tranquil Kaloko Fishpond is being rebuilt so that fish can be harvested here once again.

Elsewhere in the mostly trackless expanse of the park, several more *heiaus* as well as a *hōlua* ("land-surfing") slide and fields of petroglyphs lie scattered. Descendants of Kamehameha the Great took pains to reserve this area for themselves, which suggests that one of its countless caves may still hold his bones.

Kekaha Kai State Park

One of the Big Island's least-known but most beautiful beaches, designated as **Kekaha Kai State Park** but also widely known by its old name of Kona Coast State Park, lies a couple of miles north of Kona International Airport (daily except Wed, 9am–7pm; free). You need to keep your eyes peeled to spot the driveway, halfway between mileposts 90 and 91, and then be prepared to bump your vehicle for 1.5 miles over rippling *pāhoehoe* lava, on a virtually unsurfaced but just about passable track that takes a good fifteen minutes to drive each way.

At the bottom of the track, there's a parking lot; from its *mauka* end take the obvious path that sets off northwards across 200 yards of bare lava towards a dense grove of coconut palms. When you come to two portable toilets, you can either cut in through the trees to reach the beach directly, or follow the path round until it emerges in the middle of a perfect horseshoe-shaped bay. All around you is an exquisite beach of coarse golden sand, lightly flecked with specks of black lava – what the locals call "salt and pepper" sand. Each of the headlands jutting to either side is a spur of rougher ʻaʻā lava, topped with its own clump of palms. Immediately behind the beach is the looming bulk of Hualālai, and at this point Mauna Kea becomes visible far inland, as does Haleakalā across the sea on Maui. The calm waters of the bay are ideal for swimming, or boogie boarding when they get a bit rougher in winter. Local surfers ride the tumbling waves offshore, while divers delve into submarine caves and tunnels.

Kekaha Kai State Park has **no food and drink** facilities for visitors.

Kaʻūpūlehu

The area known as **KAʻŪPŪLEHU**, five miles north of the airport, consists of a forbidding expanse of rough, jet-black lava that was deposited by an eruption of the Hualālai volcano in 1801. Its utter inaccessibility led it to be chosen as the site of the *Kona Village Resort* in 1961 – at first, in the absence of a road, all guests and employees alike had to be flown in – though since the appearance of the *Four Seasons Resort* it has felt significantly less secluded.

Four Seasons Resort at Hualālai

First opened in 1996, but still the newest major resort on the Big Island, the sprawling **Four Seasons Resort at Hualālai** (☎808/325-8000 or 1-888/340-5662, ⓦ www.fourseasons.com/hualalai; ⊚) was originally designed as a conventional high-rise hotel. Construction was delayed for several years when the intended site was found to be an ancient Hawaiian burial ground, however, and it was built instead as a complex of smaller units, known as "bungalows" despite being two stories high. On first impression, they're not wildly prepossessing, but the individual rooms inside justify the minimum $700-per-night rate. Each holds a four-poster bed plus a bath and shower, and many have an additional outdoor, lava-lined shower. Set on an exposed headland, the *Four Seasons* stands a bit too close to the ocean for comfort, and unlike the neighboring *Kona Village Resort* it lacks a proper beach – although high surf can unceremoniously dump sand into its three swimming pools. The resort makes up for this, however, with a world-class spa.

The real architectural success of the *Four Seasons* is its gorgeous *Pahuiʻa* **restaurant**, comprising several interlinked wooden pavilions with sliding panels that open them to the ocean. Sea breezes waft in, and spotlights play on the surf, while the food itself is excellent, with a wide range of Asian and American dishes. Appetizers such as a sashimi and *tako poke* combo cost around $20; entrees average around $40.

Kona Village Resort

If you cherish a fantasy of staying in a paradise where every whim is anticipated – and you have unlimited funds – you could do no better than to stay at the oldest of the Big Island's luxury resorts, the ⚐ *Kona Village Resort* (☎808/325-5555 or 1-800/367-5290, ⓦ www.konavillage.com; ⊚). Supposedly it's a re-creation of the Polynesian past, but its main appeal lies in the very fact that it bears so little relation to reality of any kind. Set in the black Kona desertscape, the resort consists of 125 thatched South Pacific–style *hales*, or huts, most of which are surrounded by bright flowers. The huts have no phones, TVs, or radios, but each has a private *lānai*, a hammock, and an alarm clock that wakes you by grinding fresh coffee beans. Beach gear, such as masks, fins, and even kayaks, is provided free for guests, as are tours on outrigger canoes or glass-bottomed boats, while scuba equipment and instruction are also available for a fee. The daily rates of $625 to $1130 for two include all meals at the *Hale Moana* and *Hale Samoa* restaurants; for nonresidents, a four-course dinner at the *Hale Moana* costs $75 and consists of a seafood appetizer, soup, salad, and fresh fish prepared to your exact specifications. Most outsiders visit on *lūʻau* night – Friday – when $85 buys an atmospheric beachside feast plus Polynesian entertainment; advance reservations are essential. While the general upkeep of the resort has slipped somewhat in recent years, and a certain amount of upgrading is clearly overdue, extensive and possibly unwelcome changes may well be in the offing, as the *Kona Village* was sold in February 2007 to Ty Warner of Beanie Babies fame, who also owns the nearby *Four Seasons*.

The resort sits on sandy **Kaʻūpūlehu Beach**, which is superb for snorkeling; stately turtles cruise by, and manta rays billow in at night. Anyone is entitled to visit this isolated strand, though the resort's security guards do their best to discourage nonresidents. There's also a self-guided petroglyph trail on the property.

Kīholo Bay

Bit by bit, as road construction increases along the Kona and Kohala coasts, spots that were previously hidden are coming to the attention of tourists. Among the finest is the superb lagoon at **KĪHOLO BAY**, which until recently most visitors merely glimpsed from afar, from a tantalizing Hwy-19 overlook immediately north of the crest of a small hill, halfway between mileposts 82 and 83.

Kīholo Bay is now easy to reach by car, and it's such a magical spot that it's well worth setting aside half a day to enjoy it to the full. To get there, look out for an unmarked gravel road that heads *makai* (oceanward) from the highway just south of the crest described above. If heading north, be sure not to miss the turning – it's another five miles before you can turn around and head back. The gravel road itself is an easy .8-mile drive; don't stop at the gate on the right near the bottom, but keep going straight, and don't fork left.

From the parking lot at the end of the road, walk to the ocean and head right, and views will soon open up to the north. Three hundred yards along, before a lovely little bay dominated by a private home, a couple of home-made ALOHA signs mark one of the many spots known as **Queen's Bath**, just inland from the beach. This natural freshwater swimming pool, created from a lava tube and entered via a short ladder, offers a chance for a cooling salt-free dip, but really it's one of those places that's more exciting to locals than visitors, for whom the appeal of swimming in the sea seldom wears off.

It takes another twenty minutes or so of following the shoreline to reach the major reason for coming here: a spellbinding crescent lagoon, dotted with black-lava islets that are studded with coconut palms. This idyllic landscape was shaped by an unusual succession of events. First came a lava flow from Hualālai in 1801; then came a huge communal effort by the Hawaiians to enclose the bay to form a shallow fishpond; and finally another lava flow in 1859 breached the walls, filled in much of the pond, and let the sea back in. As well as looking utterly magnificent, the shallow turquoise waters here provide some of the finest swimming and snorkeling in all Hawaii – the only snag is that there's no beach to enter from, so you have to clamber over the rocks instead.

△ Green sea turtle on Kīholo Beach

The South Kohala coast

Though the whole of the western seaboard of the Big Island tends to be referred to as the Kona coast, the most famous of its resorts are in fact situated in the district of **South Kohala**, which starts roughly 25 miles north of Kailua. To confuse matters further, **Kohala Mountain** itself, the oldest and now at around 5000 feet high also the smallest of the island's five volcanoes, forms only the northernmost spur of the island, known as North Kohala (see p.212). South Kohala as it exists today was created by lava flowing from the newer peaks of Mauna Kea and Hualālai; the only vestiges of the original mountain to survive here are the offshore **coral reefs** with which it was once ringed. Erosion from those reefs is the reason why this region boasts the finest of the Big Island's few **white-sand beaches**, and also explains why it's now the Big Island's most prestigious resort destination.

Overlooked by the volcanoes of Mauna Kea, Hualālai, and Kohala – and on clear days by Mauna Loa, to the south, and even Haleakalā on Maui – South Kohala was all but inaccessible by land until the 1960s. The only visitors to the inlets along the shore were local fishermen and the occasional intrepid hiker or surfer. The Hawaiian villages that had once flourished here were long gone, and only wealthy landowners maintained a few private enclaves.

In the forty years since Laurance Rockefeller realized the potential that lay in South Kohala's status as the sunniest area in all Hawaii, the landscape has undergone an amazing transformation. Holes large enough to hold giant hotels have been blasted into the rock, and turf laid on top of the lava to create lawns and golf courses. **Queen Ka'ahumanu Highway** (Hwy-19) pushed its way across the bare lava slopes, and multi-property resorts appeared in quick succession at **Waikoloa** and then **Mauna Lani**, a couple of miles further north.

Most of South Kohala's beaches were probably destroyed by lava early in the 1800s – so the *Hilton*, for example, had to build its own beach from scratch – but as you head north toward Kawaihae you come to some of the finest expanses of sand on the island. These were prime targets for the developers: the first of the luxury hotels was the *Mauna Kea Beach Hotel*, which went up at Kauna'oa in the 1960s, while what may well be the last was the *Hāpuna Beach Prince Hotel*, erected on beautiful Hāpuna Beach in 1994, despite strong local opposition.

Since it's illegal for anyone to deny access to the Hawaiian shoreline, both locals and visitors not staying at the Kohala resorts are entitled to use all the beaches along the coast. Some hotels make things difficult by restricting the number of parking permits they issue to nonguests – as few as ten per day – but so long as you can get to the sea, you're entitled to stay there. For **information** on South Kohala as a whole, and especially on accommodations, contact the Kohala Coast Resort Association (☎1-800/318-3637, ⓦwww.kohalacoastresorts.com).

Waikoloa

For the ancient Hawaiians, the fundamental division of land was the *ahupua'a*, a wedge-shaped "slice of cake" reaching from the top of the mountain down to a stretch of coastline. The name "Waikoloa" referred to such a division, which is why modern visitors are often confused as to where exactly **WAIKOLOA** is.

The community called Waikoloa, generally referred to as **Waikoloa Village**, lies six miles *mauka* of Queen Ka'ahumanu Highway, halfway up to the Belt Road, while the **Waikoloa Beach Resort** – reached by a mile-long approach road that leaves the highway a little way south of mile marker 76, 25 miles north of Kailua – is, unsurprisingly, down by the sea. It holds little more than a couple of hotels and shopping malls, but it's still almost certainly where you want to go if you're looking for Waikoloa.

Hilton Waikoloa Village

The 1240-room ⚐ *Hilton Waikoloa Village*, 425 Waikoloa Beach Drive (☎808/886-1234 or 1-800/445-8667, ⓦwww.hiltonwaikoloavillage.com; garden view ⑥, ocean view ⑦), is almost a miniature city. Guests travel between its three seven-story towers on a light rail system, in canal boats, or along a mile-long network of walkways lined with works of art. While there's no access to the coastline itself, it boasts a four-acre artificial lagoon, complete with waterfalls and a beach of imported sand lined by coconut palms, some of which were flown here by helicopter from Kalapana on the south coast, just before it was engulfed by lava. This synthetic tropical paradise cost a fortune to build, but opened (as the *Hyatt Regency*) in 1988, just in time to be hit by the Gulf War economic downturn. Hilton bought out the original developers in 1993, for a rumored 25¢ on the dollar, and it's now the most popular of the Kohala resorts. If you book through a package-tour operator, it can also work out to be one of the cheapest. However, it can feel a bit like staying in a theme park, and thus appeals most to families with young children and those who are quite happy to see nothing of the rest of the island.

One of the resort's highlights is its independently run "swim with a dolphin" program; although time in the lagoon with your favorite sea mammal can cost anything from $165 for half an hour, the experience is so much in demand that it's essential to reserve, which is possible up to sixty days in advance (Dolphin Quest ☎808/886-2875, ⓦwww .dolphinquest.org).

Surprisingly, neither of the most formal of the *Hilton's* seven **restaurants** – the north Italian *Donatoni's* and the Japanese sushi and teppan-yaki specialists *Imari*, both of which

KOHALA RESORTS

serve dinner only – offers sea views, though they are set in very pleasant buildings, and their food is every bit as good as you'd expect. Immediately above *Donatoni's*, near the Palace Tower towards the northern end of the resort, *Kirin* is a high-quality Chinese restaurant that's open for great, well-priced dim-sum lunches as well as dinner, and has a nice balcony. The breezy *Palm Terrace* in the nearby Ocean Tower presents a different $39 dinner buffet every night, plus breakfast buffets at

$20 and $28. At the opposite end of the property, the *Kamuela Provision Company* offers excellent "Hawaiian Regional" dinners in a relatively casual atmosphere.

Waikoloa Beach Marriott

Although it stands closer to the highway than the *Hilton*, the **Waikoloa Beach Marriott**, 69-275 Waikoloa Beach Drive (☎808/886-6789 or 1-888/236-2427, Ⓦwww.marriotthawaii.com; ⑤), is also set closer to the ocean. Unlike its flamboyant neighbor, it enjoys access to a proper beach, the lovely 'Anaeho'omalu Beach, where available watersports include snorkeling, kayaking, scuba diving, and excursions in glass-bottomed boats and catamarans. The resort used to be a budget alternative to the *Hilton*, but over the years it has upgraded, and it's now a classy and very elegant upscale hotel. Sadly, in the process it has also lost almost all of its former appealing Hawaiian touches, so it can feel a little soulless. All of the 500-plus well-equipped rooms have private balconies, most with ocean views. The principal **restaurant**, *Hawaii Calls* (daily 6–11am & 5.30–9.30pm), offers fine but unexciting all-American dining in the evenings, with entrees priced at up to $35. Beside the pool, *Nalu's Bar & Grill* serves sandwiches and salads alfresco, and there's a twice-weekly *lū'au*, open to all (Wed & Sun 5.30pm; $75 adults, $38 under-12s).

'Anaeho'omalu

The *Waikoloa Beach Marriott* stands at the northern end of a sheltered white-sand beach, which shelves very gradually out to sea. This is a favorite spot with snorkelers and windsurfers, and bathing is generally considered safe. To reach the beach, however, you first have to follow the landscaped walkways that skirt the two ancient fishponds to which this area owes its name. **'ANAEHO'OMALU** means "protected mullet," in recognition of the fact that the mullet raised in the fishponds here were reserved for the use of chiefs alone – *ali'i* voyaging around the island would stop here to pick up supplies. The beach itself also witnessed one moment of high drama, when an unpopular king of Hawaii, Kamaiole, was slain by his rival Kalapana. The ambushers took advantage of the tradition whereby, when the king set off on an expedition, his canoe was always the last to leave the beach.

The Kings' Shops

As a shopping destination, the forty-store **Kings' Shops** mall (daily 9.30am–9.30pm), sited at the point where the approach road splits off to the different hotels, can't begin to compete with Kailua – let alone Honolulu. It is an attractive little spot, however, arrayed along one side of an artificial lake, and its open courtyard features interesting plaques explaining Big Island geology and history. An easy walk from the *Marriott*, if a little far from the *Hilton*, it's regularly thronging with resort guests.

Though the mall holds a number of upscale clothing stores and even a tiny *Macy's* department store, it's best known as a dining venue. As well as Chinese and Japanese restaurants and a small food court with a *Starbuck's*, it's home to *Merriman's Market Café* (daily 11am–9pm; ☎808/886-1700), a casual bistro where $20–30 entrees like tagine roasted mahimahi with lemon couscous have a strong Middle Eastern and Mediterranean flavor. *Merriman's* has plenty of outdoor seating, so it makes a good lunch spot, for salads and sandwiches at $9–14.

The finest food in the Kings' Shops, however, is to be found in the Big Island's only outlet of *Roy's* gourmet restaurant chain (daily 5.30–9.30pm; ☎808/886-4321).

Flamboyant Pacific Rim dinners – best enjoyed in the moonlight on the lakeside terrace – feature dim-sum-style appetizers, designed to share, at $10–14, and entrees such as *shutome* (swordfish) with lemongrass and Thai curry and Waikoloa roast duck at $28–34.

Outrigger Fairway Villas

The rolling green lawns of the Beach Golf Course lie across the lake from the Kings' Shops, but a little closer at hand, along the lake's inland shore, there's another **accommodation** option. The **Fairway Villas**, 69-200 Pohakulana Place (☎808/886-0036 or 1-800/688-7444, ⓦwww.outrigger.com; 2-bed ❻, 3-bed ❽), a condo development operated by Outrigger, is particularly suited to families and larger groups, for whom renting a two- to three-bedroom apartment, each capable of sleeping at least six guests, works out cheaper than staying in one of the hotels. The apartments are spacious and furnished to a high standard, have daily housekeeping service, and share use of a pool and small gym. Check-in is at an office in the Kings' Shops.

The Queens' Marketplace

The latest sign of the South Kohala boom is the construction of the large **Queens' Marketplace** shopping mall, just off Queen Ka'ahumanu Highway at the start of Waikoloa Beach Drive. This book went to press ahead of its scheduled opening, but the new mall had announced that it would focus on the upscale Island Gourmet Market foodstore, and feature a similar range of clothing and accessory stores to the Kings' Shops. As well as a food court and Thai, Mexican and Asian restaurants, expect it to hold the Big Island's first **Sansei's** restaurant, a fabulous Japanese and sushi place that's well established on Oahu and Maui.

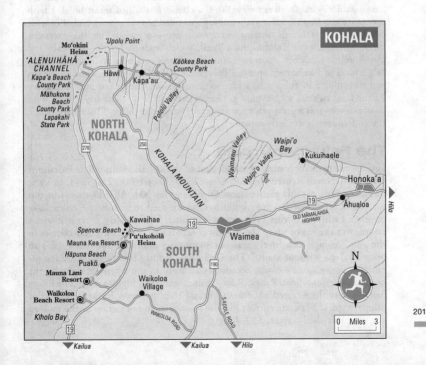

Waikoloa Village

Most visitors to the Waikoloa resorts never head the eight miles up to **WAIKOLOA VILLAGE** itself. Should you want to do so, take the road that leaves Queen Ka'ahumanu Highway a short distance north of the resort turnoff, halfway to Mauna Lani. A small lot at this otherwise desolate inter-section is the base for **helicopter** trips run for resort guests by Blue Hawaiian (℡ 808/961-5600). See p.167 for more on helicopter trips. There's nothing to the village apart from a supermarket, a gas station, a golf course, and the **Waikoloa Highlands Village** mall, which features a couple of snack places.

Mauna Lani Resort

A mile or so north of the Waikoloa Village turnoff, another approach road *makai* of Queen Ka'ahumanu Highway heads through lurid green lawns down to the plush **Mauna Lani Resort**. Two major resort hotels face the sea here in splendid isolation, sharing the use of two golf courses; each has its own small artificial beach, not worth visiting unless you're a guest. The name *Mauna Lani*, a modern coinage, means "mountains reaching heaven," and refers to the misty volcanoes that loom in the distance to the north, south, and east.

Mauna Lani Bay Hotel

With its central building thrusting like an arrow into the Pacific, and an oceanfront golf course to either side, the gleaming white **Mauna Lani Bay Hotel**, 68-1400 Mauna Lani Drive (℡ 808/885-6622 or 1-800/327-2323, Ⓦ www.maunalani .com; garden view ❽, ocean view ❾), is a classic, unabashed resort hotel. Lavish rooms are accessed via a waterfall- and lagoon-filled central atrium, and offer wide ocean views. Traces of ancient occupation are everywhere on the extensive grounds, though the **Kalahuipua'a Trail**, which leads back from the beach and the shoreline fishponds, soon turns into a grueling two-mile walk across craggy 'a'ā lava. The flamboyant open-air Polynesian-style *CanoeHouse*, close to the sea and surrounded by fishponds, serves some of Hawaii's finest but most expensive Pacific Rim cuisine, with typical entrees priced at $35–40. The *Bay Terrace*, with its ocean views, is a great place for breakfast, while the *Gallery* (Tues–Sat), beside the golf course, is similarly superb.

The Fairmont Orchid

Perhaps the most sophisticated and elegant of the Kohala giants is **The Fairmont Orchid**, 1 North Kaniku Drive (℡ 808/885-2000 or 1-800/257-7544, Ⓦ www .fairmont.com/orchid; garden view ❽, ocean view ❾). All 539 rooms in this spacious complex of six-story buildings, which used to be a *Ritz-Carlton*, have en-suite bathrooms with "twin marble vanities," and enjoy extensive views either over the sea or up to the volcanoes across one of the two golf courses in the area. As well as a lovely seafront swimming pool and hot tub, there's an open-air "spa without walls." The *Orchid*'s gloriously breezy signature restaurant, ⚹ *Brown's Beach House*, set almost entirely in the open air right by the beach, serves excellent Pacific Rim cuisine, with the highlights at lunchtime being a succulent seared *ahi poke* ($19) and the "gourmet burger" ($16). For dinner, typical à la carte entrees like the *kiawe*-grilled pork chop or the sautéed *moi* with soft-shell crab are $30–40.

Puakō

An impressive array of ancient **petroglyphs** is located between the *Fairmont Orchid* and the small community of **PUAKŌ**. The Malama Trail to Puakō Petroglyph Park heads inland from the *mauka* end of the Holoholo Kai Beach Park parking lot; there's no drinking water along the mile-long trail which, though not difficult, crosses rough terrain.

For the first 150 yards, the trail is paved, crossing open lava to some replica petroglyphs set up so visitors can take rubbings. From these, you plunge into a tinderbox-dry *kiawe* forest. Five hundred yards in, a few petroglyphs can be discerned on nearby rocks. Many visitors turn back here under the impression that they've seen all there is to see, but you should continue another 250 yards and cross an unpaved track. A short way beyond this track, a fenced-off viewing area brings you to a halt in front of a slightly sloping expanse of flat, reddish rock. This is covered with simple stick figures, most a couple of feet tall, still lying where they were left to bake centuries ago. Laboriously etched into bare *pāhoehoe* lava, the petroglyphs range from matchstick warriors to abstract symbols and simple indentations where the umbilical cords of newborn babies were buried. They're easiest to see early in the morning or late in the evening, when the sun creates shadows.

Holoholo Kai Beach Park is a mixture of black lava and white coral, and not especially good for swimming. Puakō itself is beyond it to the north, but there's no through road from here. It's more of an exclusive residential area than a town, and all you'll see if you turn on to Puakō Beach Drive from Hwy-19, three miles down the road, is a long succession of private villas.

Waialea, Hāpuna, and Kauna'oa beaches

The best of the natural white-sand beaches of South Kohala are along the coast just south of Kawaihae Harbor. Such beaches are formed from the skeletal remains of tiny coral-reef creatures; they're found in the most sheltered areas of the oldest part of the island, because that's where reefs have had the longest time to grow. That they're now at the foot of Mauna Kea rather than Kohala Mountain is because lava from Mauna Kea has progressively swamped its venerable neighbor and redrawn the contours of the coastline.

Of the three best-known beaches, which are separated by short stretches of *kiawe* forest, only the southernmost one, **Waialea**, remains in anything approaching a pristine state. Comparatively small, and sheltered by jutting headlands, it's a perfect base for recreational sailing, while the gentle slope into the sea makes it popular with family groups. The magnificence of both **Hāpuna** and **Kauna'oa** to the north has been marred by the addition of mighty resort hotels.

Hāpuna Beach

With its gentle turquoise waters, swaying palm groves, and above all its broad expanse of pristine white sand, **HĀPUNA BEACH** has often been called the most beautiful beach in the United States. Though in summer it's the widest beach on the Big Island, capable of accommodating large crowds of day-trippers, it always seems to retain an intimate feel, thanks in part to the promontory of black lava that splits it down the middle and cuts it entirely in two when the sands retreat in winter. However, its northern end is dominated by the giant *Hāpuna Beach Prince Hotel*, which opened in 1994 despite bitter opposition from campaigners who treasured Hāpuna's status as an unspoiled state recreation area. Although the hotel is forbidden to leave unoccupied furniture on the beach, to serve food or alcohol there, or to discourage public access to any area below the tree line, hotel guests inevitably dominate the sands north of the promontory.

Nonetheless, Hāpuna Beach remains a delightful public park, well equipped with washrooms and pavilions. To protect body-surfers, who consider this the best spot on the island, surfboards are forbidden. There's always the chance of unruly weather between October and March, so look for the warning flags that fly outside the hotel before you enter the water.

The *Paradise Grill*, perched above the beach, is a simple kiosk that sells burgers, shave ice and other snacks (daily 10am–5pm) and also rents out boogie boards and snorkel sets (daily 9am–4pm). Although tent **camping** is not permitted, six simple A-frame shelters, set well back from the beach itself, above the parking lot, and capable of holding up to four people, can be rented for $20 per night through the state parks office in Hilo (☏ 808/974-6200).

Hāpuna Beach Prince Hotel

Standing roughly six miles north of Mauna Lani, the luxurious ⚐ *Hāpuna Beach Prince Hotel*, 62-100 Kaunaʻoa Drive (☏ 808/880-1111 or 1-888/977-4623, ⓦ www .hapunabeachprincehotel.com; limited view ❽, ocean view ❾), is molded into the hillside north of Hāpuna Beach, but is inevitably somewhat intrusive. The prospect from the inside looking out is superb: the hotel's giant central lobby is open to cooling sea breezes, while the turquoise pool is set flush with a broad patio, complete with whirlpool spa. Few resorts in the world can offer the same combination of opulent accommodation and idyllic situation. Of its two dinner-only gourmet restaurants, the circular ⚐ *Coast Grille* (closed Wed & Thurs); occupies by far the better location, down by the pool in a very stylish two-tier space; it specializes in adventurous Pacific Rim fish dishes, such as *opah* in a ginger and pistachio crust, at up to $40 per entree. At the elegant but viewless Japanese *Hakone* (Fri–Sun), you can get a full sashimi or chicken dinner for $35–50 (though the appetizer may amount to no more than a piece of tofu), or enjoy a copious buffet for $49.

Kaunaʻoa Beach

A mile north of Hāpuna Beach, barely a hundred yards beyond the turn for the *Hāpuna Beach Prince*, and a mile south of the point where Hwy-19 meets Hwy-270, a separate approach road cuts down to reach the ocean at Kaunaʻoa Beach. Like its neighbors, it offers superb conditions for much of the year, but is exposed to very strong winds and high surf in winter, when much of the sand is washed away and swimming becomes very hazardous. The construction here of the *Mauna Kea Beach Hotel*, which opened for business in 1965 as the first of the Kohala resorts, was almost as controversial as the more recent development on Hāpuna Beach. Although local Hawaiians fought and won an eight-year legal battle to have their rights of access respected, Kaunaʻoa Beach swiftly became in effect the hotel's own exquisite private beach.

Mauna Kea Beach Hotel

The forty-year-old **Mauna Kea Beach Hotel**, 62-100 Mauna Kea Beach Drive (☏ 808/882-7222 or 1-888/977-4623, ⓦ www.maunakeabeachhotel.com), was the one major casualty of the October 2006 earthquake on the Big Island. A structural survey early in 2007 revealed its roof to have become unstable, and it was closed for an indefinite period. The property had in any case been showing its age. It was built much closer to the beach than current planning regulations would allow, which meant that any upgrading or reconstruction could only take place on its exact original "footprint." Whether that will now happen, and how long it will take, remains to be seen. Certain facilities remained open as this book went to press, including a weekly *lū'au*, but all its restaurants were closed, and its future seems very uncertain.

Kawaihae

For the ancient Hawaiians, the natural harbor at **KAWAIHAE**, a couple of miles north of Hāpuna Beach, was one of the most important landing points along the coast of the Big Island. Over the last sixty years, massive earthmoving projects have destroyed any beauty that it once possessed, but in terms of population it remains no more than a tiny settlement. That may change from 2009 onwards, when Kawaihae is scheduled to be the point of arrival for regular **Superferry** services from Oahu (see p.32). All kinds of facilities, from accommodation and dining to permanent residential developments, are expected to spring up in the vicinity.

Samuel M. Spencer Beach County Park

The last significant beach along the Kohala coast, **'Ohai'ula Beach**, is one of the few still geared toward low-tech, low-budget family fun. Better known as **SPENCER BEACH PARK**, it offers the best oceanfront campground on the island, as well as full day-use facilities, but it can get very crowded, and with the access road extending along its full length it's seldom peaceful either. No cabins are available: campers are expected to bring their own tents or trailers and to obtain permits in advance from the Hawaii County Parks office in Hilo (T 808/961-8311).

The beach itself, sheltered by a long reef and backed by some amazing gnarled old trees, is popular with recreational swimmers as well as more serious snorkelers and scuba divers, but kayaks are forbidden. It takes a major storm to render bathing unsafe.

Pu'ukoholā Heiau National Historic Site

PU'UKOHOLĀ HEIAU has to be the single most dramatic and imposing Hawaiian temple still standing on any of the islands (daily except holidays 7.30am–4pm; free; T 808/882-7218, W www.nps.gov/puhe). Its construction between 1790 and 1791 by the future Kamehameha I is one of the greatest – and most horrific – epics of Big Island history, and it's well worth allowing an hour of your time to explore the site.

The history of Pu'ukoholā Heiau

The story of this *luakini*, a "war temple" fed by human sacrifice, began in 1782, when the young warrior **Kamehameha** seized control of the northwest segment of the Big Island. Over the years that followed, he conquered Maui, Lanai, and Molokai, but failed to defeat his rivals on the rest of his home island of Hawaii. Eventually, when he heard that his cousin Keōua wanted to expand out from Ka'ū, in the southwest of the Big Island, Kamehameha sent his aunt to consult the prophet **Kapoukahi** of Kauai, who suggested that building a *luakini* at Pu'ukoholā and dedicating it to his personal war god Kūkā'ilimoku would guarantee success in the coming conflict.

Kapoukahi himself came to the Big Island to oversee the construction of the new temple, on the site of a ruined *heiau* erected two centuries before by the legendary Lonoikamakahiki. The process was accompanied throughout by exacting ritual: in the words of an old Hawaiian proverb, "the work of the *luakini* is like hauling *ohia* timber, of all labor the most arduous." First of all, the entire island had to be purified, by means of clearing the circle road and erecting altars at regular intervals.

For Kamehameha's rivals, the start of work was a clear announcement of impending war. They set out to sabotage the project, knowing that its completion would give Kamehameha irresistible *mana*, or spiritual power. Not only Keōua, but also the defeated chiefs of Maui, Lanai, and Molokai, and even the rulers of Kauai and Oahu, joined forces to attack, but Kamehameha managed to hold them all off and pressed on with construction.

When the *heiau* was completed, in the summer of **1791**, the prophet ordained a great feast, involving the sacrifice of 400 pigs, 400 bushels of bananas, 400 coconuts, 400 red fish, 400 pieces of *oloa* cloth, and plenty of human beings, preferably those possessing considerable *mana*. Kamehameha therefore invited Keōua to attend the dedication and make peace. Like a figure from Greek tragedy, Keōua accepted the invitation.

The moment Keōua stepped ashore on the beach, he was slain with a spear thrust by Kamehameha's trusted warrior Ke'eaumoku (the father of Queen Ka'ahumanu). All his companions were also killed before Kamehameha, who later insisted that he had not sanctioned the slaughter, called a halt upon recognizing the commander of the second canoe as his own son Kaoleioku. Keōua's body was the main sacrifice offered, together with those of ten of his associates (the war god, who did not like blood on his altar, preferred his victims to have been killed elsewhere).

As sole ruler of the Big Island, Kamehameha went on to reconquer first Maui, Lanai, and Molokai, then Oahu, all of which had been recaptured by their original rulers during the building of the temple. Finally he exacted tribute from Kauai, whereupon the whole archipelago took on the name of Kamehameha's native island, and thus became known as Hawaii.

The altar and idols at Pu'ukoholā were destroyed in 1819 on the orders of Kamehameha's successor Liholiho, shortly after the breaking of the ancient *kapu* system (see p.534).

Visiting Pu'ukoholā Heiau

The parking lot for the *heiau* stands just off Hwy-19, at the start of the approach road to Spencer Beach Park and next to a small visitor center. The temple's three colossal tiers of black stone are not immediately visible from here, so follow the signed trail for a couple of hundred yards down toward the sea.

As the path rounds "the hill of the whale" after which the *heiau* was named, the vast platform of the temple – 224ft long by 100ft wide – looms above you, commanding a long stretch of coastline. Disappointingly, this is as close as you'll get; access is forbidden, in part because this remains a sacred site, but also because recent earthquake damage has rendered it unstable. No traces survive of the thatched houses and other structures that originally stood upon it – the Hale Moi, the smaller Hale Kahuna Nui for the priest, the oracle tower and drum house, and the lava altar that once held the bones of human sacrifices are all gone.

A little further toward the sea stands the subsidiary **Mailekini Heiau**, narrower but longer, and much older, than the main temple. It, too, is inaccessible to visitors. Both *heiaus* loom large above **Pelekane Beach**, which you are free to walk along, although nowadays it's not all that spectacular. In Kamehameha's era the beach was far longer, and there was a royal compound in the palm grove just back from the sea. The land that now lies immediately to the north is infill created during the construction of Kawaihae Harbor, when the beach itself was largely obliterated.

Breeding sharks still circle the **Haleokapuni Heiau**. Dedicated to the shark deities, it was built under water and still lies beneath the waves around 100ft out. The voracious beasts would devour offerings beneath the watchful gaze of the king, who would stand beside the stone Leaning Post that's still visible – though now in a sorry state – above the shore. Swimming is neither permitted nor particularly desirable: if the sharks aren't enough to put you off, the water is also clogged with gritty silt, which has completely obscured, and probably damaged, the underwater *heiau*.

Kawaihae Harbor and Shopping Center

Despite remaining without a wharf until 1937, **KAWAIHAE HARBOR** has long been the most important anchorage on the leeward coast of Hawaii. It was always the major port for the cattle of the Parker Ranch (see p.210); in the old days, intrepid cowboys would swim both cows and horses from the beach out to sea, then lasso them in the water and lash a dozen of them to the outside of flimsy whaleboats, which in turn rowed them to larger vessels anchored offshore.

The bay was finally dredged by the military during the 1950s. Casualties of the process included an assortment of delightful, grassy islands, each of which held a thatched shack or two, and most of the Big Island's best coral reef. Nevertheless, the port has long remained relatively low-key, poorly protected from occasional violent storms, and with few services nearby. Its biggest flurry of activity for many years came with the much-troubled filming of the Kevin Costner blockbuster *Waterworld* in 1994–95, during which the movie's centerpiece, a floating "slave colony," sank at least once to the bottom of the harbor.

Assuming the **Superferry** does commence sailings from Oahu to the Big Island in 2009 – which rather depends on how successful its services to Maui and Kauai prove to be – Kawaihae may well be transformed beyond recognition in the years to come. For the moment, however, what few shops and restaurants it holds are concentrated in the **Kawaihae Shopping Center**, a small, two-story mall at the junction of Hwy-19 and Hwy-270. As well as a few clothes stores and the high-quality Harbor Gallery of fine arts, there's a *Café Pesto* (Mon–Thurs & Sun 11am–9pm, Fri & Sat 11am–10pm; ℡808/882-1071), serving the same menu of delicious calzones and pizzas as the branch in Hilo (see p.229). Upstairs and around the back, you'll find a Mexican bar-restaurant and the very "local" *Kawaihae Grindz* (Mon–Fri 6am–8pm, Sat & Sun 7am–3pm; ℡808/882-7776), which serves cooked breakfasts and plate lunches.

Nearby on Hwy-19, the *Kawaihae Harbor Grill* (daily 11.30am–2.30pm & 5.30–9.30pm; ℡808/882-1368) is a fine-dining restaurant where dinner entrees like Thai chicken, red curry, or straightforward steaks cost $20–30. It makes a somewhat cheaper alternative to the resort restaurants, but it's hard to see why you'd drive out here (rather than, say, Waimea) in the dark. That said, its large *lānai* makes a good spot for an early-evening cocktail.

Waimea and the Kohala uplands

The only town of any significant size in Kohala, **Waimea**, is poised between north and south, a dozen miles up from the sea on the cool green plains between Kohala

Mountain and Mauna Kea. For many of the visitors who climb inland from Kawaihae on Hwy-19, the interior of Hawaii comes as a surprise. These rolling uplands are cowboy country, still roamed on horseback by the *paniolos* of the United States' second largest private cattle ranch, the **Parker Ranch**. Only when you look closely at the occasional rounded hills that dot the landscape do you spot signs of their volcanic origin; many are eroded cinder cones, topped by smoothed-over craters. The fact that temperatures are distinctly cooler here than by the sea is one reason why locals are moving to Waimea in ever-increasing numbers; visiting sun-worshippers tend not to be quite so keen.

Waimea

Kohala's largest community, **WAIMEA**, is no longer the company town it used to be; the Parker Ranch now employs just one hundred of its eight thousand inhabitants. While still proud of its cowboy past – memorabilia of the much-mythologized *paniolos* (see p.211) are prominent everywhere – Waimea has become more of a sophisticated country resort and is now home to a diverse community that includes international astronomers from the Mauna Kea observatories and successful entrepreneurs from the mainland. Poised halfway between the contrasting Kohala and Hāmākua coasts, Waimea has "wet" and "dry" sides of its own; it's the drier Kohala side, not surprisingly, where real estate is at a premium.

There's not all that much to Waimea as a destination; most visitors simply while away an afternoon or so enjoying its dramatic setting between the volcanoes. What town there is consists of a series of low-slung shopping malls lining Hwy-19 to either side of the central intersection, where the road makes a sharp turn toward Honoka'a and Hilo. The most interesting gift and souvenir shopping is to be had at little **Parker Square**, on the west side of town, which holds several intriguing specialty stores. The much larger **Parker Ranch Shopping Center** is home to the local post office and the visitor center for the ranch itself (see opposite); head a quarter-mile east from here to see an appealing little cluster of clapboard churches, set well back from the road.

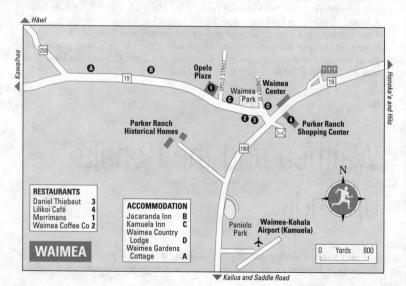

RESTAURANTS
Daniel Thiebaut 3
Lilikoi Café 4
Merrimans 1
Waimea Coffee Co 2

ACCOMMODATION
Jacaranda Inn B
Kamuela Inn C
Waimea Country
Lodge D
Waimea Gardens
Cottage A

WAIMEA

To avoid confusion with other Waimeas on Kauai and Oahu, the post office calls the Big Island's Waimea "Kamuela." Neither older nor more authentic, this name is simply a nineteenth-century corruption of "Samuel," one of the many scions of the house of Parker.

Arrival and accommodation

Waimea's tiny **airport**, in the rolling ranchlands just south of town, sees very little use. The only airline offering scheduled service is **Pacific Wings** (☎808/887-2104 or 1-888/575-4546, ⓦwww.pacificwings.com), which operates daily flights to Honolulu and Kahului on Maui.

Few visitors spend the night in Waimea, although it's one of the most pleasant towns on the island; the chief drawback is that the nights are significantly colder here than down by the ocean. For Hawaii residents, that's a plus point, so accommodation is often booked well in advance.

Jacaranda Inn 65-1444 Kawaihae Rd ☎808/885-8813, ⓦwww.jacarandainn.com. Once the home of a Parker Ranch manager, this century-old house is now a charming luxury B&B, with eight en-suite guest rooms and a lavish separate three-bedroom cottage. Rooms ⑤, cottage ⑨

Kamuela Inn 65-1300 Kawaihae Rd ☎808/885-4243 or 1-800/555-8968, ⓦwww.hawaii-bnb .com/kamuela.html. Former motel, set back from the road a half-mile west of the central intersection, within easy walking distance of several restaurants. Refurbished and given an extra wing, it holds rooms of generally high quality, all with private baths, and some "penthouse suites" with kitchenettes. Rates include basic continental breakfast. The same owners also operate the five-room *Log Cabin B&B*, a lovely rural lodge just outside Āhualoa on the Old Māmalahoa Highway (see p.212). Rooms ❷, suites ❸, *Log Cabin* shared bath ❷, en-suite ❸

Waimea Country Lodge 65-1210 Lindsey Rd ☎808/885-4100 or reserve through Castle Resorts ☎1-800/367-5004, ⓦwww.castleresorts.com. Simple motel backing onto the Kohala slopes, at the start of the road to Kawaihae from the junction in the center of Waimea. It may look a little shabby from the outside, but the rooms themselves are large and perfectly acceptable. There's also a run-of-the-mill steakhouse on-site. ❹

Waimea Gardens Cottage PO Box 563, Kamuela HI 96743 ☎808/885-4550, ⓦwww.waimea gardens.com. Upmarket and hospitable B&B two miles west of central Waimea, with two large and comfortable guest cottages; one has kitchen facilities and both have private bathrooms. Both are furnished with antiques and a library of Hawaiiana; the cottages boast views toward the rolling Kohala hills. Three-night minimum stay; reservations essential. ❺

Parker Ranch Visitor Center and Historic Homes

The small **Parker Ranch Visitor Center**, hidden away at the back of the Parker Ranch Shopping Center in central Waimea (reach it via the food court), provides an overview of Parker family history as well as the general history of Hawaii. Its primary focus is upon displays of old ranching equipment, with a hut from the ranch crammed with saddles, spurs, bottles, and cowboy paraphernalia. A short video evokes the atmosphere of ranch life, with footage of cattle being swum out to waiting steamers, and of a dawn round-up high on Mauna Kea. Closer to the front of the mall, the *Parker Ranch Store* sells *paniolo* accoutrements like belts, checked shirts, and Stetsons as well as more conventional island crafts and souvenirs.

You may find your interest in the Parker family starting to flag at the so-called **Historic Homes**, half a mile out of Waimea toward Kailua, on Hwy-190. Construction of the stately **Puʻuʻōpelu** started in 1863, but it was completely remodeled in 1969 and now lacks any apparent connection with things Hawaiian. Its pastel yellow rooms are filled instead with minor European paintings, while

△ Horses grazing in North Kohala

through the air waft the melodious tones of its last owner, Richard Smart, in recordings he made as a Broadway musical star.

The **Mana House** alongside looks like an ordinary white clapboard house, but the interior gleams with dark, heavy *koa* wood, which groans under your every step. These timbers were the only components robust enough to be moved in 1970, when it was decided to reconstruct the house here, twelve miles from the site where it originally went up during the 1840s. The walls of the tiny building are packed with family documents and fading photographs.

Five hundred yards beyond the Historic Homes toward Kailua, **Paniolo Park** hosts the **Parker Ranch Rodeo** every July 4 (for information, contact ☎ 808/885-7655 or ⓦ www.parkerranch.com).

The Parker Ranch

At its largest, in the nineteenth century, the **Parker Ranch** spread across more than half a million acres of the Big Island. It still covers around ten percent of the island, currently holding around 50,000 cattle on over 150,000 acres. The bulk of the land is divided into three huge parcels: one takes up most of North Kohala, one curves around the higher Hāmākua reaches of Mauna Kea, and the largest runs for forty miles up the western slopes of Mauna Kea from the ocean at Kawaihae.

It all dates back to **John Palmer Parker**, a ship's clerk from Massachusetts, who jumped ship in Kawaihae Harbor in 1809 and soon came to the attention of King Kamehameha, who gave him the job of maintaining the fishponds at Hōnaunau (see p.188).

In February 1793, Captain George Vancouver of the *Discovery* had presented Kamehameha with six cows and a bull and suggested that a *kapu* be placed on the cattle to allow a population to grow. By 1815, wild cattle had become a serious problem, destroying crops and terrorizing villages, and wild mustangs too were roaming unchecked. Kamehameha gave Parker permission to shoot the cattle, and from a base near Pololū he set out to impose discipline on the unruly beasts. With the decline of the sandalwood trade, the supply of fresh beef and hides to visiting

Parker Ranch practicalities

Visitor Center	daily except holidays 9am–4.45pm, last entry 4pm, $6.50, under-12s $5.50.
Historic Homes	Mon–Sat except holidays 10am–5pm, last entry 4pm, $9/7.
Combined ticket, sold	9am–3pm only, $15/11.50.
Wagon Tours	hourly Tues–Sat 10am–2pm, $15/12.
Parker Ranch Experience	all the above $27/20.50.
Horse Rides	daily 8.15am (2hr), 12.15pm (2hr), & 4pm (1hr 30min), $80.

For more information, contact ☎808/885-7655 or ⊛www.parkerranch.com.

whalers became crucial to the Hawaiian economy. Parker managed the business for the King, and by taking his pay in live animals built up his own herds. Marrying Kamehameha's granddaughter **Kipikane**, he soon integrated into local society and was one of only two foreigners present at the famous banquet in 1819 when Liholiho broke the age-old *kapu* on men and women dining together (see p.534). He moved to the village of Waimea in 1835, where he established his homestead at Mana and built a separate house there for his son, John Palmer Parker II.

The ponchos, bandanas, and rawhide lassos of the Mexican, Native American, and Spanish *vaqueros* who were brought to work on the ranch were adopted by the Hawaiian cowboys they recruited and trained. They called themselves **paniolos** (from *Españoles*, or Spaniards).

Like many outsiders, Parker seized his opportunity in the Great Mahele of 1847, when private land ownership was first allowed (see p.537). He was granted two acres, and his wife, Kipikane, received 640 more. Soon he was in a position to buy another thousand acres and to lease the entire *ahupua'a* (see p.542) of Waikoloa.

After Parker's death, the ranch was divided among his immediate heirs, and much of it then frittered away by the high-living **Samuel Parker**, before the property was reunified under Thelma Parker in 1906. Attempts to diversify into sugar production and beekeeping came to nothing, but the cattle ranch went from strength to strength for the rest of the twentieth century. When the last Parker to control the operation, the sixth-generation **Richard Smart**, died in 1992, he chose to leave just one percent of his holdings to his family. The ranch now belongs to a charitable trust, with assorted schools and health-care facilities in the Waimea area among the beneficiaries of its profits.

Restaurants

To befit its status as one of the Big Island's most exclusive residential areas, Waimea holds a couple of gourmet **restaurants**. In addition, a few old-style cowboy places are still piling up meaty mountains of ribs, while the Waimea Center mall, down the road toward Hilo, is the place to head for fast food, with *McDonald's, TCBY,* and *Subway* outlets.

Daniel Thiebaut 65-1259 Kawaihae Rd ☎808/887-2200. Classy, beautifully styled Mediterranean-Pacific restaurant in the timber-framed "Historic Yellow Building," a short way up from Parker Square, which specializes in Asian-style searing and spicing but combines them with rich European sauces. Appetizers like Hilo sweetcorn crab cakes or chicken wontons cost under $10; prices for entrees such as wok-fried scallops and five-spice-dusted duck breast run to $30. There are also vegetarian options, while the lunch menu combines modern Hawaiian staples like tuna salad niçoise ($11.50) with "*paniolo* favorites" like meatloaf ($8.50). Mon–Fri 11.30am–2pm & 5.30–9pm, Sat 5.30–9pm.

Lilikoi Cafe Parker Ranch Center ☎ 808/885-1686. Clean, busy deli next to the Parker Ranch Visitor Center, which serves salads and sandwiches for $6–10, and daily lunch specials such as meatloaf for $10. Mon–Sat 7.30am–4pm.

Merrimans Opelo Plaza, 65-1227A o Rd ☎ 808/885-6822, ⊛ www.merrimanshawaii .com. This gourmet restaurant, with its emphasis on organic produce, has regularly been voted the best on the Big Island. Lunches are simple, with a $10 bowl of saimin on the menu. Dinner entrees,

priced at $24–35, tend to be much richer, but the signature wok-charred *ahi* is superb. Check out their website for details of farm tours, combined with tastings. Mon–Fri 11.30am–1.30pm & 5.30–9pm, Sat & Sun 5.30–9pm.

Waimea Coffee Co Parker Square ☎ 808/885-4472. Lively café where the fresh coffee is complemented by an array of inexpensive soups, salads, and sandwiches, all priced at $7–8. Mon–Fri 7am–5pm, Sat 8am–5pm, Sun 9am–4pm.

Onwards from Waimea

Whichever direction you head from Waimea, there's spellbinding scenery just a few miles down the road. Heading east toward Hilo on Hwy-19 brings you to Honoka'a in less than twenty minutes, with Waipi'o Valley not far beyond (see p.237). From an intersection just six miles south of Waimea, the **Saddle Road** starts its dramatic climb across the heart of the island between Mauna Kea and Mauna Loa – a journey covered in detail on p.242. The most attractive drive of all is **Hwy-250** along Kohala Mountain to Hāwī. However, the transition from the dry to the wet side of the Big Island can be experienced at its most pronounced if you make a slight detour off Hwy-19 three miles east of Waimea and follow the atmospheric and little-used **Old Māmalahoa Highway**.

Old Māmalahoa Highway

Once part of Kamehameha's round-island trail, the **Old Māmalahoa Highway** was known to the ancient Hawaiians as "mudlane" and was notorious as a site where '*oi'o*, or processions of the souls of the dead, might be encountered at night as they headed for the underworld said to lie below Waipi'o Valley. Now it's a minor road, somewhat slow and sinuous, but not difficult, even for cyclists.

The road heads first through treeless volcanic uplands where the rolling meadows, misty when they're not windswept, are grazed by horses and cattle. After about eight miles, you abruptly plunge into a magnificent avenue of stately old ironwoods. Thereafter, the vegetation is tropical and colorful, and homes with glorious gardens dot the hillside. Soon after passing through the residential community of **Āhualoa**, you rejoin the Belt Road near Honoka'a.

North Kohala

The district of **North Kohala**, which officially starts four miles or so north of Kawaihae, to all intents and purposes comprises the low-rise flanks of Kohala Mountain itself. Spreading across both sides of the mountain, it's a microcosm of the whole island, with its dry leeward side separated by rolling uplands from the precipitous wet valleys of the eastern coastline. The road that curves around the

Kohala Mountain adventures

Perhaps the best way to experience the unique backcountry of Kohala Mountain is on a guided **adventure tour**. Two companies offer daily **4WD tours** into the hills, at prices ranging upwards from $100 for ninety minutes: Hummer Safari Tours, based in Hāwī (☎808/889-6922, ⓦwww.bigislandhummertours.com), and ATV Outfitters in Kapaʻau (closed Sun; ☎808/889-6000 or 1-888/288-7288, ⓦwww.atvoutfittershawaii.com).

You can also see the mountain on **horseback**. Naʻalapa Stables (☎808/889-0022, ⓦwww.naalapastables.com) sets off daily into the uplands from the ironwoods of Kahua Ranch on Hwy-250 (2hr 30min ride at 9am, $90 per person; 1hr 30min ride at 1.30pm, $70). Paniolo Riding Adventures (☎808/889-5354, ⓦwww.panioloadventures .com), based at Ponoholo Ranch on Hwy-250, offers similarly priced rides. Dahana Ranch, on the Old Māmalahoa Highway outside Waimea (☎808/885-0057, ⓦwww .dahanaranch.com), features 1hr 30min rides for $60, plus the more unusual experience, on demand, of joining a 2hr 30min cattle drive for $130.

north comes to an end at **Pololū Valley**, the last of a chain of valleys that begins with Waipiʻo (see p.237). Like Waipiʻo, Pololū was home to generations of ancient taro farmers; in fact, two centuries ago this region was the original powerbase of Kamehameha the Great, and several sites associated with Hawaii's first monarch can still be seen. The traditional Hawaiian way of life came to an end in 1906, when the waters from Pololū were diverted for irrigation. By 1975, the last of the sugar plantations had closed down, and these days the area is relatively unpopulated, scattered with tiny and characterful communities that are attempting to diversify into coffee and macadamia nut production.

Though North Kohala holds some of the most beautiful of all the Big Island's scenery, few visitors take the time to explore it. Its major drawback is that access to the sea is restricted on both the leeward side, which is almost entirely devoid of beaches, and the rugged windward coast. While little accommodation is available, several local businesses are encouraging day-trippers to take adventure expeditions up into the hills, and there are a number of appealing little restaurants and snack bars.

Across the mountain: Hwy-250

With a maximum elevation of 5408 feet, Kohala Mountain is considerably lower than its younger Big Island rivals. Its summit is always green, never covered by snow, and its smooth velvet knobs betray few traces of their violent volcanic past. This landscape might not conform with what's usually thought of as Hawaiian, but the varying views you get of it from a trip along **Hwy-250** are among the most sublime in the entire state.

For the first four miles or so out of Waimea, as the highway climbs the west flank of Kohala Mountain, a panorama of the Kohala coast gradually unfolds. At first the rolling lava landscape is covered with wiry green turf. Then scattered trees start to appear, together with clumps of flat-bladed cactus, often growing straight out of bare outcrops of chunky black lava. Higher still you enter proper ranching country; for a while the road becomes an avenue lined with two rows of splendid ironwood trees, between which you catch glimpses of undulating pastureland grazed by sleek horses. At various points along the way, vivid green turf-covered cinder cones bulge from the meadows, speckled with black and brown cattle.

Unfortunately, you never get the chance to turn off the road and explore the magnificent scenery higher up the mountain. As well as large landholdings of the Parker Ranch, concentrated at the northern end, there are several other private estates and even one or two old-style cattle-ranching communities hidden away along the northern half. The top of the mountain is a surreal landscape of eroded hillocks, which across the watershed become so thickly forested as to be almost impenetrable. Rudimentary trails lead down to valleys such as Waipi'o, and the rough terrain is still cut through in places by irrigation channels such as the famous **Kohala Ditch**, constructed in the early 1900s to service the sugar industry.

Along the coast: Hwy-270

The only alternative to Hwy-250 if you want to see North Kohala is the coastal **Hwy-270**, which heads north from Kawaihae Harbor. Most visitors drive a circular route that takes in both; the shoreline road is not as immediately attractive, but it does offer a handful of interesting historic sites, the occasional beach park, and, in winter, the possibility of spotting humpback whales in the waters of the 'Alenuihaha Channel.

For its first dozen miles Hwy-270 has no access to the ocean; the only practical way to snorkel in the bays at the foot of the low cliffs is to join a boat excursion from South Kohala.

Lapakahi State Historical Park

Fourteen miles north of Kawaihae, the first turning *makai* of the highway leads a short way down to **Lapakahi State Historical Park** (daily 8am–4pm; free). The ancient village of Koai'e that stood here is thought to have been inhabited for more than five hundred years until it was abandoned during the nineteenth century.

A hot, exposed, but fascinating one-mile-long trail leads through what appears to have been a sizeable subsistence-level community of ordinary Hawaiians. They probably chose this site because of its white coral beach and lack of cliffs, which made it the safest year-round canoe landing for many miles. Sustaining a population on such barren land must always have been hard, and the struggle seems to have been defeated in the end by a combination of a drop in the water table and the economic changes taking place in the islands as a whole.

You pass the villagers' dwelling places – not necessarily roofed, their low walls served primarily as windbreaks – as well as assorted traces of their day-to-day life. Most of these are simply hollowed-out rocks; some were used to hold lamps, others served as salt pans of varying depths, and there's even a little indented stone, holding scattered black and white pebbles, used to play the game *konane*. Beside a fish shrine, where offerings would have been left to ensure a successful catch, a carved decoy rests on an open net; the shy *ahu* fish was captured when it attempted to make friends with its wooden counterpart.

The **beach** at Lapakahi is composed of medium-sized boulders rather than fine sand. This is a marine conservation area, and the water is very clear, with parrotfish and darting yellow shapes visible in its turquoise depths. The one place visitors are allowed to enter the water is north of the ancient village, and even there the use of sunscreen and towels is forbidden. Strictly speaking, you're only permitted to snorkel here, not swim, though quite how you can do one without the other is not specified. From the bluff near the end of the trail, you can see Maui's towering Haleakalā Volcano.

Mo'okini Heiau and the Kamehameha Birthplace

At the island's northernmost tip, beyond the nondescript Mahunukona and Kapa'a beach parks (both of which are seldom suitable for casual swimming), a long, straight road drops down to the perimeter fence of 'Upolu's barely used military airport. From there, an unpaved road winds west along the coastline, degenerating frequently into semi-permanent pools of mud; only very rarely, when it has recently received one of its occasional regradings, is its full length fully passable in an ordinary rental car. There are no trees along this exposed and windy stretch, where the rolling meadows halt a few feet up from the black lava shoreline.

One of Hawaii's remotest but most significant ancient temples, **Mo'okini Heiau**, is roughly two miles from the airport. It's accessible from a rudimentary parking lot, via a footpath up a small bluff. Though the gate is usually locked, visitors can go through the gap in the low walls. The *heiau*, in the center of a large green lawn, is a ruined but impressive pile of lichen-covered rocks; you can enter the structure and discern the traces of separate rooms, as well as a boulder on which victims were prepared for sacrifice.

Two conflicting legends make the temple's origins obscure. Its current guardians state that it was built between sunset and sunrise on a single night in 480 AD by Kuamo'o Mo'okini, using water-worn basalt stones passed from hand to hand along a fourteen-mile human chain from Pololū Valley. Alternative sources suggest it was created by the Tahitian warrior-priest Pa'ao seven centuries later, as a temple to Kū, the god of battle. The most likely explanation, though, is that Pa'ao simply rededicated an existing temple to Kū; it may even have been the site where the practice of human sacrifice was first introduced to Hawaii. The Kahuna Nui, the hereditary priesthood of Kū, has maintained an unbroken descent; the traditional *kapu* barring female priests has long since been broken, however, and the current Kahuna Nui, Leimomi Mo'okini Lum, is the seventh woman to hold the position. She rededicated the *heiau* to the children of Hawaii in 1977, and crowds of schoolchildren now come here to learn about ancient Hawaiian spirituality.

A few hundred yards further along, the **Kamehameha Akahi Aina Hanau** is a low, double-walled enclosure that slopes down a little closer to the sea. Kamehameha the Great is said to have been born here in 1758 – the date is known thanks to the appearance of Halley's Comet – at a time when his parents were in the retinue of King Alapa'i, who was preparing to invade Maui. Whisked away in secret and brought up in Waipi'o Valley, he returned to live in Kohala in 1782. The entrance to the large compound is from the south, *mauka* side; you can't go into the central enclosure, which amounts to little more than a patch of scrubby soil scattered with a few boulders. One rock marks the precise birthsite; visitors still leave offerings to Hawaii's greatest ruler on the walls nearby.

Hāwī

Thirty years after the closure of its *raison d'être* – the Kohala Sugar Company mill – the tiny town of **HĀWĪ**, a mile beyond the 'Upolu turnoff, is hanging on as one of the nicest little communities in Hawaii. It's an attractive place, with its all-purpose stores, galleries, and snack outlets connected by old creaking boardwalks, and every yard bursting with bright flowers.

Once you've filled up with gas at the intersection of highways 250 and 270, there's nothing to see or do in Hāwī beyond strolling across the village green and along the hundred yards of its main street. However, the spacious 🌿*Bamboo Restaurant and Bar*

(Tues–Sat 11.30am–2.30pm & 6–9pm, Sun 11am–2pm; ☏808/889-5555) ranks as one of the Big Island's best **restaurants**, serving "island-style" cuisine in a dining room furnished with bamboo and rattan furniture and festooned with tropical plants. A lunchtime salad, burger, or plate of stir-fried noodles costs $7–14, while dinner entrees ($15–30) include fish cooked to your specification in a range of styles such as "Hawaii Thai," as well as chicken, beef, and lamb from local farms. A colossal plate of barbecued ribs costs $19. There's live Hawaiian music on Friday and Saturday evenings, and the attached store-cum-gallery sells attractive *koa*-wood gifts and other crafts. A few yards further up the street, in the Hāwī Hale building, *Sushi Rock* is a tiny, funky **sushi** restaurant (Mon, Tues, Thurs & Sun noon–3pm & 5.30–8pm; Fri & Sat noon–3pm & 5.30–9pm; ☏808/889-5900), where rolls like the ten-piece Pele's Inferno, containing *ahi* and white fish and chili, cost $6–15. If you're just after a light snack, the *Kohala Coffee Mill* (Mon–Fri 6.30am–6pm, Sat & Sun 7am–5.30pm; ☏808/889-5577), across the street, has fresh Kona coffee plus burgers, bagels, and ice cream.

Hāwī also holds a very well-priced **accommodation** option, in the appealing shape of the 🏠 *Kohala Village Inn*, 55-514 Hāwī Rd (☏808/889-0404, 🌐www .kohalavillageinn.com; rooms ❷–❸, suites ❹). Tucked away just off the highway intersection, it's a single-story, timber "plantation-style" building, which means that all the simple but tastefully furnished rooms, all of which have en-suite facilities, open onto an internal veranda and open courtyard. The two-bedroom suites are especially good value. An adjoining Pacific Rim restaurant, run by the same management, was not yet open at press time.

Kapaʻau

The main feature in the even smaller hamlet of **KAPAʻAU**, a couple of miles east of Hāwī on Hwy-270, is its **statue** of King Kamehameha. The original of the one facing ʻIolani Palace in Honolulu (see p.89), it was commissioned from an American sculptor in Florence for the coronation of King Kalākaua in 1883, lost at sea, and then miraculously recovered after the insurance money had paid for a replacement. Kamehameha had established his headquarters in Hāawa in 1782, in order to prepare for the imminent contest over the right to succeed the ageing King Kalaniopuʻu. All traces of Hāawa were ploughed over to plant cane many years ago, but it was very close to where modern Kapaʻau now stands, and so this sleepy town seemed a reasonable alternative location for the surplus statue.

Immediately behind the statue, the former courthouse now serves as the **Kohala Information Center** (Mon–Fri 10am–4pm). Staffed by local senior citizens, it holds a few rudimentary exhibitions, but it's basically a place to hang out. *Kohala Rainbow Café*, opposite (daily 10am–6pm; ☏808/889-0099), serves sandwiches, salads, wraps, smoothies, and all sorts of ice cream. In the restored Nanbu Hotel building, just up the street, the smart little *Nanbu Courtyard* (Mon–Fri 6.30am–4pm, Sat 8am–1pm; ☏808/889-5546) sells espresso coffees and lunchtime deli sandwiches, while the well-stocked and welcoming *Kohala Book Shop* (Mon–Sat 11am–5pm; ☏808/889-6400, 🌐http://kohalabooks.big808.com) claims to be the largest used bookstore in Hawaii.

Not far to the east of town, a narrow road *mauka* of the highway squeezes between some spectacular old banyans and coconut palms to reach the four-square stone and shingle **Kalāhikiola Church**, built in 1855.

Blue Hawaii

Defined and shaped, wooed and caressed by the Pacific Ocean, the Hawaiian islands make an irresistible destination for anyone who loves the sea. Some set out to master it atop a surfboard; some simply play in it, swimming or boogie-boarding; and some dive to explore coral caverns or snorkel on the surface. Others are happy to admire it from a distance, strolling the golden sands of long, empty beaches. All have to share it with other species, like the mighty migrating humpback whales who spend their winters here, and the spinner dolphins that wheel in and out of the water.

▲ Punalu'u Beach, Big Island

Hawaii's best beaches

Whether you're a swimmer, a snorkeler, or just a snoozer, Hawaii has the perfect beach for you. For the safest swimming, pick a beach with a sandy, slowly shelving floor and consistently gentle waves; obvious examples are resort beaches such as **Waikīkī** on Oahu, and **Kā'anapali** and **Wailea** on Maui, but they inevitably tend to get very crowded. Quieter alternatives include the gorgeous **Kailua Beach** on Oahu, and **Kekaha Kai** and **Hāpuna** beaches, for most of the year at any rate, on the Kona coast of the Big Island. Keen snorkelers prefer to swim in shallow waters with a rocky or coral floor, in which case Oahu's **Hanauma Bay** and **Kē'ē Beach** on Kauai's North Shore offer the perfect combination of a lovely sandy shoreline with fish-filled waters.

The exposed western coasts of each island hold spectacularly long beaches of deep golden sand, which are fabulous to walk on but far too dangerous for swimming; these include **Mākena** or **Big Beach** on Maui; **Pāpōhaku Beach** on Molokai; Polihua on Lanai;

▼ Mākena Beach, Maui

and the longest of the lot, Polihale or Barking Sands on Kauai. The surfing beaches of Oahu's **North Shore** are similar, except on the calmest summer day – great to look at, but deadly to swim in.

Then there are the **black-sand beaches**. Genuine black sand is created when fragments of fresh lava are washed ashore; such beaches seldom survive for long, as they're either simply washed away again, or engulfed by further lava flows. The Big Island has lost some incredible jet-black strands to the current Kīlauea eruption, but can still boast ravishing little **Kehena Beach**, deep in the Puna rainforest, and larger **Punalu'u Beach** further west, while Maui has lovely **Wai'ānapanapa Beach**. And finally, a couple of real oddities: the tiny **Red Sand Beach**, reached by a precarious footpath from Hāna on Maui, and the remote **Green Sand Beach** near the Big Island's South Point.

▲ Tribute to the legendary surfer Duke Kahanamoku, Oahu

Kings of the surf

While the peoples of Polynesia invented **he'e nalu**, or "wave-sliding," as much as four thousand years ago, it was the ancient Hawaiians who turned it into a fine art. It truly was the sport of kings; only the *ali'i*, of noble blood, were permitted to **surf** using the largest boards – huge *koa*-wood planks, measuring sixteen feet or more and weighing up to 150 pounds – or to surf the finest breaks. Great fortunes were staked on contests in which several surfers would catch the same wave and race to a fixed point. Ancient descriptions say they mostly lay on raised elbows, like modern boogie-boarders, and it was relatively unusual to stand erect; they even had an equivalent to tow-in surfing, whereby a surfer would leap with his board from a speeding canoe.

Hawaiian surfing all but died out during the nineteenth century, discouraged by the missionaries both because of its spiritual significance and because it was fun. Its re-emergence at the start of the twentieth century was spearheaded by the iconic Waikīkī Beach Boys, led by Olympic gold-medalist **Duke Kahanamoku**, but it took major changes in technology from the 1950s onwards, such as the development of fins and lightweight fiberglass boards, to win it true international popularity. If you fancy learning, surfing lessons are available at all the major tourist resorts, with the best beginners' breaks at Waikīkī on Oahu, Lahaina on Maui, and Po'ipū on Kauai. Whatever previous experience you may have, familiarize yourself with conditions elsewhere on the islands before tackling the premier-league sites.

The best breaks

Pilgrims flock from all over the world to test their skills in the home of surfing, and each of the major islands holds its own legendary sites. Oahu's North Shore is perhaps the finest of all, with mighty tubular waves breaking just a few feet out from gorgeous sandy beaches like Waimea Bay, backed by a lovely valley, and Sunset Beach, home to the fabled Banzai Pipeline. On Maui, Honolua Bay at the northern tip of West Maui is a magnificent bay where spectators can watch the action from the fields above, while the colossal waves at Jaws, east of funky Pā'ia, are only accessible via jet-ski. Kauai's greatest site is spectacular Hanalei Bay, in view of the spectacular NāPali cliffs, while on the Big Island, surfers paddle out from the lush rivermouth at Honoli'i Beach outside Hilo.

▶ Surfing at Sunset Beach, Oahu

Humpbacks on holiday

Between two and five thousand **humpback whales** migrate south from Alaska each year to winter off the shores of Hawaii; that's around half of the total North Pacific population, the rest of whom head for Mexico and Japan. Measuring up to 45ft long, and weighing up to 45 tons, they don't eat at all while they're in Hawaiian waters. Instead they come to court, and mate, and then a year later, all being well, to give birth and introduce their calves to the world. Experts believe they've only been wintering in Hawaii since the early nineteenth century, partly because Hawaiian myth and legend make so little reference to them. And although Hawaii was once a gathering place for the great whaling fleets, humpbacks were never hunted here, because unlike the "right" whale their bodies would sink when they were killed.

The whales are especially fond of the shallow channels between Maui, Molokai, and Lanai, which since 1992 have formed the center of the **Hawaiian Islands Humpback Whale National Marine Sanctuary**. Between late November and early April, they make themselves astonishingly conspicuous, through such display behaviors as slapping the water with their tails and pectoral fins, or "breaching" – leaping right out of the water. During that time, **whale-watching** boats set off from all the major islands, and on Maui in particular you're all but certain of a sighting. In fact you'll probably see them even if you stay on shore, whether from roadside vantage points or simply from the beach. Very few people get to see whales underwater – although you can clearly spot them from a helicopter, suspended in the turquoise ocean – but you may well hear them. Snorkelers at Kāʻanapali, for example, frequently hear the whistles and grunts of singing whales, whose "song" changes each year and is common to all the humpbacks in the Pacific.

▼ A humpback off the coast of Maui

Kēōkea Beach County Park

The road on from Kapaʻau runs past the site of Hāawa; a huge wayside boulder at this tight curve is known as **Kamehameha Rock**, as the future king is said to have demonstrated his right to rule by having sufficient *mana*, or spiritual power, to raise it above his head.

Immediately beyond, a lane leads, via a Japanese cemetery dotted with small black steles, down to **Kēōkea Beach County Park**. Here, in the center of a rocky bay, a small stream flows into the ocean, and the surrounding hillsides have been pounded to pieces by high surf. An open-sided lookout shelter, exposed to the winds on a small hillock, makes a nice picnic spot, but there is no beach.

A short way along the side road to the beach, *Kohala's Guest House*, PO Box 172, Hāwī HI, 96719 (℡808/889-5606, ⓦwww.kohalaguesthouse.com; ❷), doubles as both a **B&B** for short visits and a longer-term vacation rental. Each of the two separate houses has three guest rooms, and there's also a separate studio with kitchenette. The rooms are clean and comfortable, the rates are excellent, fruit trees fill the yard, and owner Nani Svendsen delights in sharing her extensive knowledge of North Kohala with her guests.

Pololū Valley

As Hwy-270 reaches its dead end at a tiny parking lot, you get a view over one final meadow to the open cliff face that abuts the sea. Stretching away into the distance, it's punctuated by a succession of valleys, only accessible to visitors on foot and each therefore progressively less frequented and wilder than the last. The last of the chain, not visible from here, is Waipiʻo (see p.237); the first, spread out beneath you, is **POLOLŪ VALLEY.**

If not quite on the scale of Waipiʻo, Pololū was also once heavily planted by taro farmers. Regular tsunamis did little to encourage a stable population, however, and the death knell came when completion of the Kohala Ditch in 1906 drained the valley's previously plentiful water supply off for use on the nearby sugar plantations.

△ Pololū Valley

Pololū Valley remains a magnificent spectacle, and nowhere more so than from the initial overlook. If you take the time to explore it close up you may well find the hike down less strenuous, and more private, than its better-known equivalent further east. The pedestrian-only trail from the end of the parking lot takes twenty minutes without ever being steep, but when it's wet – which is almost always – it's an absolute quagmire of gloopy brown mud. Conditions are at their worst at trail's start, which drops immediately into dense, head-high grasses. From there you wind down the hillside among ironwood, guava, and *hala* trees. Occasionally the trees yield to stretches of loose lava pebbles, a welcome relief from the prevailing mud with glimpses of the shore below.

Once on the valley floor, the trail remains thoroughly mucky as it approaches the broad river-cum-lake that meanders across the terrain, surrounded by marshy reeds. Hikers who try to head inland are swiftly confronted by "Private Property" signs warning you to go no further.

Though Pololū's **beach**, like the one at Waipiʻo, is commonly referred to as being black sand, it's basically gray grit, littered with decaying detergent bottles and pulverized flotsam. More welcome touches of color are added by the yellow and purple blooms backing the black lava rocks. In winter, the shore is prone to strong winds and heavy surf; there's no question of swimming even at the best of times. Depending on whether the rocks are currently piled up to block its mouth, you may have to wade across the shallow but fast-flowing stream to reach the longer segment of the beach; take care if so, as high water is capable of carrying hikers out to the sharks offshore. On the far side of the stream, the beach is lined by gentle woodlands of pine-needle-covered hillocks that are grazed by mules and horses.

Onwards from Pololū

A conspicuous but virtually impossible-to-follow trail switchbacks eastwards from Pololū over to the next valley, **Honokāne Nui**, and on to Honokāne Iki beyond that. The track doesn't go all the way through to Waipiʻo, so at some point the few suicidal hikers who attempt it have to double back. As a rule the path follows the contours of the hillsides and doesn't drop back down to the sea each time, but it's in roughly the same bedraggled condition as the trail down to Pololū and is certainly no easier. Only experienced wilderness backpackers should even consider an expedition into this remote and uninhabited terrain.

Hilo

Until a couple of decades ago, windward Hawaii's major city, **HILO**, was the economic and political powerhouse of the island. It's still the capital, and home to forty thousand people, but with the sugar mills closed and the scale of Kona-side tourism growing ever greater, it now feels more like a rather traditional small town. As a place to visit, it's relaxed and attractive, spread over a surprisingly large area but with an appealingly old-fashioned downtown district where you can stroll between friendly cafés, street markets, and historic sites.

Hilo made its first bid to become a major tourist center in the early 1970s, and is still trying hard, having expanded its harbor facilities to attract more cruise ships and constructed a major new astronomy museum. Thus far, however, mass tourism has never taken off; quite simply, it rains too much. Hilo averages 130 inches of rainfall annually, with fewer than ninety rain-free days per year. Most mornings, however, start out clear and radiant; the rain falls in the afternoon or at night, leaving America's wettest city ablaze with wild orchids and tropical plants.

As well as having the only **airport** along the Hāmākua coast, Hilo holds all its **hotels**. There are no sizeable sandy beaches, and tourists who come here are drawn either by the beauty of the nearby coast, or the relative proximity of Volcanoes National Park. The fifty-mile excursion up to Waipiʻo Valley is hard to resist, but nearer at hand you can enjoy the delightful Pepeʻekeo Scenic Drive, or the mighty ʻAkaka and Rainbow falls.

A brief history of Hilo

Hilo stands where the Wailuku and Wailoa rivers empty into an enormous curving bay, named "Hilo" by ancient Hawaiians in honor of the first crescent of the new moon. In 1796, Kamehameha the Great chose the best natural harbor on the island to build his *peleleu*, a fleet of eight hundred war canoes for his campaigns against the other Hawaiian islands. Characterized by his enemies as "monstrosities," these hybrid Western-influenced vessels carried mighty armies of warriors; some say they were never destroyed and still lie hidden in caves along the Kona coast.

Thanks to a strong missionary influence, the port prospered in the nineteenth century as a clean-living alternative to dissolute Honolulu. In the words of the evangelist Titus Coan in 1848:

No man staggers, no man fights, none are noisy and boisterous. We have nothing here to inflame the blood, nothing to madden the brain. Our verdant landscapes, our peaceful streets, our pure cold water, and the absence of those inebriating vials of wrath which consume all good, induce wise commanders to visit this port in order to refresh and give liberty to their crews.

Hilo became the center of the Big Island's burgeoning sugar industry, shipping out raw cane and serving as the arrival point for immigrants from around the world, and in the process acquired an unusually radical labor force. From the 1930s onwards, local workers spearheaded successive campaigns against the "Big Five" companies that had long dominated the Hawaiian economy (see p.537). Fifty people were injured in the "Hilo Massacre" of August 1, 1938, when strikers were attacked by armed police, and strikes in 1946 and 1949 helped to end the long-term Republican domination of state politics.

The innermost segment of the bay, encompassing both port and town, is protected by a long breakwater. In principle, this is a very calm stretch of water, but its funnel shape means that during great storms it can channel huge waves directly into the center of town. Cataclysmic tsunamis killed 96 people in April 1946, and an additional 61 in May 1960. Lava flows have also repeatedly threatened to engulf Hilo; in 1881 Princess Ruth Keʻelikūlani summoned up all her spiritual power (see p.259) to halt one on the edge of town, while in 1984 another flow stopped eight miles short.

Arrival

Compact and walkable, downtown Hilo focuses on the junction of seafront Kamehameha Avenue and Waiānuenue Avenue, which heads toward the Saddle Road across the island. However, the urban area extends for several miles, and

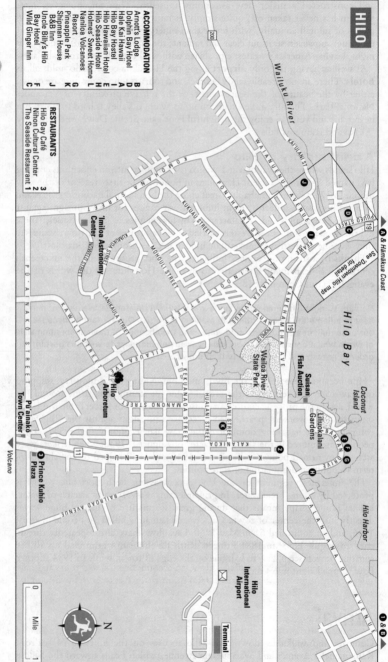

Saddle Road & **L** ▲

▲ Rainbow Falls

ACCOMMODATION
Arnott's Lodge — B
Dolphin Bay Hotel — D
Hale Kai Hawaii — A
Hilo Bay Hostel — I
Hilo Hawaiian Hotel — E
Hilo Seaside Hotel — H
Holmes' Sweet Home — L
Naniloa Volcanoes
  Resort — G
Pineapple Park — K
Shipman House
  B&B Inn — J
Uncle Billy's Hilo
  Bay Hotel — F
Wild Ginger Inn — C

RESTAURANTS
Hilo Bay Café — 3
Nihon Cultural Center — 2
The Seaside Restaurant — 1

Wailuku River

See Downtown Hilo map for detail

▲ & Hamākua Coast

KAI'ULANI ST

WAIĀNUENUE AVENUE

PONAHAWAI STREET

PŪʻUEO STREET

19

200

KAMEHAMEHA AVENUE

KUKUAU STREET

KINOOLE STREET

KĪLAUEA AVENUE

MOHOULI STREET

KĪLAUEA AVE

LANIKAULA STREET

KAWILI STREET

PĪ ʻO ʻA ʻN ʻA ʻK ʻO ʻ S T R E E T

KILAUEA AVE

'Imiloa Astronomy Center

Hilo Arboretum

KEKŪANAOA STREET

MANONO STREET

PAUAHI STREET

KALĀKAUA STREET

HUALANI STREET

PILANI STREET

KĪNOʻOLE STREET

Wailoa River State Park

Suisan Fish Auction

Hilo Bay

Coconut Island

BANYAN DRIVE

Liliʻuokalani Gardens

KALANIANAʻOLE AVENUE

Hilo Harbor

19

KAMANA STREET

Pūʻāinakō Town Center

▲ Volcano

KANOELEHUA AVENUE

11

KALANIKOA STREET

RAILROAD AVENUE

Prince Kūhiō Plaza

Hilo International Airport

Terminal

N

0   Mile   1

▲ L & B

Hilo–Kona bus timetable

	From Hilo	To Hilo
Hilo Prince Kūhiō Plaza	1.10pm	10.05am
Hilo Mooheau Bus Terminal	1.30pm	9.45am
Pepe'ekeo	1.45pm	9.30am
Honomu	1.50pm	9.25am
Laupāhoehoe	2.10pm	8.55am
Honoka'a	2.40pm	8.30am
Waimea Parker Ranch	3.20pm	8.05am
Waikoloa	3.45pm	7.25am
Kailua Lanihau Center	4.25pm	6.45am
Keauhou *Kona Surf*	4.50pm	6.25am
Kainaliu	5.05pm	6.15am
Captain Cook	5.15pm	6.00am
Hōnaunau	5.20pm	5.55am
Kealia	5.30pm	5.45am

Mon–Sat only; fares 75¢–$6. Call ℡808/961-8744 for more details.

Hilo International Airport (℡808/935-4782), on the eastern outskirts, is well beyond walking distance. If you're not renting a car at the airport, you'll need to take an $8 taxi ride into town.

Limited **bus** service is offered by the Hele On Bus Company (℡808/961-8744). Its base, **Mooheau Bus Terminal**, is an open-air bayfront pavilion on Kamehameha Avenue, between the two highways. In addition to city routes geared to commuters, and the Kona service detailed in the box above, there are a few longer-distance services. On weekdays only, the "9 Pāhoa" leaves Hilo at 8.45am, 1.30pm, 2.40pm, 4.45pm, and 9pm, to reach Pāhoa, twenty miles southeast of Hilo, just over an hour later; the "7 Downtown Hilo" leaves Pāhoa five times between 6am and 5.40pm. Several daily buses also run from Hilo to Honoka'a and Waimea, but almost all are extremely early in the morning. The bus to Hawaii Volcanoes National Park and Ocean View, which leaves Mooheau Bus Terminal at 2.40pm on Monday through Friday only, is detailed on p.254.

Details of helicopter and fixed-wing **flight-seeing** operators based at Hilo International Airport appear on p.167; there are, however, no boat trips on this side of the Big Island.

Information and services

The **Hawaii Visitors Bureau** is at 250 Keawe St, one block up from the bayfront in the center of downtown (Mon–Fri 8am–4.30pm; ℡808/961-5797, ⓦwww.bigisland.org). Its helpful staff can advise on accommodation and tours and have piles of brochures available. The rival Hilo Information Center, run by the county, forms part of the Mooheau Bus Terminal on Kamehameha Avenue (daily 8am–5pm).

Hilo's main **post office** (Mon–Fri 8.15am–4.45pm, Sat 8.30am–12.30pm) is on the approach road to the airport, but there's another one downtown in the Federal Building on Waiānuenue Ave (Mon–Fri 8am–4pm). **Banks** are dotted all over town and in the malls, with the most central branch of the Bank of Hawaii based at 117 Keawe St.

Accommodation

Although downtown Hilo is short of **hotels**, several options line the oceanfront crescent of **Banyan Drive**, a mile or so southeast. Sadly, although the state has promised to provide incentives for regeneration, most of these have become rather rundown in recent years. In addition, there are also a number of B&Bs in the vicinity, while a couple of welcoming and inexpensive inns can be found north of the Wailuku River, a short walk from downtown.

Room rates are lower on this side of the island, in part because hotel owners assume that you'll be out exploring the volcanoes or the Hāmākua Coast during the day and therefore don't supply lavish on-site amenities. If that is what you're going to be doing, there's no great reason to spend more than a couple of nights in Hilo.

Arnott's Lodge 98 Apapane Rd ☏808/969-7097, ⓦwww.arnottslodge.com. Laid-back but safe and clean budget accommodation in a two-story, motel-style lodge just off the road to Onekahakaha Beach, a couple of miles southeast of downtown. Shared dorms hold twelve beds for $25 each, while they also have semi-private double rooms, sharing bathrooms, for $60, and fancier en-suite rooms in nearby buildings for $72. You can also camp in the grounds for $10. There's a tree house and bar, and Internet access, but no food except a free Sat-night pizza feast. Also available are one free airport shuttle daily, "clunker" bike rental for $3 per day, and assorted van day-trips; excursions to the lava flows in Volcanoes National Park cost $65, while the summit of Mauna Kea is $70. Those same trips are available to non-guests at considerably higher rates. ❶–❸

Dolphin Bay Hotel 333 Iliahi St ☏808/935-1466 or 1-800/935-1466, ⓦwww.dolphinbayhilo.com. Very friendly little hotel within walking distance of downtown across the Wailuku River, set out like a motel on two levels. All the spotlessly clean studios and one- and two-bedroom suites are equipped with TV, bathroom, and kitchen, but not phones. No pool or restaurant, but free papayas and bananas dangle enticingly, and the owner is a mine of useful advice. ❸–❹

Hale Kai Hawaii 111 Honoli'i Pali ☏808/935-6330, ⓦwww.halekaihawaii.com. Small, comfortable B&B, perched above the ocean a couple of miles north of downtown. Each of the three rooms in the main building has its own bath and shares a living room; the adjacent guest cottage has a living room and kitchenette. All share use of pool and hot tub. No credit cards; reservations essential; two-day minimum stay. ❹

Hilo Bay Hostel 101 Waiānuenue Ave ☏808/933-2771, ⓦwww.hawaiihostel.net. Smart hostel, upstairs in an attractive and extremely central building in the heart of town. Assorted rooms are entered off a central landing that holds a seating area with terminals for Internet access; a dorm bed costs $22, a private room with no bathroom $55, and a more comfortable en-suite room $65. ❶–❷

Hilo Hawaiian Hotel 71 Banyan Drive ☏808/935-9361; or reserve through Castle Resorts, ☏1-800/367-5004, ⓦwww.castleresorts.com. This upmarket hotel, in a superb setting, is the only Banyan Drive property still maintaining truly high standards. The long, white crescent-shaped building directly faces Coconut Island, out in the bay, but there's no beach. All rooms fall within price code ❹, but those with the best ocean view cost $30 extra, and online discounts are often available. ❹

Hilo Seaside Hotel 126 Banyan Drive ☏808/935-0821 or 1-800/560-5557, ⓦwww.sand-seaside.com. Simple, well-priced rooms in low motel-style units near Kamehameha Avenue. Part of a small Hawaiian-owned chain, the hotel has a tiny pool and offers discounts for seniors and on car rental. ❸

Holmes' Sweet Home 107 Koula St ☏808/961-9089, ⓦwww.hilohawaiibandb.com. Two comfortable en-suite B&B rooms in a welcoming private home with extensive views, a mile off the Saddle Road and three miles up from downtown Hilo. ❸

Naniloa Volcanoes Resort 93 Banyan Drive ☏808/969-3333, ⓦwww.naniloaresort.com. This high-rise hotel, built in the 1970s, has the potential to return to its former status as Hilo's grandest option, but for the moment, as soon as you get beyond the impressive ocean-view lobby, it's seriously showing its age. The guest rooms are thin-walled and long overdue for refurbishment; hence the surprisingly low prices. At least the pool is good. Rooms ❸, suites ❺

Pineapple Park Pi'ilani and Kalanikoa 96760 ☏808/968-8170 or 1-877/865-2266, www.pineapple-park.com. New budget hostel, in a spruce, clean bungalow a mile or so from the airport, too far from downtown to walk. Bunks in six-person dorms for $25 each, plus semi-private rooms, sharing bathrooms, for $65, and one family room, with a double bed and two bunks, for $105. Kayak rental available. There are other *Pineapple Parks* in South Kona (see p.191), and in Kurtistown on the way up to Hawaii Volcanoes National Park (see p.268). ❶–❹

Shipman House B&B Inn 131 Kai'ulani St ☎808/934-8002 or 1-800/627-8447, www.hilo-hawaii.com. Magnificent, turreted Victorian mansion, in a quiet but central location, which once hosted author Jack London and Hawaiian royalty, and has now been converted by descendants of the original owners into a plush B&B. There are three grand antiques-furnished en-suite rooms in the main house, which has a lovely *lanai*, and two more in a guest cottage. None has a TV or private phone. Rates include a gorgeous breakfast and afternoon tea. ❻

Uncle Billy's Hilo Bay Hotel 87 Banyan Drive ☎808/961-5818 or 1-800/367-5102, www.unclebilly.com. The oldest of the Banyan Drive hotels, run by Uncle Billy and his family. The thatched chandeliers in the lobby set the tone: everything is relentlessly, but enjoyably, Polynesian. Two wings of basic rooms, not particularly well priced considering their fading charms, spread to either side of a tropical garden that's filled at sunset with birdsong. There's a small pool and a free nightly *hula* show (see p.230). Very popular with visitors from the other Hawaiian islands, it also offers car-rental discounts. ❸

Wild Ginger Inn 100 Pu'u'eo St ☎808/935-5556 or 1-800/882-1887, www.wildgingerinnhilo.com. Pink-painted, somewhat spruced-up inn in a quiet residential area just across the Wailuku River from downtown. While second-best to the nearby *Dolphin Bay*, it remains a good-value option for budget travelers. About thirty basic but adequate en-suite rooms arranged around attractive gardens, plus a few slightly more secluded "deluxe" rooms with TVs. Those closest to the main highway, with its traffic noise, sleep four. Rates include a simple breakfast buffet. ❷–❹

▲ *Hāmākua Coast*

RESTAURANTS
Bears Coffee	2
Café Pesto	5
Kaikodo	1
Naung Mai Thai	4
Ocean Sushi Deli	3

DOWNTOWN HILO

LEHUA STREET
ILIAHI STREET
AMAU'ULU RD
'OHAI STREET
WAINAKU AVENUE
PU'U'EO STREET
Wailuku River
WAILUKU DRIVE
KAI'ULANI ST
Maui's Canoe
Public Library
KEKAULIKE ST
SHIPMAN ST
Pacific Tsunami Museum
W A I Ā N U E N U E   A V E N U E
BAYFRONT
KEAWE STREET
KINO'OLE STREET
KALAKAUA STREET
Mission House
Lyman Museum
KAPI'OLANI STREET
HAILI STREET
ULULANI STREET
KILAUEA AVE
FURNEAUX LANE
KAMEHAMEHA HIGHWAY
Mokupāpapa Museum
Mooheau Bus Terminal
MAMO ST
KAMEHAMEHA AVENUE
P O N A H A W A I   S T R E E T

Rainbow Falls ◀

Hilo Bay

0   Yards   250

ACCOMMODATION
Dolphin Bay Hotel	A
Hilo Bay Hostel	D
Shipman House B&B	C
Wild Ginger Inn	B

Banyan Drive and Airport ▼

The City

There is a simple and tragic reason why **downtown Hilo** seems so low-key, with its modest streets and wooden stores: all the buildings that stood on the *makai* side of Kamehameha Avenue were destroyed by the tsunamis of 1946 and 1960. Furthermore, the large gap between downtown and Banyan Drive, now occupied by the Wailoa River State Park, is there because the city was literally cut in two by the inundation of 1946. After the waters returned in 1960, all hope was abandoned of rebuilding the "little Tokyo" of Japanese-owned family stores that lined Kamehameha Avenue all the way to the Wailoa River. Instead, the destroyed area was cleared as a "buffer zone," creating a new administrative complex above the high-water mark.

Little in central Hilo today bears witness to its long history, but it's a pleasant place to amble around. Regular influxes of cruise passengers keep a myriad small novelty and souvenir stores open, especially along Keawe Street a block up from the highway. On Wednesdays and Saturdays, a colorful **open-air market** takes place on Mamo Street, across the highway from the ocean. As you wander past stalls selling orchids, tropical fruits, and coffee fresh from the farm, it's hard to believe you're still in the USA.

The Pacific Tsunami Museum

The high-tech **Pacific Tsunami Museum** is housed downtown in a former bank at the corner of Kamehameha Avenue and Kalākaua Street (Mon–Sat 9am–4pm; adults $7, under-18s $2; ☎808/935-0926, ⓦwww.tsunami.org). Although its primary emphasis is on the causes and effects of the two lethal tsunamis of the last century, and of similar and potential events throughout the Pacific, it also documents the entire history of Hilo. A scale model, complete with a running train, shows how the city looked before the 1946 disaster; contemporary footage and personal letters bring home the full impact of the tragedy. The section devoted to the wave of 1960, which hit just 53 days after the official reopening of Hwy-19, is even more poignant. It was caused by an earthquake off Chile, so locals had several hours' warning that it was on its way. Amazingly enough, many flocked down to the seafront to watch it come in; photos show them waiting excitedly for the cataclysm that was about to engulf them. A total of 61 people were killed.

The Mokupāpapa Museum

A small office in the S. Hata building, a little further south at 308 Kamehameha Ave and best known as home to *Café Pesto*, has been converted into the fascinating **Mokupāpapa Museum**, devoted to the coral reefs and birdlife of the Northwestern Hawaiian Islands (Tues–Sat 9am–4pm; free; ☎808/933-8195, ⓦwww.hawaiireef.noaa.gov). There's a little aquarium, and one tiny room is mocked up to represent the interior of a submersible. Films create the illusion that you're under water, and it's even possible to manipulate the submersible's "grabber."

The Lyman Museum and Mission House

The two-part **Lyman Museum**, at 276 Haili St, a few blocks up from the ocean, is downtown Hilo's principal historic site and offers an interesting introduction to the Big Island (Mon–Sat 9.30am–4.30pm; adults $10, ages 6–17 $3; ☎808/935-5021, ⓦwww.lymanmuseum.org). Its main focus is the original **Mission House** of Calvinist missionaries David and Sarah Lyman, built in 1839. Guided tours of the oldest surviving wooden house on the island start at regular intervals from the adjacent museum.

The Lymans waited until they felt Christianity was firmly established in Hilo before constructing this, the finest home in the city, fit to welcome Hawaiian royalty and foreign dignitaries alike. It had neither kitchen – for fear of fire – nor bathroom, but stood three stories high, with a towering thatched roof, a roomy *lānai* running around the first two levels, and a spacious attic. Most of the furniture is made of dark *koa* wood, as are the floors, whose broad planks are up to nineteen inches wide.

The modern museum alongside traces the history of Hawaii from its earliest settlers, with a map of the Pacific showing the routes they followed, as well as a relief model of the Big Island, complete with black lava flows. A thatched hut holds the basic utensils of the ancient Hawaiians, among them stone tools and fish hooks, rounded calabashes of *kou* and *koa* wood, and ornaments of dogs' and whales' teeth, and even human bone (believed to transmit the spiritual power of the original owner to the wearer).

After a history of the missions comes a fascinating section on Hilo's different ethnic groups. By way of example, the Japanese are represented by an ornate wooden "wishing chair," the Chinese by a resplendent red and gilt Taoist shrine rescued from a temple destroyed by the tsunami of 1960, and the Portuguese by the little four-string *braginha* guitar that was to become the *ukulele*.

Most of the space upstairs is occupied by the **Earth Heritage Gallery**, focusing on the island's geology and astronomy. A model of the summit of Mauna Kea shows the various international observatories – computer-savvy visitors can tap into their latest discoveries – while a brief account of Polynesian techniques of stellar navigation mentions that the Ahua'umi Heiau on Mauna Kea, now badly damaged, was probably the first observatory to be built up there. A huge sonar map of the entire archipelago shows how alarmingly prone Hawaii is to massive landslides, and pinpoints the fiery submarine volcano of Lo'ihi thrusting its way to the surface just off the southeast coast of the Big Island. Another collection contains corals, shells – including those of some unique indigenous land snails – a few stuffed birds and fossils, and colorful minerals from around the world, some of which glow in the dark. The small **Shipman Collection of Chinese Art**, also displayed upstairs, consists mostly of delicately painted but uninspiring porcelain.

'Imiloa Astronomy Center of Hawaii

A five-minute drive from downtown Hilo – turn left onto Komohana Street a couple of miles up Waiānuenue Avenue – brings you to the gleaming new **'Imiloa Astronomy Center of Hawaii**, 600 'Imiloa Place in the University of Hawaii Hilo Science and Technology Park (Tues–Sun 9am–4pm; adults $14.50, ages 4–12 $7.50; ☎808/969-9700, ⓦwww.imiloahawaii.org). A lavish museum complex for such a small, out-of-the-way city, **'Imiloa** is designed to meet a rather strange brief, and one that may puzzle visitors from beyond Hawaii.

Whereas scientists see the summit of Mauna Kea as the world's finest location to build astronomical observatories, many argue that according to traditional Hawaiian beliefs such observatories desecrate a sacred site. Largely funded by NASA, this museum is an attempt to reconcile those two views. Thus it combines highly informative displays on the Hawaiian creation chant, the *Kumulipo*, and the ongoing practice of burying the *piko* or umbilical cord of newborn infants in a secret family location, with computerized updates of the latest readings from the mountaintop telescopes. It's all very fascinating, and when the scientific and traditional viewpoints dovetail convincingly, as for example in the stargazing techniques used by Polynesian navigators, it makes a lot of sense; elsewhere, though, it feels like a chalk and cheese museum, vainly attempting to persuade visitors that the two are actually one and the same.

Wailuku River and Rainbow Falls

The **Wailuku River**, which defines the western limit of downtown Hilo, is at eighteen miles the longest river in the Hawaiian archipelago. Now safely channeled and crossed by three road bridges, it once had a fearsome reputation; *wailuku* means "destroying water," as it was considered extremely dangerous during periods of high rain.

A large rocky outcrop in the riverbed, visible upstream from the bridge that connects Puueo and Keawe streets, is known as **Maui's Canoe**. In legend, it was abandoned by the mighty warrior after he'd raced it back from Haleakalā on his namesake island (with just two paddle strokes). Maui was hurrying to rescue his mother, Hina, who lived in a cave further up the river and had become trapped by rising waters engineered by a dragon.

Maui's route is now followed by Waiānuenue ("rainbow seen in the water") Avenue, and the site of Hina's cave, two miles out from downtown, is known as **Rainbow Falls**. Sightseers drive out to admire this broad waterfall from a safe distance; short trails lead to different viewpoints, but don't let you anywhere near the actual water. From the fenced-off viewing area to the right of the parapet wall of the parking lot, you can see the falls square-on as they shoot over a thick shelf of hard rock. In the pool down below, the water has progressively scooped out the hollow that was supposedly home to Maui's mother. Climbing a small but often very muddy and slippery staircase off to the left brings you level with the streambed at the top of the falls, behind which the summit of Mauna Kea looms high in the distance.

Almost two miles on up the road, the **Boiling Pots** are a succession of churning, foaming pools in the river as it drops toward the ocean, accompanied by another, smaller, set of falls. A treacherous ungraded path to the right of the viewing area allows you to approach the maelstrom, but you'd be crazy to swim.

Wailoa River State Park

Wailoa River State Park, created in the aftermath of the 1960 tsunami in what had been downtown Hilo, is a tranquil – if marshy – landscaped park of lawns, coconut palms, and dazzling orange-blossomed *lehua* trees. It's a little hard to find your way in: turn down Pauahi Street, which runs between Kīlauea and Kamehameha avenues, and then take curving Piopio Street halfway along. Paved footpaths cross the river and clear-watered lagoons on double- or even triple-humped footbridges, with one pair leading to and from a tiny island, and another one connecting with Kamehameha Avenue and the seafront. A moving memorial, dedicated to all victims of Big Island tsunamis, consists of two low, black-lava ridges that shield a central tiled design.

Banyan Drive

Green, semi-rural **Banyan Drive**, a mile east of downtown Hilo and not far from the airport, has become the prime hotel district for the city since being spared by the tsunamis. Though the hotels themselves are deteriorating, it's an attractive area, graced by curving rows of the eponymous giant drooping banyan trees. Incredibly, these magnificent specimens are little more than seventy years old, having been planted in the 1930s by the celebrities after whom they're named – Franklin Roosevelt, Babe Ruth, and King George V among others.

The best place for a stroll among the trees is **Liliuokalani Gardens**, an ornamental Japanese park built to honor Japanese migrants to Hawaii. A slender footbridge stretches out to **Coconut Island**, now just a green speck on the edge

The Merrie Monarch festival

Since 1963, the city of Hilo has celebrated the week-long **Merrie Monarch** *hula* festival in the week that follows Easter Sunday. The festival's centerpiece is a royal parade down the main street in honor of the "Merrie Monarch" himself, King David Kalākaua. He was largely responsible for the revival of *hula* following decades of missionary disapproval, when, at the time of his coronation in February 1883, he staged a performance of women dancers and male drummers on the lawns of Honolulu's 'Iolani Palace.

Performers from around thirty different *hula halau* (schools) – of which eighteen tend to be female and twelve male, and not all are necessarily from Hawaii – compete for awards in both *kahiko* (ancient) and *'auana* (modern) styles of *hula*. Official events take place in the evenings at the six-thousand-seat **Kanaka'ole Stadium**, named after Auntie Edith Kanaka'ole, one of the Big Island's best-loved twentieth-century *kumu hulas* (hula teachers). In addition, informal demonstrations and other events are held during the daytime in the *Hilo Hawaiian* and *Naniloa Volcanoes Resort* hotels.

Full schedules are available from the Merrie Monarch office at 101 Aupuni St, Hilo (℡808/935-9168, ⍟www.merriemonarchfestival.org). Tickets go on sale each year on January 1 but sell out almost immediately.

of the bay but once, as Mokuola ("healing island"), the site of a *pu'uhonua* or "place of refuge," like that at Hōnaunau (see p.187). There was also a *luakini*, where human offerings were killed by having a huge stone dropped on their chests while lying bound to a rock. When the temple was dismantled during the 1870s, its stones were used to build a quarantine hospital, but that was in turn destroyed almost immediately by a tsunami.

A small covered market area next to the quayside on Lihiwai Street, just off Kamehameha Avenue, is the site (daily except Sun) of the **Suisan Fish Auction**. You have to arrive at around 7am to be sure of seeing anything; a nearby coffee stall will help wake you up. Suisan is a large operation, and fishing vessels from all over the island come here to sell their catch. Most of the trays are packed with glistening tuna, but you can also see red snapper, parrotfish, squid, ripped-up multicolored reef fish speared by scuba divers, and the occasional unfortunate shark. Though it's a hectic and lively spectacle, there's no dramatic shouting: buyers simply inspect the shiny rows of fish and write down their bids.

Panaewa Rainforest Zoo

The little-known **Panaewa Rainforest Zoo** (daily 9am–4pm; free; ℡808/959-9233, ⍟www.hilozoo.com) is home to a relatively small menagerie of animals, few of them all that unusual. The main pleasure of stopping here en route to the volcanoes is the chance to roam beneath the zoo's canopy of tropical vegetation. Coming south from Hilo on Hwy-11, turn right just after mile marker 4, along the signed turning a short way beyond Stainback Highway.

On weekdays you may find that you're the rarest species of all, and that the animals will go out of their way to have a closer look at you. Walkways through the dense, steamy undergrowth lead past various enclaves inhabited by a pigmy hippo (with giant-sized teeth), a Shetland pony, an ominously rotund American alligator, iguanas from South America, giant land turtles from the Seychelles, and wide-eyed lemurs and bushy-tailed colobuses from Madagascar. Several impressive peacocks wander the grounds at will, displaying their plumage, while rare Hawaiian owls and hawks are confined in rusty cages. The largest, lushest enclosure holds a white Bengal tiger, though the vegetation is so thick that you may not spot him unless you're here for his indoor feed at 3.30pm or are prepared for a long wait by his watering hole.

❷ Hilo's beaches

If neither sharks nor pollution bother you, you could in theory swim out among the canoes and fishing boats from the **Hilo Bayfront Park**, across the highway from downtown Hilo. This was one of the finest black-sand beaches in all the islands, before the construction of the breakwater in 1908 and the dredging of the harbor in 1913. Now it's a pleasant place for a picnic, but the only spot nearby where you might be tempted to swim is at Coconut Island, off Banyan Drive (see p.226).

All Hilo's **beach parks** lie southeast of downtown, facing Mauna Kea across the bay and reached by following Kalaniana'ole Avenue beyond Banyan Drive. As few have any sand – they consist of shallow pools in the black lava at the ocean margin, usually backed by small grass clearings ringed with coconut palms – they attract local families rather than tourists, and so are only crowded on weekends. You'll notice also that Kalaniana'ole Avenue is lined with blue signs indicating the "Evacuation Route" in the event of a tsunami; not surprisingly, the idea is to get away from the sea as fast as possible.

Probably the best spot for family groups is **Onekahakaha Beach Park**, a mile and a half down Kalaniana'ole Avenue. Here a solid breakwater of boulders has created a calm lagoon for swimming, while the spacious lawns alongside are good for picnics. The open ocean beyond the breakwater can, however, be extremely dangerous, while fifty yards or so back from the sea the park acquires from time to time a sizeable population of homeless people. That's the main reason why none of Hilo's beach parks currently allows camping.

Leleiwi Beach Park, a couple of miles further along, is a little more exposed, with no sandy beach and some dangerous currents. Away from the open sea, the lagoon is so supremely still and tranquil as to appeal primarily to anglers, who stand in quiet contemplation almost entirely undisturbed by bathers.

△ Surfer at Honoli'i Beach

Just beyond Leleiwi, and four miles from downtown, Kalaniana'ole Avenue comes to a dead end at **Richardson Ocean Park**, where a tiny black-sand beach among the coconut groves is very popular with young children. Some venture out to play in the surf as it sweeps into the bay, beyond the snorkelers exploring the rock pools. Behind the sea wall there's a larger "beach" area – more of a sandpit, really – while the adjacent gardens are laid out around some ancient fishponds, with a few explanatory labels.

One other beach that's well worth visiting is located a couple of miles **north** of downtown Hilo. Reached by taking Nanaha Street, the first oceanward turning three quarters of a mile north of a prominent roadside lookout that offers views of all Hilo Bay, **Honoli'i Beach** is a beautiful curve of black sand at the mouth of the Honoli'i Stream. Though not safe for swimming, it's as spectacular a spot for **surfing** as you can imagine, and thus throngs with locals at weekends. The northern side of the bay is flanked by a steep wall of deep-green vegetation, making a great backdrop for action photos.

Restaurants

Hilo offers an unusually varied assortment of **restaurants**, most of which are aimed more at locals than at visitors, and thus tend to have more at stake in satisfying their customers than some of the fly-by-night Kona-side joints. **Downtown** is at its busiest during the working week, however, and you may be surprised at how quiet things are on weekends. If you're looking for crowds, you're probably better off spending the evening along **Banyan Drive**.

As for **fast food**, a wide selection of national chain outlets can be found at malls such as the Prince Kūhiō Plaza and the Puainako Town Center.

Bears Coffee 110 Keawe St ☏ 808/935-0708. Hilo's coolest breakfast hangout, one block from the ocean downtown. All kinds of coffees are available, plus bakery goodies, freshly squeezed juices, and a menu of specials such as souffléd eggs on a muffin with spinach ($5). Lunch consists of $5–8 burgers, sandwiches, salads, and simple fish and chicken dishes. Mon–Fri 5.30am–4pm, Sat 5.30am–1pm, Sun 6.30am–noon.

Café Pesto S. Hata Building, 130 Kamehameha Ave ☏ 808/969-6640. A large and modern Pacific-influenced Italian restaurant at the southern end of downtown. For a substantial snack, the lunchtime sandwiches, such as the Japanese eggplant Sandalwood and the shrimp Miloli'i, are excellent value ($9–11). There's a wide selection of pizzas and calzones, with tasty, inventive fillings such as lime-marinated fish. The dinner menu also features fresh fish, and a risotto with lobster, shrimp, and scallops ($25). There's another *Café Pesto* at Kawaihae Harbor; see p.207. Mon–Thurs & Sun 11am–9pm, Fri & Sat 11am–10pm.

Hilo Bay Café 315 Maka'ala St ☏ 808/935-4939. Smart, good-value café in the same mall as Borders, well south of the ocean, which serves much the same deli-style menu for lunch and

dinner, although at midday salads and sandwiches are also served. Most dishes are pretty rich, from the French onion soup ($6) and the "Blue Bay Burger" ($9) to entrees like lemongrass pork tenderloin or seared scallops ($15–24). Mon–Sat 11am–9.30pm, Sun 5–9pm.

Restaurant Kaikodo 60 Keawe St ☏ 808/961-2558. Very classy, very upscale restaurant on the first floor of a stunningly restored century-old building in the heart of downtown Hilo. At the edge of the large, high-ceilinged dining room, a transplanted antique Chinese bedroom serves as a very ornate private dining area for a party of four. The food itself is modern Hawaiian with an even more eclectic reach than that usually implies; there's exquisite sushi and sashimi, notably the "*Ahi* 3-Ways" appetizer ($12), while entrees range from five-fragrance pork and baby-back ribs to grilled filet mignon ($25–34). For lunch, served weekdays only, the menu ranges from crab cakes and quesadillas to burgers, at $10–14. Mon–Thurs 11am–2pm & 5.30–9pm, Fri 11am–2pm & 5.30–9.30pm, Sat 5.30–9.30pm, Sun 5.30–9pm.

Nihon Cultural Center 123 Lihiwai St ☏ 808/969-1133. Just off Banyan Drive, this Japanese restaurant has delicate, succulent fresh fish and fine

Shopping

Although **downtown Hilo** is an enjoyable district to walk around, few of its stores are worth going out of your way for. Those that are tend to be concentrated along sea-facing Kamehameha Avenue, and the parallel Keawe Street one block inland, including several shops selling Chinese and Japanese crafts and novelties, plus assorted outlets selling clothes, T-shirts, and souvenirs. By far the best of the downtown stores, indeed the finest source of *aloha* wear in the entire state, is **Sig Zane's**, selling designs inspired by native Hawaiian plants, at 122 Kamehameha Ave (℡ 808/935-7077, ⓦ www.sigzane .com). More generally, the most appealing times for a stroll are Wednesday and Saturday mornings, to coincide with the **market** on Mamo Street.

Most locals do their shopping at the various **malls**, of which **Prince Kūhiō Plaza** (Mon–Fri 10am–9pm, Sat 9.30am–7pm, Sun 10am–6pm), just south of the airport on Hwy-11, is the most extensive. As well as Sears, J.C. Penney, and Woolworth department stores, it has its own movie theater (℡ 808/959-4955), two bookstores, and a music store. The **Waiakea Center**, across the street, holds a large Borders bookstore (℡ 808/933-1410). **Banyan Drive** has a very limited selection of convenience stores.

views. Lunch specials cost under $10. Reservations are required for dinner, when full meals starting at $19 are served until 9pm; the sushi bar remains open later. Mon–Sat 11am–1.30pm & 5–10pm.

Ocean Sushi Deli 250 Keawe St
℡ 808/961-6625. Large and very popular Japanese cafeteria, serving good and inexpensive sushi (from $2.50 for two pieces) and great-value bento meals to the downtown crowd. Mixed sushi plates start at $11, sashimi at $17. Mon–Sat 10.30am–2pm & 5–9pm.

Naung Mai Thai 86 Kīlauea Ave ℡ 808/934-7540. Excellent little Thai café in central Hilo, with a full menu of $10 Thai curries, spiced to taste, plus pad Thai and other noodle dishes, and zestful appetizers like a green papaya salad ($6). Mon, Tues, & Thurs 11am–2pm & 5–8.30pm, Wed 5–8.30pm, Fri 11am–2pm & 5–9pm, Sat 5–9pm.

The Seaside Restaurant 1790 Kalaniana'ole Ave ℡ 808/935-8825. The full name of this lively restaurant continues "and Aqua

Farm," which has to be a good sign. Located just over two miles out of town, opposite Kealoha Beach, it's almost entirely surrounded by water, with its 30-acre fishponds full of trout, mullet, and catfish. In addition to the plain main dining room, there are a few outdoor tables. The fish is great, with the basic choice being steamed or fried as an entree, and also sushi-style as an appetizer. Unless you opt for the more expensive imported specials, you'd be hard-pressed to spend much over $20 on a full fish supper. Daily, except Mon, 5–8.30pm.

Uncle Billy's *Hilo Bay Hotel*, 87 Banyan Drive ℡ 808/935-0861. Themed Polynesian restaurant, where most of the menu consists of steak and breaded fish entrees for $14–24; the $25 seafood platter is great value. Free nightly Hawaiian music and *hula* dancing from 6pm, often presided over by the beaming Uncle Billy himself, and featuring members of his extensive family. Mon–Sat 7–10am & 5.30–9pm, Sun 7–11.30am & 5.30–9pm.

The Hāmākua coast

The **Hāmākua coast** extends for fifty ravishing and colorful miles north and west from Hilo up to Waipi'o Valley. This spectacular landscape has been carved by the torrents of rain unleashed when the trade winds hit Mauna Kea after crossing two thousand miles of open ocean. Countless streams and waterfalls cascade down the cliffs and gullies, nourishing jungle-like vegetation filled with multicolored blossoms and iridescent orchids. Hāmākua farms once fueled the economy of the

Big Island. Now agribusiness has all but pulled out – the last sugar mill closed in 1994 – and no one knows quite what might take its place.

For most of this stretch of shoreline, the Belt Road (Hwy-19) follows the original route of the sugar-company railroad, which carried local produce to ships waiting in Hilo and other smaller harbors. Barely rising or falling, the highway clings to the hillsides, crossing a succession of ravines on slender bridges. Damage to these bridges in the 1946 tsunami put the railroad out of business, but they were sufficiently repaired to be able to carry the road instead.

The drive is neither difficult nor particularly tortuous, but it's so beautiful that you may find it impossible to exceed the posted minimum speed of 40mph. Each little bridge offers its own glimpse of the verdant scenery – sometimes close to the ocean but high above it, sometimes winding further in to follow the contours of the gorges and passing babbling streams and waterfalls.

At first, the fields are crammed into narrow, stream-carved "gulches," and there are few places to stop and enjoy the views. The two most popular off-road sight-seeing spots are the **Hawaii Tropical Botanical Garden**, just a few miles north of Hilo, and the impressive **'Akaka Falls**, another ten miles on, where a short loop trail through the rainforest offers a rare view of the interior. Otherwise, if you just want to pause and take a few photos along the way, look out for the bridge just north of mile marker 18 (and south of Ninole), from which you can watch the **Waikaumalo River** crash into the sea amid dramatic orange-blossomed trees and giant fanning palms, and the deeply indented **Maulua Gorge** at mile marker 22.

Further north, beyond **Laupāhoehoe**, the land spreads out, allowing room for larger plantations. The Belt Road veers inland toward Waimea just before the old-fashioned sugar town of **Honoka'a**, but keeping on another eight miles on dead-end Hwy-240 brings you out at one of the most unforgettable viewpoints on all the islands – the **Waipi'o Valley** overlook.

Pepe'ekeo Scenic Drive

PEPE'EKEO SCENIC DRIVE, a small side road that drops toward the sea four miles north of Hilo, then curves for four miles before rejoining Hwy-19 at Pepe'ekeo, makes a worthwhile detour from the Belt Road. Until the highway came through, this was part of the Old Māmalahoa Highway that once encircled the island (see p.212). That explains why the trouble was taken to plant what has become its most impressive stretch, a superb avenue of overhanging Alexandra palms imported from Queensland, Australia. They make their appearance just beyond a delightful gorge that bursts with African tulip trees. Close to the north end of the road, beyond the garden described below, *What's Shakin* (daily 10am–5.30pm; ☎808/964-3080) serves the best fresh-fruit **smoothies** on the island ($6), plus sandwiches for around $7, and has a nice veranda overlooking its own orchards.

Hawaii Tropical Botanical Garden

Occupying almost the entirety of **Onomea Bay** – one of the lushest, prettiest bays of the Hāmākua coast – is the Big Island's premier showcase for tropical trees, orchids, and flowering plants, the **Hawaii Tropical Botanical Garden** (daily 9am–5pm; adults $15, under-17s $5; ☎808/964-5233, ⓦwww.htbg.com). The collection includes specimens from Brazil, Malaysia, Madagascar, and Guatemala, alongside endemic Hawaiian species, and is garnished with flamingos and macaws. Though a major stop on the tour-bus circuit, with crowds and prices to match, it

THE HĀMĀKUA COAST

still comes closer than anywhere on the island to matching the popular conception of what a tropical rainforest should look like.

From the garden headquarters, halfway along the Pepe'ekeo Scenic Drive, a signposted self-guided trail drops around 500ft to the ocean. Insect repellent and drinking water are on sale at the start, and if it's raining you should be able to borrow an umbrella. It takes roughly an hour to complete the trail's full length.

Striking features during the descent include views of a tall waterfall, on the innermost wall of the valley, visible at the upper end of the "palm jungle" of Alexandra palms. A little lower, a huge Cook pine is surrounded by spectacular heliconia and vast spreading "travelers' trees," said always to hold a little water at the base of their leaves. Most of the plants are labeled, and there's a heady succession of gingers, bromeliads, dramatic orange and yellow heliconia, coconut palms with their writhing worm-like roots, and *hala*, or pandanus trees, whose roots serve as stilts that seem to lift the trunk off the ground. Perhaps the most prominent of all is the red-leafed *obake*, which with its lurid white or yellow "prong" is something of an island trademark.

When garden owner Dan Lutkenhouse purchased this entire valley in 1977, it was so overgrown that it was all but impossible to get down to the ocean. Once it was cleared, however, local people asserted the right of access to the shoreline, which is guaranteed throughout Hawaii. Following bitter legal disputes, the state constructed a footpath that runs through the middle of the garden. That has left visitors with a moral dilemma. Halfway through your garden visit, you pass through a gate onto the state footpath, where strict notices insist you MUST turn right to re-enter the garden via another gate, and must not under any circumstances turn left. However, if you do turn left, a very short walk brings you out at the mouth of the Onomea Stream, in the centre of the bay. Similarly if you turn right but keep going rather than immediately re-entering the garden, you'll quickly come to a lovely little black-sand beach. What's more, there is actually a free roadside parking lot at that end of the footpath, so you could if you choose simply walk the path to see the bay itself without paying admission to the garden at all.

△ Hawaii Tropical Botanical Garden

'Akaka Falls

Three or four miles up Mauna Kea from the Belt Road, and fifteen miles out of Hilo, **'Akaka Falls** is one of the Big Island's most photogenic sights. Though not the highest waterfall on the island, its setting is unrivaled – a sheer drop through a chasm overrun by tropical vegetation and orchids. An easy and enjoyable half-mile trail leads visitors through a dense "jungle" and past other falls, culminating at a viewpoint looking upstream to 'Akaka itself. You don't get close to the riverbed, let alone the falls, so the only dangers to contend with are the steamy heat and persistent mosquitoes. If possible, come in the morning, when the sunshine, assuming there is any, directly hits the falls.

The trail starts from a parking lot that's reached by following a straightforward series of signs off the highway, through Honomū (see below) and up Hwy-220 via a small belt of meadowland. If you're pressed for time, head left from the trailhead for a shorter round-trip hike that will only take you to 'Akaka Falls. Otherwise, follow the signs and descend a narrow staircase that swiftly plunges you into dense tropical foliage, where thickets of bamboo soar from the gorge below to meet high above your head. Few of the plants lining the route are native to Hawaii, and the whole forest is a battleground of vivid blossoms. Among the most lurid are the fiery "lobster-claw" heliconia and birds of paradise, bedecked in either orange and blue, or white.

Shortly after you cross a narrow stream, the canopy opens up and you reach an overlook facing across a gorge to spindly **Kapuna Falls**. Mighty trees stand alongside the path, festooned with thick green mosses, fern, and creepers, with all kinds of parasitic plants sprouting from their branches and trunks. To the left, a vast banyan drips with tendrils.

Across the next bluff, you get your first view of 'Akaka Falls itself, foaming through a narrow channel to plunge around 450 feet down a mossy cliff face and disappear in a cloud of spray into the pool below. After leaving the viewing area, you recross the stream at a higher point, where a small waterfall bubbles beneath another overhanging bamboo grove.

Honomū

Were it not for the steady flow of visitors to 'Akaka Falls, tiny **HONOMŪ**, on the *mauka* side of Hwy-19, a mile or so south of Kolekole Beach Park, would probably have been swallowed up by the rainforest by now. As it is, the village consists of a row of little timber-framed galleries and crafts stores, a couple of which sell sodas, juices, and snacks as well as run-of-the-mill souvenirs. To sample the flavor of the place, stop by *Ishigo's General Store*, an authentic plantation store that has been run by the same family since 1910.

Kolekole Beach Park

Having cascaded over 'Akaka Falls, Kolekole Stream reaches the ocean a mile or so north of Honomū, at the only sizeable seafront park between Hilo and Laupāhoehoe. Look out for a small turning on the left of the highway, just before a tall, narrow bridge. The road down to **Kolekole Beach Park**, lush even by Hāmākua standards, doubles back to end at the foot of the bridge struts, far below the highway. On both sides, the gorge is thick green, half-swallowing the rusting tin-roofed pavilions of the park. There's no beach, however, and while local youths thrill to ride the breakers back into the mouth of the river, lesser mortals should be wary of submitting themselves to the high surf that lies just a few yards beyond the rounded black boulders of the shoreline.

Umauma Falls

Heading inland from Hwy-19 along any of the little access roads around milepost 16, roughly two miles north of Kolekole, enables you to join the minor road, parallel to the main highway, that leads to **Umauma Falls**. These previously little-known falls have become more prominent on tourist itineraries since 1995, when the surrounding land was opened to the public as the **World Botanic Gardens** (daily 9am–5.30pm; adults $13, ages 13–17 $6, ages 5–12 $3; ⊕808/963-5427, ⓦ www.wbgi.com). So far, the gardens themselves are relatively unenthralling, but visitors who drop in at their roadside headquarters and pay the high admission fee are given directions for reaching an overlook beside the Umauma Stream that commands a superb prospect of the tripled-tiered falls themselves. They're not nearly as dramatic as ʻAkaka Falls, but that doesn't make them bad.

Laupāhoehoe

For most of the Hāmākua coast, the shoreline cliffs are too abrupt to leave room for settlements by the sea. Hence the significance of **LAUPĀHOEHOE**, twelve miles up the coast from Kolekole, where a flow of lava extruding into the ocean has created a flat, fertile promontory (*lau* means leaf, and *pāhoehoe* is smooth lava).

As the best canoe landing between Hilo and Waipiʻo, Laupāhoehoe has long been home to a small community; the location has its perils, however. On April 1, 1946, a ferocious tsunami destroyed the school at the tip of the headland, killing 24 teachers and children. Rescue attempts were delayed as all boats and canoes in the vicinity were wrecked by waves up to thirty feet high.

As the approach road to Laupāhoehoe rounds the first tight corner on its way to the sea, you're confronted by a stunning view of the green coastal cliffs stretching away to the south. After rain, countless small waterfalls cascade from crevices in the rock. The narrow road winds down past the **Jodo Mission**, a temple built by Japanese immigrants in 1899, and arrives at a flat spit of land at the bottom of the cliffs. Most of the space here is taken up by a large lawn, fringed with tall coconut palms that have an alarming tendency to shed their fruit in high winds. A number of seafront parking lots are squeezed in before the forbidding black-lava coastline and its pounding surf, in which swimming is definitely not advisable. To the right is the small boat-launching ramp of Laupāhoehoe Harbor, so dangerous that it's usually sealed off from public access, while round to the left an open-sided beach pavilion tends to be the preserve of locals around sunset.

Until the tsunami of 1946, the main coastal road passed through Laupāhoehoe at sea level. Part of the village had already relocated higher up the hillside in 1913, however, when the sugar company **railroad** reached this far up the Hāmākua coast. Both the lower road and the railroad were destroyed by the tsunami – the railroad lost not only much of its track and its trestle bridges, but also the actual engines. The whole community, including a new school built to replace the one lost in the storm, subsequently shifted to the top of the cliffs.

Since the last of the local sugar mills closed, Laupāhoehoe has been facing an uncertain future. A few people still live along the various backroads in the district, but there's no town for visitors to explore, and no accommodation is currently available. The one concession to tourism is the little **Laupāhoehoe Train Museum**, housed in the former ticket agent's residence alongside the highway (Mon–Fri 9am–4.30pm, Sat & Sun 10am–2pm; $3; @ www.thetrainmuseum .com). Enthusiastic volunteers explain the history of the railroad, aided by a plethora of photos and artifacts, and can tell you how far they've got with their schemes to restore some of the rusted-up old machinery.

Kalōpā Native Forest State Park

A final opportunity to explore the upland slopes of Mauna Kea comes a couple of miles south of Honoka'a and a mile *mauka* of Hwy-19, in the **Kalōpā Native Forest Park**. Though the park covers 615 acres, and holds a network of rugged backcountry hiking trails, the only readily accessible part is the **Nature Trail**, a loop of less than a mile that starts from the parking lot and winds through variegated woodlands. Most of what you see is planted rather than natural, but it still provides an interesting introduction to the native flora of the island. By the end of the trail you should be able to spot the difference between the *'ōhi'a* and *kopiko* trees, be familiar with ferns such as the *hāpu'u* and the *niani'au*, and be appalled by the evil ways of the aggressive strawberry guava plant. The *'io* (Hawaiian hawk) and the tiny but melodious *'elepaio* make their nests in this area, but you may not see creatures larger than voracious mosquitoes.

The park has a small, tent-only **campground**, charging $5 per night, as well as four eight-bunk cabins, each equipped with bath, bed linen, and blankets, and sharing the use of a central kitchen and communal area. The cabins are let for up to five nights, at $55 per night. Reserve on the spot by finding the caretaker before 4pm, or call the state parks office in Hilo (☎808/974-6200).

Honoka'a

The largest and most characterful of the Hāmākua towns is rough-and-tumble **HONOKA'A**, forty miles north of Hilo where the Belt Road curves west to run across the island to Waimea. Consisting largely of a row of quaint timber-framed stores set on the wooden boardwalks of Mamane Street, it stands a couple of miles back from the ocean and is surrounded by rolling meadows.

Just over two thousand people live in Honoka'a, whose economy depended on a mill belonging to the Hāmākua Sugar Company from 1873 until it finally shut down in 1994. However, this is one of several Big Island communities to have been spruced up and revitalized by federal funding, and its historic downtown district makes it an appealing port of call.

The most conspicuous landmark along Mamane Street is the Art Deco **Honoka'a People's Theater**, built as a movie theater in 1930 by the Tanimoto family (who were also responsible for the Aloha Theater in Kainaliu; see p.184). Restored and repainted, it is now used for occasional movie performances and musical events, including a "Jazz Getaway" in May and October's **Hāmākua Music Festival**, which largely but not exclusively focuses on Hawaiian performers (@ www .hamakuamusicfestival.org).

If you're lucky enough to find it open – afternoons are a better bet than mornings, but that's as far as regular hours go – be sure to drop in on *Kimo's Collection*, at 45-3611 Mamane Street. At first glance it looks like a typical junk store, but many of the artifacts piled high on all sides are anthropological museum pieces.

The place heaves with Buddhas, bottles, stuffed hog's heads, carved-lava Hawaiian deities, and swathed mummies, and, more significantly, idols, fertility symbols, and masks from Papua New Guinea. If nothing takes your fancy, you'll find plenty more antique, crafts, and junk stores stretching for another couple of hundred yards up the road toward Hilo.

Practicalities

The only **accommodation** in central Honoka'a is the *Hotel Honoka'a Club*, on Mamane Street at the Hilo end of town (T 808/775-0678 or 1-800/808-0678; W www.hotelhonokaa.com; ❶–❸). A rambling, thin-walled, and spartan old wooden structure, it offers appealing antique-furnished en-suite rooms on the upper floor with sweeping ocean views, and much more basic alternatives downstairs, some of which serve as hostel-style dorms with $18 beds. Two miles out of Honoka'a toward Waipi'o, the *Waipi'o Wayside* **B&B** (T 808/775-0275 or 1-800/833-8849, W www.waipiowayside.com; ❹–❺) has five themed en-suite rooms in an attractive old plantation house.

The best place to **eat** in Honoka'a is *Jolene's Kau Kau Korner* (Mon, Wed, & Fri 10am–8pm, Tues & Thurs 10am–3pm; T 808/775-9498), next to the Lehua–Mamane intersection in the center of town. A lunchtime burger or stir-fry in this attractive Hawaiian-style diner will set you back $4–9; more substantial dinner entrees, such as the tasty seafood platter of breaded fish, cost $12–19. For something a little lighter, try the *Mamane Street Bakery Café* next door (Mon–Fri 6am–noon; T 808/775-9478) for sandwiches, croissants, and espresso coffee; the excellent health food deli a little further along, *Simply Natural* (Mon–Sat 8am–3.30pm; T 808/775-0119), which sells fabulous sandwiches; or the decent Italian place opposite, *Café Il Mondo*, which sells soup and focaccia ($7) and calzones ($10), plus substantial lasagnas and pizzas (Tues–Sat 11am–8pm; T 808/775-7711). Locals also rave about the filling 95¢ *malasadas* (donuts) at *Tex Drive-In*, where Mamane Street meets Hwy-19 (Mon–Sat 7am–8pm, Sun 7am–6pm; T 808/775-7711).

Kukuihaele

The village of **KUKUIHAELE**, on a looping spur road off Hwy-240, less than a mile short of the Waipi'o overlook, is the nearest community to the valley. Its name, meaning "traveling light," is a reference to the lights carried by the ghostly nocturnal processions that head for the underworld below Waipi'o (see overleaf). As well as the *Waipi'o Valley Art Works* (T 808/775-0958), the appealing crafts store and snack bar that serves as the base for the Waipi'o Valley Shuttle and other tours described on p.241, it's home to a delightful **B&B**, *Hale Kukui*, at 48-5460 Kukui-haele Rd (T 808/775-7130 or 1-800/444-7130, W www.halekukui.com; ❹–❺). Set in lush gardens above the ocean, with views of the valley mouth, the guest cottage here stands a couple of hundred yards off the loop road as you head toward Waipi'o. Accommodation is in a one-bedroom studio or a two-room unit.

Waipi'o Valley

Beyond Honoka'a, Mamane Street continues north as Hwy-240, and comes to an abrupt end after nine miles at the edge of **WAIPI'O VALLEY**. The southernmost of a succession of deeply indented, sheer-walled valleys stretching away up the coast to Pololū (see p.217), Waipi'o is the only one accessible by road. It's as close as the Big Island gets to the classic South Seas image of an isolated and self-sufficient valley, sparkling with waterfalls, dense with fruit trees, and laced by footpaths leading down to the sea. More dramatic examples of this kind of scenery abound on older islands such as Kauai, but as the Big Island is the newest in the chain, it's only here on the flanks of Kohala – its oldest volcano – that rainwater has had the necessary eons to gouge out such spectacular chasms.

Between its high walls, the valley has a surprisingly broad floor, filled with rich silt carried down from the Kohala slopes by the meandering **Waipi'o Stream** (also known as Wailoa Stream). Visitors might not appreciate quite how unusual such large areas of prime agricultural land are in the Hawaiian islands. This was probably the leading taro-farming valley of the entire archipelago; its produce alone could feed the whole population of the island in times of famine.

The valley is now far more overgrown than it was in its heyday, and inhabited by just a few farmers who squelch their way across paddy-like taro fields (known as *lo'i*, these have a consistency that has been likened to a "semi-jelled chocolate pudding"). They've been joined by assorted get-away-from-it-all *haoles*, including a sizeable population of latter-day hippies in the remoter reaches.

Only a small proportion of the steady trickle of visitors who admire the view from the Waipi'o overlook make their way down into the valley itself. It's a very strenuous hike, so most of those who do join a motorized or horseback tour (see p.241 for details). Facilities at the bottom are minimal; there's nowhere to eat or sleep, and **camping** is no longer permitted. However, it's a magical spot, and one that deserves to figure on even the most breakneck Big Island itinerary.

The history of Waipi'o

Wai being Hawaiian for "water," and *pi'o* meaning "a loop, bow, or thing bent on itself," Waipi'o Valley was named "curving water" to describe the sinuous course of the Waipi'o Stream across its floor. This beautiful and enormously productive area occupies a crucial place in Big Island history and retains great cultural significance.

The Hawaiian word for "law," *kanawai*, literally means "the equal sharing of water," and the system to which it refers is said to have been instigated in Waipi'o at some indeterminate time by **'Umi-a-Liloa**. The first ruler to unite the entire Big Island, he was responsible as a taro farmer for the development of the valley's highly complex network of irrigation channels. Many remain in use to this day. 'Umi also had his nastier side, as one of the first major practitioners of large-scale human sacrifice. Victims, such as his rival high chief and half-brother Hakua-a-Liloa, were baked in an *imu* pit and their remains placed on the altar of Waipi'o's Moa'ula Heiau.

Both 'Umi and Hakua were the sons of the previous chief, Liloa. 'Umi, the product of a secret liaison, was raised in obscurity near Laupāhoehoe. As an adult, he revealed himself to his father in Waipi'o by swimming across the stream and climbing the walls of his stockade – an offense that would have been punishable by death had he not been able to prove his birthright.

Another Waipi'o legend states that a pit at the mouth of the valley (now plowed over) marked the entrance to the underworld known as Kapa'aheo, the Hawaiian equivalent of ancient Greece's Hades. This insubstantial and barren wasteland was said to be populated by famished ghosts gnawing on lizards and butterflies; dead souls could occasionally be seen making their way to it at night, in stately processions along the Old Māmalahoa Highway (see p.212).

Waipi'o was also the boyhood home of **Kamehameha the Great**, another future chief brought up in secrecy for his own safety. It was here that chief Kalaniopu'u granted Kamehameha custody of the war god Kūkā'ilimoku in 1780, thereby sanctioning his ambitions to become ruler. Eleven years later, his warriors fought Kahekili of Maui just offshore in the inconclusive but bloody "Battle of the Red-Mouthed Gun," in which, for the first time, Hawaiian fleets were equipped with cannons, operated by foreign gunners.

All sorts of estimates have been made of the population of Waipi'o in different eras. In Kamehameha's day, there may have been as many as 7500 inhabitants; within a century that was down to more like 2000, but you may still meet people brought up in the valley who can point out overgrown spots where Catholic, Protestant, and Congregational churches, and a Chinese temple, were thriving as recently as the 1930s.

△ Waipi'o Valley

However, large-scale settlement of Waipi'o came to an end after the tsunami of April 1, 1946, which scoured the valley from end to end. No one died, but few felt much inclination to rebuild their devastated homes. The busiest Waipi'o has been since then was during the 1960s, when it was used by the Peace Corps to train volunteers heading to work in Asia. These days, sixty percent of the land is owned by one landlord – Kamehameha Schools – which leases it to private farmers. So far, all threats to "develop" Waipi'o have come to nothing – tourists, and golfers in particular, don't like the rain.

Exploring the valley

If you just want to say you've seen Waipi'o, the view from the **overlook** is more comprehensive than any you get down below. Assuming that you've driven here, you must in any case leave your vehicle at the top. A few yards down from the parking lot, a pavilion stands in a small grassy area on the very lip of the cliff, about 900ft above the sea. Off to your left is the green floor of Waipi'o, with terraced fields but barely a building in sight as it reaches back toward misty Kohala Mountain. As you look straight up the coast, across the beach at the mouth of the valley, you should be able to make out three distinct headlands. The first is etched with the zigzagging trail that climbs up toward Waimanu Valley. The second is Laupāhoehoe Iki, while Kauhola, beyond that, is up in North Kohala, near the town of Kapa'au on the road route to Pololū (see p.217). Unless you are the hardiest of hikers or kayakers or take a flight-seeing tour, you'll never see the hidden valleys that lie in between. On clear days, Maui is visible in the far distance.

A paved road heads down the side of the *pali* from the parking lot, but don't try to drive it yourself. Without four-wheel-drive it's suicidal – as the rusting relics in the undergrowth at the foot of the slope attest – and even if you do have four-wheel drive you need to know exactly what you're doing. That leaves you with the choice of either taking a **tour** – see opposite – or **hiking** down. It takes little more than fifteen minutes to reach the floor, but be warned, the 25 percent gradient makes the return trip heavy going, and you need to have at least two hours to spare to make it worth the effort.

One thing the tour operators don't mention is that they're not allowed to take visitors to the seashore. On foot, however, you're free to make your own way there. As soon as you come to the yellow warning sign at the bottom of the slope, well before you reach the stream, double back onto what swiftly becomes a muddy lane. Don't stray off this path; the taro fields to either side are strictly private.

It takes about five minutes, walking through a fine avenue of ironwood trees, to reach the flat **beach** of gray sand that's fronted by small black lava boulders. You may have heard stories about the black-sand beaches of Hawaii, but whatever people say, this isn't one of them. The sand here is simply silt washed down the mountainside, whereas a true black-sand beach is absolutely jet black and composed of tiny glass-like fragments of freshly spewn lava. The wide mouth of Waipi'o Stream cuts the beach in two; usually it's not too difficult to wade across, but you shouldn't attempt it if the water is any deeper than your thighs. Neither should you drink it, as it's liable to carry diseases from wild animals in the hills. **Leptospirosis** in particular is a major problem here, so don't let the water come into contact with the smallest open wound (see p.46). Surfers and boogie-boarders while away days on end playing in the white breakers, but it's no place for a casual dip.

If, instead of heading for the beach, you keep going at the foot of the slope, toward the back of Waipi'o, you soon come within sight of the 1200-foot **Hi'ilawe waterfall**, with the parallel but slimmer **Nani** cascade plummeting to its left. Both were finally restored to full strength in 2004, after a century of having their waters diverted to quench the thirst of the sugar plantations, and feed Waipi'o Stream as it emerges into the heart of the valley. Hi'ilawe, which is celebrated in one of Hawaii's best-known songs, made famous by Gabby Pahinui in particular, is further away than it looks. Walking to its base takes an hour and a half and involves scrambling up a channel of giant boulders. This spot was once the site of Nāpo'opo'o, Waipio's main village, which was said to have had several thousand inhabitants.

A disused, century-old trail runs on a ledge behind, halfway up Hi'ilawe, following the line of the ditches and tunnels that formerly carried water to the sugar farms. The square building to the left of the falls, conspicuous for its mirrored paneling, is also empty. It was built as a restaurant in the 1960s, but local protests at the developers' ever more grandiose plans, which included installing a cable-car ride to the top of the falls, led to the project being abandoned.

Waipi'o tours

Various **organized tours** take visitors around the floor of Waipi'o Valley, offering the chance to learn more about the valley from local people. Many of the guides were born in Waipi'o and are eager to share stories of the old days. However, regulations as to what each operator is allowed to do tend to change from year to year. The beach is off-limits and the waterfalls are too remote, so most tours consist of anecdotal rambles through the taro fields and along the riverbank.

The Waipi'o Valley Shuttle, which runs ninety-minute **van trips** from the overlook, is based at the *Waipi'o Valley Art Works* (see p.237) in Kukuihaele, a mile from the end of the road. They prefer that you call ahead to reserve a trip, but there's often a driver hanging around the overlook itself waiting to fill up his vehicle (Mon–Sat, departures usually at 9am, 11am, 1pm, & 3pm; $55, under-12s $28; T808/775-7121). Likewise working out of the *Waipi'o Valley Art Works,* Waipi'o Na'alapa Trail Rides runs two-hour **horseback expeditions** around the valley (Mon–Sat 9am & 12.30pm; $90; T808/775-0419, Wwww.naalapastables .com). The Last Chance Store, also in Kukuihaele, is the headquarters for Waipi'o Valley Wagon Tours, which takes groups of up to twelve people down into the valley for hour-long **covered-wagon excursions** (Mon–Sat, up to four tours daily, usually at 9.30am, 11.30am, 1.30pm, & 3.30pm; $55, under-12s $28; T808/775-9518, Wwww.waipiovalleywagontours.com).

In addition, various tours explore the backcountry close to and along the upper rim of Waipi'o without making the descent into the valley itself. Waipi'o Ridge Stables (T808/775-1007 or 1-877/757-1414, Wwww.waipioridgestables.com) offer both **horse rides** ($85 for 2hr 30min, $165 for 5hr) and, as Kukui ATV & Adventures (T808/775-1450, Wwww.kukuiatv.com), **off-road vehicle tours** in individual all-terrain buggies ($135 for 3hr). Hawaiian Walkways organizes none-too-strenuous **guided hikes** ($95 for 4–5hr; T808/775-0372 or 1-800/457-7759, Wwww.hawaiianwalkways.com).

Hiking beyond Waipi'o

The moment you arrive at Waipi'o overlook and look across to the trail that climbs the far wall of the valley, you'll probably start wondering what lies **beyond Waipi'o**. Very few people ever find out – it's one of the most difficult hikes in all Hawaii, way beyond what it's possible to achieve in a single day. In addition, the trail only continues as far as **Waimanu Valley**, eleven miles away. The four more valleys before Pololū (see p.217) are inaccessible from this side; a trail from Pololū reaches two of them, but that too is an extremely demanding undertaking.

Because it involves wading through at least two deep and fast-flowing streams, the trail to Waimanu – officially known as the **Muliwai Trail** – is generally only passable between May and October. Only consider setting off from Waipi'o if you're equipped with a camping permit (see below) and everything necessary for a backcountry expedition – most notably a rainproof tent and clothing, and some kind of water purification system.

Start by heading slightly inland from the far end of Waipi'o beach, and you'll soon pick up the uphill path. From the third switchback up, you get a tremendous view looking back across Waipi'o Valley, but for most of the way beyond that, the trail passes through thick woodlands, offering barely a glimpse of either sea or the valley ahead. It doesn't drop to sea level again until Waimanu, but climbs up and down through what feels like an endless succession of gullies.

Waimanu itself is a sort of miniature Waipi'o, with even more waterfalls. It, too, was once densely populated by taro-farmers and only abandoned after the tsunami of 1946. The beach itself is made up of large boulders, which means that not only is it not safe for swimming, you can hardly even walk along it. The main **campground** is on the far side of Waimanu Stream. Camping is free but limited to nine sites, and you can stay a maximum of six nights. Obtain a permit from the Department of Forestry in Hilo, at 1643 Kīlauea Ave (☎808/974-4221).

Local experts advise that the easiest way to get to Waimanu and beyond is not by hiking at all, but by **kayak**. Naturally, only experienced kayakers should attempt such an expedition.

The Saddle Road

From a glance at the map, the **SADDLE ROAD** looks the quickest route from one side of the Big Island to the other. What no map can convey, however, is quite how high and remote it is, involving a long slow haul to an altitude of well over 6000ft in order to cross the "saddle" of land that lies between **Mauna Kea** to the north and **Mauna Loa** to the south. The fifty-mile stretch from Hilo to the point where it rejoins the Belt Road – six miles south of Waimea, and more than thirty northeast of Kailua – is one of the bleakest stretches of road imaginable, utterly unlike anything you'd expect to encounter in the middle of the Pacific Ocean.

Even if the Saddle Road is not much use as a short cut, it is an enjoyable adventure in its own right. Despite the elevation, it passes a long way below the summits of the two mountains, so you probably won't see the snowcaps, but there's some memorable scenery en route. The trouble is, all the car-rental chains **forbid** drivers to take their vehicles along the Saddle Road, on pain of forfeiting your insurance cover and all rights to emergency rescue. The only way around this is to rent a 4WD vehicle (see p.166).

The rental-car ban was originally imposed because the road was poorly surfaced, and narrowed in several sections to a single lane. These days, the surface is always reasonable, and even at its narrowest cars traveling in opposite directions can pass each other comfortably. Certain dangers remain, however: the road was built to serve the military bases in the high stretches and still sees a lot of uncompromising military traffic – it's frequently closed to non-military vehicles for hours at a time – and also the weather is often atrocious, so visibility can be very bad. Above all, there are no facilities of any kind for the entire 85 miles from Hilo to Kailua, so if you do get stuck or break down, rescuing you is a difficult and expensive job. If you choose to risk it, fill up with gas, take it slowly and be sure to allow time to complete your journey in daylight.

Leaving Hilo, along first Waiānuenue Avenue and then Kaumana Drive, the Saddle Road seems to go on climbing forever, straight from the ocean. Beyond the suburbs with their tropical gardens, it heads up into the clouds, winding through a moist and misty heathland of spindly trees, then undulating across bare lava fields, until with any luck it emerges into the sun, on what feels like a wide grassy plain between Mauna Loa and Mauna Kea.

Gradually the road then curves to the north, circling Mauna Kea and bringing Hualālai into view. Various plans have been put forward over the years to cut a more direct course down to Kailua, saving perhaps twenty miles on the total distance, only to be stymied by the presence of environmentally or archeologically important sites. Federally funded work finally started in 2004, however, to upgrade the Saddle Road along its existing course in its entirety. A further spur may come with the opening of the Superferry service to Kawaihae Harbor, which will give Hilo residents the chance to take their vehicles off-island, and it seems likely that the Saddle Road will in the next few years finally become serviceable as the fastest cross-island route.

Mauna Kea

For the moment, **MAUNA KEA** is, at 13,796ft, the highest mountain in the entire Pacific. Being extinct, however, and therefore already eroding away, it's steadily losing ground to still-active Mauna Loa, 25 miles southwest. Nonetheless its height and isolation make Mauna Kea one of the very best sites for **astronomical observatories** on earth. Its summit is an otherworldly place, not just because of the surreal ring of high-tech telescopes trained out into the universe, but because it's so devoid of life, its naked hillocks composed of multicolored minerals. A spur road ascends to the summit from the Saddle Road, though its last nine miles are restricted to 4WD vehicles only, and the observatories are seldom open to casual visitors.

The ancient Hawaiians named Mauna Kea the "white mountain," as it is capped by snow for over half the year. That didn't deter them from climbing right to the top, however. Like Mauna Loa, Mauna Kea is a shield volcano (see p.253), so most of its slope is very gentle. It differs from its neighbor in having been here during the last Ice Age, making it the only spot in the central Pacific to have been covered by **glaciers**. The ice had the effect of chilling its molten lava to create the best basalt in the islands. Incredibly, there's an ancient **adze quarry** 12,400ft up the mountain. Dating as far back as 1100 AD, it was probably the major source of the stone used for all the islanders' basic tools.

Ellison Onizuka Visitor Center

The turnoff to the summit of Mauna Kea comes at mile marker 28 on the Saddle Road. At first the road passes through grazing land, covered with wiry grass but devoid of trees. Most of this land is open cattle range – a broad swathe of this flank of Mauna Kea, just like the northern side, belongs to the Parker Ranch (see p.210). The road surface is good for the nine miles to the **Ellison Onizuka Visitor Center**, a small facility that houses displays about the observatories and also has its own much more basic telescope, used for the nightly stargazing sessions (center open daily 9am–10pm; stargazing daily 6–10pm; free; ☎808/961-2180, ⓦwww .ifa.hawaii.edu/info/vis). Every Saturday, there's a special program of some kind, perhaps an astronomer describing some aspect of the observatories' work, or a Hawaiian cultural talk.

Whether or not you plan to continue on to the summit, the eerie views here, at 9000ft, make it worth coming this far. Bizarre reddish cinder cones and other volcanic protrusions float in and out of the mists that swathe the grasslands; in the afternoon, the clouds usually obscure Hilo and the coast altogether. In any case, to help prevent **altitude sickness** and related problems, you should remain for at least an hour at this level before going any higher. It's also important to drink as much water as possible – and not to come this high within 24 hours of **scuba diving**.

The road to the summit

The road on from the visitor center is kept in reasonably good condition; the astronomers who work at the top have to commute this way. It's only safe to attempt it in a **4WD vehicle**, though it has to be said that many locals do go up in ordinary cars. The surface is unpaved for the first five miles, largely to deter visitors; for its final four miles the road is paved once more, in order to avoid churning up dust that might interfere with the telescopes.

Locals delight in driving to the top of Mauna Kea to fill their pickup trucks with snow. Most tourists, however, are keen to see the inside of the observatories. If that's your goal, the best day to come is either Saturday or Sunday, when staff at the visitor center coordinate **free summit tours**. Participants are required to bring their own 4WD vehicles. If you don't have one, you could try to hitch a ride, but you can't arrange it in advance and it's a big favor to ask, as you'll be dependent on your new friend for several hours. The tour parties assemble at 1pm to watch a video presentation about the observatories, and then set off in a convoy at around 2pm.

In addition, several operators run **guided tours** to the summit of Mauna Kea, which usually include the after-dark stargazing sessions and therefore require afternoon pickups at either Kona coast or Waimea hotels. A typical tour lasts around eight hours and costs $170 or more per person; operators include Mauna Kea Summit Adventures (℡ 808/322-2366 or 1-888/322-2366, Ⓦ www.maunakea .com), Hawaii Forest & Trail (℡ 808/331-8505 or 1-800/464-1993, Ⓦ www .hawaii-forest.com), Jack's Tours (℡ 808/969-9507 or 1-800/442-5557, Ⓦ www .jackstours.com), and the much cheaper *Arnott's Lodge* in Hilo (℡ 808/969-7097, Ⓦ www.arnottslodge.com; see p.222), which charges hostel guests just $70 for a trip to the summit.

Alternatively, if you're feeling *really* energetic, you can **hike** up. This involves a grueling haul up six miles of exposed road, with an elevation increase of 4000ft, before you're rewarded with your first glimpse of the summit.

Weather conditions at and near the summit can be absolutely atrocious. Wind speeds of over 170 mph have been measured (at which point the anemometer snapped), twelve feet of snow has fallen in a single night, and visibility is always liable to drop to zero. It's essential to bring very warm, windproof clothing, sunscreen, and sunglasses.

The observatories

When you finally reach the top of Mauna Kea, it's far from obvious which of the many rusty red and gold cinder cones in the vicinity is the actual summit. In fact, out of deference to Hawaiian sensibilities, all the gleaming golf-ball-shaped **observatories** are clustered on slightly lesser eminences; the highest mound of all is topped only by a small Hawaiian shrine.

Mauna Kea was first opened up to astronomical use in the 1960s and now holds a total of thirteen observatories. Each is leased to a different academic institution or consortium, but the entire site remains under the auspices of the University of Hawaii. No further telescopes will be built, though existing ones can be replaced as they become outdated. The most technologically advanced facilities are the two identical domes of the **Keck** observatories, which function in tandem, and the giant **Subaru Observatory**, which boasts the world's largest glass mirror, at 8.3meters (about 27ft 5inches) across. (Subaru is the Japanese name for the Pleiades, or "Seven Sisters" stars.)

Some observatories, such as the Keck pair, are remote-controlled by technicians in Waimea and Hilo, while others require human operators to be on hand. Working at this altitude brings unique problems; however often you come here, the thin air is liable to render you light-headed and greatly affects your ability to concentrate. As a result, the weekend guided tours (see opposite) tend to be rather surreal, with guides and visitors alike unable to string coherent thoughts together. Those tours take you into three or four different observatories; if you arrive alone, the original Keck installation, Keck I, is the only one with a visitor gallery (Mon–Fri 10am–4pm; free).

Don't expect to be able to peer through the eyepieces of the telescopes; all information is digitally processed and can only be seen on computer screens. Astronomers from all over the world, including amateur hobbyists, can, however, submit proposals to use the telescopes for their pet projects, at typical fees of around $1 per second.

The summit of Mauna Kea

The summit of Mauna Kea, the cinder cone officially known as **Puʻu Wōkiu**, stands off to the right of the observatory access road. It can only be reached via a short, steep hike up the crumbling slope. Alongside the geodesic plate at the top you'll find a simple cairn of rocks, erected as a Hawaiian shrine. The view, of course, is awesome, with assorted natural cones and craters nearby and the mighty shapes of Mauna Loa and Haleakalā on the horizon. If there's any snow on the ground, you may well find yourself sharing this magnificent spot with groups of teenagers, rendered silly by the altitude, who come up here to **snowboard** down the rough surrounding slopes.

Mauna Kea holds one last surprise. Reached by a ten-minute hiking trail that leaves the main road at a hairpin bend just below the summit, **Lake Waiʻau** is a permanent lake set in a cinder cone 13,020ft above sea level. Some visitors swim in its icy waters, which are replenished by thawing permafrost. It makes more sense to wander over to the brass plaque by the shore, which marks where the ashes of Ikua Purdy, the 1908 World Rodeo champion, were scattered. He and his fellow Parker Ranch cowboys (see p.210) would come all the way up here when roping wild horses.

Mauna Kea State Park

Once past the summit approach road, the Saddle Road starts to head slightly north, and views begin to open up of the whole Kona coast. Close to mile marker 35, a short but very tiring two-mile hike in **Mauna Kea State Park** can bring you to superb views of the island's three largest volcanoes.

From the parking lot, head past the wooden cabins – available for rent through the state parks office in Hilo ($55 per night; ☎808/974-6200) – and follow a jeep track toward Mauna Kea. Having made your way as far as three pale-blue water towers, continue along the track until just before you reach an older and rustier tower. So far the trail has all been flat, but now a footpath leads straight up a small-looking mound to the right. The next few hundred yards are chest-thumpingly steep. Climbing across a loose surface of powdery brown dust, you pass a wide range of brittle high-altitude plants, including desiccated shrubs and a few native silverswords. Though far below the top of Mauna Kea, the crest of the mound makes a perfect vantage point for views of the entire slope of Mauna Loa across the saddle, Huālalai away to the west, and the sprawling army camp below.

Puna

With the compelling attractions of Hawaii Volcanoes National Park nearby, few tourists bother to leave the highway as they pass through the district of **PUNA**, which takes up the southeastern corner of the Big Island. The county government too seems to see it as a land apart, a quirky enclave that doesn't quite fit in with the

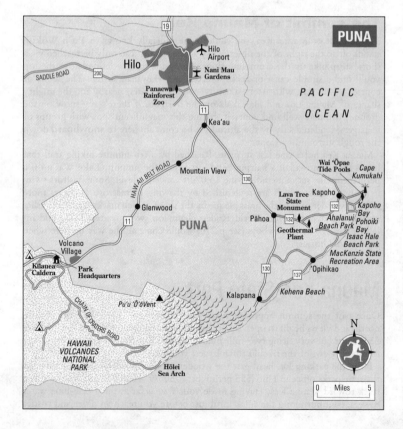

rest of the island. In the 1960s and 1970s, large portions of the region were rezoned for residential development, but it still lacks the infrastructure that you – and the thirty-thousand-plus people who live here – would expect. The volcanoes haven't helped matters either, incinerating newly built homes and cutting the coastal road to leave poor, traffic-ridden **Kea'au** as the only point of access to the whole region.

Although the eleven-mile stretch of oceanfront highway that has so far survived the volcanoes makes an attractive drive, there's no great reason to spend more than a couple of hours in Puna. Stop for lunch in the self-consciously outlaw town of **Pāhoa**, dominated by hippies and back-to-the-landers, but don't expect to swim from any of Puna's photogenic but dangerous beaches. And while Puna has long had the reputation of being the Big Island's main center for the cultivation of *pakololo* ("crazy weed"), also known as marijuana, police crackdowns have put an end to most large-scale activity.

Kea'au

The town of **KEA'AU** lies just south of Hwy-11 as it climbs toward the volcanoes, little more than three miles beyond Hilo's city limits. As a dormitory for Hilo's workers, and the gateway to Puna, it's choked morning and evening by huge traffic jams.

Kea'au consists of little more than the large parking lot for the **Kea'au Shopping Center**. This low-key wooden shopping mall holds the Sure-Save supermarket and its funkier rival, Kea'au Natural Foods, as well as a farmers' market, a laundromat, a raucous sports bar, and a couple of small Asian fast-food diners.

Pāhoa

With its false-front stores and rudimentary timber boardwalks, tiny **PĀHOA**, a dozen miles southwest of Kea'au, is a distinctive blend of Wild West cowboy town and Shangri-la. Life here moves so slowly that it hasn't quite kept up with the rest of America; the streets seem to be filled with refugees from the 1960s – even if most of them were born a decade or two later – watched by occasional, and equally incongruous, groups of *aloha*-shirted tourists. The only building of any size is the venerable Akebono Theater, founded in 1917, where the parking lot is the scene of a lively Sunday morning flea market.

Practicalities

Pāhoa's one **accommodation** option, the *Island Paradise Inn* at the north end of town (℡808/959-9070; ⓦwww.vrbo.com/23179; ➋), consists of a group of simple but very neat and clean one- and two-bedroom wooden cottages, rented at exceptionally low rates. Pāhoa also holds a handful of **restaurants**, plus an ever-changing cast of coffee-house hangouts filled with barefoot, tie-dyed locals. The best food around is served at *Ning's*, a small Thai diner on the boardwalk (daily except Wed noon–8.30pm; ℡808/965-7611), which offers the same delicious menu at both lunch and dinner, with tom yum soup ($7–12) in vegetarian or seafood versions, and red, green, and yellow curries for around $10. The *Aloha Outpost*, 15 Pāhoa Kalapana Rd (Mon–Fri 8.30am–10pm, Sat 10am–10pm, Sun 9am–10pm; ℡808/965-8333), is a **cybercafé** in a small mall at the main highway intersection just north of town.

Lava Tree State Monument

Set back in the rainforest just off Hwy-132, almost three miles out of Pāhoa, **Lava Tree State Monument** (daily dawn–dusk; free) preserves the petrified record of a double catastrophe that took place two centuries ago. First, a fast-flowing lava stream destroyed the underbrush and lapped against the 'ō'hia trees of the forest, clinging to their trunks and cooling as it met resistance. Then an earthquake opened fissures in the ground into which the liquid rock quickly drained. They left the landscape scattered with upright columns of lava, hollow inside where the trees themselves had burned away.

It takes around half an hour to walk the level, paved trail that loops around the finest specimens, which look like black termite mounds or gnarled old candles. While this landscape may be unusual and striking, if your time is limited it's best to push on to the main attractions of Hawaii Volcanoes National Park.

The Puna coast

Halfway down to the sea from Pāhoa on Hwy-130, the "scenic point" to the left of the road at mile marker 15 marks the start of a short trail to a cluster of natural **steam vents**. Locals climb into these small cones to use them as steam baths, but you'd be crazy to follow suit; see p.256 for a salutary warning.

A thick layer of shiny black lava, unceremoniously dumped by Kīlauea in 1988, brings Hwy-130 to a halt close to mile marker 21, just under ten miles from Pāhoa. Some trees are still visible beyond, and new plant growth is starting to appear, but barely a trace survives of the extensive Royal Gardens residential area that once stood here.

Almost all of the coastal village of Kalapana, to which the highway originally led, has also been destroyed. Fortunately, however, roughly half a mile short of its own dead end, Hwy-130 still joins up with Puna's main coast road, Hwy-137. That enables you to complete an enjoyable loop drive back to Pāhoa that takes you about as far off the usual tourist track as you can hope to get on the Big Island.

Kaimū

Hwy-137 reaches the ocean slightly to the east of the former site of **KAIMŪ** black-sand beach, which until it was obliterated in 1990 was one of the most photographed spots on the island. Only *Verna's* grocery and deli, alongside, was spared by the lava, though some of the coconut palms from the beach were rescued and airlifted to the *Hilton Waikoloa* hotel in Kohala.

Assuming new lava flows haven't changed the topography of this area since this book went to press, it's possible to set off walking from the end of the road. The most obvious target is to head straight for the ocean, roughly four hundred yards away and marked by a line of young coconut palms. Reach that across the bare lava field, and you may well find a new black-sand beach beyond. If so, it makes a wonderful spectacle, but don't even dream of swimming here. It's equally possible that at the time you visit active lava flows from Kīlauea may be entering the ocean at some point, in which case the plume of steam where it hits the water may well be visible from this end, as it is from the bottom of Chain of Craters Road (see p.262). However, unless you know exactly where you're going, which in this ever-changing lavascape is all but impossible, you could easily get yourself into very serious danger. Several visitors attempting short strolls from the road have become totally disoriented and ended up stranded all night in the wilderness.

Kehena Beach

Driving east along Hwy-137 takes you through scenery that varies from one minute to the next, depending on the age of the lava flow you're crossing. In places the undergrowth thins out to bare black rock, but most of the route is dripping with tropical vegetation. From time to time you get glimpses of the ocean and successive palm-bedecked headlands, but only rarely is it possible to get down to the seashore.

The best spot to do so is **Kehena Beach**, close to the 19-mile marker, where a cluster of parked cars usually betrays the presence of a small path down the cliffs. At the bottom you'll find an absolutely stupendous little **black-sand beach**, backed by coconut palms that are home to a colony of wild parrots, and forever battered by spectacular crashing surf. Boogie-boarding and body-surfing can only be recommended if you know exactly what you're doing – locals do both naked – while from the jet-black shoreline it's often possible to watch dolphins at play in the water.

Mackenzie State Recreation Area

Another four miles on Hwy-137, beyond the tiny community of **'Opihikao**, **Mackenzie State Recreation Area** is a large, level picnic ground in a grove of ironwood on the oceanfront cliffs, where the earth underfoot is crisp with shed needles. Access to the seashore here is all but impossible: high surf scoops inexorably at the shallow cliff faces, hollowing them out to the extent that even walking to the edge is foolhardy. This tranquil forest glade is popular with locals, though tourists may feel it's not quite "Hawaiian" enough to be worth a stop.

Isaac Hale Beach Park

Just north of where Hwy-137 meets a minor road from Pāhoa, **Isaac Hale Beach Park** finally lets you get down to the sea. Set in Pohoiki Bay, with a small beach of black and white pebbles, overhanging green vegetation, and high surf, the park is popular with surfers, anglers, and picnickers, though it's not a place for family bathing or for anyone inexperienced in the ways of rough Hawaiian seas. A small boat ramp, protected by an army-built breakwater, is used by local vessels; surfers occasionally hitch rides out into the breakers from here.

Not far from Pohoiki Bay, the *Pamalu Hawaiian Country House* (T 808/965-0830, W www.apeacefulenclosure.net; three-night minimum stay; 4–5) is a gay-friendly **B&B**. The five-acre property offers four en-suite guest rooms and has its own swimming pool.

Ahalanui Beach Park

A mile past Isaac Hale Park, **Ahalanui Beach Park** is a spot that can sound perfect on paper – a sheltered oceanfront lagoon, filled with water that's naturally heated by volcanic action to 90°F, and surrounded by coconut palms. In reality, it feels more like an open-air swimming pool, having been shaped into a neat rectangle and surrounded by walls of cemented black lava boulders, complete with several small staircases into the water and attendant lifeguards. Strangely enough, when the construction work was done the water was cold; only later did the volcano step in to heat things up. At weekends, Ahalanui gets very crowded with local families. There have also been alarming reports of dangerous bacteria thriving in the hot water; at least one bather has died, so at the very least don't go in the water if you have an open wound.

Wai 'Ōpae Tide Pools

As a paved road, Hwy-137 comes to an end four miles on from Pohoiki Bay, where it meets Hwy-132 from Pāhoa. To reach this spot, you pass over the site of

Kapoho, yet another town swallowed up by the lava, this time in January 1960. One of the Big Island's best **snorkeling** spots can be found if you turn oceanwards on Kapoho Kai Drive, just over a mile south of the intersection, where "Vacationland" is spelled out on a row of coconuts. Turn left at the far end of Kapoho Kai Drive, and you'll come within a few yards to a sign announcing the **Wai 'Ōpae Tide Pools Marine Life Recreation Area**. A succession of natural lava-walled lagoons here offers great and usually very safe fish viewing, though they're much too shallow to swim in for pleasure.

A dirt road east from the intersection leads in just over a mile to the rudimentary lighthouse at Cape Kumukahi, which is not open to visitors. Much of the land in this area is entirely new, though at the edge of the vegetated zone you may spot an old Japanese cemetery and a *heiau* platform.

Hawaii Volcanoes National Park

HAWAII VOLCANOES NATIONAL PARK may well be the most dynamic, unpredictable place you'll ever visit, and it's one where normal rules just don't seem to apply. What you see, and how long it takes to see it, is beyond all human control. The raw power of an active volcano is not something that can be tamed and labeled to suit those who like their scenery to stay still and their sightseeing to run to schedule. **Kīlauea**, at the heart of the park, is often called the "drive-in volcano"; it's said to be the only volcano in the world where news of a fresh eruption brings people flocking *toward* the lava flows. Only very rarely does the lava claim lives, but much of the excitement of coming here stems from the ever-present whiff of danger.

The park's sole entrance is roughly a hundred miles southeast of Kona, thirty miles southwest of Hilo, and ten miles (as the crow flies) from the ocean. Driving from the west of the island takes at least two hours, with the last thirty miles or so spent ascending through barren lava landscape similar to that in the Kona airport region. The road from Hilo, on the other hand, climbs more steeply through thick, wet rainforest.

You arrive at the park headquarters, beside the caldera (summit crater) of Kīlauea, with no real sense of being on top of a mountain. That's because Kīlauea, at only four thousand feet high, is a mere pimple on the flanks of **Mauna Loa** (13,677ft), which, despite its deceptively gentle incline, stands almost ten thousand feet taller. Furthermore, for all its trails and overlooks, the crater area is a long way from the park's most compelling attraction. Somewhere down the side of Kīlauea, molten lava is bursting out of the ground and cascading down to the sea – assuming that the eruption that has been going nonstop ever since 1983 has not died down by the time you visit.

In total, the irregular boundaries of the National Park take in around 550 square miles. At the start of the twentieth century, it only occupied the Kīlauea Caldera area. Now it incorporates the summit craters and most of the eruption-prone rift

HAWAII VOLCANOES NATIONAL PARK

N

0 — Miles — 3

▲ Puna and Hilo

▲ Mauna Loa Summit Trail

Volcano Village

Kīlauea Visitor Center

Thurston Lava Tube

Volcano House

Jaggar Museum

Kīlauea Caldera

CRATER RIM DRIVE

MAUNA LOA RD

Kīpuka Puaulu

Nāmakani Paio

See Kīlauea Caldera map for details

11

Pu'u 'Ō'ō ▲

Nāpau Crater

Makaopuhi Crater

Pu'u Huluhulu

Puhimau Crater

Panahi Crater

CHAIN OF CRATERS ROAD

CHAIN OF CRATERS ROAD

HILINA PALI ROAD

Kulanaokuaiki

HILINA PALI

HILINA PALI

KA'Ū DESERT

Hilina Pali Overlook

Pu'u Kapukapu

Keauhou Shelter

Halapē Shelter

Ka'aha Shelter

Pepeiao Cabin

KA'Ū DESERT TRAIL

KA'Ū DESERT TRAIL

FOOTPRINTS TRAIL

Ka'ū Desert Trailhead

HŌLEI PALI

PUNA COAST TRAIL

Hōlei Sea Arch

Pu'u Loa

Ka'ena Point

'Āpua Point

KA'Ū DESERT

KA DĪKI PALI

▲ Ka'ū and Kailua

251

zones of both volcanoes – an area that is largely desert but includes scattered pockets of rainforest and even one or two beaches – as well as the 200-square-mile Kahuku Ranch above South Point, which was added to the park in 2003 and remains closed to visitors. From being a solely geological park, its brief has expanded to cover responsibility for preserving the vestiges of pre-contact occupation in the region and protecting indigenous wildlife such as the Hawaiian goose, the **nēnē**. Although the most recent lava flows have been beyond the official boundaries of the park, its rangers still control public access to the danger spots.

Ever since the early missionaries, with their images of the fires of hell, Western visitors have tended to see the volcanoes as purely destructive. The ancient Hawaiians, whose islands would never have existed without the volcanoes, were much more aware of their generative role, embodied in the goddess **Pele**. It may take longer to create than it does to destroy, but fresh lava is rich in nutrients, and life soon regenerates on the new land. On a single visit to the park, it's impossible to appreciate the sheer rapidity of change. What is a crackling, flaming, unstoppable river of molten lava one day may be a busy hiking trail the next. Come back twenty years later, and you could find a rich, living forest.

Planning a visit

Generally speaking, visiting Hawaii Volcanoes National Park involves one or more of the following activities. First of all, there's the eleven-mile loop tour around Kīlauea Caldera from the visitor center, on **Crater Rim Drive**; second, you may choose to **hike** into or near the caldera, from one or more points along the way; and finally comes the fifty-mile round-trip down the **Chain of Craters Road** to the ocean, ending at the site of the current eruption. If you have the time, two additional areas are open to exploration. Getting right to the **summit of Mauna Loa** involves a four-day hike, but it's possible to drive the first 3000ft of the route to gain a different perspective on the region. Away to the west, the **Ka'ū Desert** offers more trails into a harshly beautiful moonscape.

Few people allow enough time to see the park properly. In a single day you'd be hard pushed to drive the two main roads, let alone hike any trails. Worse still,

The shield volcanoes of Hawaii

According to the classic popular image, a volcano is a cone-shaped mountain, with a neat round crater at the top that's filled with bubbling lava and spouts columns of liquid fire.

Hawaiian volcanoes aren't like that. Although you may be lured to the park by photos of pillars of incandescent lava, you're unlikely to see any such thing. These are **shield volcanoes**, which grow slowly and steadily rather than violently, adding layer upon layer as lava seeps out of fissures and vents all along the "**rift zones**" that cover their sides. The result is a long, low profile, supposedly resembling a warrior's shield laid on the ground.

Mauna Loa and Kīlauea are simply the latest in the series of volcanoes responsible for creating the entire Hawaiian chain. Like all the rest, they are fueled by a "**hot spot**" in the earth's crust, way below the sea floor, which has been channeling magma upwards for seventy million years. As the continental plates drift northwest, at around three inches per year, that magma has found its way to the surface in one volcano after another. Each island in turn has clawed its way up from the depths, emerged above the waves, and then ceased to grow as its volcanoes became ever further removed from the life-giving source. In time, erosion by rain and sea wears away the rock, sculpting the fabulous formations seen at their most dramatic on Kauai, and eventually the ocean washes over it once more, perhaps leaving a ring of coral – an **atoll** – to bear witness. Though Kauai is the oldest Hawaiian island of any size, the oldest of all are by now 3500 miles away, mere specks in the Emperor chain, off the coast of Japan.

Look at the gentle slope of **Mauna Loa**, project that gradient down through almost 20,000 feet of ocean, and you'll see why its Hawaiian name, "long mountain," is so appropriate. It's the most massive single object on earth; its summit is, at 13,677ft, very slightly lower than Mauna Kea, but its volume of 10,000 cubic miles makes it a hundred times larger than Washington's Mount Rainier. It took two million years for Mauna Loa to swell from the bed of the Pacific into the air, and for another million years it has continued to climb. In the last 150 years, the world's highest active volcano has erupted every three or four years – in a single hour in 1984, it let forth enough lava to pave a highway from Honolulu to New York. Geologists predict that every spot on its surface will receive at least one more coating of fresh lava before the fires die down.

Only around once a century does Mauna Loa erupt simultaneously with **Kīlauea**, however. Of late the younger upstart – its name means "much spewing" – has been grabbing the attention, having been in a record-breaking continuous state of eruption since 1983. Although fed by a separate conduit from the fires below, Kīlauea emerged as a lump on the side of Mauna Loa, so you can hardly tell it's a separate mountain. Its lava tends to flow consistently in the same direction, down toward the ocean. Since 1983, it has added well over 500 acres of new land to a nine-mile stretch of the Puna coastline.

Meanwhile the next volcano is on its way. Scientists are monitoring the submarine "seamount" of **Loʻihi**, twenty miles southeast of the Kaʻū coast. Were you to stay around for three thousand years, you might see it poke its head out for the first time. One day it may seem no more than a blemish on the vast bulk of Mauna Loa – or it may be destined to overrun its older sisters altogether.

you'll probably miss the most spectacular experience of all – watching the **eruption after dark**. Much the best option is to spend the night nearby, either in the park itself, at the *Volcano House* hotel (see p.256), at the campgrounds (p.257 and p.262), or in a B&B in the village of Volcano (p.268). Failing that, at least base yourself in Hilo, thirty miles away, rather than distant Kona. Be sure in any case to bring some **food** with you; none is available anywhere near the eruption, while *Volcano House* has the only, rather poor, restaurant inside the park.

Although the best way to explore the park is in your own vehicle, you can at least get there by **public bus** from Hilo. On Monday through Friday only, the Hele On Bus Company (☎808/935-8241) runs a service that leaves Hilo's Mooheau Bus Terminal at 2.40pm and calls at the park visitor center around an hour later. The return ride is in the morning, leaving the visitor center at 8.10am. Buses continue beyond the park as far as Ocean View (see p.274), but not all the way to Kailua. Alternatively, you could opt for an organized **bus tour** (some are listed on p.166), but generally these are not a good idea. They'll show you Kīlauea Caldera from above, but are unlikely to give you the flexibility to approach the eruption.

Inevitably, what you do will depend on conditions on the day you arrive. The active lava flow might be right there at the end of the road, it might be an hour's hike away, it might be somewhere else entirely or it might have stopped altogether. If it *is* flowing, then seeing it should be your top priority; why linger over photos in a museum when you can see the real thing?

Crater Rim Drive and the park headquarters

The **park entrance** is just off Hwy-11, the Belt Road, about a mile west of the village of **Volcano** (see p.167). If you're coming from the Kona side you can visit the park without ever passing through Volcano, though as it holds the only gas station for miles, you may well have to anyway. From the **Visitor Center**, on the right within a few yards of the main gate, **Crater Rim Drive** takes eleven miles to loop around the summit crater ("caldera") of Kīlauea – for safety reasons, not always in sight of the edge.

Looking from a distance like a large oval of predominantly gray lava, roughly three miles long by two miles wide, **Kīlauea Caldera** is flanked on two sides by a steep *pali*, around 400ft high. On those sides, and in places down below the wall as well, patches of rainforest have escaped the fires; off to the south and east, however, the cliff dwindles to almost nothing, and strong-smelling sulphur drifts across the plains to ensure that nothing living can find a foothold. It's possible to walk right to the edge of the main center of activity within the caldera, **Halemaʻumaʻu Crater**, either from a parking lot on Crater Rim Drive or all the way across from *Volcano House* (see p.256).

Kīlauea Visitor Center

Though **Kīlauea Visitor Center** does not overlook the crater of Kīlauea, call in as soon as you arrive to pick up the latest information on the eruption and advice on hiking trails (daily 7.45am–5pm; ☎808/967-7311, ⓦwww.nps.gov/havo). The center also has a bookstore and a small museum, and provides lots of excellent free literature. Every hour on the hour, from 9am to 4pm, it shows a ten-minute video that's packed with eruption footage. Frequent lectures explain aspects of local geology, botany, and environmental issues; at 7pm on most Tuesdays, the center reopens for a series of talks called "After Dark in the Park." Note that if you plan to camp in the backcountry, you must register here.

Just beyond the visitor center, set a little way back from the road, the **Volcano Art Center** (daily 9am–5pm; ☎808/967-7565) is a nonprofit gallery and crafts store that sells the work of local artists. Prices are slightly higher than elsewhere, but the standard of the artwork – ranging across sculpture, prints, paintings, and photographs, and not all volcano-related – tends to be much higher as well.

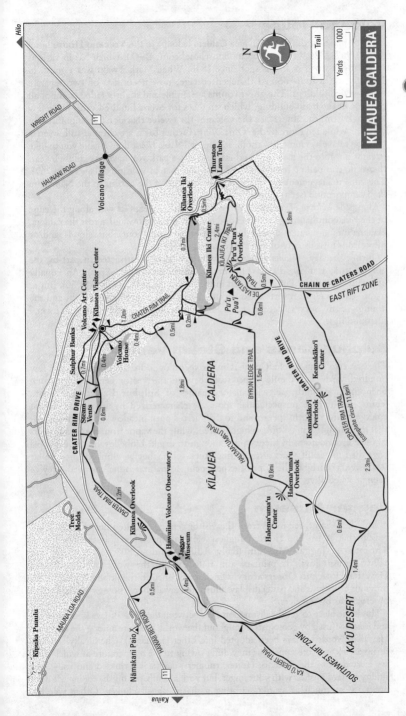

KĪLAUEA CALDERA

N

Trail

0   Yards   1000

Hilo

WRIGHT ROAD

HAUNANI ROAD

11

Volcano Village

Thurston Lava Tube

Kīlauea Iki Overlook

1.5mi

Kīlauea Iki Crater

0.7mi   2.4mi   KĪLAUEA IKI TRAIL   Pu'u Pua'i Overlook

Volcano Art Center

Kīlauea Visitor Center

Sulphur Banks

CRATER RIM DRIVE

1.0mi   CRATER RIM TRAIL   0.2mi   DEVASTATION TRAIL   0.5mi

0.7mi   0.4mi   Pu'u Pua'i   0.6mi

Steam Vents   Volcano House   0.5mi   CHAIN OF CRATERS ROAD

0.6mi   EAST RIFT ZONE

0.4mi   1.8mi   KĪLAUEA   CALDERA   BYRON LEDGE TRAIL   1.5mi   CRATER RIM DRIVE   Keanakāko'i Crater

Kīlauea Overlook   HALEMA'UMA'U TRAIL   KĪLAUEA   Keanakāko'i Overlook

.2mi   CRATER RIM TRAIL   Tree Molds   MAUNA LOA ROAD

Hawaiian Volcano Observatory   0.6mi   Halema'uma'u Overlook   CRATER RIM TRAIL (complete circuit 11.6mi)   2.3mi

Jaggar Museum   Halema'uma'u Crater   0.6mi

Kīpuka Puaulu   .4mi   0.5mi   1.4mi

HAWAII BELT ROAD   KA'Ū DESERT   SOUTHWEST RIFT ZONE   KA'Ū DESERT TRAIL

Nāmakani Paio   11

Kailua

Volcano House

Pride of place on the lip of Kīlauea Caldera belongs to the **Volcano House** hotel
(℡808/967-7321, Ⓦwww.volcanohousehotel.com; ❸–❻), which has in various
incarnations stood near this spot since 1846. When Mark Twain was a guest, in
1866, it was a four-roomed thatched cottage; now it consists of two separate
motel-style buildings. The **guest rooms** are simple and slightly faded, and not all
of those in the main building, which stretches for over a hundred yards just a few
feet back from the abyss, face the volcano; the twelve that don't are significantly
cheaper, while ten more in the ʻŌhia Wing, further back, are cheaper still. Even if
you don't have a crater-view room, staying at *Volcano House* does enable you to hike
straight out into the park, but as this is basically a park you have to explore by car,
there's no compelling reason to stay here rather than in Volcano village (see p.267).
The same management is also responsible for renting the **cabins** in the Nāmakani
Paio campground (see opposite).

Alongside *Volcano House*, the **Crater Rim Trail** squeezes its way along the edge
of the *pali*, commanding views beyond the rainforest below and across the caldera.
Halemaʻumaʻu Crater should be visible, three miles out, but clouds and/or
sulphurous mist usually obscure Mauna Loa on the far side.

During the day, *Volcano House* fills with day-trippers, attracted in part by the
hurried and, frankly, dismal $14 lunch buffet (daily 11am–2pm). An equally
unexciting breakfast buffet is served in the morning (7–10.30am; $11.50). But at
night, *Volcano House* reverts to something like its old, more intimate self, and the
dining room serves decent pasta and meat entrees ($17–30) in formal
surroundings.

Sulphur Banks and Steam Vents

The first two stops on the Crater Rim Drive, on opposite sides of the road a few
hundred yards and a mile respectively beyond the visitor center, are natural
phenomena with the self-explanatory names of **Sulphur Banks** and **Steam
Vents**. Both these unspectacular spots are characterized by white fumes that
emerge from cracks in the ground to drift across open meadows; the difference is
that the Sulphur Banks stink to high heaven, while the vapor from the Steam Vents
is, once it condenses, in theory pure enough to drink. Unbelievably, two people
have died in recent years after getting stuck when they've climbed into similar
steam vents nearby in the hope of experiencing a "natural sauna"; instead, they've
been poached alive.

Jaggar Museum

A little less than three miles from the visitor center, and sited here for the good
reason that it has the clearest, highest view of the caldera, is the fascinating
Thomas A. Jaggar Museum (daily 8.30am–5pm; ℡808/967-7643, Ⓦhttp
://hvo.wr.usgs.gov). Its primary aim is to explain the work of the adjacent
Hawaiian Volcano Observatory, which is not open to the public. Videos show
previous eruptions and panel displays illustrate Hawaiian mythology and historical
observations by travelers.

This is the place to get the distinction clear between the kinds of lava known as *ʻaʻā*
and *pāhoehoe* (used by geologists throughout the world, these are among the very few
Hawaiian words to have been adopted into other languages). Chemically the two
forms are exactly the same, but they differ owing to the temperature at which they
are ejected from the volcano. Hotter, runnier *pāhoehoe* is wrinkled and ropy, like
sludgy custard pushed with your finger, but with a sandpaper finish; cooler *ʻaʻā* does
not flow so much as spatter, creating a sharp, jagged clinker. Other volcanic

Controlling the flow

When ancient Hawaiians found their homes threatened by approaching lava, they usually attempted to propitiate Pele with offerings (see p.259), but if in the end they had to move away they were not greatly inconvenienced. Unlike their modern counterparts, they did not own the land on which they lived, and could simply rebuild elsewhere. They could also load their possessions into canoes and paddle out of harm's way.

A full-scale emergency in Puna today would be very different, with hundreds of vehicles attempting to flee along the one road out, which might be rendered impassable at any moment. What's more, anyone unfortunate enough to lose a home may face economic ruin.

That sort of scenario loomed in the mind of **Thomas Jaggar** when he founded the **Hawaiian Volcano Observatory** in 1911. Its Latin motto, *ne plus haustae aut obratae urbes*, means "no more swallowed up or buried cities," and one of its main goals was to understand the behavior of the volcanoes in an effort to control them.

In both 1935 and 1942, when Hilo appeared to be under threat from eruptions of Mauna Loa, attempts were made to **bomb** the lava flow. Angled walls have also been constructed at strategic points on the slopes, in the hope of channeling the stream away from specific targets. A military installation high on Mauna Loa seems to have been spared as a result, though a similar scheme in the Kapoho district (see p.250) could not prevent the town's destruction.

These days the emphasis is much more on prediction than containment; the emergency services are briefed to stop fires but not to try to divert the flow. Only partly is that out of respect for Pele – more important is the fear of **litigation**. Directing lava away from one site might have the effect of "aiming" it at another; aggrieved homeowners who lost their property could then blame – and sue – the authorities responsible.

by-products on display in the museum include **Pele's hair** – very fine filaments made of glass that really do look like hair – and the shiny droplets called **Pele's tears**.

Outside, a viewing area looks down into Kīlauea, and Halema'uma'u Crater in particular, which is 360ft deep at this point. By now you're on the fringes of the Ka'ū Desert, so there are no trees to block the view. The trade winds have for millennia blown the noxious emissions from the crater southwest, so despite receiving large quantities of rainfall the land in this direction supports no growth.

Namakani Paio

A ten-minute walk from the Jaggar Museum parking lot, away from the caldera, brings you to the only **campground** in the main area of the park, **Nāmakani Paio**. It's actually just across the Belt Road, so if you're driving straight to it you don't enter the park proper. The pleasant wooded sites are free and available on a first-come, first-served basis for maximum stays of seven nights (in any one year).

Basic **cabins**, sharing use of the campground's restrooms and showers, can be rented for $50 per night through *Volcano House* (see opposite; ☏808/967-7321, ⓦ www.volcanohousehotel.com; ❷). Each holds one double bed and two bunk beds, and has a picnic table and barbecue area. Bed linen is provided, but despite the fact that it can get very cold at night, there's no heating, so bring a sleeping bag or extra blanket.

Halema'uma'u Crater

Kīlauea may be extremely active, but currently it's unusual for eruptions to take place up here at the summit. Since 1980, it's happened only twice, both times for less than a day. Such eruptions can create smaller craters within the caldera; the most conspicuous of these, **Halemaʻumaʻu Crater**, is just over a mile from the museum.

Although you can see the crater from the roadside parking lot, you'll get a better idea of it by walking a couple of hundred yards across the caldera floor. The trail is clearly marked and there's a handrail, but with gusts of white mist spouting from crevices in the rock you feel as if you're taking your life in your hands.

As you look from the rim into a steaming abyss heavy with the stench of white and yellow sulphur, it's easy to see where sections of the wall have collapsed, as well as the yawning cracks where they will do so in future. In the 1830s, Halemaʻumaʻu was described as a dome rising out of the lava field; when Mark Twain saw it in 1866 it was a "heaving sea of molten fire," with walls a thousand feet high. Since a huge explosion in 1924, however, it's been shallower and quieter, and it's now a circular depression that drops about 400ft below the rest of the caldera. If this walk whets your appetite, you might be tempted to brave the entire three-mile length of the **Halemaʻumaʻu Trail**, right across the caldera from *Volcano House* (see p.256).

Keanakākoʻi and Puʻu Puaʻi

From time to time, the route of the Crater Rim Drive has had to be redrawn, as fresh lava paves over the road and a new layer of tarmac is in turn laid down on top of the lava. The stretch immediately to the east of Halemaʻumaʻu was cut in two in 1982 and now passes in between the sites of two recent eruptions.

Until it was filled almost to the brim by new outpourings, **Keanakākoʻi Crater**, south of the road, was the site of an ancient adze quarry, a source of the hard stone used by Hawaiians to make tools and weapons. **Puʻu Puaʻi**, farther along, is a bare, rust-colored cinder cone thrown up in 1959 and accessible along the Devastation Trail (see p.261).

Thurston Lava Tube

Once past the Chain of Craters turnoff (see p.262), Crater Rim Drive plunges back into dense rainforest. This much less intimidating landscape is the location of the only short walk attempted by most tour groups, into the **Thurston Lava Tube**.

As soon as you cross the road from the parking lot, a mile or so short of the visitor center, you're faced by a large natural basin bursting with huge *ʻōhiʻa* trees. Beneath it is the tube itself, created when the surface of a lava stream hardened on exposure to the air and the lava below was able to keep flowing with only a slight loss of temperature. When the lava eventually drained away, it left behind a damp, empty tunnel, an artificially lit portion of which is now open to the public. If you've ever descended into a subway system, the basic concept and appearance will be familiar.

It takes less than ten minutes to walk to and through the main section of the tube, which is remarkable only for the smoothness of its walls and its conveniently flat natural floor. Occasionally roots from the gigantic ferns that grow up above have worked their way through cracks in the rock to dangle from the ceiling. If you've brought a flashlight, it's worth continuing beyond the official exit at the end of the illuminated portion, to explore the tube in a much rawer state. Back outside, the native red-billed *ʻiʻiwi* bird can always be heard, if not seen.

Hiking in Kīlauea Caldera

Laying a road across the unstable surface of the caldera itself would be ludicrous even by the standards of this topsy-turvy park, so the sole way to experience the

Pele: The volcano goddess

Every visitor to Hawaii Volcanoes National Park soon hears the name of **Pele**, the "volcano goddess" of the ancient Hawaiians. The daughter of Haumea the Earth Mother and Wākea the Sky Father, she is said to have first set foot in the Hawaiian chain on Kauai. Pursued by her vengeful older sister, the goddess of the sea, she traveled from island to island and finally made her home in the pit of Kīlauea. As well as manifesting herself as molten lava, she appeared sometimes as a young woman, sometimes as an elderly crone. Small acts of charity to her human forms could spare the giver a terrible fate when she returned as fire.

Imbued as they are with poetry, legend, history, and symbolism, it's impossible now to appreciate all that the tales of Pele meant to those who once recounted them by the distant glow of Kīlauea. Certainly these were a people who studied the volcanoes carefully; specific places appear in the chants describing Pele's progress through the archipelago in the exact order of age agreed by modern experts. However, the destructive power of the volcanoes was just one small aspect of the goddess; she was also associated with the *hula*, with fertility, and with creation in general.

Talk of Hawaiian religion as a single system of belief ignores the fact that different groups once worshipped different gods. The god Kū, to whom human sacrifices were made in the *luakinis* (see p.205), was probably the chosen deity of the warrior elite; Pele may have been far more central to the lives of most of the islanders. She seems to have been a Polynesian deity whose worship became prominent in Hawaii around the thirteenth century. That may be because, together with Kū, she was brought to the islands by the wave of migrants who arrived at that time from Tahiti, or it may be that that was when Kīlauea entered the period of high activity that still continues today.

The earliest Christian missionaries to the Big Island were disconcerted to find that even after the *kapu* was broken and the old ways supposedly abandoned, belief in Pele endured. They made great play of an incident in 1824, when Queen Kapi'olani, a recent convert to Christianity, defied the goddess by descending into the caldera (probably on what's now known as the Byron Ledge), reading aloud from her Bible, eating the *kapu* red *'ōhelo* berries and throwing their stones into the pit. Less fuss was made in 1881, when an eight-month flow from Mauna Loa had reached within a mile of central Hilo, Christian prayers had elicited no response, and Princess Ruth Ke'elikōlani was called in from Oahu to help. Under the gaze of journalists and missionaries, she chanted to Pele at the edge of the molten rock and offered her red silk handkerchiefs and brandy. By the next morning, the flow had ceased. Well into the twentieth century, inhabitants of Puna and Ka'ū brought up in the old traditions would state that their families were directly descended from Pele and that, in a sense, each individual *was* Pele.

crater floor is by **hiking**. The only safe trails are those maintained by the park service and shown on their free handouts; venturing off these would be suicidal. To embark on even the most popular trails requires an act of faith verging on the superstitious: they're no more than ill-defined footpaths across the bare, steaming lava, guided only by makeshift rock cairns known as *ahus*. Frequent cracks reveal a crust that is on average around four inches thick – though considering the many such layers of lava piled up beneath you, that's not as alarming as it may sound. Geologists estimate that the molten lava here is two miles down.

The caldera is not for agoraphobics; you can't assume that anyone will be on the same trail as you. Mundane accidents happen frequently, and trying to hike at night is a very bad idea.

The longest trail in the caldera area, the 11.6-mile **Crater Rim Trail**, is not described in detail here because it so closely parallels the Crater Rim Drive, though it generally runs nearer the edge than the road. It is an exciting, dramatic walk, and a level and easy one too, but it shows you very little that you can't see from a car. All the trails in this section start from or cross the Crater Rim Trail, however, so you're likely to walk at least a short section of it. Note that there's no need to register for any of the caldera hikes. You must do so, however, if you're heading into the backcountry (see p.254).

The Halemaʻumaʻu and Byron Ledge trails

Two separate hiking trails – the **Halemaʻumaʻu** and the **Byron Ledge** – cross the main floor of Kīlauea Caldera. However, as they meet each other twice, it makes sense to combine the two into one single round-trip, of roughly seven miles and around four hours.

The obvious place to start is along the Crater Rim Trail from *Volcano House*. Heading northwest (away from the park entrance), the path drops slightly for a hundred yards, until a signpost points to the left down the **Halemaʻumaʻu Trail**. From there, a clear, easy walkway descends through thick **rainforest**, where the bright orange heliconia growing to either side is interspersed with delicate white-blossomed shrubs and green *hāpuʻu* ferns. Except when the odd helicopter passes overhead, the only sounds are the chatter of the tiny bright birds that flit through the canopy, and the steady drip of rain falling from the highest branches. Soon a sheer wall of rock to your left marks the abrupt fault line of the outermost crater rim. Less than half a mile down, from a small rain shelter, views open out across a small gorge filled with gently stirring jungle.

Not far beyond are the massive rock slides left by an earthquake in November 1983; the giant cubic boulders that tumbled down the cliff face now reach to the very edge of the path. Thereafter the vegetation thins out, and shortly after the first intersection with the Byron Ledge Trail, which you can ignore at this point, you come to the edge of the vast black expanse of the **crater floor**. The trail from here on is nowhere near as distinct as you might expect. At first the passage worn by the feet of previous hikers is clear enough, but before long you're gingerly picking your way from cairn to crude cairn, the schoolyard game of not treading on the cracks taking on a real urgency when you think of the lake of molten lava somewhere beneath your feet. The state of the trail depends on the age of the flow at each precise spot. Different vintages overlap in absurd profusion, and from time to time the path becomes a jumble of torn, cracked, and uplifted slabs of rock.

For at least half an hour you cross a plain where tiny ferns have taken root in every fissure, creating a green latticework of fault lines. Here and there *ʻōhelo* bushes bearing the dew-glistening red berries sacred to Pele have established themselves. Then the ground begins to rise again, the cairns become harder to pick out against the general chaos, and wisps of sulphurous steam gust across the path with ever-greater regularity.

In due course you're confronted by what appears to be a low ridge of sharp, rough hills, with no indication of what lies behind. A single clear footpath leads up to a gap; through that gap, a similar landscape opens up once again. If you don't know what a **spatter cone** is yet, turn around; on this side the walls of most of the castellated hillocks are hollow, exposing fiery red interiors. They were created by the eruption of April 1982, when hikers in this lonely spot had to be evacuated immediately before a nineteen-hour onslaught.

This spot is clearly marked as the intersection of the Halemaʻumaʻu and Byron Ledge trails, which head on together for a couple of hundred yards to the very lip of **Halemaʻumaʻu Crater**. At this point you'll probably encounter other sightseers who have got here the easy way, via the short trail from the Crater Rim Drive; that walk, and the actual crater, are described on p.257. If you can arrange to be picked up at the parking lot, you can end your hike here. Alternatively, double back and take your choice as to your return route.

If you decide to head back along the **Byron Ledge Trail**, you'll find it considerably easier to follow, with a shorter distance across the crater floor; the walk to the edge of the crater from the junction of the two trails takes around half an hour. This trail is more even underfoot, although once or twice it requires you to step across narrow (roughly nine inches) but alarmingly dark cracks in the ground, including one with a small tree in it.

The ascent to **Byron Ledge** (named after the cousin of the poet, who came here in 1825) is quite precipitous. The surface of the path is unstable gravel, of the same sharp shards of black glass as a new "black-sand" beach, and occasionally the scree slope plunges away below your feet. It can be very vertiginous; from this close, the black crater floor is so huge and featureless that the brain can't really take it in. The rainforest at the top is gloomier and less lush than on the Halemaʻumaʻu Trail.

At one point along the ledge, you pass a spur trail that leads within minutes to the Kīlauea Iki Trail. Sticking to the Byron Ledge Trail involves dropping right back down to cross a small segment of the caldera floor, in order to rejoin the Halemaʻumaʻu Trail back to *Volcano House*.

The Kīlauea Iki Trail

Just east of Kīlauea Caldera proper, but still within the Crater Rim Drive, the subsidiary crater of **Kīlauea Iki** ("little Kīlauea") took on its current shape during a gigantic eruption in 1959. Prodigious quantities of lava, shooting 1900ft high, raised the crater floor by around 350ft; some of it is still thought to be red-hot, a few hundred feet below the surface. Though Kīlauea Iki may not have quite the same sense of scale as the main caldera, it offers in some ways an even more spectacular assortment of terrain, which can be explored along the two-hour, four-mile **Kīlauea Iki Trail**.

The loop trail is most easily done as a counterclockwise hike from the **Thurston Lava Tube** (see p.258), a mile south of the visitor center. Start by following the Crater Rim Trail for about a mile, as it circles close to the lip of the gulf. At a three-way junction with the spur to Byron Ledge (see above), signs point left to the Kīlauea Iki Trail proper. Now the rainforest becomes especially dense, with startled wild gamebirds running along the path ahead, and songbirds overhead.

Soon you glimpse the far wall of Kīlauea Iki, tinged with pastel greens and yellows against the general darkness. Views of the crater floor thus far have made it appear smooth, but after a half-mile or so the path drops abruptly down to reach a primeval mess of jagged *ʻaʻā* lava. Follow the line of cairns for a few hundred yards before arriving at the vent where the 1959 eruption took place. This sudden, gaping maw in the hillside, filled like an hourglass with fine reddish-orange sand, is seen across an open scar in the lava; do not approach any closer.

The trail then descends slightly to a more even, but no less alarming, expanse of undulating *pāhoehoe*, punctuated by white- and yellow-stained cracks that ooze stinking plumes of white vapor. You have to step across the odd fissure and, once again, it takes an act of faith to follow the scattered cairns that mark the way. Eventually, however, you pass through a final chaos of rocks into the dripping, dank bosom of the rainforest. The path then zigzags back up to the rim; the gradient is never steep, but it's a fair walk and can get pretty muddy.

Devastation Trail

Much of the lighter debris from the 1959 Kīlauea Iki eruption (see above) was blown clear of the crater itself, then carried by the wind to pile up as a **cinder**

cone near its southwestern edge. This is **Puʻu Puaʻi**, which can be reached along the half-mile **Devastation Trail** between two parking lots on Crater Rim Drive.

If you set out from the Devastation parking area, opposite the top of Chain of Craters Road, you start by following the old route of Crater Rim Drive, which was severed at this point by the eruption. A paved pathway snakes through low, light-pink undergrowth – a favorite haunt of the park's population of **nēnē** geese. Most of what you see is new growth, though a few older trees survived partial submersion in ash by developing "aerial roots" some way up their trunks. Puʻu Puaʻi itself is just a heap of reddish ash, while the barren land around it is scattered with bleached branches.

Chain of Craters Road

CHAIN OF CRATERS ROAD winds down to the ocean from the south side of Crater Rim Drive, sweeping around successive cones and vents in an empty landscape where only the occasional dead white tree trunk or flowering shrub pokes up. From high on the hillside, the lava flows look like streams of black tarmac, joining in an ever-widening highway down to the Pacific. Long **hiking trails** and the minor **Hilina Pali Road** lead to sites of geological and historic interest all the way down, but the real reason to head this way is to see what may be at the end – the ongoing **eruption of Kīlauea**.

Chain of Craters Road used to run all the way to Puna, then loop back up to the highway. The scale of the damage since 1983 has been too great to repair, however, so now it's a dead end, and getting shorter year by year. One by one, the landmarks along its seafront stretch – such as **Wahaʻula Heiau**, another temple believed by some to have been where human sacrifice was introduced to Hawaii, and the gorgeous black-sand beach at **Kamoamoa**, whose short existence lasted only from 1988 until 1992 – have been destroyed, and before long the road may not follow the shoreline at all.

Check current conditions at the visitor center when you arrive and make sure you have enough gas. The end of the road is a fifty-mile round-trip from the park entrance, and there are no facilities of any kind along the way, while it's impossible to buy gas even in Volcano after 7.30pm.

Hilina Pali Road

Four miles down Chain of Craters Road, a sign to the right points out **Hilina Pali Road**. This crosses the bleak Kaʻū Desert for nine miles, to reach an overlook above the main 1200-foot drop of Hilina Pali. *Pali* is the Hawaiian word for cliff; you may be used to hearing it applied to the lush razorback hills of the Hāmākua coast, but Hilina is much starker and rawer than that, being the huge wall left behind when a piece of the island dropped into the sea. The views are immense, but desolate in the extreme. Infrequent clusters of battered palms in the distance show the locations of former coastal villages; the hillock of Puʻu Kapukapu, near the shore to the southeast, however, obscures the most popular of the park's backcountry campgrounds, at Halapē.

Halfway along the road, **Kulanaokuaiki** is one of the park's two fully equipped, drive-in **campgrounds**. Smaller and somewhat more basic than Nāmakani Paio (see p.257), it's free and available on a first-come, first-served basis for up to seven nights in any one year.

All **hiking** in this area involves extended periods of walking across barren, exposed, and baking-hot lava flats. If you want to get to the shoreline, it makes more sense to hike the **Puna Coast Trail** (see p.265), than to climb up and down the *pali* as well. However, gluttons for punishment have a choice of two trails to the sea. Both the **Hilina Pali** and **Ka'aha trails** start by zigzagging down the cliff along the same poorly maintained footpath; the Ka'aha leads for just under four miles to **Ka'aha Shelter** (see p.266), while the Hilina Pali covers the eight miles to the **Halapē Shelter**, joining the **Halapē Trail** from Kīpuka Nēnē. In addition, you can even walk to the Hilina Pali overlook from the Jaggar Museum, along the eighteen-mile **Ka'ū Desert Trail** (the "Footprints" section of which is detailed on p.267).

Mauna Ulu Trail and Pu'u Huluhulu

Another three miles along Chain of Craters Road beyond the Hilina Pali turnoff, a small approach road on the left leads to the **Mauna Ulu Trail**. A couple of miles along, this becomes the **Nāpau Trail**, then runs for ten miles to the open **Pu'u 'Ō'ō** vent, far out along Kīlauea's East Rift Zone – the culprit responsible for most of the lava flows since 1983. At present, it's illegal to continue along the trail any further than the basic campground at Nāpau Crater, three miles short of the end. If you plan to spend the night here, you must register at the visitor center; see p.254.

Most hikers content themselves with the three-mile round-trip to **Pu'u Huluhulu**, an ancient cinder cone that has somehow escaped inundation for several millennia. It owes its name (*huluhulu* means "very hairy") to the dense coating of unspoilt, old-growth rainforest that surrounds it as a result. Following the footpath to the top of this small mound enables you to peer into its inaccessible hollow interior, circled by craggy red rocks and filled with primeval-looking green ferns and darting birds. The sensation of being in a real-life "Lost World" is enhanced by the wasteland visible all around.

Pu'u 'Ō'ō itself is extremely unstable; gaping holes regularly split its sides to release floods of liquid rock, and there have been several major collapses. With luck, you should be able to spot its smoldering cone from Pu'u Huluhulu, while views to the south are dominated by the miniature shield volcano of **Mauna Ulu**, created between 1971 and 1974 and already home to native trees and shrubs like the *'ōhi'a* and *'ōhelo*.

Pu'u Loa petroglyphs

Ten miles beyond Mauna Ulu, and just after its descent of the 1000-foot Holei Pali, Chain of Craters Road passes within a mile of the most extensive field of **petroglyphs** – ancient rock carvings – on the island.

The level trail east to Pu'u Loa ends at a circular raised boardwalk. Most of the petroglyphs visible from here are no more than crude holes in the lava, and only inspire any wonder if you're aware that each was probably carved to hold the umbilical cord of a newborn infant. *Pu'u loa* means "long hill," and by extension "long life," so this was considered a lucky spot for the traditional ceremony. The purpose of the boardwalk is not to display the most elaborate petroglyphs, but to discourage you from exploring further, for fear that you might damage such irreplaceable works of art as the images of pre-contact **surfers**, said to lie somewhere in the area.

Hōlei Sea Arch

Chain of Craters Road currently comes to an end just beyond mile marker 20, with the small parking lot near **Hōlei Sea Arch** used as a turnaround point for all vehicles. Less than two miles survive of the road's previous eleven-mile shoreline route to Kalapana, and soon it may not reach the coast at all.

Until recently, few visitors bothered to pause at the sea arch; now it's the only named feature left in what was once a very scenic area. From the parking lot, cross a few yards of sparsely grassed lava and you'll see a chunky pillar of basalt blocks to your right, tenuously connected to the rest of the island by the top slab. The thudding of the waves against the cliffs makes the ground reverberate beneath your feet – clear evidence of the fragility of this coastline, most of which is too dangerous to approach.

Approaching the eruption

It's impossible to do more than generalize as to what might lie beyond the end of Chain of Craters Road. Assuming that the eruption is still continuing, somewhere high on the hillside one or more fissures in the earth will be spilling out large quantities of molten lava, which then sets off toward the ocean. En route it may or may not have to pour over fault scarps (cliffs formed by minor earthquakes), and its surface may or may not harden to create an underground stream. You can only view the lava itself if the nearest active flow has reached a point you can walk to from the road; if it is flowing directly into the ocean, which is easy to spot because the contact produces great plumes of steam; or if it is crossing or flowing along the road itself.

Find out if any of these scenarios apply by calling the park's **Volcano Update line** (℡808/985-6000); the Hawaiian Volcano Observatory's website (🌐http ://hvo.wr.usgs.gov) also carries up-to-date information. The Kīlauea visitor center (℡808/967-7311) can offer more detailed advice and implores all visitors to view a three-minute safety video. Since the early 1990s, at least twelve visitors have died in separate incidents, and many more have had to be rescued after becoming stranded out on the lava at night. The most dangerous situation occurs when lava flows directly into the **ocean**, when there's a risk of inhaling toxic fumes that contain not only acids but even tiny particles of glass. In addition, new land is extremely unstable; it may be no more than a thin layer of solidified lava resting on seawater – a "bench" – and thus liable to collapse at any moment. Swirling mists can make it hard to keep your bearings and can also mean that only

△ Obsolete sign at the end of Chain of Craters Road

264

occasionally do you see the actual lava. According to rangers, most problems arise when walkers attempt to approach the eruption from the east, from the foot of Hwy-130, as described on p.248.

The park service maintains a wooden **information shack** (on wheels, for obvious reasons) at the end of the road, where they hand out alarming leaflets explaining that new lava is unstable and may collapse at any time, and that it's best to avoid clouds of hydrochloric acid. When safety permits, rangers lead **guided hikes** to the site of the eruption. A daily schedule is posted at the visitor center; as a rule they start in the early afternoon, in order to get back to the road before nightfall.

Walking across flaky, crumbling, new lava is an extraordinary experience. Every surface is like sandpaper, a fall can shred your skin and, even far from the apparent center of activity, the ground can be too hot to touch. Heavy rain dries off without penetrating your clothing. The sight of liquid rock oozing towards you, swirling with phlegmy gobbets and destroying all it touches; the crackle as it crunches across previous layers of lava; the sudden flash as a dried-out tree bursts into flame: all leave you with a disconcerting sense of the land itself as a living, moving organism.

After dark, the orange glow of the eruption becomes even more apparent. Pinpoint incandescent lights become visible all across the slopes and leave the mountain looking like the proverbial city on a hill. Without official sanction or approval, and heedless of the immense risks, many visitors stay out all night to marvel at the glowing rivers of molten rock. If you try it, be sure to carry a flashlight for the walk back across the lava.

Finally, it's only fair to warn you that when current activity is occurring several miles beyond the end of the road, as it often is, you may well feel a profound sense of **anticlimax** at the little you see. Children in particular, excited by photographs of lava fountains, are liable to be very disappointed by the reality. On the other hand, they may see something that one day they will tell their own kids about.

Puna Coast Trail

The **southern coastline** of the Big Island is now very sparsely populated; the villages that once stood along its central section were abandoned around 150 years ago, following a succession of devastating tsunamis. Underground upheavals make this region extremely prone to **earthquakes**; in 1960 the entire south coast dropped by three feet, and campers in backcountry sites were washed out to sea after another major landslide in 1975.

The only way to explore the area is on foot, by means of the **Puna Coast Trail**. This starts roughly a mile up from the sea, at the Pu'u Loa parking lot (see p.263), setting off west, away from the eruption area, towards the coastal campgrounds at **Keauhou** and **Halapē**.

Also known as the **Puna Ka'ū Trail**, this long and very challenging hike is only worth attempting if you have several days to spare. It's possible to get to 'Āpua Point and back in a single day, but that's a thirteen-mile round-trip that still stops a long way short of the more interesting spots along the trail. If you plan to camp out, you must register at the Kīlauea visitor center, as this area is prone to landslides and tsunamis. Collected rainwater is available at the shelters, but carry plenty more yourself. All three huts consist of three-walled shelters, so you'll need a tent as well.

From Chain of Craters Road, the trail makes its way across a patchwork of lava flows, the new ones glistening in the sun and crunchy underfoot, the older ones worn and smooth. Roughly four miles along, you reach the low seafront cliffs, which you follow for a couple more miles to **'Āpua Point**. From a distance it's a welcome flash of green against the relentless grays and blacks of the lava; when you arrive it turns out to have just a few coconut palms emerging from a tangled carpet of the ivy-like native *naupaka* shrub.

With no water, shelter, or other facilities at 'Āpua, you either have to turn back to the road or continue along the coast. Heading west, you're faced by the massive fault scarp of Hilina Pali looming ever larger inland. As well as releasing cascades of rock and even lava toward the ocean, landslides like those that created the *pali* also produce tsunamis that flood the coastal plains, so little is left standing along this stretch of the shoreline. Both the **Keauhou** and **Halapē** campgrounds, three and five miles respectively from 'Āpua, remain visibly scarred by the battering they received in 1975 (when two campers lost their lives at Halapē). However, the park service has been replanting coconut palms to restore their lost beauty, and Halapē still has the feel of a little oasis beside the sea. Unfortunately, so many campers trek out to its white-sand beach that the cabins at both campsites are infested with ants and cockroaches. The tidal pools are excellent for snorkeling, but the open sea can be very dangerous. In theory these are nesting grounds for sea turtles, though the regulations against disturbing them seem to be a case of too little, too late and few are thought to land here any more.

To get to the final oceanfront campground, at Ka'aha, requires a very difficult six-mile hike from Halapē, up and along the top of a lesser *pali*. You can also climb down, with equal effort, from Hilina Pali Road (see p.262). Either way, it too is riddled with insects and even more dangerous for swimming.

Mauna Loa

If you're interested in seeing a bit more of **Mauna Loa**, as opposed to Kīlauea, leave the caldera area by the park's main entrance and head west for a couple of miles. The third turning on the right, **Mauna Loa Road**, winds up toward the summit from there, although it stops a long way short and only very rarely allows you views either up the mountain or down toward Kīlauea and the sea.

Kīpuka Puaulu

Most visitors take the drive of less than a mile up Mauna Loa Road to see the enchanting little forest sanctuary of **Kīpuka Puaulu**. Known as the "bird park," this enclave is an utter contrast to the raw landscape elsewhere in the National Park. A *kīpuka* is a patch of land that has been left untouched by lava, and thus forms a sort of island in a sea of lava. Kīpuka Puaulu's well-preserved rainforest serves as a sanctuary for rare native birds such as the *'elepaio* flycatcher and the *'amakahi* honey-creeper.

A woodland stroll around the two-mile loop path takes you past some huge old *koa* trees and through sun-dappled clearings, with birds audible on all sides. However, unless you have a lot of patience – and binoculars – you may not manage to see more than the odd flash of color. Your best bet is to walk slowly and quietly and hope to surprise a group on the ground. At lunchtime, the covered **picnic area** makes this a popular stop for park visitors.

The Mauna Loa Summit Trail

Beyond Kīpuka Puaulu, Mauna Loa Road climbs through thick woodland virtually all the way to the end, fourteen miles up, crossing only a single stray lava flow. Its width varies between one and two lanes, but it's driveable if not exactly conducive to a quick journey. The surrounding tree-cover gradually changes from tropical to high-altitude before the road finally stops in a small clearing, 6662ft up.

The parking lot here is the trailhead for the **Mauna Loa Summit Trail**. As the very explicit signs in the small pavilion explain, this is no trail to attempt on a whim. The summit is a gradual but exhausting nineteen miles further on across bleak, barren lava, with a round-trip usually taking four days. There's no shelter along the way except for two crude cabins – check with the Park Service, with whom you must register anyway, to see whether they are stocked with water. Hypothermia is a very real threat, as the higher slopes are prone to abominable weather conditions. If you make it to the top, you're confronted by the **Moku'āweoweo Caldera**, similar to Kīlauea's, which last erupted in 1984.

The Ka'ū Desert

All the land in the National Park that lies to the south and west of Kīlauea Caldera is officially known as the **Ka'ū Desert**. By the conventional definition of a desert, it should therefore receive no rain: in fact it receives almost as much as the rainforest to the east, but here it falls as a natural acid rain, laden with chemicals from Kīlauea. Only a few desiccated plants ever managed to adapt to this uncompromising landscape, and most of those have in the last century been eaten away by ravenous wild goats.

Walking the eighteen-mile **Ka'ū Desert Trail** can bring you into close contact with this region if you so desire; there's one overnight shelter, the three-bed **Pepeiao Cabin**, about nine miles along the trail's great curve from the Jaggar Museum down to Hilina Pali Road. From the cabin you can choose instead to hike another six miles down to **Ka'aha Point** and connect with the Puna Coast Trail (see p.265).

The Footprints Trail

Ten miles west of the park entrance on the Belt Road, an inconspicuous roadside halt marks the start of the **Footprints Trail**, which leads due south for just under a mile across rough 'a'ā lava. A small shelter at what might seem like a random spot covers a bunch of depressions in the rock, which popular legend says are human footprints. Whether or not you agree, the factual basis for the story is bizarre.

In 1790, Keōua, a rival of Kamehameha, was returning to his own kingdom of Ka'ū after two major battles in Puna. As his armies, complete with attendant women and children, traversed this stretch of desert, he divided them into three groups. The first group got safely across; then Kīlauea erupted, and the third group found the members of the second strewn across the pathway. All were dead, poisoned by a cloud of gas from the volcano. Supposedly, their footprints in the falling ash solidified and can still be seen, alternately protected and exposed as sand blows across the desert.

Keōua himself, incidentally, met a no less dramatic end: see p.206.

Volcano village

Unless you stay in *Volcano House* (p.256) or the park-service campgrounds (p.257 and p.262), the village of **VOLCANO** offers the only **accommodation** in the vicinity of the park. Though it's just a mile or so east of the park entrance, toward

Hilo, it would be easy to drive straight past it without realizing it's there. The main street runs parallel to the highway, on the *mauka* (uphill) side, but it's well hidden by a roadside fringe of trees. Along it you'll find nothing much of interest other than a small post office, a couple of general stores, and two gas stations, both of which close by 7.30pm nightly.

Accommodation

The strange thing about staying in Volcano is that there's nothing to suggest you're anywhere near an active volcano – only *Volcano House* in the park can offer crater views. Instead, the village's crop of small-scale **bed and breakfasts** are tucked away in odd little corners of a dense rainforest. Be warned that it rains a *lot* in Volcano.

Carson's Volcano Cottages 505 Sixth St ☎808/967-7683 or 1-800/845-5282, ⊛www .carsonscottage.com. A friendly, romantic little place, south of the highway, with three en-suite guest rooms, furnished according to varying themes, and three private garden cottages, plus an open-air hot tub. They also offer three separate rental cottages. ④

The Chalet Kīlauea Collection PO Box 998, Volcano HI 96785 ☎808/967-7786 or 1-800/937-7786 (US), ⊛www.volcano-hawaii.com. This assortment of B&Bs and vacation rentals, all under the same management, offers accommodation for all budgets. The owners' original property, now known as the *Inn at Volcano* (④–⑧), is a very plush, lavishly furnished B&B, set well north of the highway on Wright Road, with themed individual rooms in the main house and separate cottages, including a "tree house," on the grounds. Their cheapest alternative is the simple *Volcano B&B* (②), where six rooms share two bathrooms and use of a common lounge. ②–⑧

🏃 **Hale Ohia** PO Box 758, Volcano HI 96785 ☎808/967-7986 or 1-800/455-3803, ⊛www.haleohia.com. Very attractive and tastefully furnished accommodation, ranging from studio apartments in a lovely converted water tank (really) to a three-bedroom cottage. The buildings are scattered across the ravishing rainforest gardens of a former plantation estate, south of the highway across from the village. ③–⑤

HoloHolo Inn 19-4036 Kalani Honua Rd ☎808/967-7950, ⊛www.enable.org/holoholo. Volcano's cheapest option, this HI-AYH-affiliated

"Japanese-style" hostel consists of a rambling rainforest home, half a mile up from the highway, that offers beds in rudimentary but adequate single-sex dorm rooms for $19, and one private double for $44. ①–②

Kīlauea Lodge PO Box 116, Volcano HI 96785 ☎808/967-7366, ⊛www.kilauealodge.com. Imposing former YMCA on the main street, now converted into an upmarket B&B, with some of its seventeen en-suite bedrooms in secluded chalets and cottages dotted across the grounds. The central lodge building holds a good restaurant (see below). ⑤

My Island PO Box 100, Volcano HI 96785 ☎808/967-7216, ⊛www.myislandinnhawaii.com. Several different grades of accommodation in individual buildings set amid dense tropical vegetation. The friendly owner, an island expert, lives in the central lodge; guests can use his library and a communal TV lounge. ③–⑤

Pineapple Park Volcano PO Box 639, Kurtistown HI 96760 ☎808/968-8170 or 1-877/800-3800, ⊛www.pineapple-park.com. Despite the name, this large, modern budget hostel is not actually located in Volcano, but fifteen miles up from Hilo, in a remote area south of Hwy-11. For the moment, it no longer boasts the nighttime views of the erupting volcano that accounted for its location, but if you have your own transport it's not a bad option. Bunks in its 18-person dorms cost $25 each, and it also offers comfortable en-suite private rooms for $85. There are other *Pineapple Parks* in South Kona (see p.191), and in Hilo (see p.222). ①–③

Restaurants

Although *Volcano House* (see p.256) holds the only **restaurant** within the National Park itself, Volcano village offers a good range of nearby alternatives, plus a couple of stores where you can pick up picnic supplies.

Kīlauea Lodge 19-3848 Old Volcano Rd, Volcano ☎808/967-7366. Large inn dining room, with rich

wooden furnishings and a blazing log fire. A full range of strong-flavored European-style meat and game entrees for $20–40, including *hasenpfeffer*, a braised rabbit dish not found on many Big Island menus, plus house specialties such as *Seafood Manua Kea* (seafood and mushrooms on pasta). Nonresidents should reserve well in advance. Daily 5.30–9pm.

Lava Rock Café 19-3972 Old Volcano Rd, Volcano ☎808/967-7969. Funky local café, behind the *Aloha* gas station on Volcano's main street, which serves inexpensive snacks, plate lunches, and espresso coffees, and also offers Internet access. Mon 7.30am–5pm, Tues–Sat 7.30am–9pm, Sun 7.30am–4pm.

 Thai Thai 19-4084 Old Volcano Rd, Volcano ☎808/967-7969. Unassuming but high-quality dinner-only Thai place on the main village road. Most entrees, which include salads as well as green and yellow curries, a tasty Massmana curry with coconut and peanut, and pad Thai noodles, cost around $12. Daily 5–9pm.

Volcano Golf & Country Club Pi'i Mauna Drive, off Hwy-11 ☎808/967-7331. Up a side road two miles west of the park entrance, this daytime-only golf course restaurant serves a conventional but adequate menu of steaks, fish, and salad at around $12 per entree. Its large picture windows look out across unexpected, but boring, meadows. Mon–Fri 8am–3pm, Sat & Sun 6.30am–4pm.

Ka'ū

The district of **KA'Ū** occupies the southern tip of the Big Island, which is also the southernmost point of the United States. Stretching for roughly fifty miles along the southern side of the immense west flank of the "long mountain," Mauna Loa, it ranges from the bleak Ka'ū Desert area, across fertile, well-watered hillsides, to the windswept promontory of **South Point** itself. Situated downwind of the acrid volcanic fumes emitted by both Mauna Loa and Kīlauea, it's far from being the most enticing area of the island. Nonetheless, it may well have been home to the first Polynesian settlers, and remains one of the last bastions in the state of anything approaching the traditional Hawaiian way of life.

Ka'ū was a separate kingdom right up to the moment of European contact. Its last independent ruler was Kamehameha the Great's arch-rival, Keōua, some of whose warriors met a bizarre end in the Ka'ū Desert (see p.267) and who was himself killed during the dedication of Pu'ukoholā Heiau (see p.205).

The population today is very sparse, and it's likely to get sparser now that the sugar mill at **Pāhala**, the last working mill on the island, has closed. All the towns in the area are absolutely tiny; on the map the grid of streets at **Hawaiian Ocean View Estates** may look impressive, but this forty-year-old residential development is still only minimally occupied, even if the real-estate boom in the rest of the island has finally pushed up land values here as well.

In recent years, the state government has repeatedly come up with schemes to revitalize the local economy. After environmental campaigners managed to thwart proposals to develop a vast new luxury resort below Ocean View, the state vigorously promoted a plan to build a commercial **spaceport** at Palima Point, just three miles outside the National Park, to launch satellites and the Space Shuttle. That would supposedly have created ten thousand jobs, but the concept of positioning such a facility on the tsunami-battered slopes of an active volcano attracted so much derision that it now seems to have been quietly abandoned. The spaceport was due to be named after the late *Challenger* astronaut and local hero Ellison Onizuka, who came from Ka'ū, until enterprising journalists uncovered remarks he made before his death opposing the plan.

Although it has a handful of accommodation options, few people spend more than a day at most exploring Ka'ū. Access to the sea is limited, as the highway curves around the ridge of Mauna Loa roughly ten miles up from the shoreline. The two most obvious stops are **South Point**, to admire the crashing waves and perhaps hike to **Green Sand Beach**, and **Punalu'u**, which since the demise of Kalapana boasts the island's finest black-sand beach.

As you pass through Ka'ū, look out for the strange, eroded cinder cones that dot the landscape. Some of these craters are so steep-sided as to have been forever inaccessible to man or beast, and paleobotanists are intrigued by the pre-contact vegetation that is thought to survive within.

Huge **Kahuku Ranch**, which stretches inland from the Belt Road near South Point Road almost to the summit of Mauna Loa, was in 2003 incorporated into Hawaii Volcanoes National Park. Much of it is scheduled to remain as wilderness, but some of the areas immediately up from the highway may well open up to hiking and backcountry exploration.

Pāhala and Wood Valley

As the vegetation reasserts itself after the bleak Ka'ū Desert, 23 miles west of the National Park entrance, little **PĀHALA** stands just *mauka* of the highway. Apart from its tall-chimneyed sugar mill, a gas station, and a small shopping mall that's home to an outlet of the *malasada* (donut) specialist *Tex Drive-In* (Mon–Sat 7am–8pm, Sun 7am–6pm; ☎808/928-8200), there's nothing to catch the eye here, but a drive back up into the hills to the northwest takes you through some appealing agricultural scenery.

Just when you think the side road is about to peter out altogether, it enters a grove of huge eucalyptus trees and you're confronted with one of the Big Island's least likely buildings: on top of a hill, and announced by streamers of colored prayer flags, stands a brightly painted Tibetan temple. Originally built by Japanese sugar laborers, the **Wood Valley temple** (or Nechung Dryung Ling) was rededicated by the Dalai Lama in 1980 and now serves as a retreat for Tibetan Buddhists

△ Punalu'u black-sand beach

from around the world (☎808/928-8539, ⓦwww.nechung.org; ❷–❸). Priority is given to religious groups, but when there's room, travelers can stay in the simple dormitory accommodation or private rooms at the temple.

Punalu'u

Five miles beyond Pāhala, at the point where the highway drops back down to sea level, **PUNALU'U** has been flattened by tsunamis so often that it's given up trying to be a town any more. A single road loops from the highway to the ocean and back, running briefly along what is now the largest **black-sand beach** on the island.

Black sand is a finite resource, as it's only created by molten lava exploding on contact with the sea, and at any one spot that happens very rarely. Even those beaches not destroyed by new lava usually erode away within a few years. Each time the coastline of Punalu'u Bay gets redrawn, however, its black sand washes in again, piling up to create a new beach. At the moment it's gorgeous, a crescent of jet-black crystals surrounding a turquoise bay and framed by a fine stand of coconut palms.

On the north side of the bay, you can make out the remains of an old concrete pier. Until a century ago tourists used to disembark from their ships at Punalu'u for the ride up to the volcanoes by horse; later it became the terminus of a short railroad from Pāhala and was used for shipping sugar. In 1942, by which time it had fallen into disuse, the military destroyed it as a potential landing site for Japanese invaders.

Swimming in these rough waters is out of the question, but many people come to Punalu'u to **camp**. Hawksbill turtles drag themselves ashore on the main beach at night, so camping on the sand is forbidden, but there's a pleasant, if incredibly windy, campground tucked into the rolling meadows of Punalu'u Beach Park, immediately to the south. Permits can be obtained from the Department of Parks and Recreation in Hilo ($5 per day; ☎808/961-8311).

The dilapidated complex of pseudo-Polynesian buildings behind the palms in the center of the beach, facing the sea across its own private lagoon, holds a restaurant that has been closed since the early 1990s downturn in tourism. Plans have repeatedly been announced to construct **new hotels** here; the latest scheme, unveiled in April 2007, envisages two hotels with a total of 350 rooms. The smaller of the two will be run as an ecotourism center, under the auspices of Jean-Michel Cousteau.

For the moment, however, the only **accommodation** nearby is in the *SeaMountain at Punalu'u* condo complex, a few hundred yards from the beach on the southern segment of the loop road (☎808/928-6200 or 1-800/333-1962, ⓦwww.vrivacations.com/resorts/seamountain; ❹–❺). It's an incredibly remote and often very windy place to stay, but most of its studios and one- and two-bedroom apartments, arrayed along what looks like a typical suburban residential street, are well equipped and comfortable. A two-night minimum stay is required. Alongside it, but a separate entity, is the *SeaMountain* **golf course** (☎808/928-6222), where the $50 green fees are among the lowest on the island. The name "Sea Mountain," incidentally, refers to the underwater volcano of Lo'ihi, just twenty miles offshore (see p.253).

Nā'ālehu

You can't miss **NĀ'ĀLEHU** as you drive through Ka'ū. Eight miles south of Punalu'u, it lines each side of the highway for around half a mile, without stretching very far away from the central ribbon. Although it bills itself as "America's southernmost town," Nā'ālehu offers little to induce drivers to stop. Whittington Beach Park, a couple of miles outside it to the north, is not so much a beach as a picnic ground, and the only reason to call in at Nā'ālehu is for a quick lunch.

Nā'ālehu holds a handful of **restaurants**, which change names with monotonous regularity. The best of the bunch is the *Hana Hou Bakery*, 95-1148 Spur Rd (℡808/929-9717), open for all meals daily and serving high-quality diner food as well as fresh baked goods. The *Shaka Restaurant* is a reasonable alternative (daily except Mon 10am–9pm; ℡808/929-7404), and there's also an espresso place, *Keoki's Café*, and a Japanese takeout counter.

Wai'ohinu

Having climbed away from the sea for two miles west of Nā'ālehu, the highway makes a sweeping curve around the small settlement of **WAI'OHINU**. This held a dozen houses when Mark Twain passed through in 1866, and boasts barely more than that today. Twain planted a monkey-pod tree here, but even that has now been dead for forty years. Alongside what may or may not be its descendant, a few hundred yards east of the center, *Mark Twain Square* is a gift shop that also sells sandwiches, cakes, and coffee (℡808/929-7550). Nearby, the rather rundown *Shirakawa Motel* (℡808/929-7462, ⓦwww.shirakawamotel.com; ❷) is gradually being overwhelmed by trees, while just around the highway bend you pass a pretty chapel, the white-and-green clapboard 1841 **Kauaha'ao Church**.

Half a mile south of the church, *Macadamia Meadows Farm*, 94-6263 Kamaoa Rd (℡808/929-8097 or 1-888/929-8118, ⓦwww.macadamiameadows.com; ❸), is a large modern home that offers four comfortable, spacious **B&B** rooms. Guests have use of the on-site pool and tennis courts.

South Point Road

As you circle the southern extremity of the Big Island on the Belt Road, you're too far up from the ocean to see where the island comes to an end. It is possible, however, to drive right down to the tip along the eleven-mile **SOUTH POINT ROAD**, which leaves the highway six miles west of Wai'ohinu.

Car rental agencies forbid drivers from heading to South Point because vehicle damage is more likely on the poor road surfaces and providing emergency recovery is inconvenient. Like the similarly proscribed Saddle Road, however, it's not a difficult or dangerous drive. Most of the way it's a single-lane paved road, with enough room on either side for vehicles to pass comfortably.

The road heads almost exactly due south, passing at first through green cattle-ranching country. As it starts to drop, the landscape takes on a weather-beaten look, with pale grass billowing and the trees bent double by the trade winds. It comes as no surprise to encounter the giant propellers of the Kamoa wind farm, though you're unlikely to see many of them turning: the winds have proven too gusty and violent for the farm to be a commercial success.

Ka Lae

After ten miles from the wind farm, the road forks 100 yards beyond a sign announcing the **Ka Lae National Historic Landmark District**. The right fork ends a mile later at a red-gravel parking lot perched above a thirty-foot cliff. Local people fish over the edge, and ladders drop down the cliff face to boats bobbing at a small mooring below. Watch out for the large hole in the middle of the parking lot, which plummets all the way down to the sea.

Walk a couple of minutes south and you come to **Ka Lae**, or **South Point**, where you can ponder over the fact that everyone in the United States is to the north of you. The earliest colonizers of Hawaii battled against the winds to reach this spot long before the Pilgrims crossed the Atlantic, and in doing so traveled a far greater distance from their homes in the distant South Seas. Abundant bone fishhooks found in the area are among the oldest artifacts unearthed in Hawaii, dating as far back as the third century AD. At the restored **Kalalea Heiau**, at the very tip, offerings wrapped in *ti* leaves are still left by native Hawaiians. Beyond that is a ledge of black lava, steadily pounded by high surf.

The deep waters offshore were renowned not only for holding vast quantities of fish, but also because they're prey to such fierce currents that it can take days on end for human- or sail-powered boats to negotiate the cape. An old legend tells of a king of Ka'ū who became deeply unpopular after stealing fish from fishermen and forcing his people to build heavy-walled fishponds for his benefit. He was finally abandoned by his warriors after he plundered a fleet of canoes near Ka Lae and stole so much fish that his own canoe began to founder. The currents swept him away to a lonely death.

Among the rocks at the headland, you can still see holes drilled for use as **canoe moorings**. In ancient times, fishermen would tie their canoes to these loops by long cords so that they could fish in the turbulent waters without having to fight the sea. Looking inland, you can follow the grey outline of Mauna Loa in the distance; on a cloudless day, you might even make out its snow-capped peak. Nearer at hand, across a foam-flecked sea to the northwest, is the stark shoreline cinder cone of **Pu'u Waimānalo**.

As you head back to the fork, a side turning toward the ocean leads swiftly to more dramatic views up the coast. Don't drive too fast here though; the road ends almost immediately where it simply crumbles with no warning into the sea.

Green Sand Beach

GREEN SAND BEACH, a couple of miles northeast of Ka Lae, doesn't quite live up to its name. It is a beach, and it is greenish in a rusty-olive sort of way, but if you're expecting a dazzling stretch of green sand backed by a coconut grove you'll be disappointed. The only reason to venture here is if you feel like a bracing, four-mile hike along the oceanfront, with a mild natural curiosity at the end. Without great expectations, and on a rain-free day, it's worth the effort.

If you want to try it, start from the junction on South Point Road a mile short of Ka Lae, and drive down the left fork as far as you can go, which is a turnaround point just beyond some military housing. If conditions are dry enough, you might continue down to the boat landing below on any of the many rutted mud tracks that criss-cross each other down the slope. However, you'd have to have a very high-clearance 4WD vehicle to follow the two-mile track from there to the beach.

Apart from one or two heavily-rutted sections, the walk itself is very easy, although on the way out you can expect to be pushing into a stiff tradewinds breeze. For most of the route you cross rolling, pastel-green meadows – an oddly pastoral landscape considering the mighty surf pummeling at the lava rocks alongside.

Your destination comes in sight after just over a mile – the crumbling **Pu'u O Mahana** cinder cone that forms the only significant bump on the line of the coast.

273

As you approach you can see that half the cone has eroded away, and the resultant loose powder has slipped down the cliffs to form a long sloping beach. You can see all there is to see from up above, but with care it's possible to scramble down to the seashore and examine handfuls of the "green sand." Close inspection reveals shiny green-tinged crystals of various sizes – this is in fact a mineral called **olivine**, which once formed part of a lava flow. Green Sand Beach is, however, much too exposed for swimming – or even walking too close to the sea – to be a good idea.

Hawaiian Ocean View Estates

West of South Point Road, you can't get down to the sea again in the twelve miles before the Belt Road reaches South Kona. The road does, however, run past a few isolated buildings and communities where you can get a snack or fill up with gas.

The residential zone of **HAWAIIAN OCEAN VIEW ESTATES**, also known as "Ocean View" or "HOVE," was designated for development during the 1960s. Intricate grids of roads were planned, and some sites were sold that were no more than patches of bare lava. People are slowly moving in, but only a small proportion of the lots have been built on, and many of the roads still don't exist. The center of Ocean View consists of two small malls: one has an Aloha gas station and the *Ohia Cafe* espresso bar, while the other is home to the friendly little *Desert Rose* (daily 7am–7pm; ☏808/939-7673), which serves simple breakfasts and highly recommended lunchtime sandwiches and salads. Just off the highway a couple of hundred yards north, the takeout counter at *Mr Bell's* (daily 7am–9pm; ☏808/929-9291) offers breakfast ($6) and basic plate lunches taken on a shady *lānai*.

Places to **stay** nearby include the four-roomed *Bougainvillea B&B*, two blocks down from the *Desert Rose* (☏808/929-7089 or 1-800/688-1763; ⓦwww.hi-inns .com/bouga; ❸).

Manukā State Park

Ka'ū comes to an end half a dozen miles west of Ocean View, as you finally cross the long ridge of Mauna Loa. The former royal lands on the border with Kona, once the *ahupua'a* of **MANUKĀ**, remain set aside to this day as the **Manukā Natural Area Reserve** – at 25,000 acres, the largest natural reserve in the state.

Only a small segment of the reserve is open to the public – **Manukā State Park**, three miles west of Ocean View on the *mauka* side of the highway. From its leafy roadside parking lot, equipped with a picnic pavilion, restrooms, benches, and rolling lawns, the one-hour, two-mile **Manukā Nature Trail** leads into peaceful woodlands. Almost all the terrain is *'a'ā* lava, and although there's no great climb, the path can be very rough underfoot. Humans aren't the only ones who find it hard to cross lava flows, so pigs and exotic plants alike are relatively scarce, and the area remains a haven for native plants. One of the main features of long-established native species tends to be that they've lost unnecessary defences against predators; thus you'll see a mint with no smell and a nettle with no sting. The trail's only dramatic feature is a collapsed lava pit, whose sides are too steep to permit access to wild pigs (see p.551), and which gathers enough moisture to feed plants such as the *'ie 'ie* vine, which normally only grows in much wetter areas.

Free maps, available at the trailhead, explain how the vegetation varies with the age of the lava flow. Some of the ground is new and barren, and some is around two thousand years old, but those areas that date back four thousand years have managed to develop a thick coating of topsoil.

About eight miles beyond Manukā, as the road heads due north toward Kailua, you come to the turnoff down to **Miloli'i Beach** – see p.191.

Maui

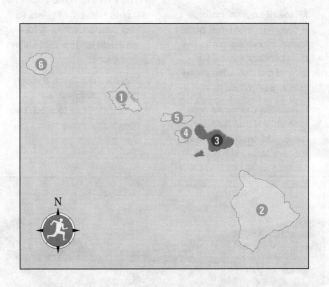

CHAPTER 3 **Highlights**

＊ **Sunset in Lahaina** Best admired from the seafront of this West Maui town, the setting sun sinks behind the russet island of Lanai.
See p.290

＊ **The Feast at Lele** A sumptuous banquet of Polynesian specialties to beat any *lū'au* in the state.
See p.299

＊ **Molokini snorkel cruises** A daily flotilla of small boats ferries snorkelers out to see the abundant marine life around this tiny submerged crater. See p.325

＊ **Haleakalā Crater** An eerie moonscape that feels far removed from the bustle of modern Maui. See p.346

＊ **Downhill biking** Free-wheeling down the forty-mile Haleakalā Crater Road offers amazing views at every turn.
See p.348

＊ **Ho'okipa Beach Park** The world's premier windsurfing destination hosts the sport's top competitive events.
See p.357

＊ **The Road to Hāna** Legendary day-trip drive that twists its way past dozens of hidden waterfalls and verdant valleys.
See p.359

＊ **Pīpīwai Trail** Climb through the lush rainforest of southeast Maui to reach two spectacular waterfalls.
See p.371

△ Haleakalā Crater

3

Maui

W idely trumpeted, not least by its own inhabitants, as the world's most glamorous vacation destination, the island of **Maui** has long proclaimed its charms with the slogan *Maui Nō Ka 'Oi* – "Maui is the Best." Perhaps the claim owes something to Maui's apparent habit of coming in second: the island ranks a distant second to Oahu in terms of annual visitors and is the second largest of the Hawaiian chain. And the state itself is called "Hawaii" rather than "Maui," because just when Maui seemed set to conquer all its neighbors, it was itself overrun by warriors from the island of Hawaii.

Maui does, however, have a lot to boast about, starting with the sheer variety of its landscapes. The windward flanks of its two mountains are ravishingly beautiful, with the east-coast **road to Hāna** winding below them through fifty miles of quintessentially tropical scenery, while cool, green **Upcountry Maui** is an unexpected pastoral idyll, and the volcanic desert on top of **Haleakalā** offers an unforgettable spectacle at sunrise. The drier, less photogenic western coastlines of the island hold some of Hawaii's most popular **beaches**; resorts like Kā'anapali and Kīhei may not be attractive in their own right, but they perfectly meet the needs of tourists who come specifically for sun, sand, and swimming. In West Maui, you can walk the streets of old **Lahaina**, once the capital of Hawaii and rendezvous for the hell-raising Pacific whaling fleet, while atmospheric smaller towns elsewhere, such as **Makawao** and Hāna, evoke the island's plantation and ranching heritage.

Aside from its natural attractions, Maui entices a younger, more dynamic crowd than Waikīkī by offering Hawaii's most exhilarating range of vacation **activities**, including surfing, windsurfing, diving, sailing, snorkeling, cycling, hiking, and horse riding.

A brief history of Maui

Ancient Maui was not the fertile island it is today; both the central isthmus and the upcountry slopes were arid wastelands, and the population was crowded into scattered coastal valleys. For its first thousand years of human occupation, the island consisted of several independent regions, each constantly at war with the rest. Both the two main centers were in **West Maui** – one was the northwestern shoreline, the other was the region of **Nā Wai 'Ōha**, which stretched northwards from 'Īao Valley – while remote Hāna on the east coast was a lesser chiefdom, prone to fall under the control of Big Island invaders.

The first chief to rule over all of Maui was **Pi'ilani**, who is thought to have reigned during the fifteenth or sixteenth centuries. He conquered all the way

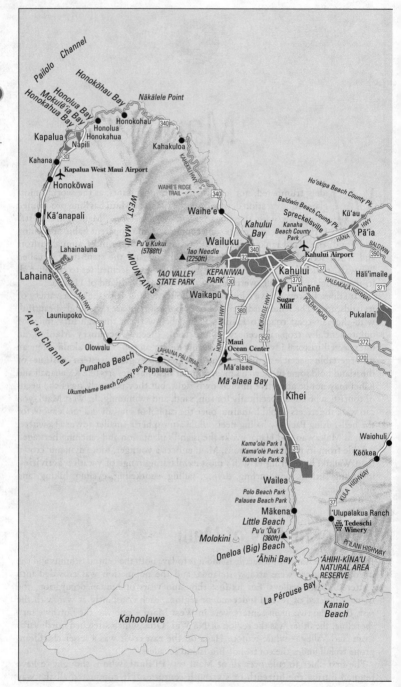

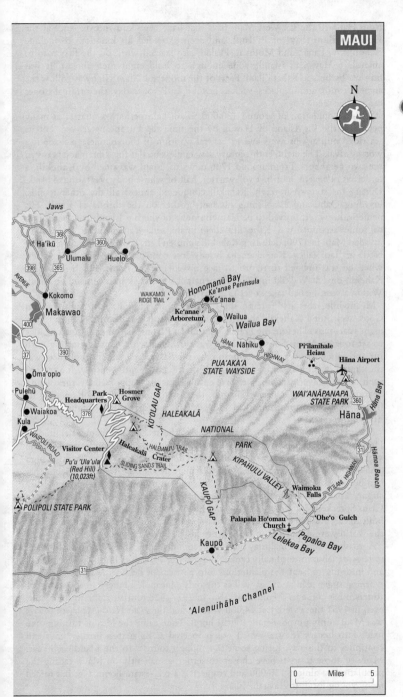

from Hāna to the six West Maui bays that have been known ever since as the **Honoapi'ilani** (bays of Pi'ilani), and even extended his kingdom to include Kahoolawe, Lanai, and Molokai. Pi'ilani also started work on the first road to encircle a Hawaiian island; wide enough to hold eight men abreast, it was finished by his son Kihapi'ilani. Parts of the modern Pi'ilani Highway follow the ancient route, and in places, such as beyond La Pérouse Bay, the original stones can still be seen.

With a population of around 120,000, Maui held perhaps a quarter as many people as the Big Island of Hawaii by the time the Europeans arrived, but its warriors' military prowess and its central position in the archipelago made it a worthy rival. The eighteenth century saw endless battles for supremacy between the two neighbors. From around 1736 onwards, Maui was ruled by **Kahekili**, a ferocious *pahupu* or "cut-in-two" warrior, half of whose body was tattooed black. During his sixty-year reign, Kahekili conquered almost all the other islands, invading Oahu and establishing his half-brother on the throne of Kauai. His nemesis, however, proved to be **Kamehameha** of the Big Island, who according to some accounts was Kahekili's illegitimate son. Kamehameha successfully invaded Maui in 1790, defeating Kahekili's chosen heir, Kalanikūpule, in a bloody battle at 'Īao Valley. Kamehameha briefly lost control of the island thereafter, when he was obliged to return to face his enemies at home, but by the time Kahekili died at Waikīkī in 1794, Kamehameha was back in command on Maui. Within a year, he had taken over Oahu as well.

Meanwhile, the first foreign ships had reached Hawaii. Although Captain Cook welcomed Kahekili aboard the *Discovery* off Wailuku in 1778, another eight years passed before the French admiral La Pérouse became the first outsider to set foot on Maui. Soon the island was swamped with visitors, starting with fur and sandalwood traders. **Lahaina**, by now a favored chiefly residence, was the capital of all Hawaii in the first half of the nineteenth century. It attracted such an intensive missionary effort, enthusiastically supported by the island's devoutly Christian Governor Hoapili, that, within a few years of opening its first school and printing press in 1831, Maui had achieved the highest rate of literacy on earth.

After Hoapili died in the early 1840s, and the seat of government shifted to Honolulu, Lahaina spent twenty raucous years as the "**whaling capital of the world**." When the whaling trade finally died down (see p.537), Maui was left high and dry, with its population reduced to a mere 12,000. However, the lands that had been used to grow food for the sailors turned toward other crops, especially **sugar**. Thanks to the frenzied efforts of entrepreneurs such as the German-born Claus Spreckels, Samuel Alexander, and Henry Baldwin, irrigation channels were built to carry water from East Maui to the isthmus, and immigrants from all over the world were shipped in to work the fields.

Agriculture was the mainstay of Maui's economy until after World War II, when state-wide labor unrest finally broke the power of Hawaii's "Big Five" (see p.537), and in doing so, sent the plantations into permanent decline. Maui still has one working sugar plantation, as well as the only pineapple cannery in the state, but **tourism** has come to dominate all else. In 1927, 428 tourists came to the island; even in 1951 there were just 14,000 visitors, and the *Hotel Hāna-Maui* (see p.367) was Maui's only purpose-built tourist hotel. Then came the idea of turning cane fields into luxury resorts, which was pioneered at Kā'anapali in the 1950s and continues to this day, luring some 2.4 million tourists to the island each year. Many of those tourists have chosen to settle permanently on Maui, raising the population to almost 150,000 and triggering a real-estate boom that has forced many young locals to leave the island.

Maui overview

The island of Maui is what's known as a "volcanic doublet," consisting of two originally separate but now overlapping volcanoes. The older of the two, known to geologists as Mauna Kahalawai, has eroded to become a serrated ridge that's usually referred to as the **West Maui Mountains**; it's now dwarfed by the younger **Haleakalā** to the southeast. Haleakalā itself stood several thousand feet taller around 400,000 years ago and dominated the landmass of Maui Nui, which took in what are now Kahoolawe, Molokai, and Lanai. Although the ocean has flowed in to create four distinct islands, the channels between them are the shallowest, and the calmest, in the state of Hawaii. That's one reason why the western coastlines of both parts of Maui are its most popular tourist playgrounds, with safe, sandy beaches and good sailing conditions.

When you've tired of the rather sterile atmosphere of resorts such as **Lahaina** and **Kāʻanapali** in West Maui, or **Kīhei** in South Maui, there's plenty to explore elsewhere on the island. The central isthmus, or "neck," between the volcanoes can be so flat in places that you fear the waves will wash right over it. It holds **Kahului**, the main commercial center, and the faded but somehow appealing older town of **Wailuku**, standing guard over the once-sacred **ʻĪao Valley**.

To the east, **Upcountry Maui**, on the lower slopes of Haleakalā, is a delight, its meadows and flower farms offering a pastoral escape from the bustle below. Higher up, beyond the clouds, you can look out across the many-hued volcanic wasteland of the vast **Haleakalā Crater** or dwindle into cosmic insignificance by hiking down into it.

Tortuous, demanding roads wind right around the **windward coasts** of both halves of the island. The better known of the two, the **road to Hāna** in the east, does not quite merit its legendary status, but its countless waterfalls and ravines make for a wonderful day-trip, culminating at lush **ʻOheʻo Gulch**. West Maui's equivalent, **Kahekili Highway**, enables visitors to explore the remote Waiheʻe Valley and offers a glimpse of how Maui must have looked before the tourists arrived.

Getting to Maui

Of the three airports on Maui, **Kahului** (see p.314) is by far the largest and is the only one capable of handling trans-Pacific flights. For full details of flights to

Maui favorites: beaches			
Swimming beaches			
Kāʻanapali Beach	p.302	Polo Beach	p.334
Kapalua Beach	p.306	Waiʻānapanapa Beach	p.364
Oneloa (Big) Beach	p.336		
Snorkel spots			
Honolua Bay	p.309	La Pérouse Bay	p.337
Kāʻanapali Beach	p.302	Molokini	p.325
Surfing and windsurfing			
Honolua Bay	p.309	Jaws	p.358
Honomanū Bay	p.360	Kanahā Beach	p.315
Hoʻokipa Beach	p.357	Māʻalaea Bay	p.324

Maui favorites: hikes			
Halemau'u Trail	p.354	Sliding Sands Trail	p.352
Kaupō Trail	p.356	'Ula'ino Road	p.363
Pīpīwai Trail	p.371	Waihe'e Ridge Trail	p.310
Pu'u 'Ōla'i	p.337	Waikamoi Nature Trail	p.360

and from the state of Hawaii, and contact details for the airlines mentioned below, see pp.27–32.

The route between Honolulu and Kahului is the busiest domestic route in the entire United States, with over three million passengers per year. Both of the two major local airlines, Hawaiian and Aloha, fly this way at least ten times every day. In addition, Aloha operates two daily nonstop flights between Kahului and both Kona and Hilo on the Big Island, as well as two to Kauai, while Hawaiian offers one nonstop service on each of those routes. Aloha's affiliate, Island Air, also connects Kahului with Molokai twice daily. In addition, Pacific Wings (℡808/873-0877 or 1-888/575-4546, ⓦwww.pacificwings.com) operates scheduled flights that connect both Lanai City, and Waimea on the Big Island, with Kahului, while Paragon Air (℡1-866/946-4744, ⓦwww.paragon-air.com), an on-demand charter service, links Molokai with any airport on Maui.

Kapalua in West Maui – see p.307 – receives around five Island Air flights from Honolulu each day. Scheduled flights to and from **Hāna**, the third, tiny airport, are currently only available on Pacific Wings (see above), which operates three or four daily round-trip flights between Kahului and Hāna, and also one or two nonstop flights between Honolulu and Hāna.

At the time this book went to press, high-speed **ferries** were about to start operating between Honolulu and Kahului on Maui, with a one-way fare of $42 per passenger, plus $55 per vehicle. For the latest news, check ⓦwww.hawaii superferry.com. In addition, smaller-scale ferries connect Lahaina with Lanai and Molokai; see p.293.

Getting around Maui

Although you can't really make the most of a Maui vacation without renting your own vehicle, the island does offer a **public transport** network. Maui Bus (℡808/871-4838, ⓦwww.mauicounty.gov/bus) operates scheduled **bus** services from the Queen Ka'ahumanu Center in Kahului to both Lahaina – where you can connect with separate services on to Kā'anapali, as detailed on p.293 – and South Maui – running down South Kīhei Road and into Wailea; see p.326. Both routes run via the Maui Ocean Center at Mā'alaea, meaning that with one change of bus you can get from Lahaina to Wailea. Another route also connects **Kahului Airport** with downtown Kahului and Pā'ia and Haikū. In addition, Akina Aloha Tours (℡808/879-2828 or 1-800/977-2605, ⓦwww.akinatours.com) runs shuttle vans on demand from the airport to all the resorts, as does Speedishuttle (℡808/661-6667 or 1-877/242-5777, ⓦwww.speedishuttle.com). Typical rates start at around $15 to Kīhei, $28 to Lahaina, and $36 to Nāpili.

All the national **rental car** chains are represented at Kahului Airport and at or near Kapalua Airport; in addition, Avis has branches in Kīhei, Wailea, and Kapalua; Budget has an office in Wailea; and Dollar is in Hāna. In the absence of adequate roads to cope with its volume of tourists, the **traffic** on Maui is consistently bad.

Flight-seeing tours

All the **helicopter** companies listed below run tours from Kahului Airport; none currently operates from Kapalua. Maui is large enough for a full round-island flight to take more than an hour and cost around $200; if you'd prefer a shorter flight, try a 20- or 30-minute loop over West Maui. Aim to pay around $75 for a 20-minute jaunt, something over $150 to fly over Haleakalā and Hāna, and more than $200 to fly over to Molokai or Lanai as well. Visibility is almost always best in the early morning.

It's also possible to take an **airplane** or "fixed-wing" tour, with Volcano Air Tours (☏808/877-5500, ⊛www.volcanoairtours.com), which flies across to the active volcano on the Big Island from Kapalua or Kahului for around $300.

Helicopter tour operators

Air Maui	☏808/877-7005 or 1-877/238-4942, ⊛www.airmaui.com
Alexair Helicopters	☏808/871-0792 or 1-888/418-8455, ⊛www.helitour.com
Blue Hawaiian Helicopters	☏808/871-8844 or 1-800/745-2583, ⊛www.bluehawaiian.com
MauiScape	☏808/877-7272, ⊛www.mauiscape.com
Sunshine Helicopters	☏808/871-5600 or 1-800/469-3000, ⊛www.sunshinehelicopters.com

The worst area is the narrow **Honoapiʻilani Highway** around West Maui, where drivers habitually make sudden stops in winter to watch whales in the ocean. At least the snail's pace along the **Haleakalā** and **Hāna** highways is owing to the natural obstacles en route, and gives you a chance to appreciate the scenery. Rental companies forbid their clients to drive off-road, which can lead to trouble if you're heading for obscure beaches or surf sites. In the past, those strictures have applied to both the **Kahekili Highway** in West Maui, and the remote **Piʻilani Highway**

Horse riding

Ironwood Ranch ☏808/669-4991, ⊛www.ironwoodranch.com. Riding excursions up to the forest above Kapalua, at $60 for 1hr (available seasonally), $90 for 1hr 30min, $120 for 2hr, or $300 for the advanced "Ironwood Odyssey."

Mākena Stables ☏808/879-0244, ⊛www.makenastables.com. Two- to three-hour morning or evening rides along the coastline from ʻĀhihi Bay, south of Big Beach, to La Pérouse; $145–170. No credit cards. Mon–Sat.

Maui Horseback Tours ☏808/248-7799, ⊛www.mauistables.com. Three-hour riding tours with an emphasis on Hawaiian history and spirituality, in the remote but beautiful Kīpahulu district, west of ʻOheʻo Gulch in East Maui. Departs 9.30am and 1pm daily, $150.

Mendes Ranch ☏808/871-5222, ⊛www.mendesranch.com. Half-day tours of this cattle ranch in East Maui's Waiheʻe Valley, with barbecue lunch; $130 per person or $280 with a 30min helicopter flight. Mon–Sat.

Lahaina Stables ☏808/667-2222, ⊛www.mauihorse.com. Horseback adventures on the slopes of the West Maui Mountains above Lahaina; two-hour morning rides for $110 or sunset rides for $120, 3hr 30min morning rides for $135.

Pony Express Tours ☏808/667-2200, ⊛www.ponyexpresstours.com. 1hr 30min ($90) or 2hr ($105) tours of Haleakalā Ranch, Maui's largest cattle ranch (Mon–Fri), or 5hr 30min descent to Ka Moa O Pele junction in Haleakalā Crater ($175), with picnic lunch (Mon–Sat).

along the southern coast of East Maui (which was closed due to earthquake damage when this book went to press), but they seldom do so any longer.

The most popular **bus tours** on the island run around East Maui to Hāna (typically costing $80–100 per person), and up the volcano to Haleakalā Crater ($70–80). Operators include Akina Aloha Tours (☎808/879-2828, ⓦwww.akinatours.com), Polynesian Adventure Tours (☎808/877-4242 or 1-800/622-3011, ⓦwww.polyad .com), and Ekahi Tours (☎808/877-9775 or 1-888/292-2422, ⓦwww.ekahi.com).

Among companies renting out **mountain bikes**, typically at $25–30 per day or up to $120 per week, are South Maui Bicycles, 1993 S Kīhei Rd, Kīhei (☎808/874-0068, ⓦwww.stirflux.com/smb); West Maui Cycles, 1087 Limahana Place, Lahaina (☎808/661-9005, ⓦwww.westmauicycles.com); and Island Biker, 415 Dairy Rd, Kahului (☎808/877-7744, ⓦwww.islandbiker.com). Chris' Bike Adventures (☎808/871-2453) can arrange customized **bike tours** of Maui to your specifications. A full list of operators running **downhill bike rides** on Haleakalā appears on p.348.

Finally, **Pacific Wings** flies between Kahului and Hāna; see p.366.

Where to stay

Even more so than on the other Hawaiian islands, most of the tourist accommodation on Maui is situated in the drier and less scenic parts of the island. The majority of its hotels and condos are located either along the leeward coast of **West Maui**, in the highly developed strip that runs from Lahaina up to Kapalua, or on the southwest shoreline of the eastern half of the island, between Kīhei and Mākena in what's known as **South Maui**. If beaches or golf are your main priority, you'll be well situated in these areas; most of Maui's historic sites and most attractive landscapes, however, are a long way away.

Travelers looking for a paradise-island hideaway would do better to consider one of the many plush **B&Bs** tucked away in the meadows of Upcountry Maui and in the rainforests around Hāna in the east. (Don't expect to spot any as you drive around, though; county regulations forbid B&Bs to display signs.) If you're not planning on renting a car, **Lahaina** is the only place where you can stay in a real town with sightseeing, beaches, and restaurants within easy walking distance. For **budget travelers**, the cheapest options of all are in faded downtown Wailuku.

Opportunities to **camp** on Maui are very limited, with the best sites in **Haleakalā National Park**, up near the crater (see p.349), and also at Kipahulu on the southeast shore (see p.372). Cabins and tent camping are also available at Maui's

Maui favorites: accommodation

Banana Bungalow, Wailuku (①–②)	p.318
Old Lahaina House, Lahaina (③–④)	p.294
Best Western Pioneer Inn, Lahaina (④–⑤)	p.294
The Mauian, Nāpili (⑤)	p.307
Old Wailuku Inn, Wailuku (⑤)	p.318
Hāmoa Bay Bungalow, Hāna (⑥–⑦)	p.366
Nāpili Kai Beach Resort, Nāpili (⑦)	p.307
Fairmont Kea Lani Maui, Wailea (⑧–⑨)	p.332
Hyatt Regency Maui, Kāʻanapali (⑧–⑨)	p.304
Hotel Hāna-Maui, Hāna (⑨)	p.367

two **state parks**, **Polipoli** (see p.343 for updates on recent closure) and the much nicer **Waiʻānapanapa** (see p.364); $5 permits are issued, by mail or in person, by the Department of Land and Natural Resources, 54 S High St, Wailuku, HI 96793 (Mon–Fri 8am–3.30pm; ☎808/984-8109, ⓦwww.state.hi.us/dlnr). As detailed on p.315, the only **county park** currently open to campers is at **Kanahā Beach** outside Kahului; for information and reservations, contact the Department of Parks and Recreation, 1580 Kaʻahumanu Ave, Wailuku, HI 96793 (Mon–Fri 8am–4pm; ☎808/270-7389, ⓦwww.co.maui.hi.us).

When to go

Maui basks in the usual balmy Hawaiian **climate**, rarely experiencing temperatures along the coast below the mid-seventies Fahrenheit or higher than the mid-eighties. The busiest tourist season, between December and February, coincides with the "rainiest" time of year. You can be unlucky, but as a rule the main leeward tourist areas seldom receive more than the occasional light shower even then.

Unless you have specialized interests, there's no overriding reason to visit the island at one time rather than another. To avoid the crowds and take advantage of lower room rates, come between March and June or from September through November. The best **swimming** conditions are between April and September, but the peak **surfing** season arrives with the higher winter waves, from November through March – which is also the time when there's every chance you'll see humpback whales. The **flowering trees** along the Hāna Highway reach their peak in June, while July and August are the best months to see the extraordinary blossoming **silversword** plants of Haleakalā.

Watersports and other activities

From the moment you arrive on Maui, you'll be inundated with handouts and free magazines that detail the island's vast range of tours and activities. **Activities operators** in all the tourist areas offer **cut-price deals** well below the advertised rates. Tom Barefoot's Cashback Tours, 250 Alamaha St, Kahului (☎1-800/895-2040, ⓦwww.tombarefoot.com), is one of the few that don't also try to sell time-shares, and its website details every imaginable island activity, along with the latest prices.

In addition to the activities detailed below, you'll find lists of Molokini **snorkel cruises** on p.325; downhill **bike rides** on p.348; **helicopter tours** on p.283; and **horse riding** trips on p.283.

Diving

Maui and its immediate neighbors offer probably the best **scuba diving** in the Hawaiian islands. The most popular spots are in the vicinity of **Molokini Crater**, off South Maui. Learners and inexperienced divers start by exploring the sheltered, shallow "Inside Crater" area, and eventually progress to the "Back Wall," with its huge drop-offs. There's also good **shore diving** at Black Rock in Kāʻanapali and in La Pérouse Bay, while the most spectacular dives of all lie off southern Lanai, within easy reach of a day's boat-trip from Maui.

A huge number of companies arrange **diving excursions** in the waters off Maui and Lanai, with the largest operator being **Maui Dive Shop**; full listings appear in the box, overleaf. Prices generally start at around $80 for a one-tank trip, $100 for two tanks, with equipment rental costing an additional $25 or so. Almost all offer multi-day packages for beginners, leading to PADI certification; a typical price would be $220–250 for three days, and $300 for four. Bear in mind that many of the Molokini snorkel cruises listed on p.325 actually offer diving as well as snorkeling.

Be sure not to dive within 24 hours of flying or ascending to any significant altitude. The summit of Haleakalā is certainly out of bounds, while you should ask your dive operator for advice before even driving into the Upcountry.

Snorkeling

Maui offers some of the finest conditions for **snorkeling** in all Hawaii. Although the volcanic islet of Molokini is the most compelling destination of all, you can only get there if you pay for a snorkel cruise (see p.325), while plenty of great alternatives are accessible by car. When conditions are calm, the turquoise waters of magnificent **Honolua Bay**, at the northern tip of West Maui, are teeming with fish, while the rocky shores of **La Pérouse Bay**, at the southern end of South Maui, are preserved as a marine sanctuary and offer almost infinite scope for underwater exploration. Even in the major resorts the snorkeling can be great, as for example at Kāʻanapali and Wailea beaches.

Ocean activities

Dive operators
Ed Robinson's Diving Adventures Kīhei, ☏808/879-3584, ⊛www.mauiscuba.com
Extended Horizons Lahaina, ☏1-888/348-3628, ⊛www.scubadivemaui.com
Maui Dive Shop Island-wide, ☏808/879-1775, ⊛www.mauidiveshop.com
Maui Dreams Kīhei, ☏808/874-5332, ⊛www.mauidreamdiveco.com
Mike Severn's Kīhei, ☏808/879-6596, ⊛www.mikesevernsdiving.com
Pacific Dive Lahaina, ☏808/667-5331, ⊛www.pacificdive.com
Prodiver Kīhei, ☏808/875-4004, ⊛prodivermaui. com
Trilogy Lahaina, ☏1-888/225-6284, ⊛www.sailtrilogy.com

Boat tours
Atlantis Submarines ☏808/667-2224 or 1-800/548-6262, ⊛www.atlantisadventures .com. One-hour underwater excursions off Lahaina ($80; look for discounts online).
Maui Princess ☏808/661-8397 or 1-877/500-6284, ⊛www.mauiprincess.com. Dinner ($84) and whale-watching ($27 and $34) cruises from Lahaina, plus one-day excursions to Molokai (from $80).
Pacific Whale Foundation ☏808/249-8811 or 1-800/942-5311, ⊛www.pacificwhale .org. This nonprofit organization offers 2–3hr whale-watching cruises from Lahaina or Māʻalaea (Nov–April; $20 and $32), plus snorkeling and dolphin-watching tours to Molokini ($55–80) or Lanai ($80).
Reefdancer ☏808/667-2133. Sixty- or ninety-minute cruises ($33/$45) in a semi-submersible from Lahaina; passengers view the reef from an underwater cabin.
Trilogy Ocean Sports ☏808/661-4743 or 1-888/225-6284, ⊛www.sailtrilogy.com. Day-long sailing trips from Lahaina to Lanai, including snorkeling, beach barbecue, and Lanai van tour ($179). They also offer diving and snorkeling at Molokini and off Lanai.
For a list of Molokini snorkel cruises, see p.325.

Parasailing

Parasailing, which is a bit like waterskiing, except you suddenly find yourself several hundred feet up in the air, has become very popular in the waters just off Kā'anapali and Lahaina in West Maui. To avoid disturbing humpback whales during their winter migrations, however, it's only permitted between mid-May and mid-December. Expect to pay $45–55 for a fifteen-minute flight with operators such as Parasail Kā'anapali (☎808/669-6555), UFO Parasail (☎808/661-7836 or 1-800/359-4836, ⓦwww.ufoparasailing.com), and Lahaina West Maui Parasail (☎808/661-4060).

Surfing

Surf aficionados rate several Maui sites as equal to anything on Oahu's fabled North Shore, with **Honolua Bay** on the northern tip of West Maui, and **Jaws** off Ha'ikū in the east, as the greatest of all. You need to be a real expert to join the locals who surf there, however – beginners would do better to start out at Lahaina and Kā'anapali beaches. The peak **season** is between November and March. Companies that offer surfing **lessons** in the Lahaina area include the Goofy Foot Surf School (☎808/244-9283, ⓦwww.goofyfootsurfschool.com) and the Nancy Emerson School of Surfing

Kayak tours

Kelii's Kayak Tours ☎1-888/874-7652, ⓦwww.keliiskayak.com. Two-hour kayak tours ($54) from Lahaina, plus several more options in West, North and South Maui.

South Pacific Kayaks Rainbow Mall, 2439 S Kīhei Rd ☎808/875-4848 or 1-800/776-2326, ⓦwww.southpacifickayaks.com. An extensive range of kayaking tours, from 2hr 15min whale-watching trips ($65; in season only) via 3hr guided excursions at Mākena or Lahaina, up to extended tours in South or West Maui for up to $99.

Equipment rental

Auntie Snorkel 2439 S Kīhei Rd, Kīhei ☎808/879-6263 or 1-877/256-4248, ⓦwww.auntiesnorkel.com. Choose from snorkels and kayaks.

Boss Frog's Dive Shop 1215 S Kīhei Rd, Kīhei (☎808/891-0077); 2395 S Kīhei Rd, Kīhei (☎808/875-4477); 150 Lahainaluna Rd, Lahaina (☎808/661-3333); 3636 Lower Honoapi'ilani Rd, Kā'anapali (☎808/665-1200); 4310 Lower Honoapi'ilani Rd, Kahana (☎808/669-6700); and Nāpili Plaza, Nāpili (☎808/669-4949); ⓦwww.bossfrog.com. Activity center that also rents out scuba, snorkeling and surf gear.

Maui Dive Shop. 1455 S Kīhei Rd, Kīhei (☎808/879-3388); Honokōwai Marketplace, 3350 Lower Honoapi'ilani Rd (☎808/661-6166); and five other Maui locations; ⓦwww.mauidiveshop.com. Dive specialists who rent scuba and snorkeling equipment.

Snorkel Bob's 1279 S Kīhei Rd, Kīhei (☎808/875-6188); 2411 S Kīhei Rd, Kīhei (☎808/879-7449); Dickenson Square, Dickenson St, Lahaina (☎808/662-0104); and Nāpili Village Hotel, 5425C Lower Honoapi'ilani Rd, Nāpili (☎808/669-9603); ⓦwww.snorkelbob.com. Snorkel gear that can be returned on any island.

South Pacific Kayaks Rainbow Mall, 2439 S Kīhei Rd ☎808/875-4848 ⓦwww.southpacifickayaks.com. Choose from kayaks, surfboards, snorkels, boogie boards, beach chairs, and the like.

West Maui Cycles 1087 Limahana Place, Lahaina ☎808/661-9005, ⓦwww.westmauicycles.com. Besides mountain bikes, you'll find snorkels, boogie boards, and surfboards.

(☎808/244-7873, ⓦwww.mauisurfclinics.com). South Maui instructors include Hawaiian Style Surf School (☎808/874-0110), while Maui Waveriders (☎808/875-4761, ⓦwww.mauiwaveriders.com) operate in both locations.

Windsurfing and kitesurfing

Maui is renowned as the world's most sublime **windsurfing** and **kitesurfing** destination. Legendary **Ho'okipa Beach Park**, just east of Pā'ia on the central isthmus, is a mecca for devotees and plays host to major championships throughout most of the year. Strong winds are of greater importance to windsurfers than high surf, so summer is the peak season for the sport. Between December and February the winds tend to drop for days on end, but even then conditions are usually good enough somewhere on the island; **Mā'alaea Bay** on the south shore of the isthmus is the likeliest spot.

The best place to **learn** is Kanahā Beach near Kahului, a few miles west of Ho'okipa. Expect to pay around $80 for a 2hr 30min lesson (including equipment rental) with operators such as Action Sports Maui (☎808/871-5857, ⓦwww.actionsportsmaui.com), Alan Cadiz's HST Windsurfing School (☎808/871-5423 or 1-800/968-5423, ⓦwww.hstwindsurfing.com), Hawaiian Island Surf & Sport (☎808/871-4981 or 1-800/231-6958, ⓦwww.hawaiianisland.com), or Maui Ocean Activities (☎808/667-2001, ⓦwww.mauiwatersports.com). Maui Windsurfari specializes in putting together all-inclusive **packages** (☎808/871-7766 or 1-800/736-6284, ⓦwww.windsurfari.com).

Nightlife and entertainment

Although it can't compete with the big-city atmosphere of Honolulu, and island residents jokingly refer to the hour of 10pm as "Maui midnight," by Hawaiian standards Maui offers visitors a reasonably lively **nightlife**.

As ever, most of the activity is confined to the tourist enclaves, and the resort hotels in particular, but if you enjoy wandering the streets from bar to bar the oceanfront at **Lahaina** provides almost the same buzz as Waikīkī. The south coast, from **Kīhei** on down, is too spread out to have the same intensity, but it's always party time somewhere along the strip.

Lovers of traditional **Hawaiian music** should head to the *Ritz-Carlton* in Kapalua, which stages a superb series of weekly slack key guitar concerts, masterminded by

Maui favorites: eating	
These are not so much the ten best restaurants on Maui as ten very good places to eat, drawn from all price categories and arranged in ascending order of price.	
Nāhiku Fruit Stand, Nāhiku	p.362
Soup Nutz and Java Jazz, Honokōwai	p.308
Cilantro Fresh Mexican Grill, Lahaina	p.298
AK's Café, Wailuku	p.320
Hula Grill, Kā'anapali	p.305
Sansei Seafood Restaurant, Kapalua	p.308
Sansei Seafood Restaurant, Kīhei	p.330
Roy's Kīhei Bar and Grill, Kīhei	p.330
Hali'imaile General Store, Hali'imaile	p.341
The Feast at Lele, Lahaina	p.299

Maui festivals and events

Jan 1	New Year's Day (public holiday)
Jan	Maui Pro Surf Meet; surfing competition, Honolua Bay and Hoʻokipa Beach
3rd Mon in Jan	Martin Luther King Day (public holiday)
3rd week in Jan	Hula Bowl Football All-Star Classic; college football tournament, War Memorial Stadium, Wailuku
early Feb	Whale Fest Week; whale-related events, Lahaina and Kāʻanapali
3rd Mon in Feb	Presidents' Day (public holiday)
late Feb	Maui Classical Music Festival, Maui Arts & Cultural Center
March	Run to the Sun; foot race, Pāʻia to Haleakalā
March 26	Prince Kuhio Day (public holiday)
March/April	East Maui Taro Festival, Hāna
Easter Monday	Public holiday
late April	David Malo Day, Lahainaluna High School, Lahaina
late April	Maui County Agricultural Trade Show, Ulupalakua Ranch
May 1	Lei Day (public holiday)
late May	Bankoh Hoʻomanaʻo Challenge; outrigger canoe race, Kāʻanapali to Waikīkī; International Festival of Canoes, Lahaina
last Mon in May	Memorial Day (public holiday); In Celebration of Canoes, Lahaina
June 11	Kamehameha Day (public holiday)
mid-June	Maui Film Festival, Wailea
late June	Kihoʻalu; slack-key guitar festival, Maui Arts & Cultural Center
July 4	Independence Day (public holiday); Makawao Rodeo, Makawao
early July	Quicksilver Cup; windsurfing competition, Kanahā Beach
early Aug	Hawaii State Championships; windsurfing competition, Kanahā Beach
3rd Fri in Aug	Admission Day (public holiday)
1st Mon in Sept	Labor Day (public holiday)
mid-Sept	A Taste of Lahaina; food festival, Lahaina
late Sept	Maui Marathon, Kahului to Kāʻanapali
2nd Mon in Oct	Columbus Day (public holiday)
early Oct	Maui County Fair, Wailuku
mid-Oct	Aloha Festival
Oct 31	Halloween Mardi Gras of the Pacific, Lahaina
Late Oct/early Nov	Aloha Classic World Wavesailing Championships; windsurfing competition, Hoʻokipa
Nov 11	Veterans Day (public holiday)
4th Thurs in Nov	Thanksgiving Day (public holiday)
Dec 25	Christmas Day (public holiday)

Note that the exact dates of surfing contests, and in some cases the venues as well, depend on wave conditions.

virtuoso George Kahumoku, Jr (late Dec to April Wed 6pm & 8.30pm, May to late Dec Wed 7.30pm; $45; ☎808/669-3858 or 1-888/669-3858, ⓦ www .slackkey.com). Each week sees a different guest star, from the very biggest names of the genre – regulars include Cyril Pahinui, Led Kaʻapana, and Dennis Kamakahi – and live recordings of the concerts have twice won Grammys. During renovations at the *Ritz-Carlton* in 2007, the concerts relocated to a more congenial setting at the nearby *Napili Kai Beach Resort*; check to make sure they've now returned.

Maui lū'aus

The **lū'aus** listed below charge anything from $60 to $95 per adult and $28–60 per child; you can buy discounted tickets (perhaps $10 off the usual price) from activities operators all over the island. While *The Feast at Lele* offers the best food (see p.299), it's not quite a *lū'au* in the usual sense of the word, so the *Old Lahaina Lū'au*, in a splendid oceanfront setting close to the Lahaina Cannery Mall, is generally considered to be the best value. Note that all times listed below may vary slightly, to take advantage of changing sunset times.

Drums of the Pacific *Hyatt Regency Maui*, Kā'anapali ☎808/661-1234. Daily 5pm.

The Feast at Lele 505 Front St, Lahaina ☎808/667-5353, ⓦwww.feastatlele.com. April–Sept daily 6pm, Oct–March daily 5.30pm.

Maui Sunset Lū'au *Maui Prince*, Mākena ☎808/875-5888. Tues & Thurs 5.30pm. $83.

Old Lahaina Lū'au Lahaina Cannery Mall, Lahaina ☎808/667-1998 or 1-800/248-5828, ⓦwww.oldlahainaluau.com. April–Sept daily 5.45pm, Oct–March daily 5.15pm.

Royal Lahaina Lū'au *Royal Lahaina Resort*, Kā'anapali ☎808/661-9119. Daily 4.45pm.

Wailea's Finest Lū'au Outrigger Palms at Wailea, Wailea ☎808/879-1922. Mon & Thurs–Sat 5pm.

Away from the resorts, the local community of rock exiles and ex-Californians makes *Casanova's* in upcountry **Makawao** an amazingly happening venue for such a tiny town. There's also the Maui Arts and Cultural Center by the harbor in **Kahului**, which attracts big-name touring bands.

Lahaina

Seen from a short distance offshore, **LAHAINA**, the only true town in West Maui, is one of the prettiest communities in all Hawaii. During the early nineteenth century it served as capital of the entire Kingdom of Hawaii, but it has barely grown since then and could almost be mistaken for a peaceful, tropical village. Its main oceanfront street is lined with timber-frame buildings; yachts bob in the harbor; coconut palms sway to either side of the central banyan tree; surfers swirl into the thin fringe of beach to the south; and the mountains of West Maui dominate the skyline, ringed as often as not by beautiful rainbows. Up close, however, many of Lahaina's decrepit-looking structures turn out to be fakes, housing T-shirt stores and tacky themed restaurants, while the crowds and congestion along **Front Street** can seem all too reminiscent of Waikīkī.

Even so, Lahaina makes an attractive base, sandwiched between the spectacular ocean and spellbinding hills. Early evening is especially unforgettable, with the sun casting a rich glow on the mountains as it sets behind the island of Lanai. Lahaina is lively and by Maui standards inexpensive, with a huge range of activities and little rainfall, but above all it's the only town on Maui to offer lodging, sightseeing, nightlife, and an abundance of restaurants within easy walking distance of each other.

A brief history of Lahaina

Although there's little left to show for it nowadays – you can easily see all the town has to offer in a couple of hours – Lahaina boasts a colorful past. By the time the first foreigners came to Hawaii, it was already the residence of the high *ali'i* of Maui. **Kamehameha the Great** sealed his conquest of Maui by sacking Lahaina in 1795, then returned in 1802 and spent a year preparing for what was to be an unsuccessful invasion of Kauai (see p.436). His successors, Kamehamehas II and III, made Lahaina their **capital** between the 1820s and 1840s, ruling from the island of **Moku'ula**, in a lake in what is now Malu'ulu o Lele Park, south of downtown.

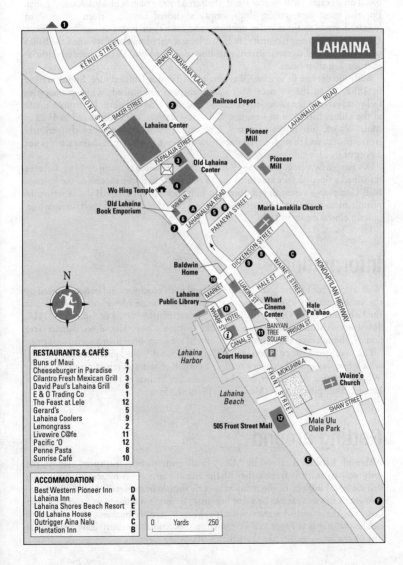

LAHAINA

Railroad Depot

Lahaina Center

Pioneer Mill

Pioneer Mill

Old Lahaina Center

Wo Hing Temple

Old Lahaina Book Emporium

Maria Lanakila Church

Baldwin Home

Lahaina Public Library

Wharf Cinema Center

Hale Pa'ahao

Banyan Tree Square

Court House

Lahaina Harbor

Lahaina Beach

Waine'e Church

505 Front Street Mall

Mala Ulu Olele Park

N

RESTAURANTS & CAFÉS

Buns of Maui	4
Cheeseburger in Paradise	7
Cilantro Fresh Mexican Grill	3
David Paul's Lahaina Grill	6
E & O Trading Co	1
The Feast at Lele	12
Gerard's	5
Lahaina Coolers	9
Lemongrass	2
Livewire C@fe	11
Pacific 'O	12
Penne Pasta	8
Sunrise Café	10

ACCOMMODATION

Best Western Pioneer Inn	D
Lahaina Inn	A
Lahaina Shores Beach Resort	E
Old Lahaina House	F
Outrigger Aina Nalu	C
Plantation Inn	B

0   Yards   250

When **whaling** ships started to put in during the 1820s, seeking to recuperate from their grueling Pacific peregrinations, fierce struggles between the sailors and Lahaina's Christian **missionaries** became commonplace. Whaling crews, incensed by missionary attempts to control drinking and prostitution, repeatedly attacked the home of Reverend William Richards, but in due course chose to head instead for the fleshpots of Honolulu. In the 1840s, however, following the death of Maui's devout Governor Hoapili, the whalemen returned en masse to Lahaina. For the next two decades, it was a lawless and rip-roaring frontier town, described by another missionary as "one of the breathing holes of Hell."

Surprisingly, Lahaina has never been a true deep-water port. Its prosperity was based on its calm, shallow roadstead, sheltered by the islands of Molokai and Lanai. For the most part, sailing ships simply anchored anything from a couple of hundred yards to three miles offshore, and sent their crews ashore by rowboat. During the nineteenth century, in fact, a long covered marketplace lined the banks of a canal parallel to the seafront, enabling seamen to buy all they needed without ever leaving their boats.

With the decline of whaling, Lahaina turned toward agriculture. **Sugar** arrived in 1862, when the Pioneer Mill Company was established, while **pineapples** followed early in the twentieth century. The roadstead had never been quite as safe as the sailors had liked to imagine, and a new harbor was constructed in 1922 at Mala Wharf, just north of town. Unfortunately it proved to be dangerously storm-prone, and though cruise ships now anchor far offshore, Lahaina itself is not a port of call for ships of any size.

Devastated by a huge fire in 1919 and by the state-wide tsunami of 1946, Lahaina remained a sleepy backwater until the 1970s. Only with the success of the Pioneer Mill Company's resort development at neighboring **Kā'anapali** did it return to prominence, as the hectic tourist destination of today. The mill itself, meanwhile, quietly closed down in 1999.

Information

Walk along Front Street and you'll be deluged with brochures and leaflets hawked by the various activity kiosks. Somewhat more dispassionate advice can be obtained at the **Lahaina Visitor Center** (daily 9am–5pm; ☎808/667-9193 or 1-888/310-1117, ⓦwww.visitlahaina.com), inside the Old Lahaina Court House on Banyan Tree Square, though even that is more of an official souvenir store than a useful resource.

The main **post office** (Mon–Fri 8.30am–5pm, Sat 9am–1pm; zip code 96761), which handles general delivery mail, is a couple of miles north of town past Mala Wharf, near the civic center, but there's a smaller branch at 132 Papalaua St, in the Lahaina Shopping Center (Mon–Fri 8.15am–4.15pm).

Getting around

Although Lahaina is served by Maui's fairly basic **public transport** system, the only way to reach it from either of the island's airports is by renting your own vehicle or taking one of the many taxi-style shuttle buses detailed on p.282. Once you get to town, a car can be a real nuisance. If you're staying here, leave it at your hotel, as the cramped streets make **parking** a terrible business. The only free public parking is at Front and Prison streets, or you can usually leave your car at one of the larger malls, like the Lahaina Shopping Center.

If you'd prefer to **cycle**, West Maui Cycles, behind *Pizza Hut* off Honoapi'ilani Hwy at 1087 Limahana Place (☎808/661-9005, ⊛www.westmauicycles.com), rents out mountain bikes at around $30 for 24 hours or about $120 per week; it also has snorkel equipment, boogie boards, and surfboards.

Buses

Maui Bus (☎808/871-4838, ⊛www.mauicounty.gov/bus) runs hourly **buses** between Lahaina and **Kahului** ($1; departs Queen Ka'ahumanu Center in Kahului daily 5.30am–7.30pm, Wharf Cinema Center in Lahaina daily 6.30am–8.30pm). All those services call at Mā'alaea, where you can change for buses to Kīhei and Wailea. They also offer frequent connections between Lahaina and **Kā'anapali**, leaving from Lahaina Harbor hourly from 6.30am until 8.30pm daily.

The Lahaina Kā'anapali Railroad

Also known as the Sugar Cane Train, the **Lahaina Kā'anapali Railroad** (adults $21 round-trip, under-13s $15; ☎808/667-6851 or, in the US only, 1-800/499-2307, ⊛www.sugarcanetrain.com) is a restored locomotive (complete with "singing conductor") that runs a six-mile, half-hour long excursion through the cane fields along the tracks of the old Lahaina & Kā'anapali Railroad. It travels from Lahaina to Kā'anapali and then half a mile beyond to turn around at Pu'ukoli'i. For anyone other than a small child, it's not an exciting trip. The first departure from Lahaina is at 11.05am daily and the last at 4pm; from Kā'anapali, the first is at 10.25am daily, the last at 3.10pm. There's also a weekly dinner train, setting off from Pu'ukoli'i at 5pm on Thursday (adults $79, under-13s $49). Free shuttle buses connect the Lahaina and Kā'anapali stations with the Wharf Cinema Center and the Whaler's Village, respectively.

Ferries

Lahaina Harbor is home to a couple of **inter-island ferry services**. *Expeditions* (☎808/661-3756 or, from outside Maui, 1-800/695-2624, ⊛www.go-lanai.com) sails from in front of the *Pioneer Inn* to Manele Bay on **Lanai** daily at 6.45am, 9.15am, 12.45pm, 3.15pm, and 5.45pm. Departures from Lanai are at 8am, 10.30am, 2pm, 4.30pm, and 6.45pm; the adult fare is $25 each way, while under-12s go for $20. The trip takes approximately fifty minutes. It's also possible to make a 1hr 30min ferry crossing between Maui and **Molokai** on the *Molokai Princess* (adults $40 one-way, children $20; ☎808/662-3535 or 1-877/500-6284, ⊛www.mauiprincess.com). The boat leaves Lahaina at 7.15am and 6pm daily, and returns from Kaunakakai Harbor on Molokai at 5.30am and 4pm.

Accommodation

In terms of **accommodation**, Lahaina has nothing to rival the opulence of Kā'anapali and Kapalua, further north up the coast. However, the *Pioneer Inn* harks back romantically to the old days of Hawaiian tourism, and there are also a couple of classy B&B inns, plus a few central but quiet hotel-cum-condos.

Best Western Pioneer Inn 658 Wharf St ☎808/661-3636 or 1-800/457-5457, ⊛www.pioneerinnmaui.com. Maui's oldest hotel, on the seafront in the very center of Lahaina, makes a historic and highly atmospheric place to stay – though not as luxurious as the modern resorts – and often has last-minute availability. All the tastefully furnished rooms have private baths and a/c, and open onto lovely *lānais*; the quieter ones face an inner courtyard, the rest overlook Banyan Tree Square. There's a small pool, but no on-site parking. Rooms ❹, suites ❺

Lahaina Inn 127 Lahainaluna Rd T 808/661-0577 or 1-800/669-3444, Ⓦ www.lahainainn.com. Set slightly back from Front Street above the *Lahaina Grill*, this sumptuous, antique-furnished re-creation of how a century-old inn ought to look was actually built as a store in 1938. The twelve rooms of varying sizes have a/c, private bathrooms (most with showers rather than baths) and phones, but no TV. No children under 15 years. ❹–❺

Lahaina Shores Beach Resort 475 Front St T 808/661-3339 or 1-800/642-6284 (US & Canada), Ⓦ www.lahaina-shores.com. Large, airy, shorefront hotel facing a pretty little beach a few hundred yards south of central Lahaina, next door to the 505 Front Street mall. Two-, three-, and four-person rooms and suites, all with kitchens and *lānais*; an ocean view costs around $30 more than a mountain view. Rooms ❺, suites ❼

Old Lahaina House PO Box 10355 T 808/667-4663 or 1-800/847-0761, Ⓦ www.oldlahaina.com. Good-quality B&B accommodation in a friendly private home with pool, a

few hundred yards south of downtown Lahaina. There's one guest room in the house and four more in a separate garden wing; all are en-suite, with refrigerators, TVs, and a/c. Rates include breakfast on the *lānai*. ❸–❹

Outrigger Aina Nalu 660 Waine'e St T 808/667-9766, 1-800/688-7444, Ⓦ www.outrigger.com. This sprawling but low-key condo complex, a couple of blocks from the sea in central Lahaina, has been through many incarnations over the years. Completely rebuilt and revamped in 2005, it now offers smart, well-equipped rooms in two X-shaped blocks, though with no beach and just a small pool, it's not a place to linger all day. Check online for the best rates. ❻

Plantation Inn 174 Lahainaluna Rd T 808/667-9225 or 1-800/433-6815, Ⓦ www.theplantationinn .com. Luxury B&B hotel, not far back from the sea and styled after a Southern plantation home, complete with columns and verandas and a twelve-foot-deep pool. All 19 rooms have bathrooms and *lānais*, while the suites also have kitchenettes. Guests get a discount at the downstairs restaurant, *Gerard's* (see p.299). Rooms ❺, suites ❻

Downtown Lahaina

Almost all the activity of modern Lahaina is concentrated along **Front Street**, where a few historic buildings, such as the Baldwin Home and Wo Hing Temple, hang on amid an awful lot of shopping malls, souvenir stores, and fast-food outlets. The very heart of town is **Banyan Tree Square**, an attractive public space that's often rendered too busy for comfort by busloads of tourists.

For respite, locals and visitors alike gravitate toward the **waterfront**. The views are superb, whether you look straight across to the island of Lanai, where you'll probably be able to make out the crest of Norfolk pines along its topmost ridge, or north toward Molokai, where the west-end mountain of Mauna Loa is visible on a clear day. Closer at hand, fishermen angle for sand fish in the inshore waters, boats and yachts rock beyond the placid roll of white surf fifty yards out, and parasailers peer down upon all this activity from on high.

If you're looking for **shops**, the two largest malls are the modern **Lahaina Center**, three blocks north of downtown and still a long way short of filling up – despite its own reproduction Hawaiian village, the **Hale Kahiko**, which stages *hula* shows and is open for explanatory tours (daily 11am–4pm) – and the Lahaina Cannery, a long walk further north near Mala Wharf.

Banyan Tree Square

A magnificent banyan tree, planted on April 24, 1873, almost completely fills **Banyan Tree Square**. It consists of at least twenty major trunks, plus any number of intertwined tendrils pushing back down into the ground. A phenomenal number of chirruping birds congregate in the branches, while portrait artists tout for customers in the shade below.

Here and there on the surrounding lawns, a few outlines mark the former extent of **Lahaina Fort**, started by Governor Hoapili in 1832. Its walls once held as many as 47 cannons, salvaged from assorted shipwrecks throughout Hawaii; a drum was beaten on its ramparts at nightfall as a signal for all foreign seamen to return to their ships. The fort was demolished in 1854, but one small corner has been reconstructed, at the southwest end of the square.

The stolid, four-square **Court House**, on the harbor side of Banyan Tree Square, was constructed in 1859 after a storm had destroyed most of Lahaina's previous official buildings. Downstairs, you'll find the small local visitor center (see p.292), as well as the Banyan Tree Gallery, which hosts interesting, free **art exhibitions** (daily 9am–5pm). Up on the second floor, the town's former courtroom, last used in 1987, now serves as the **Lahaina Heritage Center** (same hours; $2 suggested donation), where the displays and photographs on local history include illuminating sections devoted to the whaling and plantation eras.

Across Hotel Street from the Court House, the **Pioneer Inn** has, since it was moved en masse from the island of Lanai in 1901, been the main social center of Lahaina. Its original owner, a Canadian "Mountie" who had pursued a criminal all the way to Maui, decided to stay on and go into the hotel business, catering to passengers on the Inter-Island Steamship line. It makes an atmospheric – and busy – place to stop in for a beer.

Lahaina Harbor

On the waterfront, across from the *Pioneer Inn*, a simple and modern white structure has replaced what was the oldest **Pacific Lighthouse**, built to serve the whaling fleet in 1840. Shielded by a breakwater of boulders, **Lahaina Harbor** now serves as an overworked pleasure-boat marina, and is also the base for ferries to Molokai and Lanai (see p.293). Although the harbor wall has kiosks for most local **boat operators**, it's not much of an area to stroll around, and you can usually get better prices from the activity centers along Front Street.

The Brick Palace and the Hauola Stone

Lahaina Public Library, immediately north of the *Pioneer Inn*, stands on the site of the former royal taro patch, personally tended by the first three Kamehamehas. A line of bricks set into the grass on its seaward side traces the foundations of the **Brick Palace**, the first Western-style building in Hawaii. Two stories high and measuring 20ft by 40ft, it was built for Kamehameha the Great in 1798 by an English convict who had managed to escape from Australia; the palace survived until the 1860s.

Poking out from the waves beyond the seawall to the north is the approximately chair-shaped **Hauola Stone**, a "healing rock" where Hawaiian women would give birth. In thanks for a trouble-free labor, the umbilical cord (*piko*) of the infant would be left under the rock.

Lahaina Beach

Immediately south of the marina, **Lahaina Beach**, with its shallow water, sandy bottom, and gentle breaks, is where companies such as the Goofy Foot Surf School (T 808/244-9283, W www.goofyfootsurfschool.com) and the Nancy Emerson School of Surfing (T 808/244-7873, W www.surfclinicsmaui.com) teach their clients the rudiments of **surfing**, and beginners and old-timers alike swoop back and forth. The beach itself is too narrow for long days of family fun, but it's fine for a stroll.

Baldwin Home

The **Baldwin Home**, on Front Street just north of Banyan Tree Square, is the oldest surviving building in Lahaina. Dating from the days when this was Hawaii's royal capital, it was built as the Maui base of the Sandwich Islands Mission and is now a reasonably interesting museum of missionary and local history (daily 10am–4pm; $3 per person, $5 per couple or family; ☏808/661-3262). The admission price includes a brief narrated tour, after which visitors are free to take a closer look around.

Constructed in 1834, with 24-inch-thick walls made of plastered lava and coral, the house is named for Reverend Dwight Baldwin, who took it over when his predecessor fell sick three years later. Baldwin remained as pastor of Lahaina's Waine'e Church until 1871, and much of his original furniture is still in place. Oddly frivolous touches among the chairs, quilts, and memorabilia include an inlaid *koa* gaming table and a table-top croquet set. On one wall hangs a "Native Doctor's License" from 1865, with a scale of charges ranging from $50 down to $10, according to whether the patient had a "Very great sickness," "Less than that," "A Good Deal Less," a "Small sickness," or a "Very Small."

The **Masters' Reading Room**, next door to the Baldwin Home, is the headquarters of the Lahaina Restoration Foundation, which manages most of Lahaina's historic sites, but it's not open to the public.

Wo Hing Temple

The distinguished-looking building with the unmistakably Oriental facade, a short walk north of downtown Lahaina on Front Street, is known as the **Wo Hing Temple** (daily 10am–4pm; $1). It was built in 1912 as the meeting place for the Wo Hing Society, a mutual-aid organization established in China during the seventeenth century. Until the 1970s it housed elderly members of the society, but it's now a fine little museum devoted to Chinese immigration to Hawaii, with a small Taoist altar on its second story.

Amid the faded signs and battered pots and pans in the decrepit adjacent **cookhouse**, you can watch scratchy film footage shot by Thomas Edison in Hawaii in 1898, and shown in a continuous loop.

Hale Pa'ahao

At the corner of Prison and Waine'e streets, the plain one-story **Hale Pa'ahao** replaced the Fort as Lahaina's prison during the 1850s; in fact, as the Fort came down, the prison went up, using the same stones. Now a public hall, it's usually left open, and you're free to wander into the former cells, which hold a few exhibits about the days when they were filled to bursting with drunken sailors.

Waine'e Church

The first church on Maui, built in 1828 after five years of open-air services, was **Waine'e Church**, one block back from the sea. Twice destroyed by hurricanes, and burned down in 1894 amid protests against the overthrow of the Hawaiian monarchy, this less-than-enthralling edifice has been officially known as Waiola Church since it was last rebuilt in 1953.

Tombs in the sun-scorched graveyard alongside, however, include some of the greatest names in early Hawaiian history. A simple monument commemorates the last king of Kauai, **Kaumuali'i**, who was buried here in 1825 after being kidnapped by Liholiho and forced to live out the rest of his life in exile (see p.436).

Warren and Annabelle's Magic Show

Apart from eating and drinking, Lahaina is short on evening entertainment. Well worth recommending, therefore, is **Warren and Annabelle's Magic Show**, presented in a purpose-built theater in the oceanfront Lahaina Center (900 Front St; ☏808/667-6244, ⊛www.warrenandannabelles.com; Mon–Sat 5pm & 7.30pm; adults only, $50, or $82 with food and two cocktails, or $86 with dessert as well). The whole experience has been very thoughtfully designed. Each group of guests must solve a puzzle to gain admission to the pre-show bar, where cocktails and a large selection of appetizers and desserts are served while an invisible pianist (the ghostly "Annabelle") plays show tunes. The whole audience then moves to the intimate showroom, where they're treated to a wonderful display of sleight-of-hand magic by Warren Gibson, many of whose tricks are truly mind-boggling. There's nothing particularly Hawaiian about the show, but for a fun night out it's unbeatable. Note that the two shows overlap; the entire evening lasts four hours.

Nearby are **Queen Keopuolani**, one of the many wives of Kamehameha the Great, who was of such distinguished *ali'i* blood that her husband could only enter her presence naked on all fours; the governor of Maui, **Hoapili Kane**, who died in 1840; and his widow and successor **Hoapili Wahine**, who passed away two years later.

Lahainaluna

High above Lahaina town, reached by a winding two-mile climb up Lahainaluna Road past the Pioneer Sugar Mill, **Lahainaluna Seminary** was founded by American missionaries in 1831. Its goal was to teach Hawaiians to read and write, in the hope of producing future teachers and ministers. In 1850, however, the seminary passed into government control, and it eventually became Hawaii's most prestigious public **high school**. Although when it was built Hawaii did not belong to the US, it's regarded as being the first American educational institution west of the Rockies, and in the Gold Rush years many Californians sent their children here rather than risk the long journey East.

Visitors are welcome to take a quick look around the high school grounds; pause to identify yourself at the gate first. The only building you can enter is the seminary's small printing house, **Hale Pa'i** (Mon–Fri by appointment only; free; ☏808/661-3262). Dating from 1837, it holds some of Hawaii's first printed books, as well as a replica of the press that produced them.

Among Lahainaluna Seminary's earliest pupils were Hawaii's most famous native historians, **Samuel Kamakau** and **David Malo**. Malo had been brought up at the court of Kamehameha the Great on the Big Island and was 38 when he first came here. Although he became a Christian, and was a minister at the old village of Kalepolepo in what's now Kīhei, he was also a passionate defender of the rights of the Hawaiian people. At the time of the Great Mahele – the disastrous 1848 land division that made the American takeover of Hawaii possible (see p.537) – Malo was regarded as the firebrand behind native Hawaiian resistance. Before he died in 1853, he asked to be buried "beyond the rising tide of the foreign invasion." His gravesite, above Lahainaluna at **Pu'u Pa'upa'u**, is marked with a huge letter "L" (for Lahainaluna) etched into the hillside and visible from all over Lahaina.

Restaurants

Dozens of places to **eat** line the waterfront in Lahaina, with sophisticated gourmet **restaurants** mingling with national and local chain outlets and takeout places, so you should find something to suit you within a few minutes' wandering. For a quick snack, the best local **fast-food court** is in the Lahaina Cannery mall, a mile north of downtown, while there are several cheap Asian diners in the more central Old Lahaina Center.

For a full listing of Maui's *lū'aus*, see p.290.

Inexpensive

Buns of Maui 878 Front St ☎808/661-5407. Tucked away just behind Front St, this appealing little bakery serves fresh pastries, muffins, and of course sumptuous cinnamon buns in the morning, and switches to sandwiches later on. It doesn't have espresso coffee, but there's a *Starbucks* nearby. Daily 7.30am–8.30pm.

Cilantro Fresh Mexican Grill Old Lahaina Center, 170 Papalaua Ave ☎808/667-5444. Simple but clean and very appetizing Mexican diner, where you order at the counter in front of the open kitchen and either take it away or eat on site with plastic utensils. The food is uniformly tasty and fresh, with enchiladas, burritos and so on for $7–13, whole rotisserie chickens for $15, and specials like a chicken or fish taco plate for just over $10. There's no liquor license, but you can bring a bottle from the nearby *Foodland* supermarket. Mon–Sat 11am–9pm, Sun 11am–8pm.

Livewire C@fe 612 Front St ☎808/661-4213. The staff can be a little ditzy, but this roomy, tidy café, just south of Banyan Square, serves good coffees, snacks and smoothies, and makes a convenient place to hang out and check your email. Daily 6am–9pm.

Penne Pasta 180 Dickenson St ☎808/661-6633. Cheerful Italian café, with sidewalk and indoor seating, serving straightforward but tasty pastas, salads, and pizzas for under $10. The thin, crispy flatbread topped with olives, capers, basil, oregano, and roasted peppers is particularly good. Lunch is served on weekdays only. Mon–Fri 11am–9.30pm, Sat 5–9.30pm, Sun 5–9pm.

Sunrise Café 693A Front St at Market St ☎808/661-8558. Small, laidback, and very central café-cum-restaurant, with outdoor seating beside its own tiny patch of beach. Coffees, smoothies, and full cooked breakfasts are served from dawn onwards, plus $6–9 sandwiches, plate lunches, and salads later on. No credit cards. Daily 6am–6pm.

Moderate

Cheeseburger in Paradise 811 Front St ☎808/661-4855. Busy, crowded seafront restaurant, perched on stilts above the water. The great

views, buzzing ambience, and seafaring bric-a-brac are more of a draw than the food, which is very much what the name suggests, though in addition to meaty $8–10 cheeseburgers they have fish sandwiches and tofu nut-burgers at similar prices. There's live music nightly. Daily 8am–midnight.

Lahaina Coolers 180 Dickenson St ☎808/661-7082. Central bistro serving eggy breakfasts for around $10, then lunch specials like *kalua* pig tacos for around $10, or the same extensive menu of salads, pastas, pizzas, tortillas, steaks and fresh Hawaiian fish for lunch and dinner (entrees $17–22). A couple of blocks from the sea, but it's open and breezy, with a pleasant atmosphere. Live English soccer games shown regularly. Daily 8–2am.

Lemongrass 930 Waine'e St ☎808/667-6888. Bright little Vietnamese/Thai restaurant, behind the Lahaina Center. In addition to soups and noodle dishes such as beef *phó* ($7) and pad Thai with shrimp or chicken ($10), there's a full menu of meat and seafood entrees, including plenty of curries, almost all under $15. Daily 10am–9pm.

Expensive

David Paul's Lahaina Grill Lahaina Inn, 127 Lahainaluna Rd ☎808/667-5117. Upmarket, dinner-only restaurant serving some of Maui's finest Pacific Rim cuisine, just off Front Street in downtown Lahaina. The setting is slightly cramped, but the food is excellent. Of the appetizers, try the superb Kona lobster crabcake ($18). Entrees include rack of lamb flavored with coffee ($41), *kālua* duck ($32), and various fish dishes, while the fruity desserts are wonderful. A five-course tasting menu costs $76. Daily 6–10pm.

E&O Trading Company Lahaina Cannery Mall, 1221 Honoapiilani Highway ☎808/667-1818. This pan-Asian restaurant, part of a Californian/Hawaiian chain, occupies a large indoor and outdoor space on the inland side of a mall at the northern end of Lahaina. A lunch of pad Thai noodles or spicy fish costs $10–15. The dinner menu is divided between "small plates" such as Thai *ahi poke* at $7–15, and larger $17–35 plates, like a whole fish, intended for sharing. The nan bread is nothing special, but on the whole the meat and fish dishes are nicely varied and flavored. Reserve early to dine in one of the three tent-like indoor "pavilions." Happy hour daily 4–6pm, live music Thurs & Fri 6–8pm. Daily 11am–10pm.

The Feast at Lele 505 Front St ☎808/667-5353 or 1-866/244-5353, ⓦwww.feast atlele.com. An inspired cross between a *lū'au* and a gourmet restaurant that, for once, lavishes as much care on the food as on the entertainment. Among the Polynesian specialties are *kālua* pork from Hawaii, *fafa* (steamed chicken) and *e'iota* (marinated raw fish) from Tahiti, and grilled fish in banana leaves from Samoa. Each of the excellent and unusual five courses consists of at least two dishes, while the very romantic beachfront setting has individual tables set out facing the ocean at sunset. Music and *hula* performances punctuate the evening, culminating in a Samoan fire dance. Though steep, the $105 adult charge includes unlimited cocktails and other beverages; for children, it's $75. Reservations are essential. April–Sept daily 6pm, Oct–March daily 5.30pm; schedules may vary.

Gerard's *Plantation Inn*, 174 Lahainaluna Rd ☎808/661-8939. This upscale dinner-only restaurant adds a Hawaiian twist to traditional French cuisine, to create a menu of appetizers ($13–25) such as snails with wild mushrooms or *foie gras* with truffles, and entrees (up to $40) like veal sweetbreads, or *opakapaka* (snapper). Desserts include *profiteroles* and other classic pastries. Daily 6–9pm.

Pacific 'O 505 Front St ☎808/667-4341. Attractive oceanfront mall restaurant, serving Pacific Rim cuisine on a beach-level terrace with indoor dining above. The relatively simple lunch specials ($10–15) include a bleu burger, a chicken wrap, and delicious sesame fish. In the evening, try appetizers ($9–16) such as the shrimp wontons in Hawaiian salsa, and entrees like "Thai dye duck" – a coconut curry ($25) – or tempura blocks of fish ($30). For vegetarians, the "leaning tower of tofu" costs $14 at lunch, $26 for dinner. Leave room for the huge, delicious chocolate desserts. Daily 11am–4pm & 5.30–10pm; live jazz Fri & Sat from 9pm.

West Maui

Over the eons, the older of Maui's two volcanoes has eroded away to create a long, curving ridge known collectively as the **West Maui Mountains**. The highest point – Pu'u Kukui, barely six miles inland from Lahaina – is deluged by around 400 inches of rain per year and is almost always obscured by clouds. However, the leeward (western) slopes are consistently dry, and for eight miles north of Lahaina the sun-baked beaches are lined with a seamless succession of hotels and condos, in purpose-built resorts such as **Kā'anapali**, **Honokōwai**, and **Kapalua**. Lahaina itself may be appealing and historic, but none of its neighbors to the north hold the slightest interest in their own right. They do, however, offer superb facilities for family vacations, although room rates tend to be too high for budget travelers.

No road crosses the mountains; in fact, parts of the all-but-impenetrable wilderness of the interior have never been explored. The main road to Lahaina from central Maui – **Honoapi'ilani Highway**, named after the six northwestern bays conquered by the great Maui chief Pi'ilani – is forced to loop laboriously around the southern end of West Maui. Thanks to a sensible policy allowing development only on its *makai* (oceanward) side, the route makes for an attractive drive, with views of inland hills and valleys left largely untouched; it's also a very slow one, thanks to horrendous and ever-growing traffic problems.

At the northern end of West Maui, beyond Kapalua, the weather becomes progressively wetter; the coast is more indented with bays; and driving conditions grow increasingly difficult. Honoapi'ilani Highway eventually gives up altogether around Nākālele Point. Sinuous, undulating **Kahekili Highway** beyond narrows to a single lane for several miles, but it's possible to complete a full circuit of West

Maui, and the extravagant beauty of the windward coast – best seen from hiking trails in and above **Waiheʻe Valley**, which is more easily accessible from Wailuku – should not be missed.

South of Lahaina

Few people live along the parched coastline to the **south of Lahaina**, where ditches in the hillside still irrigate extensive green cane fields. There are no significant settlements, but the only road, Honoapiʻilani Highway, is prone to hideous traffic congestion, especially as it narrows to climb around Papawai Point in the far south and head back to Māʻalaea (see p.322).

Launiupoko State Wayside Park

While always scenic, the beaches that lie immediately south of Lahaina are not nearly as appealing as those to the north, consisting as a rule of narrow strips of sand deposited atop sharp black rocks. The first one you come to, Puamana Beach County Park, offers no visitor facilities, but **Launiupoko State Wayside Park**, three miles out, makes an attractive picnic spot. Coconut palms lean out from the shoreline, while larger trees shade the tables on the lawn; the only snag is that it's very much in earshot of the highway. From the center of the park, boulder walls curve out to enclose a shallow artificial pool, suitable for small children, with two narrow outlets to the sea. South of that is a small beach of gritty sand, while to the north the lava rocks create a sea wall, alive with scuttling black crabs. The offshore waters here are a good spot for beginners to practice their surfing skills, and there are also showers and restrooms in the park, but camping is forbidden.

Olowalu

There's little more to **OLOWALU**, six miles south of Lahaina, than a tiny row of stores *mauka* of the highway. The most noteworthy of these is *Chez Paul* (☎808/661-3843), an incongruous and very expensive French bistro set behind a pretty little brick wall. It's open for dinner only, nightly except Sunday, with two sittings, at 6.30pm and 8.30pm. Most of the appetizers cost at least $10, though there's caviar for $95, while entrees such as fish poached in champagne or Tahitian duck are well over $30.

There's no public access to the ocean on the promontory across the road, but you can take a short hike toward the mountains to a cluster of ancient **petroglyphs**. Start by heading round to the left behind the stores and then continue inland, following the dirt road that starts immediately left of the nearby water tower. After about ten minutes' walk through the cane fields, you'll notice that the nearest side of the cinder cone straight ahead of you has sheared off, leaving behind a flat wall of red rock. Fresh-painted red railings a few feet up the rock mark the site of the petroglyphs, but the stairs and walkways that once enabled visitors to climb up to them have largely vanished. So too have many of the petroglyphs, and others have been vandalized. However, you should still spot several wedge-shaped human figures etched into the rock, together with a sailing canoe or two, characterized by their "crab-claw" sails. Looking back, you'll also get good views across to Lanai.

Ukemehame and Pāpalaua

South of Olowalu, the cane fields come to an end, and Hwy-30 skirts the shoreline only a few feet above sea level. It's possible to park just about anywhere,

The Olowalu Massacre

Olowalu was the site of the worst **massacre** in Hawaiian history, perpetrated by **Captain Simon Metcalfe** of the American merchant ship *Eleanora* in 1790. After Hawaiians had killed a member of his crew as they stole one of the ship's boats off East Maui, Metcalfe set fire to the nearest village and then sailed for Olowalu, which he was told was the home of the chief culprit. Offering to continue trading, he lured more than two hundred canoes out to the *Eleanora*, many of them filled with children coming to see the strange ship. Metcalfe placed a *kapu* on the port side of the vessel, so all the canoes flocked to starboard and then, without warning, bombarded them with his seven cannons. More than a hundred Hawaiians died.

Ironically, Captain Metcalfe's 18-year-old son, **Thomas**, was to pay for his father's sins. Metcalfe had previously antagonized a Big Island chief, Kame'eiamoku, who vowed to kill the next white man he met. Ignorant of events at Olowalu, Thomas Metcalfe landed his tiny six-man schooner *Fair American* at Kawaihae on the Big Island a few days later and was killed when it was stormed and captured by Kame'eiamoku and his men. Of its crew, only **Isaac Davis** was spared, for putting up such valiant resistance.

In due course, the *Eleanora* arrived at Kawaihae in search of the younger Metcalfe, and first mate **John Young** was sent ashore to investigate. Kamehameha the Great himself prevented Young from rejoining his vessel with the news of the killings, whereupon Captain Metcalfe concluded that his envoy had been killed and sailed away. Metcalfe himself was killed soon afterwards and never learned of the death of his son; both Davis and Young, however, remained on the islands for the rest of their lives, taking Hawaiian names and becoming valued advisors to the king. They were responsible for teaching the Hawaiians to fight with muskets and cannon – the royal arsenal began with two guns seized from the *Fair American* – and personally directed Kamehameha's armies at battles such as 'Iao Valley on Maui (see p.321) and Nu'uanu Pali on Oahu (see p.107).

and in whale-watching season that's exactly what people do – often with very little warning.

Ukemehame Beach County Park, three miles along, consists of a very small area of lawn between the highway and the ocean, with picnic tables and a couple of portable restrooms, fringed by a small strip of sand. Lots of trees have been planted here, but they remain very short so far. By this point, the mountains begin to rise just inland of the road and are much drier and barer than further north.

Pāpalaua State Wayside, which leads on south from Ukemehame, is a long dirt strip used as a parking lot, separated from the sand by a thin line of scrubby trees. Local surfers and snorkelers – snorkeling is best around the rocks beyond the south end of the beach – set up tents among the trees, but there are virtually no facilities here. Immediately beyond Pāpalaua, the highway starts its climb over (and through) the headland of **Papawai Point**, where a roadside lookout is one of Maui's best **whale-watching** sites. From there it's less than two miles to Mā'alaea (see p.322) and the isthmus.

The Lahaina Pali Trail

Until the hard labor of convicts constructed the first road around the southern coast of West Maui, in 1900, the only way to reach Lahaina via dry land was to follow the centuries-old *alaloa*, or "long road," across the mountains. A five-mile stretch is now open as the **Lahaina Pali Trail** – a grueling hike that climbs 1600 feet above sea level and, being situated at the dry, exposed southern tip of the island, is also a very hot one. Don't expect to penetrate into the mysterious green heart of the interior; for that, the Waihe'e Ridge Trail (see p.310) is a better bet. Your rewards instead will be the sight of some ravishing upland meadows, carpeted with magnificent purple, yellow, and red flowers, and long-range views out to the islands of Lanai and Kahoolawe and down across the isthmus. You'll also get a close-up look at the turbines recently erected to convert the powerful winds into electricity.

Both ends of the trail are a long way from the nearest town, so you'll need a car to reach either trailhead and, unless you can arrange to be picked up at the far end, hiking its full length necessitates a ten-mile round trip. The path leaves Honoapi'ilani Highway from a parking lot near the 11-mile marker at Ukemehame and rejoins it five miles south of Wailuku, via a dirt road immediately south of the off-white bridge that lies between its intersections with highways 31 (to Kīhei) and 380 (to Kahului).

Whichever end you start – the eastern slope near Wailuku is the steeper – you'll have at least a mile of stiff climbing before the trail levels out, still far below the mountain tops. The trail then meanders through successive gulches to cross Kealaloloa Ridge, with almost the only shade being provided by the occasional native dryland sandalwood tree.

North from Lahaina: Kā'anapali

When American Factors (Amfac), the owners of the Pioneer Sugar Mill, decided in 1957 to transform the oceanfront cane fields of **KA'ANAPALI** into a luxury tourist resort, they established a pattern that has been repeated throughout Hawaii ever since. There had never been a town at Kā'anapali, just a small plantation wharf served by a short railroad from the sugar mill at Lahaina. What Kā'anapali did have, however, was a superb white-sand **beach** – far better than anything at Lahaina – backed by a tract of land that was ripe for development and more than twice the size of Waikīkī.

△ Kā'anapali Beach

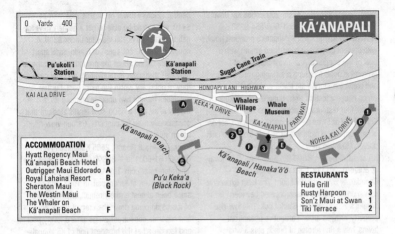

Kā'anapali's first hotel opened in 1963 and has been followed by half a dozen similar giants, whose four thousand rooms now welcome half a million visitors each year. There's still nothing else here apart from the central, anodyne **Whaler's Village** mall, though. Kā'anapali is a pretty enough place, with its two rolling **golf courses** and sunset views of the island of Lanai filling the western horizon, but there's little to distinguish it from any number of similar purpose-built tropical resorts around the world.

As for **Kā'anapali Beach**, it's divided into two separate long strands by the forbidding, three-hundred-foot cinder cone of Pu'u Keka'a, known as the **Black Rock**. The sand shelves away abruptly from both sections, so swimmers soon find themselves in deep water, but bathing is usually safe outside periods of high winter surf. The rugged lava coastline around the Black Rock itself is one of the best **snorkeling** spots on Maui.

Whether or not you're staying at one of Kā'anapali's hotels, you're free to use the main beach, but there are also a couple of **public beach parks** just around the headland to the south. Both **Hanaka'ō'ō** and **Wahikuli** are right alongside Hwy-30; swimming is generally safer at Wahikuli, but the facilities and general ambience are more appealing at Hanaka'ō'ō.

Public transport

Maui Bus (☎808/871-4838, ⓦwww.mauicounty.gov/bus) runs hourly **buses** from Kā'anapali both south to **Lahaina** ($1; departs Whaler's Village daily 6am–9pm) and northwards to **Honokōwai**, **Kahana** and **Nāpili** ($1; departs daily 6am–8pm).

Accommodation

Kā'anapali is far from being a budget destination, but its lavish **hotels** do offer cut-price deals on rental cars or longer stays, and all feature kids' activities. Be warned that many hotels have taken to adding a daily "resort charge" of up to $20 to their room rates, and quite possibly a $10 parking fee on top of that. It all seems to be part of a trend towards providing fewer of the services traditionally offered, which is epitomized by the transformation of the former *Maui Marriott* into an exclusively time-share condo property. For the latest offers, and general information on Kā'anapali, call the Kā'anapali Beach Resort Association (☎808/661-3271 or 1-800/245-9229, ⓦwww.kaanapaliresort.com).

Hyatt Regency Maui 200 Nohea Kai Drive ☏808/661-1234 or 1-800/554-9288, ⊛www.maui.hyatt.com. Kā'anapali's grandest hotel, with opulent gardens, a palm-filled atrium with a pool of live penguins, and a vast labyrinth of swimming pools including a swinging rope bridge and bar. A ten-story main tower and subsidiary wings house a total of eight-hundred-plus luxurious rooms, four restaurants including the sumptuous Son'z *Maui at Swan* (see opposite), and a full-service oceanfront spa; a nightly *lū'au* is held alongside (see p.290). Mountain view ⑧, ocean view ⑨

Kā'anapali Beach Hotel 2525 Kā'anapali Parkway ☏808/661-0011 or 1-800/262-8450 (US & Canada), ⊛www.kbhmaui.com. The least expensive option on Kā'anapali Beach, located between Whaler's Village and the Black Rock. This low-rise property, arrayed around attractive oceanfront lawns, has a fine stretch of beach plus a whale-shaped swimming pool complete with *tiki* bar. All of its large, well-equipped rooms have balconies or patios, though some offer showers rather than a bath. A strong commitment to preserving Hawaiian culture is reflected in regular classes and performances. Garden view ⑥, ocean view ⑦

Outrigger Maui Eldorado 2661 Keka'a Drive ☏808/661-0021 or 1-888/339-8585, ⊛www.outrigger.com. Condo property consisting of several low buildings ranged up the hillside, well back from the shoreline; shuttle buses run to the resort's private beachfront area. All units offer a/c, *lānai*, maid service, washer/dryer, and a kitchenette or full kitchen. Garden view ⑤, ocean view ⑥

Royal Lahaina Resort 2780 Keka'a Drive ☏808/661-3611 or 1-800/280-8155, ⊛www.2maui.com. One of Kā'anapali's two original resorts, commanding a long strip of perfect sand at the north end of the beach; it's been extensively upgraded during the last few years, but remains significantly cheaper than its neighbors provided you book online. While rack rates for its

central 12-story tower of plush suites start at $410, you should be able to get a garden view for half that, and an ocean view for under $300. A couple of dozen "cottages" of condo-style apartments are dotted about the grounds, though these may well disappear in renovation, and any case they're not really worth the extra cost. Further amenities include two upscale restaurants, a nightly *lū'au*, and a 3500-seat tennis stadium that's occasionally used for concerts. Garden view ⑥, ocean view ⑦

Sheraton Maui Resort 2605 Kā'anapali Parkway ☏808/661-0031 or 1-866/716-8109, ⊛www.sheraton-maui.com. This large luxury resort was the first to open at Kā'anapali, in 1963, and has since been almost entirely rebuilt, with five tiers of rooms dropping down the crag of Black Rock and separate oceanfront wings, plus a lovely pool and lagoon, all at the broadest end of Kā'anapali Beach. ⑨

The Westin Maui 2365 Kā'anapali Parkway ☏808/667-2525 or 1-866/716-8112, ⊛www.westinmaui.com. High-rise hotel in the center of Kā'anapali Beach, immediately south of Whaler's Village, where the five swimming pools are fed by artificial waterfalls and feature some great waterslides, and there's a lagoon of live flamingos to match the predominantly pink decor. Not surprisingly, it's a major favorite for families with young children, so other guests can find it too noisy and hectic. Bright, modern, luxurious hotel rooms, all with private *lānai*. ⑨

The Whaler on Kā'anapali Beach 2481 Kā'anapali Parkway ☏808/661-4861 or 1-888/211-7710, ⊛www.the-whaler.com. Just north of Whaler's Village, this condo resort holds comfortable one- and two-bedroom units, each with lavish bathroom, *lānai*, and full kitchen. Though most of the rooms don't face the ocean, the accommodation itself is good, and there's also a small pool. Garden view ⑥, ocean view ⑦

Whale Museum

A pavilion at the main (inland) entrance to the Whaler's Village mall shelters the articulated skeleton of a sperm whale, whose vestigial "fingers" are visible in its flippers. Nearby, a mock-up of a small nineteenth-century whaleboat is fully labeled with its various esoteric components and gadgets. Both serve by way of introduction to the gripping, if somewhat grisly, **Whale Museum**, which takes up half the mall's uppermost floor (daily 9am–10pm; free).

This free exhibition is devoted to Maui's former heyday as a whaling center, illustrating the tedium and the terror of the seamen's daily routine through scrimshaw, shellwork valentines, logbooks, tools, letters, and bills. The largest single exhibit is a cast-iron "try pot"; though used for reducing whale blubber at sea, they gave rise to the stereotyped but not entirely untrue image of cannibals cooking missionaries in big black cauldrons. Contrary to what you might imagine, no actual killing of whales took place in Hawaiian waters. Hawaii was simply the place where the whaling ships came to recuperate after hunting much further north in the Pacific. What's more, the humpback – the whale most commonly found in Hawaiian waters – was not hunted at all during the nineteenth century; the target for the fleets was instead the right whale, so named, logically enough, because it was deemed the "right" whale to kill.

Restaurants

All Kāʻanapali's hotels have at least one flagship **restaurant**, though catering on such a large scale makes it hard for staff to pay much attention to detail. Away from the hotels, the only alternative is to eat at the **Whaler's Village** mall. In addition to its more formal oceanfront restaurants, it holds a **food court**, set back on the lower level, featuring Korean, Japanese, and Italian outlets, plus an espresso bar and a *McDonald's*.

Hula Grill Whaler's Village ☎ 808/667-6636. This large, long oceanfront restaurant, open to the sea breezes and offering great views at lunchtime, features live Hawaiian music nightly. Chef Peter Merriman, who is known for his distinctively Hawaiian take on things, prepares some interesting appetizers, such as a Hawaiian ceviche, marinated in lime, Maui onion, and coconut milk ($8), along with plenty of dim sum and sashimi, while the entrees ($18–34) include a $27 coconut seafood chowder. Daily 11am–9.30pm.

Rusty Harpoon Whaler's Village ☎ 808/661-3123. Mall restaurant, set slightly back from the sea but enjoying good views from both terrace and covered seating. The lunch menu combines inexpensive standards like burgers and sandwiches with inventive specials, such as a seafood curry casserole ($20); traditional dinner entrees such as steaks, ribs, and fresh fish cost $23–33. A $17 set dinner menu is served 5–6pm only. Daily 8am–10pm.

Son'z Maui at Swan Court *Hyatt Regency Maui*, 200 Nohea Kai Drive ☎ 808/667-4506. The *Hyatt's* sublimely romantic *Swan Court* restaurant, laid out

around a lagoon populated by live swans and flamingos, has been revamped under this clumsy name to signal its desire to serve "classic cuisine for the next generation." The food is as good as ever, but now the menu is part Pacific Rim, with appetizers like tiger-eye sushi ($17) and New Zealand mussels ($14), and some great fish entrees at $32–40, and part Mediterranean, with standards like *coq au vin* ($32) or grilled steak for two ($79). Sun–Thurs 5–10pm, Fri & Sat 5–10.30pm.

Tiki Terrace *Kāʻanapali Beach Hotel*, 2525 Kāʻanapali Parkway ☎ 808/667-0124. This unassuming hotel restaurant attempts to serve traditional Hawaiian foods, meaning plenty of fish, plus local ingredients like *taro* and sweet potato, and much of it steamed in *ti*-leaf parcels. In the evening, when there's somewhat cheesy Hawaiian entertainment, the set Hawaiian dinner menu costs $23, or you can order rather more Westernized entrees like BBQ ribs or New York steak ($19–45). However, the open-air "tiki grill" section makes it a favorite with families with young kids, and as a result it tends to be both hectic and messy. Daily 7–10am & 5–9.30pm.

North of Kāʻanapali: from Honokōwai to Kapalua

If you found Kāʻanapali dull, just wait until you follow the road further north. A mile or so out of Kāʻanapali, Lower Honoapiʻilani Road branches down toward the ocean from the main highway, to undulate its way through **Honokōwai**, **Kahana**, and **Nāpili**.

None of these barely distinguishable, purpose-built communities holds an ounce of interest for casual visitors. Even though they do have some great **beaches** – Nāpili

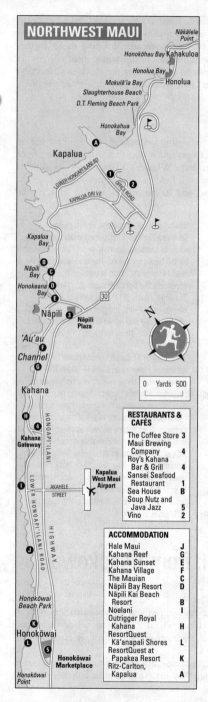

NORTHWEST MAUI

Nākālele Point
Honokōhau Bay Kahakuloa
Honolua Bay
Mokulē'ia Bay Honolua
Slaughterhouse Beach
D.T. Fleming Beach Park

Honokahua Bay

Ⓐ

Kapalua

LOWER HONOAPI'ILANI RD
❶ OFFICE ROAD
❷
KAPALUA DRIVE

Kapalua Bay
Ⓑ
Nāpili Bay Ⓒ
Honokeana Bay Ⓓ
Ⓔ
30
Nāpili ❸ Nāpili Plaza
'Au'au Ⓕ
Channel
Ⓖ

Kahana

HONOAPI'ILANI

Ⓗ

❹

Kahana Gateway

LOWER HONOAPI'ILANI ROAD
AKAHELE STREET
Kapalua West Maui Airport

Ⓘ

HIGHWAY

Ⓙ

Honokōwai Beach Park

Ⓚ

Honokōwai

Ⓛ
❺
Honokōwai Marketplace

Honokōwai Point

N

0   Yards   500

Bay in particular is well worth seeking out – you'll hardly get a glimpse of them unless you're staying at one of the innumerable condo buildings that line the entire road. There are few shops or restaurants nearby, which is why the highway is always busy with traffic heading south to the hot spots of Lahaina and beyond.

KAPALUA, at the end of Lower Honoapi'ilani Road in Maui's far northwest corner, is West Maui's equivalent of the exclusive resort of Wailea, at the southwest tip of East Maui. Few ordinary tourists stray into this pristine enclave, whose luxurious hotels were sited here mainly because of the proximity of **Kapalua Beach**. A perfect little arc of white sand, set between two rocky headlands, it is frequently voted the best beach in the US. Besides being pretty, it's also one of Maui's safest beaches, especially good for snorkeling and diving, and even receives occasional visits from monk seals. The one drawback to Kapalua is that the climate is undeniably worse even this short distance north of Lahaina, with rain and cloud more likely to drift in from the northeast.

Accommodation

The **condo** properties along Lower Honoapi'ilani Road make reasonable cut-price alternatives to the Kā'anapali and Kapalua resort hotels, though if you don't rent a car you could feel very stuck indeed. Bear in mind that the lower the street number in the addresses below, the closer the property is to Kā'anapali. The *Kapalua Bay Hotel*, long a byword for luxury, is omitted from the following listings because it is closed for total rebuilding, and will probably reopen as a timeshare property rather than a hotel.

Tiny **Kapalua Airport** – a short distance above Hwy-30, halfway between Kapalua and Kāʻanapali – is too small to be served by anything other than commuter flights, principally Island Air service from Honolulu, and Pacific Wings connections with Honolulu and Waimea on the Big Island. For details of flight frequencies, see p.282. All the major car-rental chains have outlets at the airport – see p.33 – but there's no public transport.

Hale Maui 3711 Lower Honoapiʻilani Rd, Honokōwai ☏ 808/669-6312, ⊛ www.maui .net/~halemaui. Small family-run "apartment hotel" in Honokōwai, offering one-bedroom suites that sleep up to five guests, with kitchens, washer-dryers, and *lānais*, but have no phones; maid service is limited. ❸

Kahana Reef 4471 Lower Honoapiʻilani Rd, Kahana ☏ 808/669-6491 or 1-800/451-5008, ⊛ www.mauicondo.com. Four-story row of well-furnished – if characterless – studios and one-bedroom units, right next to the sea, though there's little beach here. The rates are reasonable, but there's no a/c. Discounted car rental available. ❺

Kahana Sunset 4909 Lower Honoapiʻilani Rd, Kahana ☏ 808/669-8011 or 1-800/669-1488, ⊛ www.kahanasunset.com. Luxury condos, spacious inside but squeezed close together, in lush gardens by a lovely sandy beach that's effectively restricted to guests only. Only the larger two-bedroom units have ocean views. Garden view ❺, ocean view ❻

Kahana Village 4531 Lower Honoapiʻilani Rd, Kahana ☏ 808/669-5111 or 1-800/824-3065, ⊛ www.kahanavillage.com. Large and very comfortable two- and three-bedroom condos, right beside the ocean if not a beach. The views are great, and the rooms good value for small groups, but the pool is small and the loft-like second bedrooms in the upper-level apartments can seem like an afterthought. Five-night minimum stay. ❻

🏃 **The Mauian** 5441 Lower Honoapiʻilani Rd, Nāpili ☏ 808/669-6205 or 1-800/367-5034 (US & Canada), ⊛ www.mauian.com. Very friendly, laid-back little resort, in vintage 1950s architectural style, facing ravishing Nāpili Beach and consisting of three two-story rows of tastefully furnished studio apartments with kitchenettes. The only phone and TV are in the communal lounge and library, which is also where the complimentary breakfast is served. ❺

Nāpili Bay Resort 33 Hui Drive, Nāpili; reserve through Maui Beachfront Rentals, ☏ 808/661-3500 or 1-888/661-7200, ⊛ www.mauibeachfront.com. Small, fairly basic individually owned studio apartments, each with kitchenette and *lānai*, and

capable of sleeping four guests, in a superb ocean-front location on Nāpili Beach. ❹

🏃 **Nāpili Kai Beach Resort** 5900 Lower Honoapiʻilani Rd, Nāpili ☏ 808/669-6271 or 1-800/367-5030 (US & Canada), ⊛ www.napilikai .com. While upgraded to the highest modern standards, this forty-year-old resort was built much closer to the ocean than would ever be allowed these days, so guests can enjoy breathtaking Nāpili Bay right on their doorstep. Rates aren't low, but it's an independent property with a friendly old-time feel and a wonderful location; the on-site *Sea House* restaurant is reviewed below. ❼

Noelani 4095 Lower Honoapiʻilani Rd, Kahana ☏ 808/669-8374 or 1-800/367-6030 (US & Canada), ⊛ www.noelani-condo-resort.com. Fifty condo apartments of all sizes, set on a promontory, so all units enjoy views across to Molokai. Amenities include cable TV and VCR, plus use of two ocean-front pools, a hot tub, and laundry facilities. ❹

Outrigger Royal Kahana 4365 Lower Honoapiʻilani Rd, Kahana ☏ 808/669-5911 or 1-800/447-7783 (US & Canada), ⊛ www.outrigger .com. This oceanfront condo building, standing twelve stories high in central Kahana, enjoys views of Molokai and Lanai. While it's less intimate than the family resorts of Nāpili, it's undeniably smart, and all the a/c units, which include studios as well as one- and two-bedroom suites, have kitchens, washer-dryers, and private *lānais*. ❺

ResortQuest Kāʻanapali Shores 3445 Lower Honoapiʻilani Rd, Honokōwai ☏ 808/667-2211 or ☏ 1-877/997-6667, ⊛ www.kaanapalishores.com. Grand oceanfront condo development, right on the beach at the south end of Honokōwai, with two nice pools and a/c throughout. Booked online, typical rooms, which are on the small side, start at $180, while the large family suites are good value, costing from $205. Tennis is free, but parking costs $9 per night. ❺

ResortQuest at Papakea Resort 3543 Lower Honoapiʻilani Rd, Honokōwai ☏ 808/669-4848 or ☏ 1-877/997-6667, ⊛ www.resortquesthawaii .com. Oceanfront Honokōwai complex of privately owned, and thus widely varying condo suites of all sizes, priced from $200 for the smallest. They're housed in eleven buildings arranged around two matching gardens, each of which has a pool, spa, lagoon, and putting course. ⑥

Ritz-Carlton, Kapalua 1 Ritz-Carlton Drive, Kapalua ⓣ 808/669-6200 or 1-800/241-3333, ⓦ www.ritzcarlton.com. The sheer elegance of this opulent, marble-fitted *Ritz-Carlton* can make it feel a bit formal for Maui, but there's no disputing the level of comfort, with three swimming pools, a nine-hole putting green to complement the three nearby golf courses, a spa, and a croquet lawn. See p.288 for details of the regular Wed evening slack key guitar concerts. ⑧

Restaurants

Considering its vast number of visitors, the Honokōwai-to-Kapalua stretch of northwest Maui is notably short of places to **eat**. Barely any of the hotels and condos have restaurants, so the few options are concentrated in the three highway-side **malls**. In addition to the restaurants listed below, the southernmost, the **Honokōwai Marketplace**, holds some smaller snack places, while the next, the **Kahana Gateway**, offers an *Outback Steakhouse*, a *McDonald's*, and an ice-cream parlor. Further on, the **Nāpili Plaza** has *Maui Tacos* as well as the *Coffee Store*.

The Coffee Store Nāpili Plaza, 5095 Nāpili Hau St, Nāpili ⓣ 808/669-4170, ⓦ www.mauicoffee.com. Small espresso bar, busy with active locals from 6.30am daily, offering pastries, sandwiches and Internet access. Daily 6.30am–11pm.

Maui Brewing Company Kahana Gateway, 4405 Honoapi'ilani Hwy ⓣ 808/669-3474. Large mall complex consisting of a pub serving pilsners, stouts, and wheat beers brewed on the premises, and an open restaurant area dominated by a *kiawe* grill and an oyster bar. The food is surprisingly good for mall fare, with grilled ribs or chicken for under $20, a one-pound prime rib for $28, and fresh fish prepared in various styles for around $28. A lighter, limited menu is served during the afternoon and until 1am nightly. Daily 11am–1am.

🏃 **Roy's Kahana Bar & Grill** Kahana Gateway, 4405 Honoapi'ilani Hwy ⓣ 808/669-6999. Celebrity chef Roy Yamaguchi's Maui showcase is open for dinner only – which is just as well, given its lack of views. The aromas of its superb "Euro-Asian" food waft from its open kitchen as you walk in. Signature dishes such as hibachi salmon, "butterfish" (black cod) steamed with *miso*, and "Roy's 'Original' Blackened Rare *Ahi*" appear on the menu as both appetizers (around $12) and entrees ($25–30); there are also several mouth watering specials each night. Daily 5.30–10pm.

🏃 **Sansei Seafood Restaurant** 600 Office Rd, Kapalua ⓣ 808/669-6286. Top-quality, dinner-only seafood specialist, which also has outlets in Kīhei (see p.330), and on Oahu and the Big Island. Now ensconced in spacious new premises, *Sansei* is fundamentally Japanese, though there's a strong Pacific Rim element as well. The fresh sushi selection includes a mouth-watering mango crab salad roll ($8), while entrees include a delicious prawn and scallops pasta ($20) and daily fish specials ($25). There's also karaoke until 1am on Thurs and Fri nights. Mon–Wed, Sat & Sun 5.30–10pm, Thurs & Fri 5.30pm–1am.

Sea House *Nāpili Kai Beach Resort*, 5500 Lower Honoapi'ilani Rd, Napili ⓣ 808/669-1500. Very popular seafront restaurant, right on Nāpili Beach at the most upscale of the oceanside hotels. The food is good without being exceptional – conventional American breakfasts for around $10; lunchtime soups, salads, sandwiches, or sushi rolls for $9–14; and steak or seafood dinner entrees costing anything from $23 to $40 – but the views from the oceanside tables are fabulous. Every Tuesday at 5.30pm, local kids put on a display of *hula* and Hawaiian culture, in a separate marquee, for $10. Mon & Wed–Sun 8–10.30am, 11.30am–2pm, & 6–9pm; Tues 5.30–9pm.

🏃 **Soup Nutz and Java Jazz** Honokowai Marketplace, 3350 Lower Honoapi'ilani Rd ⓣ 808/667-0787. At first glance, you'd think this funky, arty mall hangout is just a juice and espresso bar, but it actually serves pretty good food throughout the day, and with lots of comfy seating and a steady jazz soundtrack you may well feel tempted to linger despite the lack of views. The menu includes omelets ($8–12); smoothies ($5); falafel and other lunchtime sandwiches (under $10); and evening specials that range up to steak and lobster ($22–33). Mon–Sat 6am–9pm, Sun 6am–5pm.

Vino Kapalua Village Golf Course Clubhouse, Office Rd, Kapalua ⓣ 808/661-8466. This superb restaurant, just off the main highway above the Ritz-Carlton, is the creation of the Japanese chef/owner of the nearby *Sansei*. The specialty is Italian with a definite Hawaiian tinge, meaning ingredients like Kona lobster and raw *ahi* feature alongside the pasta and gnocchi dishes. A large selection of *tapas*-sized portions, most costing $7–10, enable you to sample several very disparate dishes, and particular attention is afforded to wine, with special pairings devised for most dishes. If you prefer a more conventional meal, a full-sized entree, such as *osso bucco* or horseradish-crusted short rib, costs $19–25. The one drawback is that its golf-course clubhouse setting lacks atmosphere. Daily 5.30–9.30pm.

Beaches beyond Kapalua

Honoapi'ilani Highway sweeps down beyond Kapalua to rejoin the ocean at **D.T. Fleming Beach Park**, in Honokahua Bay. The dunes here, knitted together with ironwood trees, drop sharply into the sea, and swimming can be dangerous – though surfers love the big waves. Full park amenities, including showers, restrooms, picnic tables, and the presence of lifeguards, make this a popular destination for local families.

From here, the highway climbs again to cross a rocky headland. You can't see it from the road, but **Mokule'ia Bay** lies at the foot of the cliffs. At several points along the highway, the landowners, Maui Pineapple, have built fences to stop people from clambering down through the undergrowth to shaded, sandy Slaughterhouse Beach. Keep your eyes peeled instead for the top of the concrete stairway that provides safe access; look for cars parked on the verge. Winter conditions usually preclude bathing, but nude sunbathing carries on year-round.

Both Mokule'ia Bay and **Honolua Bay**, just past the point, have been set aside as a Marine Life Conservation District, and in summer offer some of the island's best **snorkeling**. Honolua's major claim to fame, however, is as Maui's most heralded **surfing** spot, and between September and April, the waters regularly swarm with surfers. As long as the swell remains below five feet, intermediate surfers can enjoy some of the longest-lasting and most predictable waves in all Hawaii. By the time they exceed ten feet, however, only absolute experts can hope to survive; perils include not only a fearsome cave that seems to suck in every passing stray, but cut-throat competition from other surfers. Parking for surfers is at several ad hoc lots along the graded dirt roads that line the fields covering the headland on the far side of the bay. Large galleries of spectators assemble on the clifftop to watch the action, while the surfers themselves slither down to the ocean by means of treacherous trails.

To reach the **beach** at Honolua, park instead beside the road at the inland end of the bay and walk down. The access path is the width of a road, but the surface is terrible and driving on it is illegal. Taking it will lead you through a weird, lush forest with the feel of a Louisiana bayou; every tree, and even the barbed-wire fence, has been throttled by creeping vines. Across a (usually dry) streambed lies the neat, rocky curve of the beach itself, consisting largely of dark black rocks, with the eastern end of Molokai framed in the mouth of the bay. This was the departure point of the *Hōkule'a* canoe, on its first epic voyage to Tahiti in 1976 (see p.546). The **snorkelers** who congregate at Honolua whenever the waves die down generally ease themselves in from the beach, but then have to swim a fair way out beyond the clear turquoise inshore waters to reach the coves and coral on the left side of the bay.

Beyond here Honoapi'ilani Highway runs past one final beach, at **Honokōhau Bay**. You're still only five miles out of Kapalua here, but it feels like another world. The entire valley is swamped by a dense canopy of flowering trees; there's a hidden village in there, but it's hard to spot a single building. The beach itself is a small crescent of gray pebbles, used only by fishermen.

Kahekili Highway

Although on the map the **Kahekili Highway** looks like a good route to continue around northwest Maui and back to Wailuku, rental car companies generally advise their customers not to use it. Those warnings should be taken seriously: it's unquestionably a dangerous drive. It's certainly not a shortcut; Wailuku is little more than twenty miles beyond Honokōhau Valley, but you have to allow well over an hour for the journey.

While not quite on a par with the road to Hāna (see p.359), the Kahekili Highway can be exhilaratingly beautiful, and it provides a rare glimpse of how Maui must have looked before the advent of tourism. Often very narrow, but always smoothly surfaced, it appears to wind endlessly along the extravagantly indented coastline, alternating between scrubby exposed promontories, occasionally capable of supporting a pale meadow, and densely green, wet valleys.

Nākālele Point

Kahekili Highway begins at Maui's northernmost limit, **Nākālele Point**, 6.5 miles out of Kapalua, at milepost 38. This rolling expanse of grassy heathland fell victim a few years ago to a bizarre craze that swept most of Hawaii. In remote spots all over the islands, people suddenly started erecting miniature stone cairns, under the impression that they were maintaining an ancient tradition. Stacks of perhaps a dozen small rocks are dotted all over the landscape, and many visitors have also used pebbles to spell out their names or other messages – much to the displeasure of Maui Pineapple, which still owns the land.

Various deeply rutted dirt roads drop away from the highway toward the sea in this area, starting both from the parking lot at milepost 38 and from another more makeshift lot half a mile further on. Hiking in that direction enables you to inspect the small **light beacon** that warns passing ships of the rocky headland, and an impressive natural **blowhole** in the oceanfront shelf. Be exceedingly wary of approaching the water, however; several hikers have been swept off the rocks by rogue waves in recent years.

Kahakuloa

A few miles after Nākālele Point, the huge and very un-Hawaiian crag of **Kahakuloa Head** towers 636ft above the eastern entrance to Kahakuloa Bay. The name means "tall lord," on account of its supposed resemblance to a member of the chiefly class, the *aliʻi*, wearing a feathered cape; alongside it stands his attendant, a lesser peak known as Puʻu Kāhuliʻanapa. The verdant valley that stretches back from both once ranked among the most populous on Maui, and still looks like a classic *ahupuaʻa* – the fundamental ancient land division, reaching from the sea to the mountain via low-lying taro terraces and groves of palms and fruit trees.

The perfect little village of **KAHAKULOA** is poised just behind its beach of black and gray boulders. Close to the green clapboard church as you drive in, a couple of fruit stands, laden with fresh pineapples and other goodies, make tempting places to stop. The streambed nearby is lined with trees, while dirt roads crisscross the valley between the fields and the ramshackle houses. A little further back nestles the **St Francis Xavier Mission**, built in 1846.

Waiheʻe Ridge Trail

One of Maui's most enjoyable hikes, the **Waiheʻe Ridge Trail**, starts a mile up a spur road that branches *mauka* (inland) from Kahekili Highway at mile post 7, opposite the Mendes Ranch and roughly seven miles south of Kahakuloa. Signposted to *Camp Maluhia*, a scout camp, the dirt road is 2.8 miles north of the village school in **Waiheʻe**, which is in turn four miles north of Wailuku, the logical way to come if you're driving from central or south Maui.

△ Kahakuloa Head

This gorgeous climb, best done in the morning before the clouds set in, takes you as deep into the West Maui Mountains as it's possible to go; allow at least two hours, and preferably three, for the round trip. From the easily spotted parking lot where the road makes a sharp curve right towards the camp itself, the trail starts off as a very clear cement path beyond a barred gate. This is its steepest section, but it soon comes to an end, when you turn left to find yourself in a pine and eucalyptus forest. Before long you emerge from that in turn, to enjoy views down into Waihe'e Valley, over to a double waterfall embedded in the next ridge to the north, and back across the isthmus to Haleakalā Highway snaking up the volcano.

For all this first stretch of the trail, which totals 1.5 miles, it looks as though you're heading for the crest of the ridge ahead. Ultimately, however, the path sidesteps across a brief razorback to reach an unexpected high mountain valley. The terrain here is extremely marshy, but you're soon climbing again, this time through treeless uplands that feature a much greater preponderance of native Hawaiian plants and shrubs, including some spectacular orchids and also stunted red- and orange-blossomed *lehua* trees.

The trail ends at an unsheltered picnic table in a clearing 2.25 miles up. The chances are that by now you're well above the cloud line. If you're lucky enough to be here on a clear morning, however, you can see most of northern Maui from this spot, which is the summit of Lanilili ("Small Heaven") Peak but still well short of the overall summit of West Maui. Towering cliffs and waterfalls lie ahead, while as you look north towards the ocean the island of Molokai is clearly visible beyond the rocky pinnacle of Kahakuloa.

Waihe'e Valley

Beyond Waihe'e Ridge, the road drops steadily down to Waihe'e, by which time you're clearly out of the backwoods. The traffic picks up again, and the highway broadens for the final four miles to Wailuku.

At times during the past few years, it has been possible to drive half a mile inland from Waiheʻe on Waiheʻe Valley Road, and then take a two-hour hike up into the rainforest of **Waiheʻe Valley** itself. When this book went to press, however, the major local landowner, Wailuku Agriculture, had chosen to deny all access to the area. The hike used to be one of Maui's finest, so it's worth calling them on ☏ 808/244-9570, or simply driving in, to see whether the trail has been reopened.

Central Maui: the isthmus

The plains of **central Maui**, overshadowed by mighty Haleakalā to the east and the West Maui Mountains to the west, were formed as a narrow "neck" when eroded rock washed down the slopes of the island's two volcanic massifs and fused them together. Measuring just seven miles north to south, this is the economic heartland of Maui. In ancient times, only **Wailuku**, on the western fringes, held much of a population. From a royal enclosure at the mouth of the stunning ʻĪao **Valley**, its chiefs ruled a region known as Nā Wai ʻŌha, watered by four rivers that flowed down from the West Maui Mountains.

The rest of the isthmus was described by the nineteenth-century British traveler Isabella Bird as "a Sahara in miniature, a dreary expanse of sand and shifting sand hills, with a dismal growth of thornless thistles and indigo." Only since the sugar barons created irrigation channels to carry water from the eastern flanks of Haleakalā has the land been capable of supporting the agriculture that now makes it so green. As a result, Wailuku and its upstart neighbor **Kahului** are now home to nearly half of Maui's 140,000 inhabitants – the workers who keep this fantasy island going.

Kahului

Although **KAHULUI** is the largest town on Maui – it holds the island's principal harbor and airport, and most of its major shopping centers – it's not an interesting, let alone historic, place to visit. A couple of inexpensive hotels stake a claim for Kahului as a convenient central base on the island, but there's next to nothing to see here, and you could miss it altogether with a clear conscience.

Having started the nineteenth century as a small cluster of grass shacks, Kahului grew in tandem with the expansion of commercial agriculture. After the Kahului and Wailuku Railroad opened in 1879, it channeled the sugar and pineapple crops of central Maui down to the wharves of Kahului. At first Kahului was an unsanitary place: a major outbreak of plague in 1900 forced the authorities to burn down the oceanfront Chinatown district and ring the whole town with rat-proof fences. When it was rebuilt, the harbor was greatly expanded and dredged to provide the only deep-water anchorage on the island.

Kahului thereafter supplanted Lahaina as Maui's main port and has remained so to this day. It was further boosted after World War II, when newly built, low-cost housing in "Dream City" lured laborers away from plantation towns such as Pāʻia with the promise that they would have their own homes.

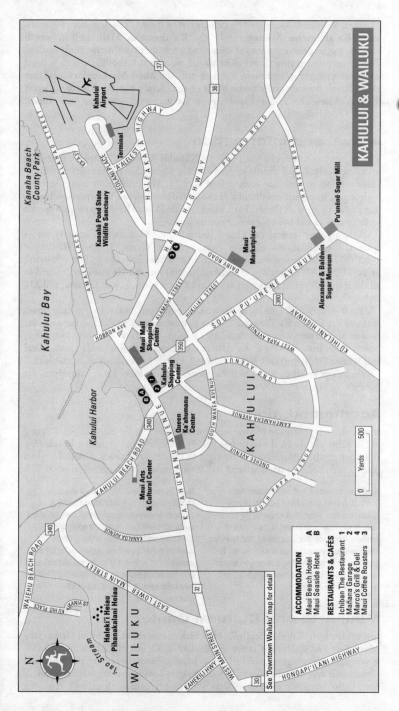

ACCOMMODATION
Maui Beach Hotel A
Maui Seaside Hotel B

RESTAURANTS & CAFÉS
Ichiban The Restaurant 1
Mañana Garage 2
Marco's Grill & Deli 4
Maui Coffee Roasters 3

See 'Downtown Wailuku' map for detail

0   Yards   500

313

Central Kahului is dominated by a characterless sprawl of ageing shopping malls along **Ka'ahumanu Avenue**. Only the **Ka'ahumanu Mall** itself is worth visiting, for its generic upmarket stores and a few more distinctive crafts outlets. There's no point trying to get close to the **waterfront**, though, which is lined with factories and warehouses. Further out, the **Maui Marketplace** mall, on Dairy Road, is noteworthy as the home of the island's best **bookstore** – a giant Borders (Mon–Thurs 9am–11pm, Fri & Sat 9am–midnight, Sun 9am–10pm; ℡808/877-6160).

Arrival and information

The majority of visitors to Maui arrive at **Kahului Airport**, a couple of miles east of town. See p.27 for details of trans-Pacific flights that use the airport; inter-island services to Maui are summarized on p.31. The main lobby area is surprisingly small, though it does hold a **Hawaii Visitors Bureau information booth** that's open to greet all flights. For a snack or a drink, you have to pass through the security checks and head for the departure gates.

All the national **rental car** chains (see p.33) have offices immediately across from the terminal. In addition, Akina Aloha Tours (℡808/879-2828 or 1-800/977-2605, Ⓦwww.akinatours.com) and Speedishuttle (℡808/661-6667 or 1-877/242-5777, Ⓦwww.speedishuttle.com) run **shuttle vans** on demand to all the resorts. Typical rates start at around $15 to Kīhei, $28 to Lahaina, and $36 to Nāpili.

Maui Bus (℡808/871-4838, Ⓦwww.mauicounty.gov/bus) runs five daily **buses** between the Queen Ka'ahumanu Center in downtown Kahului and the **airport**; two of the airport buses continue on to Pā'ia. The same company also offers hourly buses from the Queen Ka'ahumanu Center to **Lahaina**, and to both **Kīhei** and **Wailea** ($1; departures daily 5.30am–7.30pm). All services call at Mā'alaea.

Kahului's **post office** is at 138 S Pu'unōnō Avenue (Mon–Fri 8.30am–5pm, Sat 9am–noon; zip code 96732).

Accommodation

If you plan to spend most of your time on Maui touring the island or windsurfing at Ho'okipa just down the coast (see p.357), Kahului's pair of ageing **hotels** may suit your needs. Although both are right in the center of town, Kahului is not a place you'd choose to stroll around and doesn't make a lively overnight stop.

Maui Beach Hotel 170 W Ka'ahumanu Ave ℡808/877-0051 or 1-888/649-3222, Ⓦwww .elleairmaui.com. Although it's right on the ocean-front, this veteran hotel is also in the middle of Kahului's downtown business district, and following a long-overdue renovation has wisely decided to pitch itself at bargain-hunting business travelers rather than tourists. Its 150 rooms are small and simple, but adequate. ❹

Maui Seaside Hotel 100 W Ka'ahumanu Ave ℡808/877-3311 or 1-800/560-5552 (US & Canada), Ⓦwww.mauiseasidehotel.com. Bland but reasonably well-kept waterfront hotel, with a swimming pool and its own artificial beach. The location, across from the shopping malls, is hardly romantic, but at least it is by the sea and makes a convenient and relatively inexpensive base. For the best room rates, try booking online. ❸

Maui Arts and Cultural Center

Just off the busy Kahului Beach Road, which curves around Kahului Harbor, the **Maui Arts and Cultural Center** (℡808/242-2787, box office ℡808/242-7469, Ⓦwww.mauiarts.org) opened in 1994 as Maui's premier venue for the visual and performing arts. In addition to a four-thousand-seat open-air amphitheater, it houses two separate indoor theaters and an art gallery that hosts changing temporary exhibitions. Those big-name musicians who make it as far as Maui – more than you might expect, as it's a favorite final stop for trans-America touring bands – play here, and the Maui Symphony Orchestra (℡808/244-5439) puts on half a dozen concerts each winter.

In addition, the center's Castle Theater operates as a **movie theater** in conjunction with the **Maui Film Festival** (℡808/579-9244, ⓦwww.mauifilmfestival .com). The festival itself takes place in Wailea each June, but every Wednesday evening the Castle Theater shows a current release, and each December it also puts on nightly "Academy Screenings" of potential Oscar contenders.

Kanahā Pond State Wildlife Sanctuary

Half a mile west of Kahului Airport, just before Hwy-36A meets Hwy-36, a tiny roadside parking lot marks the only public access to the **Kanahā Pond State Wildlife Sanctuary**. This marshy saltwater lagoon – used as a fishpond until it was choked by the mud dredged up from Kahului Harbor – is now set aside for the protection of endangered bird species, among them the black-necked *ae'o* stilt and the *'auku'u* (night heron).

There are no official opening hours; visitors simply make their way through the gate and follow a pedestrian causeway for fifty yards out to a windy, open-sided viewing shelter. Although it's not a very prepossessing spot, with the factories of Kahului Harbor clearly visible off to the left, and planes passing low overhead as they descend into the airport, it's surprisingly peaceful, and waterfowl do indeed seem to like it. Wading birds can almost always be spotted picking their way through the shallow waters, though when it comes to smaller species you're likely to hear more than you actually see.

Kanahā Beach County Park

Due east of central Kahului, Amala Place runs through an industrial area behind Kanahā Pond. Even on the ocean side of the airport, before the road joins Alahao Street, you'll find plenty of places where you can park beside the road and walk through the trees to find a long strip of empty beach.

However, the most popular oceanfront spot is the large **Kanahā Beach County Park** which, despite its proximity to the runways, is completely undisturbed by all the comings and goings and feels comfortably far from Kahului. Its shallow, choppy turquoise waters are ideal for novice **windsurfers**, who come from all over the world to swirl back and forth against the backdrop of 'Īao Valley and the West Maui Mountains. Among companies offering windsurfing lessons here (at around $80 for 2hr 30min, including equipment rental) are Action Sports Maui (℡808/871-5857, ⓦwww.actionsportsmaui.com), and Alan Cadiz's HST Windsurfing School (℡808/871-5423 or 1-800/968-5423, ⓦwww.hstwindsurfing.com). Windsurfers ready for the big time graduate to **Ho'okipa**, just a few miles east but light-years away in terms of difficulty; see p.357.

For its full, considerable length, the beach is fringed by pine trees, with countless shoots sprouting from the dunes, and fallen needles creating a soft carpet just behind. Local clubs keep their outrigger canoes here, and you're likely to see them practicing. The lawns under the trees have picnic tables, though to buy food or drink you have to drive back into Kahului.

There is a **campground** here, administered by the county parks office (see p.285), with seven individual sites ($3 per night; three-night maximum stay). However, the combination of being right next to the airport, with all the noise that entails, and also the potential exposure to crime, thanks to nearby Kahului, makes it hard to recommend.

Alexander & Baldwin Sugar Museum

There's no missing the rusty red hulk of the **Puʻunēnē Sugar Mill**, which forces Hwy-350 to make a sharp right turn a mile south of Kahului. Still belching smoke as it consumes cane from the surrounding fields, this was the largest sugar mill in the world when it was built in 1902. Only two such mills are still operational in the state of Hawaii; the other is on Kauai. Easily overlooked, however, is the smaller building just across from the mill, at the intersection with the minor Hansen Road, which houses the **Alexander & Baldwin Sugar Museum** (daily 9.30am–4.30pm; adults $5, under-18s $2).

The museum relates the history of sugar production on Maui, a tale of nineteenth-century scheming and skullduggery that, a century later, may not be capable of holding your interest for very long. Alexander & Baldwin was one of the original "Big Five" companies at the heart of the Hawaiian economy – see p.537 – and remains a prominent island name to this day. **Samuel T. Alexander** and **Henry Baldwin** started growing sugar at Pāʻia in 1869 and were responsible for constructing the first irrigation channel in 1878 to carry water from East Maui to the central isthmus. Their great rival was **Claus Spreckels**, who used his royal connections (he underwrote King Kalākaua's gambling debts) to acquire land and water rights at "Spreckelsville" near Pāʻia and all but controlled the Hawaiian sugar industry before losing favor with the king and being forced to return to California. Alexander and Baldwin were then free to expand their operations across Maui, centered on the processing facilities at Puʻunēnē.

Scale models in the museum include a whirring but incomprehensible re-creation of the main mill machinery, and a relief map of the whole island. More illuminating displays focus on the lives of the plantation laborers, showing the thick clothes they wore to protect against the dust and poisonous centipedes, and the numbered *bango* tags by which they were identified in place of names. No bones are made of the fact that the multi-ethnic workforce was deliberately, but ultimately unsuccessfully, segregated to avoid solidarity. The museum store is well stocked with books on ethnic and labor history, as well as souvenir packets of raw sugar.

Restaurants

Kahului is disappointingly short of **restaurants**, and few people would choose to drive here from elsewhere on Maui in search of a good meal. There are, however, a few possibilities scattered around the town's lesser malls, while the breezy **Queen's Market** area, upstairs at the **Queen Kaʻahumanu Center**, holds a wide assortment of fast-food counters, as well as a good, cheap deli counter at the *Tamakawaya* Japanese department store. There's another, smaller food court at the Maui Marketplace, as well as a large *Starbucks*.

Ichiban The Restaurant Kahului Shopping Center, 47 Kaʻahumanu Ave ☏ 808/871-6977. Large mall eatery, which serves American and continental breakfasts, then devotes itself for the remainder of the day to Japanese cuisine. For lunch there's *saimin* for $6, *donburi* bowls for $7, and teriyakis for $6–9; at dinner you can get shrimp or chicken stir-fries, *udon* noodles, and sushi rolls for under $10. Mon–Fri 7am–2pm & 5–9pm, Sat 10.30am–2pm & 5–9pm.

Mañana Garage 33 Lono Ave ☏ 808/873-0220. This Latin American–Mexican restaurant, kitted out with a cheery, vaguely post-industrial decor and located in an office building right on Kaʻahumanu

Ave, serves a creative but somewhat overpriced menu ranging from fish tacos to guava salmon to paella. It's popular with locals for lunch, and, thanks to a spacious (albeit viewless) terrace, for after-work drinks. Typical entrees cost around $12 for lunch, up to $30 in the evening. Live music and dancing most nights. Mon 11am–9pm, Tues–Fri 11am–10.30pm, Sat 5–10.30pm, Sun 5–9pm.

Marco's Grill & Deli 395 Dairy Rd ☏ 808/877-4446. Lively Italian restaurant, in a modern mall not far from the airport. Once the breakfast omelets, pancakes, and espressos have finished, the lunch and dinner menus feature deli sandwiches, pizzas (from \$12), and rich meat and seafood pastas, including rigatoni with prosciutto in a vodka sauce (\$19). Daily 7.30am–10pm.

Maui Coffee Roasters 444 Hana Hwy ⊤808/877-2877. This relaxed, daytime-only espresso bar with hand-painted tables is a popular hangout for windsurfers from the nearby beaches. Vegetarian wraps and sandwiches, like focaccia with mozzarella, are \$6–8; try the fabulous raspberry-and-white-chocolate scones. Mon–Fri 7am–6pm, Sat 8am–5pm, Sun 8am–2.30pm.

MAUI | Wailuku

Wailuku

The center of **WAILUKU** is barely two miles west of Kahului, and there's no gap in the development along Ka'ahumanu Avenue to mark where one town ends and the other begins. However Wailuku, located as it is at the mouth of the fertile and spectacular 'Iao Valley and within a few miles of the lush valleys that line the windward coast of West Maui, has a very different geography and a much more venerable history. This was what might be called the *poi* bowl of Maui, at the heart of the largest taro-growing area in Hawaii, and was home to generations of priests and warriors in ancient times.

Well into the twentieth century, Wailuku was the center of the island's nascent tourist industry, housing the few visitors Maui received and equipping their expeditions up Haleakalā. Much of its administrative and commercial role was then usurped by Kahului, and Wailuku went into something of a decline. These days, with the construction of various new county offices and even a few stores, Wailuku appears to be on the way back, but it remains a sleepy sort of place, easily seen in less than half a day. Nonetheless, it's one of the few towns on Maui that still feels like a genuine community, and can serve as a welcome antidote to the sanitized charms of the modern resorts elsewhere.

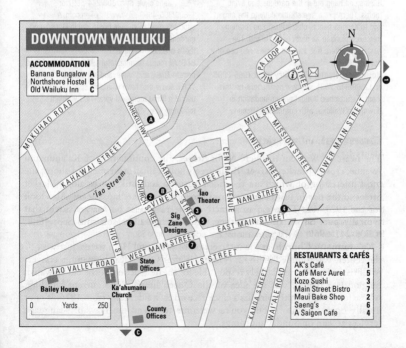

317

Information

The main Maui office of the **Hawaii Visitors Bureau** (Mon–Fri 8am–4.30pm; ☎808/244-3530 or 1-800/525-MAUI, ⓦwww.visitmaui.com) is tucked away at 1727 Wili Pa Loop, half a mile northeast of central Wailuku – they can provide lots of printed material on all of Maui County, which also includes the islands of Molokai and Lanai. Wailuku's **post office** is nearby at 250 Imi Kala St (Mon–Fri 8am–4.30pm, Sat 9am–noon; zip code 96793).

Camping permits for Maui's state parks are available from the Department of Land and Natural Resources, opposite Ka'ahumanu Church at 54 S High St (Mon–Fri 8am–3.30pm; ☎808/984-8109, ⓦwww.state.hi.us/dlnr), while the county parks office is at Baldwin High School, just east of central Wailuku at 1580 Ka'ahumanu Ave (Mon–Fri 8am–4pm; ☎808/270-7383, ⓦwww.co.maui.hi.us).

Accommodation

As Wailuku has Maui's only **hostels** – and no hotels – the only people who spend the night here tend to be backpackers and surfers. One drawback for budget travelers is that the nearest beaches are several miles away, but the *Banana Bungalow* runs inexpensive mini-van trips to them.

Banana Bungalow 310 N Market St ☎808/244-5090 or 1-800/846-7835, ⓦwww.mauihostel.com. Friendly independent hostel, open to non-Hawaiian residents only, in a rundown light industrial area not far from central Wailuku. Beds in two- and three-bed dorms are $26.50, while basic private rooms, without en-suite facilities, cost from $54 single, $65 double. Guests can hang out in the gardens and living rooms. There's one free shuttle daily to the airport and to Kanahā beach, plus a changing rotation of free excursions to all parts of the island. The hostel also offers free Internet access and use of a hot tub. ❶–❷

Northshore Hostel 2080 Vineyard St ☎986-8095 or 1-866/946-7835, ⓦwww.northshore-hostel .com. Refurbished budget accommodation in downtown Wailuku, with communal kitchen facilities. Beds in plain, four- and six-bed dorms cost $25, or $20 with leaflets available at the airport, while equally plain private rooms – each with just a bed or two bunks, and a closet – go for $50 single, $65 double. Popular with European travelers, who leave their surfboards propped against the giant banyan in the courtyard. ❶–❷

Old Wailuku Inn at Ulupono 2199 Kaho'okele St ☎808/244-5897 or 1-800/305-4899, ⓦwww.mauiinn.com. A spacious plantation-style home, set in landscaped gardens a short walk south of central Wailuku, that's been converted into a luxurious ten-room B&B. All rooms have tasteful 1930s-era furnishings, private *lānais* and baths, and are equipped with VCRs; some also have whirlpool spas. Guests share use of a living room and veranda. Two-night minimum stay. ❻

Central Wailuku

The heart of Wailuku is where **Main Street**, the continuation of Ka'ahumanu Avenue, crosses **Market Street**. Both streets hold a small assortment of shops, the most interesting of which are the faded **antique** and **junk stores** along Market Street to the north, just before it drops down to cross the 'Īao Stream. Also look for the 1929 **'Īao Theater**, an attractive little playhouse on Market Street that typically puts on six Broadway-type shows each year (season runs Sept–June; ☎808/242-6969, ⓦwww.mauionstage.com).

Ka'ahumanu Church, at the intersection of Main and High streets just west of the center, was founded in 1832. Naming it after Queen Ka'ahumanu, a convert to Christianity who was largely responsible for the destruction of the old Hawaiian religion (see p.368), was the idea of the Queen herself. The current building, whose four-story white spire has a clock face on each side, dates from 1876. It's not usually open to visitors, but you're welcome to attend the Hawaiian-language services at 9am on Sunday mornings.

Bailey House

The **Bailey House**, to the left of Main Street as it starts to climb west out of Wailuku as 'Iao Valley Road, is the best museum of general history on Maui (Mon–Sat 10am–4pm; adults $5, ages 7–13 $1, under-7s free; ☎808/244-3326, Ⓦwww.mauimuseum.org). The oldest house on the island, it sits on what was once Maui's most highly prized plot of land: the site of a royal compound that controlled access to the sacred 'Iao Valley. Local chiefs donated it during the 1830s so the Central Maui Mission could build day schools to teach both adults and children to read. From 1837 until 1849, it was also the site of the **Wailuku Female Seminary**, a boarding school designed to produce "good Christian wives" for the male graduates of the Lahainaluna Seminary (see p.297).

The first occupant of the house was Reverend Jonathan Green, who resigned from the mission in 1842 to protest the fact that the American Board of Commissioners for Foreign Missions accepted money from slave-owners. For the next fifty years, it was home to Edward Bailey and his wife Caroline Hubbard Bailey. He was a minister, schoolmaster, carpenter, and amateur painter, while she is remembered in the name of the long "Mother Hubbard" dresses, also known as *mu'umu'us*, that she made for local women.

After an entertaining introductory talk, visitors can wander through rooms filled with period furniture, none of which originally belonged here. The largest room focuses on ancient Hawaiian history, with archeological finds from Maui, Lanai, and Kahoolawe, including bones, clubs, shark's-tooth weapons, and *leis* of shells and feathers. One large wooden platter was used for serving boiled dog – a popular dish for native Hawaiian women, who were forbidden to eat pork. There's also a copy of the only carved temple image ever found on Maui, a likeness of the pig-god Kamapua'a that was discovered in a remote sea cave. As the label points out, both the Baileys and the ancient Hawaiians alike would be appalled to see such a sacred item on public display. On the wall there's a portrait of the unruly chief Boki, who sailed to the South Seas in 1829 in search of sandalwood to replace Hawaii's vanished crop and died in an explosion at sea (see p.536).

A separate gallery downstairs is reserved for local landscapes painted by the white-bearded Edward Bailey in his old age, while the upstairs rooms are preserved more or less as the Baileys would have known them, though presumably they'd disavow the opium pipe and paraphernalia displayed at one point. A very solid wooden surfboard that once belonged to Duke Kahanamoku (see p.83) hangs outside the restrooms in the garden.

Haleki'i and Pihanakalani heiaus

A mile from central Wailuku – but over three miles by road – the twin ancient temples of **Haleki'i** and **Pihanakalani** guard the Wailuku Plain from two separate hillocks near the mouth of the 'Iao Stream (both open daily 7am–7pm; free). They can only be reached via a very convoluted route; follow Hwy-333 all the way out of Wailuku to the north, double back south along Waiehu Beach Road, turn inland at Kuhio Place, and take the first left, Hea Place.

With rows of low-budget housing to the north and the industrial area of Kahului to the south, this is not the most evocative of sites, but raising your gaze toward the horizon provides fine views of the ocean and the turquoise waters of the **harbor** and, in the early morning, mighty Haleakalā can often be seen in its entirety. The short trail from the parking lot leads through scrubby soil – these hillocks are, in fact, lithified sand dunes – to **Haleki'i Heiau**. Maui's ruling chief, Kahekili, lived at this "house of images" during religious ceremonies in the 1760s, when its uppermost platform would have held thatched huts interspersed with carved effigies of the gods. The hilltop is now bare, and the only remnants of the *heiau* are the lower stone terraces dropping down the side toward Kahului.

Both Haleki'i and **Pihanakalani Heiau**, on the far side of the gulch to the west, were *luakinis*, or temples dedicated to the war god Ku that were the site of human sacrifices. Pihanakalani seems to have been originally constructed sometime between 1260 and 1400 AD, and reoriented to face toward the Big Island during the eighteenth century, which archeologists see as a sign that the chiefs of Maui must have been preparing an attack. When Kamehameha the Great's Big Island warriors finally conquered Maui, they celebrated their victory at 'Iao Valley with a rededication ceremony at Pihana that included its final human sacrifice. Like all ancient Hawaiian temples, it was stripped of its images and largely dismantled after the death of Kamehameha, which coincided with the arrival of the first Christian missionaries. Significantly more traces survive than of Haleki'i, however, so it's worth continuing this far, by following the main path to the far side of the gulch and then turning left.

Maui Tropical Plantation

The **Maui Tropical Plantation**, two miles south of Wailuku below the entrance to Waikapū Valley, may be a principal stop on round-island bus tours, but it's of minimal interest (daily 9am–5pm; free). Visitors are free to walk into the main "Marketplace," where the stalls are piled with plants, fruits, and souvenirs, and then pass into the lackluster gardens beyond to explore pavilions describing the cultivation of macadamia nuts, sugar, coffee, and other local crops. You can see a few more unusual plants on forty-minute tram tours (daily 10am–4pm, every 45min; $10), then take in the spectacular orchids in the nursery before you leave.

The indoor *Tropical Restaurant* (daily 9am–3pm) serves unremarkable $15 buffet lunches between 11am and 2pm (expect long lines), and sandwiches and salads the rest of the day.

Restaurants

Wailuku may not have any particularly outstanding **restaurants**, but it does have a wide assortment of inexpensive options. Most are downtown, with the rest strung along Lower Main Street as it loops down toward Kahului Harbor – these are too far to walk to from the center.

AK's Cafe 1237 L Market St ☎808/244-8774, ⓦwww.akscafe.com. This bright, clean and highly recommended little restaurant, well away from downtown on the road up from Kahului Harbor, has a mission to improve the health of local residents, with an emphasis on steaming or grilling rather than frying. Great-value lunch specials at $7–9, such as the succulent baked *ono*, and $12–18 dinner entrees like crab cakes, seared *ahi* or lemongrass duck breast, come with two sides, such as *taro* or *ulu* (breadfruit). Tues–Fri 11am–2.30pm & 5–9pm, Sat 5–9pm.

Café Marc Aurel 28 N Market St ☎808/244-0852. Smart and very popular sidewalk café, serving espressos, smoothies, and pastries, and also offering Internet access. Mon–Sat 7am–9pm.

Kozo Sushi 52 N Market St ☎808/243-5696. Attractive central sushi place that

mainly provides takeout for local office workers, but also has a couple of tables where you can enjoy tasty and very well priced individual rolls ($2 or less), a *nigiri* lunch box ($6.50), or Hawaii's very own spam *musubi* – spam, seaweed, and rice ($1.30). Mon–Sat 10am–6pm.

Main Street Bistro 2051 Main St ☎808/244-6816. The chef/owner of this simple, roomy lunch-only café on Wailuku's somewhat neglected Main Street has an impressive record with Maui's top restaurants, and now prepares good-value, healthy but filling meals for appreciative locals. Salad choices include an *ahi tataki* fresh tuna salad for $13, Southern fried chicken costs $8, and daily specials like Thursday's beef brisket run $8–14. Mon–Fri 11am–3pm.

Maui Bake Shop & Deli 2092 Vineyard St ☎808/244-7117. French-style *patisserie*, serving healthy deli breakfasts and lunches, close to the *Northshore Hostel*. Choose from a wide assortment of soups, salads, and quiches as well as wonderful fresh-baked breads, including focaccias, calzones, whole-grain loaves, and sweet brioches. You can eat well for $5 or less. Tues–Fri 6.30am–2.30pm, Sat 7am–1pm.

Saeng's 2119 Vineyard St ☎808/244-1567. Pleasant Thai restaurant, serving high-quality food at bargain prices. Plate lunches, on weekdays only, include honey-lemon chicken and garlic shrimp for $6–9, while selections from the full dinner menu cost a few dollars more. Mon–Fri 11am–2.30pm & 5–9.30pm, Sat & Sun 5–9.30pm.

A Saigon Cafe 1792 Main St ☎808/243-9560. Vietnamese restaurant with a wide-ranging and unusual menu, most of it very tasty. Hot and cold noodle dishes and soups, a lot of curries and seafood stews – even a "Vietnamese bouillabaisse" – plus simpler steamed fish specials, and plenty of vegetarian options. A filling noodle dish costs under $10, though some entrees range over $20, while appetizers like "Vietnamese burritos" are around $5. Even though its address is on Main Street, it's actually below the raised section of the highway, so you have to approach via Central Ave. Mon–Sat 10am–9.30pm, Sun 10am–8.30pm.

ʻĪao Valley

Main Street heads due west out of Wailuku to enter the high-walled cleft carved by ʻĪao Stream into the West Maui Mountains, with waterfalls dropping down pleated grooves in the rock on either side. For ancient Hawaiians, the gorgeous **ʻĪao Valley** (pronounced "ee-ow") was the equivalent of Egypt's Valley of the Kings: they buried their royal dead in the long-lost Olopio cave, and access was barred to commoners.

Kamehameha the Great conquered Maui in a battle here in 1790. The local armies were driven back into the valley from the shoreline, where they could be bombarded with impunity by the great cannon *Lopaka*, directed by John Young and Isaac Davis (see p.301). While the defeated general, Kalanikupule, the son of Maui's chief Kahekili, fled across the mountains, the corpses of his men choked ʻĪao Stream. Hence the name by which the battle became known – **Kepaniwai**, "the water dam."

ʻĪao Valley is now one of Hawaii's most famous beauty spots, easily explored along a three-mile road that dead-ends at the stunning **ʻĪao Needle**, a 1200-foot pinnacle of green-clad lava. Owing to the crumbly nature of the rock, climbing the needle itself would be a physical impossibility, but you can admire it from various short trails that meander around its base.

Tropical Gardens of Maui

Less than a mile out of Wailuku, the **Tropical Gardens of Maui** (daily 9am–5pm; free) spread away below and to the right of what by now is ʻĪao Valley Road. This small commercial garden displays and sells a colorful assortment of tropical plants from all over the world and mails specimens to the continental US. It also holds a small snack bar.

Kepaniwai County Park

Just after the road crosses ʻĪao Stream, a mile past the Tropical Gardens, **Kepaniwai County Park** (daily dawn–dusk; free) is an attractive public garden set amid dramatic, curtain-like folds in the mountains. Its lawns and flowerbeds are laid out in themed areas paying tribute to Maui's Japanese, Chinese, and Portuguese immigrants, among others. Wandering the grounds you'll come upon a traditional thatched *hale*, ornamental pavilions, and miniature pagodas, as well as statues of anonymous sugarcane workers and even Dr Sun Yat Sen.

Hawaii Nature Center

The **Hawaii Nature Center**, immediately adjoining Kepaniwai County Park, is largely an educational facility for schoolchildren and holds simple exhibitions on Hawaiian flora, fauna, and handicrafts (daily 10am–4pm; adults $6, under-13s $4; ⑦808/244-6500, ⑩www.hawaiinaturecenter.org). In addition, however, staff members conduct guided **hikes** in the ʻĪao Valley area (Mon–Fri 11.30am & 1.30pm, Sat & Sun 11am & 2pm; adults $30, ages 8–12 $20). As the high-mountain trails are otherwise closed to visitors, these provide the only access to the wilderness beyond the Needle. The cost of the hikes includes admission to the center and a souvenir T-shirt.

John F. Kennedy Profile

The next stop along ʻĪao Valley Road is a wayside lookout at the mouth of a small side valley. A natural rock formation a couple of hundred yards up the valley was for many years known as the **John F. Kennedy Profile**, although tree growth often obscures JFK's chin. Signs that formerly pointed out the likeness have been changed to read "A Changing Profile" and studiously avoid mentioning the assassinated president. The official line now is that the face belongs to Kuakaʻiwai, a sixteenth-century chief.

ʻĪao Valley State Park

ʻĪao Valley Road meanders to a dead end three miles out of Wailuku, at the parking lot for **ʻĪao Valley State Park** (daily 7am–7pm; free), which in all truth is more of a viewpoint than a park in its own right. Although you can clearly see ʻĪao Needle from here, a short but steep footpath crosses the stream and climbs up a nearby knoll for even better views from a covered rain shelter. Two very short trails, paved but potentially slippery, loop down to the stream from the main footpath, one on either side of the stream. Gardens laid out with native plants line the one closer to the parking lot, and the small waterlogged *loʻi* or taro patch here, similar to a paddy field, offers one of the best angles for photographs, as you look up past the footbridge toward the Needle itself.

Despite appearances, the velvety **ʻĪao Needle** is not freestanding, but simply a raised knob at the end of a sinuous ridge. Towering, head usually in the clouds, at the intersection of two lush valleys, it's what geologists call an "erosional residual" – a nugget of hard volcanic rock left behind when the softer surrounding rocks were eroded away. From this side, the Needle is an impressive 1200-feet tall, but no higher than the ridges that surround it. The ancient Hawaiians, with their usual scatological gusto, named it Kukaʻemoku, which politely translates as "broken excreta."

This whole area owes its existence to the phenomenal amount of rain that falls on West Maui; the 5788-foot peak of **Puʻu Kukui**, just over two miles from here, receives more than four hundred inches per year. Unless you come early in the morning, it's likely to be raining in ʻĪao Valley, but even when it's pouring you can usually look straight back down the valley to see the dry sunlit plains of the isthmus. After a series of accidents, the **trails** that lead beyond ʻĪao Needle can now only be seen on the guided hikes run by the Hawaii Nature Center.

Māʻalaea

The direct road south from Wailuku, **Honoapiʻilani Highway** (Hwy-30), is joined as it crosses the isthmus by highways from Kahului and Kīhei and carries

△ Īoa Valley State Park

virtually all the traffic heading for Lahaina and the West Maui resorts. At the point where it reaches the south coast, six miles out of Wailuku, **MĀ'ALAEA** is a former commercial port that has been given a new lease of life as the preferred marina of Maui's cruise and pleasure boats. The largest contingent are the Molokini snorkel boats (see p.325), which collectively bring Mā'alaea to life very early in the morning, when the day's passengers assemble. At this time it also offers great views of Haleakalā, whose summit pokes out above the ring of clouds that usually obscures it from Kīhei.

Swimming anywhere near Māʻalaea is not recommended, but there are good **surfing** breaks just to the south, while **windsurfers** hurtle out into Māʻalaea Bay from the thin and unexciting strip of sand that stretches all the way east to Kīhei.

For an account of the Lahaina Pali Trail, which sets off across the southern tip of West Maui from just north of Māʻalaea, see p.301. The remainder of Honoapiʻilani Highway's route around West Maui to Lahaina is covered on p.299 onwards.

Maui Ocean Center

While Māʻalaea is still not a town in any meaningful sense, it has acquired a center of sorts, in the form of the **Māʻalaea Harbor Village** mall. That in turn focuses on the **Maui Ocean Center**, a state-of-the-art **aquarium** providing a colorful introduction to the marine life of Hawaii (Sept–June daily 9am–5pm, July & Aug daily 9am–6pm; adults $23, ages 3–12 $16; ℡808/270-7000, Ⓦwww.mauioceancenter.com). It's not quite as large as you might expect from the size of the entrance fee, but its exhibits are well chosen and very well displayed, and it has rapidly established itself as Maui's most visited paying attraction.

The most spectacular section comes first. The coral groves of the **Living Reef** (some of them fluorescent) hold such species as camouflaged scorpionfish, seahorses, octopuses, and bizarre "upside-down jellyfish." Eerie garden eels poke like blades of grass from the sandy seabed, but the star, of course, is the little *humuhumunukunukuapuaʻa* – literally, "the triggerfish with a snout like a pig."

Open-air terraces perched above the harbor hold tanks of huge rays and green sea turtles; as a rule, each turtle is kept at the aquarium for just a few months before being fitted with a tracking device and released into the ocean. Further on, additional displays cover the life cycle of **whales**, and the relationship between **Hawaiians and the sea**, illustrating traditional fishing techniques and equipment. A final huge tank holds **pelagic**, or open-ocean, sea creatures; its walk-through glass tunnel means that you can stand beneath mighty sharks and rays as they swim above your head. Certified scuba divers can arrange to take an accompanied **dive** into the tank for a one-on-one shark encounter (Mon, Wed & Fri 8.30am; $200); some divers have even been married in the tank.

Practicalities

Māʻalaea has acquired half-a-dozen characterless **condo** buildings, lined up beyond the harbor along Hauʻoli Street. Most enjoy broad sea views, but Māʻalaea is a decidedly windy and insect-prone spot, and staying here is only likely to appeal to fanatical sailors. If you do want to book a condo locally, contact Māʻalaea Bay Rentals (℡808/244-7012 or 1-800/367-6084, Ⓦwww.maalaeabay.com). Typical rates start at around $100 per night.

Māʻalaea is, however, home to a handful of good **restaurants**. Perched above the harbor at the seaward end of Māʻalaea Harbor Village – with an ocean-view terrace that comes into its own at lunchtime – the *Māʻalaea Grill* (Mon 10.30am–5pm, Tues–Sun 10.30am–9pm; ℡808/243-2206) serves conventional meat and seafood entrees at reasonable prices, and specializes in salads at midday. Nearby, the menu at the equally large and scenic *Māʻalaea Waterfront Restaurant*, 50 Hauʻoli St (daily 5–9.30pm; ℡808/244-9028), focuses on expensive freshly caught fish, with a *cioppino* stew priced at $38. You can also buy fish for yourself at the Māʻalaea Fish Market (Mon–Sat 10am–4pm), just around the harbor.

Molokini snorkel cruises

Maui's best-known **snorkeling** and **diving** spot is the tiny crescent of **Molokini**, three miles off Mākena. Created by a volcanic eruption some 230,000 years ago, it rises about 500ft from the underwater flank of Haleakalā, though only the southern half of the circular crater still pokes above the waves, to a maximum height of 162ft. There's no beach or landfall of any kind, but it's a real thrill to enter the water, and see the steep crater wall dropping far into the abyss beneath you, and you're certain to see a staggering array of multi-colored fish, including deep-water species.

Countless cruises leave early each morning from **Māʻalaea Harbor**. It's also possible to take a significantly longer and more expensive cruise from Lahaina, while the very shortest crossing departs from Mākena's *Maui Prince* hotel (see p.333). Strong ocean currents off the South Maui coast render it too dangerous to try to swim or kayak to Molokini.

All the boats listed below operate out of Māʻalaea. For virtually all, you should be able to find **discount prices** from activities operators such as those listed on p.285. Snorkelers can pay anything from $50 to $110 for a five- to six-hour morning trip, depending on the size and comfort of the boat and the refreshments offered, and from $35 for a shorter afternoon jaunt; scuba divers pay around $40 extra. Note that between November and April, many companies stop running Molokini trips and concentrate on lucrative **whale-watching** cruises instead; for full details, see p.286.

Boat	Phone	ⓦwww.	Passengers
Four Winds II	☎808/879-8188	mauicharters.com	130
Frogman II	☎808/661-3333	bossfrog.com	52
Hokua	☎808/249-2583	alohabluecharters.com	20
Lahaina Princess	☎877/500-6284	mauiprincess.com	100
Lani Kai	☎808/244-1979	mauisnorkeling.com	70
Ocean Odyssey	☎808/249-8811	pacificwhale.org	149
Ocean Spirit	☎808/249-8811	pacificwhale.org	142
Paragon II	☎808/244-2087	sailmaui.com	35
Pride of Maui	☎808/242-0955	prideofmaui.com	140
Prince Kuhio	☎808/242-8777	mvprince.com	149
Quicksilver	☎808/661-3333	bossfrog.com	142

South Maui

The area generally referred to as **South Maui** is in fact the western shoreline of East Maui, stretching south of Māʻalaea Bay. Until well after World War II, this was one of the island's least populated districts, a scrubby, exposed, and worthless wasteland. Since then, a largely unattractive and almost unchecked ribbon of resort development has snaked down the coast, with the mass-market hotels and condos of **Kīhei** in the north being joined more recently by far more exclusive luxury properties at **Wailea** and **Mākena**.

Almost all the way down, narrow strips of white sand fill each successive bay, so most hotels are within easy walking distance of a good stretch of beach. So far, the development stops just short of the best beach of all, **Oneloa** or **Big Beach**, while the coastal highway peters out not far beyond. This final stretch, and the ocean-front trail to secluded **La Pérouse Bay**, is the only part of South Maui worth visiting on a sightseeing tour of the island; none of the resort communities holds any interest in itself.

Kīhei

If you've always thought of Hawaii as Condo Hell, then **KĪHEI** probably comes closer to matching that image than anywhere else in the state. Stretching for seven miles south from Mā'alaea Bay, it's a totally formless sprawl of a place, whose only landmarks consist of one dull mall or condo building after another. That said, it can be a perfectly pleasant place to spend your vacation, with abundant inexpensive lodging and dining options and plentiful beaches. Just don't come to Kīhei expecting a town in any sense of the word.

During the 1960s, Kīhei spread for just a hundred yards to either side of the point where Mokulele Highway (Hwy-50) reaches Mā'alaea Bay. **North Kīhei Road** is still a hundred yards long, but **South Kīhei Road** now keeps on going for around five miles. It's not totally built up, but the occasional half-mile gaps of derelict land are fast being developed; Kīhei was until recently ranked as the second-fastest-growing community in the United States. Traffic congestion is so rife that for all journeys of any length, you'd do better to follow the parallel

Condo rentals

Individual apartments in virtually all the properties listed here, and a great many more besides, can also be booked through various specialist agencies. Broadly speaking, typical prices start around $100 per night in low season, rising towards $150 between Christmas and March; be sure to check whether you're expected to pay an additional one-time "cleaning fee," which is usually around the $50 mark.

AA Oceanfront Condominium Rentals 1279 S Kīhei Rd, Kīhei ☎808/879-7288 or 1-800/488-6004, ⓦwww.aaoceanfront.com

Condominium Rentals Hawaii 362 Huku Li'i Place, #204, Kīhei ☎808/879-2778 or 1-800/367-5242, ⓦwww.crhmaui.com

Kīhei Maui Vacations PO Box 1055, Kīhei, HI 96753 ☎808/879-7581 or 1-888/568-6284, ⓦwww.kmvmaui.com

Maui Condominium and Home Realty 2511 S Kīhei Rd, Suite H, Kīhei ☎808/879-5445 or 1-800/822-4409, ⓦwww.vacationweb.com/mchr

Pi'ilani Highway, half a mile or so up the hillside. There's even talk of building another, third highway still further up the slope.

The largest of Kīhei's shopping malls are the matching pair of **Azeka Makai**, on the ocean side of the street at 1280 S Kīhei Rd, and **Azeka Mauka**, opposite. Between them they hold the local **post office**, a large Bank of Hawaii with ATMs, and lots of fast-food places. Otherwise, the newer **Pi'ilani Village Shopping Center**, not far away on the upper highway, is expanding rapidly and holds a huge Safeway supermarket, while **Kukui Mall**, opposite Kalama Park, has a four-screen movie theater and more takeout options.

Accommodation

There's little difference between Kīhei's countless **condos** and **hotels**, with standards in even the cheapest options tending to be perfectly adequate. Very few visitors simply pass through for a single night; there are no rock-bottom budget

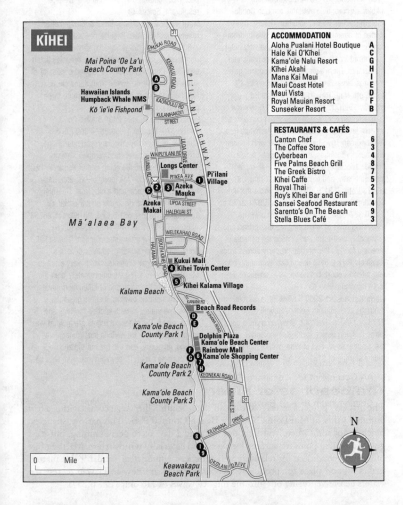

KĪHEI

ACCOMMODATION
Aloha Pualani Hotel Boutique	A
Hale Kai O'Kīhei	C
Kama'ole Nalu Resort	G
Kīhei Akahi	H
Mana Kai Maui	I
Maui Coast Hotel	E
Maui Vista	D
Royal Mauian Resort	F
Sunseeker Resort	B

RESTAURANTS & CAFÉS
Canton Chef	6
The Coffee Store	3
Cyberbean	4
Five Palms Beach Grill	8
The Greek Bistro	7
Kīhei Caffe	5
Royal Thai	2
Roy's Kīhei Bar and Grill	1
Sansei Seafood Restaurant	4
Sarento's On The Beach	9
Stella Blues Café	3

Mai Poina 'Oe La'u Beach County Park

Hawaiian Islands Humpback Whale NMS
Kō 'ie'ie Fishpond

Longs Center
Pi'ilani Village
Azeka Mauka
Azeka Makai

Mā'alaea Bay

Kukui Mall
Kīhei Town Center
Kīhei Kalama Village

Kalama Beach

Beach Road Records

Kama'ole Beach County Park 1

Dolphin Plaza
Kama'ole Beach Center
Rainbow Mall
Kama'ole Shopping Center

Kama'ole Beach County Park 2

Kama'ole Beach County Park 3

N

0   Mile   1

Keawakapu Beach Park

MAUI | Kīhei

alternatives or B&Bs, and most places insist on a minimum stay of at least three nights. Rates on the whole are low, but Kīhei is more seasonally sensitive than most destinations, and in peak season (mid-Dec to March) you can expect to pay at least $30 over the price code given below.

Aloha Pualani Hotel Boutique 15 Wailana Place ☏808/875-6990 or 1-866/870-6990 (US & Canada), 🖳www.alohapualani.com. Five two-story suites across from Mā'ā'alaea Bay at the north end of Kīhei, providing luxurious personalized accommodations. Each suite has a living room, kitchen, bedroom, and *lānai*, and they're clustered around a central pool and bar. On-site owners provide breakfast and advice. Two-night minimum stay. **❼**

Hale Kai O 'Kīhei 1310 Uluniu Rd ☏808/879-7288 or 1-800/457-7014 (US & Canada), 🖳www.hkokmaui.com; also available through Condominium Rentals Hawaii (see box, p.326). Three stories of straightforward one- and two-bedroom condos, in an absolutely stunning and very quiet beachfront location, near Kīhei's best malls and restaurants. There's also a private coconut grove, spacious *lānais*, and discounted car rental. **❹**

Kama'ole Nalu Resort 2450 S Kīhei Rd ☏808/879-1006 or 1-800/767-1497, 🖳www.kamaolenalu.com. Large beachfront complex set on neat lawns at the south end of Kama'ole Park 2. Two-bedroom, two-bath condos, all with kitchen and laundry facilities; the long, private *lānais* provide spectacular sunset views. Five-night minimum stay, and discounts on car rental. **❺**

Kīhei Akahi 2531 S Kīhei Rd; available through Condominium Rentals Hawaii ☏808/879-2778 or 1-800/367-5242, 🖳www.crhmaui.com. The ascending rows of unexciting but low-priced and reasonably well-furnished condos (all capable of sleeping four) in this garden property across from Kama'ole Park 2 have use of two swimming pools and a tennis court, but no views to speak of. Four-night minimum stay. **❹**

Mana Kai Resort 2960 S Kīhei Rd; available through Condominium Rentals Hawaii ☏808/879-2778 or 1-800/367-5242, 🖳www.crhmaui.com. Large building beside lovely Keawakapu Beach at the grander south end of Kīhei, with small hotel rooms starting at $132 and full-blown condo apartments from $212, plus a pool and the excellent *Five Palms* grill restaurant (see p.330). Rooms **❹** , apartments **❻**

Maui Coast Hotel 2259 S Kīhei Rd ☏808/874-6284 or 1-800/895-6284, 🖳www.mauicoasthotel.com. Tasteful, upscale, and reasonable-value modern hotel, set slightly back from the highway opposite Kama'ole Park 1. Standard hotel rooms, as well as pricier one- and two-bedroom suites, with good deals on car rental, plus an attractive pool with poolside bar, and an above-average restaurant, *Spices*. **❺**

Maui Vista 2191 S Kīhei Rd ☏808/879-7966; reserve through Marc Resorts, ☏808/922-9700 or 1-800/535-0085 (US & Canada), 🖳www.marcresorts.com; or through Kīhei agencies listed on p.326. Comfortable, well-equipped condos of all sizes, on the hillside across from Kama'ole Park 1. Not the best views, but amenities include three pools and six tennis courts. **❹**

Royal Mauian Resort 2430 S Kīhei Rd ☏808/879-1263 or 1-800/367-8009 (US & Canada), 🖳www.royalmauianresort.com. Huge, luxurious, oceanfront condo complex, though lacking a/c, beyond the south end of Kama'ole Park 1. Highlights include the lovely views, especially from the roof terrace, and a nice pool. Five-night minimum stay, and discounts on car rental. **❺**

Sunseeker Resort 551 S Kīhei Rd, Kīhei HI 96753 ☏808/879-1261 or 1-800/532-6284 (US & Canada), 🖳www.mauisunseeker.com. This small hotel-cum-condo building, which caters to a predominantly gay clientele, stands very close to Mā'alaea Bay beach (and, unfortunately, also the main road) at the north end of Kīhei. As renovated by its enthusiastic owners, it offers great-value rooms and suites, all with kitchen facilities and ocean views. The cheapest rooms are in what was formerly the separate Wailana Inn, immediately behind; all guests can use the hot tub and deck on that building's roof. Three-night minimum stay. **❹**

The beaches of Kīhei

The first easy point of access to the ocean along South Kīhei Road comes within a few hundred yards, at **Mai Poina 'Oe Ia'u Beach County Park**. This narrow, shadeless beach is not somewhere you'd choose to spend a day, or to go swimming, but it's a good launching point for surfers, kayakers, and especially **windsurfers**. Mā'alaea Bay offers ideal conditions for relatively inexperienced windsurfers – and, for that matter, makes a good place for proficient sailboarders who are new to Hawaii to test the waters before venturing out into the mighty waves of Ho'okipa (see p.257).

To the naked eye, and especially to guests staying at oceanfront properties such as the *Hale Kai O' Kīhei* and its neighbors, the beaches of northern Kīhei look attractive enough, if rather narrow. However, thanks to the output of a **sewage treatment facility** above the next formal roadside beach park, at **Kalama Beach**, three miles south of Mai Poina, this entire stretch is best admired from dry land. Swimming is not recommended. Nonetheless, the large lawns and sports fields on the promontory at Kalama remain popular with locals, especially in the evenings, and there's a pretty coconut grove as well.

Much the busiest of the Kīhei beaches – and for good reason – are the three separate, numbered segments of **Kama'ole Beach County Park**, immediately beyond. All boast clean white sand and are generally safe for swimming, with lovely views across the bay to West Maui, and all are constantly supervised by lifeguards. Most of beautifully soft **Kama'ole 1** beach is very close to the road, but it also curves away out of sight to the north, which is where you're likely to find the best snorkeling conditions. Little **Kama'ole 2**, cradled between two headlands, is a bit short on shade, and very near a large concentration of condos, which leaves long, broad **Kama'ole 3** as the pick of the bunch. Families gather under the giant trees on its wide lawns, while the beach itself, which is especially popular with boogie-boarders, is shielded from the road at the bottom of a ten-foot grassy slope.

In high season, **Keawakapu Beach Park**, at the far south end of South Kīhei Road, makes an inviting and less crowded alternative. Swimming is best in the center, while there's good snorkeling off the rocks to the south, thanks to an artificial offshore reef made up mostly of old automobile parts that were submerged in the hope of boosting the local fish population.

Hawaiian Islands Humpback Whale National Marine Sanctuary

At the northern end of Kīhei, squeezed onto a minor headland not far south of Mai Poina 'Oe Ia'u Beach, a small compound at 726 S Kīhei Rd serves as the headquarters of the **Hawaiian Islands Humpback Whale National Marine Sanctuary** (Ⓣ808/879-2818 or 1-800/831-4888, Ⓦwww.hihwnms.nos.noaa.gov). The organization was created to protect and study the estimated three thousand humpback whales that annually winter in Hawaiian waters. Enthusiastic volunteers can explain its work and talk you through the displays in the garage-like **Education Center** (Mon–Fri 10am–3pm; free). The organization's offices, located in the larger blue house on the seafront, is not open to the public. Its spacious veranda, however, is equipped with free binoculars and makes an ideal spot for watching whales in Mā'alaea Bay.

A six-acre tract of ocean immediately offshore from the sanctuary headquarters is enclosed by the ancient lava walls of the **Kō'ie'ie Fishpond**, which dates originally from the sixteenth century. This area was then the site of the village of **Kalepolepo**, whose inhabitants left after the fishpond became silted up during the 1860s, thanks to runoff caused by the expansion of agriculture further up the slopes.

Restaurants

The **restaurants** listed overleaf represent just a small selection of what's available in Kīhei. Virtually all the malls also hold at least one budget diner or takeout place, and most have an espresso bar, too. The best places for **food shopping** are the Safeway supermarket at Pi'ilani Village Shopping Center on the upper highway (where there's also a *Starbucks*), and the *Hawaiian Moons* wholefood store at the Kama'ole Beach Center, 2411 S Kīhei Rd.

Inexpensive

The Coffee Store Azeka Mauka, 1279 S Kīhei Rd
☏ 808/875-4244. Cheery mall café serving
espressos of all kinds, plus breakfast pastries,
lunch salads, pizzas, and sandwiches. Mon–Sat
6am–7pm, Sun 6am–5pm.

Cyberbean Kīhei Town Center, 1881 S Kīhei Rd
☏ 808/879-4799. Internet café that, as well as
specialty coffees, provides the usual array of
inexpensive pizzas, salads, and sandwiches. Mon–
Sat 7am–9pm, Sun 8am–8pm.

Kīhei Caffe 1945 S Kīhei Rd ☏ 808/879-2230.
Friendly café offering espressos, flavored lattes,
and smoothies, plus breakfast eggs and pancakes
and $7 lunchtime sandwiches or burgers, to take
out or eat at a shaded roadside gazebo. Daily
5am–3pm.

Royal Thai Azeka Makai, 1280 S Kīhei Rd
☏ 808/874-0813. Small place, tucked away at the
back of the mall, serving Kīhei's best Thai food.
Choose from red, yellow, and green curries in
vegetarian, meat, and fish versions; *tom yum* (spicy
and sour soup) and long-rice soups; and mussels in
black-bean sauce – all for $8–12. Mon–Fri 11am–
3pm & 4.45–9.30pm, Sat & Sun 4.45–9.30pm.

Moderate

Canton Chef Kama'ole Shopping Center, 2463 S
Kīhei Rd ☏ 808/879-1988. Roomy Chinese restaurant, with $8 lunch specials and a dinner menu
bursting with chicken, shrimp, scallop, and fish
entrees ($8–22), including several served in a
tangy black-bean sauce. With advance notice,
they'll prepare a whole Peking duck for $43. Daily
11am–2pm & 5–9pm.

The Greek Bistro 2511 S Kīhei Rd ☏ 808/879-
9330. Friendly, dinner-only Greek place on a garden
terrace set back from the road and crammed with
coconut palms and a banyan tree. The food is OK
without being wonderful, but makes a welcome
and potentially healthy change. Appetizers like feta
and olive salad, or stuffed grape leaves go for $8–
12; entrees include *moussaka* and *souvlaki* for
under $20, while a mixed platter costs $25 per
person. Daily 5–10pm.

Stella Blues Café Azeka Mauka, 1279 S Kīhei Rd
☏ 808/874-3779. California-style café, complete
with ponytailed waiters and Grateful Dead posters,
and centering on a huge wood-burning grill. The
menu includes continental and cooked breakfasts
($6–10); burger, salad, and sandwich lunches ($8–
15; try the special of grilled and roasted vegetables
on herb bread); dinners like fettuccini Alfredo,
Cajun chicken, crab cakes, and ribs ($15–24); as
well as an assortment of smoothies and espressos.
Daily 7.30am–10pm.

Expensive

Five Palms Beach Grill *Mana Kai Resort*, 2960 S
Kīhei Rd ☏ 808/879-2607. Beachfront restaurant in
a spectacular setting on the ground floor of a
condo building, with open terraces within earshot
of the waves, and live music nightly. An à la carte
brunch menu is served until 2.30pm daily, including
an eggs Benedict with seared-tuna for $18, or
salad or lunch specials for $13–20. Dinner items –
mostly Pacific Rim, along with standard ribs and
steaks – are delicious and beautifully presented,
with appetizers such as soft-shell crab cakes in
Japanese tartare sauce ($16) and entrees like fresh
opah (moonfish), and Szechuan glazed rack of
lamb ($28–43). Daily 8am–9.30pm.

Roy's Kīhei Bar and Grill Pi'ilani Village,
303 Pi'ikea Ave ☏ 808/891-1120. Large,
always busy and very highly recommended dinner-
only outlet of the upscale island chain, beside the
upper highway in a mall half a mile up from Kīhei
Road. Signature Roy's dishes such as lemongrass-
crusted *shutome* (swordfish) and blackened rare
ahi stream from the open kitchen, at around $10–
13 for an appetizer and $25–30 for an entree. The
steamed fresh catch ($30) is irresistible, while half
a Mongolian roasted duck or honey-mustard short
rib is $26. Rather than bread, they provide a dish of
edamame beans. A three-course set menu costs
$40. Daily 5.30–10pm.

Sansei Seafood Restaurant Kīhei Town
Center, 1881 S Kīhei Rd ☏ 808/669-6286.
Sensational Japanese–Hawaiian, dinner-only restaurant, also found in Kapalua (see p.308). Individual
appetizers and entrees are invariably delicious, but
the special Omakase Tasting Menu, at $68 for two, is
fabulous value, offering copious portions of signature
dishes such as *miso* butterfish and the Asian rock
shrimp cake. It's all pretty hectic, so don't expect to
linger over a romantic dinner, and there are no views,
but it's a dynamic spot and the food is out of this
world. Laser karaoke until 2am at weekends. Mon–
Wed & Sun 5.30–10pm, Thurs–Sat 5.30pm–1am.

Sarento's on the Beach *Best Western Oceanfront
Inn*, 2980 S Kīhei Rd ☏ 808/875-7555. This dinner-
only Italian restaurant is very much a special-
occasion kind of place, at Kīhei's southern end in an
open-sided pavilion adjoining Keawakapu Beach,
which is gently spotlit once the sun goes down.
Everything is scrupulously tasteful, from the complimentary focaccia breads to the Sinatra soundtrack,
but with starters like gazpacho with crab or the
house salad costing $12–18, and entrees such as
tiger shrimp at over $30, or *fra diavolo* seafood
stew for $45, the check can be gargantuan,
especially if you buy your souvenir photo from the
house photographer. Daily 5.30–10pm.

Wailea and Mākena

Both South Kīhei Road and Piʻilani Highway end on the southern fringes of Kīhei. The only road south from here, branching off Okolani Drive halfway between the two, is **Wailea Alanui Drive**, which becomes **Mākena Alanui Drive** after a couple of miles. It's forced to run several hundred yards inland by a sequence of half a dozen colossal resort hotels, constructed on a scale to rival any in Hawaii. Neither **WAILEA** nor **MĀKENA** is a town as such; were it not for the resorts, the names would not even appear on island maps. The only **shops** in the area are congregated in the very upmarket **Shops at Wailea** mall, whose target audience can be guessed from the presence of Louis Vuitton, Cartier, and Dolce & Gabbana stores.

Until the 1950s, what is now Wailea was just barren oceanfront acreage belonging to the ʻUlupalakua Ranch (see p.340). It was then bought by Matson Cruise Lines, who planned to turn it into the "City of Roses," but nothing happened until control of Matson passed to Alexander & Baldwin in the 1970s.

Mākena, which blends imperceptibly into the south end of Wailea, was developed even more recently: its first hotel appeared at the end of the 1980s. For a period in the late nineteenth century, however, it ranked as Maui's second port after Lahaina, thanks to the comings and goings at ʻUlupalakua Ranch, just two miles higher up the gentle slope of Haleakalā. These days, in the absence of any direct road, getting to the ranch requires a forty-mile drive.

Wailea and Mākena together constitute a luxurious enclave of

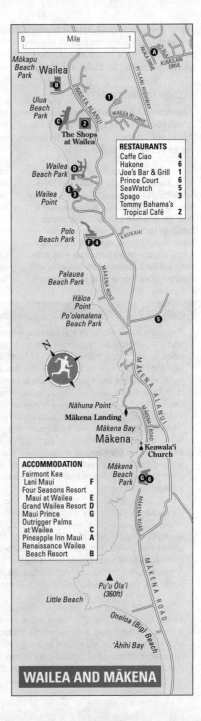

RESTAURANTS

Caffe Ciao	4
Hakone	6
Joe's Bar & Grill	1
Prince Court	6
SeaWatch	5
Spago	3
Tommy Bahama's Tropical Café	2

ACCOMMODATION

Fairmont Kea Lani Maui	F
Four Seasons Resort Maui at Wailea	E
Grand Wailea Resort	D
Maui Prince	G
Outrigger Palms at Wailea	C
Pineapple Inn Maui	A
Renaissance Wailea Beach Resort	B

WAILEA AND MĀKENA

velvet golf courses and pristine beaches, where nonguests feel distinctly unwelcome. In theory, outsiders are free to use any of the beaches; although few bother, with the exception of magnificent Oneloa Beach (see p.336) just beyond Mākena, glorious strands like **Polo** and **Maluaka** really should not be missed.

Accommodation

The moment you see the manicured lawns of Wailea, let alone its gleaming resorts, it will become clear that you need a *lot* of money to **stay** at this end of South Maui. There are one or two little B&Bs nearby, but otherwise rooms can rarely be found for under $250 a night.

Fairmont Kea Lani Maui 4100 Wailea Alanui Drive, Wailea ☎ 808/875-4100 or 1-800/257-7544, ⑩ www.kealani.com. Locals call it the Taj Mahal, but this dazzling white resort is more like something from the *Arabian Nights*. Despite its flamboyant domed silhouette, the interior is characterized by smooth unadorned curves, and you can see through the lobby to lily ponds and the lagoon-cum-pool, crossed by little footbridges. Two huge wings of plush rooms (all

equipped with TVs, DVD and CD players), 37 garden villas, and some excellent restaurants are all focused on lovely Polo Beach; there's also a great Italian deli. Garden view ⑧, ocean view ⑨

Four Seasons Resort Maui at Wailea 3900 Wailea Alanui Drive, Wailea ☎ 808/874-8000 or 1-800/334-6284, ⑩ www.fourseasons.com/maui. Lavish resort property at the south end of Wailea, with a large, beautiful, white-sand beach on view beyond the open lobby, and a gorgeous,

Kahoolawe

The uninhabited island of **Kahoolawe** is clearly visible from all along Maui's south and west coasts, and especially around Wailea and Mākena. Measuring just eleven miles by six, and a maximum of 1477 feet above sea level, it's the eighth-largest Hawaiian island, with its nearest point a mere eight miles off Maui. From a distance, Kahoolawe looks like a barren hillock; at sunset it glows red, thanks to a haze of red dust lifted by the winds. Trapped in the rainshadow of Haleakalā, it receives thirty inches of rain a year. Agriculture is now all but impossible, but a few green valleys, invisible from the other islands, cut into the central plateau.

Whether Kahoolawe ever held much of a population has become a controversial issue, thanks to the protracted campaign by **native Hawaiians** to claim the island back from the **US Navy**. The Navy used it for target practice for almost fifty years, arguing that it had no value as a home to humans; the Hawaiians claimed that it held great spiritual significance to their ancestors, and that access to it remained their inalienable birthright.

Both sides marshaled archeologists and anthropologists, and Kahoolawe has consequently been more thoroughly probed and excavated than anywhere else in Hawaii. The consensus seems to be that, although it was principally used as a seasonal base by fishermen, the presence of house sites, *heiaus*, and petroglyphs proves that it also held permanent agricultural settlements. In addition, Kealaikahiki Point at its southwest corner was a marker for navigators sailing to and from Tahiti. A "navigator's chair" of shaped boulders still stands atop the island's second-highest peak, the 1444-foot Moa'ulaiki, which is thought to have served as a school and observatory for apprentice navigators.

The whole island was probably covered by forest until 1450 AD, when it was swept by a bushfire. The trees have never grown back, and Captain Cook's expedition described Kahoolawe as "altogether a poor Island" in 1779. The process of erosion was completed by sheep and goats imported during the nineteenth century. For a short period during the 1840s, Kahoolawe was a penal colony; several ranchers then eked out a living there. The last of them was

palm-ringed pool. Rooms have private *lānais*, bamboo furnishings, and 24-hour room service, and you can choose from several restaurants, including *Spago* (see p.335). **⑨**

Grand Wailea Resort 3850 Wailea Alanui Drive, Wailea ☏808/875-1234 or 1-800/888-6100, ⓦwww.grandwailea.com. Large and very ostentatious resort hotel, with a five-level swimming pool ("Wailea Canyon") that's linked by waterslides and features a swim-up bar, hot-tub grottoes, and even a water elevator back to the top. There's also a luxurious spa, half a dozen restaurants, a nightclub, and tropical flowers everywhere. Check for online discounts. **⑨**

Maui Prince 5400 Mākena Alanui Drive, Mākena ☏808/874-1111 or 1-888/977-4623, ⓦwww.mauiprince.com. South Maui's southernmost resort is a secluded and stylish low-rise facing gorgeous, sandy Maluaka Beach, and just about within walking distance of the even more wonderful Big Beach (see p.336). The main hotel block focuses inwards around a central courtyard; the rooms are spacious,

pared-down, and elegant; and there are trickling ponds filled with koi carp everywhere you look. Top-quality Japanese and Pacific Rim restaurants, golf packages, pilates, and yoga on the beach, and early-morning snorkel cruises to nearby Molokini. Look for great room-and-car deals online. **⑦**

Pineapple Inn Maui 3170 Akala Drive ☏808/298-4403 or 1-877/212-6284, ⓦwww.pineappleinnmaui.com. Small, luxurious purpose-built inn, high on the Wailea hillside, that makes a wonderfully affordable alternative to the giants down below. The pastel-yellow main building holds four guest rooms with private baths and ocean-view *lānais*, and there's a separate two-bedroom cottage. Rooms **④**, cottage **⑤**.

Outrigger Palms at Wailea 3200 Wailea Alanui Drive, Wailea ☏808/879-1922 or 1-888/294-7731 (US & Canada), ⓦwww.outrigger.com. Though Wailea's first resort hotel has been thoroughly upgraded to match its neighbors, it retains its original open-air appeal. Comprising of several small buildings in landscaped gardens and a larger

summarily evicted after the 1941 attack on Pearl Harbor, so that the island could be used by the Navy.

After World War II, the military declined to return Kahoolawe to the state of Hawaii. In 1953, President Eisenhower granted the Navy control over the island, with the proviso that it should be cleaned up at Federal expense and returned when no longer needed. For forty more years, Kahoolawe was blasted by thunderous explosions that could be seen and heard from Maui.

Intermittent Hawaiian efforts to reclaim Kahoolawe crystallized in 1975 with the formation of the **Protect Kahoolawe 'Ohana**, a group of young activists that saw Kahoolawe as a unifying cause for all native Hawaiians, the most obvious symbol of the way in which Hawaiian lands had been seized and desecrated by the United States. The PKO organized the first of a series of illegal occupations of the island in January 1976, at the start of Bicentennial year.

The PKO eventually turned to the courts. Accusing the Navy on several fronts – water, noise, and air pollution; the threat to endangered marine mammals and historic sites; and the infringement of religious freedoms – they won restrictions on bombing and gained "visiting rights" of up to ten days per month. President George H.W. Bush finally called a halt to the bombing in 1990, and Kahoolawe was handed back to the state of Hawaii in May 1994. The Navy continued to control access to the island for a further ten years, while it struggled to fulfill its commitment to remove all unexploded ordnance. In the end, when control passed to the state in November 2003, an estimated seventy percent of the island's surface had been cleared, although only ten percent had also been checked for explosive materials buried beneath the soil. Open access to native Hawaiians, let alone casual visitors, still therefore seems a long way off, though there are at least plans to develop a safe "perimeter trail" around the shoreline, and a program of reforestation is achieving some success. The situation is further complicated by the fact that Kahoolawe is ultimately due to pass into the hands of a native Hawaiian government, but consensus on the creation of any such government has yet to be achieved.

central tower, all with spacious, comfortable rooms, the hotel offers three pools, two restaurants, plus Hawaiiana lectures and four weekly *lū'aus* (see p.290). The nearest beach is however ten minutes' walk away. Garden view ⑥, ocean view ⑦

Renaissance Wailea Beach Resort 3550 Wailea Alanui Drive, Wailea ☎ 808/879-4900 or 1-800/992-4532, ⓦ www.renaissancehotels .com.

A highly luxurious resort, stacked in seven tiers above twin crescent beaches and boasting swimming pools set amid lush gardens. Sumptuous rooms come with DVD players and *lānais* angled toward the ocean. The *Hāna Gion* serves good Japanese food, and there's also a thrice-weekly *lū'au* (see p.290). Mountain view ⑧, ocean view ⑨

The beaches

Five separate little bays indent the coastline of Wailea, with two more at Mākena. All hold crescent beaches of white sand that, in all but the worst winter conditions, are ideal for swimming.

A short access road just past the *Renaissance Wailea* leads down to **Ulua Beach**, where the surf is usually at its highest along this stretch of coast and which is therefore popular with body-surfers and boogie-boarders. There's also great snorkeling around the rocky point that separates it from **Mōkapu Beach**, a short walk to the north.

Although **Wailea Beach** itself, reached by a spur road between the *Grand Wailea* and the *Four Seasons*, is the most overshadowed by the resorts of all the beaches in the vicinity, the hotels are here for a reason. A superb broad expanse of curving sand, it offers safe swimming virtually year-round, with a gentle ripple at the southern end to please first-time boogie-boarders, and easy snorkeling around the rocks at either extremity. The views are great too, looking across the bay with its busy pleasure-boat traffic and whales in winter to East Maui on the far side.

Polo Beach, the next along, is the best of the lot for swimming. A pleasant, paved coastal trail connects it to Wailea Beach, while there's plenty of parking just off Kaukahi Street, on the south side of the *Fairmont Kea Lani*. The path down from the parking lot hits the sand at Polo Beach's northern end, which, being right beneath the hotel, can feel rather like a goldfish bowl, crammed with loungers and short on shade. Double back south, however, and you'll come to two much less crowded stretches, which in winter become distinct beaches.

Ten minutes' walk south from Polo Beach, **Palauea Beach** is the quietest of the Wailea beaches, well away from the built-up areas. Surfers and boogie-boarders predominate, but it's also a good spot for a family day by the sea and for snorkeling. In 1994, Palauea Beach was where the US Navy held a ceremony formally handing control of the island of Kahoolawe, clearly visible out to sea, back to the people of Hawaii.

Mākena Road, which leaves Mākena Alanui Drive a little over a mile south of the *Kea Lani*, skirts the shoreline of **Mākena Bay**. This was once the site of busy **Mākena Landing** harbor, which was superseded by the creation of Kahului's new docks in the 1920s. The jetty has now gone, leaving behind a sleepy black-lava bay with little sand.

A little further on, the **Keawala'i Congregational Church** stands on an ocean-front patch of lawn that doubles as a graveyard, surrounded by trees with multi-colored blossoms. It's a plain cement structure, topped by a pretty, wood-shingled belfry, and painted with a neat green trim; the coconut palms beyond front a tiny beach. Visitors are welcome to the 7.30am and 10am Sunday services, which incorporate Hawaiian language and music.

Keawala'i Church is opposite the parking lot for **Maluaka Beach** – also known as **Mākena Beach Park**, which naturally leads to confusion with Mākena State Park, described on p.337 – a hundred yards down the road.

Somewhat overshadowed by the *Maui Prince*, it's still an attractive little half-moon beach, with reasonable snorkeling. Its combination of relative tranquility and superb sunset views over to Molokini and Kahoolawe also makes it a favorite spot for wedding ceremonies.

Restaurants

Neither Wailea nor Mākena holds many alternatives to the resort hotels' own **restaurants**, but there are enough excellent ones to choose from, provided you don't mind paying $40 per head per night for dinner. For cheaper meals, you'll just have to head back to Kīhei (see p.330).

Caffe Ciao *Kea Lani Maui*, 4100 Wailea Alanui Drive, Wailea ☎ 808/875-2225. Very good, if pricey, Italian bakery/deli/trattoria, downstairs and to the left of the *Kea Lani*'s imposing lobby. The deli section sells pastries and espressos all day, plus massive sandwiches like a hummus wrap for $8.50 or a pesto sandwich for $9, while the trattoria serves more formal meals on an open-air terrace, with lunchtime sandwiches or pasta specials for $14–20, and dinners ranging from $17–19 pizzas up to a veal *saltimbocca* $31 or a $36 *cioppino* seafood stew. Daily 6.30am–10pm.

Hakone *Maui Prince*, 5400 Makena Alanui Drive, Makena ☎ 808/875-5888. Classic dinner-only Japanese restaurant, upstairs in the *Prince*, with tastefully minimal decor – but for the odd framed vintage aloha shirt – and no views. On Saturdays, there's a $45 dinner buffet; otherwise the seven-course Rakuen Kaiseki set menu costs $60, but you can also order sushi or sashimi dinners for around $40, smaller set menus for more like $35, or simply individual dishes from the sushi bar. Tues–Sat 6–9pm.

Joe's 131 Wailea Iki Place, Wailea ☎ 808/875-7767. One of Maui's most fashionable restaurants, owned by the same top-notch team as the *Hali'imaile General Store* (see p.341). Neither the tennis-club setting nor the decor – dull rock-music memorabilia – will grab you, but the food is heavenly, a fusion of cutting-edge Pacific Rim cuisine with down-home local favorites. Appetizers ($8–20) include *ahi* tartare with wasabi aioli, while entrees ($20 and up) range from meatloaf with garlic mashed potatoes to a smoky, applewood-grilled salmon. Daily 5.30–9pm.

Prince Court *Maui Prince*, 5400 Makena Alanui Drive, Makena ☎ 808/875-5888. Relatively formal, somewhat solemn resort restaurant. Appetizers include oysters on the half-shell ($14), and a tower of Hawaiian tuna and *foie gras* ($14). Apart from fish dishes like the tempura *moi* (threadfish) for $28, the entrees tend to be rather predictable,

though caramelized Maui onions lift options like roast lamb or venison. Sunday morning sees a buffet brunch for $43, and Friday night a prime rib and seafood buffet, also costing $43. Mon–Sat 6–9pm, Sun 9am–1pm & 6–9pm.

SeaWatch 100 Wailea Golf Club Drive, Wailea ☎ 808/875-8080. Daily 8am–3pm & 5.30–9pm. Grand terrace restaurant in the clubhouse of the Wailea Golf Club, a few hundred yards uphill from the highway, open daily for all meals and enjoying stupendous ocean views during daylight hours. Lunch is the best time to come, with well-priced specials like the $9 *kālua* pork sandwich; at night the cuisine is Pacific Rim, with $8–15 appetizers such as five-spice crab cakes, and $26–36 entrees including fish, grilled chicken, and lamb with onion torte.

Spago *Four Seasons*, 3900 Wailea Alanui Drive, Wailea ☎ 808/879-2999. Celebrity chef Wolfgang Puck spreads himself a little thin these days, but as befits the stunning ocean-view location in this grandest of resorts, the buzzy *Spago* pulls out all the stops. It serves dinner only, with an assured and irresistible Pacific-Rim menu that includes a great scallop *ceviche* with Kula onions ($23), delicious *ahi poke* (spicy cubes of raw tuna) served in sesame-miso cones ($18), and entrees like whole steamed *hapu'upu'u* (sea bass) for $40, or grilled lamb chops with chili-mint vinaigrette for $49. Daily 5.30–9.30pm.

Tommy Bahama's Tropical Café The Shops at Wailea, 3750 Wailea Alanui Drive, Wailea ☎ 808/875-9983. Pricey but pretty good bar and restaurant adjoining the upscale clothes store of the same name. At lunch, you can tuck into huge fishy sandwiches or pasta specials for $15–20 – try the tasty Habana Cubana barbecue pork sandwich – while enjoying sweeping (if distant) ocean views from the terrace. The dinner entrees are more overtly Caribbean, including a Port au Prince spiced pork chop ($35) and Trinidad tuna with cilantro and lemongrass ($40). Sun–Thurs 11am–11pm, Fri & Sat 11am–midnight.

Beyond Mākena

Once past the *Maui Prince*, you're finally clear of South Maui's resorts and can enjoy some of the island's finest beaches and most unspoiled scenery. The road gives out altogether before long, but it's possible to hike on beyond the end.

Oneloa Beach - "Big Beach"

Maui's most spectacular sweep of golden sand stretches for over half a mile south of the landmark cinder cone of Pu'u 'Ōla'i, just south of Mākena. There's not a

△ Big Beach

building in sight at **Oneloa Beach** (literally "long sand," and widely known as **Big Beach**), just perfect sands and mighty surf, backed by a dry forest of *kiawe* and cacti. During the 1970s, it was home to a short-lived hippy commune; nowadays it's officially **Mākena State Park**, with two paved access roads.

The very first turn off the main road south of Mākena, though labeled "Mākena State Park," is a dirt track that leads via an orange gate to a scrubby gray-sand beach. Instead, keep going on the main road until you reach the paved turnoff to Oneloa, three quarters of a mile beyond the *Maui Prince*. A footpath from the parking lot here leads through the trees to a small cluster of portable toilets and picnic tables, and then emerges at the north end of Big Beach. While the clear blue ocean across this broad expanse of deep, coarse sand is irresistible, Big Beach is actually extremely **dangerous** because it faces straight out to sea and lacks a reef to protect it. Huge waves crash right onto the shoreline, and fearsome rip currents tear along the coast just a few feet out. Although it's been the scene of many drownings, all lifeguards were controversially withdrawn several years ago, to cut costs.

Despite its perils, Big Beach remains busy most of the time with enthusiastic swimmers, boogie-boarders, and even snorkelers. Non-locals tend to congregate at its northern end, where in calmer periods the red-brown cliffs provide enough shelter to create a little turquoise "lagoon" of relatively placid water. Walk right to the end of the beach here, and as if by magic a natural cleft in the cliff reveals the "stairway" across the rocks that enables you to reach the much smaller, and significantly safer, **Little Beach**. Shielded once again by the rocky headland, and shaded by the adjacent trees, this is perhaps the most idyllic swimming spot on Maui, with views of Molokini and Lanai. The winter surf can still get pretty high, however, so it helps if you're into bodysurfing. One relic of the hippy days is that it's still widely known as an (illegal) **nudist** beach; even if you don't go naked yourself, some of your fellow beachgoers certainly will. As a result, they can be extremely sensitive to intruders carrying, let alone using, cameras.

Pu'u 'Ōla'i

Halfway along the easy trail between Big and Little beaches, where the ground levels off at the top of the first cliff, another trail doubles back to climb **Pu'u 'Ōla'i** itself. This crumbling cinder cone was produced by one of Maui's very last volcanic eruptions, perhaps two centuries ago, and is barely held together by scrubby grass and thorns. The ascent is so steep that strongly worded signs warn against making the attempt. If you do try, you may find you have to advance on all fours. Scrambling over the raw red – and very sharp – cinders is extremely painful in anything other than proper hiking boots.

The summit of Pu'u 'Ōla'i – which is not the peak you see at the start of the climb – is a wonderful vantage point for watching humpback whales in winter. It commands views all the way up the flat coast to Wailea and Kīhei, down the full length of Big Beach, inland to the green uplands of Haleakalā, across the ocean to the low ridge of Molokini – circled by cruise boats from dawn onwards – and beyond to glowing red Kahoolawe, the West Maui Mountains, and Lanai.

La Pérouse Bay

Mākena Road continues for another three miles south from Big Beach, as a narrow, undulating road that often narrows to a single lane. During the initial stretch, it runs right beside the ocean, clinging to the coastline of **'Āhihi Bay** around several small coves lined by very rough, jagged *'a'ā* lava, before setting out across a wide, desolate field of yet more chunky lava. **La Pérouse Bay** lies beyond.

In theory, this southernmost point of Maui is the driest part of the island, meaning it receives heavy traffic on those days when it seems to be raining everywhere else. That can make reaching it a long, slow process, with no guarantee that it won't be raining here too. Most visitors either park or turn around at what looks like the end of the road, where a cairn bearing a bronze plaque commemorates the voyages of the French Admiral Jean-François Galaup, Comte de la Pérouse. In fact, however, you can turn right at the cairn and continue for another couple of hundred yards to the shoreline, where there's much more parking space.

By spending three hours ashore here on May 30, 1786, la Pérouse became the **first foreigner** to set foot on Maui. He was under orders to claim the island for the King of France but, unusually for a European, considered that he had no right to do so. As he put it, "the customs of Europeans on such occasions are completely ridiculous." His ships, the *Astrolabe* and the *Boussole,* simply sailed away, and were lost with all hands in the Solomon Islands two years later.

La Pérouse encountered a handful of coastal villages in this area. Its inhabitants knew it as *Keone'ō'io,* or "bonefish beach," and still told of how chief Kalani'opu'u of the Big Island had landed a fleet of canoes here during an attempted invasion of Maui a few years earlier. However, the villages were largely destroyed just four years after la Pérouse's visit by the last known eruption of Haleakalā. A river of lava two miles wide flowed into the sea at the center of what had been one long bay, to create the two separate bays seen today. Look inland from here to see several russet cinder cones that are relics of the eruptions.

The waters around the headland at the east end of La Pérouse Bay are set aside as the **'Āhihi-Kīna'u Natural Area Reserve**, notable for its large numbers of dolphins. All fishing is forbidden; **snorkeling** is allowed, but it's easier to enter the water in the inlets around La Pérouse Bay itself than to go in off the sharp rocks of the headland. The very best snorkeling areas can only be reached on foot, by following along a trail that follows the shoreline around to the right when you reach the end of the road, to a succession of successively clearer little coves. **Scuba divers** too enter the water straight from the shore, most usually from 'Āhihi Bay. In addition, the **kayak** operators listed on p.257 run excursions here. The trail from the road meanders alternately across the sands and among the scrubby *kiawe* trees to follow the whole curve of the bay. The lichen-covered walls of ancient dwellings can often be glimpsed in the undergrowth.

Kanaio Beach

At the far end of La Pérouse Bay, you come to another field of crumbled, reddish-brown lava. A separate trail – not the obvious coastal path, which soon peters out, but one further inland – heads onwards from here. While it's of some historic interest, tracing the route of the King's Highway footpath that once ringed the entire island is extremely rugged, hot, and exposed. As archeologists and environmentalists alike are keen to minimize the impact of visitation on this area, it's probably best not to bother. If you do decide to keep going, little-visited **Kanaio Beach**, a pretty cove of turquoise water two miles along, is as far as it makes any sense to go, and even that's not a hike to undertake lightly.

Upcountry Maui

The lower western slopes of Haleakalā, which enjoy a deliciously temperate climate a couple of thousand feet above the isthmus, are known as **Upcountry Maui**. Most visitors simply race through on their way up the mountain, but the upcountry is among the most attractive regions in the state. A narrow strip that stretches for at most twenty miles, it varies from the wet, lush orchards and

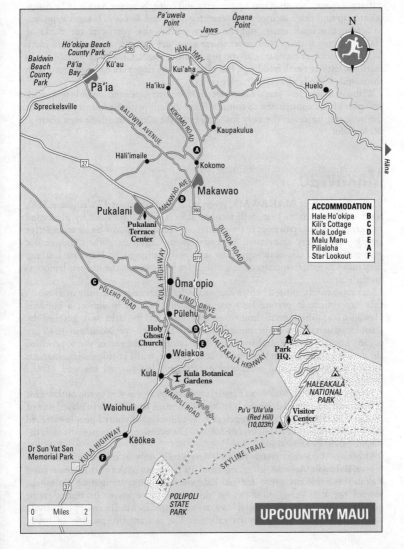

ACCOMMODATION	
Hale Ho'okipa	B
Kili's Cottage	C
Kula Lodge	D
Malu Manu	E
Pilialoha	A
Star Lookout	F

rainforests around **Makawao** in the north to the parched cattle country of the venerable **'Ulupalakua Ranch** twenty miles to the south. It holds few significant towns and even fewer tourist attractions, but the whole region is laced with quiet rural lanes that make for relaxing explorations. Although commuter traffic up and down Haleakalā Highway attests to its status as one of the most popular residential districts on the island, accommodation for visitors is limited to a handful of pretty, small-scale **B&Bs**.

At this altitude, the pineapple and sugar plantations of the isthmus give way to smaller private farms. In the past these grew the white potatoes that first lured the whaling fleet to Maui, as well as coffee, cotton, and Maui onions, but the most conspicuous crop now is flowering plants, especially dazzling **protea blossoms**.

If you expect a nonstop riot of greenery and color, however, you may be disappointed to find that much of the upcountry is dry and desolate. It takes irrigation to render this land fertile, and the many gulches that corrugate the flanks of Haleakalā only manage to support sparse grass, dry stunted trees, and even cacti. That becomes ever more true as you head further south. Clumps of high old trees mark the sites of ranch buildings, but otherwise the slopes are bare, scattered with the rounded knolls of ancient cinder cones.

Within the next few years, a new stretch of highway, or even a whole new road, will possibly be constructed to connect Kīhei directly with Upcountry Maui. For the moment, however, the only route up from the island's south or west coasts is via Kahului.

Makawao

The small town of **MAKAWAO**, seven miles up from coastal Pā'ia (see p.356), represents Maui at its best. Still recognizable as the village built by plantation workers and *paniolo* cowboys in the nineteenth century, it's now home to an active artistic community dominated by exiles from California. When they're not giving each other classes in yoga, feng shui, belly dancing, and Hawaiian healing, they make its galleries, crafts stores, and coffee bars some of the liveliest hangouts on the island.

Makawao barely existed before Kamehameha III chose it as the site of Hawaii's first experiment in private land ownership in 1845, when almost a hundred Hawaiians acquired small homesites, but most of the area was grabbed by outsiders when they were permitted to buy land by the Great Mahele of 1848 (see p.536). Local timber-yards, harvesting the rainforest to the east of town, provided the dark *koa* wood used in Honolulu's 'Iolani Palace, while Portuguese immigrants arrived to work on the neighboring cattle ranches toward the end of the nineteenth century.

The moment when Makawao's lawless cowboy past gave way to the outlaw chic of today can be pinned down to July 30, 1970, when **Jimi Hendrix** played one of his last concerts, barely a month before he died, to eight hundred people gathered in a field above Seabury Hall private school. The occasion was immortalized in the turgid movie *Rainbow Bridge*.

Although Makawao extends for well over a mile, only its central intersection – where **Baldwin Avenue**, climbing from Pā'ia, meets **Makawao Avenue** from Pukalani – holds any great interest. Baldwin here points straight up Haleakalā, toward the lush green meadows on the slopes above town. Its timber-frame buildings, painted in fading pastel hues, are connected by a rudimentary boardwalk and hold half a dozen quirky art galleries. The real artistic epicenter of town, however, is the Hui No'eau Visual Arts Center, a country estate a mile south at 2841 Baldwin Ave (Mon–Sat 10am–4pm; ☎808/572-6560, ⓦwww.huinoeau .com). As well as offering classes in practical arts and crafts, it houses its own small store and a gallery for temporary exhibitions.

Makawao's *paniolo* days are commemorated on July 4 each year by the Makawao Rodeo, which includes a parade through town as well as competitive events at the Oskie Rice Arena.

Restaurants

There's very little **accommodation** in or near Makawao; see the accommodation listings for the Upcountry as a whole, on p.342, for B&Bs within a few minutes' drive. The town does, however, boast an excellent selection of friendly **restaurants**, good for inexpensive lunch stops, and a lively night-time scene focused on *Casanova's*. For supplies, head for *Down to Earth Natural Foods* at 1169 Makawao Ave, a wholefood store with a deli counter.

Café del Sol 3620 Baldwin Ave ☎ 808/572-4877. Off-street café in the Courtyard Mall, serving espressos, pastries, salads, sandwiches, and blue plate specials, all for under $10, at shaded garden tables. Mon–Sat 8am–5pm, Sun 8am–3pm.

Casanova's 1188 Makawao Ave ☎808/572-0220, ⓦwww.casanovamaui.com. The 1970s Art Nouveau–style lettering and faded exterior of this single-story wooden building in the heart of Makawao belies its status as one of Maui's hottest nightspots. There's a dance floor and bar just inside the door, a romantic Italian restaurant stretches further back, and the breakfast deli/espresso bar is alongside. Lunchtime salads, pastas, and sandwiches range $6–16, while in the evening, wood-fired pizzas cost $12–20, pasta entrees are $12–18, and specials are $22–28. Portions are huge. The $5 cover charge on dance nights (unless you dine) can rise to $10 when there's live music (typically Fri and Sat). Mon & Tues 5.30–12.30am, Wed–Sun 5.30am–1am.

Hali'imaile General Store 900 Hali'imaile Rd ☎808/572-2666. One of Maui's very best restaurants, serving gourmet Hawaiian food in a large, bright and smart former store in the village of Hali'imaile, which is two miles down Baldwin Avenue from Makawao and then a mile west towards Haleakalā Highway. Appetizers (up to $20)

include an Asian pear and duck taco, and fresh island fish cakes; entrees, like Szechuan barbecued salmon or rack of lamb Hunan style, can cost over $30; and there's also a raw bar. Lunch is served on weekdays only. Mon–Fri 11am–2.30pm & 5.30–9.30pm, Sat & Sun 5.30–9.30pm.

Kitada's Saimin 3617 Baldwin Ave ☎808/572-7241. Old-fashioned diner, only open from dawn until lunchtime, where $5 buys a huge bowl of *saimin*. Burgers, sandwiches, and plate lunches cost only a bit more. Mon–Sat 6am–1.30pm.

Makawao Sushi & Deli 3647 Baldwin Ave ☎808/573-9044. This smart little place on the main drag started out as a coffee bar, and still serves panini, espressos, and smoothies, but these days it's better known for its good, inexpensive sushi, with individual rolls from $3, eight-piece specialty rolls at $15–18, and sashimi plates from $17. Good-value lunches include a chef's bento box for $8. Mon–Thurs 11.30am–3pm & 5–9pm, Fri & Sat 11.30am–3pm & 5–10pm, Sun 3.30–9pm.

Polli's 1202 Makawao Ave ☎808/572-7808. Busy, good-value Mexican restaurant at Makawao's central crossroads, open for all meals. All the usual menu items are on offer, from chimichangas to fajitas (under $10), and they also do barbecue chicken and ribs on Mondays. Mon–Sat 7am–10pm, Sun 8am–10pm.

Pukalani

Now that a new bypass carries traffic on the busy Haleakalā Highway (Hwy-37) around, instead of through, **PUKALANI**, seven miles up from Kahului, there's no reason for tourists ever to see the town at all. This shapeless sprawl is home to six thousand people, but has no appreciable downtown area. The run-down Pukalani Terrace Center mall holds the closest gas station to the summit of Haleakalā, as well as a big Foodland supermarket, a *Subway* sandwich shop, and several budget diners.

△ Cattle grazing in Upcountry Maui

Kula and the heart of the Upcountry

Immediately beyond Pukalani, Hwy-37 changes its name to **Kula Highway**, while **Haleakalā Highway**, now Hwy-377, branches off up the mountain. It meets the route to the summit, **Haleakalā Crater Road**, after six miles, and then, as **Kekaulike Highway**, swings back to rejoin Kula Highway.

This general region is known as **Kula**. None of the four separate communities – from north to south, **Ōmaʻopio**, **Pūlehu**, **Waiakoa**, and **Kula** itself – amounts to very much, but the views they afford are superb. Far below, the curve of the ocean bites into either side of the flat, green isthmus, while on the horizon, clouds squat on the West Maui Mountains. In the light of the morning sun, you can make out the condo buildings lining the Kīhei coast, but by afternoon, apart from the odd glint from a car, the long gentle slopes seem predominantly rural.

Accommodation

Driving across the Kula district, you probably won't notice any **accommodation** apart from the *Kula Lodge*, but tucked away on the backroads are a wide assortment of lovely little B&Bs. All require advance reservations, and some can only be booked through specialist B&B agencies.

Hale Hoʻokipa 32 Pakani Place, Makawao ☏808/572-6698 ⓦwww.maui-bed-and -breakfast.com. Tucked away on a quiet residential street, this lovely timber-built plantation-style home abounds in tasteful architectural detail. Its three well furnished, en-suite B&B rooms share a common living room, where good breakfasts are served in a friendly atmosphere. ❹–❺
Kiliʻs Cottage Kula; reserve through Hawaii's Best B&B ☏808/263-3100 or 1-800/262-9912, ⓦwww.bestbnb.com. A real bargain: a comfortable three-bedroom, two-bathroom house, set in

beautiful upland gardens below Pūlehu, equipped with TV, VCR, and full kitchen, and rented for less than the price of most Maui hotel rooms. Three-night minimum stay. ❹
Kula Lodge RR1 ☏808/878-1535 or 1-800/233-1535, ⓦwww.kulalodge.com. Upmarket board and lodging in a Hawaiian approximation of an Alpine inn, *makai* of Haleakalā Highway, just before the Haleakalā Crater Road turnoff. Accommodation is in five chalets, four of which can sleep family parties: all are comfortably furnished, though they don't have phones or TV. ❹–❺

Malu Manu 446 Cooke Rd ☎ 808/878-6111 or
1-888/878-6161, ⓦ www.maui.net/~alive/. Two
short-term rentals in seven acres of gardens,
enjoying magnificent views, 4000 feet up the flanks
of Haleakalā. Besides a fully furnished two-bedroom
house, there's a smaller "writer's retreat" cabin;
both are furnished with antiques and share use of
an outdoor hot tub. Three-night minimum stay. ❺

Star Lookout 622 Thompson Rd, Kula
☎ 808/878-6730, reservations on
☎ 907/346-8028, ⓦ www.starlookout.com.
Gorgeous rental cottage perched high on the green
Upcountry slopes just above Kula, offering comfortable accommodation for four for $200 per night.
There's a full kitchen, and a long *lānai*, with
stupendous views. Two-night minimum stay. ❻

Holy Ghost Church

Five miles south of the point where it branches away from the route up to
Haleakalā, the lower Upcountry road, the Kula Highway, passes just below the
white octagonal **Holy Ghost Church**. Portuguese Catholics came to Maui from
1878 onwards, and by 1894 were prosperous enough to construct their own
church, shipping the hand-carved high-relief gilt altar from Austria, and capping
the structure with a gleaming silver-roofed belfry. The interior is very light,
with pink-painted walls, and features the Stations of the Cross labeled in Portuguese. Not surprisingly, this was the only octagonal structure built in nineteenth-
century Hawaii; it's thought to be eight-sided either because the crown of the
Portuguese Queen Isabella was octagonal, or because the German parish priest
came from near Aachen, the site of a similar octagonal chapel built by
Charlemagne.

Kula Botanical Garden

A couple of miles beyond the foot of Haleakalā Crater Road, on Kekaulike
Highway, the **Kula Botanical Garden** offers self-guided tours through large and
colorful landscaped gardens (daily 9am–4pm; adults $5, kids 6–12 $1). Among its
broad range of plants are proteas, hydrangeas, lurid yellow and red cannas, and
spectacular purple and yellow birds of paradise from South Africa. Many of its
species betray their Pacific origins by bearing the Latin name *banksia*, in honor of
Sir Joseph Banks, the pioneering botanist who sailed with Captain Cook; perhaps
the finest is the red and white "Raspberry Frost" from Australia.

Polipoli State Park

Although Maui residents rave about thickly wooded **Polipoli State Park**, set high
above the Upcountry, visitors from beyond Hawaii may feel that as an "ordinary"
temperate forest it has little they can't see at home. Unfortunately, thanks to a
major forest fire in January 2007, Polipoli Park was **closed** at the time this book
went to press. The following account is included in the hope that it will once more
be accessible by the time you read this, but check locally before you visit.

The park stands at the top of the ten-mile Waipoli Road – *not* nearby Polipoli
Road, oddly enough – a fun drive that climbs away from Kekaulike Highway just
south of the Kula Botanical Garden. The first six miles, in which you do all the
climbing, are paved, passing through tough, springy ranchland where cattle graze
on the open range. This is Maui's best launching spot for **hang gliders**, which you
may see sharing the winds with circling Hawaiian owls (unique in that they fly by
day, rather than night).

It shouldn't be too difficult to coax a rental car along the rough, but level, dirt
road that meanders along the hillside above the ranch. After three miles, the road
surface improves; drop right at the fork half a mile further along, and after another
half a mile you'll come to Polipoli's **campground** in a grassy clearing, which offers
neither showers nor drinking water. Tent camping here ($5), and overnight stays

in the simple cabin nearby ($45 for up to four people; closed Tues), can be arranged through the state parks office in Wailuku (see p.285).

The entire Polipoli area was planted with Californian redwood trees by the Civilian Conservation Corps during the 1930s. The **Redwood Trail**, which leads down from a hundred yards before the campground, burrows through such thick forest that the persistent rain can barely penetrate it, and very little light does either. The forest floor is too gloomy even to support a light scattering of moss, and many of the tightly packed trees are dead. It comes as a huge relief when the trail emerges from the bottom-most strip of eucalyptus after 1.5 miles to show expansive views across the ranchlands.

Various other trails crisscross throughout Polipoli, including some to lava caves hidden in the woods, but the only one likely to interest visitors from outside Hawaii is the **Skyline Trail**. This epic thirteen-mile trek follows the southwest rift zone of Haleakalā right the way up to Science City, at the summit (see p.351); it too was closed following the 2007 fire, so check with the park service if you're hoping to make the hike. It climbs a dirt track that heads off to the left two miles along the left fork from the junction 9.5 miles up Waipoli Road, described above. Unless you arrange a pickup at the far end, it's too far for a day-hike, and the higher you get the more exposed to the biting winds you'll be. Alternatively, you can take a **mountain bike** along the trail.

Kula region restaurants

There are very few **eating options** in the Kula region. The wood-furnished dining room of *Kula Lodge* (see p.342; ☏808/878-1535) is open daily from 6.30am until around 9pm; it's busiest at the start of the day, when customers are already on their way back *down* Haleakalā after watching the sunrise. The food is American, with a definite Pacific Rim tinge; the lunch menu consists of sandwiches and a few selections from the dinner menu ($11–18), while evening offerings include a *miso* oysters Rockefeller appetizer ($16), and lamb *osso buco* or *lilikoi* prawns (upwards of $30). Protea blossoms adorn the tables, and the views are immense. A couple of hundred yards higher up, *mauka* of the highway, *Kula Sandalwoods* (☏808/878-3523) offers a similar menu for breakfast and lunch only. Hidden away on Lower Kula Rd, just above the Holy Ghost Church, *Café 808* (daily 6am–8pm; ☏808/878-6874), with just a few plastic tables and chairs scattered across its large bare floor, feels much like a village hall. Upcountry residents gather here all through the day; breakfast pancakes run $5, while later on local favorites – "island grinds" like loco moco, *saimin*, teriyaki beef, or chicken katsu – cost well under $10.

For smaller **snacks**, or an espresso fix, call in at *Grandma's Coffee Store* in Kēōkea (daily 7am–5pm; ☏808/878-2140). You're unlikely to see "Grandma," but there's plenty of her fresh Maui-grown coffee, plus avocado sandwiches, salads, macnut pesto, taro burgers, and killer home-made cookies or desserts such as blueberry cobbler.

Kēōkea

A couple of miles south of the intersection of the Kekaulike and Kula highways, the village of **KĒŌKEA** consists of a small cluster of roadside stores, together with green and white **St John's Episcopal Church**. All were built at the end of the nineteenth century to serve the local Chinese community, which also supported three Chinese-language schools and, it's said, a number of opium dens.

Alongside *Grandma's Coffee Store* (see opposite), one room of Henry Fong's general store houses the appealing little **Kēōkea Gallery** (Tues–Sat 9am–5pm, Sun 9am–3pm), where you'll find arts and crafts displayed.

The wife and children of Sun Yat Sen, the first president of China, stayed on his brother's ranch here during 1911 and 1912, while Sun was away fomenting revolution. Hence the statue of Sun, guarded by Chinese dragons, that looks out over Wailea and Kahoolawe from the somewhat neglected **Dr Sun Yat Sen Memorial Park**, which lies at the intersection of Hwy-37 and Kealakapu Road, less than two miles beyond Kēōkea. Thanks to its healthy elevation, Kēōkea was also the site of **Kula Sanatorium**, which opened in 1910 to treat tuberculosis sufferers, and was soon joined by a "Preventorium" that set out to reduce the incidence of the disease.

'Ulupalakua Ranch

Six miles on from Keokea, the six tin-roofed, single-story wooden buildings of the **'Ulupalakua Ranch** headquarters nestle into a shady bend in the road. Comings and goings are overseen by the three carved wooden cowboys stationed permanently on the porch of the 'Ulupalakua Ranch Store (daily 9am–4.30pm); inside, you can buy sodas and snacks, *paniolo* hats, T-shirts, and limited basic supplies.

'Ulupalakua Ranch started out in the middle of the nineteenth century as **Rose Ranch**, owned by an ex-whaling captain, **James McKee**. Originally its main business was sugar, but the focus soon shifted to cattle, and it employed expert *paniolo* cowboys such as Ike Purdy, a former world rodeo champion. In his huge mansion, McKee played host to Robert Louis Stevenson and King David Kalākaua among others, who took advantage of Hawaii's first ever swimming pool. Spotting ships arriving at Mākena Landing (see p.334), McKee would fire a cannon to signal that he was sending a carriage down to meet his guests. The mansion burned down during the 1970s, but the ranch itself is still going, raising elk and sheep as well as cattle.

Tedeschi Winery

Around the corner beyond 'Ulupalakua Ranch, one of the ranch's co-owners has established the **Tedeschi Winery** as a successful sideline on the site of James McKee's original Rose Ranch. It uses two annual grape harvests from a small vineyard in a fold below the highway, a mile to the north, to produce 30,000 cases a year of white, red, and rosé wines, as well as *Maui Brut* champagne and a "sparkling pineapple" wine. They're on sale in the new **King's Cottage**, which also houses an entertaining little museum of ranch and cowboy history and serves as the assembly point for fifteen-minute guided **tours** (store and museum daily 9am–5pm, free tours daily 10.30am, 1.30pm & 3pm; ☎808/878-6058, ⓦ www.mauiwine.com). The converted and imitation ranch buildings used for processing and bottling are less than enthralling, but you do at least get to see some amazing trees, including a pine drowning in multicolored creeping bougainvillea, and a giant camphor.

Pi'ilani Highway

South of 'Ulupalakua, Kula Highway confusingly becomes the **Pi'ilani Highway**, despite having no connection with the parallel road of the same name that runs through Wailea and Mākena down below. For all the strictures of the rental companies – see p.283 – it takes appalling weather to render it unsafe, and in principle, for most of the year, it's possible to drive all the way along the south coast to Hāna, 37 miles away. However, as a result of the October 2006 earthquake that primarily affected the Big Island, the road was **closed** at the time this book went to press. If it remains closed, the fifty-mile round-trip to the point where you'd have to turn back, roughly 26 miles east of 'Ulupalakua, is not worth making. Just in case it has reopened by the time you read this, a detailed description of the route, coming in the opposite direction, begins on p.373.

Haleakalā

Although the briefest glance at a map shows the extent to which mighty **Haleakalā** dominates Maui, it's hard to appreciate its full majesty until you climb right to the top. Hawaiian-style shield volcanoes (see p.253) are not as dramatic as the classic cones of popular imagination, and with its summit often obscured by clouds, Haleakalā can seem no more than a gentle incline rising a short distance above the rest of Maui.

By ascending more than ten thousand feet above sea level in just 38 miles from Kahului, **Haleakalā Highway** is said to climb higher, faster than any road on earth. En route, it crosses a bewildering succession of terrains, equivalent to a drive from Mexico to Alaska. Beyond the exclusive homes and white clapboard churches of Upcountry Maui, it leads through purple-blossoming jacaranda, firs, and eucalyptus to reach open ranching land, and then sweeps in huge curves to the volcanic desert and the awe-inspiring **Haleakalā Crater** itself. Almost eight miles across, this eerie wasteland would comfortably hold Manhattan.

To the ancient Hawaiians, Haleakalā was "the House of the Sun." They told of how at one time the sun crossed the sky much faster than it does today, until the demi-god Maui captured it here in a web of ropes, and only released it on the condition that it travel slowly enough to give his mother time to dry her *tapa* (bark-cloth). Pre-contact Hawaiians trekked to the summit in search of basalt for adzes, to hunt birds, to use in religious ceremonies and to bury their dead; traces have even been found of a paved trail that crossed the crater and led down through the Kaupō Gap (see p.356).

The higher reaches of the mountain joined with the volcanoes of the Big Island to form Hawaii Volcanoes National Park in 1921, and became the independent **Haleakalā National Park** in 1961. It now ranks as the tenth most visited national park in the US, with around a million people a year reaching the summit. The most popular time to come is for sunrise – described by Mark Twain as "the sublimest spectacle I ever witnessed" – but don't let that give you the impression that it's not worth coming later in the day. The views of the crater itself are at their best in mid-afternoon, when the sun lights up its staggering array of russet cinder cones, ashen slopes, pockmarked craters, and craggy cliffs, but you can enjoy superb views from the roadside lookouts along the way up whatever time you arrive. It's also possible to hike into the crater, and even to spend the night there.

Officially, Haleakalā National Park also includes Kīpahulu Valley and 'Ohe'o Gulch, on Maui's southeast coast. However, no hiking trail, let alone direct road, connects those areas with Haleakalā Crater.

Haleakalā Crater Road

From all the major accommodation centers on Maui, the quickest route to the top of Haleakalā is to head for Kahului, and then follow **Haleakalā Highway** into the Upcountry (see p.339). Also known from there on as **Haleakalā Crater Road**, it continues all the way to the summit, entering the park after a twisting twelve-mile climb through the meadows, and reaching the park headquarters shortly after that. With another ten miles to go before the summit, you should allow two full hours to get to the top from Lahaina, Kāʻanapali, or Kīhei, or one and a half hours from Kahului or Wailuku. The last gas station before the summit is at Pukalani, 28 miles below; the last food and lodging is at *Kula Lodge* (see p.342), 22 miles short.

Downhill biking

For over twenty years, one of Maui's most unusual and popular tourist activities has been to take a minivan to the top of Haleakalā – especially at dawn – and then climb onto a **bike** and ride, or rather roll, back down the mountain. It's possible to make it all the way down to the ocean at Pāʻia, a 39-mile ride, without pedaling. Approaching 100,000 people make the descent each year. It can be great fun, although some tend to find it a bit pointless, as to comply with park-service regulations most operators make their groups ride together, at the pace of the slowest member. Other drawbacks include the chilly temperatures on the mountain (though all the companies supply protective gear) and the very early starts for the sunrise tours; hotel pick-ups can be as early as 2am – hardly conducive to a happy family atmosphere.

The usual activities desks, such as Tom Barefoot's (see p.285) offer discount rates on biking trips: typical rates range from around $85 for a daytime ride up to $130 to go at sunrise. Unguided trips, or shorter routes, cost about $20 less. All riders must have at least some biking experience, and be aged 12 or over.

Only four operators are currently permitted to start their trips from the crater itself. All offer fully guided group trips only, and include hotel pick-ups from West or South Maui.

Cruiser Phil's ☎808/893-2332 or 1-877/764-2453, ⊛www.cruiserphil.com. Sunrise and daytime tours, all the way to Pāʻia.

Maui Downhill ☎808/871-2155 or 1-800/535-2453, ⊛www.mauidownhill.com. Long tours, including hotel pickup and usually lunch as well, to Pāʻia or Kula.

Maui Mountain Cruisers ☎808/871-6014 or 1-800/232-6284, ⊛www.mauimountain cruisers.com. Sunrise or morning downhill rides to Pāʻia.

Mountain Riders Bike Tours ☎808/242-9739 or 1-800/706-7700, ⊛www.mountain riders.com. Sunrise and morning tours down Haleakalā, with or without guides, and ending at Pāʻia or Kula.

Though it's not always clear from their brochures, the following companies offer trips on which you only see the summit itself as part of a van tour, and you actually start cycling from the edge of the park, eleven miles below. This makes for a warmer, cheaper and potentially shorter ride, and as you don't necessarily have to be guided or accompanied, can also mean that you get to do some genuine cycling around the Upcountry.

Aloha Bike Tours ☎808/249-0911 or 1-800/749-1564, ⊛www.mauibike.com. Small-group tours, starting below the summit and ending at Tedeschi Winery rather than the sea.

Haleakalā Bike Co ☎808/575-9575 or 1-888/922-2453, ⊛www.bikemaui.com. Unguided tours; they provide the bikes and a van tour to the top, then drop you at the park entrance, from where you descend at your own pace.

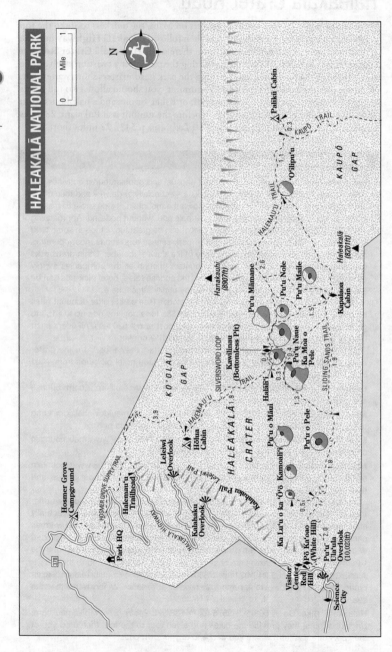

HALEAKALĀ NATIONAL PARK

N

0   1
Mile

Assuming you join the majority in attempting to drive up to Haleakalā Crater to witness the **sunrise** (around 5.50am in midsummer and 6.50am in midwinter) – and don't feel that you have to as the views can be wonderful at any time of day – you'll need to make a very early start and a long hard drive in the dark. If you do end up late for the dawn, be warned that you'll be driving straight into the dazzling sun, and watch out for the endless posses of downhill bikers coming the other way. If you're here during the 38-mile Run-to-the-Sun **foot race** up Haleakalā each spring, the record time to beat is an incredible 4hr 45min.

Hosmer Grove

Just beyond the **park entrance** – the gates never close, though there's not always a ranger on duty – a short road off to the left leads to the park's main **campground**, at **Hosmer Grove**. Set almost exactly at the mountain's tree line, this may look like a pleasant wooded copse, but in fact it marks the failure of an early-twentieth-century experiment to assess Maui's suitability for timber farming. Out of almost a hundred different tree species planted by Ralph Hosmer, only twenty survived, though that's enough to provide a nice thirty-minute **nature trail**.

By way of contrast, **Waikamoi Preserve**, adjoining Hosmer Grove, is a five-thousand-acre tract of upland rainforest that's home to a wide assortment of indigenous Hawaiian **birds**. You can only hike through it with an authorized

Backcountry camping and cabins at Haleakalā

Hosmer Grove is the only Haleakalā campground accessible by car, and the only one for which campers do not need to obtain permits. Backcountry camping, in the sense of simply pitching your tent in some remote spot, is not permitted anywhere in the park. There are, however, three rudimentary, but sound, **backcountry cabins** within Haleakalā Crater, which can only be reached on foot. All are on the grassy fringes of the crater, sheltered by the high surrounding cliffs, and are padlocked to deter casual backpackers from wandering in. Each is rented to one group only per night, and has twelve bunk beds, with no bedding, plus a kitchen, a stove for heating, and an outhouse. **Hōlua** and **Palikū** cabins offer **tent camping** in the adjacent meadows – the 25 daily permits are issued on a first-come, first-served basis at the park headquarters, between 8am and 3pm daily – but **Kapalaoa Cabin** does not. Water is normally available, but it's up to you to purify it before you drink it.

Permits to stay in the cabins are heavily oversubscribed, and limited to three days in total, with no more than two days at any one cabin. In a system that prioritizes island residents, you have to apply in writing at least three months in advance, stating the exact dates you want, to Haleakalā National Park, PO Box 369, Makawao, HI 96768 (contact ☎808/572-4400 or ⊛www.nps.gov/hale for more information). A lottery at the start of each month decides the schedule for the month ahead; at that point successful applicants are requested to pay $75 per cabin per night. To check on possible cancellations, call ☎808/572-4459 between 1pm and 3pm daily.

guide, so call ahead to see when the next of the Park Service's regular free **Waikamoi Cloud Forest Hikes** is scheduled (see p.350 for contact details).

There's **tent camping** in a soft sloping meadow surrounded by tall pines; a small open pavilion holds basic washing facilities. The fifty sites are available free on a first-come, first-served basis. No advance reservations are taken, and no permit is required, but there's a three-night maximum stay.

It's possible to walk all the way into Haleakalā Crater from Hosmer Grove; a supply trail up the mountain meets the Halemau'u Trail after 2.5 miles, just short of the crater rim.

The park headquarters

The **park headquarters** looks out across central Maui from the right of the highway, three quarters of a mile up from the park entrance (daily 8am–4pm; ☏808/572-4400 information, ☏808/871-5054 weather; ⊕www.nps.gov/hale). This is the place to enquire about the day's quota of backcountry camping places (see box, p.349) or to register if you've managed to reserve a cabin. It holds little by way of exhibits or printed information, but you can pick up a basic park brochure and buy detailed hiking maps; the best topo map of the park is published by National Geographic/Trails Illustrated.

The roadside lookouts

Beyond the park headquarters, Haleakalā Crater Road zigzags for another ten miles up the mountain, repeatedly sweeping toward the lip of the crater and then doubling back. The three closest approaches are each marked by a roadside parking lot.

The first of these, 2.5 miles up from the park headquarters, is the **Halemau'u Trailhead**. One of the park's two main hiking trails begins its long descent into the crater from here, as described on p.352, but the edge of the *pali* is almost a mile away; there's nothing to see at the parking lot.

Another 4.5 miles up the road, **Leleiwi Overlook** is set a couple of hundred yards beyond its parking lot. It offers views across the isthmus to West Maui, as well as a first glimpse into Haleakalā Crater, but you'll probably have seen enough of West Maui from the Crater Road, and better vantage points over the crater lie ahead.

It's only legal to stop at the **Kalahaku** or **"Silversword" Overlook**, a couple of miles short of the visitor center, as you drive *down* rather than up the mountain; in fact it's easy to pass by without noticing it at all. That's a shame, because this sheltered viewpoint provides perhaps the best overall prospect of Haleakalā Crater. Mauna Kea on the Big Island is often visible through the Kaupō Gap in the ridge to the right, and when the clouds clear you can also see down to the north coast of Maui. Unless you hike into the crater, this may be the only place you see any **silverswords** (see p.354); in theory, there should be a few in the small enclosure below the parking lot, across from the overlook.

Haleakalā Visitor Center

Although the highway continues beyond it, most visitors consider they've reached the top of Haleakalā when they get to the **Visitor Center**, eleven miles up from the park entrance (summer daily 6am–3pm, winter daily 6.30am–3pm; no phone). The railed open-air viewing area beside the parking lot commands great views of Haleakalā Crater. In the pre-dawn chill, however, many people prefer to admire the procession of red-brown cinder cones, marching across the moonscape far

The geology of Haleakalā

Dramatic, multicolored **Haleakalā Crater**, 10,023 feet above sea level at the summit of Haleakalā, and measuring more than seven miles long, two miles wide, and half a mile deep, is often hailed as the largest extinct volcanic crater in the world. As far as geologists are concerned, however, it's none of these things. They insist that not only is the "crater" not a crater at all – in shape, size, origin, and location it bears no relation to any summit crater Haleakalā may once have possessed – but strictly speaking it's not even volcanic, having been created by erosion rather than eruption.

Fueled by the same "hot spot" that has created all the volcanoes of Hawaii – see p.253 – Haleakalā originally thrust its way from the ocean around 800,000 years ago. In the 400,000 years that followed, it first fused with, and eventually came to dominate, the West Maui Mountains. At its highest, it may have stood 15,000 feet tall, which is higher than Mauna Kea and Mauna Loa on the Big Island today. It towered over the land mass geologists call "**Maui Nui**," or Big Maui, which also incorporated the present-day islands of Kahoolawe, Molokai, and Lanai.

The volcano then slumbered for several hundred thousand years, during which time torrential rainfall eroded away its topmost 6000 feet and sculpted vast canyons into its flanks. Two of these valleys, **Keanae** to the north and **Kaupō** to the east, cut so deeply into the mountain that they met in the middle, creating a huge central depression. When the "hot spot" beneath Haleakalā finally reawakened, a series of smaller eruptions poured another 3000 feet of lava into that cavity, and gushed out of the Ko'olau and Kaupō gaps to refill the valleys. Peppering the summit with raw red cones of cindery ash, it made it look to the untrained eye like the sort of crater you might expect to find at the top of a volcano.

Although the "hot spot" today directs most of its energy into Kīlauea volcano on the Big Island, Haleakalā is merely **dormant**. It has erupted at least ten times in the last thousand years, with the most recent volcanic activity in the area being in 1790 (see p.338). That it's been peaceful for two hundred years doesn't mean it always will be – in 1979, for example, it was thought more likely to explode than Mount St Helens.

below, through the panoramic windows of the small visitor center itself. If you're feeling more energetic, follow the short paved trail to the right instead, which leads up **Pa Ka'oao**, or White Hill, for 360° views.

The exhibits inside the visitor center are pretty minimal, though there's a good 3-D model of Haleakalā to help you get oriented. Park rangers also provide hiking tips and lead free **guided hikes**, such as the **Cinder Desert** walk, which sets off from here along the Sliding Sands Trail (see p.352) and the **Waikamoi Cloud Forest Hike** from Hosmer Grove. Call the park headquarters (☎808/572-4400) for current schedules.

Pu'u Ula'ula (Red Hill)

A few hundred yards further up the highway, a smaller parking lot at a final loop in the road stands just below **Pu'u Ula'ula**, or **Red Hill** – at 10,023 feet, the highest spot on Maui. A circular shelter at the top of a short stairway offers what feel like aerial views of Haleakalā Crater. In clear conditions – soon after dawn is the best bet – you may be able to see not only the 80 miles to Mauna Loa on the Big Island, but even the 130 miles to Oahu.

Confusingly, the peak that officially bears the name of Haleakalā is five miles east, above Kapalaoa Cabin (see p.355), and a couple of thousand feet lower.

Science City

The road beyond Puʻu Ulaʻula is closed to the public, but leads in a few more yards to the gleaming white domes of **Kolekole** or **Science City**. This multinational astronomic research facility, perched at the top of the House of the Sun, monitors the earth's distance from the moon by bouncing laser signals off a prism left there by the Apollo astronauts.

Hiking in Haleakalā Crater

The only way to get a real sense of the beauty and diversity of Haleakalā Crater is by hiking down into it. Although there are just two principal trails – the **Sliding Sands** and **Halemauʻu** trails – the terrain varies far more than you could ever tell from the crater-edge viewpoints, ranging from forbidding desert to lush mountain meadows.

The obvious problem is that, once you've descended into the crater, you'll have to climb back out again, which at an altitude of 10,000 feet is never less than grueling. That said, reasonably fit hikers should be able to manage a **day-hike** that takes them down one trail and back up the other – a minimum distance of eleven miles, which is likely to take at least seven hours. More ambitiously, you could aim to take in Kapalaoa Cabin along the way, for a total of thirteen miles and more like eight hours, but heading any further east would be unrealistic. The easier route is to go down Sliding Sands and back on Halemauʻu, though since the trailheads are several miles apart, you'll need to arrange a pickup or hitch a ride between the two. A parking lot near the Halemauʻu Trailhead (see p.354) makes the ideal spot for hitchhikers hoping to get a lift back up the mountain.

If you've arranged to stay overnight in the crater (see p.349), you could see the whole thing in two days, although most hikers spend longer. It takes a hardy and very well-prepared backpacker, however, to trek out via the **Kaupō Trail** to the south (see p.356).

Don't underestimate the effects of the **altitude**. Allow an hour or so in the summit area to acclimatize before you set off on the trails; not only will that prepare you for the effort ahead, but it will also mean that you're still close to the road if you start to feel ill. By far the most effective treatment for altitude sickness is to descend a few thousand feet. **Scuba divers** should not go up Haleakalā within 24 hours of a dive; ask your dive operator for detailed advice. You should also be prepared for the **cold**. Temperatures at the summit at dawn are likely to be around freezing, while rain clouds are liable to drift into the crater at any time of the day, and seriously chill anyone without warm, waterproof clothing.

Finally, Haleakalā is such an ecologically delicate area that it's essential to practice **minimum impact hiking**. Carry out everything you carry in, take all the water you need (reckon on six pints a person a day; unfiltered water is available at the wilderness cabins), and stick to established trails. Above all, never walk on the cinder soil surrounding a silversword plant (see box, p.354).

For details of companies that organize **horse-riding** expeditions in Haleakalā Crater, see p.283.

Route 1: The Sliding Sands Trail

From the visitor center parking lot, the **Sliding Sands Trail** briefly parallels the road to skirt White Hill. It then starts its leisurely switchback sweep into the crater, down a long scree slope of soft red ash. While the *pali* to the north of the visitor center is scattered with buttresses of rock and patches of green vegetation,

△ Sliding Sands Trail

this side is almost completely barren, the smooth crumbling hillside only inter-rupted by an occasional bush. Far ahead, mists and clouds stream into the crater through the Koʻolau Gap.

For most of the way down, a close look at the ground beneath your feet reveals that it's made of tiny fragments of rock with different colors and textures; hard-baked pink clay is interspersed with tiny brown gravel and little chunks of black basalt. It takes a while to appreciate the immensity of the crater; for the first mile, you expect to arrive at the crater floor at a group of multicolored rocks in the middle distance, but when you reach them you find a longer descent ahead.

Two miles down, the trail passes between a clump of twenty-foot-high ʻaʻā rock outcroppings. A spur trail from here leads 0.4 miles, by way of a miniature "garden" of silverswords, to the smooth lip of the **Ka Luʻu O Ka ʻŌʻō Crater**. This full round cinder cone, glinting with pink, red, yellow, and ochre highlights in the bright sun, cradles a hollow core filled with tumbled boulders. From the trail above, you can see long clinker flows extending for two miles north of it, eating away at the neighboring Kamaoliʻi Crater.

Continuing on the main trail, you wind down through a rough field of ʻaʻā lava. In season, the silverswords that almost line the path shoot up above head height. For the final stretch of the total 3.8-mile descent, the desolate crater floor spreads out broad and flat ahead of you, punctuated by heaped mounds of ash.

Route 2: The Halemauʻu Trail

The alternative route down into the crater, the switchbacking **Halemauʻu Trail**, starts at a trailhead half a dozen miles down Haleakalā Crater Road from the visitor center. Toward the end of the relatively featureless 0.75-mile descent from the parking lot to the crater rim, the main trail is joined by a side trail up from Hosmer Grove (see p.349). It then passes through a gate, to run parallel to the wire fence that marks the park boundary. After a few more minutes, the trail crosses a high, narrow ridge; provided the afternoon clouds aren't passing over it, you'll get staggering views down to the north Maui coastline, as well as south into the crater.

Only the first few switchbacks cross back and forth between the north and south sides of the high bluff. Here at the tip of the **Leleiwi Pali**, it's very obvious how

---

Silverswords

Not far from the ragged edge of the crater, we came upon what we were searching for; not, however, one or two, but thousands of silverswords, their cold, frosted silver gleam making the hill-side look like winter or moonlight. They exactly resemble the finest work in frosted silver, the curve of their globular mass of leaves is perfect, and one thinks of them rather as the base of an *épergne* for an imperial table, or as a prize at Ascot or Goodwood, than anything organic.

Isabella Bird, May 1873

Haleakalā is a treasure trove of unique plants and birds, but the most distinctive of all its species is the **silversword**. A distant relative of the sunflower, presumably descended from a lone seed that wafted across the Pacific from America, this extraordinary plant has adapted perfectly to the forbidding conditions of Haleakalā Crater.

Known by the ancient Hawaiians as the *ʻāhinahina*, or "silvery-gray," it consists of a gourd-shaped bowl of curving gray leaves, a couple of feet across, and cupped to collect what little moisture is available. Slender roots burrow in all directions just below the surface of the low-quality cinder soil; merely walking nearby can crush the roots and kill the plant.

Each silversword takes between three and twenty years to grow to full size, and then blossoms only once. Between May and June of the crucial year, a central shaft rises like a rocket from the desiccated silver leaves, reaching a height of from three to eight feet, and erupting with hundreds of reddish-purple flowers. These peak in July and August, releasing their precious cargo of seeds, and the entire plant then withers and dies.

The slopes of Haleakalā no longer glow with the sheer abundance of silverswords, thanks to depredation by wild goats from the late nineteenth century onwards. In recent years a new threat has been posed by the appearance of Argentinean ants, which prey on the Hawaiian yellow-faced bee that's responsible for pollinating the silversword. However, the park authorities have so far managed to reverse the decline, and clusters of silverswords can be seen at many places along the crater trails.

the landscape below has simply poured down through the Koʻolau Gap, from the crater toward the ocean. Soon, however, the trail narrows to drop sharply down the south side of the *pali*; it never feels too dangerous, though the drop-offs are enormous. The tiny shape of the overnight Hōlua Cabin comes into view a couple of miles ahead, a speck at the foot of the mighty cliff.

The trail eventually levels out beyond a gate at the bottom of the final switch-back, then undulates its way through a meadow filled with misshapen and overgrown spatter cones toward **Hōlua Cabin**, just under four miles from the trailhead. A slight detour is required to reach the cabin itself, where the lawns are often filled with honking *nēnē* geese (for details of camping regulations, see p.349). Beyond it, the trail climbs on to a much more rugged *aʻa* lava flow, the youngest in the crater area. Indentations in the rocky outcrops are scattered with red-berried *ʻōhelo* bushes, nurtured by the wet clouds that drift in through the Koʻolau Gap.

As you climb slowly toward the heart of Haleakalā Crater, you can branch away to the left to follow the brief **Silversword Loop**, which holds the park's greatest concentration of silversword plants.

The crater floor

At the point where the **Halemauʻu Trail** reaches the crater floor, almost six miles from its start, a bench enables weary hikers to catch their breath while contemplating the onward haul around the north side of the **Halāliʻi** cinder cone. If you continue south, and turn right after 0.3 miles, you'll come to the foot of the Sliding Sands Trail 1.3 miles after that.

Keep going to the left, however, and within a couple of hundred yards the Halemauʻu Trail follows the crest of a low ridge to make a serpentine twist between Halāliʻi and the nameless cinder cone to the north. Known as **Pele's Paint Pot**, this gorgeous stretch is the most spectacular part of Haleakalā Crater, the trail standing out as a lurid red streak of sand against the brown and yellow mounds to either side. You can tell that Halāliʻi is of relatively recent origin by the fact that its rim has not yet worn smooth; looking back you'll see the park visitor center framed far away on the crater rim.

It's possible to loop right around Halāliʻi and head back along either trail, but the Halemauʻu Trail continues east for another four miles. Immediately north of the junction where you're forced to decide, you'll see the fenced-off hole of **Kawilinau**, also known, misleadingly, as the **Bottomless Pit**; in fact, this small volcanic vent is just 65 feet deep. Spatters of bright-red rock cling to its edges, but it's not especially remarkable. Ancient Hawaiians are said to have thrown the bones of important chiefs into it, to ensure their remains would never be disturbed. Half a mile further east, you have the additional option of cutting south across the crater, between Puʻu Naue and Puʻu Nole, to meet the Sliding Sands Trail near Kapalaoa Cabin (see below).

Those hikers who choose, on the other hand, to take the **Sliding Sands Trail** down from the visitor center know they've reached the crater floor when they reach the south end of the clearly marked spur trail that connects the two main trails. Turning left toward the Halemauʻu Trail involves a fairly stiff climb across the flanks of the ruddy **Ka Moa O Pele** cinder cone; over to the right, the trian-gular mountain peak of **Hanakauhi** can be seen rising beyond Puʻu Naue.

If instead you continue east along the Sliding Sands Trail, you enter a landscape that resembles the high mountain valleys of the western United States. The trail runs at the foot of a steep *pali*, on the edge of a delightful alpine meadow carpeted with yellow flowers, including the primitive native *moa*. Two miles along, shortly after two successive turnoffs to the left – one is an official trail, one a "trail of use," but it's impossible to tell which is which, and in any case they soon join to cut across to the Halemau'u Trail – you come to **Kapalaoa Cabin**. This small, wood-frame, green-roofed cabin, on a slight mound tucked beneath the peak that's officially named Haleakalā, is the only overnight shelter in the crater that doesn't have its own campground; for details of how to make a reservation, see p.349.

East of Kapalaoa, the Sliding Sands Trail has two more miles to run before it finally merges with the Halemau'u Trail at the 'O'ilipu'u cinder cone, and the two then run together a further 1.4 miles to **Palikū Cabin**. The hike all the way here from the crater rim and back up again is too far to attempt in a single day; only press on if you've arranged to stay overnight. The last three miles along either trail involve a gentle descent through sparsely vegetated terrain that turns progressively greener as you approach Palikū. There are actually two cabins at Palikū, one for public use and one for the rangers; both are nestled beneath a sheer cliff, where an attractive, but generally dry, meadow gives way to a well-watered strip of forest.

Kaupō Trail

The very demanding, nine-mile **Kaupō Trail** heads south from Palikū Cabin, first through the Kaupō Gap to the edge of the park, and beyond that all the way down to meet the Pi'ilani Highway on Maui's remote south coast. It takes a couple of miles to escape the pervasive cindery dryness of the crater flow, but once past it you find you've crossed to the rain-drenched eastern side of the island.

As the walls of the Kaupō Gap rise to either side, the trail drops through dense forest, then, once out of the park, descends steeply through lush grazing land. Now that you're on Kaupō Ranch land, be scrupulous about staying on the correct trail; free-ranging bulls roam on the other side of many of the fences. After several hours of extravagant switchbacks, you finally reach the highway 200 yards east of the Kaupō Store (see p.373). Unless you've arranged to be picked up, your problems may just be beginning – little traffic passes this way. If Pi'ilani Highway is still closed, as it was at the time this book went to press (see p.373), the only safe way to make the hike would be to leave a vehicle of your own parked at the Kaupō Store, having driven it there via Upcountry Maui.

Some people make the entire hike from the summit to Kaupō in a single day, on the basis that doing so means that they don't have to reserve a cabin or campsite or carry heavy equipment. That's a very, very long and demanding day-hike, however, and not one you should attempt without prior experience of hiking in Haleakalā.

East Maui

Exposed to the full force of the trade winds and sculpted by rainwater flowing back down the northern slopes of Haleakalā, Maui's **northeast coast** holds the most inspiring scenery on the island. From Kahului, the **Hāna Highway** takes fifty miles to wind its way round to the time-forgotten hamlet of **Hāna** at the easternmost tip. This memorable drive forms an essential part of most Maui itineraries, but is almost always done as a day-trip. Devoid of safe beaches, and too wet to build resorts, East Maui has very little overnight accommodation, and thus remains the **least spoiled** region of the island.

Pā'ia

PĀ'IA, four miles east of Kahului on the Hāna Highway, is a friendly, laid-back town whose two distinct sections both began life serving the sugar plantations in the 1870s. **Upper Pā'ia**, concentrated around the sugar mill half a mile inland, was built on plantation land and held the camps that housed the laborers, as well as company stores and other facilities. Meanwhile, freebooting entrepreneurs set up shop in **Lower Pā'ia**, at sea level, operating stores, theaters, restaurants, and anything else that might persuade their captive clientele to part with a few pennies.

Both parts of Pā'ia declined apace with the collapse of agriculture, especially after the post-World War II drift to Kahului (see p.312). The name "Pā'ia" today refers almost exclusively to what used to be Lower Pā'ia, which has re-emerged in recent years as a center for windsurfers and beach bums. The paint-peeling wooden buildings around the bottom end of Baldwin Avenue give it a very similar feel to Makawao, at the top of the road – see p.340 – while its role as the gateway to the Hāna Highway keeps its gift stores and galleries busy with browsing tourists. Look out in particular for *Alice in Hulaland*, 19 Baldwin Ave (☎808/579-9922), which is by far the best store on Maui to buy *tiki*-themed gifts and novelties.

Narrow footpaths thread their way toward the ocean from the Hāna Highway, passing between ramshackle houses with colorful gardens, to reach a short, tree-lined, and sandy **beach**. Swimming here in Pā'ia Bay is rarely appealing, thanks to shallow, murky water and abundant seaweed, so locals head instead to the **H.A. Baldwin Beach County Park**, a mile west. Named after Harry Baldwin, son of Henry Baldwin of Alexander & Baldwin fame (see p.315), this was once the official sugar-company beach, and the chimneys of the sugar mill, which closed down in 2000, remain visible for the moment a few hundred yards off the highway, across the still-active cane fields. The beach itself is reached by a short approach road lined by a graceful curve of palm trees. Perfect bodysurfing waves crash onto its long unprotected stretch of sand, with safer swimming areas at either end.

△ Downtown Pā'ia

Jaws

Thanks to mouthwatering photo spreads in many a surfing magazine, Maui's most famous **surf site** these days is **Jaws**, a highly inaccessible spot east of Pā'ia where 70ft waves have occasionally been recorded. Surfing there has only become at all practicable since the advent of tow-in surfing, using jet skis, in the early 1990s, and Hawaii's premier surfers now flock here in winter to do battle with monsters that typically measure around 50ft. If you want to watch the action, you can reach Jaws by turning left toward the ocean five miles east of Ho'okipa, between mileposts 13 and 14 on Hwy-36, following Hanaha Road until your vehicle can take no more, which will probably be soon in an ordinary rental, and then hiking oceanwards between the pineapple fields.

Ho'okipa Beach County Park

The best **windsurfing** site in Maui, if not the world, is **Ho'okipa Beach County Park**, just below the highway two miles east of Pā'ia. Thanks to a submerged rocky ledge that starts just a few feet out, the waves here are stupendous, and so are the skills required to survive in them – this is no place for beginners. The peak season for windsurfing is summer, when the trade winds are at their most consistent. By longstanding arrangement, sailboarders can only take to the water after 11am each day. In the early morning, and on those rare winter days when the wind dies down, expert **surfers** flock to Ho'okipa to ride the break known as "Pavilions" near the headland to the east.

As a beach, Ho'okipa is not hugely attractive. There's little shade for most of its length, apart from a nice big grove of trees at the western end. Picnic shelters, showers, and restrooms are ranged along a platform of lava boulders raised above the small shelf of sand. In summer, the surf can be low enough for swimming, but you still have to negotiate the seaweed-covered ledge to reach deep enough water.

Ho'okipa is so busy that you can only approach it along a one-way loop road, which starts beyond its far eastern end; the auxiliary parking lot on the headland here is a great place from which to watch or photograph the surf action.

Accommodation in the Pā'ia area

There's very little **accommodation** in Pā'ia itself. Windsurfers on a tight budget tend to stay at the *Banana Bungalow* in Wailuku (see p.318), while those limited to around $75 per night head for Kahului or a cheap Kihei condo. If you can pay more, try one of the plush **B&Bs** scattered along country lanes in and around nearby villages such as **Kū'au** and **Ha'ikū**. Long-term visitors should be able to find a room through the **bulletin boards** outside *Mana Foods Deli* on Baldwin Avenue, which advertise rates of around $250 per week, or from $700 to $850 per month.

Both the county parks near Pā'ia that used to offer **camping** – **Baldwin Beach County Park** and **Rainbow Park**, up the road toward Hali'imaile – no longer do so.

Aloha Maui Cottages PO Box 790210, Pā'ia
☎808/572-0298, ⓦwww.alohamauicottages.com.
Very rural B&B, not far off Hwy-360 and thirteen miles east of Pā'ia, consisting of four simple but attractive and comfortable cabins. The cheapest, which share a bathroom, are a bargain for budget travelers. The helpful owner can lend you a bike, but you'll need a car to get here. Three-night minimum. ❸–❹

The Inn at Mama's Fish House 799 Poho Place, Pā'ia ☎808/579-9764 or 1-800/860-4852, ⓦwww.mamasfishhouse.com. Six fully equipped, tropically styled rental apartments right beside Kū'au Beach, and alongside a popular restaurant. Three have two bedrooms and look out over the ocean, the others have one – but can still hold four guests – and are set slightly back in lush gardens. ⑥

Pilialoha 2512 Kaupakalua Rd, Ha'ikū ☎808/572-1440, ⓦwww.pilialoha.com. Small cottage in the gardens of a private home above Ha'ikū, with kitchen, bathroom, and space enough to sleep four comfortably. Three-night minimum stay. ④

Pā'ia restaurants

Pā'ia may fall down on lodging, but as far as **restaurants** are concerned it comes up trumps. Though fresh fish is the local specialty, there's something for all tastes, for once even including vegetarians.

Anthony's Coffee Co 90C Hāna Hwy ☎808/579-8340. Small, early-opening coffee bar just west of central Pā'ia, fitted with a churning coffee roaster and serving espressos, pastries, soups, bagels, and deli sandwiches at a handful of indoor tables, plus $5 smoothies and a wide range of ice creams to go. Daily 5.30am–6pm.

Cafe Mambo 30 Baldwin Ave, Pā'ia ☎808/579-8021. Pale orange diner, just off the highway, serving espressos plus $7–10 burger or sandwich lunches and $9–19 dinner-time fajita specials. Picnics to go cost from $8.50 per person, $15 for two. Daily 8am–9pm.

The Flatbread Company 89 Hāna Hwy ☎808/579-8989. If you suspect "flatbread" is a fancy way of saying "pizza", you're dead right. Call them what you will, these ones, cooked in a wood-fired clay oven, are delicious, courtesy of a small New England-based chain that places its emphasis on free range and organic ingredients. The restaurant itself is lively but unhurried. Twelve-inchers cost $9–11.50, and toppings include *kālua* pork and mango BBQ. Daily 11.30am–10pm.

🏃 **Fresh Mint** 115 Baldwin Ave ☎808/579-9144. Formerly a hippy vegan hangout, this place has spruced itself up considerably to become a smart, even cool, but still vegetarian Vietnamese restaurant. Lots of delicious noodles, stir-fries, soups, or curries, some with soy chicken or soy fish, others with tofu or just eggplants. All entrees cost around $10. Daily 11am–9pm.

Livewire C@fe 137 Hāna Hwy ☎808/579-6009. Buzzing central coffee bar, with Internet access and a wide selection of drinks, snacks and smoothies. Daily 6am–10pm.

Mama's Fish House 799 Poho Place ☎808/579-8488. Upmarket and wildly popular fish restaurant, in breezy beachfront gardens a mile east of downtown Pā'ia. At lunch, you can opt for fish sandwiches and burgers for around $12, or go for full-scale fish entrees, each identified with the name of the fisherman who caught it. Dinner offers similar choices, along with even more fancy gourmet-Hawaiian dishes like *mahi-mahi* steamed in a *ti* leaf with coconut milk, costing anything from $30 upwards. While the views are sublime, if you come after sunset you may feel you're paying premium prices for little added value. Daily 11am–9pm.

Milagros 112 Hāna Hwy at Baldwin Ave ☎808/579-8755. Friendly terrace café, serving all meals at parasol-shaded tables at Pā'ia's main intersection. Salads and deli sandwiches for around $8; burgers, tacos, and burritos for more like $10. Daily 8am–10pm.

Moana Bakery & Cafe 71 Baldwin Ave ☎808/579-9999. Smart, tasteful café/restaurant not far off the main highway, with mosaic tables and large windows. Fancy breakfasts, lunchtime *saimin* or sandwiches ($7–10), and dinner entrees ($14–29) that range from green or red Thai curries to chili-seared *ahi* to *opakapaka laulau* (snapper wrapped in *ti* leaves). Daily 8am–9pm.

Pā'ia Fish Market 110 Hāna Hwy at Baldwin Ave ☎808/579-8030. Informal, inexpensive place with wooden benches, where fresh fish – sashimi or blackened – is $14, while scallops, shrimp, and calamari cost a bit more, and a fish or meat burger is just $8. Fish'n'chips is $10 for lunch, $12 for dinner. Pasta entrees include chicken ($15) and seafood ($16), and there's a sideline in quesadillas, fajitas, and soft tacos. Daily 11am–9.30pm.

Pauwela Café 375 W Kuiaha Rd, Ha'ikū ☎808/575-9242. Occupying one corner of the rusting gray hulk of Pauwela Cannery, a mile off Hwy-36 and roughly five miles east of Pā'ia, this cheerful, classy neighborhood café serves delicious, inexpensive breakfasts – try the *pain perdu* – plus salads, sandwiches, and lunch specials all priced close to $6. Mon 7am–2.30pm, Tues–Fri 7am–2.30pm & 5–8pm, Sun 8am–2pm.

The road to Hāna

The endless rains that fall on Haleakalā cascade down Maui's long windward flank, covering it with impenetrable jungle-like vegetation. Ancient Hawaiians allowed up to two days for the canoe trip from the isthmus round to the far eastern settlement of **Hāna**. Now the **Hāna Highway**, hacked into the coastal cliffs by convicts during the 1920s, has become a major attraction in its own right, twisting tortuously in and out of gorges, past innumerable waterfalls and over more than fifty tiny one-lane bridges. All year round, and especially in June, the route is ablaze with color from orchids, rainbow eucalyptus, and orange-blossomed African tulip trees, while characteristic little fruit stands and flower stalls make tempting places to stop. In fact, although many people make a big point of taking a **picnic** with them, it's more fun to pick up whatever food you need along the way.

The usual day's excursion is roughly fifty miles each way, from Pā'ia to 'Ohe'o Gulch beyond Hāna. While not as hair-raising as popular legend would have it, driving is slow going, taking around three hours each way, and demands serious concentration. If you'd prefer to keep your eyes on the scenery rather than on the road, consider taking an **organized tour**, available from around $80 per person with the operators detailed on p.284.

Huelo

Although the coastal road around East Maui is called Hāna Highway from the moment it leaves Kahului, it changes from Hwy-36 to Hwy-360 ten miles east of Pā'ia, at the foot of Hwy-365 from Makawao, and that's where you'll find **mile marker 0**.

The first potential distraction on the drive to Hāna is the unsigned turnoff, marked by a double row of mailboxes at a bend in the highway roughly 3.5 miles along, that leads down to the village of **HUELO**. The dirt road soon passes the plain **Kaulanapueo** ("resting-place of the owl") **Church**, built of coral cement on a black lava base and usually kept locked. It continues for a couple of miles, but neither it nor its many side roads offer access to the sea. Like many local communities, Huelo has become an uncertain mixture of Hawaiians and wealthy *haoles*. The clifftop *Huelo Point Flower Farm* (☎ 808/572-1850, ⓦ www.mauiflower farm.com; ❺) offers luxury **accommodation** with spectacular views over Waipi'o Bay, plus an on-site waterfall and open-air waterfront hot tub. It consists of two separate cottages – either of which would make a lavish, private honeymoon retreat – plus larger houses appropriate for four or six guests.

Not far beyond the road down to Huelo, the picnic table immediately below the *Huelo Lookout* fruit stand offers an opportunity to stop and admire the views of the forested slopes and the ocean beyond.

Waikamoi Nature Trail

Your one opportunity to explore the forested ridges above the Hāna Highway comes just over half a mile beyond the 9-mile marker, where the short but enjoyable **Waikamoi Nature Trail** sets off from an obvious roadside pull-out. The one-mile loop trail starts beyond a small picnic shelter, gently zigzagging up a muddy ridge (some hikers go barefoot). Despite the stone benches along the way, there are no views – it's barely possible to see beyond the tight-packed *hala* trees and green rustling bamboos hemming the track – but sunlight dapples down through the overhead canopy to magical effect. Here and there, you pass a variety of eucalyptus trees whose bark peels like fine tissue paper. The trail tops out at a smooth grassy clearing, with another picnic shelter, and a large mosquito population. It makes little difference whether you return by the same route, or down the adjacent jeep road that drops directly to the parking lot.

A little further along the highway, **Waikamoi Falls** tumbles down toward the road at a tight hairpin bend. If you want a closer look, the only place to park is immediately before the bridge – a spot that's all too easy to overshoot. Not far beyond Waikamoi Falls, at mile 10.5, the small and privately-owned **Garden of Eden Arboretum** (daily 8am–3pm; $10; T 808/572-9899, W www.mauigardenofeden.com) displays an attractive assortment of colorful flowers and orchids. It also offers a slightly distant waterfall view, and has picnic tables with a panoramic prospect of the coastline.

Honomanū Bay

Shortly after mile marker 13, the highway drops down to sea level for the first time since Ho'okipa Beach, and you finally start to get the long coastal views for which it's famous. The Ke'anae Peninsula appears on the horizon, but much closer at hand – where the gorgeous, uninhabited **Honomanū Valley**, lit up by tulip trees, gives way to the ocean – you'll see the black gravel beach at **Honomanū Bay**. Swimming and snorkeling here is only advisable on the calmest of summer days, but it's a popular site with local **surfers**.

Two separate dirt tracks cut down to the shore from the road as it sweeps around the narrow valley. The first, at 13.5 miles, leads down to the north shore of the stream; the second, just after the 14-mile marker on the far side of the stream, is paved for the first few yards, but then becomes steeper and muddier. It comes out at the longer side of the beach.

Ke'anae Arboretum

From a wooded bend in the road a few hundred yards before the 17-mile marker, a paved level trail heads inland to the attractive public gardens of the **Ke'anae Arboretum** (daily dawn–dusk; free). Following the course of a stream you can hear but not see, it leads into a lush, narrow valley and reaches the arboretum within a quarter of a mile.

Fifty-foot-high clumps of "male bamboo" guard the entrance, with tropical plants beyond including Hawaiian species such as torch ginger and wet and dry taro. Beyond the taro fields, a mile into the park, the trail becomes a wet scramble through the rainforest, crossing up and over the valley ridge by way of tree-root footholds. Along with lots of small waterfalls and swarms of tiny flies feasting on fallen guava and breadfruit, there's a good chance of spotting rare forest birds and even wild boar.

Ke'anae Peninsula

Not far beyond the arboretum, a side road twists down to the flat **Ke'anae Peninsula**, the site of a small, and still predominantly Hawaiian, village. It's said that this windswept promontory consisted of bare rock until a local chief forced his followers to spend two years carrying baskets of soil down the mountainside; thereafter it became a prime taro-growing region, and supported a large population.

The taro fields are still here, surrounded by abundant banana trees and birds of paradise, and there's also a fine old **church** among the tall palms. The edge of the ocean is as bleak as ever, with *hala* trees propped up along the shoreline and the surf crashing onto headlands of gnarled black lava; swimming here is out of the question.

A small pavilion nearby holds the best **public restrooms** on the whole route to Hāna.

Almost the only **food** and **lodging** along the main stretch of the Hāna Highway is in the Keʻanae area. The renovated *YMCA Camp Keʻanae*, on the highway shortly before the arboretum, served as a prison once but now offers **cabin** accommodation and also has its own grassy **campground** (☎808/248-8355, ⓦwww.mauiymca.org/campk .htm). Whether you stay in your own tent or in a cabin, it costs $17 per person or $35 per family. Not surprisingly, the facilities tend to be reserved way in advance.

Simple snacks are sold at two roadside kiosks – *Halfway to Hāna* and *Uncle Harry's*, before and after the **18-mile marker** respectively. The specialty at *Halfway to Hāna* (which has its own ATM machine) is the banana bread; at *Uncle Harry's*, opposite a dazzling bed of flowers, try the banana and pineapple smoothie. Neither keeps very regular hours, but both claim they're open daily for lunch.

Wailua

Within a mile of Keʻanae, as the highway veers inland, the arrow-straight Wailua Road plunges down to another traditional village, **WAILUA**. Unlike Keʻanae, its ancient rival, Wailua has always been fertile and still holds extensive taro terraces.

The lower of the two churches that stand a short way down from the turnoff is known as the **Coral Miracle**. Local legend has it that, in 1860, just as its builders were despairing of finding the stone to complete it, a freak storm washed up exactly enough coral on the beach below. It's a simple but attractive chapel, painted white, with turquoise stenciling around the porch and windows. Look back across the valley as you leave the building for a superb view of the high **Waikani Falls**, garlanded by flowering trees at the head of the valley.

Wailua Road ends just above the tranquil mouth of Wailua Stream, which makes a sharp contrast with the ocean pummeling the beach of black pebbles beyond. Don't drive down to the stream – there's no room to turn round – and don't even consider a swim.

Wailua viewpoints

Lookouts on either side of the highway beyond the Wailua turnoff offer scenic views up and down the coastline. From the inconspicuous *mauka* parking lot of **Wailua Valley State Wayside**, steps climb through a tunnel of trees to a vantage point overlooking Wailua Valley as it reaches the sea, and also inland across Keʻanae Valley, to towering waterfalls, undulating ridges, and endless trees.

A little further on, immediately after the 19-mile marker, Wailua Valley spreads like a little oasis beneath **Wailua Lookout**. The taller of Wailua's two churches, **St Gabriel's**, pokes its head above the sea of trees, while the thickly wooded gorge stretches away to the right. At the next bend, just around the corner, a big cascade roars beside the road; you have to react quickly to stop.

Puaʻakaʻa State Wayside

The spacious parking lot of **Puaʻakaʻa State Wayside**, 22.5 miles along Hāna Highway, is every bit as big as the park itself. In fact, this is a favorite stop for bus tours, because so little effort is required to negotiate the park's few yards of paved trails. If you brave the crowds, you'll see a pretty but far from spectacular sequence of small waterfalls, with picnic tables dotted on either side of a stream.

Nāhiku

Not far after the 25-mile marker, a narrow unmarked road takes about three miles to wind down to the ocean. The few houses along the way constitute **NĀHIKU**, though there's no town, just a jungle of trees and vines, some of which all but engulf the abandoned vehicles left here. The road comes out at **Ōpūhano Point**, from where you can look back toward Wailua atop the tree-covered cliffs reaching down into the water.

Early in the twentieth century, Nāhiku was the site of the first, albeit unsuccessful, rubber plantation in the US. Subsequently, ex-Beatle George Harrison had a home here, but in his later years he only visited occasionally, following a bitter legal dispute with his neighbors that centered on the construction of a beach-access footpath.

Just before the 29-mile marker, the ⚓ *Nāhiku Fruit Stand* (daily 6.30am–4.30pm) is a funky, friendly roadside shack that sells delicious espressos and smoothies, along with home-made lunches such as banana bread and fish specials. There's a small crafts gallery alongside, as well as an open-air grill, *Up In Smoke BBQ*, that serves baked breadfruit and smoked fish to no discernible schedule.

'Ula'ino Road

The first sign that you're finally approaching Hāna is when you pass Hāna **Gardenland**, a not very exciting commercial nursery, on the right. Immediately afterwards, **'Ula'ino Road** drops away to the left of the highway, leading both to the largest ancient *heiau* (temple) in all Hawaii, and – if ongoing disputes over access have been settled – what's potentially one of the best **hikes** on Maui.

Kahanu Garden

Three-quarters of a mile down 'Ula'ino Road, the paved surface gives out where the road crosses a minor ford. On the far side, you'll find the entrance to **Kahanu Garden**, a nonprofit facility belonging to the National Tropical Botanical Garden (Mon–Fri 10am–2pm; adults $10, under-13s free; ☎808/248-8912 or 332-7234, ⓦwww.ntbg.org). This holds over a hundred acres of tropical plants, but is of most significance as the site of **Pi'ilanihale Heiau,** the largest ancient *heiau* (temple) not merely in Hawaii but quite possibly in the entire Pacific. A *luakini*, or temple where human sacrifice took place, its original construction has been dated to the late thirteenth century, but it's thought to have been enlarged and re-dedicated by Pi'ilani around 1570 AD to celebrate his then-recent conquest of the

△ Pi'ilanihale Heiau

entire island. It was rebuilt once more in the late eighteenth century, and extensively restored and reconstructed during the 1990s.

A mile-long loop trail through Kahanu Garden begins by skirting the edge of an extensive forest of splay-footed *hala* trees. A free booklet describes the traditional uses of several different species of indigenous and imported plants that have been cultivated along the way. Your first sight of the *heiau* itself presents it towering above the lush oceanfront lawns. Constructed from black lava boulders, intricately slotted into place, and set on a natural lava flow, it's an impressive spectacle. Measuring 174 meters by 89 meters, it covers almost three acres and consists of five separate tiers on its oceanward side. As usual at such sites, however, in deference to ongoing Hawaiian religious beliefs, visitors are not allowed to set foot on the actual structure and can only admire it from a distance. As a result, you're not likely to spend more time here than the half-hour it takes to walk the trail, which also offers some gorgeous views along the coast.

The Blue Pool

'Ula'ino Road continues beyond the garden as a much rougher but still mostly paved track, almost always negotiable with care in an ordinary rental car as it undulates gently through the woods for another 1.4 miles. The road ends abruptly in a shady grove a hundred yards short of the ocean, just above a stream whose outlet is blocked by a natural wall of heavy black boulders.

In recent years, the existence of a fabulous **waterfall** a short walk from here, popularly known as the **Blue Pool**, has become common knowledge among visitors to Maui. The area has therefore become rather too popular for its own good, and local residents have been infuriated by the sheer quantity of day-trippers who find their way down here. Some have succumbed to the inevitable by turning their gardens into parking lots, while others have confronted visitors and refused to let them through. If you do come this way, it's currently impossible to predict what your reception will be. Assuming the situation has been resolved by the time you read this, don't expect to park for free right at the bottom of the road, but keep going in any case as far as you can – prices get cheaper further down, so you can expect to pay around $2 rather than the $4 on offer higher up.

To reach the shimmering Blue Pool itself, make for the shoreline, then head left for a hundred yards. Less than twenty yards from the sea, the pool is constantly replenished by water cascading from the *hala*-covered ridge above. It's set in a grotto that's festooned with ferns, vines, and *hala* trees, its mossy walls bursting with tiny pinks and peonies. As you sit on the rocks, fresh water from the falls splashes your face, while you can feel the salt spray of the ocean on your back. It's also possible to walk to the right along the beach, where coconuts lie among the boulders. Atop a spit of rough 'a'ā lava, five minutes along, you can watch the surf crashing and grinding the black rocks to hollow out little coves, while a jungle of *hala* trees lies, unreachable, beyond.

Wai'ānapanapa State Park

Within two miles of Hāna, beyond the turnoff to Hāna Airport (see p.366), a clearly signed road *makai* of the highway leads through a "tunnel" of overhanging trees to the shoreline at **Wai'ānapanapa State Park**. To reach the main parking lot, perched above a tiny **black-sand beach**, turn left when you reach the park cabins at the end of the first straight stretch of road. A short and easy trail descends from the parking lot to this beautiful little cove, where the beach changes from shiny black pebbles to fine black sand as it shelves into the ocean. It looks wonderful, and barely has room to hold its daily crowd of sunbathers, but swimming is deadly, with heavy surf and deep water just a few yards out.

At the right-hand side of the beach as you face the sea, look for a hollow cave in the small cliff that you just walked down. Squeeze your way through its narrow entrance and you'll find that not only does it widen inside, it is, in fact, a **tunnel**. The far end, where it's open to the ocean, is a truly magical spot.

By contrast, a very short loop trail to the left of the parking lot back at the top leads down and through **Wai'ānapanapa Cave**. A few yards back from the sea, this "cave" is actually a collapsed lava tube, holding two successive grotto-like pools. It's slightly stagnant and smells rather like a public restroom, but you do see some nice clinging flowers.

Coastal **hiking trails** in both directions make it easy to escape the throngs at the beach. Heading **northwest** (left), you're soon clambering over a headland of black lava through a forest of *hala* and *naupaka*. Inlets in the jagged shoreline harbor turquoise pools, while the surf rages against the rocks; in places, where the sea has hollowed out caverns, you can feel the thud of the ocean beneath you. A painting of a natural "lava bridge" here, executed in 1939 by Georgia O'Keeffe, now hangs in the Honolulu Academy of Arts. A mile or so along, the trail ends at the fence of Hāna Airport.

Southeast of the beach, the footpath crosses smoother, firmer lava, passing the park campground, a cemetery, and an impressive blowhole. After around a mile, it reaches the ruined **Ohala Heiau**, the walls of which remain clear despite ivy-like *naupaka* growing inside. You can continue four miles on to Hāna; the scenery is invigorating all the way, but the trail gets progressively harder to follow.

Wai'ānapanapa is by far the nicest place on Maui to **camp** beside the ocean. In addition to tent camping, at $5 per person, it has basic cabins, each holding up to four people, at $45 per cabin. Permits are available from the state parks office in Wailuku (see p.285), but the cabins are usually reserved far in advance.

Hāna

For some visitors, the former sugar town of **HĀNA** comes as a disappointment after the splendors of the Hāna Highway. Certainly, the point of driving the road is to enjoy the scenery en route, rather than to race to Hāna itself; having said that, it's a pleasant enough little town that's home to just a few hundred inhabitants. In ancient times, Hāna controlled a densely populated region, and modern locals have long resisted any concept of "development" for its own sake, proudly viewing themselves as one of the most staunchly traditional communities in the state.

When the local sugar plantation closed in 1943, most of its land was bought by **Paul Fagan**, a Californian businessman. He established not only the **Hāna Ranch**, whose cowboys still work cattle herds in the fields above town, but also modern Maui's first **hotel**, the *Hotel Hāna-Maui*. Fagan died in 1959 – he's commemorated by a large white cross on the hillside – but the town remains dominated by the businesses he founded. Most of the town's central area is taken up by the *Hotel Hāna-Maui*, while the Hāna Ranch headquarters on the main highway houses its most conspicuous restaurant and other utilities.

Both the ranch and the hotel, and thus effectively most of the town itself, have repeatedly changed hands over the last few years. In the 1990s, Japanese corporate owners published alarming plans to turn Hāna into an exclusive resort much like Wailea, complete with a new oceanfront hotel above Hāmoa Bay, an upscale shopping and restaurant complex, a golf course, and acres of residential properties. None of those schemes ever left the drawing board, however. Hāna has since

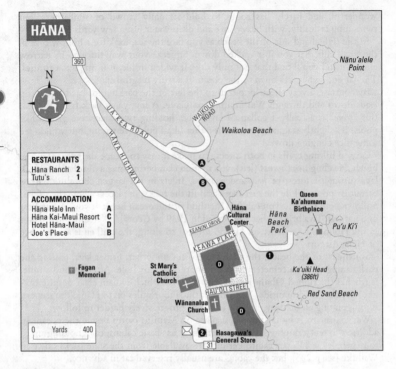

Within the map:

HĀNA

360

UA'KEA ROAD

HĀNA HIGHWAY

WAIKOLOA ROAD

Nānu'alele Point

Waikoloa Beach

RESTAURANTS
Hāna Ranch 2
Tutu's 1

ACCOMMODATION
Hāna Hale Inn A
Hāna Kai-Maui Resort C
Hotel Hāna-Maui D
Joe's Place B

Hāna Cultural Center

KEANINI DRIVE

KEAWA PLACE

Queen Ka'ahumanu Birthplace

Hāna Beach Park

Pu'u Ki'i

Fagan Memorial

St Mary's Catholic Church

Ka'uiki Head (386ft)

Red Sand Beach

HAU'OLI STREET

Wānanalua Church

0 Yards 400

31

Hasagawa's General Store

passed back into American ownership, and remains one of the most relaxing places on Maui to spend a few days, short on swimmable beaches and golf, perhaps, but very long indeed on character, history, and beauty.

Arrival and information

The principal user of Hāna's small **airport**, perched beside the ocean three miles north of town, is the tiny Pacific Wings airline (☎808/248-7700 or 1-888/575-4546, ⓦwww.pacificwings.com). It operates daily round-trip flights between Kahului and Hāna – taking just fifteen minutes and timed to connect with flights to and from Honolulu and Lanai – plus one or two nonstop flights to Honolulu. Only Dollar offers **car rental** at **Hāna**.

The town has no public transport of any kind, but the Hāna Ranch Center holds a **post office** (Mon–Fri 8am–4.30pm; Hāna, HI 96713) and a Bank of Hawaii (Mon–Thurs 3–4.30pm, Fri 3–6pm). In addition, Hang Gliding Maui is a one-man operation that provides (powered) **hang-gliding lessons** at $130 for 30min, $220 for 1hr (☎808/572-6557, ⓦwww.hanggglidingmaui.com).

Accommodation

More **accommodation** is available around Hāna than is immediately apparent. As well as the *Hotel Hāna-Maui*, small-scale B&Bs are scattered all over town, and many of the houses along the shoreline are for rent. You can also **camp** at Wai'ānapanapa State Park (see p.365).

Hāmoa Bay House and Bungalow PO Box 773, Hāna, HI 96713 ☎ 808/248-7884, 🖥 www.hamoabay.com. Two fabulous rental properties, splendidly isolated – even from each other – two miles south of Hāna. Perched on stilts in a jungle-like setting, and with an open-air hot tub on its wooden *lānai*, the bungalow makes an idyllic honeymoon hideaway, while the house is large enough for two couples. Both have Balinese bamboo furnishings, and require a three-night minimum stay. Bungalow ❻, house ❼

Hāna Aliʻi Holidays ☎ 808/248-7742 or 1-800/548-0478, 🖥 www.hanamauitravel.com. Choose from some twenty apartments and cottages in and around Hāna, many by the ocean, and some absolutely gorgeous. Rates range from $90 to $450 a night, but $125–150 should get you a spacious and attractive cottage.

Hāna Kai-Maui Resort 1533 Uaʻkea Rd ☎ 808/248-8426 or 1-800/346-2772, 🖥 www .hanakaimaui.com. Small condo building, set in lovely multilevel gardens overlooking Hāna Bay, a short way north of Hāna Beach County Park. Each well-equipped studio and one-bedroom unit has a kitchen and private *lānai*; the larger ones sleep four. Studios ❹, apartments ❺

Hāna Hale Inn 4829 Uaʻkea Rd ☎ 808/248-7641, 🖥 www.hanahaleinn.com. A cluster of distinctive rainforest-style timber buildings, not far up from the ocean and overlooking an attractive fishpond that actually belongs to the neighbors. All are very luxurious, with hot tubs and bamboo furnishings; the more expensive ones can comfortably sleep four. ❹–❼

Hotel Hāna-Maui 5031 Hāna Hwy ☎ 808/248-8211 or 1-800/321-4262, 🖥 www.hotelhanamaui.com. Secluded luxury hotel, built in the 1940s as Hawaii's first self-contained resort and integrated into the community to create a unique atmosphere. In addition to the older rooms in the Bay Cottages near the lobby, rows of plantation-style Sea Ranch cottages are arranged across the lawns that drop down to the ocean. They have no TVs, but boast every other creature comfort, with kitchenettes and private *lānais* that have individual hot tubs and enjoy great views. As well as regular shuttles to Hāmoa Beach for activities, hotel guests have use of tennis courts and a pitch-and-putt golf course, and there's regular live music in the lounge. ❾

Joe's Place 4870 Uaʻkea Rd ☎ 808/248-7033, 🖥 www.joesrentals.com. Joe himself passed away some years ago, but his ordinary Hāna home, opposite the Hāna Kai-Maui Resort, still offers eight simple rooms, sharing a kitchen and communal lounge. All cost $45 except the one that has its own en-suite bath, priced at $55; there are no sea views, but this is Hāna's best option for budget travelers. ❷

Downtown Hāna

None of the buildings along the main highway, which passes through Hāna a hundred yards up from the ocean, is especially worth exploring, though **Wananalua Church**, whose square, solid tower contrasts appealingly with the flamboyant gardens surrounding it, makes a photogenic landmark. Across the road, the **Hāna Ranch Center** is a dull mall, designed to feed and water the daily influx of bus tours, but given a flash of color by the odd *paniolo* cowboy. **Hasegawa's General Store**, stocked with every item imaginable, burned down in 1990. It's been rehoused in a charmless former theater, but is still a friendly place to pick up supplies. The **Hāna Coast Gallery**, at the northern end of the lobby of the *Hotel Hāna-Maui*, sells an unusually good, if expensive, assortment of Hawaiian crafts and paintings of East Maui landscapes.

Local history is recalled by the low-key exhibits – gourds, calabashes, fish hooks, and crude stone idols – at the **Hāna Cultural Center** (daily 10am–4pm; $2 suggested donation; ☎ 808/248-8622), on Uaʻkea Road, down from the highway and above the bay. It also holds art exhibitions and is amassing a comprehensive collection of photos of past and present Hāna residents. Nearby stands a tiny nineteenth-century jail-cum-courthouse; on the grounds alongside it, a replica living compound has been constructed, of the kind used by the ancient Hawaiian *makaʻainana* (common people). As well as a thatched stone dwelling and a canoe house, it features garden terraces planted with taro and *ti*.

Queen Ka'ahumanu: scenes from a life

She is prodigiously fat, but her face is interesting . . . her legs, the palm of her left hand, and her tongue, are very elegantly tattooed.

Jacques Arago, 1823

Returning from town, I saw Queen Ka'ahumanu in her four-wheeled cart being dragged to the top of a small hill by natives. The cart was afterwards pushed off at the top and allowed to roll down hill by itself, with her in it. This ludicrous sort of amusement was always accompanied with much shouting on the part of the natives.

James Macrae, 1825

At the Sandwich Islands, Kaahumannu, the gigantic old dowager queen – a woman of nearly four hundred pounds weight, and who is said to be still living at Mowee – was accustomed, in some of her terrific gusts of temper, to snatch up an ordinary sized man who had offended her, and snap his spine across her knee. Incredible as this may seem, it is a fact. While at Lahainaluna – the residence of this monstrous Jezebel – a humpbacked wretch was pointed out to me, who, some twenty-five years previously, had had the vertebrae of his back-bone very seriously discomposed by his gentle mistress.

Herman Melville, *Typee*

No figure encapsulates the dramas and paradoxes of early Hawaiian history as completely as **Queen Ka'ahumanu**, the daughter of Nāmāhana, a chiefess from East Maui, and Ke'eaumoku from the Big Island. Her parents' strategic alliance presented such a threat to Kahekili, the ruling chief of Maui, that they were fleeing for their lives when Ka'ahumanu was born at Hāna, around 1777.

Chief Ke'eaumoku was one of Kamehameha the Great's closest lieutenants; it was he who killed Kamehameha's rival Keōua at Pu'ukoholā (see p.205). His daughter may have been as young as eight when she first caught the eye of the king; soon afterwards, she became the seventeenth of his twenty-two wives.

Captain Vancouver described Ka'ahumanu in 1793 as "about sixteen ... [she] undoubtedly did credit to the choice and taste of Kamehameha, being one of the finest women we had yet seen on any of the islands." According to nineteenth-century historian Samuel M. Kamakau, "Of Kamehameha's two possessions, his wife and his kingdom, she was the most beautiful."

Ka'ahumanu was Kamehameha's favorite wife. As a high-ranking *ali'i*, she possessed great spiritual power, or *mana*; she herself was a *pu'uhonua* (see p.186), meaning that *kapu*-breakers who reached her side could not be punished. She was also an expert surfer and serial adulterer. Among her paramours was the dashing Kaiana, killed commanding the armies of Oahu against Kamehameha at Nu'uanu Pali, in 1795.

It was after Kamehameha's death, in 1819, that Ka'ahumanu came into her own. Announcing to her son Liholiho that "we two shall rule over the land," she proclaimed herself Kuhina Nui, or Regent, and set about destroying the system of *kapus*. This elaborate system of rules denied women access to certain foods and, more importantly, to the real source of power in ancient Hawaii – the *luakini* war temples. At first Ka'ahumanu's goal was to break the grip of the priesthood, but in 1825 she converted to Christianity, after being nursed through a serious illness by Sybil Gingham, the wife of Hawaii's first missionary. Meanwhile, in 1821, she had married both the last king of Kauai, Kaumuali'i, and his seven-foot-tall son, Keali'iahonui.

Ka'ahumanu outlived Liholiho, who died in England in 1824, and remained the effective ruler of Hawaii when his younger brother Kauikeaouli succeeded to the throne as Kamehameha III. Her achievements included selecting Hawaii's first jury, presiding over its first Western-style trial, and enforcing its first law on marriage and divorce. After seven years spent proselytizing for her new faith, she died on June 5, 1832. Her last words were reported as "Lo, here am I, O Jesus, Grant me thy gracious smile."

Hāna Bay

Hāna's reputation for beauty relies largely upon broad **Hāna Bay**, a short walk below the north end of the town center. Much the safest place to swim in East Maui, it's also the only protected harbor in the area.

The small gray-sand beach known as **Hāna Beach County Park** spreads to the south, at the foot of Keawa Place, backed by lawns that hold picnic tables, restrooms, and changing rooms. The park's long terraced pavilion, pressed against the curving hillside across the road, houses *Tutu's* takeout counter (see p.369). *Hāna-Maui Seasports*, based at the *Hotel Hāna-Maui*, offer daily kayak and snorkel "eco adventures," and surfing lessons, in the bay (℡808/248-7711, @www.hana-maui-seasports.com).

Thrusting into the ocean further south, the high cinder cone of **Ka'uiki Head** is the most prominent feature of the bay. Now covered with trees, it used to be just a bare rock, and served as a fortress for the ancient chiefs of Maui; Kahekili is said to have repelled an invasion from the Big Island here in 1780. Its far side – only seen easily from the air – collapsed into the sea long ago.

A short **hiking trail** – hard to spot at first, but soon clear enough – heads off around Ka'uiki Head from beyond the jetty, offering excellent views across the bay and up to Hāna itself. Soon after a tiny red-sand beach, it reaches a bronze plaque, set into a slab of rock near a couple of small caves in the base of the hill. This marks the birthplace of the great Hawaiian queen **Ka'ahumanu**, though she was probably born later than the year it says, 1768 (see box opposite). Continuing on, you discover that the rocky point beyond is in fact an island. Known as **Pu'u Ki'i**, it was once topped by a giant *ki'i* (wooden idol), erected by the Big Island chief, Umi; an automated lighthouse now stands in its place. Around the next corner, the trail is blocked by an impassable red scree slope.

Red Sand Beach

A precarious coastal footpath leads along the south flank of Ka'uiki Head to a lovely little cove that shelters one of Maui's prettiest beaches, **Red Sand Beach**. The Hāna Ranch, which owns the land here, considers the walk so dangerous that it makes every effort to discourage visitors; the path is often closed due to serious erosion, and should only be attempted after seeking local advice as to current conditions. To find it, walk left from the south end of Ua'kea Road, below a small, neat Japanese cemetery. Approximately a five-minute walk, the path follows, and in places spans, a narrow ledge around a hillside of loose red gravel, but at this low elevation it's not too nerve-racking.

Behind a final promontory, the beach lies angled toward the rising sun, shielded by a row of black dragon's-teeth rocks, kept well flossed by the waves. Hawaiians knew this canoe landing as Kaihalulu Beach. It's only ever safe for swimming in the tiny inshore area, and even then the razor-sharp rocks beneath the surface make it essential to wear reef shoes. The origin of the beach's coarse reddish cinders – the eroded red cliffs above it – is very obvious, and it's equally obvious that you can hike no further.

Restaurants

For a town with so many daytime visitors and overnight guests, Hāna has remarkably few **places to eat**.

Hāna Ranch Hāna Hwy ℡ 808/248-8255.
Bland quick-fire restaurant in the heart of Hāna, specializing in dull lunches for the daily hordes of bargain-seeking day-trippers. Mostly it's fries with everything – a half-pound burger made from local beef costs $13 – and they do a vegetarian taro burger too. Dinner is served on Wednesday, Friday and Saturday only, and is slightly more interesting;

$18–35 entrees, such as barbecue ribs or teriyaki chicken, include a salad bar. A cheaper takeout counter sells *saimin* for $3.50 and plate lunches for around $8. Restaurant Sun–Tues & Thurs 8–10am & 11am–3pm; Wed, Fri & Sat 8–10am, 11am–3pm & 6–8.30pm; takeout daily 6.30am–4pm.

Ka'uiki *Hotel Hāna-Maui*, Hāna Hwy ☎ 808/248-8211. The deluxe resort's open-sided, wicker-furnished dining room ranks among the most expensive restaurants in Hawaii, which can make its downhome ambience and local-style service seem a little odd. Thanks to recent improvements in the kitchen, however, the food is truly superb. A commitment to local ingredients and techniques results in magnificent fish dishes in particular, such as *hapu* (sea bass) steamed with coconut in *ti* leaves as an entree, or a *ceviche* appetizer of *onaga* (red snapper). A changing three-course dinner menu costs $60; lunch is much simpler, centering on classy burgers and sandwiches for around $18, while breakfast is a relaxed delight. Daily 7.30–10.30am, 11.30am–2.30pm & 6–9pm.

Tutu's Hāna Bay ☎ 808/248-8244. Beachfront takeout counter, whose indifferent sandwiches, burgers, plate lunches, sodas, and lemonades attract long queues at lunchtime. Daily 8.30am–4pm.

South of Hāna

South of Hāna, Hāna Highway gives way to **Pi'ilani Highway**, but the scenery is, if anything, even more gorgeous than before. In those stretches where the road is not engulfed by magnificent flowering trees, you can look up beyond the ranch-lands to the high green mountains, while Mauna Kea on the Big Island comes into view across the 'Alenuihaha Channel.

Kōkī Beach Park

A couple of miles south of Hāna, the Haneo'o Loop Road heads left from the highway. After half a mile, it reaches the ocean alongside the white sands of **Kōkī Beach Park**. Local surfers and boogie-boarders love this spot, but unless you're a very confident swimmer and all-round watersports expert, take heed of the many signs that warn of a very dangerous rip-current just offshore. It's a great place for a coastal stroll, in any case. The exposed red cinder cone dominating the beach is named **Ka Iwi O Pele**, or "the bones of Pele", as the volcano goddess was suppos-edly killed here by her sister, the goddess of the sea. Oprah Winfrey, who has purchased a number of lots in the vicinity of the Hāna Ranch, has built herself a home on a hundred-acre plot immediately north.

Just south of Kōkī Beach, tiny **Ā'lau Islet** stands just out to sea. Ancient Hawaiians reshaped the lava rocks along the promontory closest to the island to create artificial fishponds, and fishermen are still frequent visitors.

Hāmoa Bay

Not far beyond Kōkī Beach, a 1.5-mile detour down the Haneo'o Loop Road takes you to the white-sand beach at **Hāmoa Bay**, used by *Hotel Hāna-Maui* for all its oceanfront activities, including a weekly *lū'au*. There was a small settlement here until it was destroyed by the tsunami of 1946; it's a good surfing spot, and holds a nice picnic area, but it's unsafe for swimming. The highway continues south through a succession of tiny residential villages, where, apart from the odd roadside fruit stand and countless crystal-clear waterfalls, there's no reason to stop.

'Ohe'o Gulch

Almost all the day-trippers who reach Hāna press on to beautiful **'Ohe'o Gulch**, ten miles beyond, where a natural rock staircase of waterfalls descends to the oceanfront meadows at the mouth of the **Kīpahulu Valley**. This far-flung outpost

△ ʻOheʻo Gulch

of Haleakalā National Park, sometimes spuriously known as "Seven Sacred Pools," tends to be jam-packed in the middle of the day, but, as one of the few places on Maui to offer easy access to unspoiled Hawaiian rainforest, it shouldn't be missed. If you hike a mile or two into the hills, you'll soon escape the crowds to reach cool rock pools, which so long as it's not raining are ideal for swimming.

The national park at ʻOheʻo Gulch remains open 24 hours per day, and charges its standard **admission fee** of $10 per vehicle to all users of the roadside parking lot. That covers access to the entire park for three days, so unless you manage to visit ʻOheʻo Gulch and the summit crater within two days of each other, you'll have to pay twice. A **ranger station** just down the slope from the lot has up-to-date information on local roads and hiking trails (daily 9am–5pm; ☏808/248-7375). **Guided hikes** to different destinations set off daily except Saturdays at 9.30am; for details of trips on **horseback** in the vicinity, see p.283.

Access to the upper reaches of the **Kīpahulu Valley**, regarded as one of the most pristine and environmentally significant regions in all Hawaii, is barred to the public. The park is, however, hoping to purchase large tracts in the valleys to the west, in order to open more hiking trails and remote beaches.

The lower trail

The paved footpath that leads **downhill** from the ʻOheʻo Gulch parking lot – officially, **Kōloa Point Trail** – is so busy that it's forced to operate as a one-way loop. Get here early if you want to enjoy it before the onslaught, but don't avoid it otherwise. After ambling through the meadows for five minutes, the trail winds past ancient stone walls on the low oceanfront bluff, and then down to a tiny gray-grit beach, where the shark-infested ocean is far from tempting.

However, upwards from the ocean, a "ladder" of stream-fed pools climbs the craggy rocks, an ascent negotiated by suckerfish in breeding season. Several of the pools are deep and sheltered enough for swimming, and on calm sunny days the whole place throngs with bathers. It's impossible to follow the stream as far up as the high road bridge; by that point, the gorge is a slippery, narrow water chute.

The higher waterfalls

The **Pīpīwai Trail**, into the mountains above 'Ohe'o Gulch, ranks as one of the very best hikes in Hawaii (though one on which it's essential to carry mosquito repellent). Occasionally it's closed by bad weather, but the construction of two sturdy footbridges has ensured that the first mile or so is almost always accessible. It starts beside the ranger station, but swiftly crosses the highway and heads uphill through steep fields, where thick woods line the course of the 'Ohe'o Stream. After the first half-mile, which is by far the most demanding stretch of the hike, a spur trail cuts off to the right to reach a railing that overlooks the towering 200-foot **Makahiku Falls**. A deep groove in the earth nearby leads to a series of shallow bathing pools just above the lip of the falls, where the stream emerges from a tunnel in the rock. As well as commanding magnificent views, it's an utterly idyllic spot for a swim on rain-free days.

Continuing by means of a gate in a fence along the main trail, you emerge into an open guava orchard and soon hear the thundering of smaller waterfalls to your right. There's no way to get to the water, but you'll see it framed through the thick jungle, together with the gaping cave mouth it has hollowed out on the far side. A little further on, you may be lured off the trail again by a pair of twin falls near a small concrete dam, which can be admired from a rocky outcrop in the streambed below.

Beyond that lies a lovely meadow, with views to the high valley walls in the distance, laced by huge waterfalls. A mile up, the trail crosses high above the stream twice in quick succession, over the bridges. It then follows a dark and narrow gap through a forest of huge old bamboo interspersed with sections of level wooden boardwalk. Eventually, two miles up from the road, you'll spot the spindle-thin, 400-foot **Waimoku Falls** ahead. Reaching its base requires a lot of scrambling, and close to the end you have to cross the stream itself on stepping stones. Despite the obvious danger of falling rocks, many hikers choose to cool off by standing directly beneath the cascade. Allow a good two hours to complete the entire round-trip hike.

Camping

The first-come, first-served National Park **campground** at 'Ohe'o Gulch is extremely rudimentary – it's just a field, with pit toilets and no drinking water – but it stands in the ruins of an ancient fishing village, and enjoys superb ocean views. Permits are not required, and it's free, with a three-night maximum stay.

Kīpahulu

Within a mile of 'Ohe'o Gulch, the highway passes through the village of **KĪPAHULU**. Time seems to have stood still in this attractive little spot since the local sugar mill closed down eighty years ago. The only sign of life these days comes from the occasional lunchtime fruit stand selling the produce of the roadside orchards.

A quarter-mile beyond **milepost 41** at Kīpahulu, a paved road branches left off the highway. After a couple of hundred yards, turn left again onto a dirt road through a "tunnel" of trees, and park by the giant banyan tree at the end that guards the **Palapala Ho'omau Church**. Founded in 1864, it has whitewashed coral walls and a green timber roof, and is set in pretty clifftop gardens. The interior is utterly plain and unadorned.

Visitors make their way to this tranquil spot because the fenced-off platform of black lava stones in the churchyard holds the grave of **Charles Lindbergh** (1902–74), who won fame in 1927 as the first man to fly the Atlantic. Less appetizingly,

Lindbergh was also a notorious Nazi sympathizer, who once told *Reader's Digest* that aviation is "one of those priceless possessions which permit the White Race to live at all in a sea of Yellow, Black and Brown." President Roosevelt told a friend in May 1940, "If I should die tomorrow, I want you to know this. I am absolutely convinced that Lindbergh is a Nazi." Philip Roth's recent novel *The Plot Against America* envisages an alternative history in which Lindbergh defeated Roosevelt in that year's presidential election. In real life, Lindbergh retired to Maui in his old age, and died within a couple of years.

Leading off from the cemetery, and only accessible through it, **Kīpahulu Point Park** is a small, shaded lawn, fringed with bright orange-leafed bushes, where the picnic tables command wonderful ocean views.

Along the South Maui coast

Until recently, anyone who had driven the Hāna Highway and had a congenital aversion to going back the same way they came could choose in normal weather to follow Pi'ilani Highway right around the whole barren coastline of southern Maui and into the upcountry above Wailea. Roughly five miles of the road is unpaved; it's a bumpy ride, no faster than the Hāna Highway, and not as spectacular, but it does offer a glorious sense of isolation. However, when this book went to press, Pi'ilani Highway was **closed to all traffic** as a result of an earthquake in October 2006. The problem was said to be that boulders had become perched in dangerous positions above the road itself, and county authorities therefore barricaded the Kukulula Bridge, near Kālepa Point, a couple of miles west of 'Ohe'o Gulch towards Kaupō. Enquire locally to find out whether it has reopened; the account below appears on the basis that it surely must do so at some point.

The entire stretch of coast used to be known as **Kahikinui**, or Tahiti Nui; the equivalent part of Tahiti, which has the same outline as Maui, bears the same name. The countryside immediately beyond Kīpahulu is lovely, dotted with exclusive homes whose owners are no doubt happy that this is not yet a standard tourist loop.

After less than two miles from Kīpahulu, the road returns to sea level – for the first time in several miles – and skirts the long gray pebble beach at **Lelekea Bay**. As you climb the cliffs at the far end, look back to see water spouting out of the hillside above an overhang in the rock, forceful enough to be a gushing jet rather than a waterfall.

The pavement gives out after the second of the two little coves that follow. An overlook 2.3 juddering miles further on looks down on the small flat promontory holding the 1859 **Huialoha Church**. A mile after that, the solitary **Kaupō Store** is an atmospheric general store that's normally open on weekdays only. By now, the landscape has become much drier, and you're starting to get views up to the **Kaupō Gap**, where a vast torrent of lava appears to have petrified as it poured over the smooth lip of Haleakalā Crater. To the east, you can peek into the lushness of the upper Kīpahulu Valley, but the slopes to the west are all but barren.

Beyond **St Joseph's Church**, which stands below the highway a mile beyond the Kaupō Store, the pavement starts up again and the road begins to mount the long southern flank of Haleakalā at the gentlest of angles. There's no tree cover on the deeply furrowed hillside – where some of the cracks seem like incipient Waimea Canyons – so cattle gather beneath the occasional shade tree beside the road.

Naked russet cinder cones lie scattered to either side of the road, some bearing the traces of ancient Hawaiian stone walls, while rivers of rough black *a'a* lava snake down to the sea. An especially vast hollow cone, near the 20-mile marker, marks the spot where small huts and ranch buildings start to reappear. Soon Mākena becomes visible below, with Molokini and Lanai out to sea, and three miles on it's a relief to find yourself back in green woodlands. The Tedeschi Winery (see p.354) is a little over a mile further on, with another 23 miles to go before Kahului.

4

Lanai

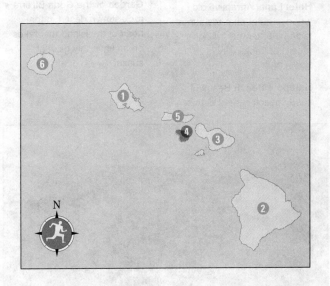

N

CHAPTER 4 # Highlights

* **Expeditions ferry** Much the best way to reach Lanai; in winter, whales are usually spotted on the ocean voyage from Maui. See p.380

* **4WD adventures** Careering down Lanai's sand-logged backroads in a rented jeep makes an exhilarating day's adventure. See p.380

* **Hotel Lanai** Attractive old wooden hotel-cum-restaurant, facing the tranquil "village green" of Lāna'i City. See p.384

* **Hulopoʻe Beach** Beautiful sandy beach shared between locals, campers, and guests at the adjoining *Mānele Bay Hotel*. See p.388

* **Shipwreck Beach** Flotsam and jetsam lie strewn across the sands of this atmospheric beach, where trans-Pacific voyagers have been coming to grief ever since the sixteenth century. See p.390

* **Garden of the Gods** Bizarre rock-strewn desert in the heart of the island that takes on an unearthly glow at sunset. See p.393

△ Shipwreck Beach

Lanai

The sixth largest Hawaiian island, and the last to open up to tourism, **Lanai** stands nine miles west of Maui and eight miles south of Molokai. Firmly in the rainshadow of its two neighbors, it's a dry and largely barren place, measuring just thirteen miles wide by eight miles long. Right up until the twentieth century, ancient Hawaiians and modern settlers alike barely bothered with it; then began its seventy-year reign as the world's largest **pineapple** producer.

Lanai's days as the "Pineapple Island" are now long over. Widely known as the "Private Island," it has become the personal fiefdom of **David H. Murdock**, a Californian businessman who in 1985 became chairman of Castle & Cooke – one of Hawaii's original Big Five, which officially reverted to the name of **Dole** in 1991 – and thus acquired control of 98 percent of the land on Lanai. Deciding that the island's future lay with tourism and not agriculture, he shut down the pineapple plantation and set about redeveloping Lanai as an exclusive resort. Since 2000, Murdock has reaffirmed his commitment to the island first by buying **a controling share in Dole** for $675 million, and then by purchasing the remaining shares for $2.5 billion and turning it into a private, delisted company. Among the former shareholders who benefited from the deal was Bill Gates, who was married on Lanai and until that point was rumored to be hoping to buy the island himself.

Prospective visitors (or purchasers) should not picture Lanai as the ultimate unspoiled Hawaiian island. In many ways, it's very un-Hawaiian, largely lacking both the lush scenery and the safe sandy beaches of the other islands. Instead it's a vast flat-topped mound of red dirt, with a low wooded mountain ridge running down the center as its "backbone." Almost all the island's three thousand inhabitants – half of whom are of Filipino ancestry, descended from laborers who were shipped here to work the fields – live in the former plantation village wildly misnamed **Lāna'i City**, 1600ft above sea level. This is also the site of all the island's hotels, restaurants, and other businesses, except for the *Mānele Bay Hotel*, which stands on the south coast near Lanai's only swimming beach.

Lanai can be a very relaxing place to visit, with plenty of wilderness trails to explore by jeep, bike, or on foot, as well as world-class golf and diving. The clientele at the two major hotels, however, tend to be either rich *kama'āinas* (residents of other Hawaiian islands), for whom the damp upland forests make a welcome weekend break, or mega-rich jet-setters, who either place a great premium on privacy or want to have stayed on every Hawaiian island. It's hard to imagine why an ordinary visitor from outside Hawaii would choose Lanai over the other islands, even though it does have one inexpensive hotel, one B&B rental, and even a campground to make it affordable. Most visitors simply come for the day, on the ferry from Maui.

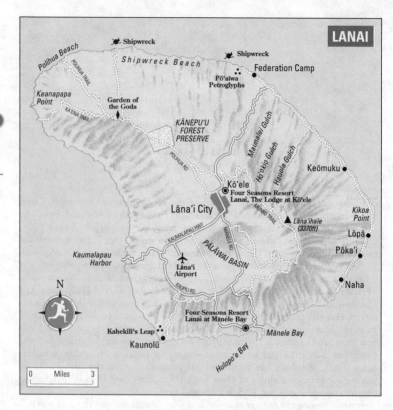

A brief history of Lanai

For the thousand years after the Polynesians first reached Hawaii, they are said to have given Lanai a wide berth, believing it to be the abode of evil spirits. Its first permanent inhabitants came across from **Maui** during the fifteenth century, and the island has remained subordinate to its larger neighbor ever since. Ancient legends say that most of the interior was used for raising pigs, and the annual tribute demanded from West Maui was paid in hogs. However, the population never rose much over three thousand, concentrated in small coastal villages such as Kaheʻa in the east and Kaunolū in the far southwest, who lived primarily by fishing.

Although European explorers dismissed Lanai as worthless and barren, it was wetter and more fertile before imported animals deforested the hillsides. Even so, early attempts by outsiders to establish commercial agriculture ended in failure. In 1802, a Chinese immigrant set up Hawaii's first sugar mill, but failed to grow enough cane to keep it going. In 1899, a similar experiment at Keōmuku, on the east coast, lasted just two years.

The main flurry of activity on Lanai in the nineteenth century came around 1850, with the establishment of Hawaii's first **Mormon church**. Mormon missionaries came here to escape the antagonism they encountered in Honolulu; when they were called back to Utah in 1857, they left the church in local Hawaiian control. In 1861, a recent Mormon convert, **William Gibson**, arrived on Lanai proclaiming himself to be "Chief President of the Islands of the Sea," and galvanized the congregation into collecting enough money (around $2500) to buy the entire Pālāwai Basin. Three years later, it was revealed that Gibson had registered all the 10,000 acres in his own name. He was excommunicated, while his flock moved on to Lāʻie on Oahu (see p.143). Not only did Gibson hold onto the land but, as the self-appointed spokesman for all native Hawaiians, he went on to become the most powerful politician in the kingdom, winding up as King David Kalākaua's prime minister.

Gibson's heirs eventually sold his holdings and, following abortive attempts to rear sheep and cattle, Lanai's population had dwindled to around 75 by 1920. After entrepreneur **Jim Dole** bought Gibson's ranch, the Lanai Ranch, for $1.1 million in 1922, he set out to grow **pineapples**, which require remarkably little water, and housed his predominantly Filipino labor force in newly built Lānaʻi City. Castle & Cooke became majority shareholders in the Dole Corporation in 1932, but the Dole name remained in use, and the Pālāwai Basin became the world's largest pineapple plantation. Its workers were expected to pick a ton of fruit per day – they were paid bonuses if they managed more – and well into the 1980s Lanai was shipping out a million pineapples a day. However, the statewide struggle to win decent wages for farm laborers eventually made it cheaper to grow pineapples in Thailand and the Philippines, and Lanai's last official harvest took place in 1992. There are still a couple of show fields near the airport, and a few plants have managed to run wild.

What's particularly surprising about the program to turn Lanai into a **tourist destination** is that it has focused as much on the pinewoods at **Kōʻele**, just outside Lānaʻi City, as on the shoreline. *The Lodge at Kōʻele* opened in 1990, followed by the more traditional beachfront *Mānele Bay Hotel* the next year, and luxury condo developments have been appearing in the vicinity of both hotels ever since. However, although Murdock has so far invested well over a billion dollars, he has yet to make the slightest profit. It's estimated that in 2005, for example, the total running cost of his operations on Lanai was around $100 million, with visitor spending totalling only $58 million. With hotel occupancy declining and condos said to be selling poorly, Murdock therefore decided to rebrand both the hotels as **Four Seasons** properties, sprucing them up a bit but with no real major changes.

As for the future, most people on Lanai feel they've debated the issue of development into the ground. Given the choice between almost total unemployment or massive investment in new leisure-industry jobs, few speak out against the changes, but there remains an undercurrent of resentment at being told they live on a "private island," as exemplified by Murdock's willingness to seal off the island and arrest intruders in 1993, to ensure that Bill Gates could get married in privacy at Mānele Bay.

On the positive side, the hotels have a policy of retraining local workers rather than bringing in outsiders – although most earn much less than they did in the fields – and young people have started to return to Lanai after completing their education elsewhere. Despite the optimistic self-restraint of the planners, who aim to limit the island's population to fifteen thousand, it remains just twenty percent of that target figure. The biggest fear on Lanai is not that development will run rampant, but that it might fizzle out altogether.

Getting to Lanai

Tiny **Lanai Airport**, perched on the western edge of the central plateau around four miles southwest of Lānaʻi City, is served by two airlines. Island Air connects it around six times daily with **Honolulu**, and also offers one weekly flight, early on Monday mornings, to **Kahului** on Maui and on to Hilo on the Big Island; all flights can also be booked through Hawaiian Airlines. Pacific Wings, under the name PW Express (☏808/873-0877 or ☏1-888/866-5022, ⓦwww.flypwx.com), operates one daily flight from Honolulu to Lanai, and also a daily connection between Lanai and Molokai, with a one-way fare of $30.

The airport holds a small store, but no café, and since the plantations closed down, it seems to have become home to all the fruit flies on the island. Guests at the major hotels are picked up by bus; for details of taxis and rental cars, see below.

It's also possible to get to Lanai by **boat**. The *Expeditions* ferry (☏808/661-3756 or 1-800/695-2624, ⓦwww.go-lanai.com) sails from Lahaina on **Maui** (see p.293) to Mānele Bay daily at 6.45am, 9.15am, 12.45pm, 3.15pm, and 5.45pm. Departures from Lanai are at 8am, 10.30am, 2pm, 4.30pm, and 6.45pm; the adult fare is $25 each way, while under-12s go for $20. The trip takes approximately 50 minutes. *Expeditions* intend to add extra sailings to Lanai from Mā'alaea on Maui's central isthmus in the near future.

Although *Expeditions* also arranges discounted golf packages and overnight stays, most ferry passengers simply come for the day. **Shuttle buses** meet each arriving ferry at the harbor and charge a $5 flat fare even for the 500-yard hop to the *Mānele Bay Hotel*. Nonetheless, if you're staying at the hotel, don't try walking instead; it's quite a distance to trundle your baggage uphill along the hot dry road.

Finally, many visitors also come to Lanai on day trips from Maui with **Trilogy Ocean Sports** (☏808/661-4743 ext 2387 or ☏1-888/225-6284, ⓦwww.sailtrilogy.com), whose **Discover Lanai** tour includes a barbecue picnic beside Hulopo'e Beach (adults $180, ages 3–15 $90).

Getting around Lanai

Lanai has the most rudimentary **road** system imaginable, with less than thirty miles of paved highway, none of which runs along the coast. As far as most visitors are concerned, the only significant stretches are the eight-mile **Mānele Road** from Lāna'i City down to Mānele Bay, and the four miles of **Kaumalapau Highway** between Lāna'i City and the airport. Free **shuttle buses** ferry guests at the three hotels along these routes. Buses between the *Mānele Bay Hotel* and *The Lodge at Kō'ele* run every half-hour until the late evening via *Hotel Lanai* in the heart of Lāna'i City; nonguests who look confident enough should have no problem hopping a ride.

There are two **car rental** outlets: **Lāna'i City Service**, affiliated with Dollar, which is based on Lāna'i Avenue a short walk south of *Hotel Lanai* in Lāna'i City (daily 7am–7pm; ☏808/565-7227 ext 23 or 1-800/JEEP-808), and the **Adventure Lanai Ecocenter** (☏808/565-7373, ⓦwww.adventurelanai.com), which doesn't have an office but will deliver a vehicle to anywhere you choose. There's no point in renting an ordinary car; the only way to explore the island at all is with a **4WD vehicle**, along a network of rough-hewn, mud-and-sand jeep trails. Furthermore, following heavy rain, many of those trails are closed to all traffic; both companies advise customers as to which roads they consider open, with the Lāna'i City Service being much the stricter of the two. Don't rent a vehicle unless you're sure you can take it where you want to go.

A basic Wrangler Jeep costs around $140 per day – the prices are high partly because there are such limited repair facilities on the island – so most visitors cram all their sightseeing into a single 24-hour period. Both companies provide full instruction if you've never driven 4WD before, plus useful booklets of suggested routes. Be warned, however, that neither offers any extra insurance; you're liable for any damage to your vehicle, which can easily amount to several thousand dollars for a basic mishap in the sand.

Lāna'i City Service also runs the island's only **taxis** (when there's a vehicle to spare), charging around $5 to the airport or Mānele Bay from Lāna'i City, and $10 from the airport to Mānele Bay.

In addition, Adventure Lanai Ecocenter offers guided **jeep tours** of the island, which involve some active hiking, at around $100 for a half-day trip. They also arrange half-day **kayaking**, **quad-biking**, and **diving** excursions; **surfing** lessons for kids; and rent out **mountain bikes**.

Where to stay

Apart from a **B&B** in Lāna'i City and **camping** at Hulopo'e Beach (see p.388), the only accommodation on Lanai is in **three hotels**. *The Lodge at Kō'ele* (see p.384) is modeled on a European country inn, while the *Mānele Bay Hotel* (see p.388) is a full-fledged Hawaiian beach resort; both are run by Four Seasons, with room rates starting at around $300. The *Hotel Lanai*, in sleepy Lāna'i City (see p.384), is lower-key and much less expensive.

When to go

There's no real reason to visit Lanai in any particular season. Room rates stay constant all year, and as a rule the island receives so little rainfall that the supposed rainy season of September to November is barely noticeable. The only beach where swimming is safe is Hulopo'e Beach, below the *Mānele Bay Hotel*, and it remains so in winter, barring the occasional *kona* (leeward) storm. The climate, however, varies between sunny Mānele Bay and cooler Lāna'i City, which is often overcast and can get chilly (down to around 50° F) in the evenings.

Nightlife and entertainment

Although **nightlife** is not something anyone would associate with Lanai, the two resort hotels make great efforts to keep guests entertained. In particular, they run a successful **visiting artists** program, offering leading writers, musicians, directors, and the like a few complimentary days on Lanai in return for readings or recitals; contact the resorts for the latest schedules. You can also hear gentle Hawaiian music at the poolside of the *Mānele Bay Hotel* most evenings, and they hold occasional *lū'aus* down by the beach. In addition, the island boasts a **movie theater** – the Lāna'i Playhouse, at Seventh and Lāna'i in Lāna'i City (☎808/565-7500).

Apart from statewide public holidays (see p.49), Lanai's major annual event is its **Aloha Week**, which usually comes in mid- to late October and features an open-air concert at Dole Park in Lāna'i City.

Meanwhile, **golf** is the island's biggest single attraction, with a course at Kō'ele designed by Greg Norman, and one at Mānele Bay by Jack Nicklaus. Both charge $190 to guests and $225 to outsiders. The nine-hole Cavendish course in Lāna'i City, between *The Lodge at Kō'ele* and the *Hotel Lanai*, is free to all comers, but doesn't offer club rental.

Lāna'i City

To think of **LĀNA'I CITY** as a town requires a stretch of the imagination; that it should call itself a "city" is little short of absurd. This neat, pretty community of just 2500 people, centered on a village green, was laid out on a basic grid pattern

△ Dole Park

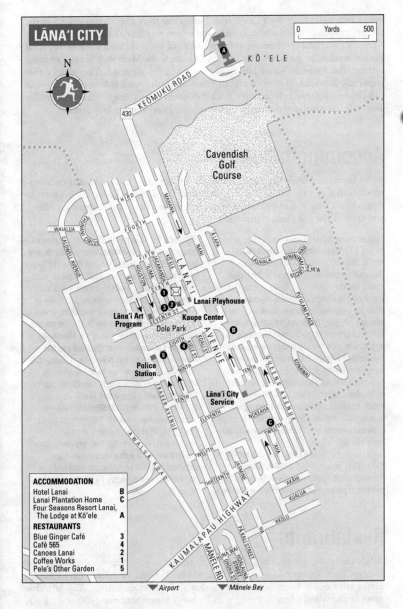

LĀNA'I CITY

0   Yards   500

N

KŌ'ELE

KEŌMUKU ROAD

430

Cavendish
Golf
Course

THIRD

FOURTH

WAIALUA

PANNING

CALDWELL AVENUE

CIRCUS

FIFTH

GAY

HOUSTON

ILIMA

KŪ'ELE

SIXTH

LĀNA'I

MAHINA

'ALAPA

MANI

LAUHALA

NĪNĪWAI 'O 'O HI'A

PU'U LANI PLACE

SEVENTH ST

Lāna'i Art
Program

Dole Park

AVENUE

KOALI ST

'ILIMA ST

Lanai Playhouse

Kaupe Center

Police
Station

EIGHTH

NINTH

TENTH

FRASER AVENUE

AWALUA ROAD

TENTH

ELEVENTH

QUEEN'S AVENUE

KONAWAI

**Lāna'i City
Service**

NOKEAHA

TWELFTH

'AHA

C

TWELFTH

THIRTEENTH

JASMINE

'AKĀHI

KUAILA

'AKOLU

KAUMALAPAU HIGHWAY

MĀNELE RD

HŪNA WAI
STREET

HI'ALAINA
STREET

OHONA ST

PA'AU STREET

ACCOMMODATION

Hotel Lanai	**B**
Lanai Plantation Home	**C**
Four Seasons Resort Lanai, The Lodge at Kō'ele	**A**

RESTAURANTS

Blue Ginger Café	**3**
Café 565	**4**
Canoes Lanai	**2**
Coffee Works	**1**
Pele's Other Garden	**5**

▼ Airport   ▼ Mānele Bay

in 1924 to house laborers from the newly opened pineapple plantations, and it has barely changed since then. You have to search to find a two-story building: the leafy backstreets hold rows of simple plantation cottages, identical but for the colors they're painted and the rampant flowers in their gardens.

Virtually all the daily business of Lanai revolves around **Dole Park**, at the heart of Lāna'i City. The main road, **Lāna'i Avenue**, runs along the eastern end, while over a hundred ninety-foot Cook Island pines rise from the wiry grassland in the center, towering over the stores, cafés, and offices that line all four sides.

Lanai's government offices are at the west end of the park, with the low-key local **police station** at the southwest corner. Officers from Maui staff it on a rotation system; the outhouse-sized **jail** alongside is seldom occupied. The island's two **supermarkets** take up most of Eighth Street, along the south side of the park – like old-fashioned general stores, they stock just about everything – while the smaller *Pele's Garden* **wholefood store** is tucked around the corner on Gay Street.

Accommodation

Apart from the *Mānele Bay Hotel* on the south shore (see p.388), all Lanai's **accommodation** is in Lāna'i City. In the seclusion of *The Lodge at Kō'ele*, there's little to remind you that you're in Hawaii at all, but the smaller-scale alternatives offer a real taste of the old plantation days.

Four Seasons Resort Lanai, The Lodge at Kō'ele 1 Keōmoku Hwy, Lāna'i City HI 96763 ☎808/565-4000 or 1-800/919-5053, ⓦwww .fourseasons.com/koele. Quite why *The Lodge* should win the *Condé Nast Traveler* readers' poll as the world's best tropical resort is anyone's guess, since the gorgeous, immensely luxurious hotel is several miles from the ocean, 1600ft up in a pine forest reminiscent of the Scottish Highlands. The ambience is pure country-house, and most of the one hundred rooms – tucked away in the low bungalows around the "executive putting course" and croquet lawns – are comfortably furnished rather than opulent. Guests have full privileges and beach access at the *Mānele Bay Hotel*, while special offers include a fourth night free, or a five-night combination with the *Mānele Bay* with one night free. ❼

Hotel Lanai 828 Lāna'i Ave ☎808/565-7211 or 1-877/665-2624, ⓦwww .hotellanai.com. Appealing wooden bungalow hotel, perched at the edge of the woods above Dole Park.

Built for Jim Dole in the 1920s, it's now run as an inexpensive, low-key alternative to the resorts, and consists of a long central veranda flanked by two wings of tasteful, comfortable but simple en-suite rooms, plus a self-contained cottage. Rates include a self-service continental breakfast abounding in pineapple. There's also a good restaurant, while guests have free access to the facilities at the two resort hotels (except the pool at the *Mānele Bay Hotel*) and can make use of the same free bus services. At the time this book went to press, *Hotel Lanai* was about to change hands, however, so changes may be imminent. Rooms ❹, cottage ❺

Lanai Plantation Home 547 Twelfth St ☎808/565-6961 or 1-800/566-6961, ⓦwww .dreamscometruelanai.com. This restored plantation home, set in nice gardens a short walk southeast of Dole Park, has four very comfortable guest rooms, each with a luxurious en-suite bathroom, that can be rented out individually, or you can also rent the entire house. Room ❹, house ❾

Restaurants

While the restaurants at *The Lodge at Kō'ele* set out to match any in the world, and *Henry Clay's Rotisserie* is a worthy alternative, the rest of Lāna'i City's eating places offer down-home atmosphere rather than gourmet cuisine. The fact that most of the island's food is brought in by barge means that most dishes start out frozen or tinned.

Blue Ginger Café 409 Seventh St ☎808/565-6363. Simple café-restaurant alongside Dole Park. It's a favorite local rendezvous, though the food is just basic plate lunches and pizzas, all for $7–10. Daily 6am–8pm.

Café 565 408 Eighth St ☎808/565-6622. As well as pizzas and calzones, this small café, with open-air seating alongside Dole Park, serves sandwiches, plate lunches, and even sushi. Mon–Fri 10am–3pm & 5–8pm, Sat 10am–3pm.

Canoes Lanai 419 Seventh St ☎808/565-6537. A local-style diner, complete with swivel stools and soda fountain, serving burgers, saimin, and big breakfast fry-ups. Daily 6.30am–1pm.

🏃 **Coffee Works** 604 Ilima St ☎808/565-6962. Spacious coffee bar a block north of Dole Park, behind the post office. Besides the espressos, they also sell a few cheap sandwiches, smoothies, and ice cream, which you can enjoy on the large *lānaʻi*. Mon–Sat 6am–4pm.

Formal Dining Room *The Lodge at Kōʻele* ☎808/565-4580. Extremely formal restaurant, with a lofty reputation and silver-service treatment. Reserve early and savor the presentation as much as the food, which is a richer, meatier version of the usual upscale Hawaiian resort cuisine. Typical appetizers include *carpaccio* of venison and *foie gras*, both priced at around $20; entrees, upwards of $42, include rack of lamb, steak, and seafood; and there are some amazing chocolate desserts. Daily 6–9.30pm.

🏃 **Henry Clay's Rotisserie** *Hotel Lanai*, 828 Lānaʻi Ave ☎808/565-7211. Friendly, intimate dining room, open for dinner only, but with an adjoining bar that remains open late each night. Under the keen supervision of its New Orleans–born chef/manager, the Cajun-influenced menu makes full use of local ingredients, with entrees ranging all the way from pizza ($18) to local venison ($46). Almost anything you choose, from an oyster in a shot glass ($1.50), to an appetizer of mussels in saffron broth ($12), to a fish entree ($27), is likely to be excellent. Be warned, however, that a change in the hotel's ownership may well mean that the restaurant too changes in the near future. Daily 5.30–9pm.

🏃 **Pele's Other Garden** Eighth Street and Houston ☎808/565-9628. Bustling health-food deli, with juices and wholesome $7 sandwiches to take out or eat in at lunchtime, which turns into a full-fledged Italian restaurant in the evening, with entrees like a gnocchi pasta special priced at $17–20. Mon–Sat 10am–2.30pm & 5–8pm.

The Terrace *The Lodge at Kōʻele* ☎808/565-4580. *The Lodge*'s somewhat less formal restaurant, with indoor and outdoor seating overlooking the lawns, serves health-conscious food, but still at quite high prices: even an egg-and-ham breakfast costs $14. Lunch is the best value, with $10 fresh-made soups and $15 grilled meat and fish dishes. Typical dinner entrees include slow-roasted lamb shank on couscous, and roasted chicken (both $30). Daily 6am–9.30pm.

The Munro Trail

The only way to explore the mountainous ridge that forms Lanai's "backbone" is along the ill-defined **Munro Trail**, as a loop trip from Lānaʻi City. This rutted track climbs through the forest to the 3370-foot summit of **Lānaʻihale**, also known as "The Hale," which on clear days becomes the only spot in Hawaii from which it's possible to see five other islands.

Although it's often promoted as a **hiking** trail, even if you manage to walk the shortest possible route – which is difficult, in the absence of signposts – it's at least twelve miles long. Most visitors prefer instead to see it from the comfort of a rented **four-wheel-drive vehicle**, which allows for detours while making it much easier to reach the summit before the clouds set in. It's also possible to take a **horseback** trip; contact *The Lodge at Kōʻele* (see opposite) for details.

Even the start of the trail is far from obvious. Basically, you head east into the woods from the main road as it heads north beyond *The Lodge*. If you're driving, it's easiest to wait until the road curves east and climbs into the woods, and turn right after a mile or so onto the paved Cemetery Road. Otherwise, simply turn right as soon as you get the chance – there are at least two options a short way along – and then, once on the ridge, turn right again. Either way, you should come to a Japanese cemetery, where the only sign on the whole route sets you off. Turn left soon after and then follow your nose; as a rule of thumb, fork left whenever you're in doubt, look for the most-used path, and don't worry about dropping down because you'll soon be heading back up again. As you climb through the fresh pine forest, look up ahead to see if clouds are sitting on the ridge; if they are, consider coming back on a day when you'll be able to make the most of the view.

George Munro's pine trees

The Munro Trail was named after **George Munro**, a naturalist from New Zealand who was employed by the Lāna'i Ranch around 1917. Having calculated that the leaves on a single tall tree on Lanai can collect forty gallons of water per hour that would not otherwise have fallen as rain, he set to work covering the island with Cook Island and Norfolk Island pines. They're recognizable partly by the knobbly bands around their trunks, and partly by their sheer abundance. The strip along the central ridge – which has turned the topmost sections of the Munro Trail into a quagmire, lined with dripping ferns – is clearly visible from Lahaina on Maui.

The first major viewpoint comes after roughly three miles, where a short spur road leads to the head of the bare, red **Maunalei Gulch**. A few sparse trees sprinkle the top of the ridge that defines its western edge, while far below you can see the jeep road that winds along the greener valley floor. Molokai should be obvious on the northern horizon, and you may even see Oahu too, to the left. Visible off to the right, the top of the connected **Ho'okia Gulch** was the site of a ferocious battle in 1778, when Big Island warriors led by Kalaniopu'u vented their spleen, after a failed bid to conquer Maui, by massacring the armies of Lanai instead.

Continuing to climb on the main trail, you soon pass some tall communications towers. Both the road and the ridge it's following narrow to the width of a single vehicle, and you find yourself driving between rounded "parapets" of mud, overhung by dense thickets of strawberry guava. Any turkeys and other gamebirds you may startle – in the absence of the usual Hawaiian mongooses, they thrive here – are forced to run shrieking up the road ahead of you.

After five miles, by which time you may well have penetrated the clouds, a clearing on the right looks out over the high, green **Waiapa'a Gulch**. For the clearest views of Lāna'i City, keep going for another muddy mile, to the very summit. It's another two miles, however, before you finally see across the ocean to West Maui, dwarfed beneath the misty silhouette of Haleakalā, while Lanai's central Pālāwai Basin spreads out behind you.

From here on, the soil reverts from dark brown mud to Lanai's more usual red earth. A rudimentary "crossroads," just beyond the exposed portion of the ridge and a total of 8.5m from the start, marks the start of **'Āwehi Road** to the left. This jeep track runs all the way to the sea at the southeast corner, between Lōpa and Naha (see p.392), but it's in far too bad a condition to recommend. As the Munro Trail drops ever more steeply, clearings on the left frame views of Kahoolawe, with Mauna Kea on the Big Island potentially visible in the endless ocean beyond.

Drivers can follow more or less any of the countless red-dirt roads that branch off at the southern end of the trail, and thread their way back to town. If hiking, you'll want to take the shortest route back to Lāna'i City, so head as directly as you can along the base of the ridge, which means generally following right forks.

South and west Lanai

The southern half of Lanai used to be the main pineapple-growing region, but now all activity revolves around the tourist industry. **Hulopoʻe Beach** is the only safe swimming beach on the island, while **Mānele Bay**, next door, is its only pleasure-boat harbor. That's as much as visitors usually bother with, though **Kaunolū** in the far southwest is Lanai's most important historical site.

Lanai's **west coast** is the one leeward shoreline in Hawaii to have sea cliffs, some of which rise over a thousand feet. These have been shorn away by wintertime *kona* storms, while the rest of the island is sheltered by Maui and Molokai. No road runs along the coast, though it is possible to drive down to Kaumalapau Harbor.

The Pālāwai Basin

It would be easy to drive repeatedly through the **Pālāwai Basin**, immediately south of Lānaʻi City, without ever noticing what it is. Once it's pointed out to you, however, it's glaringly obvious that you're in the collapsed caldera of the volcano that built Lanai. The entire 15,000-acre basin – until just a few years ago, the largest pineapple field on earth – is a bowl-shaped depression. The high mountain ridge on its eastern side stands thousands of feet taller than the low rise to the west, while the bowl spills over altogether to flow down to the ocean on the southern side. Nothing is planted now in the fields, but the occasional vivid flowering tree lights up the highway.

Luahiwa Petroglyphs

On the eastern edge of the Pālāwai Basin, a grove of trees a short way up the hillside toward the peak of Lānaʻihale marks the site of the **Luahiwa Petroglyphs**. It's hard to find, so ask for directions at your hotel or car rental outlet. Etched into a couple of dozen boulders embedded in the soil – which are thought to have formed part of a *heiau* dedicated to prayers for rain – these carvings were created during several separate eras. The earliest examples, which may be as much as five hundred years old, show simple stick figures, sometimes superimposed on each other. A couple of centuries later, the Hawaiians began to depict wedge-shaped bodies, and thereafter the human shapes have muscles and wield oars or weapons. Animals also start to appear, with images of horses produced after European contact. Some are known to have been embellished by native Hawaiian students in the 1870s.

Mānele Bay

Just under five miles from Lānaʻi City, Mānele Road drops from the southern lip of the Pālāwai Basin to wind for three more miles down to **Mānele Bay**. The word *Mānele* refers to the Hawaiian equivalent of a sedan chair, but no one knows why the long-vanished fishing village that once stood here bore that name.

As parched and barren as a Greek island, the bay is protected from the open ocean by the high flat-faced cliff on its eastern side, which glows red when it's hit by the setting sun. Until 1965, when the harbor was dredged and further shielded by a lava breakwater, there was a small black-sand beach. People fish from the rocks or picnic nearby, and the odd brave soul dodges the boats to go snorkeling, but there's nothing much here apart from an overpriced little snack bar, the *Harbor Café* (closed Sat), and the headquarters of Trilogy's dive operations (see below). Day-trippers arriving on the *Expeditions* ferry from Maui (see p.380) usually head straight for Hulopoʻe Beach, around to the left, or up to Lānaʻi City.

Mānele Bay Hotel

Despite its name, the *Four Seasons Resort Lanai at Mānele Bay*, 1 Mānele Bay Rd (℡808/565-2000 or 1-800/919-5053, Ⓦwww.fourseasons.com/manelebay; terrace view ❻, garden or ocean view ❾) is not actually at Mānele Bay, although its jade-tiled roof is visible from the harbor. It spreads itself instead across the hillside above the much nicer Hulopoʻe Beach, a few hundred yards west. Although *The Lodge at Kōʻele* is regarded as the island's flagship hotel, the *Mānele Bay* conforms far more closely to what most visitors want from Hawaii: a lovely beach, ocean views, marble terraces, cocktails by the pool and plenty of sun. Its 250 lavishly appointed rooms (some of which come with their own private butler) are arranged in two-story terraced buildings, engulfed by colorful gardens, with a golf course alongside. The whole property is themed towards Hawaiian and Pacific history, and centers on a wonderful pool. There's also a luxury spa, where Hawaiian treatments such as *lomi lomi* massage or *ti*-leaf wraps are available ($100 and up for 45min).

The less formal of the hotel's two **restaurants**, the lovely, breezy ⚓ *Hulopoʻe Court*, opens for breakfast and dinner (daily 7–11am & 6–9.30pm), charging $25 (full) or $17 (continental) for the morning buffet, and around $37 for delicious evening menu items such as steamed Hawaiian seafood *laulau*. The dinner-only *Ihilani Dining Room* serves "Mediterranean Gourmet" cuisine, with steamed and grilled island fish or roast meat for around $40. At lunchtime, your choice is restricted to sandwiches and gourmet snacks like a $16 burger, or *ahi* sashimi for $18, beside the pool.

Hulopoʻe Beach

Only accessible by road from Mānele Bay – it's just a couple of hundred yards further along, at the end of Mānele Road – but also reached via a footpath down from the *Mānele Bay Hotel*, the curving sandy strip known as **Hulopoʻe Beach** is by far the best swimming beach on Lanai. What's more, it's far enough from the hotel to retain its own individual character; apart from a small equipment kiosk at the west end, the hotel maintains no snack bars or other facilities for guests.

The beach was set aside by Castle & Cooke as a beach park in 1961, and the main users, especially at weekends, still tend to be local families rather than tourists. They come to swim, picnic, and explore the **tide pools** at the foot of **Mānele Cone**, the extinct cinder cone dividing Hulopoʻe Bay and Mānele Bay. Both the tide pool area and the bays form a Marine Life Conservation Area. **Spinner dolphins** are regular visitors, and in the morning especially, the **snorkeling** here can be excellent.

The waters off the south coast of Lanai are also recognized as among the very best **diving** sites in Hawaii. Regular dive trips are organized by **Trilogy Ocean Sports** (℡808/661-4743 ext 2387 or ℡1-888/225-6284, Ⓦwww.sailtrilogy .com), whose Discover Lanai day-trips from Maui (see p.286) include a picnic beside **Hulopoʻe Beach**.

The beach park maintains showers and restrooms just back from the sand, and it's also possible to **camp**, for up to a week, at a tiny, peaceful, six-pitch campground

(☎808/565-3982). There's a charge of $5 per person per night, plus a one-time $5 registration fee.

The black lava walls of a Hawaiian village that was occupied intermittently during the last five centuries are clearly visible between the hotel and the beach. Sometimes it held permanent residents, who grew gourds and sweet potatoes, while during other periods it served as a seasonal fishing camp. Signs here and there explain how the whole place used to look.

Pu'u Pehe

Although you can't quite see it from either Hulopo'e Beach or Mānele Bay, Mānele Cone curves around to protect a tiny, inaccessible pocket beach, with the islet of **Pu'u Pehe** just offshore. Technically, this isolated rock is a sea stack, a rocky column that was formerly part of a cliff but has become cut off. It's also known as Sweetheart Rock because, according to local legend, a jealous warrior once hid his Maui-born wife (Pehe) in a cave here, and when she was killed by a storm, he threw himself from the top of the rock. There is some sort of ancient shrine up there, but archeologists can't tell what it was used for. The best way to see Pu'u Pehe is from a boat entering or leaving Mānele Bay.

Kaunolū

No one has lived in the hot, dry valley of **KAUNOLŪ**, in Lanai's remote south-western corner, for well over a century. As a result, its ruined stone walls constitute one of the best-preserved ancient village sites in Hawaii, though some may not think it worth the long and extremely bumpy ride down. The route has deteriorated so much, in fact, that in recent years both rental companies have forbidden customers from driving their cars on it, and unless you have access to your own vehicle the only way to see it currently is on an ATV tour with the Adventure Lanai Ecocenter (see p.380).

To reach Kaunolū, take Mānele Road as far as the Mānele Bay turnoff and then follow paved Kaupili Road as it loops east to drop toward the golf course. Within half a mile, turn right where a straight red-dirt road crosses the highway, just before a fenced enclosure; water pipes can be seen on the left. As you reach a long fence on the right-hand side, turn left down a smaller dirt road. This descends beyond the irrigated area, passing rows of long-dead *wili-wili* trees, to reach two parking lots above **Kaunolū Gulch.**

Despite its narrowness and barren appearance, the gulch appealed to the ancient Hawaiians because it offered a sheltered canoe landing for fishermen in the rich inshore waters, and a freshwater spring not far inland. A trail from the upper parking lot leads through the walls of the main village, built on the gulch's eastern rim. However, they're mostly concealed by wild *pili* grass, grown originally for thatch, and it makes more sense simply to park at the end of the road and take the footpath from here down into the gulch, to a large, trash-strewn house platform that's said to have been fortified for use by the young **Kamehameha the Great** during his frequent deep-sea fishing trips to the area.

Barely thirty yards across, the floor of the gulch has a scattering of trees and a slope of black boulders at the ocean's edge. A trail climbs the far side, passing a rudimentary canoe shed, to the **Halulu Heiau**, where a large stone platform marks the site of the village's temple. You're now atop a slender headland; a gap in the stark rock columns on its western side gives access to a cliff that drops 90ft into the foaming ocean. "Cliff-jumping" was a mark of bravery among Hawaiian warriors, and this plunge – into a mere twelve feet of water – was known as **Kahekili's Leap**, in honor of the former chief of Maui. You have to be pretty brave to edge anywhere near it, but if you do so you'll see that it frames a good view of the thousand-foot Pali Koholo that lines Lanai's west coast.

Kaumalapau Harbor

West of Lanai's airport, Kaumalapau Highway winds for four miles down the coastal cliffs. En route, it offers views northwards to the sea stacks – tall, thin islands – known as the **Nānāhoa**, which have been set aside as a bird sanctuary and can't be approached more closely.

The highway ends at **Kaumalapau Harbor**, built in the 1920s to ship Lanai's pineapples to a waiting world, but now used only by local fishermen and the once-weekly ships that bring in almost all of Lanai's food supplies. It's a functional rather than a scenic port, where there's no temptation even to get out of your car.

The east coast

Most visitors who rent 4WD vehicles on Lanai set out to drive down as many of the island's roads as they can. The longest of the lot, **Keōmuku Road**, runs the full length of Lanai's east coast, a forty-mile round-trip from Lāna'i City that on island maps may appear to offer plentiful beaches, sleepy long-lost towns, and ocean views. In reality it's a long, hard drive for very little reward, and you'd be better off simply driving its paved section as far as the sea, taking the detour north to **Shipwreck Beach**, and skipping the jeep road south altogether.

Keōmuku Road heads briefly north from *The Lodge at Kō'ele*, then veers east to enter the forest and cross the lower northern end of Lanai's central ridge. As soon as it leaves the plateau, it enters a barren but spectacular landscape, meandering down a long, red, desolate hillside; Molokai is visible to the left, West Maui to the right, and Haleakalā in the distance beyond. For much of its eight-mile descent, you'll get views of the giant, ragged **Kaimuhoku meteor crater**, but the road never approaches the rim close enough to see into it. Whichever way you turn when the pavement runs out – southeast down the coast, or northwest to Shipwreck Beach – four-wheel-drive is essential.

Shipwreck Beach

Just over a mile after an obvious left turn at the foot of Keōmuku Road, the bumpy track passes the tumbledown shacks of **Federation Camp**. This recreational weekend "village," built by Filipino plantation workers in the 1950s and still occasionally used by their descendants, backs onto a little crescent of sand that's fine for fishing but not swimming. This is **Kaiolohia Beach** ("tranquil sea"), but the name has also come to refer to the whole eight-mile stretch west to Polihua.

Lanai's northern shoreline, however, is more commonly known as **Shipwreck Beach** because of its remarkable history of maritime accidents. Countless vessels have come to grief in these shallow, treacherous waters; the coast is littered with fragments, while two large wrecks remain stuck fast a few hundred yards offshore. Some historians have even suggested that a sixteenth-century Spanish galleon may have been wrecked somewhere along here; see p.532 for more details.

The sand road lurches to a halt at an informal parking lot less than half a mile beyond Federation Camp, by which time the tree cover has given out, too. Keep walking in the same direction for a few yards, and from the ruined foundations of a former lighthouse you'll be able to see the rusting orange hulk of a World War II **"Liberty Ship"** propped up on the rocks, almost completely out of the water. No one seems sure how it got there; it may have been deliberately beached.

From here, an enjoyable **hike** heads northwards for closer views of the wreck; allow at least an hour, though it's possible to make a day of it by continuing all the way to Polihua. The only viable route runs along the shorefront; if you try to set off further inland, you'll soon find yourself confronted by a succession of gullies filled with thorny *kiawe* scrub, where the only trails have been made by animals, not humans, and close over at waist height. Head instead for the mouth of the first gully you come to. A thin filament of sand, a few feet wide, runs just beyond the vegetation, but it's often so narrow that you have to sidestep the waves. As you pick your way across the tide pools sunk into the odd spit of lava, you'll soon encounter all sorts of flotsam and jetsam.

A mile or so along, you round a final corner to find a large red refrigerated container washed onto the beach. The wreck of the ship lies a hundred yards offshore – you can easily pick out the details of its deck – while the green valleys of east Molokai rise directly behind it.

The only other wreck that survives relatively intact on Shipwreck Beach is an oil tanker lost in the 1950s, some six miles further on at **Awalua**. If you're determined to see it, a far less grueling approach would be to walk a mile east from Polihua Beach (see p.393).

Pō'aīwa Petroglyphs

From the same parking lot where the trail to the lighthouse and Liberty Ship begins, a short walk directly inland leads to a gulch where the rocks still bear a handful of **petroglyphs** carved by ancient Hawaiians. As you face back down the small ramp from the lighthouse platform, follow the footpath bearing fractionally to the right, which if you're lucky will be marked with faintly discernible splashes of white paint. After about 200 yards, beyond a rock with a painted warning, you drop down into the gully itself. It's filled with large red boulders; where sections have shorn off in places to leave smooth flat surfaces, the rocks are incised with tiny stick drawings and bird-headed figures.

South along the coast

To drive **south** along the coast, simply continue along Keōmuku Road instead of taking the left turn to Shipwreck Beach described above. Be sure to check with your rental company whether the road is currently passable, however. Assuming it is, from this initial junction onwards, the road repeatedly divides into separate deep sandy channels, which then rejoin after a few hundred yards. Whichever branch you follow, you'll find yourself deep in the woods for most of the way along. Thanks to soil runoff from the hills above, the shoreline pushes further out to sea by an amazing ten feet every year; only rarely do you glimpse the ocean, let alone West Maui across the ʻAuʻau Channel. Similarly, the encroaching scrubby vegetation makes it hard even to spot the long-overgrown sites of the various abandoned villages along the way.

The windward coasts of other Hawaiian islands are usually lush and fertile, but the mountains of Maui ensure that little rain reaches Lanai. Only the valley of **Maunalei**, a mile down the road, was wet enough to grow taro, and it still supplies most of the island's fresh water; the jeep road up the valley is almost always barred.

Six miles from the turnoff, in a small grove of coconut palms, **Mālamalama Church** is all that survives of the village of **Keōmuku**. Built to serve a new sugar plantation in 1899, the village was deserted within two years, after the plantation went broke. The church is not a very evocative relic; its original wood rotted away, so it has been completely rebuilt using fresh timber.

Normally, the one difficult stretch on Keōmuku Road comes after ten miles, as it undulates across the headland at Kikoa Point. At **Lōpā**, immediately beyond, it twice passes within a few feet of the waves, and a couple of oceanfront parking lots offer views of ancient fishponds – now mostly submerged – as well as across to the island of Kahoolawe (see p.332). By the time the road ends at **Naha**, after just over twelve miles, it has made a right-angle turn and is heading along Lanai's south coast, with West Maui out of sight behind you.

North Lanai

The eight-mile drive from Lānaʻi City to the **north coast** is the best four-wheel-drive excursion on the island. En route, the scenery ranges from the dust bowl of the central plateau, through thick woodlands and multicolored desert, to one of Hawaii's emptiest and largest beaches. The main drawback is that **Polihua Road** is truly a dirt road; it's the filthiest drive imaginable, leaving you coated in thick, red mud even if you never wind down your windows. As the famed Garden of the Gods is best seen at sunset, make this your last stop of the day before heading home to wash off the grime.

Kānepuʻu Forest Preserve

For its first two miles, northwest from *The Lodge at Kōʻele*, Polihua Road runs through abandoned pineapple fields. It then passes over a cattle grid to enter the fenced-off **Kānepuʻu Forest Preserve**. This 590-acre tract, run by the Nature Conservancy of Hawaii, was set aside in the early 1990s in a belated attempt to preserve one of the few remaining vestiges of the dryland forests that once covered much of Hawaii. Many of the animals it holds are not indigenous – most obviously, the axis deer hunted by local sportsmen every weekend – but it also protects 48 native Hawaiian tree species, including gardenia (*nāʻū*) and sandalwood (*ʻiliahi*).

Not far short of the Garden of the Gods, the **Kānepuʻu Self-Guided Trail** is a ten-minute loop trail that enables visitors to get a sense of this unusual environment. Markers along the way identify the rarest species.

Garden of the Gods

Lanai's extraordinary **Garden of the Gods** looks more like the "badlands" of the American Wild West than anything you'd expect to find in Hawaii. Perched on a bleak, windblown plateau above the island's north coast, a total of five miles out from Lāna'i City, this small desert wilderness is predominantly a rich russet red, but its unearthly hillocks and boulders are scored through with layers of lithified sand of every conceivable hue – grays, yellows, ochres, browns, and even blues. At sunset, the whole place seems to glow, and the rocks lying scattered across the red sands cast long, eerie shadows.

During the 1980s, a craze swept Hawaii in which locals erected **rock cairns** in isolated places in the belief that such "shrines" were an ancient Hawaiian tradition. Garden of the Gods was until recently filled with hundreds of **cairns**, but now that the practice is officially discouraged, and the old ones have toppled, it has reverted to something like its natural state.

Although the main depression at the Garden of the Gods holds the most impressive rock formations, it's worth continuing for at least a short distance beyond. Take the right fork at the only point where the route may be hard to make out, and as the hillside starts to slope down, you come to a fabulous vantage point that looks across the bare red soil toward the island of Molokai.

Polihua Beach

A short way past the Garden of the Gods, signposts mark the junction of the Ka'ena and Polihua roads. The latter is the right fork, which gets steadily worse as it drops toward the ocean, cutting a groove into the red earth. It virtually never rains here – the clouds that drift over the plateau seldom reach this far – and the views are amazing.

At sea level, the road ends at the edge of broad **Polihua Beach**, where the red dust gives way to broad yellow sand. Over a hundred yards wide and 1.5 miles

△ Polihua Beach

long, Polihua is a magnificent sight, and the chances are you'll have it to yourself. Until the 1950s, this remote spot was a favorite laying ground for green turtles – the name means "eggs in the bosom." They rarely turn up these days, but during the winter humpback **whales** can often be seen not far offshore, in the Kalohi Channel that separates Lanai from Molokai.

Like the similar vast, windswept beaches at the western extremities of Kauai (Polihale; see p.514) and Molokai (Pāpōhaku; see p.429), Polihua is best admired from a distance. The current is always too dangerous for swimming, though there's great **windsurfing** around the headland to the east. Beyond that stretches Kaiolohia or Shipwreck Beach; as described on p.390, it's possible to hike its full eight-mile length.

Molokai

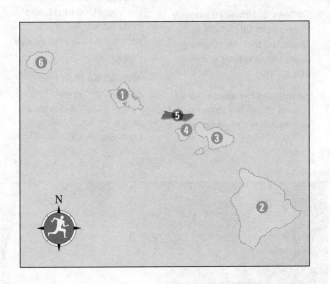

CHAPTER 5

Highlights

* **Hālawa Valley** Superb guided hikes explore this lush tropical valley, at the far eastern end of the island. See p.410

* **Kamakou Preserve** The rainforest of eastern Molokai is home to some of Hawaii's rarest birds and plants. See p.413

* **Coffees of Hawai'i** Gloriously relaxing plantation café in Kualapu'u that serves fresh-picked Muleskinner coffee. See p.416

* **Kalaupapa Peninsula** A truly special place: the former leper colony where Belgian priest Father Damien carried out his inspiring mission. See p.418

* **Molokai Mule Ride** Let a mule carry you down the steep trail to remote Kalaupapa – they've been doing it all their lives. See p.419

* **Pāpōhaku Beach** Perhaps the largest, emptiest, and most fearsomely wave-battered beach in all Hawaii. See p.429

* **Molokai Ka Hula Piko** Atmospheric annual festival held in the upland groves where the art of *hula* was born. See p.430

△ Hammock outside Hotel Molokai

Molokai

MOLOKAI is not the sort of island you'd expect to find halfway between Oahu and Maui. With a population of just eight thousand, and a mere fraction of the tourist trade of its hectic neighbors, it feels more like a small Caribbean outpost than a part of modern Hawaii. Measuring forty miles west to east, but only ten miles north to south, it doesn't have a single traffic light or elevator. No building on Molokai stands taller than a palm tree, and even the capital, **Kaunakakai**, is no more than a dusty street of wooden false-front stores.

There's some truth in the criticism that there's nothing to do on Molokai. If you like to stay in plush hotels, spend lots of money in shops and restaurants, and try out expensive sports and pastimes, this is probably not the place for you. The infrastructure for tourists is minimal, nightlife is virtually nonexistent, and the beaches may look nice but hardly any are good for swimming.

Many visitors, however, rank Molokai as their favorite island, saying it offers a taste of how Hawaii must have been fifty or sixty years ago. Until recently, Molokai was promoted under the slogan of "The Most Hawaiian Island"; now it makes more sense to think of it as "The Last Hawaiian Island." With a higher proportion of native Hawaiians than any of the major islands, it has resisted excessive development while maintaining a friendly and distinctive character. Where else in the US could an exhibition of schoolchildren's art include graffiti by a teenager who laments that he's "never seen any graffiti in person"? Spend any time exploring the island – even visiting "attractions" that might on paper sound too mundane to bother with – and you'll soon find yourself drawn into the life of the community. That said, Molokai holds some indisputable highlights as well, including unspoiled **scenery** to rival any in Hawaii – from ravishing **Hālawa Valley** in the east to gigantic, deserted **Pāpōhaku Beach** in the west – and the poignant historical relic of Father Damien's leprosy colony at **Kalaupapa Peninsula**.

A brief history of Molokai

Molokai may have been home to as many as thirty thousand people in ancient times. Lush **Hālawa Valley**, at its **eastern** end, was one of the first regions to be settled in Hawaii – remains have been unearthed of Polynesian-style dwellings dating back to the seventh century – and an almost permanent state of war seems to have existed between the Kona and Koʻolau sides of the eastern mountain.

The **western** end of the island was also extensively settled. Its proximity to the main thoroughfare used by canoes traveling between Maui, the Big Island, and

MOLOKAI

Kaiwi Channel

Kalaupapa Peninsula

Hipuapua Falls
Cape Hālawa
Pu'u o Hoku Ranch
HALAWA VALLEY
Moa'ula Falls
Papalaua Valley
Wailau Valley
Twenty Mile Beach
Pāku'o
Kamakou (4961ft)
'Ili'ili'ōpae Heiau
Our Lady of Sorrows Church
St Joseph 'Ualapu'e Church
'Ualapu'e Fishpond
Palaoa Fishpond
KAMAKOU
Pelekunu Valley
Mōkapu Island
Oka'la Island
Huelo Island
Waikolu Valley
PEPE'OPAE TRAIL
Smith-Bronte Landing
Kamalō
Ali'i Fishpond
Keawanui Fishpond
Pāka'ula Fishpond
Waikolu Lookout
Pālā'au State Park
Kalaupapa
Kauhakō Crater
Kala'e
Judd Pk.
Mule Stables
Meyer Sugar Mill
Kala'e
Awahua Beach
KALAUPAPA MULE TRAIL
Ka Ule o Nānāhoa
KUKUIOHAPU'U TRAIL
Lua Nā Moku'iliahi (Sandalwood Pit)
Kualapu'u
Kualapu'u Reservoir
Ho'olehua
MAUNALOA HWY
Pāhuhiwa
Kawela Battleground
Kala'e
Kalama'ula
Kaunakakai
One Ali'i Beach
Kahinapōhaku Fishpond
Kaloko'eli Fishpond
Kaloni'a Fishpond
Kaunakakai Harbor
Kapuāiwa Coconut Grove
Kalohi Channel
Pailolo Channel
Mo'omomi
Kawā'aloa Bay
Mo'omomi Bay
Ka'ana
Maunaloa
'Amikopala (1346ft)
MAUNA LOA
KALUAKO'I ROAD
Kaluako'i
'Ilio Point
Kāwākiu Iki Bay
Kāwākiu Nui Bay
Pu'u o Kalaka
Pāpōhaku Beach County Pk.
Pāpōhaku Beach
Dixie Maru Beach
Kaunalā Beach
Hale o Lono Harbor
La'au Point

N

0   Miles   6

Oahu made it a staging post and meeting place for travelers from all the islands. The quarries of Kalauako'i were such a valuable source of the hard stone used to make adzes that chiefs from elsewhere would come to Molokai for extended stays to build up their arsenals. Umi, the legendary ruler of the Big Island, for example, is said to have erected 2400 dwellings during one such visit. In addition, the taro farmers of the wet valleys of the north shore would spend their winters fishing at drier Mo'omomi to the west.

During the eighteenth century, the fertile valleys and rich fishponds of the east attracted a succession of foreign **invaders** to Molokai. Among the chiefs who celebrated their conquests by erecting mighty war temples (such as **'Ili'ili'ōpae Heiau**) were Alapa'inui of the Big Island, Kahekili from Maui, and Kamehameha the Great himself.

For around fifty years after the arrival of the Europeans, however, Molokai was largely ignored. That was partly because the coast held no safe anchorages for ocean-going ships, but also because the island had acquired a reputation for being a place of sorcery and black magic, as the home of the greatly feared **poisonwood gods** (see p.426).

The concept of Molokai as being God-forsaken no doubt played a role in the decision to site a **leprosy colony** at Kalaupapa during the 1860s, though this resulted in the Belgian miracle-worker **Father Damien** giving the island its only brush with world fame (for the full story, see box, pp.420–421). By the time **Robert Louis Stevenson** visited in 1889, Damien was dead; so too was the vast majority of the island's native population, wiped out by imported diseases. Stevenson wrote, "The whole length or breadth of this once busy isle I have either coasted by or ridden. And where are the people? where are the houses? where is the smoke of the fires? I see again Apaka riding by me on the leeward beach; I hear again the sound of his painful laughter and the words of his refrain: '*Pau kanaka make,*' which means 'finished; people dead.'"

Meanwhile, the **Molokai Ranch** had been established, taking over the entire western end of the island for raising **cattle**. With the construction of pipelines and tunnels to channel water across from the northern valleys, Molokai went on to prosper, producing **honey** and **pineapples**. Like everywhere in Hawaii, however, agriculture on Molokai began to turn unprofitable during the 1970s, and the island went into recession. Unemployment hit hard, and some Molokai residents found themselves having to commute to Maui each day to work in the resorts. At home, however, local resistance to development, and a perennial water shortage, combined to thwart ambitious plans to shift the economy toward **tourism**. Thus far the visitor facilities that have been created around the former pineapple town of **Maunaloa** have had little impact on the level of tourism to the island, while the construction of new luxury housing in the Kaluako'i area has yet to be matched by the development of resort facilities like hotels or restaurants. In fact, Molokai is experiencing a small-scale revival of agriculture, in the shape of a burgeoning **coffee** plantation on the central "saddle" between the two mountains, and a much more secretive, and less welcome, experimental program by Monsanto to grow **GM crops** in the fields near Kaunakakai.

Molokai overview

Like Oahu and Maui, Molokai consists of two separate volcanoes, plus the "saddle" that lies between them. At almost 5000ft, the younger mountain to the east – sometimes named after its highest peak, Kamakou, but usually referred to as simply the **Eastern Mountain** – is tall enough to capture most of the island's rain. Its north shore holds the world's highest **sea cliffs**, pierced by spectacular valleys, but it's virtually impossible to reach, and there's hardly anywhere from which you can even see it. The rainforest at the top of the mountain, protected as the **Kamakou Preserve**, can only be explored on foot.

From Molokai's principal town, tiny **Kaunakakai** in the center of the south coast, a ribbon of colorful little settlements stretches east along the shoreline, all the way to sumptuous **Hālawa Valley**. To the west, the smoother, smaller, and much drier mountain of **Mauna Loa** offers little sign of life, apart from the plantation settlement of **Maunaloa** and the oceanfront oasis of **Kaluako'i**. Molokai's central plain holds a few more farming villages, while tacked on below the cliffs to the north is the isolated **Kalaupapa Peninsula**, still home to the island's celebrated leprosy colony.

Getting to Molokai

Despite its proximity to both Oahu and Maui, Molokai has earned itself a reputation of being hard to reach. Locals may complain that it can be hard to get a seat on the weekend (because the airport is too small to cope with large aircraft), but tourists prepared to be flexible are unlikely to experience problems in reserving a flight.

Molokai's main **airport**, outside Ho'olehua in the center of the island, is currently served by direct flights from **Oahu**, **Maui**, and **Lanai** only, though it's easy enough to connect with flights from the other Hawaiian islands. Island Air (see p.32) offers the most daily flights, with around five from **Honolulu** and two from **Kahului** on Maui. Hawaiian Airlines currently operates no services of its own, but code-shares with Island Air.

Several lesser operators fly to Molokai. Pacific Wings, which offers low-cost flights under the name PW Express (℡808/567-6814 on Molokai, ℡808/873-0877 on Maui, ℡1-888/575-4546 or ℡1-888/866-5022, ⓦwww.pacificwings .com or ⓦwww.flypwx.com), operates hourly flights from Honolulu to the main airport every day between 6.20am and 7.15pm, as well as one or two flights daily from Kahului on Maui, and one from Lanai. As this book went to press, Go! (℡1-888/435-9462, ⓦwww.iflygo.com) was about to start service between Honolulu and Molokai, with standard one-way fares on both airlines set at $30. In addition, Paragon Air (℡808/244-3356 or 1-866/946-4744, ⓦwww.paragon -air.com) runs on-demand charter flights connecting Molokai with any airport on Maui or Lanai.

For details of flights direct to the **Kalaupapa Peninsula** – not a sensible option if you want to see the whole island – from Oahu, Maui, and elsewhere (or "top-side") on Molokai, see p.422.

It's also possible to make a 1hr 30min ferry crossing between Maui and Molokai on the *Molokai Princess* (adults $40 one-way, children $20; ℡808/662-3535 or 1-877/500-6284, ⓦwww.mauiprincess.com). The boat leaves Lahaina at 7.15am and 6pm daily, and returns from Kaunakakai Harbor at 5.30am and 4pm.

Getting around

There is no **public transport** on Molokai, and the airport is several miles out of town. **Taxis** are supplied by Molokai Off-Road Tours & Taxis (℡808/553-3369,

ⓌW www.molokai.com/offroad), who also run **minivan tours**, for three or more passengers, costing $49 per person for "island highlights", $41 for Hālawa Valley, and $53 for a **jeep tour** that will take you up to, but not into, the Kamakou Preserve (see p.413). Most visitors, however, will feel stranded without a car. The national **rental car** chains are Budget (Ⓣ808/567-6877) and Dollar (Ⓣ808/567-6156), both based at the airport; reserve via the toll-free numbers or websites listed on p.33. Dollar has a few 4WD jeeps, but neither company has many vehicles, and, unless you make a reservation several weeks in advance, they may have nothing at all available. Island Kine (Ⓣ808/553-5242 or 1-866/527-7368, ⓌW www.molokai-car-rental.com), located at the central intersection in Kaunakakai, is a friendly local alternative that offers a wide selection of cars and trucks at reasonable prices, and provides free airport transfers as well. Molokai Rent-A-Car (Ⓣ808/553-3929 or 1-866/239-3929) has particularly good rates for small compacts.

Where to stay

Molokai has a small stock of **accommodation** options, though those hotels that do exist tend to be reasonably priced. Despite continuing rumors as to its re-opening, the best-known resort property, the *Kaluakoʻi Hotel* at the island's western end, had been closed for six years when this book went to press. That leaves the *Hotel Molokai* and the *Molokai Shores* in **Kaunakakai** as the most obvious lodging choices. In addition, the Molokai Ranch runs the small, upscale *Molokai Ranch Lodge* up in sleepy Maunaloa and offers expensive "tentalows" on a remote west-end beach. Although a handful of pretty B&Bs are scattered along the **south-eastern coast**, there's nowhere to stay in or near Molokai's most scenic spot, Hālawa Valley, while the island's most historic area, the Kalaupapa Peninsula, can only be visited on guided day-trips.

Molokai festivals and events

You'll find what news there is on Molokai, plus listings of upcoming events, in the free weekly *Dispatch* newspaper (ⓌW www.themolokaidispatch.com), while the website ⓌW www.molokaievents.com also has an up-to-date calendar.

3rd Sat in Jan	Molokai Makahiki; festival of ancient Hawaiian sports, Kaunakakai
March 26	Prince Kuhio Day; state holiday
May 1	May Day, Lei Day; state-wide celebrations
3rd Sat in May	Molokai Ka Hula Piko; celebrations for the birth of *hula*, Pāpōhaku Beach Park
late May	Kanaka Ikaika Molokai–Oahu kayak race
June 11	Kamehameha Day, state-wide; arts and crafts fair, Kaunakakai
Aug 18	Admission Day; state holiday
late Sept	Na Wahine O Ke Kai, Molokai–Oahu women's outrigger canoe race starts at Hale O Lono
late Sept/early Oct	Aloha Festival week on Molokai, including Molokai Mule Run, Kaunakakai
early Oct	Molokai–Oahu men's outrigger canoe race starts at Hale O Lono
Nov	Friendly Isle Ultra-Marathon
Nov	He Makana Aloha Competition; day-long music, dance, and crafts festival, Maunaloa

As for traditional **camping**, the two county-run sites, at **One Aliʻi Beach Park** in the east and **Pāpōhaku Beach Park** in the west, cost $5 a day and limit campers to a three-day maximum stay; permits are issued in person only at the Mitchell Pauʻole Center on ʻĀiloa Street in Kaunakakai (Mon–Fri 8am–4pm; ☎808/553-3204). Permits for the free campgrounds at **Waikolu Lookout** and **Pālāʻau State Park**, both of which allow a maximum stay of five nights, can be picked up from the Department of Land and Natural Resources, near the post office on Puʻupeʻelua Avenue in Hoʻolehua (Mon–Fri 7.30am–4pm; ☎808/567-6891).

When to go

In terms of **climate**, it makes very little difference what time of year you visit Molokai; the west is sunny all year round, while the higher or further east you go, the greater the chance of rain. Only a few of the beaches are suited to swimming, even in summer. All else being equal, the best time to come to Molokai is in May, during the **Molokai Ka Hula Piko** festival (see p.430).

Watersports and other activities

The main **activity operator** on the island is **Molokai Fish and Dive**. The company runs a store at 63 Ala Malama St in Kaunakakai (Mon–Sat 8am–6pm, Sun 8am–2pm; ☎808/553-5926, ⓦwww.molokaifishanddive.com), as well as offices at the *Molokai Ranch Lodge* and the *Hotel Molokai*, and serves as agents for virtually every activity available on the island. Its program of outdoor pursuits includes **sightseeing cruises** along the North Shore cliffs ($150); **whale-watching** and **snorkeling** trips (both $70); **kayaking** ($90); **downhill cycling** ($60) and **bike rental** (from $40); **horse rides** ($85); and the can't-miss **Hālawa Valley hikes** described on p.411 ($75). Although **scuba diving** is also offered, the sport is not as popular on Molokai as on the other islands – the immediate offshore waters tend to be too shallow and murky on the south coast, and too rough everywhere else. The company also rents out **snorkel equipment**, boogie boards, and the like. For details on the activities they run for the Molokai Ranch, see p.427.

Many of these same activities are offered by **Molokai Outdoor Activities** (☎808/553-4477 or 1-877/553-4477, ⓦwww.molokai-outdoors.com), which also rents out – and delivers – **a similar range of** equipment. **Bike** and **kayak** rental are also available from Molokai Bicycle, 80 Mohala St, Kaunakakai (☎808/553-3931 or 1-800/709-2453, ⓦwww.bikehawaii.com/molokaibicycle).

At the eastern end of the island, the Puʻu o Hōkū Ranch organizes **horseback** riding amid idyllic scenery (see p.410). For hunting, deep-sea fishing, spear fishing, and kayaking trips on the remote north shore, contact Walter Naki of Molokai Action Adventures (☎808/558-8184). Lawrence Aki, who's responsible for the Hālawa Valley hikes, also leads customized **hiking tours** anywhere else on the island, on demand (☎808/553-5926 or 1-800/274-9303, ⓦwww.gomolokai.com).

Kaunakakai

KAUNAKAKAI, at the midpoint of the southern shoreline seven miles southeast of the island's airport, is by far the largest settlement on Molokai. Despite being home to most of the businesses that keep island life ticking over, it's really no more than a village. There's just one main street, **Ala Malama Street**, half a mile in from the ocean. Once you've ambled its full 200-yard length and scanned its array of wooden, single-story, false-front stores and the little timber-framed **St Sophia's Church**, you've seen all that central Kaunakakai has to offer. Be sure to call in at the Kanemitsu Bakery, 79 **Ala Malama St**, to pick up a loaf of their sweet Molokai bread, which is renowned throughout the islands. Molokai Island Creations – 65 **Ala Malama St** and run by the same people as Molokai Fish and Dive next door (see opposite) – is the most interesting place for clothes and souvenirs and has piles of signed copies of the owner's book of photographs, *A Portrait of Molokai*.

Arrival and information

The epicenter of the island is generally considered to be the crossroads at milepost 0 on Kamehameha V Highway, where Ala Malama Street heads away inland; at the

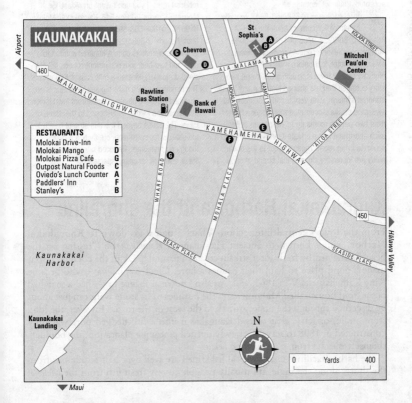

KAUNAKAKAI

RESTAURANTS

Molokai Drive-Inn	E
Molokai Mango	D
Molokai Pizza Café	G
Outpost Natural Foods	C
Oviedo's Lunch Counter	A
Paddlers' Inn	F
Stanley's	B

intersection you'll find a gas station and the Molokai branch of the Bank of Hawaii (Mon–Thurs 8.30am–3pm, Fri 8.30am–6pm). The friendly offices of the **Molokai Visitors Association** are to the east, at 2 Kamō'i St (Mon–Fri 8am–5pm; PO Box 960, Kaunakakai HI 96748; ☎808/553-3876 or 1-800/800-6367, ⓦwww .molokai-hawaii.com).

Accommodation

As the obvious base for exploring Molokai, Kaunakakai has the only inexpensive **hotel** on the island, the *Hotel Molokai*. The *Molokai Shores* makes a smarter but slightly more expensive alternative, while there are a few **B&Bs** as well. It's also possible to **camp** at One Ali'i Park; see opposite.

A'Ahi Place B&B PO Box 528, Kaunakakai, Molokai HI 96748 ☎808/553-8033, ⓦwww .molokai.com/aahi. Welcoming garden-set holiday cottage, on a low hill just east of Kaunakakai. The one bedroom has two large beds, and though there are no phones or TVs, an ample breakfast is served each morning. A "Backpackers' Cabin" on the same property is more basic but still has a decent bed and en-suite bathroom. No credit cards accepted. Cabin ❶, cottage ❸

🏃 **Hotel Molokai** ☎808/553-5347, ⓦwww .hotelmolokai.com, or book through Marc Resorts, ☎808/922-9700 or 1-800/535-0085, ⓦwww.marcresorts.com. An appealing, inexpensive beach hotel, just before milepost 2 on the highway east of town, consisting of several two-story cottages that are shaped like so many armored samurai, with very broad shoulders and sweeping cloaks. Accommodation options range from two-person rooms up to six-person suites; each apartment has a private *lānai* and bath, and a separate living room. Those closest to the ocean really are incredibly close; a thin strand of sand,

scattered with palm trees strung with hammocks, is just a single step away. There's a nice pool, and a bar open daily 3–11pm; the restaurant is reviewed opposite. Garden view ❹, ocean view ❺
Ka Hale Mala 7 Kamakana Place ☎808/553-9009, ⓦwww.molokai-bnb.com. Secluded four-room garden apartment, with kitchen and *lānai*, plus bikes and snorkel equipment, a little under five miles east of Kaunakakai. Run as a B&B, with reduced rates if you don't want breakfast. ❸
Molokai Shores PO Box 546, Kaunakakai, Molokai HI 96748 ☎808/553-5954, or reserve through Marc Resorts ☎808/922-9700 or 1-800/535-0085, ⓦwww.marcresorts.com. A hundred comfortable one- and two-bedroom oceanfront condos (all can sleep up to four), located a mile east of Kaunakakai. The buildings, which have big sea-view *lānais*, are arranged around a pleasant oceanfront lawn looking out across the Kaloko'eli Fishpond to the island of Lanai. The ocean beyond the thin strip of beach is too shallow for swimming, but there's a pool, though no restaurant. Reduced rates for longer stays, and look for online specials. ❺

Kaunakakai Harbor and the shoreline

From the town's central intersection **Wharf Road** leads down to **Kaunakakai Harbor**, a spot known to ancient Hawaiians as *Kaunakahakai* ("resting on the beach"); the nearby freshwater stream creates a natural break in the coral reef, so it made a good place to haul their canoes ashore. Chief Kapuāiwa – who became King Kamehameha V in 1863, and was also known as Prince Lot – had a thatched oceanfront home called **Malama** here; the outlines of its stone walls can just about be discerned through the undergrowth to the west of the road. However, the long stone mole, or jetty, that turned Kaunakakai into a full-fledged port was only constructed in 1898 to serve the newly opened pineapple plantation; the boulders themselves came from a dismantled *heiau*.

The harbor facilities used by local fishermen are well over half a mile out from the shore, along the mole. It's usually possible to buy fresh fish from the *Molokai*

Ice House here, a cooperative venture to which all the fishing vessels sell their catch. This is also the main dock for inter-island boats, including the daily **ferry** service between Molokai and Maui (see p.400).

None of the **beaches** near Kaunakakai is particularly suited to swimming, though walking along the shoreline to the east (around the defunct *Pau Hana Inn*) can be pleasant enough. The sea is not hazardous, but there's only a narrow strip of often rather dirty sand, and the water itself tends to be very murky, thanks to run-off from the hills.

One Ali'i Beach Park, three miles to the east, is little better, but it does at least offer some nice lawns and coconut palms, as well as the neighboring Ali'i Fishpond (see p.408). The original name of the beach was *oneali'i* or "royal sands," but what was once a spelling mistake has become the official name. The beach itself consists of two separate sections; the first one you come to, Number 2, is reserved for day use only, while the nicer Number 1, a little further on, holds a **campground** run by the county parks office (see p.402).

Kapuāiwa Coconut Grove

A couple of miles west of central Kaunakakai, on the ocean side of Maunaloa Highway, Kiowea Park is the site of the photogenic **Kapuāiwa Coconut Grove**. The more than one thousand tall palm trees were planted in the 1860s by Chief Kapuāiwa, whose name, intriguingly, means "mysterious taboo." As the coastline gradually erodes, and as the trees approach the end of their natural life spans, they are toppling one by one, but they still make a fine spectacle, especially in the glow of sunset. Coconut trees in public places in Hawaii are not usually allowed to bear fruit, but these ones do; signs warn of the obvious danger from falling nuts. Swimming from the park is not recommended. Across the highway, a neat little row of wooden chapels is the only other point of interest nearby.

Restaurants

Around eighty percent of Molokai's restaurants are located in Kaunakakai, but the choice is far from overwhelming. The island lacks the national fast-food chains, but neither is there anything that might be called fine dining. Saturday morning sees a **farmers' market** at the central intersection, stretching north from the Bank of Hawaii.

Hula Shores *Hotel Molokai*, Kamehameha V Hwy ☎ 808/553-5347. The oceanfront dining room at the *Hotel Molokai*, located just two miles east of town, has a romantic ambience and live nightly entertainment, including Aloha Fri with Na Kupuna on Fri 4–6pm, when local "aunties" sing, dance, and "talk story." The food itself is adequate, with lunch specials for under $10 and all dinner entrees except steak costing under $20. There are changing fish specials as well as a standard menu of chicken or shrimp stir-fries, prime rib (available weekends only), and barbecue pork (as part of a $16 buffet on Sun). Daily except Fri 6am–2pm & 6–9pm, Fri 6am–2pm & 4–9pm.

Molokai Drive-Inn Kamehameha V Hwy ☎ 808/553-5655. Exactly what it sounds like: a roadside diner offering simple daily specials ranging from hot dogs to prime rib. You'd be hard-pressed to spend $10. Mon–Thurs & Sun 6am–10pm, Fri & Sat 6am–10.30pm.

Molokai Mango 93D Ala Malama St ☎ 808/553-8232. Video rental store on the main shopping street with a sideline in tasty hot and cold sandwiches ($3–4). Mon–Sat 8am–8pm, Sun 8am–6pm.

Molokai Pizza Café Kaunakakai Place, Wharf Rd ☎ 808/553-3288. Good-value mall diner with a takeout counter, near Kaunakakai's central inter-section. Pizzas named after the different islands

△ Kapuāiwa Coconut Grove

range from the basic Molokai ($10) up to the Big Island ($19); at lunchtime on weekdays you can get an individual Molokini pizza for $5. The menu also features submarine sandwiches, ribs, and roast chicken, and there are evening fresh fish specials for $15 or so. Wed is Mexican night, with fajitas,

tacos, and burritos all for around $10. Mon–Thurs 10am–10pm, Fri & Sat 10am–11pm, Sun 11am–10pm.

Outpost Natural Foods 70 Maka'ena Place ☎ 808/553-3377. Lunch counter and juice bar in a wholefood store, off Ala Malama St behind the Chevron garage. Tofu sandwiches and tempeh burgers are under $5; sensational smoothies, quite possibly the best in the state, cost $4.50. Shop: Mon–Thurs 9am–6pm, Fri 9am–4pm, Sun 10am–5pm, closed Sat. Juice bar Mon–Fri 11am–3pm.

Oviedo's Lunch Counter 145 Pauli St ☎808/553-5014. Simple one-room Filipino restaurant in the heart of town where the owner cooks up delicious dishes like chicken stewed with papaya and local herbs ($8) as well as pork *adobo* (stew), roast pork, and turkey-neck stew. There's lots of ice cream to round things off. Daily 8am–5pm.

Paddlers' Inn Kamehameha V Hwy☎808/553-5256. This large restaurant-cum-bar is a major

drinking hangout for locals, but it's still a welcoming spot for visitors, with lots of outdoor space, including an open-air stage that regularly features live if not necessarily Hawaiian music. Saimin or burgers for under $10, lunch specials like *kalbi* beef or fresh *mahi mahi* for around $12, and steaks for just under $20. Mon–Fri 7am–11pm, Sat & Sun 9am–11pm.

Stanley's 125 Pauli St ☎808/558-8996. Spacious coffee bar-cum-art gallery on the main street, where you can find full breakfasts, sandwiches, and smoothies; simple snacks like saimin and hot dogs; and surf the Internet at rock-bottom rates. Mon–Sat 6.30am–3.30pm.

Eastern Molokai

Kamehameha V Highway runs along the coast for 28 miles **east of Kaunakakai** before reaching a dead end at one of the great Hawaiian "amphitheater valleys," **Hālawa Valley**. Molokai's closest equivalent to the better-known Road to Hāna on Maui (see p.359), the highway ranks among the most beautiful driving routes in the whole state.

Before you set off, be warned that it takes well over an hour to drive from Kaunakakai to Hālawa, and there are no gas stations en route. The highway remains in good condition all the way to the end, but gets progressively narrower, as finding a foothold between the hills and the ocean becomes more difficult. Eastern Molokai is the wettest part of the island; most of the rain that falls on the mountaintop flows down to the inaccessible valleys of the North Shore, but enough feeds the streams to the south to create a verdant patchwork of fields and forest.

The tiny wayside communities hold the odd church, B&B, or ancient site, but the real attraction is the lush countryside, with flowers and orchids at every turn, and horses and cows, each with its attendant white egret, grazing contentedly in the meadows. For much of the way the road lies within a few yards of the sea, but there's no good swimming in the first twenty miles, and barely a decent stretch of sand. The coast is lined instead with pre-contact **fishponds**, now largely silted up and overgrown with mangroves.

Kawela

Six miles out of Kaunakakai, a small cluster of houses constitutes the village of **KAWELA**. Kamehameha the Great invaded Molokai at this spot in around 1794, with a vast wave of canoes landing simultaneously along a four-mile length of beach. The remains of the dead killed in the subsequent **battle** in Pakuhiwa Coconut Grove are said to lie beneath a mound to the east, while the inaccessible ruins of a *puʻuhonua*, or "place of refuge" (see p.189), overlook it all from high on the ridge above. An official marker at the foot of Onini Road stands close to the battle site, but there's nothing more to see. After the battle, Kamehameha camped for a year further along the coast, growing taro, before launching his invasion of Oahu in 1795 (see p.106).

The fishponds of Molokai

Ancient Hawaiians developed the art of aquaculture, or fish farming, to standards unmatched elsewhere in Polynesia. Using intricate networks of artificial fishponds, laced around sheltered coastal areas, they are estimated to have raised around two million pounds of fish per year. In the words of the nineteenth-century Hawaiian historian Samuel Kamakau, "fishponds were things that beautified the land, and a land with many fishponds was called 'fat.'"

By that reckoning, the southeastern coast of Molokai was very fat indeed. More than fifty separate fishponds have been identified within a twenty-mile stretch – a sure sign that the area was home to many powerful chiefs, and a prime reason why Molokai was so coveted by the rulers of the other islands.

A typical fishpond consisted of a long stone wall that curved out from the beach to enclose a large expanse – as much as 500 acres – of shallow ocean. Building such a wall, which needed to poke a meter out of the water at high tide, took a great deal of labor. That work was made much easier in southern Molokai, where the inshore coral reef provided a ready-made foundation, and already all but encircled natural lagoons. When completed, the wall would have one or two gaps, or sluice gates, which were usually sealed off with wooden lattices. Small fry could enter, but once they grew to full size they'd be unable to leave, and it was a simple matter to harvest them in nets.

A fishpond connected to the sea always also held a freshwater spring, and would be used to raise fish that liked brackish water, such as 'ama'ama (mullet) and awa (milkfish). Such ponds were complemented by similar freshwater ponds, usually built near rivermouths that were sealed off from the sea by sandbars, and held such species as 'npae (shrimp) and 'o'opu (a native goby). Some smaller fish were even cultivated in the waterlogged taro fields.

The fishponds of Molokai remained in use well into the nineteenth century, and as recently as the 1960s there were attempts to revive them for commercial production. These days, most of the ponds, and also the coral reefs beyond them, are being inexorably submerged by sediment washed down from the hills. Overgrazing on the higher slopes is allowing around a foot of mud per year to settle into the ocean, and many ponds are turning into mangrove swamps.

If you'd like to take a close-up look, drop by the Ali'i Fishpond, immediately west of One Ali'i Beach Park, where an 800m wall enclosing a thirty-acre pond is currently being cleared of mangroves and painstakingly restored by a team of community volunteers under the leadership of the Ka Honua Momona organization (no fixed hours; ☏808/553-8353, ⓦ www.kahonuamomona.org).

The small **Kakahai'a Beach Park** in Kawela makes a convenient launching-point for **kayak expeditions** along the coast, as listed on p.402. Otherwise, it is significant solely because it is adjacent to the **Kakahai'a National Wildlife Refuge**, a wetland area set aside for rare waterbirds. Its main feature, the fresh-water **Kakahai'a fishpond**, stands *mauka* of the highway slightly further along, largely obscured by a protective screen of palm trees; access to both the pond and the refuge is forbidden.

Kamalō

KAMALŌ, six miles east of Kawela, served as the primary landing for vessels visiting Molokai until the end of the nineteenth century. What's left of the wharf is still in use, but Kamalō itself is now just a tiny village. It's mainly noteworthy as the site of the simple white **St Joseph Church**, built by Father Damien in 1876

Hiking in Hawaii

Hawaii is an absolute paradise for hikers. Thanks to the mighty volcanoes that formed them, even the smaller islands hold barely explored wildernesses, while the dramatic effects of erosion have produced some of the most majestic scenery on the planet. Well-maintained but nonetheless demanding trails enable visitors to escape the crowds and see Hawaii in something approaching its original pristine state.

▲ Kalalau Trail, Kauai

Choosing your trail

If hiking is among your main vacation priorities, then the two best destinations have to be the youngest of the islands, the **Big Island**, where you can watch new land forming daily as lava spills from the Kīlauea volcano, and the oldest, **Kauai**, where breathtaking trails penetrate remote North Shore valleys that no road could ever reach. Kauai's legendary **Kalalau Trail**, which clings precariously to the Nā Pali cliffs for eleven unforgettable miles, is often hailed as the greatest in the world, and offers the reward of camping beside the golden sands of Kalalau Valley at the far end. Three thousand feet up from there, in Kōke'e State Park, the **Awa'awapuhi Trail** runs along a perilous mountain ridge to reach an incredible bird's-eye view of yet another verdant hidden valley.

Rainforest trails

Several great trails explore Hawaii's lush **rainforests**, filled with unique flora and fauna – and entirely devoid of nasty reptiles or dangerous predators. Two of the finest, the **Alaka'i Swamp Trail** on Kauai and the **Pēpē'ōpae Trail** on Molokai, follow boardwalks across strange stunted swamplands at the very top of the islands, where patches of dense jungle-like vegetation are interspersed with eerie marshes scattered with orchids and twisted shrubs. Both offer alert hikers tantalizing glimpses of some of the rarest birds on earth, and culminate with fabulous views across remote, inaccessible and quintessentially Polynesian valleys.

▼ Kōke'e State Park, Kauai

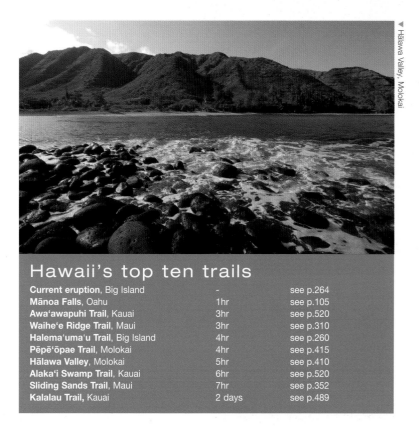

Hālawa Valley, Molokai

Hawaii's top ten trails

Pīpīwai Trail, Maui

Much lower down, starting from sea level in eastern Maui, the **Pīpīwai Trail** climbs up into the Kīpahulu section of **Haleakalā National Park**, passing through various different ecosystems, criss-crossing streams on precarious bridges, to reach two spectacular waterfalls high in the rainforest. You have to join a guided hike to see the waterfalls of glorious **Hālawa Valley** on Molokai, but this was among the very first places to be settled by humans in all Hawaii, and learning its history and traditions from a true native makes for a totally compelling experience. Even on Oahu, on the edge of Honolulu just a couple of miles up from Waikīkī, lovely rainforest trails through **Makiki and Mānoa valleys**.

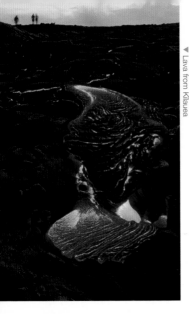

The lure of lava

The most exciting hike Hawaii has to offer is the chance to watch the ongoing eruption of Kīlauea on the Big Island, in **Hawaii Volcanoes National Park**. Whereas every other hike detailed in this book follows a well-defined trail, there's no predicting where or how far you'll have to walk to see it; the current flow might be anywhere in the desolate, ten-mile-wide lava field that stretches along the island's southeastern shoreline. As if the thrill of close-up views of torrents of molten lava were not enough, it's often possible to hike out there at night, when the hillside is alive with glowing red fire.

Even if the eruption turns out to be beyond your reach, further great hikes in the national park enable you to explore Kīlauea's currently quiescent summit caldera. The long **Halemaʻumaʻu** and **Kīlauea Iki** trails venture out across desolate, still-steaming crater floors, while the aptly-named **Devastation Trail** skirts recent cinder cones where the rainforest is clawing its way back.

On Maui, **Haleakalā** may not be active these days, and technically what looks like its summit crater is simply an eroded hilltop, but it too offers superb hiking. The wonderful dayhike that combines the **Sliding Sands and Halemaʻumaʻu** trails is a real test of stamina, being at least eleven miles long, and a wearying ten thousand feet above sea level. Unlike on the Big Island, it's also possible to spend the night atop Haleakalā, either tent camping or in a rudimentary cabin.

▼ Offerings to the goddess Pele, Hawaii Volcanoes National Park

and spruced up in 1995 to coincide with the return of his right hand to Kalaupapa. The priest's garlanded statue stands to the right of the entrance, within a boulder surround, and backed by yellow trumpet flowers.

An inconspicuous plaque less than a mile east marks the spot where **Ernest Smith** and **Emory Bronte** (no relation to the author of *Wuthering Heights*) crash-landed amid the trees to terminate the first commercial flight from California to Hawaii, in July 1927. The journey had taken 25 hours; they were heading, naturally, for Honolulu. Luckily, they survived.

An appealing **B&B**, the *Kamalō Plantation* (HC01, PO Box 300, Kaunakakai HI 96748; ☎808/558-8236, ⓦwww.molokai.com/kamalo; cottage ➌, beach house ➎), stands in superb tropical gardens across from St Joseph's, a short way beyond milepost 10. There's guest accommodation for two in a private cottage, with its own kitchen and outdoor deck, away from the main house, and the same owners also offer a lovely two-bedroom beach house further along the coast. Credit cards are not accepted.

'Ili'ili'ōpae Heiau

The second-largest *heiau* in all Hawaii is tucked away in Mahulepu Valley, a mile past Our Lady of Sorrows Church. Hardly anyone lives around here now, but when the **'Ili'ili'ōpae Heiau** took its final form in the eighteenth century, it served as a robust proclamation of the power of a mighty warrior chief. A *luakini*, or temple of human sacrifice, it was probably erected on the site of several previous temples; its four colossal tiers, rising to a stone platform that measures almost 300 feet long by 87 feet wide, may well stand atop its predecessors.

Although 'Ili'ili'ōpae Heiau stands on private property, individual walkers are sometimes allowed to hike up to it; check with the Molokai Visitors Association or at your hotel before you set off. Assuming you get permission, park just before Mapulehu Bridge, half a mile beyond milepost 15, and then follow the track that leads inland from the silver mailbox no. 520. Following a dry riverbed, this track enters a cool and colorful woodland filled with fruit trees, before coming to an end after ten minutes at a solitary house on the right. A footpath to the left crosses the stream, where it meets four massive layers of the *heiau*, which looks as if it was approached by a ramp at this southeastern corner. The *heiau* is located at the foot of a ridge, where the valley walls begin to rise. Trees surround it, but only the odd shrub or tiny flower punctuates the flat expanse of lichen-speckled boulders on top. Not a trace survives of its sacred buildings, towers, and altars, and the whole place now has a very tranquil air.

According to the local version of a myth common to most *luakinis*, 'Ili'ili'ōpae Heiau was originally constructed, during a single night, with boulders passed from hand to hand along a chain of *menehune* from Wailau Valley on the North Shore. Until recently a hiking trail from here ran right across the island to Wailau; more stone walls are scattered in the hills behind the *heiau*, but the undergrowth is virtually impossible to penetrate.

For an account of Hawaii's biggest *luakini*, Pu'ukohola Heiau on the Big Island, see p.205.

Pūko'o

Beyond the *heiau*, the village of **PŪKO'O** was, like Kamalō, an important port during the nineteenth century. It, too, all but withered away following the development of Kaunakakai. Today, Pūkoʻo marks the point where traffic along the coast is forced to slow down by a succession of narrow curves, but sightseers are rewarded by some delightful little pocket beaches. The only place along Kamehameha V Highway where you can **eat** is just before milepost 16 in Pūkoʻo. The *Neighborhood Store 'n' Counter* (daily except Wed 8am–6pm; T808/558-8498) serves appetizing breakfasts and lunch specials, with plate lunches costing around $7.

Twenty-Mile Beach

The prettiest of the south coast beaches, and almost the only one where swimming and snorkeling are consistently safe, can be found at milepost 20. Officially Murphy Beach Park, it's more commonly known as **Twenty-Mile Beach**. There's room to park on the grass verge at the headland just beyond.

After that, the twin islets of **Moku Hoʻoniki** and **Kanaha Rock** – both bird sanctuaries – become visible ahead, and the speed limit drops to just 5mph as the road twists in and out around the rocky headlands.

Puʻu o Hōkū Ranch

Each of the three lush little valleys beyond Twenty-Mile Beach holds a house or two and a patch of sand. As the rocky silhouette of Kahakuloa Head, at the very tip of western Maui, looms into view across the water, the highway climbs up into the rolling meadows of the **Puʻu o Hōkū Ranch**. The scenery by now is absolutely gorgeous, with the ranchlands stretching a long way back from either side of the road.

The ranch headquarters stands to the right of the highway near mile marker 25 (T808/558-8109, Wwww.puuohoku.com). As well as coordinating the daily work of the ranch, staff here organize an extensive program of **horseback riding** in the vicinity; charges range from $55 per person for a one-hour ride to up to $120 for an all-day "beach adventure" to the waterfalls above Hālawa Valley. In addition, two fully equipped **guest cottages** in the heart of this pastoral idyll are available for rent (●). One has two bedrooms, and the other four; both cost $140 per night for two people.

Hālawa Valley

Twenty-six miles out of Kaunakakai, beyond a series of progressively wider and deeper gulches, Kamehameha V Highway reaches an overlook poised 750ft above the full spread of **HĀLAWA VALLEY**. The view from here is staggeringly beautiful, with the stream far below meandering to meet the foaming ocean, the rich green valley stretching away to either side, and the distant waterfalls shimmering in the valley's innermost recesses, half-hidden by clouds.

For its final 1.5 miles, the highway drops down the walls of the valley, providing more tremendous views at each of its hairpin curves, before coming to an end on the south side of the stream. At the spot where the road reaches the valley floor, a tiny wooden **church**, the chapel of Jerusalema Hou, is always unlocked and open for quiet meditation. The dirt road just beyond leads back upstream, but the only way to pass through its locked gate is on one of the **guided hikes** described below.

Continuing a hundred yards or so on towards the shoreline, the road becomes too pitted for ordinary vehicles just across from a rather derelict county picnic pavilion and restroom facility. Walk a little further and you'll reach the mouth of the stream. To the right there's a **beach** of grayish sand, accessible beyond a carpet of creeping flowers and barely sheltered from the force of the ocean. Off the low rocky promontory to the left, where the waves sweep in toward the rivermouth, is Molokai's most popular **surfing** site. Large numbers of local kids may be in the water, but that's no sign that it's safe for outsiders.

Across the stream on the far side of the bay, you can see another pretty little crescent **beach**, backed by a line of palm trees and made up of sand rendered somewhat grubby by soil washed down the valley walls. Currently the only road there is blocked by a gate bearing the stern warning "KEEP OUT – NO TRESPASSING," and you'll be made very unwelcome if you try to reach it.

Hiking in Hālawa Valley

It's only possible to **hike** into the depths of Hālawa Valley as part of an organized tour, run by Molokai Cultural Hikes ($75; reserve through Molokai Fish and Dive, ☎808/553-5926, ⊛www.molokaifishanddive.com). Don't let that put you off, however; this is the best such tour you can take anywhere in Hawaii.

Access to the inland portions of Hālawa Valley has for many years been very restricted, thanks to the presence of 64 separate landowners. Now, however, Lawrence Aki, whose extended family includes the great majority of those landowners, has instigated these tours to raise awareness of – and funds for – an ambitious attempt to restore **taro production** in the valley. Much like rice, taro grows in walled fields, known as *lo'i*, that for most of its life cycle have to be kept submerged in water. Step by step, aided by community volunteers and visiting students from throughout Hawaii, a cooperative venture spearheaded by Aki and his family is rebuilding the ancient *lo'i*, and clearing the irrigation channels. It's all part of the same process of revitalizing Hawaiian cultural traditions that's the inspiration for the reconstruction of the fishponds described on p.408.

The tours set off at 9.30am daily; reserve well in advance, wear good walking shoes, plus a swimsuit beneath your clothes, and bring insect repellent and a picnic. Lawrence himself doesn't lead every tour, but all are designed to introduce visitors to the heritage of the valley. The family trace their history here back to the very first Polynesian settlers, and speak in a way that's extremely rare in modern Hawaii of their identity as being specifically Marquesan, as opposed to the Tahitian belief system introduced by subsequent invaders.

The trail back through the valley soon leaves the cultivated areas to magnificent tropical rainforest, crossing streams and passing numerous ruined homesites and *heiaus*. At one such temple, dedicated to Lono, the only practicable route leads straight through the most sacred area, necessitating a chant that asks for permission. The ultimate goal, the dramatic 250-foot **Moa'ula Falls**, is said in legend to be the dwelling place of a giant lizard or *mo'o*. Swimming in the chilly pool beneath the falls is only safe if a *ti* leaf tossed into the water floats; otherwise, it is said, you'll be dragged down by the *mo'o*.

While it's barely two miles up to the falls, the round-trip hike can easily take five hours, allowing time for a swim, a picnic (you have to bring your own), and lots of stops to "talk story" along the way. Note also that any other operator who offers the hike for a lower price is almost certainly trespassing.

△ Moa'ula Falls

The history of Hālawa Valley

When the Polynesians first arrived in Hawaii, they always chose to settle in the lush windward valleys of the islands. Its sheltered sandy inlet, abundant rainfall, and year-round streams made Hālawa an ideal home. Excavations have revealed the remains of round-ended huts, of a kind otherwise unknown in Hawaii, but resembling those on Easter Island and in eastern Polynesia, which have been dated to before 650 AD.

Hālawa went on to become the major population center of Molokai, home to perhaps a thousand people. Archeologists have identified over a thousand distinct taro ponds (*lo'i*), irrigated by a system of canals that stretched over half a mile back into the hills, while the fertile slopes were terraced into stone-walled fields. In addition to many *heiaus* dedicated to agricultural deities, it also held a *pu'uhonua* (see p.189), and twelve of Molokai's eighteen human-sacrifice *luakinis*. One of these, the Mana *Heiau* on the northern slope, was erected around 1720 by chief Alapa'inui of the Big Island to celebrate his conquest of the island.

Taro production in Hālawa continued throughout the nineteenth century – when most of the crop was exported to feed the whaling fleet at Lahaina on Maui – and well into the twentieth, as Chinese laborers left the plantations to start their own taro farms. In 1935, Californian businessman Paul Fagan, based at the Pu'u o Hōkū Ranch, bought up much of the valley in the hope of revitalizing its traditional lifestyle. However, most of the *lo'i* were destroyed by the tsunami of 1946, and Fagan turned his attentions to Hāna on Maui instead (see p.365).

During the 1960s, when only three families still lived in Hālawa, the waterfalls started to flow so fiercely that they destroyed the remaining *lo'i*, and made the river channel too deep to be used for irrigation. Photographs reveal that until the 1950s the floor of the valley was virtually treeless, but now it swiftly became overgrown. Squatters moved in, many of whom planted marijuana in the backcountry, and Hālawa became a byword for lawlessness. Only recently has the situation appeared to stabilize and the residents to set about restoring the *lo'i*.

Central Molokai

West of Kaunakakai, Maunaloa Highway follows the coast for a couple of miles before turning inland to climb the "saddle" between Molokai's two volcanoes. The southwest shoreline of the island belongs almost entirely to the Molokai Ranch, and the only road access is via Maunaloa at the western end (see p.426).

The **central plain** of Molokai used to nourish extensive pineapple plantations, but apart from the island's main airport it holds little to interest visitors today. Villages such as **Kualapu'u** and **Ho'olehua** are sleepy little places, and although any stay on Molokai is likely to involve passing this way several times, there's no compelling reason to stop.

The rainforest

The summit of eastern Molokai remains covered by some of the state's most pristine **rainforest**. Owned by the Molokai Ranch, but run by the private, nonprofit Nature Conservancy of Hawaii as the **Kamakou Preserve**, it's a sanctuary for native plants and animals, the last-known haunt of rare indigenous birds such as the Molokai thrush (*olomāo*) and the Molokai creeper (*kakawahie*). Most of the area is completely inaccessible even on foot, and the authorities prefer outsiders to venture in only with experienced local guides such as those listed on p.402.

There is, however, a rough dirt road that climbs right to the top of the mountain from central Molokai. It's virtually always raining up there, and even at its best the track tends to be a deep wet furrow in the earth, where anything other than a high-clearance 4WD vehicle will slither uncontrollably. If you have a jeep and are determined to make your own way up, ask for advice on the latest conditions at the Nature Conservancy of Hawaii office, which is located in the upper section of the Molokai Technology Park, to the left of Maunaloa Highway, 2.5 miles up from Kaunakakai (Mon–Fri 8am–3pm; ☎808/553-5236, ⓦwww.nature.org). The Nature Conservancy also organizes occasional **guided hikes** (usually but not always on the first Saturday of each month; call for details) and welcomes volunteers prepared to spend a day participating in regular maintenance trips.

Finally, it's also possible to hike up into the preserve from Molokai's south coast, along a trail that sets off from Kamehameha V Highway opposite One Ali'i Beach Park (see p.405). Head through the small gate alongside the locked jeep-road gate here; a climb of around ninety minutes along the line of the ridge brings you onto the dirt road at the top, a short way east of the Waikolu Lookout (see below) in Pelekunu Valley. The total round-trip hike to the valley and back to the ocean takes at least six hours.

The Forest Reserve road

Less than four miles from Kaunakakai, just before Maunaloa Highway crosses a bridge, the **Forest Reserve jeep road** heads off to the right and soon reaches the dusty Homelani Cemetery. The long, straight, red-dirt track from here may seem innocuous at first, but it becomes heavily rutted as you climb higher.

By the time you pass the sign announcing the Molokai Forest Preserve, you'll probably have penetrated the mountain's semi-permanent cloud cover. Within half a mile, you'll spot the largely abandoned scout camp that's home to sculptor Robin Baker, who has carved totem poles, sharks, octopuses, and cobras into the living trees. Well beyond that, the imported eucalyptus starts to give way to a pine forest that's interspersed with bright-blossomed native *ohia* trees.

The Sandalwood Pit

In a grassy clearing on the very crest of the Kamakou ridge, a deep groove in the ground betrays the site of Lua Nā Moku'iliahi, or the **Sandalwood Pit**. This is one of the few surviving examples of a *"picul* pit," dug early in the nineteenth century to the exact size and shape of a ship's hull. Hawaiian commoners were sent up into the mountains by their chiefs to cut down precious sandalwood trees; once they had filled one of these pits with logs (weighed in units called *piculs*), they then had to carry them back down to the sea on their naked backs and load them onto ships bound for China.

You're unlikely to see any living sandalwood here now, though a small stand is said to survive somewhere in the vicinity. Legend has it that the exploited laborers deliberately uprooted sandalwood saplings to ensure that their children would not have to do the same cruel work.

Waikolu Lookout

Around ten miles from the highway – 45 minutes' driving on a good day – the jeep road reaches **Waikolu Lookout**. This dramatic viewpoint commands a majestic prospect of the verdant Waikolu Valley, which drops 3700ft down to the ocean. Tiny Huelo Island stands offshore, while the Kalaupapa Peninsula is just out of sight around the headland to the left.

The **north coast** of Molokai boasts the tallest **sea cliffs** in the world, measuring up to four thousand feet high. Geologists once believed these sheer green walls were created by gigantic landslides, perhaps along volcanic fault lines. While such landslides have pared away much of the coastline of Hawaii, it's now known that the cliffs of Molokai were created by the power of the Pacific alone.

Few visitors ever see the cliffs or the mighty **amphitheater valleys** – so called for the unclimbable walls that soar to either side and meet in a high encircling ridge at the head – that cut deep into them. **Hālawa** to the east is accessible by road (see p.410), while **Waikolu** in the west can technically be reached on foot from Kalaupapa (though you'd never get permission to do so), but **Pelekunu**, **Wailau**, and **Pāpalaua** valleys are completely sealed off from the rest of Molokai.

All of these valleys held substantial populations in pre-contact times. The name of the largest, Pelekunu, means "moldy smell," a frank acknowledgment of the fact that, even when it's not raining, the valley floor receives less than five hours of direct sunlight each day. Pelekunu's taro farmers are thought to have abandoned the valley each winter, when the seas grew too rough to permit canoe landings, and migrated west to Mo'omomi to catch and dry fish in relative comfort. The last permanent population had left by 1917, though for a few years after that the valley was infested by wild water buffalo abandoned by Chinese farmers.

These days most of the land in the North Shore valleys is privately owned. Some back-to-nature enthusiasts camp out on their properties in summer, but there's no formal agriculture. Meanwhile, the state is gradually buying up as much of the area as it can, in the hope of turning the whole shoreline into a vast nature reserve.

Most of Molokai's drinking water comes from Waikolu, flowing to the reservoir at Kualapu'u along a tunnel that pierces the valley wall almost directly below this spot. Access is denied to the general public, but if you have the right connections, it's said to be possible to hike through the tunnel and reach the Waikolu Valley.

The meadow across from the lookout is equipped with a few picnic tables and latrines and also holds a rudimentary **campground** that lacks running water. Free permits, for a maximum five-night stay, can be picked up from the Department of Land and Natural Resources (see p.402).

The Pēpē'ōpae Trail

Commercial off-road tours (see p.401) tend not to go beyond Waikolu Lookout, which marks the start of the **Kamakou Preserve**. For most of the year, the jeep road beyond is impassable for vehicles of any kind, but it's always possible to continue **on foot**. As it winds its way through a succession of minor gulches, it soon leaves the last vestiges of the dryland forest behind and plunges into the jungle.

After about five minutes, you can cut through a gap in the dense greenery to your left and join the **Hanalilolilo Trail**, which sets off up and over a steep hillock. That trail is, however, just a very soggy way of getting to the Pēpē'ōpae Trail, and it's much simpler to continue on the road for the full 2.5 miles to the official Pēpē'ōpae trailhead.

The **Pēpē'ōpae Trail**, the only track to penetrate into the heart of the preserve, is an absolutely wonderful hike. To protect the various fragile ecosystems through which it passes, it consists of a slender wooden boardwalk, seldom more than a plank wide. It begins by pushing its way through thick rainforest, where every tree is festooned with dangling vines and spongy, fluorescent moss, and dazzling orchids glisten amid the undergrowth of tightly coiled ferns. Between wisps of mountaintop mist, you might just glimpse unique native birds such as the Molokai creeper or the Molokai thrush.

The trail eventually emerges into an eerie patch of windswept bog. Amazingly, the red-blossomed, stunted shrubs scattered across the desolation are *'ohia*, the same species that grows as full-sized trees in the neighboring forest. A viewpoint here enables you to look back across the island to the west end, before the trail plunges once more into the jungle. After a final steep climb, the boardwalk ends abruptly at another incredible view of the north coast, this time over **Pelekunu Valley**.

In total, it takes over an hour to walk the full length of the Pēpē'ōpae Trail, to the overlook and back, and more like four hours to hike from the Waikolu Lookout.

Kualapu'u

In its sixty-year existence, the fortunes of the former plantation town of **KUALAPU'U**, two miles east of Maunaloa Highway along Kala'e Highway (Hwy-470), have fluctuated immensely. Dole stopped growing pineapples in this area in 1982, but Kualapu'u has been experiencing something of a comeback since the Malulani Estate set out to produce **coffee** here instead. Brands such as its Muleskinner Coffee have gained a foothold as somewhat cheaper rivals to the Big Island's long-established gourmet crop (the only coffee entitled to call itself "Kona"; see p.183).

The headquarters of the coffee estate is just to the right of Farrington Avenue as it turns left from Kala'e Highway at the eastern end of Kualapu'u. Here, a bakery and **café** called ☕ *Coffees of Hawaii* (Mon–Fri 7am–4pm, Sat 8am–4pm, Sun 8am–2pm; ☎808/567-9490, ⓦ www.coffeesofhawaii.com) serves free percolated coffee and inexpensive espressos, as well as preparing sandwiches and takeout box lunches, while the attached Plantation Store sells Muleskinner and other coffees, plus souvenirs and local crafts. Sitting on their open terrace, looking out across Molokai, is as enjoyable and relaxing an experience as the island has to offer. If you'd like to explore the plantation in more detail, you can join either a **walking tour** ($20; Mon–Fri 10am, Sat 11am) or a mule-drawn **wagon tour** ($35; Mon–Fri 8am & 1pm, Sat 10am). In the afternoon, you can take a self-guided **hike** across the fields to the top of Kualapu'u Hill, for sweeping island views ($7; Mon–Fri 3–5.30pm).

A few hundred yards west, an attractive timber building houses the ☕ *Kualapu'u Cookhouse* (Mon 7am–2pm, Tues–Sat 7am–8pm; ☎808/567-9655), a popular diner with indoor seating and an adjacent garden terrace. Breakfast eggs cost around $8, and burgers and plate lunches are $6–9, but the place really comes into its own in the evening, when high-quality dinner specials like stuffed shrimp, seared *ahi*, or rack of lamb are more like $20, and unless you arrive by 6.30pm you may well have a long wait to be seated, let alone served.

The lake-like expanse of water visible to the south of Farrington Avenue is the largest rubber-lined **reservoir** in the world, holding over a billion gallons of water piped from the North Shore valleys.

Ho'olehua

There's even less to **HO'OLEHUA** – a mile west of Kualapu'u along Farrington Avenue, or a mile north of Maunaloa Highway to the east of the airport – than there is to its neighbor.

Anywhere else in the world, the lone attraction, **Purdy's Nut Farm**, a little way up Lihi Pali Avenue, might not seem a big deal. If you take the time to stop, however, you can while away an inconsequential but thoroughly enjoyable half-hour (Mon–Fri 9.30am–3.30pm, Sat 10am–2pm; free). In a nutshell, Tuddie Purdy – the grandnephew of Ikua Purdy, who was World Rodeo Champion in 1908 (see p.245) – stands at a counter amid a small grove of macadamia nut trees, telling whoever drops by about the trees, cracking nuts with his hammer, and handing out slices of coconut to dip in honey. With any luck he'll also sell a few nuts, some fruit from his orchard, or a little honey. Because Tuddie does not use pesticides, which preclude visits to macadamia nut orchards elsewhere, you can stroll among the 75-year-old trees. They're rooted in bare red earth, which is swept clean every day and kept clear of grass, to make the fallen nuts easy to spot.

Mo'omomi Beach

Farrington Avenue heads west through Ho'olehua and out the far side almost before you'd notice. After another 2.5 miles, the road surface turns to red dirt, but usually remains in good enough condition to make it worth driving the final two miles down to **Mo'omomi Bay**. There's a little sandy **beach** to the left of the end of the road, and tide pools in the jagged sandstone to the right, formed in the rounded depressions left by long-gone lava boulders. Local kids choose this side of the bay to go surfing and boogie-boarding.

Mo'omomi Bay is one of several small indentations in the three-mile stretch of solidified sand dunes known as **Mo'omomi Beach**. The shallow offshore waters were once highly prized fishing grounds, and countless ancient octopus lures and fishhooks have been found nearby, but the dry coastline has probably never hosted much of a permanent population. As often seems to be the case in such marginal districts, the land is now set aside as Hawaiian Home Lands and reserved for those with a certain percentage of Hawaiian blood; the precise figure is revised downwards from time to time.

Walking along the coastal track a mile west of Mo'omomi Bay brings you to prettier **Kawa'aloa Bay**, where the large sandy beach is slightly safer for swimming. The dunes here are an ecological treasure-trove, with not only the fossilized remains of extinct flightless birds, but also rare living species of plants. Casual strolling is not encouraged, but the Nature Conservancy of Hawaii in Kualapu'u (see p.414) organizes monthly **guided hikes**, on different Saturdays to those on which it runs trips up to the Kamakou Preserve.

Kala'e

The tiny residential area of **KALA'E** is located two miles northeast of Kualapu'u, 1500ft above sea level as Kala'e Highway climbs toward the top of the *pali* above Kalaupapa. Its rich wet farmland – the best on Molokai – was acquired in the 1850s by a German migrant, **Rudolph Meyer**, when he married the local high chiefess, Kalama. Soon after establishing a ranch up here, he fell victim to an extensive cattle-rustling operation. All the men of Pālā'au village, down on the southern coast, were sent to jail in Honolulu, and the village was abandoned – not the sort of thing that gets forgotten on Molokai.

During the 1870s, Meyer ventured briefly into the sugar business. The roadside **R.W. Meyer Sugar Mill** operated only from 1878 until 1889, before Meyer returned to cattle ranching and went on to found the Molokai Ranch (see p.427). Hawaii's smallest sugar mill then lay rotting for almost a century, but it has now been laboriously restored to full working condition. Outside the main shed stands the original mule-powered cane crusher, while inside you can see the furnace, boiler, and the elaborate steam engine. So far, it's all quite underwhelming, but the modern hall in the field behind is slowly evolving into the **Molokai Museum and Cultural Center** (Mon–Sat 10am–2pm; $6), which tends to show temporary exhibitions of Hawaii-related photographs. Meyer and many of his descendants were buried in a peaceful garden cemetery beyond.

Pālā'au State Park

A couple of miles beyond the sugar mill, and less than a mile past the mule stables and Kalaupapa trailhead (see opposite), Kala'e Highway ends its climb across Molokai in the forested parking lot of **Pālā'au State Park**.

A short walk to the right from the far end of the lot brings you to a railed **overlook** that faces east along the coast. Kalaupapa Peninsula lies spread out far below, with the village of Kalaupapa clear on the near side, and the slight upswell of the central Kauhakō Crater behind it. The pinnacle of Mokapu island juts from the ocean beyond, but the original settlement of Kalawao (see p.423) is obscured by the slight curve of the *pali*. Captioned photographs explain the local topography, as well as the history and treatment of Hansen's disease (see p.422). A footpath continues left from the lookout, offering a pleasant half-hour **hike** but no better views.

To the left of the parking lot, a broad and very well-worn trail, which at first leads downward through the woods, takes five minutes to reach the top of the Pu'u Loa knoll, known for its **Phallic Rock**. This reshaped and much-fondled stone outcrop was in ancient times a fertility shrine known as Ka Ule O Nānāhoa – "the penis of Nānāhoa" – and used to stand fully exposed to the plains below, rather than deep in the forest. Women who brought offerings here and then spent the night were said to return home pregnant; the furrowed tip still holds cigarettes, dollar bills, flowers and other gifts. Ancient petroglyphs are concealed beneath an overhanging rock nearby, while an extremely old *heiau* on a rocky point two miles to the west is surrounded by phallic emblems.

Camping near the parking lot at Pālā'au State Park is free; contact the Department of Land and Natural Resources, as detailed on p.402.

The Kalaupapa Peninsula

They were strangers to each other, collected by common calamity, disfigured, mortally sick, banished without sin from home and friends. Few would understand the principle on which they were thus forfeited in all that life holds dear; many must have conceived their ostracism to be grounded in malevolent caprice; all came with sorrow at heart, many with despair and rage. In the chronicle of man there is perhaps no more melancholy landing than this of the leper immigrants among the ruined houses and dead harvests of Molokai.

Robert Louis Stevenson

The **KALAUPAPA PENINSULA** is a dramatic volcanic afterthought, tacked on to Molokai's forbidding north coast and almost completely cut off by towering 2000-foot cliffs. It was created long after the cliffs had been shaped by the force of the sea, when lava from a minor eruption lapped against the vast bulk of the island to form a flat and exposed spit of land.

This remote outpost became world famous in the nineteenth century as the grim place of exile for Hawaiian sufferers from **leprosy**, and the site of the ministry of the saintly **Father Damien** (see box, pp.420–421). Although there is no longer any risk of the disease spreading, the peninsula is still reserved for former leprosy patients. Under the joint administration of the National Park Service and the Hawaii State Department of Health, it's run as the **Kalaupapa National Historic Park**. It's also a somewhat anomalous county in its own right, although it has no official county government, and all the other counties in Hawaii consist of one or more entire islands. As no one under the age of 16 is allowed on the peninsula, this is the only **child-free** county in the US.

Kalaupapa is an inspiring place to visit, but you can only do so with a reserved ticket for an official **park tour**. These are operated (though sadly no longer personally led) by the residents as Damien Tours, and are not open to children. Other than **flying** down to the peninsula, the only means of access is the long but perfectly safe **trail** that zigzags down the *pali*, which you can either **hike** or descend by **mule**.

If you don't have the time to visit the peninsula itself, it's possible to get a distant overview from the overlook in **Pālā'au State Park** (see opposite), at the top of Kala'e Highway.

The trail to Kalaupapa

The trailhead for the precipitous descent to Kalaupapa, the three-mile **Kukuiohapu'u Trail** (also known as the Pali Trail), is located to the right of Kala'e Highway, almost three miles north of Kualapu'u and just beyond the barn that's the headquarters of the **Molokai Mule Ride**. Molokai's most popular tourist attraction – famous for its bumper-sticker slogan *Wouldn't You Rather Be Riding a Mule on Molokai?* – is a wonderfully escapist experience, though in essence it's simply an expensive, if enjoyable, means of transportation. Once at Kalaupapa, the riders dismount and join the same motorized tours of the peninsula (see p.422) as all other visitors.

Each day except Sunday, mule riders rendezvous by 8am to set off at 8.30am, and return at around 3.30pm. All riders must be aged 16 or over; the fee of $165 per person includes the ground tour and a picnic lunch, while round-trip airport transfers are $25 extra. For reservations, call ☏808/567-6088, 808/336-0802, or 1-800/567-7550, or email via ⓦ www.muleride.com, as far in advance as possible.

If you prefer to **hike**, there's nothing to stop you from walking the full length of the trail and then climbing back up again, but you can only enter the peninsula itself if you meet up with a pre-arranged tour. Most hikers set off around 8.30am to coincide with the 10.15am Damien Tours tour.

Hiking down to the bottom of the cliffs takes around an hour and a quarter, while the mules take more like an hour and a half. For the first few hundred yards from the highway, the trail winds through bucolic meadows and guava orchards; then, suddenly, it comes to the edge of the cliff, above a sheer 1644-foot drop. The section that follows is the narrowest of the lot, with the yawning abyss in full view to your left. Soon, however, you enter the shade of the forest and continue dropping steeply down 26 numbered switchbacks. The majestic *pali* stretches away to the horizon in both directions, with rainbows floating beneath the clouds and the plain of Kalaupapa laid flat at your feet.

The whole trail was rebuilt during 1994 and 1995, when the mule ride was closed by legal and insurance wrangles. Rather than ferrying tourists, the hard-working mules were obliged instead to assist in the renovation project, making up

Father Damien and the story of Kalaupapa

Within a century of its first contact with the outside world, the population of Hawaii dropped from around one million to just over fifty thousand. Among the main reasons was the susceptibility of native Hawaiians to imported **diseases**, none of which was more feared than **leprosy**.

Hawaii's first case of leprosy was diagnosed in 1835, at Kōloa on Kauai. Believed to have spread with the arrival of plantation laborers from China, it became known as *ma'i Pake*, or the "Chinese disease." In 1865, when one in fifty Hawaiians was said to have contracted leprosy, King Kamehameha V saw no alternative but to pursue a policy of rigorous **isolation**.

All persons deemed to be suffering from the disease – which, given the state of medical knowledge in rural Hawaii, effectively meant anyone with a visible skin blemish – were obliged to surrender themselves for shipment to the Kalaupapa Peninsula, to live out their days in permanent **exile**. Apart from one voluntary *kokua* (helper), they were separated forever from their homes and families. There was no right of appeal against the diagnosis, and as bounty hunters scoured the islands in search of potential victims, some sufferers, such as the legendary Koolau on Kauai (see p.495), turned outlaw to escape their fate.

Although nowhere in Hawaii is more isolated than the Kalaupapa Peninsula, numerous shrines, *heiaus*, and gravesites – now mostly buried in the undergrowth – attest to extensive ancient occupation. There was a substantial settlement here in the 1860s, but the villagers swiftly relocated "top-side" once shipments of sufferers began to arrive at nearby Kalawao Bay to the east.

In its **early years**, the colony at Kalaupapa was a God-forsaken place. Intended to be self-sufficient, it rapidly dissolved into anarchy. The first boatload of people were left to divide all the land among themselves; as additional exiles followed, it had to be re-divided again and again, occasioning bitter disputes each time. The strong dominated the weak, to be supplanted in turn as each succumbed to the disease. For fear of contagion, ships often refused to pull in closer to shore than Mokapu island, and many new arrivals were forced to swim for their lives through the rough surf. Legend has it those that made it to the shore were greeted with the words, "*A'ole kanawai ma keia wahi*" ("There is no law in this place") and stripped of their few possessions.

The people of Kalaupapa were not regarded as patients; receiving no treatment, they were simply abandoned to die. There was little sympathy from the white-dominated government, which held the view that the natives had brought disease upon themselves by wanton promiscuity.

Matters only began to change in 1873, when the Belgian Catholic priest **Father Damien Joseph de Veuster** – who had worked for nine years on the Big Island – was posted to Kalaupapa. Initially he was assigned for a brief tour of duty, but his appointment received so much international publicity that his superiors felt that for him to leave Molokai within a few months would have seemed like a retreat. Only 12 of the 822 residents at that time were Catholic, but Father Damien dedicated himself to improving conditions for all. He was to spend the remaining sixteen years of his life on Molokai, in a sustained outpouring of sheer physical effort that doomed him to an early grave.

to four round-trips per day as cement stairways were set into the earth, and parapets placed along the occasional hair-raising stretch.

Eventually the trail levels out to run the full length of **'Awahua Beach**, which you will have repeatedly glimpsed to the west of the peninsula on your way down. In winter, this broad expanse of slightly grimy sand can be stripped completely bare overnight. As on all the beaches at Kalaupapa, swimming is strictly forbidden.

Damien's daily routine consisted in nursing, bathing, and dressing the sores of the sick, and in due course carrying their corpses for burial with his bare hands. Although determined to build a new church at Kalawao, he regarded that task as intrinsically less important and only allowed himself to work on its construction after dark. He also built three hospitals and over three hundred houses to replace the previous crude windbreaks, and constructed a pipeline to carry fresh water along the coast from high in Waikolu Valley.

One Sunday morning, in June 1885, Damien began his sermon with the words "**We lepers . . .**" rather than the usual "my brethren." Out of more than a thousand helpers to have worked at Kalaupapa, he remains the only one ever to contract leprosy, through sustained physical contact and general exhaustion. His 82-year-old mother died the day after news of his illness reached Belgium; Damien himself died in Kalaupapa in April 1889, at the age of 49, having previously stated that "I would not have my health restored to me at the price of my having to leave the island and abandon my work here."

Damien has been eulogized ever since his death, by figures as disparate as the future King Edward VII of Britain and Mahatma Gandhi. One famous note of criticism, however, was sounded by Reverend Charles Hyde, a Protestant minister in Honolulu, who wrote of him as "a coarse, dirty man, headstrong and bigoted . . . not a pure man in his relations with women." Robert Louis Stevenson, who visited Kalaupapa a month after Damien's death, sprang to his defense in an "Open Letter" that was reproduced all over the world.

Although Damien made it very clear that he wished to remain buried at Kalaupapa, his body was exhumed and taken to Belgium in 1936; his right hand was, however, returned to Molokai in 1995. Evidence of the miraculous cure of a nun in 1895 has been accepted by the Vatican, and in 1994 Damien was officially beatified as "the Blessed Damien," the last step on the road to eventual sainthood. A poll conducted in Belgium in 2005 declared him to be the Greatest Belgian of all time.

Meanwhile, the work at Kalaupapa has been carried on by such followers as Brother Joseph Dutton and Mother Marianne Cope. Over the years, the entire population shifted across the peninsula to the village of Kalaupapa itself, and Kalawao was abandoned altogether in 1932. Decades of false hopes and spurious treatments finally came to an end in the 1940s, with the appearance of the first effective treatment. The formal separation of patients at Kalaupapa finally ended in 1969.

In all, a total of more than eight thousand patients made their homes on the peninsula, with the population during its heyday varying between the mid-700s and something over a thousand. As of 2007, 33 of those patients were still alive, with the youngest being aged 66. Five live on Oahu, while the rest remain at Kalaupapa, together with around forty health workers and another forty park employees. No doctors live on the peninsula; they simply visit for the day from Honolulu. As the saga gently draws to a close, the peninsula is turning into a historical monument; when the last patient dies, it will become wholly owned by the park service.

Flying to Kalaupapa

Four daily **flights** to Kalaupapa's tiny airstrip from Molokai's main airport at Ho'olehua are operated by Pacific Wings (℡808/567-6814 or 1-888/575-4546, ⓦwww.pacificwings.com). This seven-mile, nine-minute hop, currently priced at around $60 for the round-trip, claims to be the shortest scheduled air service in the world, and carries the added bonus of a close-up view of the world's tallest sea cliffs, along Molokai's otherwise inaccessible northern coastline. Pacific Wings also offer direct flights to Kalaupapa from both Honolulu and Kahului. All passengers landing at Kalaupapa must have tour reservations. However, if you've walked down to the peninsula and can't face the hike back up again, just ask the tour guide, and you may well be able to catch a flight back up again – the only problem is, that will take you to the airport rather than where you've left your car.

The Molokai Mule Ride (℡808/567-6088 or 1-800/567-7550, ⓦwww .muleride.com) arranges day-trips to Kalaupapa, including round-trip flight, mule ride, and ground tour, from any hotel in Waikīkī, or from either airport on Maui. Oddly, they'll also sell you a day-trip whereby you fly to and from Kalaupapa and tour the peninsula without taking the mule ride. Precise rates depend on current airline prices and schedules, which vary enormously.

Touring Kalaupapa

All **tours** of Kalaupapa Peninsula are organized by Damien Tours (for reservations, call ℡808/567-6088 or 1-800/567-7750), at a cost of $40 per person. Every day except Sunday, their rickety minibuses or four-wheel-drive vehicles pick up tourists either from the airstrip or at the east end of 'Awahua Beach, just outside the settlement of **KALAUPAPA**, where the trail from Kala'e ends. Visitors are not allowed to wander unaccompanied, or to take photographs of residents. Even if you're on the mule ride, bring plenty of **water**; it can be a long hot day.

Exactly what is included on any one tour depends on the whim of that day's guide. Until recently, the guides were themselves former patients, who provided a fascinating and often very moving link with the history of the colony, but as the

---

Hansen's disease

The disease familiar from the Bible as **leprosy** is known to scientists as "**Hansen's disease**," in honor of the Norwegian Gerhard Hansen, who first identified the leprosy bacillus in February 1873. Despite popular misconceptions, Hansen's disease is not in fact particularly contagious, and only around one person in twenty is even susceptible to it.

Any need for the isolation of patients, as practiced at Kalaupapa, was rendered obsolete by the development of **sulfone drugs** in the 1940s. These arrest the development of the disease in sufferers and eliminate the possibility of contagion. Nonetheless, although the disease has been all but eradicated both in Hawaii and the US as a whole, there are still two million sufferers worldwide, and some 600,000 new cases diagnosed each year.

In the last sixty years, Hawaiian state law regarding the official name of the disease has alternated three times between the terms "Hansen's disease" and "leprosy." While "Hansen's disease" is the current official choice, many of the patients at Kalaupapa continue to prefer "leprosy." Some are even content to be referred to as "lepers," despite what may seem to outsiders to be the negative connotations of the word.

△ Father Damien's grave

patients age and decline in health it seems unlikely that will ever again be the case. Indeed, as the tours come past at pretty much the same time every day, many of the residents choose to stay behind closed doors for the duration rather than face scrutiny, and it's quite possible you won't see any at all.

The guides now tend to be "top-siders," as inhabitants of the rest of Molokai were traditionally known, who are not always as knowledgeable or indeed sympathetic as you might expect. As a rule, you can expect to spend the first hour in Kalaupapa village, probably with stops at both *Fuesaina's* bar for drinks and ices, and at the **Kalaupapa National Historic Park Museum and Bookstore** (Mon–Sat 10.30am–12.30pm). The latter is a fancy name for a small house that holds ornaments and artifacts made by the patients, plus utensils that they adapted for their own use, and a fine selection of books.

Among other likely stops are a memorial to Father Damien; the gravesite of his successor Mother Marianne Cope; the church, where an outbuilding displays historical photos; and the small **boat landing** where all local supplies arrive. Just one barge per year now delivers cargo to Kalaupapa, including a hundred cases of Spam and 2700 cases of beer. The essentials of life are so hard to obtain in Kalaupapa that most residents have two of everything – cars, TVs, etc – in case one breaks down. This cautious approach proved ineffective in 1991, however, when the old wooden hospital burned down, with all its medical records. Both fire engines had failed to start.

Kalaupapa is located on the sheltered, drier, western side of the peninsula. As you cross to the east, the vegetation grows rapidly thicker and greener, and groves of fruit trees start to appear. To the left of the one dirt road, the mound of **Kauhakō Crater** – the volcanic vent that created the peninsula – rises gently to a height of 400ft. White crosses stand on its rim, while the brackish lake inside is more than 800ft deep, reaching far below sea level. In the early years of the colony, residents are said to have sheltered overnight in caves down in the crater. Off to the right of the road, the *pali* soars up into the clouds. After heavy rain, all the clefts in the cliff face become waterfalls; one, which runs red at first from the mud, takes twenty minutes to work its way down, filling six successive pools en route.

As you enter the original settlement of the "Lazaretto" (leper colony), **KALAWAO**, you pass the unobtrusive "**birthing stone**" where the chiefs of Molokai were traditionally supposed to be born. The tasseled Australian casuarina tree alongside it was planted by Father Damien in front of the third hospital he built in Kalawao – the first he was permitted to construct away from the exposed shoreline.

Nothing now remains of the hospital. Indeed the only building left standing in Kalawao, which was inhabited from 1866 to 1932, is **St Philomena's Church**, sited where the road meets the sea. Shipped from Honolulu in 1872, this was greatly expanded by Damien in the years that followed and is widely known as "Damien's Church." The rectangular holes in the floorboards beneath the pews were cut by Damien himself, when he realized that the sickest patients were not attending Mass because they were afraid of despoiling the church by spitting. Before his body was taken to Belgium, Damien was buried in the gardens to the right; his grave remains decorated with *leis* and now contains his right hand once more.

Despite the horrific tales of misery and squalor, Kalawao is an extraordinarily beautiful place. From the lawns beyond the church, and especially from **Judd Park** at the end of the road, the views of the coast are superb. Mists swirl beneath the gigantic *pali* to the east, occasionally parting to offer glimpses of the remote valleys that pierce it, while stark, rocky islands poke from the churning ocean. Daredevil ancient Hawaiians are said to have swum out to **'Okala Island**, the closest to the shore, to leap from its 400ft summit with the aid of braided palm-leaf "parachutes."

Western Molokai

Western Molokai consists of what remains of the older of the island's two volcanoes, **Mauna Loa**. Similar in profile to its Big Island namesake, but much lower, the "long mountain" lies within the rainshadow of the larger East Molokai volcano, in that almost all the moisture carried by the prevailing winds has already fallen as rain before they reach this far. As a result, this end of the island is much drier, and there's been little erosion to dissect it into valleys.

Nonetheless, recent archeological research has revealed that western Molokai had a considerable population in ancient times. As well as having the mysterious woodlands that witnessed the emergence of the *hula* and the fearsome apparition of the poison-wood gods (see p.426), the upper slopes of its mountain were one of Hawaii's best sources of the ultra-hard basalt used for making adzes – a precious commodity in a world without metal. Hence the region's name: **Kaluako'i**, "the adze pit."

In 1898, the entire west end of Molokai was sold for $251,000 to the consortium that became the **Molokai Ranch**. The ranch remains a totally dominant presence, although it has long since shifted its focus away from cattle-ranching and pineapple-farming and toward real estate and tourism. During the 1970s, it unveiled plans for the development of Kaluako'i that envisioned the population growing to ten thousand within twenty years. Not only has that failed to happen, but the **hotel** that was supposed to be the centerpiece of the coastal resort area – which has itself come to be called **Kaluako'i** – has now been closed for several years, leaving just a smattering of smaller condo properties, a handful of private homes, no restaurants, and only the most basic of local stores. At root, the problem is **water** – there simply isn't enough for that scale of growth to happen.

Western Molokai has some magnificent **beaches**, such as the phenomenal **Pāpōhaku Beach**, but almost all are subject to surf that is too fierce for swimming. Instead, those few visitors who come this way tend to be here for the **golf**, or simply the seclusion. As the base of the Molokai Ranch, which has an unfailing capacity to surprise visitors with its latest initiatives, the hillside plantation village of **Maunaloa** is also worth visiting.

The Struggle for Lā'au Point

At the time this book went to press, Molokai was sharply divided over the latest in a perennial series of controversies surrounding the Molokai Ranch's development plans. The current issue focuses on a scheme to build an exclusive residential community of two hundred luxury homes at **Lā'au Point**, at the far southwestern tip of the island. To the ranch owners, it's the one way to get a return on their investment now that agriculture is no longer viable, and would create jobs and stimulate the island economy. To local activists, Lā'au Point is one of the last surviving pristine wildernesses in Hawaii, home to rare plant and marine species, while the arrival of two hundred super-rich new residents, with the spending power to influence elections, would permanently reshape the politics of the island. From that standpoint, even a new hotel would be better, because it would require a local labor force and guests would simply visit rather than stay. No doubt the debate will have moved on by the time you read this, but feelings are running very high and the one thing on which both sides seem to agree is that however the issue is finally settled, Molokai will never be the same again.

Maunaloa

Together with Kēʻē on Kauai (see p.489), **MAUNALOA** is one of two Hawaiian sites that claim to be the birthplace of *hula*. This tiny place also plays a prominent role in the myths and legends of ancient Molokai. Only a few stone ruins, near the adze quarry on the hillock of ʻAmikopala, remain of the pre-contact settlement, but a thriving community existed here until little over a decade ago, when Maunaloa was among the most picturesque plantation villages in the state.

Perched high on the red-dirt flanks of western Molokai, enjoying views all the way to Diamond Head and Waikīkī on Oahu, modern Maunaloa took shape after Libby leased the nearby land to grow pineapples in the 1920s. At that time, it consisted of a cluster of simple timber cottages, shielded from the winds by stately rows of tall trees. The fence of the lowermost home was a line of discarded surfboards wedged into the soil. Soon after passing into the hands of the Dole corporation in the 1970s, the pineapple fields were abandoned, the land reverted

The poisonwood gods

Maunaloa was renowned throughout ancient Hawaii as the home of the dreaded **Kālaipāhoa**, or **"poisonwood gods."** According to legend, sometime in the sixteenth or seventeenth centuries a Molokai man called **Kāneiākama** lost everything he possessed playing ʻulumaika, which involved bowling stone disks down a hillside. As he was about to concede defeat, a god appeared to him in a dream and encouraged him to stake his life on the next throw. Upon winning, Kāneiākama sacrificed a pig to the mysterious god, who reappeared and gave his name as **Kāneikaulanaʻula**. Kāneiākama then watched as a grove of tall trees suddenly appeared in the hills above Maunaloa, and each different kind of tree was entered by a different deity.

When the then-chief of Molokai decreed that some of these magical trees should be chopped down and carved into images of the gods, it was found that the woodcutters died as soon as they were touched by flying chips or sap. Kāneiākama revealed how, with the appropriate sacrifices and ceremonies, the images could be created in safety; they passed into the control of the rulers of Molokai, while Kāneiākama became their *kahuna*, or priest.

For many years, access to the images was ruthlessly restricted, and fear of them kept Molokai safe from attack. Eventually, however, Molokai was conquered by the other islands, and the *Kālaipāhoa* passed first to Kahekili of Maui and then to Kamehameha the Great. According to nineteenth-century Hawaiian historian Samuel Kamakau, Kamehameha kept the images by him during his final years at Kailua on the Big Island, and was the only person able to resist their power: "Not only was *Kālaipāhoa* fatal to eat or touch, but it was also fatal if one carelessly went in and out of the house in which the god-images were kept without going out backward . . . a person would drop dead instantly at the door of the house if this rule was not observed."

Meanwhile the people of Molokai, and Maunaloa in particular, had begun to use the surviving trees for their own purposes. They used splinters or shavings of wood to poison each other's food, and even created magical bundles known as *akua kumuhaka*, that flew like flaming rockets through the night sky to seek out their enemies. During the first half of the nineteenth century, Molokai became widely feared as an evil place of *poʻokoʻi* (sorcery), and was often called the ʻaina hoʻounauna, "the land where spirits were sent on malicious errands."

Knowledge of the whereabouts of the *Kālaipāhoa* images died with Kamehameha, although at least one is thought to survive in the collections of Honolulu's Bishop Museum.

to the Molokai Ranch, and Maunaloa became a sleepy enclave of ranch hands, resort employees, and alternative artists.

In 1995, however, Molokai Ranch bulldozed most of the residential district of Maunaloa and replaced it with tracts of low-income housing further up the hillside. To this day, there still seems to be few jobs on the horizon for its hoped-for future inhabitants. That said, although the destruction created considerable bitterness at the time, those villagers that remain seem grateful for the level of commitment – and investment – shown by the ranch.

Maunaloa may not be as attractive as it used to be, but the area around its **village green** is largely unspoiled, and even boasts its own three-screen movie theater (☎808/552-2707). The most interesting of its handful of stores is the Big Wind Kite Factory (Mon–Sat 8.30am–5pm, Sun 10am–2pm), whose convivial owner makes and sells colorful kites and is usually happy to demonstrate the finer points of kite-flying. The adjoining Plantation Gallery (same hours) stocks an excellent range of imported crafts from Bali, Nepal, and elsewhere, plus Molokai "Red Dirt" T-shirts and books on Hawaii, while across the road the old-style General Store (Mon–Sat 9am–7pm) is still going strong.

Molokai Ranch

The headquarters for the **Molokai Ranch**'s program of visitor activities stands on the right as you enter Maunaloa from the end of Maunaloa Highway, just above the turning to the *Lodge* (see below). Housed in what may appear to be an old barn, but is in fact a new building, the **Outfitters Center** (daily 6am–7pm; ☎808/552-0184, ⓦwww.molokaifishanddive.com) is the place to reserve or rendezvous for such things as **horseback riding** ($85), **downhill bicycle excursions** ($59), and even **archery** ($37) and **sport clay shooting** ($75).

During the early 1990s, the ranch ran safari tours into the dry savannah-like landscape that stretches from here down to the coast. Herds of zebra and Barbary sheep are still said to be down there somewhere, though the giraffes are long gone.

Accommodation

The one accommodation option in Maunaloa, the timber-built **Molokai Ranch Lodge**, is set slightly to the right of the main road (100 Maunaloa Hwy; ☎808/660-2824 or 1-888/627-8082, ⓦwww.molokairanch.com; ❼). This small, upscale hotel stretches across the hillside above an expanse of pastureland that sprawls way down toward the ocean; at night, it's often possible to see all the way to Diamond Head on Oahu. It offers just 22 very spacious, comfortable, and beautifully furnished guest rooms, with large *lānais* and access to a small swimming pool. While quiet and very tasteful and boasting extremely friendly staff, its cool upcountry location means it's not the kind of place most visitors would associate with Hawaii, and it's not so much a tropical getaway as a retreat for overheated (and affluent) Hawaiian residents.

The *Lodge* is, however, run in association with a very unusual alternative: **Kaupoa Beach Village** (❺), reached by a very dusty seven-mile drive from Maunaloa down the ranch's private dirt roads. Set by a delightful and usually deserted beach, this oceanfront complex consists of semi-permanent, canvas-walled structures known as "tentalows," each set on its own open wooden platform that holds a detached "bathroom" and a smaller "bedroom" suitable for children. As an adventurous destination for a beach and watersports family vacation, it's quite wonderful. The rates have recently dropped to around $180 per day (from the previous absurd figure of $300), though it's still no budget bargain once you factor in activities or meals (there's precious little choice about eating in the on-site dining room, where the buffet meals cost $15 for lunch and $31 for dinner). Contact details are the same as for the *Lodge*.

Eating

The *Maunaloa Room* in the *Lodge* is open for breakfast and dinner daily, plus a $25 brunch on Sundays (Mon–Sat 7–10am & 6–9pm, Sun 7–10am, 11am–1.30pm, & 5–9pm; T808/660-2725). Typical evening entrees include a $25 catch of the day prepared in Oriental (steamed), Mediterranean (with capers and olives), or local (broiled with citrus cream sauce) style, while Sunday night sees an excellent Asian buffet ($30). Lunch, served in the *Paniolo Bar* (daily 10am–4pm), is a less inspiring assortment of burgers and sandwiches at around $10. The main lobby at the *Lodge* often serves as the venue for live **music** and **hula** performances, especially on Sunday evenings.

Hale O Lono Harbor

Molokai's remote **southwestern shoreline** has long been inaccessible to visitors. However, the **Hale O Lono Harbor** reverted a few years ago to state ownership, after being leased to the Molokai Ranch for 35 years. Anyone who wants to can now drive down here, along the red-dirt road (very passable except after heavy rain) that starts just beyond the *Lodge* in Maunaloa. En route, keener eyes might spot a phallic rock in a gully to the left that marks ancient burial caves.

Hale O Lono Harbor, which was constructed to ship sand from Pāpōhaku Beach to Oahu, consists of a few concrete jetties with minimal facilities. In September and October each year, it serves as the starting point of the prestigious Bankoh men's and women's **outrigger canoe races** from Molokai to Oahu. Walking a couple of hundred yards east from the parking lot at the end of the road brings you to a small, sheltered beach.

Kaluako'i

Until construction began on the **Kaluako'i Resort** during the 1970s, just one person lived on the coast of western Molokai. That owes more to the fact that it belonged to the Molokai Ranch than to there being anything wrong with it. However, the lack of water has prevented the resort from growing to anything like the size originally envisaged. To this day, only one of its planned four hotels has ever been built, and even that one, the *Kaluako'i Hotel*, had by 2001 deteriorated to such an extent that it was forced to **close** indefinitely pending large-scale renovations. As the hotel was home to the only stores or restaurants in the area, its closure has made staying in any of the nearby condo developments a much less appealing prospect, although it's still unquestionably worth making the trip here to enjoy splendid **Pāpōhaku Beach**.

Opinion on the island appears to be unanimous in favor of reopening the hotel, and its new owners – the Molokai Ranch, of course – have declared their intention to do so. However, they have also said that any such opening is dependent on their plans for development at **Lā'au Point** getting the go-ahead, which is a much more controversial proposition (see p.425).

Accommodation

The only **accommodation** in Kaluako'i is located in the small area where Kaluako'i Road reaches the ocean, which is dominated by the defunct *Kaluako'i Hotel* on the headland. For now, the hotel remains in a strange state of limbo; its couple of little souvenir and snack stores and even its pool are still open, catering to visitors staying in the neighboring condos. In addition to the properties listed below, other privately owned properties can be rented through Swenson Real Estate (☎808/553-3648 or 1-800/367-2984, ⓦwww.molokai-vacation-rental.com).

Ke Nani Kai 50 Kepuhi Place ☎808/679-2016 or 1-800/490-9042, ⓦwww.kenanikai.com. Spacious and very comfortable one- and two-bedroom condos on the *Kaluako'i Hotel* approach road, few of which have sea views, in a small, well-kept resort with its own pool and spa. ❺

Kepuhi Beach Condo PO Box 20, Maunaloa HI 96770 ☎808/552-2222, 1-800/MOLOKAI, ⓦwww.1-800-molokai.com. A couple of upscale condos on the Kaluako'i golf course, very close to Pāpōhaku Beach, with good-value nightly or weekly rental rates. ❹

Paniolo Hale PO Box 190, Lio Place, Maunaloa HI 96770; reserve through Swenson Real Estate, ☎808/553-3648, ⓦwww.molokai-vacation-rental .com. An estate of studio apartments plus one- and two-bedroom condos, just north of the *Kaluako'i Hotel*. Some of the larger ones are complete houses and in very good condition. ❹

The West End beaches

Although the *Kaluako'i Resort* was positioned to enable guests to enjoy the long white sands of **Kepuhi Beach**, located directly in front of the *Kaluako'i Hotel*, it's only safe to swim here on calm summer days. Like most of the beaches of western Molokai, however, it looks fabulous and is ideal for sunset strolls.

A mile **north** of the resort, and reached by a very rough road – far too rough to drive – that starts by crossing the golf course beyond *Paniolo Hale*, pretty, crescent-shaped **Kawākiu Iki Bay** was a favorite fishing ground in ancient times. Mass protests in the 1970s persuaded the Molokai Ranch to grant free public access, and there's even a free but completely unequipped **campground** here, but it's almost always deserted.

Immediately **south** of the hotel, it's possible to follow a track to the summit of the crumbling cinder cone of **Pu'u O Kaiaka** for views of the entire coastline and, with luck, across to Oahu. Beyond it lies 2.5-mile-long **Pāpōhaku Beach**, one of Hawaii's broadest and most impressive white-sand beaches. It's so huge that for many years it was quarried for sand, much of which was used to build Waikīkī Beach.

Almost all the land to either side of Kaluako'i Road, which parallels Pāpōhaku a hundred yards back from the sea, was parceled off and sold for residential development many years ago. However, homes have so far only been built on a small proportion of the lots, and even those seem seldom to be occupied, so you may find that you have the full length of the beach to yourself. The relentless pounding of the surf is spectacular, but makes swimming extremely dangerous.

Three successive turnoffs connect Kaluako'i Road with the beach. The northern-most leads to **Pāpōhaku Beach Park**, a well-equipped county park that has picnic tables on its lawns and barbecue pits amid the trees. Visitors with permits from the Division of Parks in Kaunakakai (☎808/567-6083) are allowed to **camp** here. The southernmost turnoff, Papapa Place, appears as Kaluako'i Road starts to climb at the south end of the beach; it comes out near the gated tunnel through which sand destined for Waikīkī was carted off to the docks on the south coast.

Kaluako'i Road ends beyond Pāpōhaku Beach, but by turning right on to Pōhakuloa Road you can drive a couple of miles further down the coast. A couple of beach access roads along the way lead to an exposed and rocky shoreline, but

Molokai Ka Hula Piko

On the third Saturday of May, between 8am and 4pm, Pāpōhaku Beach Park hosts **Molokai Ka Hula Piko**, a day-long celebration of Molokai's role as the birthplace of the *hula*. That's a slightly contentious boast – Kēʻē on Kauai also claims to be the home of Hawaii's oldest art form – but Ka Hula Piko is universally acknowledged to be one of the most authentic traditional festivals in the islands. As well as performances by dancers, musicians, and singers from all over Hawaii, it features local crafts and food stalls. Admission is free.

On Molokai, the story runs that the goddess **Laka** was taught to dance the *hula* by her sister **Kapo** amid the verdant *'ōhi'a lehua* groves of **Kā'ana**, near Maunaloa. After traveling through the Hawaiian islands teaching *hula*, Laka returned to Molokai to die, and lies buried beneath the hill of **Pu'unānā**.

Ka Hula Piko commences each year with a dawn ceremony at a ruined *heiau* at Kā'ana, to which the public is not admitted. However, the festival's organizers have in the past offered guided tours of related sites during the preceding week. At other times, the only way to see Kā'ana and Pu'unānā would be on a guided hike; contact the Molokai Visitors Association to see if anyone is currently leading them. The fact that the area is now almost entirely denuded of trees has made it possible to identify, and in some cases excavate, countless cultural sites.

Local hotels offer all-inclusive transport and accommodation packages to Ka Hula Piko; once again, contact the Molokai Visitors Association for details (see p.404).

the final turnaround comes at the small sandy cove named **Dixie Maru Beach**, after a long-vanished shipwreck. Sparsely vegetated and relatively unattractive, the cove – whose official name, which you'll see on some maps, is **Kapukahehu Beach** – is enclosed enough to create a small lagoon of sheltered turquoise water, where the swimming is usually great.

From **Dixie Maru Beach**, it's possible to follow the coastal footpath for another mile south to reach **Kaunalā Beach**, where the ocean is muddier and much rougher. Beyond that, the remaining segment of the western coast belongs to the Molokai Ranch, though as usual in Hawaii anyone is free to walk along the shoreline below the high-water line. Another mile further on, you'll come to the Molokai Ranch's *Kaupoa Beach Village* (see p.427), while two miles after that – a laborious hike of four miles from **Dixie Maru** that can take up to four hours one-way – you'd reach **Lā'au Point**, the subject of the fierce controversy described on p.425.

Kauai

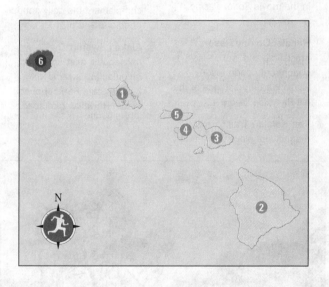

N

6

KAUAI

CHAPTER 6 # Highlights

* **Helicopter trips** There's no place quite like Kauai for a flight-seeing extravaganza of hidden canyons, remote rainforests, velvety waterfalls and uninhabited valleys. See p.439

* **Lumaha'i Beach** The sublime (if dangerous) tropical beach where Mitzi Gaynor washed that man right out of her hair in the movie *South Pacific*. See p.484

* **Hanalei Colony Resort** Irresistible and inexpensive beachfront condo resort, within walking distance of the Nā Pali cliffs. See p.485

* **The Kalalau Trail** Utterly magnificent eleven-mile trail along Kauai's northern Nā Pali coastline; just hike the first stretch if time is limited. See p.489

* **Po'ipū Beach** Snorkel, boogie-board, sunbathe or surf on Kauai's most popular family beach. See p.501

* **Waimea Canyon** An extraordinary gorge for such a tiny island, where rainbows complement the daily panoply of colors. See p.515

* **Alaka'i Swamp** The mysterious, mist-shrouded, mountaintop swamp, in Kōke'e State Park, abounds in rare Hawaiian bird species. See p.517

△ The Kalalau Trail

6

Kauai

A lthough no point on the tiny island of **KAUAI** (rhymes with "Hawaii") is even a dozen miles from the sea, the sheer variety of its landscapes is quite incredible. This is the oldest of the major Hawaiian islands, and the forces of erosion have had over six million years to sculpt it into fantastic shapes. The resultant spectacular **scenery** – celebrated in movies from *South Pacific* to *Jurassic Park* – is Kauai's strongest selling point. In addition to such showpiece beauty spots as the plunging **Nā Pali cliffs** on the North Shore and mighty **Waimea Canyon**, every humble roadside town abounds in flowers, orchids, and greenery. The Garden Island, as it's known, is also fringed with stunning **beaches** of white and golden sand, which provide a marked contrast to the island's rich, red soil. On some beaches, on the north and west coasts in particular, it's seldom safe even to approach the ocean; others, especially around the southern resort of **Po'ipū**, are ideal for family bathing.

Kauai ranks fourth not only in size among the Hawaiian islands, but also in population and number of annual visitors. With only a little over sixty thousand inhabitants scattered fairly evenly around the shoreline, it holds no large towns. The administrative center, **Līhu'e**, is functional but unenthralling, while all the main accommodation bases – **Po'ipū**, the coastal strip around **Kapa'a**, and **Princeville** – are too busy catering to tourists to possess much of an identity of their own. If you're looking for the high life, stick to Waikīkī or Maui; Kauai is more suited to a quiet family holiday or a romantic rural retreat. It's also a place to be active, on both sea and land. In addition to some of the world's most exhilarating hiking trails, it offers great **snorkeling** and **surfing**. Taking a boat trip along the North Shore is a can't-miss experience, and if you only go on one **helicopter** flight in your life, this is the place to do it.

A brief history of Kauai

Although most details of ancient Hawaiian history remain unknown, Kauai can legitimately claim to possess its own separate heritage, as the only island never to be conquered by another. Before the arrival of the Europeans, it was always an independent kingdom. Even Kamehameha the Great opted to accept tribute from Kauai, after twice staging unsuccessful invasions.

Just as it was the first of the Hawaiian islands to be "discovered" by Captain Cook, it's perfectly plausible that Kauai had been **colonized** before the rest, by a different group of Polynesian settlers. Evidence such as the design of Kauaian stone *poi* pounders, and distinctive long, narrow *heiaus*, suggests that its first

433

Kē'ē Beach   Hā'ena
Hanakāpī'ai Beach
Limahuli
Gardens   Wainiha

N   ā   P   a   l   i   C   o   a   s   t

Kalalau Beach   Kalalau Valley
Pu'u o Kila
Lookout
Honopū Val.   Kalalau   Pihea
Awa'awapuhi Val.   Lookout   (4284ft)
AWA'AWA PUHI TR.
NU'ALOLO TR.   PIHEA TR.
KŌKE'E   ALAKA'I
Kōke'e Lodge   SWAMP TRAIL

Māhaha   Valley   STATE   ALAKA'I
WAIMEA   PARK   SWAMP

Pu'u Hinahina (3636ft)

CANYON   WAIMEA
Pu'u Ka Pele (3662ft)   CANYON
POLIHALE   Waimea
Barking Sands   STATE PARK   STATE   Canyon
Lookout

PARK
Pacific Missile
Range Facility
Mānā Point

KŌKE'E ROAD

550

K   a   u   l   a   k   a   h   i   C   h   a   n   n   e   l

WAIMEA CANYON DRIVE

KAUMUALI'I HIGHWAY

50   Kekaha
Waimea   550
Kīkīaola Harbor   Russian Fort
Lucy Wright Beach County Pk.   Elizabeth St. Pk (1817)   Pākalā (Makaweli)
Ho'ahuanu Bay   Kaumakani   50
540
Hanapēpē   'Ele'ele

Hānāpēpē Bay
▲ Niihau   Port Allen

N

0   Miles   6

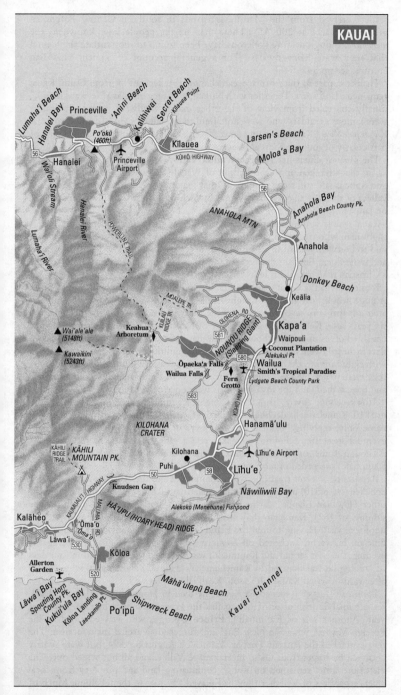

KAUAI

Lumaha'i Beach
Hanalei Bay
Princeville
'Anini Beach
Kalihiwai
Secret Beach
Kīlauea Point
Po'okū
(460ft)
Kīlauea
Larsen's Beach
Moloa'a Bay
KŪHIŌ HIGHWAY
56
Hanalei
Princeville
Airport
Wai'oli Stream
Hanalei River
POWERLINE TRAIL
Lumaha'i River
ANAHOLA MTN
Anahola Bay
Anahola Beach County Pk.
56
Anahola
MOALEPE TR.
Donkey Beach
Keālia
KUILAU RIDGE TR.
OLOHENA RD
Wai'ale'ale
(5148ft)
Keahua
Arboretum
NOUNOU RIDGE (Sleeping Giant)
Kapa'a
581
Waipouli
Coconut Plantation
Kawaikini
(5243ft)
Alakukui Pt
Ōpaeka'a Falls
580
Wailua
Wailua Falls
Smith's Tropical Paradise
Fern
Grotto
Lydgate Beach County Park
583
KŪHIŌ HWY
Hanamā'ulu
KILOHANA
CRATER
Kilohana
Līhu'e Airport
KĀHILI
RIDGE
TRAIL
KĀHILI
MOUNTAIN PK.
Puhi
58
Līhu'e
50
Knudsen Gap
Nāwiliwili Bay
KAUMUALI'I HIGHWAY
MALUHIA RD
Alekoko (Menehune) Fishpond
Kalāheo
HĀ'UPU (HOARY HEAD) RIDGE
'Ōma'o
Lāwa'i
'Ōma'o
530
Kōloa
520
Allerton
Garden
Māhā'ulepū Beach
Lāwa'i Bay
Spouting Horn
County Pk.
Kukui'ula Bay
Kōloa Landing
Laeokamilo Pt.
Shipwreck Beach
Po'ipū
Kauai Channel

settlers arrived from the Marquesas islands in southern Central Polynesia, perhaps as early as 200 AD. These may be the people later known as the *menehune*, though no tiny skeletons have been found to substantiate the legend that they were hairy dwarfs. (For a general account of ancient Hawaiian culture, see pp.542–546).

Thanks in part to the stormy ocean channel that separates it from Oahu, Kauai remained a land apart. Together with Niihau, it was regarded as a "leeward island," usually concealed from view of the other major, windward, islands. Its sailors were famous as raiders who were not afraid to sail out of sight of land. Known as Kauai *pule o'o* – "Kauai of strong prayers" – it also had a reputation as the home of particularly devout prophets and seers.

The greatest chiefs lived in the **Wailua Valley**, maintaining a chain of sacred *heiaus* that stretched up to the summit of Wai'ale'ale, where a phallic altar to the god Kane is said still to be standing. Other major population centers included the valleys of the Nā Pali coast and Waimea, which was where **Captain Cook** arrived on January 19, 1778 (see p.508).

Kauai's most famous ruler, **Kaumuali'i**, was born two years later, in 1780. A slight man who traced his genealogy back over seven centuries to Tahiti, and was said to be twenty-third in an unbroken succession of chiefs, he learned to speak and write fluent English; one foreign visitor called him "more dignified, more like a Christian than any of his fellows."

Kamehameha the Great made his first bid to **invade** Kauai in the spring of 1796. A huge fleet set off at dead of night from Oahu, but the attempt was abandoned after a storm sank several canoes. By the time he was ready for another attempt, six years later, Kaumuali'i was in charge of Kauai. This time Kamehameha's force consisted of around seven thousand Hawaiians and as many as fifty Europeans; his fleet included twenty-one schooners as well as traditional canoes and was equipped with eight cannons. As the force assembled on the eastern shore of Oahu, however, they were struck by a terrible pestilence. Many of Kamehameha's closest advisers and friends died, and the invasion plans were once more shelved.

After receiving envoys from Kamehameha, Kaumuali'i agreed to go to Honolulu in 1810. Kamehameha declined Kaumuali's face-saving offer to surrender Kauai in name only, replying "Return and rule over it. But if our young chief" – his eventual successor, Liholiho – "makes you a visit, be pleased to receive him." Although some of Kamehameha's advisers urged him to poison his rival, Kaumuali'i succeeded in returning home.

Reports of a secret treaty between Kaumuali'i and the **Russian** envoy George Schäffer (see p.510) under which a joint Kauaian–Russian fleet would invade the other Hawaiian islands, alarmed Kamehameha. Shortly after his death, in the summer of 1821, Kamehameha's son Liholiho sailed to Kauai, supposedly for an unofficial visit. Having toured the island for six weeks, he invited Kaumuali'i to dine on his yacht, anchored off Waimea, on September 16, 1821. During the evening, the boat set sail and Kaumuali'i was abducted to Oahu. Within four days of landing he was married to Kamehameha's widow, Ka'ahumanu, who shortly afterwards married Kaumuali'i's son, Keali'iahonui, as well.

Kaumuali'i never returned to Kauai; he died in Honolulu on May 26, 1824. Kauai's final flourish of resistance against the Hawaiian monarchy came later that year. Another son of Kaumuali'i, **Prince George**, who was educated at the Foreign Mission School in New England, launched an armed **insurrection**. The rebels attacked the Russian Fort at Waimea on August 8, 1824, but were swiftly cornered by forces from Oahu in Hanapēpē Valley, and all but wiped out. The victorious army remained on Kauai, confiscating land and property from local chiefs regardless of whether they had played any part in the rebellion. Much of

Kauai was parceled out among the descendants of Kamehameha, labeled by a contemporary historian as the "loafers and hangers-on of Oahu and Maui."

The **corruption** of these newcomers, the inequities of the sandalwood trade (see p.535), and the founding of Hawaii's first sugar plantation at Kōloa in 1835, combined to erode the traditional way of life on Kauai. Thereafter, Kauaian history becomes the usual Hawaiian tale of a diminishing and disinherited native population, the growth of American-owned agricultural concerns, and the influx of low-paid laborers from Asia and elsewhere.

By 1872, the island's population had slumped to just 5200. Agricultural land was increasingly given over to sugar, although there were experiments with silk and coffee in Hanalei, silk at Kōloa, and cattle-ranching along the West Shore. As indentured Chinese workers left the plantations, they converted the taro terraces of Hanalei Valley into the largest **rice** paddies in Hawaii. Subsequently, many Chinese moved on to Honolulu, and in recent decades taro production has made something of a comeback on Kauai.

Although **tourism** on any scale is relatively new to Kauai, and the island still lags far behind Oahu and Maui in terms of visitor numbers, large-scale development has caused unsightly hotel and condo sprawls along both the East and South shores, and local residents now find it hard to afford places to live. The onslaught of **Hurricane Iniki** in September 1992, which damaged an amazing 71 percent of homes on the island, slowed things for a while, but the economy soon bounced back, and little trace of the devastation remains.

For the moment, sugar production continues, and the first Hawaiian island to grow sugar commercially looks set to also become the last. With the closure of Amfac's plantations at Līhu'e and Kekaha in 2000, only Gay and Robinson's cane fields, in the southwest of the island, are still under cultivation. Farmers on Kauai have been attempting to diversify, growing crops such as corn and tropical fruits, and the **coffee** industry is also expanding rapidly. Defense remains a key element of the economy – the Pacific Missile Range Facility at Barking Sands, once targeted for closure, now has a crucial role in the National Missile Defense system (detailed on p.511).

Kauai overview

Mount Wai'ale'ale, the long-extinct volcano responsible for creating Kauai, was the biggest of all the Hawaiian shield volcanoes. Lava streamed from it in all directions, so the island is roughly circular, measuring up to 33 miles north to south and 25 miles west to east. Little of the volcano's original outline, however, remains discernible. On all sides, but especially to the north and west, it is now furrowed with deep, lush valleys, while its summit has worn down to a mere 5000ft above sea level. The wettest place on earth, the summit is perched atop steepled cliffs and permanently shrouded in mist. Even on a helicopter tour (see p.439) or while hiking to its base (see p.465), you're unlikely to glimpse the highest peak.

The largest expanse of flat land on Kauai lies in its southeast corner, where **Līhu'e** is the site of its principal airport. While the county seat does offer a small selection of hotels and an attractive little beach, most visitors head for more scenic areas almost as soon as they touch down.

Six miles up the coast, north of the Wailua River and the overrated Fern Grotto, the beach strip from **Wailua** to **Kapa'a** holds a plethora of relatively inexpensive hotels and a wide range of restaurants. The old wooden boardwalks of Kapa'a make for a diverting pause on the round-island drive, while some fine hiking trails weave through the valleys inland.

Beyond Kapa'a, the highway steers clear of a succession of pretty and barely used beaches as it cuts through to the North Shore. **Princeville** here is a luxurious but soulless resort, guarding the headland above beautiful **Hanalei Bay**. At this point the green cliffs of the **Nā Pali** coast heave into view, towering above quirky Hanalei. From here on the coast road is breathtaking, passing gorgeous golden beaches pounded by endless surf as it tunnels through the overhanging rainforest. After ten miles, the ever-taller cliffs bar all further progress. Though accessible enough by canoe to sustain large populations in ancient times, the Nā Pali valleys are now uninhabited, and can only be reached on foot on the **Kalalau Trail**.

Po'ipū, ten miles southwest of Līhu'e at Kauai's southernmost tip, is the island's most popular resort, boasting several showpiece hotels and condos. Its beaches remain the best for year-round family vacations, with great surfing and scuba-diving spots just offshore. **Waimea**, around to the west, should in theory be a fascinating historic town – it's the place where Captain Cook first arrived in Hawaii and the site of an unlikely Russian fort – but it lacks the commercial infra-structure to persuade visitors to linger.

A few miles west of Waimea, **Polihale State Park** preserves the longest beach in the state, a dangerous but compelling fifteen-mile strand that ends at the western limit of the Nā Pali coast. High above, in the narrow gap between the mile-wide **Waimea Canyon** and the start of the Nā Pali valleys, **Kōke'e State Park** combines phenomenal roadside views with tremendous hiking trails. One of the most extraordinary leads through the land-locked **Alaka'i Swamp**, the last refuge of countless unique Hawaiian plant and bird species.

Getting to Kauai

Only one airport on Kauai, located just outside **Līhu'e**, is currently served by commercial flights. Other than three daily nonstop services from **Los Angeles** (on United and American), and two from **San Francisco** (on United only), all flights come from **Honolulu**. Hawaiian, Aloha and Go! all offer frequent connec-tions to and from other Hawaiian islands; for more details and a full list of phone numbers, see p.32.

This book went to press just before the **Super Ferry** (Ⓦ www.hawaiisuperferry .com) commenced sailings from Honolulu to Nāwiliwili Harbor at Līhu'e, in the summer of 2007. Ferries were scheduled to leave Honolulu at 3pm, every day except Saturday, arrive at Nāwiliwili at 6pm, and depart again at 7pm. One-way fares were promised to start at $42 per passenger, plus $55 per vehicle.

Getting around Kauai

As Kauai's resort areas tend to be spread out, and scenic spots like Waimea Canyon and the Nā Pali cliffs are a long way from the nearest places to stay, most visitors end up **driving** more than they expect. All the major car rental chains are represented at Līhu'e airport; the relevant phone numbers are listed on p.33.

As a rule, driving on Kauai is a pleasure. There's just one main road, known as **Kaumuali'i Highway**, south of Līhu'e and **Kūhiō Highway** to the north, and only thirteen stoplights. However, all the way between Po'ipū and Princeville there's usually a fair amount of traffic; try to avoid the morning and evening "rush hours" between Līhu'e and Kapa'a, and you should be able to count on making steady progress. On both the narrow single-lane road along the North Shore – where you can be forced to a standstill as you wait for a chicken or a goose to cross the road – and the tortuous Waimea Canyon Drive up into the western hills, average speeds drop below 20mph.

By bus

The Kauai Bus operates a **bus service** to all parts of the island, with a flat fare of $1.50 (students and seniors 75¢, monthly passes available; ☏808/241-6410 or ⓦwww.kauai.gov). As with TheBus on Oahu, large backpacks and suitcases are forbidden. Of the two main routes, one runs between JC Penney's at Kukui Grove in **Līhu'e** and the Circuit Court in **Hanalei**, via Wailua, Kapa'a, Kīlauea, and Princeville (Mon–Fri 8 services daily, Sat 6 services; journey time 1hr 23min). The other connects **Līhu'e** and **Kekaha** via Hanapēpē and Waimea (Mon–Fri 12 services daily, Sat 6 services; journey time 1hr 15min). There are also four daily services from **Līhu'e** to Kōloa, on weekdays only (journey time 30min).

Helicopter flight-seeing

Kauai is the best Hawaiian island to see from the air. It's small enough, and its mountains are low enough, for a single flight to cover the whole island – and many of its most spectacular spots are impossible to reach any other way. It was, however, Kauai's bad accident rate that led to the state-wide ban on low flying (see p.34). Regulations now outlaw their previous practice of deliberately plummeting over the Nā Pali coastline, and thus, it has to be said, make trips less exciting. A further spate of accidents, in March 2007, may result in yet more stringent restrictions.

Full **island tours** start from Līhu'e and follow a clockwise route up Waimea Canyon and along the north coast; they last 45 minutes to an hour. If you're satisfied to see just the Nā Pali cliffs, take a shorter flight from Princeville (see p.476). Official rates generally range $115–135 for a 45-minute tour and $160–200 for an hour-long excursion, but many operators offer discounts for advance or online bookings, and you can also find bargains with the general activities operators listed on p.442.

For details on Niihau Helicopters, which only runs excursions to the island of Niihau, see p.512.

	Number	ⓦwww.	Departs
Air Kauai	☏1-800/972-4666	airkauai.com	Līhu'e
Blue Hawaiian	☏1-800/745-2583	bluehawaiian.com	Līhu'e
Heli USA	☏1-866/936-1234	heliusa.com	Princeville, Līhu'e
Inter-Island	☏1-800/656-5009	interislandhelicopters.com	Port Allen
Island	☏1-800/829-5999	islandhelicopters.com	Līhu'e
Jack Harter	☏1-888/245-2001	helicopters-kauai.com	Līhu'e
Safari	☏1-800/326-3356	safarihelicopters.com	Līhu'e
Will Squyres	☏1-888/245-4354	helicopters-hawaii.com	Līhu'e

Tours and taxis

Companies offering guided **minibus tours**, all based in Līhu'e but happy to pick up passengers in the Po'ipū and Kapa'a areas, include Roberts Hawaii (T 808/539-9400 or 1-866/898-2519, W www.robertshawaii.com) and Polynesian Adventure Tours (T 808/246-0122 or 1-800/622-3011, W www.polyad.com). Typical prices would be $50 for a half-day tour, $70 for a full day.

Hawaii Movie Tours (T 808/822-1192 or 1-800/628-8432, W www.hawaii movietour.com) organizes a specialized all-day tour for $100 that concentrates on scenic Kauai spots that have featured in major Hollywood films (see p.559); they also offer a 4WD tour that reaches more inaccessible locations for $115. Aloha Kauai Tours (T 808/245-8809 or 1-800/452-1113, W www.alohakauaitours.com) offers four-hour tours of the backroads of Grove Farm Plantation in 4WD vans, starting from Kilohana at 8am & 1pm daily, for $70, as well as four-hour expeditions that involve a three-mile hike near the base of Mount Wai'ale'ale.

Guided hikes, usually on Saturdays, Sundays, and at the full moon, are organized by the local chapter of the Sierra Club (W www.hi.sierraclub.org); look for details in the *Garden Island* newspaper.

Kauai **cab** operators include Kauai Taxi Company (T 808/246-9554) and Akiko's Taxi (T 808/822-7588). Expect to pay $15 from the airport to Kapa'a, $25–30 to Po'ipu, and $40 or more to the North Shore.

Where to stay

Kauai is small enough that you can base yourself pretty much anywhere and still explore the whole island, so it's more important to decide what sort of property you want to stay in than it is to choose a particular area. Away from Po'ipū and Princeville, room rates are generally lower than elsewhere in Hawaii. If finding **budget** accommodation is a priority, then the hostel or simple B&Bs in and

Kauai favorites: campgrounds

'Anini Beach County Park	p.473	Kalalau Valley	p.494
Hā'ena Beach County Park	p.486	Kōke'e State Park	p.517
Hanakāpī'ai Valley	p.492	Polihale State Park	p.514
Hanalei Pavilion Beach County Park	p.482	For details on Nā Pali permits	p.492.

around Kapa'a are your best bet (see p.462). Kauai County ordinances technically forbid B&Bs to serve breakfasts, so while virtually all do, they prefer not to advertise the fact. If you want a **beach-based** holiday in a family resort, opt for a hotel or condo in Po'ipū or Kapa'a. To rent a **tropical hideaway**, get in touch with the agencies in Princeville (see p.477).

Kauai offers some great opportunities for **camping**, especially along the North Shore and on the Nā Pali coast. Full details are available from the state and county parks offices in Līhu'e, as detailed on p.448. The **state** office (Dept of Land and Natural Resources, State Parks Division, 3060 Eiwa St, Līhu'e HI 96766; ☎808/274-3444) provides permits and information, including maps, for Kōke'e State Park, Polihale, Miloli'i and the Nā Pali coast. (See p.492 for more details on Nā Pali permits.)

Permits for camping in Kauai's **county** parks – Hā'ena, Hanalei, 'Anini, Anahola, Hanamā'ulu, Salt Pond, and Lucy Wright parks – are available by post at least a month in advance (Parks Permit Section, Dept of Public Works, Division of Parks and Recreation, 4444 Rice St #150, Līhu'e HI 96766; ☎808/241-6660). Enclose a photocopied passport, driver's license or other ID for all adults in your party, plus $3 fee per adult per night (Hawaii residents and under-18s free). Other locations where you can pick up permits are detailed on the county website, ⓦwww.kauai.gov.

When to go

If you're able to choose, the best times to come to Kauai are late spring and fall, when room rates are often slightly lower and crowds are smaller than at other times. But since Kauai rarely feels either overcrowded or overpriced, it doesn't make that much of a difference.

Seasonal **weather** variations are relatively minimal. Along the south coast, Kauai's warmest region, daily maximum **temperatures** range upwards from the low seventies Fahrenheit (around 22°C) in winter (Jan–March) to almost 80°F (27°C) in summer (Aug–Sept). Po'ipū, the most popular base for beach holidays, is marginally warmer than Līhu'e and Kapa'a, and warmer again than Princeville, but the difference is negligible.

Rainfall statistics look far more dramatic on paper than they do on the ground. Mount Wai'ale'ale, as you'll often be reminded, is the wettest place in the world – its record of 683 inches of rain in a single year is not the most ever measured, but its annual average of 451 inches beats the 428 inches of second-ranked Cherrapunji in India. Figures for the coast, just a few miles away, are very different. Waimea receives less than twenty inches per year, Po'ipū less than forty, and Kapa'a less than fifty. Princeville nears a hundred inches, but even on the North Shore you'd have to be pretty unlucky to have your vacation plans seriously affected. In all areas, significantly more rain falls in winter than in summer, but even then most of it falls at night. If your main priority is to spend time on the beach, then there's a

6

KAUAI | When to go

441

Kauai favorites: eating

These restaurants are listed in ascending order of price, not (necessarily) quality.

strong case for choosing Po'ipū above Princeville, and summer above winter, but if you plan to tour the island as a whole, then you can usually reckon that on any particular day you'll be able to escape any rain by driving far enough.

As usual in Hawaii, the state of the **ocean** changes much more than the weather. Between December and April, winter thunderstorms, often caused by tropical "kona" storms that approach from the south, can render water activities unsafe on all but the most sheltered beaches. Nā Pali coast tours are obliged to follow different itineraries in winter, and are often canceled altogether for days at a time (see p.490). However, many visitors choose to come at precisely that time, in the hope of seeing whales.

Watersports and other activities

For energetic vacationers, Kauai offers an exhausting range of both water- and land-based activities. Operators at all the major resort areas stand ready to instruct beginners or pamper experts in watersports such as diving, kayaking, and wind-surfing, while the island's stunning landscapes make it a wonderful playground for hikers, golfers, and horseback riders.

In addition to the specialized outfits listed below, several companies offer tours and activities of all kinds, often at discounted rates, and also rent out every piece of equipment you might need. At their best, they can be great sources of help and advice. Recommended businesses include Tom Barefoot's Cashback Tours (℡1-888/222-3601, Ⓦwww.tombarefoot.com), Cheap Tours Hawaii (℡1-888/822-5935, Ⓦwww.cheaptourshawaii.com), and Activity Warehouse (℡1-800/688-0580, Ⓦwww.travelhawaii.com).

One company that offers an especially wide-ranging program of adventurous activities on the island is **Outfitters Kauai**, based in Pō'ipu (℡1-888/742-9887 or 808/742-9667, Ⓦwww.outfitterskauai.com). In addition to bike and kayak rentals and guided tours, they organize expeditions on and near the Hule'ia River, close to Līhu'e, that include hikes to jungle waterfalls; rope-swinging and jumping into rivers and waterholes; and a fifty-foot-high **"Zipline"** leap, in which you cross a mountain stream suspended from a pulley. A full-day jaunt costs $165 for adults, $125 for under-15s; half a day is $120 and $94 respectively.

Cycling

Among companies that rent out **bicycles** on the island are Kauai Cycle and Tours, 1379 Kūhiō Hwy, Kapa'a (℡808/821-2115, Ⓦwww.bikehawaii.com/kauaicycle), which charges $20–35 per day and up to $150 per week, and Outfitters Kauai (☎808/742-9667), as described opposite.

For most of the way around Kauai, conditions are generally pretty flat, but only a real glutton for punishment would attempt to cycle up Waimea Canyon Road to Kōke'e State Park. It is, however, possible to be driven up to the Kalalau Lookout and then be given a bike on which to freewheel all the way back down again. Both Outfitters Kauai and Kauai Coasters (☎808/639-2412) charge about $100 for the privilege.

Deep-sea fishing

A veritable armada of **sport fishing** vessels sets off into the waters around Kauai daily from harbors on all sides of the island. Typical charter rates start at around $100 per person for a half-day trip. Operators along the South Shore include Sport Fishing Kauai in Po'ipū (☎808/639-0013, ⓦwww.fishing-kauai-hawaii.com), and Lahela Ocean Adventures in Nāwiliwili (☎808/635-4020, ⓦwww.sport-fishing-kauai.com). Both Hawaiian Style Fishing (☎808/635-7335) and Hana Pa'a Charters (☎1-866/776-3474, ⓦwww.fishkauai.com) are based in Kapa'a, while Nā Pali Sportfishing (☎808/635-9424) and Kekaha Fishing Co (☎808/337-2700) are at Waimea and Kīkīaola Harbor, respectively, on the West Shore. Sportfish Hawaii (☎1-877/388-1376, ⓦwww.sportfishhawaii.com) can arrange charters on several different vessels.

Horseback riding

Several stables offer **guided horseback excursions** on Kauai. The best of the bunch for ordinary riders are the Silver Falls Ranch in Kīlauea (☎808/828-6718, ⓦwww.silverfallsranch.com), which offers rides every day of the week, and charges $80 for ninety minutes, $100 for 2hr, and $120 for 3hr, and CJM Country Stables near Po'ipū (☎808/742-6096, ⓦwww.cjmstables.com), as described on p.502. Princeville Ranch Stables offers large-scale group rides on the North Shore (☎808/826-6777, ⓦwww.princevilleranch.com), detailed on p.474. Two smaller companies, based in Kapa'a on the East Shore, make good choices for more proficient riders. Keapana Horsemanship offers private rides tailored to your requirements at $60 per rider, per hour (☎808/823-9303), while Esprit de Corps, active on weekdays only (☎808/822-4688, ⓦwww.kauaihorses.com), charges from $120 for a 3hr ride up to $375 for 8hr.

Kayaking

Kauai is unique in Hawaii in offering **river kayaking** on several inland waterways. Guided trips are available along the Hulē'ia Stream near Līhu'e (True Blue; ☎808/246-6333, ⓦwww.kauaifun.com; from $89), the Wailua River on the East Shore (Wailua Kayak Adventures; ☎808/822-5795, ⓦkauaiwailuakayak.com; from $43), and the Hanalei River on the North Shore (Kayak Kauai; ☎808/826-9844, ⓦwww.kayakkauai.com; $60). These and other operators, including Pedal & Paddle in Hanalei's Ching Young Village on the North Shore (☎808/826-9069, ⓦwww.pedalnpaddle.com), also rent out kayaks for self-guided expeditions from as little as $15 for a couple of hours.

In general it's much safer for inexperienced kayakers to explore the rivers than it is for them to set off into the ocean. Only absolute experts should attempt to tackle the Nā Pali coast on their own; if you really want to see it, it's best to take a guided tour with Kayak Kauai (above; May–Sept only; $185).

Scuba diving

Although Kauai can't claim to be the very best of the Hawaiian islands for divers – the high North Shore seas preclude diving for most of the year, while the coast elsewhere tends to be short of spectacular coral – its waters still hold some truly superb dive sites. For novices, the best of the lot lie close to Po'ipū and are usually accessible year-round. **Sheraton Caverns**, just offshore from the *Sheraton* hotel, is a network of three massive lava tubes that shelters a large population of sea turtles and lobsters. At the slightly harder **General Store** site, colorful fish swarm through the wreckage of the steamship *Pele*, which foundered in 1895. In summer, popular North Shore snorkel sites such as **Tunnels Reef** and **Kē'ē Lagoon** also attract plenty of shore divers. The tiny islet of **Lehua**, off Niihau, is similar to Maui's Molokini (see p.325), but infinitely less crowded and polluted; however, it takes a long sea trip to reach it and considerable expertise to dive once you're there.

Dive operators based on the South Shore include Fathom Five (☎808/742-6691 or 1-800/972-3078, ⓦwww.fathomfive.com), and Mana Divers (☎808/335-0881 or 1-877/348-3669, ⓦwww.manadivers.com). Bubbles Below (☎808/332-7333 or 1-866/524-6268, ⓦwww.bubblesbelowkauai.com) and Seasport Divers (☎808/742-9303 or 1-800/685-5889, ⓦwww.seasportdivers.com) offer dives both from Po'ipū and on the East Shore, while Dive Kauai (☎808/822-0452 or 1-800/828-3483, ⓦwww.divekauai.com) are exclusively in Kapa'a. Hanalei is home to North Shore Divers (☎808/828-1223 or 1-877/688-3483, ⓦwww.northshoredivers.com). Expect to pay $65–80 for a one-tank boat dive, $100–130 for two tanks, and perhaps $150 for a two-tank, fully guided beginner's trip, with instruction.

Snorkeling

Snorkeling is more of a year-round activity on Kauai than diving, as even along the North Shore several mini-lagoons are sufficiently sheltered by offshore coral reefs to remain calm through most of the winter. Prime North Shore sites include **Kē'ē Beach** and **Tunnels Beach**, while the best spot along the East Shore is **Lydgate State Park**, just south of the Wailua River. Probably the safest and most convenient sites of all, however, are those abutting the resorts of Po'ipū, such as **Po'ipū Beach** and **Lāwa'i Beach**.

Any number of outlets rent out snorkel equipment, including the ubiquitous Snorkel Bob's (ⓦwww.snorkelbob.com), here based at 4-374 Kūhiō Hwy in Kapa'a (☎808/823-9433) and 3236 Po'ipū Road in Kōloa (☎808/742-2206); both locations are open daily 8am–5pm. Note also that most Nā Pali boat trips (see p.490) double as snorkel cruises, and equipment is provided.

Surfing and windsurfing

For surfers, conditions on Kauai are reminiscent of those on Oahu, in that southern beaches such as Kalāpakī Beach and Po'ipū Beach are ideal places for beginners to learn the ropes, while the North Shore provides some great challenges to experts. Hanalei Bay in particular is immensely popular with serious surfers, with **Tunnels Beach** a close second. The best site on the East Shore is **Lydgate State Park** near Wailua.

Among those offering **surfing lessons** on Kauai are Titus Kinimaka's Hawaiian School of Surfing, in Hanalei on the North Shore (☎808/651-1116, ⓦwww.hawaiianschoolofsurfing.com), and, in the Po'ipū area, both Kauai Surf School (☎808/651-6032, ⓦwww.kauaisurfschool.com) and Margo Oberg's Surfing School (☎808/332-6100, ⓦwww.surfonkauai.com). A two-hour group surfing lesson costs about $60 per person, a private lesson $100–150.

Kauai lū'aus

Almost all the *lū'aus* listed below charge $65–75 per adult and $25–35 per child; you should be able to get tickets for under $50 from activities operators all over the island. The Princeville Resort's is more expensive, at $100/$45, but it enjoys by far the best setting, right beside the beach at Hanalei Bay.

Grand Hyatt Kauai Lū'au *Grand Hyatt Kauai*, Po'ipū ☎808/240-6456. Thurs & Sun 6pm.

Garden Lū'au Smith's Tropical Paradise, Wailua ☎808/821-6895, ⊛www .smithskauai.com. Summer Mon–Fri 5pm, winter Mon, Wed, & Fri 5pm (see p.457).

Surf to Sunset Lū'au *Sheraton Po'ipū*, Po'ipū ☎808/742-8200, ⊛www.luaukilohana .com. Mon & Fri 5.30pm.

Lū'au Kilohana *Kilohana Plantation*, Līhu'e ☎808/245-9593, ⊛www.luaukilohana .com. Tues & Thurs 5pm.

Tihati's Hiva Pasefika Lū'au *ResortQuest Kauai Beach at Makaiwa*, Kapa'a ☎808/823-345. Daily except Mon 5.45pm.

Pā'ina 'O Hanalei, *Princeville Resort*, Princeville; ☎808/826-2788. Mon & Thurs 6pm.

With the exception of sheltered **'Anini Beach**, most of the North Shore is too dangerous for **windsurfers**. They head, instead, for the South Shore near Po'ipū. **Po'ipū Beach** is the best place to learn; the beaches of the **Māhā'ulepū** area are more favored by the already proficient. Windsurfing instruction, at about $65 per lesson, is offered by Windsurf Kauai in Hanalei (☎808/828-6838).

Kauai festivals and events

mid-Feb	Waimea Town Celebration; races and entertainment
March 26	Prince Kūhiō Day; week-long festival in Līhu'e and Po'ipū
May 1	May Day by the Bay; festival in Princeville
May 1	Lei Day; *lei*-making contests in Līhu'e
Memorial Day	Kauai Polynesian Festival; four-day dance and music festival, Līhu'e
June 11	Kamehameha Day; state-wide celebrations
July 4	Concert in the Sky; charity concert, Līhu'e
late July	Kōloa Plantation Days; week-long festival in Kōloa
mid-Aug	Na Holo Kai Canoe Race; from Oahu to Kalāpakī Bay
mid-Aug	Kauai-Tahiti Fete; weekend cultural festival, Kapa'a
Aug 18	Admission Day; state holiday
Sept 1	Kauai County Farm Fair, Līhu'e
late Sept	Kauai Mokihana Festival; week-long *hula*, music, and crafts festival
Oct	Kauai Taro Festival, Hanalei
late Oct	Aloha Week Festival, island-wide
early Nov	Hawaiian Slack-Key Guitar Festival; one-day free concert, *Kauai Marriott*, Līhu'e
mid-Dec	PGA Grand Slam, golf tournament, Po'ipū

Nightlife and entertainment

Barring the occasional big-name concert at the War Memorial in central Līhu'e, and promotional appearances by local stars at the Kukui Grove mall, virtually all Kauai's **nightlife** takes place in its hotels and restaurants. Among venues that can usually be depended upon for **live music**, especially at weekends, are the *Whaler's Brew Pub* and the *Hilton Kauai Beach Resort* just outside Līhu'e; *Keoki's Paradise* in Po'ipū; the *Hanalei Bay Resort* in Princeville; and the *Hanalei Gourmet*, *Sushi Blues*, and *Tahiti Nui* in Hanalei. The North Shore, in particular, is where the more funky local musicians tend to hang out. Kauai Community Radio, broadcasting from Hanalei on 90.9 and 91.9FM (ⓦ www.kkcr.org), is a good source of up-to-date music and entertainment listings

Līhu'e

Kauai's capital, **LĪHU'E**, will likely be the first and the last place you see on the island, and chances are you'll pass through it several times during your stay as well. Set a mile or two back from the sea in the southeast corner of the island, it's the site of Kauai's main **airport** and **harbor**, and the midpoint of the highway that circles the island.

However, Līhu'e is not an attractive or exciting town, and few tourists spend more time here than they have to. It's the administrative and commercial center of this tiny island, but with a population of just five thousand, its main effect on visitors tends to be to reveal just how rural Kauai really is. Several of the roads run through open fields without a sign of life, while downtown Līhu'e consists of a handful of tired-looking plantation-town streets lined with simple one- and two-story buildings.

That said, visitors shouldn't overlook Līhu'e completely. Its inland section offers Kauai's widest selection of **shops** and its best **museum**, while the area around **Nāwiliwili Bay** holds some good hotels and restaurants, a fine sheltered white-sand beach, and a stretch of unspoilt riverfront that serves as a sanctuary for native waterbirds.

Līhu'e cannot boast a long history. It dates from the middle of the nineteenth century, when it was a village serving the Grove Farm sugar plantation. The area's sugar-growing days finally came to an end in 2000, when Amfac/JMB's Līhu'e Plantation gave up cultivating cane in the surrounding fields. Grove Farm, which now belongs to America Online co-founder Steve Case, has long since diversified into real estate, including the large Kukui Grove shopping mall.

Until well into the twentieth century, Kauai's chief ports were Port Allen, outside Hanapēpē in the southwest, and Hanalei Bay in the north. Not until about 1930, when **Nāwiliwili Harbor** and the new airport were completed, did Līhu'e become the island's major port. That status was secured in 1939, when the Belt Highway took on its present route. Since then, Līhu'e has grown apace with the increase of road transportation; the fact that it's designed to drive around is the main reason why it's so much more spread out than other island towns.

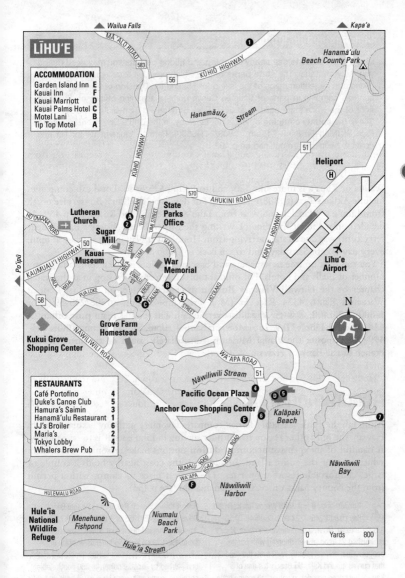

LĪHU'E

ACCOMMODATION

Garden Island Inn	**E**
Kauai Inn	**F**
Kauai Marriott	**D**
Kauai Palms Hotel	**C**
Motel Lani	**B**
Tip Top Motel	**A**

RESTAURANTS

Café Portofino	**4**
Duke's Canoe Club	**5**
Hamura's Saimin	**3**
Hanamā'ulu Restaurant	**1**
JJ's Broiler	**6**
Maria's	**2**
Tokyo Lobby	**4**
Whalers Brew Pub	**7**

Arrival and information

Līhu'e's **airport** is only two miles east of downtown, near the ocean on Ahukini Road. Apart from a fast-food coffee shop selling *saimin* and Portuguese bean soup, the main feature of its small terminal is a colorful, three-dimensional mosaic of the Nā Pali coast.

All the major car rental companies (see p.33) have offices across from the terminal. A **taxi** into Līhu'e costs around $10, while the fare from the airport to

Camping and hiking permits

Līhu'e is the place to gather any **camping** and **hiking permits** you may need during your stay on Kauai. The **state parks office**, which provides excellent, double-sided hiking and recreation maps of the island for $5, and the **Division of Forestry**, which controls camping in parts of Waimea Canyon, share adjoining offices on the third floor of the white state building at 3060 Eiwa St (Mon–Fri 8am–3.30pm; ☎808/274-3444); the **county camping office** is not far away, in the Līhu'e Civic Center at 4444 Rice St (Mon–Fri 8am–4.15pm; ☎808/241-6660). Permit requirements for Nā Pali coast expeditions are outlined on p.492.

Wailua or Kapa'a is more like $20, and to Po'ipū $35 or so. Local cab companies include Akiko's Taxi (☎808/822-7588). For details on the Kauai Bus service north from Līhu'e to Hanalei, and west from Līhu'e to Kekaha and Kōloa, see p.439. As detailed on p.438, at the time of writing the **Super Ferry** (ⓦwww.hawaiisuperferry.com) was due to start arriving from Honolulu at Nāwiliwili Harbor at 6pm, every day except Saturday, and to sail back to Oahu at 7pm.

You can pick up free newspapers and brochures galore at the airport and in any number of malls and hotels. For official tourism information, stop in at the Kauai chapter of the **Hawaii Visitors Bureau** in central Līhu'e, on the first floor at Watamull Plaza, 4334 Rice St (Mon–Fri 8am–4.30pm; ☎808/245-3971 or 1-800/262-1400, ⓦwww.kauaidiscovery.com). The island's main **post office**, at 4441 Rice St, Līhu'e HI 96766 (Mon–Fri 8am–4.30pm, Sat 9am–1pm; ☎808/245-4994) is opposite the Kauai Museum, immediately south of the most central branch of the Bank of Hawaii.

Accommodation

Although the opulent *Kauai Marriott* compares favorably with any luxury resort in Hawaii, the only other reason to consider staying in Līhu'e itself is to save money. A handful of inexpensive **accommodation** options make reasonable bases from which to tour the entire island. In addition, the coast nearby holds a couple of large, comfortable resort properties. The nearest place to **camp**, with a permit from the county parks office, is in Hanamā'ulu (see p.453).

🏃 **Garden Island Inn** 3445 Wilcox Rd, Kalāpakī Bay ☎808/245-7227 or 1-800/648-0154 (US & Canada), ⓦwww.gardenislandinn.com. Nicely refurbished 21-room motel, dripping with purple bougainvillea, and set slightly back from the road that curves around Kalāpakī Beach. It's one of Kauai's best accommodation values; all rooms have fridges and microwaves, with rates rising according to which of the three floors they're on. Those on the first have no views; on the second they have a/c and *lānais*; and on the third they're suites sleeping 3–4 guests. There's also a two-bed, two-story condo perched on the bluff behind. The restaurants of Anchor Cove are right across the street, and snorkel sets and boogie boards are available for free; the one drawback is that the traffic can be busy. Rooms ❸, suites ❹, condo ❺

Hilton Kauai Beach Resort 4331 Kauai Beach Drive ☎808/245-1955 or 1-800/445-8667, ⓦwww.kauaibeachresort.hilton.com. Smart, upscale beachfront resort, along Hwy-56 three miles north of Līhu'e, and very convenient for the airport (although undisturbed by airplane noise). Its 350 comfortable, spacious rooms and suites have plush beds and old Hawaiian prints, and are set in four low-rise wings around an enticing three-segment swimming pool, complete with simulated fern grotto. The artificial beach is a nice feature, as the natural beach alongside is seldom safe for swimmers. Nightly Polynesian show with free drinks. Look for bargain rates online. Garden view ❻, ocean view ❼
Kauai Inn 2430 Hulemalu Rd, Niumalu ☎808/245-9000 or 1-800/808-2330, ⓦwww.kauai-inn.com. This reconstructed motel-like inn, a

mile beyond Kalāpakī Beach between Nāwiliwili Harbor and the Menehune Fishpond, offers 48 good-value rooms arrayed around a small (and very shallow) pool. While far from being a destination in its own right, it makes a good central base. ❹

Kauai Marriott 3610 Rice St ☎808/245-5050 or 1-800/220-2925 (US & Canada), ⓦwww.marriott.com/lihhi. Lavish resort with 350 tower-block rooms and another 230 suites. Most rooms overlook Hawaii's largest swimming pool and its five whirlpool spas, and are along lovely Kalāpakī Beach. Condo suites are available for $20,000 a week. The property boasts two golf courses, four restaurants, eight tennis courts, and eight miles of footpaths. Garden view ❽ , ocean view ❾

🏃 **Kauai Palms Hotel** 2931 Kalena St ☎808/246-0908, ⓦwww.kauaipalmshotel.com. Plantation-style inn in a quiet spot in downtown Līhu'e, just round the corner from *Hamura's Saimin* and with views out over the fields. Appealingly converted by new owners, it holds 22 rooms; only the larger ones, capable of sleeping three, have a/c, but the smaller ones are still tasteful and good value. ❸

Motel Lani 4240 Rice St ☎808/245-2965. Rudimentary but presentable central motel, overgrown with plants, where the nine rooms lack phones and TVs. It's only worth staying here if you plan to be out all day. Cash only, with a two-night minimum stay. ❶

Tip Top Motel 3173 Akāhi St ☎808/245-2333, ⓔtiptop@aloha.net. Unprepossessing but well-equipped motel, hidden away on a back street not far from the airport. Each room has TV and a/c, a shower but no bathtub, and costs just $65 per night. There's an inexpensive bakery-cum-diner plus a sushi restaurant on-site (see p.454). ❷

The Town

At first sight, you might think that **Līhu'e** had never quite clawed its way back to normal following the hurricane of 1992. In fact, the town – a low-key assortment of plain homes, stores, and offices scattered among rusting reminders of the plantation days and hastily erected shopping malls – has always looked pretty much the same. If anything, Līhu'e is a bit prettier these days, its mountain backdrop more visible since the hurricane cleared away most of the trees that interfered with the view.

Līhu'e is divided into three distinct areas. The old **downtown**, along **Rice Street**, remains the administrative center of the island; in the middle of the day it's busy with local office workers, but barely a soul is left when evening comes. Driving a mile or so southeast beyond Rice Street brings you to **Nāwiliwili Bay**, where hotels and restaurants look out onto **Kalāpakī Beach**. The road that circles the island, running past the sugar mill at the northwest end of Rice Street, holds the bulk of Līhu'e's modern development. West of Līhu'e it bears the name **Kaumuali'i Highway**. About a mile out of town it passes the large **Kukui Grove Shopping Center**; after another mile it comes to the country-house mall **Kilohana**; from there it leads to Po'ipū and Waimea. Northeast of Līhu'e, the road is officially called **Kūhiō Highway**; for the first of the two miles that separate Līhu'e from the small but distinct community of **Hanamā'ulu**, it's lined with fast-food outlets and small malls.

Kauai Museum

The **Kauai Museum**, downtown Līhu'e's only significant attraction, occupies two buildings next to the state offices at 4428 Rice St (Mon–Fri 9am–4pm, Sat 10am–4pm; adults $7, seniors $5, ages 13–17 $3, ages 6–12 $1; ☎808/245-6931, ⓦwww.kauaimuseum.org). If you've come to the island for sun, sea, and scenery, it may not hold your interest for long, but it does a creditable job of tracing Kauaian history from the mythical *menehune* onwards.

Visitors enter the museum through the older **Wilcox Building**, which holds the core of the collection – the private memorabilia of the missionary Wilcox family. Downstairs, there's a large assortment of traditional artifacts such as oval platters, *lei* standards, and calabashes made from *koa* wood. One colossal and highly polished calabash was used as a *poi* bowl by Kamehameha III; several have been skillfully repaired with butterfly-shaped patches, a process that was held to increase their value. Exhibits upstairs cover the growth of the sugar plantations and the great era of immigration. Photographs focus especially on the island's Japanese population, recording sumo tournaments, Bon dances, and Buddhist ceremonies.

The modern **Rice Building**, alongside the Wilcox Building, has a more comprehensive collection. It too has its fair share of calabashes, decorated gourd bowls, and bottles, but it also displays some more unusual ancient relics such as stone receptacles said to have been used in the *pule ana'ana* ("praying-to-death") rite, and a huge "thrusting spear," a weapon designed to be thrust rather than thrown. A relief model of the island shows where the Hawaiians had their original settlements, as well as the trails that connected them. Among the trails that no longer exist are those that lead down to the Nā Pali valleys from the heights of Kōke'e, and paths from the summit of Mount Wai'ale'ale not only to Wailua, but also to Waimea and Hanapēpē. A diorama of Waimea at the time of Cook's first landfall depicts a settlement of a few thatched huts. Contemporary maps of Cook's voyages show tell-tale blank spaces for areas as yet unknown – Hawaii, New Zealand, and eastern Australia are absent, while the Pacific coast of North America, where Cook hoped to find the Northwest Passage, remains uncharted.

The whole history of Kauai is told in immense detail, tracing island genealogy as far back as Kamawae Lualani, who's said to have been *ali'i nui* or paramount chief in 310 AD. Illustrative exhibits include a letter from King Kuamuali'i, signing himself King Tamoree (the Hawaiian language was not yet written consistently in his day), and a soft sea otter pelt brought by the Russians during their brief sojourn in Kauai (see p.510). Other displays cover mission and plantation life, and there's also a rain gauge that stood for many years atop Mount Wai'ale'ale, the wettest place on earth. It is capable of holding 900 inches of rain, but the most it ever received in a year was 682.94.

The museum's gift store, which is packed with books, maps, and wooden craft items, can be visited without paying for admission.

Nāwiliwili Bay

As Līhu'e has been a port for even less time than it has been a town, the oceanfront area around **Nāwiliwili Bay**, reached by heading east down Rice Street, is functional and without much character. So long as you stay on or near the golden sands of **Kalāpakī Beach**, however, that probably won't bother you. Despite the ugly developments that surround it, this sheltered quarter-mile stretch in front of the *Kauai Marriott* is actually a pretty good beach. Its smooth, shelving slope makes it ideal for family swimming, and it's also a good place to learn to **surf**, though beginners should avoid venturing out too far towards the open sea.

At the western edge of the beach, across the Nāwiliwili Stream – which, when it hasn't petered out altogether, is usually shallow enough to wade across – stands the **Anchor Cove Shopping Center**, home to a handful of restaurants, stores, and tour companies. The seafront at this point is no more than a wall, popular with anglers, but the lawns of **Nāwiliwili Beach County Park** are dotted with coconut palms and make a pleasant picnic spot.

Immediately beyond the park, still within sight of the beach, stand the first structures of **Nāwiliwili Harbor**, which stretches away west at the mouth of the Hulē'ia Stream. The harbor was constructed in the 1920s to afford greater protection to large vessels than Port Allen could offer; it's also closer to Oahu than Port Allen. A long breakwater was pushed out into the bay from below Carter Point on the far side of the stream, and a combination of dredging the seabed and using the silt as infill to create new flatland permanently changed the local topography. The harbor is now deep enough to accommodate mighty cruise liners, which make an incongruous spectacle moored so closely to the low-key park facilities, as well as the Superferry. All that dredging explains why the stream itself has largely silted up, but fishermen still try their luck from the jetties. The small **Niumalu Beach Park** nearby is unlikely to tempt swimmers because of the silt and its proximity to the port.

Menehune Fishpond and Hulēʻia National Wildlife Refuge

West of Nāwiliwili Harbor, Hulemalu Road climbs a hillside beyond the village of Niumalu to reach a viewpoint overlooking a pond. Officially this is the Alekoko ("Rippling Blood") Fishpond, but its nickname, the **Menehune Fishpond**, offers a better indication of its age. Created when the ancient Hawaiians sealed off a right-angle bend in Hulēʻia Stream with a half-mile-long low wall of rounded stones, the artificial lake was originally used for rearing mullet.

In popular mythology, the *menehune* were the earliest inhabitants of the islands, said to be hairy dwarfs who were given to erecting large monuments in the space of a single moonlit night. That such tales are especially prevalent on Kauai suggests that the island may have been populated by a different group of migrants than its neighbors. Scholars now believe that the word *menehune* may be related to a Tahitian word for "commoner," and may refer to a social caste that was seen as inferior by later colonizers.

Whatever the truth, the Hawaiians developed fish farming to a greater level of sophistication than anywhere else in Polynesia, and the Menehune Fishpond is rivaled only by those on Molokai (see p.408) as the best-preserved such pond in the islands. It's now under private ownership, so unless you explore the stream by boat (guided kayak trips are offered by Outfitters Kauai, among others; see p.442) the overlook is as close as you can get to the actual pond. Most of the stone wall is overgrown with mangroves, so it's not a hugely impressive sight, but the overlook makes an appealing stop on a driving tour. The river spreads out below you, with just one little shack to interrupt the greenery along its banks.

On the far side, the jagged **Hāʻupu** (or "Hoary Head") **Ridge** is silhouetted against the skyline, its slopes thick with vegetation. Two natural columns on the hillside are said to be the remains of the royal couple who commissioned the *menehune* to build them a fishpond; they were turned to stone when they disobeyed orders by sneaking a peek at the nocturnal work. Further right, and more visible from the main highway at Puhi near Kilohana, the crest of the ridge supposedly resembles either **Queen Victoria's Profile** or, for ancient Hawaiians, the equally stern Princess Hina.

Standing at the fishpond viewpoint, you'll probably hear the cries of the water-birds wheeling above the **Hulēʻia National Wildlife Refuge** just upstream. Like its equivalent at Hanalei in the north of the island (see p.480), this area still bears traces of terraces once used to grow first taro and later rice. It's now a sanctuary for endangered Hawaiian wetland birds and the only way to see it close-up is in a **kayak**, either as part of a tour or simply rented for your own explorations.

Grove Farm Homestead

Life on the nineteenth-century plantation to which Līhuʻe owes its existence is recalled at the restored **Grove Farm Homestead**, hidden away on Nāwiliwili Road southwest of downtown (tours Mon, Wed, & Thurs 10am & 1pm; adults $5, under-12s $2; ☎808/245-3202). Although it's just a few hundred yards from Rice Street, you can only cross the deep channel of Nāwiliwili Stream down by the harbor or up at the main road, so it's too far to walk from town. Reservations are required for the tours, which fill up fast; call at least a week in advance.

The plantation was opened in 1864 by George Wilcox, who was, in classic Hawaiian fashion, the entrepreneurial son of Hanalei-based missionaries. An ascetic bachelor, he lived in a cottage on the grounds; the larger *koa*-paneled mansion that's the centerpiece of the two-hour guided tours belonged to his brother and his descendants. The tours also take in the plainly furnished home of the Japanese family who looked after the Wilcoxes, and George's personal orchard of fruit trees.

West on Kaumuali'i Highway

Kaumuali'i Highway commences its westward journey around the island from the top of Rice Street by ducking under a rusty conveyor belt built to carry sugar cane from the fields to the north into the grinders of the Līhu'e Sugar Mill. Immediately beyond the mill, a turn *mauka* onto Ho'omana Road leads up to the **Old Lutheran Church**, erected in 1885 by German immigrants. Its interior design deliberately echoes the vessels that carried the immigrants to the island, complete with slanting wooden floors and a balcony modeled on a ship's bridge. But the current church is in fact a replica of the original, which was destroyed by Hurricane Iwa in 1982. Ho'omana Road peters out amid the cane fields a little further on.

Back on the highway, you soon come to the **Kukui Grove Shopping Center**, Kauai's largest and best-equipped shopping mall. Apart from the huge Borders bookstore, with its exhaustive stock of newspapers and magazines, it holds little of interest to tourists, although its department stores and supermarkets at least ensure that you can pick up food, extra clothing, and other supplies. At 7pm on Friday evenings, its central concourse hosts free performances by island musicians.

A mile past Kukui Grove, the stately house at **Kilohana Plantation** was built in 1935 by another scion of Līhu'e's founding family, Gaylord Wilcox. Most of the ground floor and veranda of the imposing mansion, which stands at the end of a sweeping driveway, is occupied by an excellent restaurant (*Gaylord's*; see p.454), while several rooms on two stories hold upmarket crafts shops and galleries. Some of these can be rather quaint, but Kilohana is nevertheless one of Kauai's better options if you're looking for gifts to take home (shops open Mon–Sat 9.30am–9.30pm, Sun 9.30am–5pm; admission to the house is free).

Kilohana is named after the mountain peak that towers over the cane fields behind it. You can get a close-up view of the plantation itself on a formal tour in a horse-drawn **carriage** (daily 11am–5pm; adults $12, under-12s $6). Less frequent but longer **wagon** tours along the rougher cane roads cost around twice the price (contact ℡808/246-5608 or ⓦwww.kilohanakauai.com for schedules and reservations).

Wailua Falls

Just over a mile northeast of Rice Street, after the strip development along Kūhiō Highway has thinned out beyond the airport turnoff, Ma'alo Road leads away leftwards up to **Wailua Falls**. This picturesque, eighty-foot drop interrupts the south fork of the Wailua River, a couple of miles upstream from the Fern Grotto (see p.457), and may be familiar from the credit sequence of *Fantasy Island*.

A parking lot, offering a side-on view both of the falls and of the streambed below, comes after a climb of three slow and sinuous miles through the cane fields. Depending on recent rainfall, you're likely to see from one to three cascades, one of which emerges from a small tunnel a little way down the cliff face. You may

△ Wailua Falls

have heard that it's possible to climb the guardrail and hike down to the base of the falls, but don't try it: as makeshift memorials nearby attest, several would-be hikers have fallen to their deaths.

Hanamā'ulu

The small community of **HANAMĀ'ULU** is located a short way beyond the road to Wailua Falls. Apart from the attractive *Restaurant and Tea House* (see p.454), it's mainly noteworthy as the site of the **Hanamā'ulu Beach County Park**, almost a mile out of town at the wooded mouth of the Hanamā'ulu Stream. Spreading along a broad and sheltered bay, this narrow strip of sand is an attractive place to spend a peaceful afternoon. However, the breakwater at the mouth of the bay prevents the silt in the stream from being carried out to sea, and so the water is usually too cloudy for swimming. There's also a fully equipped campground, but locals tend to party at Hanamā'ulu well into the night, and visiting families usually prefer to camp elsewhere.

Restaurants

Downtown Līhu'e has a reasonable choice of **places to eat** during the day, but the highway malls offer standard fast-food chains and no more. Any quest for views or atmosphere – let alone fine dining – will take you away from the center, either as far as Kilohana or Hanamāʻulu on the main road, or down to the oceanfront. The restaurants reviewed here are marked on the map on p.447.

Café Portofino Pacific Ocean Plaza, 3501 Rice St ☏808/245-2121. Formal Italian restaurant on the second floor of a quiet mall, within easy walking distance of the beach and the *Marriott*, where the deck offers sea breezes and harbor views. Tasty pasta entrees such as chicken cannelloni and *linguine a la puttanesca* cost around $18, while veal specialties go for $24 and up. Reservations recommended. Daily 5–10pm.

Duke's Canoe Club *Kauai Marriott*, 3610 Rice St ☏808/246-9599. Cheerful, informal bar-restaurant right on Kalāpakī Beach, arranged around its own waterfall and carp pond, and enjoying gorgeous views. A burger or stir-fry lunch costs around $10, while dinner, served upstairs 5–10pm, might feature fish of the day prepared as you like for $20–30 or prime rib for $28. Dinner is accompanied by Hawaiian music on Thurs, Sat, & Sun. Daily 11am–11pm.

Gaylord's at Kilohana 3-2087 Kaumualiʻi Hwy ☏808/245-9593. Delicious food served in the very British-influenced courtyard of a former plantation home, with views of extensive gardens and the mountains of the interior. Lunch consists mainly of sandwiches and salads, such as a chicken caesar ($13); Sun sees a brunch buffet for $23; and pasta, steak, or fish dinner entrees cost $24–40. Mon–Sat 11am–3pm & 5–9pm, Sun 7.45am–3pm & 5–9pm.

🏃 **Hamura's Saimin** 2956 Kress St ☏808/245-3271. This family-run diner and takeout spot is a much-loved Kauai institution, serving tasty and good-value Japanese-style fast food at communal U-shaped counters. Just grab a seat if you spot one free. The specialty is heaped bowls of *saimin* (noodle soup) – a standard portion costs $4.50, one with shrimp tempura, $6. As a side order, try a satay skewer of barbecue chicken or beef for $1.40. Mon–Thurs 10am–11pm, Fri & Sat 10am–midnight, Sun 10am–9pm.

🏃 **Hanamāʻulu Restaurant and Tea House** 3-4253 Kūhiō Hwy ☏808/245-2511. A pleasant attempt to evoke the feel of a Far Eastern teahouse, complete with fishponds and some nice private tearooms in the gardens, a mile or so from central Lihuʻe. Surprisingly, they serve both Chinese and Japanese cuisine; both are excellent. Lunchtime specials start at around $7, while dinner options include an Oriental seafood platter with fish marinated in ginger, tempura, and crab claws for $18, and three set menus for $17–19. Sushi is served in the evening only. Tues–Fri 10am–1pm & 5.30–8.30pm, Sat & Sun 4.30–8.30pm.

JJ's Broiler Anchor Cove Shopping Center, 3416 Rice St ☏808/246-4422. Popular, breezy bar-cum-restaurant, in a prime position looking out across Nāwiliwili Bay. Burgers with avocado and other Pacific-style trimmings, sandwiches, and chunky soups cost $10–15, and there's a full dinner menu of steaks and seafood at $24–40 per entree. A good open-air seafront spot for an evening drink; reserve ahead if possible. Daily 11am–10pm.

Maria's 3142 Kūhiō Hwy ☏808/246-9122. Inexpensive and very popular Mexican restaurant in the business district, where you can pick up satisfying if slightly bland lunches and dinners for under $15. Mon–Sat 11am–9pm.

Tip Top Café and Bakery *Tip Top Motel*, 3173 Akāhi St ☏808/245-2333. Family-run diner in a quiet area of central Lihuʻe, known for its simple and very filling food. The best bet is a breakfast of fruity pancakes or *malasadas* (Portuguese donuts) for $6–7, but they also offer plate lunches, stews, and basic meat dishes, as well as breads and pastries to take out, and sushi in the separate Sushi Katsu section. Café Tues–Sun 6.30am–2pm, sushi Tues–Sun 11am–2pm & 5.30–9.30pm.

Tokyo Lobby Pacific Ocean Plaza, 3501 Rice St ☏808/245-8989. Kauai's finest Japanese restaurant is located on the ground floor of a small mall. The light, pleasant interior has a sushi bar, but the open-air *lānai* feels too close to the road. Lunch options include noodles and tempura ($10–15), or soup, salad, and your choice of chicken, beef teriyaki, or sashimi for $13; at dinner the latter combination costs about $18. Romantics should try a "Love Boat," a wooden boat full of mixed goodies for $28 per person. Mon–Fri 11am–2pm & 4.30–9pm, Sat & Sun 4.30–9pm.

Whaler's Brew Pub Kauai Lagoons Golf Course, 3132 Ninini Point ☏808/245-2000. They don't brew their own beer at Whaler's any more, but it's still a lively restaurant/bar. Set in a bright and attractive pavilion with spectacular views over the mouth of Nāwiliwili Bay, its location at the very far end of the *Kauai Marriott* driveway means it's too far to walk even from the hotel. There's a lunch menu of sandwiches and fresh fish, for around $10, and a dinner menu with $18–28 steak, fish, or pasta entrees. A giant, 20oz "Whale of a Burger" ($24) is available at both lunch and dinner. There's live music several nights per week; locals flock in on weekends for gigs by touring reggae artists or DJs. Mon–Fri 11am–9pm, Sat & Sun 11–1am.

The East Shore

Ever since Kauai was first settled, its population has been most heavily concentrated along the valley of the **Wailua River** and the nearby coastline. This region, starting roughly five miles north of Līhu'e, is now home to approaching 20,000 people, but they're so spread out that you'd barely know they were there. Much more conspicuous are the guests at the oceanfront hotels and condos, here for the sun and fun rather than the relatively poor beaches along what's collectively known as the **Coconut Coast**.

Technically, Kūhiō Highway, the main artery, passes through several separate communities as it heads north beyond the river itself. The distinctions between the overlapping towns of **Wailua**, **Waipouli**, and **Kapa'a**, however, are far less significant or even noticeable than the contrast between the malls and modern high-rises along the highway and the residential districts that lie a couple of miles inland. Tucked away behind long, low **Nounou Ridge** (the "Sleeping Giant"), which runs parallel to the coast, neat individual cottages are set amid gardens that erupt with spectacular blooms, and ramshackle farms still squeeze as much produce as possible from their few acres.

Beyond Kapa'a, there's far less development, and only rarely is access to the seashore at all easy. However, en route to Princeville you can stop at several little-known beaches.

Wailua River

Kūhiō Highway crosses the **WAILUA RIVER** five miles out from central Līhu'e, marking the start of Kauai's East Shore. For the ancient Hawaiians, the area to either side of the twin bridges here was the *Wailua Nui Hoano*, or Great Sacred Wailua. Fertile, beautiful, and sheltered from the sea, it provided some of the finest living conditions in all the islands, and served as home to Kauai's greatest chiefs. A trail known as the **King's Highway**, lined with *heiaus* and other religious sites, ran beside the river all the way from the ocean to the rain-drenched summit of Mount Wai'ale'ale.

In those days the Wailua flowed in two separate channels. It still has a South Fork and a North Fork, but they now fuse together for the last couple of miles. The resultant broad, flat stream is often called the only navigable river in Hawaii, although sandbars at its mouth usually stop vessels from entering it from the open sea. Exploring it in a kayak is one of the best ways to spend a day on this side of the island; rental outlets are detailed on p.443. (Other good rivers to kayak on Kauai include the Hanalei, see p.478, and the Kalihiwai, see p.473).

The south bank of the river has long been set aside for agriculture and is almost entirely free of buildings or even roads; it's impossible to head any further inland than the Smith's Tropical Paradise theme park, though tour boats leave regularly for the short cruise up to the **Fern Grotto**, which involves a brief walk along the south bank. Otherwise, very few vantage points offer so much as a glimpse of its rolling fields and woodlands.

It was on the Wailua's north shore that Kauai's most famous ruler, Kaumuali'i, had his own personal coconut grove and *heiau*. He had been born just a few yards away, at the Birthing Stones, as was essential to attain the highest rank on the

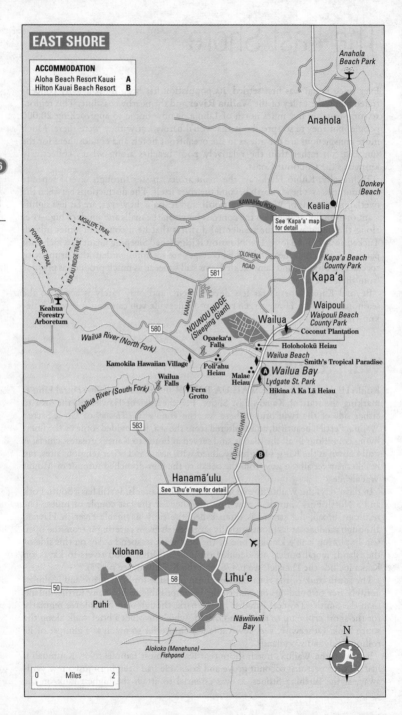

EAST SHORE

ACCOMMODATION
Aloha Beach Resort Kauai **A**
Hilton Kauai Beach Resort **B**

Anahola
Beach Park

KAUAI

Donkey
Beach

Keālia

KAWAIHAU ROAD

See 'Kapa'a' map
for detail

MOALEPE TRAIL

Kapa'a Beach
County Park

'OLOHENA
ROAD

POWERLINE TRAIL

Kapa'a

581

Waipouli

Waipouli Beach
County Park

Coconut Plantation

KUILAU RIDGE TRAIL

KAMALU RD

NOUNOU RIDGE
(Sleeping Giant)

Wailua

Keahua
Forestry
Arboretum

580

Wailua River (North Fork)

Opaeka'a
Falls

Holoholokū Heiau

Wailua Beach

Smith's Tropical Paradise

Kamokila Hawaiian Village

Poli'ahu
Heiau

Malae
Heiau

Wailua Bay

Lydgate St. Park

Wailua
Falls

Fern
Grotto

Hikina A Ka Lā Heiau

Wailua River (South Fork)

583

KŪHIŌ HIGHWAY

B

Hanamā'ulu

See 'Līhu'e' map for detail

Kilohana

50

58

Līhu'e

Puhi

Nāwiliwili Bay

Alokoko (Menehune)
Fishpond

N

0   Miles   2

456

island. Several such historic sites, in various states of repair, are now preserved in **Wailua River State Park**, together with plenty of attractive scenery.

The Fern Grotto

Some visitors consider the trip to the **Fern Grotto**, a short way up the Wailua River, to be the highlight of their stay on Kauai; others find it hard to imagine anything to which they'd less like to subject themselves. Promoted as a romantic, fern-bedecked jungle cavern, the grotto has an undeserved reputation as the island's premier beauty spot, and can only be reached as part of a large group excursion. Don't kid yourself that the grotto itself may be compelling enough to make it worth putting up with all the kitsch nonsense that surrounds it: the kitsch nonsense is the best bit.

At the time this book went to press, the Fern Grotto was **closed** to visitors, state authorities having assessed it as unsafe. Assuming that it has once more reopened by the time you read this, then the way to reach it is on a canopied barge, sent up the river by Smith's Motor Boats (℡808/821-6895, ⓦwww.smithskauai.com), from a marina *mauka* of the highway on the south bank of the Wailua. The 1hr 20min tour costs $20 for adults, $10 for under-13s; the precise schedule varies, but there are usually departures every half-hour between 9am and 3.30pm daily.

As the barge heads upriver, a commentary on the few undramatic sights along the way is interspersed with local legends. For most of the route, you see little beyond the thick trees on both banks. After a couple of miles, once you've passed the houses high on the ridge near ʻŌpaekaʻa Falls, and the Kamokila Hawaiian Village, the river divides. The Fern Grotto is just up its left (south) fork; to avoid the tour groups, most kayakers head off to the right.

Having disembarked at the grotto landing, you walk a short paved trail, lined with bananas and torch ginger plants, up to the cave. This large, natural amphitheater was hollowed out by a waterfall that has slowed to a trickle in the century since the sugar plantations diverted the stream that fed it. Until Hurricane Iniki toppled most of the tree cover up above the cave, in 1992, dense clusters of *aʻe* ferns drooped down from its lip, screening off the interior with a green curtain. As ferns hate direct sunlight, they're now much shorter than they used to be. The state has vouchsafed $440,000 to help relandscape the spot, but it has yet to return to its former splendor. Only the acoustics remain unchanged, so each tour party in turn assembles to be serenaded with the *Hawaiian Wedding Song* by the guitar-toting crew of its barge, whose concert continues on the way back downstream.

As you might expect, the Fern Grotto is also a popular site for weddings, with two or three couples getting married here each day.

Smith's Tropical Paradise

There's plenty more ersatz Polynesian posturing at **Smith's Tropical Paradise**, alongside the marina. In the daytime, you can explore its thirty acres of colorful gardens in relative peace (daily 8.30am–4pm; $6). On several evenings each week, it reopens for a reasonable buffet *lūʻau* and a cheerfully tacky "International Pageant" called *The Golden People of Hawaii*, featuring song and dance from China and Japan as well as Hawaii and Polynesia (summer Mon–Fri, winter Mon, Wed, & Fri; gates open 5pm, *lūʻau* 8pm; ℡808/821-6895, ⓦwww.smithskauai; adults $70, under 14s $30). Kauai's other *lūʻaus* are detailed on p.445.

The King's Highway

Although it's still possible to make out several of the ancient sites that once lined the Wailua River, few now amount to more than vague ruins. None has any formal opening hours or guided tours; you have to find them yourself and settle for reading whatever explanatory signs may have been erected.

Slightly back from the lava rocks of Lydgate State Park (see p.460), alongside the *Aloha Beach Resort* on the southern bank of the Wailua at the river mouth, stands the **Hikina A Ka Lā** ("Rising of the Sun") **Heiau**. Only traces survive of the hundred-yard-long, ten-foot-thick wall that once faced the rising sun here. Part of the area behind it was devoted to a "place of refuge" (see p.189), the Hauola O Hōnaunau, while the waters in front were popular, then as now, with expert surfers.

On the other, *mauka*, side of the highway, just before the marina turnoff, a large mound covered with grass and trees in the middle of a cane field marks the site of **Malae Heiau**. Roughly a hundred yards square, this was the island's biggest temple. In the 1840s, well after the death of Kaumualiʻi, his favorite wife, Deborah Kapule, is rumored to have used it as a pen for her large herd of cattle, to demonstrate her conversion to Christianity.

As soon as you cross the Wailua, you're in the area where Kaumualiʻi lived amid his grove of coconut palms. A road inland from here follows the route of the old **King's Highway** trail; it's now known as Kuamoʻo Road or Hwy-580. The first of the riverside parking lots on the left is the kayak and canoe launching ramp for **Wailua River State Park**, which encompasses the river itself and a thin strip along most of both banks. The second riverside parking lot is at the foot of the low Ka Lae O Ka Manu ("Crest of the Bird" or cock's comb) ridge, where **Holoholokū Heiau** once stood. So tiny that it could only be entered on all fours, this was a *luakini*, used for human sacrifices. A few stone walls remain, but the hill itself is overgrown.

A little way further north around the base of the hill are the **Birthing Stones**, where all the great chiefs of Kauai were born. The mother was supposed to brace her back against one stone and her legs against the other as she gave birth, though they seem a bit too far apart for that to be very likely. An even slab at the edge of the small walled enclosure nearby was used to cover the corpses of dogs sacrificed on such occasions, while the infant's umbilical cord was inserted in the crack in the boulder behind. A flight of steps from beside the stones leads up the hill. At the top you find yourself in a more recent, though now also overgrown, **Japanese cemetery**, straight across from the Fern Grotto ferry landing.

From here on, the road steadily climbs along Kuamoʻo ("Lizard") Ridge. After about a mile, a parking lot on the left commands a sweeping prospect of the broad flatlands beside a gentle curve in the Wailua. Helpful signs explain that this spot on the bluff was the site of the palace of chief Hoʻono. The broad low walls of **Poliʻahu Heiau**, constructed of smooth stones from the riverbed, still stand, though with the thatched temple structures long gone they now enclose just grass and rubble. Coconut palms sway at either end, unusually high above the sea.

The birth of a new *aliʻi* at the Birthing Stones was traditionally greeted by a hammer striking the **Bell Stone**, further upstream. To find it, head down the rutted dirt road off to the left just beyond the *heiau*, then follow a rough walkway down the hill. No one can now say for sure which among the pile of stones here is the correct one, so you'll just have to hit a few and make your own mind up.

ʻŌpaekaʻa Falls and beyond

The next parking lot, this time on the right, is the overlook for **ʻŌpaekaʻa Falls**. Set amid thick green undergrowth, this wide, low waterfall splashes into a pool stained red with eroded earth, where native shrimp could once be seen churning in the water (*ʻŌpaekaʻa* means "rolling shrimp"). The falls interrupt ʻŌpaekaʻa Stream, which flows in between Kuamoʻo Ridge and Nounou Mountain before joining the Wailua a mile back down the hill. You can't walk any closer to the falls than this – a number of hikers have died trying in recent years – but you get a slightly better view from the highway bridge a few yards further up.

Carefully cross the road at this point for a fine panorama of Wailua Valley. Immediately below, you can see the huts of **Kamokila Hawaiian Village**, a reasonably authentic re-creation of a traditional riverside settlement. Demolished by Iniki in 1992, it was subsequently restored to serve as an African village in the 1995 Dustin Hoffman thriller *Outbreak*, and has now reopened for low-key tours that focus on daily life in ancient Kauai (daily 9am–5pm; $5; ☎808/823-0559, ⓦwww.kamokila.com).

The King's Highway runs for several progressively wilder miles beyond 'Ōpaeka'a Falls, but no longer right up Wai'ale'ale. You're only likely to venture this way if you plan to do some backwoods **hiking**, along the excellent trails detailed on pp.464–467.

Wailua to Kapa'a

Although the East Shore's nicest beach, Lydgate State Park, and its top tourist attraction, the boat trip to the Fern Grotto, are both on the south shore of the Wailua River, the strip development along the coast only gets going once you cross the river and enter **WAILUA** proper. At this point, a thin fringe of trees and sand is all that divides the highway from the sea, while further on an extensive grove of palms on the *mauka* side marks the site of the **Coco Palms Resort**. Kauai's most famous hotel – the one through which Elvis and his new bride floated in *Blue Hawaii*, to the accompaniment of the *Hawaiian Wedding Song* – has remained closed ever since 1992's Hurricane Iniki. As this book went to press, however, it was finally due to reopen as an upscale condo development, which promised to retain the look of the original.

Within less than a mile, as the gap between road and ocean starts to widen, the extensive **Coconut Market Place** complex appears *makai* of the highway. This centers on a mall of rather ordinary souvenir stores, fast-food outlets, bars, and restaurants, arranged around an open-air courtyard. Behind that lie half a dozen large hotels, while out of sight to the south are several condo buildings, not strictly speaking part of the complex.

Northbound traffic along the highway from here on in can get very congested; at busy times, it's well worth taking the alternative **bypass** system that follows the former sugar-cane roads from behind *Sizzlers* in Wailua and rejoins Hwy-56 via Olohena Road in Kapa'a. Other than a few worthwhile restaurants (see p.463 for reviews), and the shops in the **Kauai Village** shopping center, halfway between Wailua and Kapa'a in **WAIPOULI**, you miss nothing if you skip the main highway altogether.

KAPA'A itself is about the only recognizable town between Līhu'e and Hanalei. The old-fashioned boardwalks at the main intersection (not important enough to boast a stop light, but a welcome interruption in the monotonous strip) hold small shops, cafés, and restaurants. Several equipment rental outlets offer kayaks, surfboards, and the like at reasonable rates, while a handful of quirky clothes and gift stores catch the eye.

The beaches

Although an almost unbroken ribbon of sand runs along the shore all the way from the mouth of the Wailua up to Kapa'a, it rarely deserves to be called a beach. The nearby mountains lend the area some scenic beauty, but the coastline is flat and

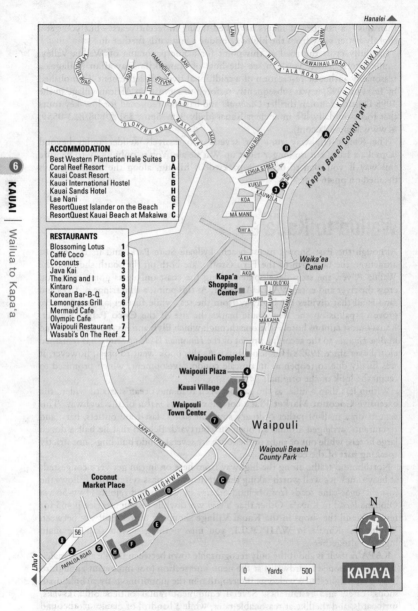

Hanalei ▲

ACCOMMODATION

Best Western Plantation Hale Suites	D
Coral Reef Resort	A
Kauai Coast Resort	E
Kauai International Hostel	B
Kauai Sands Hotel	H
Lae Nani	G
ResortQuest Islander on the Beach	F
ResortQuest Kauai Beach at Makaiwa	C

RESTAURANTS

Blossoming Lotus	1
Caffé Coco	8
Coconuts	4
Java Kai	3
The King and I	5
Kintaro	9
Korean Bar-B-Q	6
Lemongrass Grill	9
Mermaid Cafe	3
Olympic Cafe	1
Waipouli Restaurant	7
Wasabi's On The Reef	2

KAUAI | Wailua to Kapa'a

Kapa'a Shopping Center

Waika'ea Canal

Waipouli Complex
Waipouli Plaza
Kauai Village
Waipouli Town Center

Waipouli

Waipouli Beach County Park

KAPA'A BYPASS

Coconut Market Place

KŪHIŌ HIGHWAY

56

Papaloa Road

Lihu'e ▲

0   Yards   500

N

KAPA'A

dull, devoid of the sheltered coves and steepled cliffs that characterize the waterfront further north. Strong waves and stronger currents rightly deter most bathers, so the swimming pools in the major hotels are kept busy.

By far the most popular and attractive of the public beaches is the first one you come to heading north from Līhu'e. Hidden from the road, **Lydgate State Park** lies behind the *Aloha Beach Resort* (see p.462) on the southern side of the mouth of

460

the Wailua River. The murky, swirling waters where the river flows into the sea are of great interest to surfers, but for family swimming the two linked artificial pools in the park, lined with smooth lava boulders, are preferable. Regularly replenished by the sea, they are usually bursting with fish eager to be fed by snorkelers. There's a picnic spot alongside the pools, in the shade of a stand of ironwoods. The park is also the site of the **Kamalani Playground**, an intricate tangle of free-form wooden structures for children to climb on. In addition, Lydgate State Park holds the first of the trail of ancient *heiaus* that line the Wailua River, described on p.458.

From the north bank of the river, the narrow crescent of **Wailua Beach** runs for something over half a mile, until its sand peters out at the rocky headland of Alakukui Point. Fringed with palms, the beach is an attractive place to stroll – especially at sunrise – if you're staying in the vicinity. However, it offers no amenities and, apart from the sheltered patch in front of the *Lae Nani* condos, the surf is generally high.

Waipouli Beach County Park, which starts just past the exposed Coconut Market Place strip, is rather less accessible, being backed for much of its length by small residential properties. In any case, only fitful patches of sand cover the rock at the ocean's edge, and if you do go into the water, the drop-off is alarmingly steep. You can admire the Pacific from the safe distance of a paved footpath lined with ironwoods, although you'll have to return to the main road to cross the small Moikeha Canal.

Next comes **Kapa'a Beach County Park**, a short way north. Almost as soon as it gets going, the beach here is interrupted by the Waika'ea Canal, built during plantation days to drain the inland marshes. The combination of silt deposited by the canal, and the more recent blasting of the shallow reef just offshore has badly eroded the shoreline. As little sand remains and swimming from the rocks is unappetizing, the park is largely the reserve of local fishermen.

Finally, just beyond Kapa'a, comes an unexpected stretch of low sand dunes at **Keālia Beach**. These are now the only dunes along the East Shore; others, at Waipouli for example, were bulldozed to build hotels. As a result, the tremendous surf that crashes almost onto the highway makes this the area's most exciting-looking beach. You'll probably see crowds of surfers and boogie-boarders getting pummeled half to death, especially at its northern end, but like all such "shore-break" beaches – where there's no coral reef to protect you from the force of the open ocean – this is no place for inexperienced bathers.

Beaches beyond Keālia – including the beautiful sands at Anahola, just four miles north of Kapa'a – are described on p.467 onwards.

East Shore accommodation

In terms of number of beds, the East Shore or Coconut Coast ranks second to Po'ipū as Kauai's main vacation center. As for beaches, it's a distant third to both the south and north coasts. If you enjoy hanging out in seaside resorts, however, this area has a lot going for it, offering the widest range of **accom-modation** and restaurants on the island. With the *Coco Palms* still closed (see p.459), the best **hotels** and **condos** are in or near the Coconut Market Place, with little to choose between them. As bases for exploring Kauai, the homely **B&Bs** a mile or two from the coast are ideal, while downtown Kapa'a has the island's only **hostel**.

Hostel

Kauai International Hostel 4532 Lehua St, Kapaʻa ☎ 808/823-6142, ⓦ www.kauaihostel.net. Kauai's only hostel is a short walk from the highway in central Kapaʻa, and open only to those with return flights to leave Hawaii, with a maximum three-week stay. The two-story building holds eight-bed dorms ($25 per bed), one of which is reserved for women only, and a few $60 private rooms that share bathrooms, as well as a suite with its own shower plus TV and fridge. Kitchen facilities are available, and there's easy access from the airport by public bus (see p.439). 11pm curfew. ❶–❸

B&Bs

Inn Paradise 6381 Makana Rd, Kapaʻa ☎ 808/822-2542, ⓦ www.innparadisekauai.com. Great-value garden cottage, deep in the hills above Wailua, with three fully equipped en-suite B&B units. All share use of a roomy *lānai* and hot tub. ❸

Lani-Keha 848 Kamalu Rd, Kapaʻa ☎ 808/822-1605 or 1-800/821-4898, ⓦ www.lanikeha.com. Three comfortable en-suite B&B rooms in large country house tucked in behind the Sleeping Giant; all have access to the main kitchen, living room, and a large *lānai*. Two-night minimum stay, no credit cards. ❷–❸

Rosewood B&B 872 Kamalu Rd, Kapaʻa ☎ 808/822-5216, ⓦ www.rosewoodkauai.com. Spacious plantation-style house, complete with columns and veranda. There's one cozy (somewhat overly so) guest room, two fully equipped cottages in the gorgeous gardens, and a bunkhouse that holds three simple budget rooms sharing a single bathroom. The same owners serve as rental agents for several other East-Shore condos and apartments. Bunkhouse ❷, room ❸, cottages ❹

Hotels and condos

Aloha Beach Resort Kauai 3-5920 Kūhiō Hwy, Wailua ☎ 808/823-6000 or 1-888/823-5111, ⓦ www.abrkauai.com. The much-remodeled *Aloha Beach Resort* stands just off the highway immediately south of Wailua River, looking over the ocean from above Lydgate State Park. With its busy weekend dance club, regular live entertainment, and actively pro-kids policy, there's always something going on, and it's probably the liveliest of the Coconut Coast resorts. The location is especially good for families, very close to the safe swimming and great playground at Lydgate Beach, and it even offers gaming systems in every room. The actual rooms are nothing exceptional, but if you look online you should find the very acceptable

rates indicated here. They also have thirteen separate, more luxurious cottages, even closer to the ocean. Rooms ❹, cottages ❺

Best Western Plantation Hale Suites Coconut Market Place, 484 Kūhiō Hwy, Kapaʻa ☎ 808/822-4941 or 1-800/775-4253, ⓦ www.plantation-hale .com. Inexpensive and somewhat faded apartment suites, each with separate kitchen, living room, dressing room and bathroom, in several buildings facing across lawns to the sea. Take your pick of three swimming pools. ❹

Coral Reef Resort 1516 Kūhiō Hwy, Kapaʻa ☎ 808/822-4481 or 1-800/843-4659, ⓦ www .hotelcoralreefresort.com. Inexpensive suites in small, friendly, and recently renovated seafront hotel a short walk north of central Kapaʻa. All rooms have a/c, phones and safes. ❹

Kauai Coast Resort at the Beachboy 520 Aleka Loop, Kapaʻa ☎ 808/822-3441, ⓦ www.kauai coastresort.com. This renovated condo resort looks forbidding from the outside, with high lava-rock walls fronting the main road to the Coconut Market Place. Inside, it's far pleasanter. Three wings of comfortable guest rooms enclose spacious lawns and a pool; the fourth – open – side is the beach. All rooms have private *lānais* and two double beds; under-18s can share your room for free. Garden view ❺, ocean view ❻

Kauai Sands Hotel 420 Papaloa Rd, Wailua ☎ 808/822-4951 or 1-800/560-5553, ⓦ www .kauaisandshotel.com. Large and somewhat faded oceanfront property at the southern end of the Coconut Market Place, though not technically part of it. Several buildings of motel-style units are arrayed around a pool; spacious lawns lead down to the beach. Ask about discounted rates. ❹

Lae Nani 410 Papaloa Rd, Wailua ☎ 808/822-4938 or book through Outrigger ☎ 303/369-7777 or 1-800/688-7444, ⓦ www.outrigger.com. Spacious low-rise complex of luxurious one- and two-bedroom condos, all capable of sleeping at least four guests, on a headland at the northern end of Wailua Bay, just south of the Coconut Market Place. The adjacent beach is ideal for inshore swimming, and there's also a pool, plus a ruined *heiau*, in the grounds. ❼

ResortQuest Islander on the Beach 440 Aleka Place, Kapaʻa ☎ 808/822-7417 or 1-877/997-6667 (US & Canada), ⓦ www.resortquesthawaii.com. Beachfront property at the southern end of the Coconut Market Place. Seven separate guest wings – rates rise the closer you get to the sea – plus a small pool and spa. All of the appealing and spacious rooms have *lānais*, safes and refrigerators, while the *Jolly Roger* restaurant, set back from the ocean, offers live entertainment. ❺

ResortQuest Kauai Beach at Makaiwa 650
Aleka Loop, Kapaʻa ☎ 808/822-3455 or
1-866/774-2924, ⊛ www.resortquesthawaii.com.
The northernmost of the Coconut Market Place
resorts comprises several large beachfront wings
holding 311 Hawaiian-themed rooms with private
lānais, but sadly it all tends to feel a little cramped
and dark. Guests enjoy use of the pool, spa, and
free tennis courts, and can dine at the open-air
Voyager Grille restaurant. Some rates include a free
rental car; look for special discounts on the
website. ❻

East Shore restaurants

Restaurants jostle for the attention of hotel guests all along the Wailua to Kapaʻa
coastal highway. However, with one or two exceptions, the glossier-looking steak-
and-seafood places tend to be less interesting than the cheaper ethnic alternatives.
If you feel that strolling around comparing menus is an essential precursor to
eating out, only downtown Kapaʻa fits the bill. Besides the places reviewed below,
there are also any number of the usual chain fast-food outlets.

Blossoming Lotus Dragon Building, 4504 Kukui
St, Kapaʻa ☎ 808/822-7678. Hugely popular
"vegan fusion" restaurant at the central intersection in Kapaʻa, with a strong emphasis on organic
ingredients. Inspiration is drawn from all over the
world, and the large portions are pretty good,
though the Asian-influenced items, like the Thai
green curries and the tempeh vindaloo, tend to be
better than the Greek and Mediterranean dishes. All
entrees apart from the $12 "monk's bowl" mixture
cost just under $20. On the Sun brunch menu,
which does include eggs, all items are under $10.
Mon–Sat 5–9pm, Sun 10am–2pm & 5–9pm.

Caffé Coco 4-369 Kūhiō Hwy, Wailua ☎ 808/822-
7990. Attractively ramshackle café, with a laidback
hippy feel, set well back from the highway in
central Wailua. Almost all the tables are outdoors in
a graveled garden that's sometimes busy with
mosquitoes. Wholesome, though not entirely
vegetarian, lunches cost under $10; changing
dinner specials, such as grilled or roasted Italian-
style meat dishes, under $25. Tues–Fri 11am–9pm,
Sat & Sun 5–9pm.

Coconuts 4-919 Kūhiō Hwy, Kapaʻa ☎ 808/823-
8777. Bright, tropically themed restaurant on the
main highway; the large bamboo screens don't
quite keep the noise out from the closer tables. The
Pacific Rim cuisine isn't quite gourmet standard,
and the fish dishes are very the way to go.
Appetizers include "*ahi* tuna two ways" – tempura
and sushi – for $12 and a scallop salad for $13,
while entrees range from the "very tasty burger"
for $11, via fresh catch with sweet potatoes and a
lime-dashi broth for $22, up to *filet mignon* for $30.
Daily 4–10pm.

Java Kai 4-1384 Kūhiō Hwy, Kapaʻa ☎ 808/823-
6887. Lively, friendly coffee bar in the heart of
downtown Kapaʻa, serving good coffee drinks from
the crack of dawn, and fine smoothies too. Daily
6am–5pm.

The King and I Waipouli Plaza, 4-901 Kūhiō Hwy,
Kapaʻa ☎ 808/822-1642. Inexpensive but high-
quality Thai place, in a small mall just north of
Kauai Village. They're proud of growing their own
herbs, and most dishes are heaped with fresh
basil. For an appetizer you can get a bale of crispy
straw-like noodles for $7, meat or shrimp satay for
$9–12, or share a two-person portion of spicy
lemongrass or Siam coconut soup. The tastiest
entrees are the red, green, and yellow curries,
prepared with meat for $10, fish or shrimp for $12,
or as even cheaper vegetarian options. Most of the
desserts involve green tea or coconut milk. Daily
4.30–9.30pm.

Kintaro 4-3561 Kūhiō Hwy, Wailua ☎ 808/822-
3341. Friendly, informal, but exquisite restaurant,
serving reasonably priced Japanese food. Full sushi
bar, plus teppanyaki meals and more unusual
specialties such as grilled eel ($20) and *yose nabe*,
a sort of Japanese *bouillabaisse* with clams and
crab (also $20). Mon–Sat 5.30–9.30pm.

Korean Bar-B-Q Restaurant 4-3561 Kūhiō Hwy,
Wailua ☎ 808/823-6744. Modest, friendly, and very
good-value barbecue joint. The meat dishes are all
tasty, with combos costing $8–10; vegetarian
options include spicy *kimchee* vegetables. Takeout
is available. Mon & Wed–Sun 10am–9pm, Tues
4.30–9pm.

Lemongrass Grill 4-885 Kūhiō Hwy, Kapaʻa
☎ 808/821-2288. Smart, lively, upscale restaurant,
serving a predominantly Japanese and seafood
menu, and set in an attractive building close to the
highway just north of the Kauai Village shopping
center. There are some outdoor tables, plus plenty
more indoor dining space upstairs. Graze on
delicious appetizers like the *togorashi* scallops for

a lighter meal, or choose a more substantial entree such as broiled lamb loin, barbecued ribs, or grilled fresh catch ($15–28). Vegetarian options available. Daily 5.30–10pm.

Mermaids Café 1384 Kūhiō Hwy, Kapaʻa ☏ 808/821-2026. Small, partly vegetarian café in central Kapaʻa, alongside adjoining Java Kai, serving wholesome egg-and-fruit breakfasts and bargain Asian-flavored lunches and dinners such as chicken satay, tofu or *ahi* wraps, black bean burritos, and the like for under $10, washed down with lemonade or hibiscus tea. Daily 11am–9pm.

Olympic Café 4-1354 Kūhiō Hwy, Kapaʻa ☏ 808/822-5825. This large open-sided café, perched on the first floor close to the heart of Kapaʻa, makes a popular breakfast rendezvous for locals and visitors alike, with its eggs, pancakes, juices and coffee. For lunch, you can get sandwiches, burgers and burritos at similarly inexpensive prices, while fish and meat dinner entrees range up to $25. Sun–Thurs 6am–9pm, Fri & Sat 6am–10pm.

Waipouli Restaurant Waipouli Town Center, 4-831 Kūhiō Hwy, Waipouli ☏ 808/822-9311. Simple plate-lunch restaurant, in a small mall just south of Kauai Village. The menu includes roast pork, chicken and other meats (it takes a huge combo to cost as much as $10), but the specialty is filling bowls of *saimin* noodles, in different varieties ($4–8). Mon & Sun 7am–2pm, Tues–Sat 7am–2pm & 5–8.30pm.

Wasabi's on the Reef 1394 Kūhiō Hwy, Kapaʻa ☏ 808/822-2700. Bright, tiny Japanese restaurant in the heart of Kapaʻa, where the focus is on good sushi at a good price; a soft-shell crab (or "cane-spider") roll, for example, costs $9. For a little more there's a wide selection of other seafood dishes. Bring your own beer or wine, and live Hawaiian music featured Tues & Wed. Tues–Sun 11am–2pm & 5–9pm.

East Shore hikes

If you have only a few days to spend **hiking** on Kauai, then the East Shore cannot compete with the splendors of the Kalalau Trail (see p.489) or the treks in Kōkeʻe Park (see p.517). However, some very enjoyable trails do lead through the hills above Wailua and Kapaʻa. The most compelling attraction here is the awe-inspiring crater wall of **Mount Waiʻaleʻale**, which looms before you as you head inland. It's no longer possible to walk to the top, as the ancients did, but despite the claims of the helicopter companies that it can be seen only from the air, keen hikers can trek to the wilderness at its base.

Nounou Mountain – "The Sleeping Giant"

The long, sharp crest of **Nounou Mountain** parallels the shoreline between Wailua and Kapaʻa, roughly two miles back from the sea. These days it's known more often as the **Sleeping Giant**, although the only spot from which it bears much resemblance to a slumbering profile is down a side road opposite the Chevron station in Waipouli. Three separate trails lead up to the top of the ridge, where they join for a final assault on the summit.

The least demanding trail, from the **east**, starts near the end of Haleilio Road, a mile up from its junction with Kūhiō Highway. After an initial gentle zigzagging ascent through tropical vegetation, it gets a little hard to follow – head right, not left, at the fork half a mile along. Switchbacking across the northern end of the ridge, you get to see the high mountains inland as well as views back towards the ocean. Something over a mile along, the western trail links up from the right, and both continue left a short way to the picnic area.

Coming from the **west**, pick up the trail at the end of Lokelani Road, a small *makai* turn very near the northern end of Kamalu Road, which connects Hwy-580 with Olohena Road. This is a shorter but steeper hike, more or less straight up the forested hillside. The highlight is a superb avenue of poker-straight Norfolk pines, recognizable by the raised ridges at regular intervals around their trunks. Such trees were formerly in great demand as masts, though these ones are just eighty years old.

Finally, it's also possible to climb the Sleeping Giant from the **south**, along a trail that starts a few hundred yards west of the 'Ōpaeka'a Falls parking lot (see p.458). The two-mile trail is mostly in thick woodland as it meanders up the hillside, but a picnic table in a clearing along the way offers some fine inland **views**. The trail meets the western route in the stand of pines mentioned above, with plenty of climbing still to go.

Whichever way you climb, you'll know you've reached the top when you arrive at the **Ali'i Vista Hale**, a sheltered picnic table set in a little clearing. So long as it isn't raining, you'll be able to see the entire coastline, from Līhu'e to Anahola, or look inland towards the residential areas of Wailua and Kapa'a.

If you're feeling intrepid, and conditions are not too slippery, it's possible to continue beyond the picnic area along a hair-raisingly makeshift trail. Were you down on the highway, you'd know this as the Giant's Nose; up here it's a sheer razorback ridge, with long drops to either side. Scrambling up the rocks at the end brings you out at a level and even better viewpoint. The soil underfoot is a rich red loam, which explains why such mountains erode so quickly; most of the slopes below are dense with small trees, but slashes of bare earth show where mudslides have taken place. Away to the west is the main ridge of Mount Wai'ale'ale, almost permanently wreathed in mist and cloud, while to the south lies the twisting, wooded gorge of the Wailua River. Anahola Mountain runs across the northern horizon, looking much like a sleeping giant itself.

Mount Wai'ale'ale Base Trail

For most visitors to the East Shore, the mountains of the interior remain a cloud-shrouded mystery. Behind the semi-permanent veil of mist, however, lies a landscape of extraordinary beauty. The very heart of the island is **Mount Wai'ale'ale**, whose annual rainfall of around 440 inches makes it the wettest spot on earth. Its highest point is less than a dozen miles west of Kapa'a, which receives a tenth as much rain. The name *Wai'ale'ale* means "overflowing water"; as you approach it from the ocean, it appears as a curved wall of velvet-green rock, furrowed by countless waterfalls. Most of its rain falls on the Alaka'i Swamp, just behind the summit, then flows in every direction to create Kauai's major rivers. (Details of the amazing trail through the Alaka'i Swamp from Kōke'e State Park appear on p.522). The escarpments of Wai'ale'ale are far too steep to climb, but hiking to the foot of the mountain is rewarding and far from strenuous.

To get here, drive along Hwy-580 (the King's Highway) beyond 'Ōpaeka'a Falls. The road ends roughly five miles further on at the **Keahua Forestry Arboretum**, a stretch of woodlands and meadows where native trees are grown in controlled conditions. It's a pleasant enough area to stroll around, though the trees are not labeled for your benefit. Incidentally, the arboretum also serves as the trailhead for the Kuilau Ridge Trail (see p.466) and the southern end of the Powerline Trail (see p.474).

From here on, how far you can continue, first by car and then on foot, depends on the weather. Driving involves fording streams that cross the unpaved continuation of the road; if the water is at all high, don't try it. Otherwise, check your odometer, and set off across the stream at the arboretum. After 1.6 miles, a pull-out on the left offers the first clear views of Wai'ale'ale. Turn right at the T-junction after 2.2 miles, then left at the fork after 2.7 miles. Ignore the road to the left after 3.5 miles, but fork left a short way beyond that. The road ends at a yellow gate just under four miles from the arboretum, but you're free to walk on.

You're now heading directly towards Wai'ale'ale. As the track rises after about half a mile, a side trail to the left leads in a few minutes to a tranquil pool in dense, wild forest, but you'll probably want to press on ahead. Not far beyond, the dirt road reaches a small dam. This is the North Fork of the Wailua River, which has just plummeted down the face of the mountain. Upstream, its waters foam and tumble between the boulders, against the unforgettable backdrop of the high, green walls of Wai'ale'ale. If you're lucky, the cloud cover may clear long enough to offer a glimpse of the ridge at the top. The white specks of helicopters show up clearly against the green, and their engines are just about audible above the river. All the rudimentary footpaths on the far side of the dam peter out in a morass of mud, roots, ferns and water.

It's simply not possible to climb to the summit of Wai'ale'ale from here; the trail of the ancient Hawaiians followed the ridge that leads up the flank to your right. However, you may hear talk of a hike to the so-called **"Blue Hole"** at the very base of the mountain. The only way to get there is to clamber along the riverbed itself, an exercise that is fraught with danger and very likely to end in failure. At best, it's likely to involve wading chest-deep against a strong current for up to an hour. At worst, when there's been heavy rain – which is virtually always, but especially in springtime – it's simply impossible. Do not attempt to make the hike without first calling the state parks office (☎808/274-3444) for advice.

The Kuilau Ridge and Moalepe trails

Two further, less demanding trails traverse the upland forests above Kapa'a, leading through a rural landscape scattered with pink and purple blossoms and alive with birdsong. Each is a four-mile round-trip, but since they meet in the middle, you can combine the two if you arrange to be picked up at the opposite end from which you started.

A short way back down towards Wailua from the Keahua Forestry Arboretum (see p.465), a dirt road signed as the **Kuilau Ridge Trail** leads north from Hwy-580. As the name suggests, it climbs up the gradual slope of Kuilau Ridge, with views of Wai'ale'ale away to the left, and the Kamali'i Ridge of the Makaleha Mountains ahead. For much of the way it runs through dense tropical foliage, with flashes of color provided by bright-red, raspberry-like thimbleberries, 'ōhi'a lehua blossoms down in the gullies, and a rich panoply of orchids. Not far beyond the picnic area that marks its halfway point, the trail rises sufficiently to let you see all the way to Līhu'e.

After just over two miles – perhaps 45 minutes of hiking – the trail seems to double back sharply on itself from a small clearing. In fact, as a very inconspicuous sign informs you, this is officially the end. Straight ahead of you is the highest, straightest segment of the Makaleha Mountains. A tiny footpath continues for a couple of hundred yards along the crest of Kuilau Ridge. You can push your way through the thorny undergrowth to get a few more views, including down to Kapa'a to your right, but it gradually gets more and more impenetrable. There is, in any case, no outlet to the hills.

You can also reach this point by following the **Moalepe Trail**, which leads from the top of the straight section of Olohena Road, six miles up from Kūhiō Highway. Park where the road turns to dirt, with one of its two tracks curving off north. It might look possible to drive the first few hundred yards of the trail, but it soon gets very rugged, by which time it's too narrow to turn around. Coming from this direction, too, you'll find the mountains confront you like a solid wall. You climb steadily, but the main ridge remains always on your right, and you never get near the summit. After half an hour the road becomes steep and rutted, but you're unlikely to lose your way; at the one confusing point, take the steeper option, towards the hills. At times, the ridge you're on has sheer drops to either side, but you're rarely aware of it: the vegetation is thick enough to meet up overhead in places, so you can't really see out. The clearing described above comes after around an hour's hiking, just beyond a final arduous climb.

Northeast Kauai

Once north of Kapa'a, the main highway stops running along the shoreline; it barely returns to sea level until Hanalei on the North Shore, twenty miles on. That leaves **Northeast Kauai** largely undisturbed by visitors. It is, in any case, sparsely inhabited, in part because it bears the full brunt of the trade winds and winter high seas. However, there are some spots where making your way down to the shore is rewarded by fine and often deserted beaches, though few are safe for swimming.

Donkey Beach

You can't see **Donkey Beach** from the highway, but the first beach north of Keālia can be reached via a simple half-mile downhill trail. Look out for parked cars just over half a mile beyond mile marker 11 and close to a blue emergency call box. Nearby, the path sets off through the ironwoods. Traditionally, this was plantation country, to which the sugar growers strove to restrict access; nowadays there's no difficulty about using the trail, though its precise legal status remains unclear. The beach is named after the donkeys that formerly hauled cane here, and were left to graze nearby for much of the year.

By the time you get to the crescent beach, curving north of Paliku Point, the tree cover has thinned out. The final slope is carpeted with white-flowered *naupaka*, a creeping cross between an ivy and a lily, and there's no shade on the sands. The surf created by the steep drop-off attracts skilled surfers, but makes Donkey Beach unsafe for swimming. Instead it's a popular spot for nude sunbathing, and is now known (not exclusively) as a gay hangout, though there have been reports of some anti-gay intimidation by local teenagers. (Note that nudity is illegal on all Hawaii's beaches, and the Kauai Police Department have a policy of enforcing that law.)

Anahola

Beyond Kapa'a, it's not possible to turn right from Kūhiō Highway until just after the 13-mile marker, where a side road heads straight down to the sea then doglegs north. **Anahola Beach County Park** lies almost immediately below. The park is the southernmost stretch of the spellbinding curve of sand that rims Anahola Bay, sheltered by Kahala Point and therefore safe for family swimming (except in winter). Surfing is forbidden at this end, but boogie-boarders and surfers are free to enjoy the rest of the bay. There's no picnic pavilion or snack bar, but restrooms and showers are located among the palms.

Anahola has long been the focus of great controversy. Most of the area is set aside as Hawaiian Homelands, to provide affordable housing for native Hawaiians, but state authorities have interpreted that to mean that they can sell basic homes to anyone with at least half-Hawaiian blood for sums that are way beyond the means of those locals who have lived at the beach for many years. Although the beach here is a pleasant and trouble-free place to spend the day, the campground is not recommended. If you really want to stay there, contact the county camping office in Līhu'e (see p.448).

Away from the beach, Anahola holds little to entice tourists, though the **Anahola Baptist Church**, set against a green mountain backdrop *mauka* of the highway, is worth a photograph. Nearby, just after the road crosses Ka'alua Stream, a tiny cluster of stores includes *Duane's Ono Char Burger* (Mon–Sat 10am–6pm, Sun 11am–6pm; ℡808/822-9181), where you can eat substantial, high-quality beef-burgers under a spreading monkey-pod tree. A basic burger costs under $5; one with avocado is $7; and further variations include "Local Girls" and "Local Boys" burgers – the distinction is in the cheese. Be sure to try a marionberry milkshake while you're here.

The only **accommodation** around is a sophisticated, gay-owned, Japanese-style B&B, 🕱 *Mahina Kai* (4933 'Aliomanu Rd, Anahola; ℡808/822-9451 or 1-800/337-1134, ⓦwww.mahinakai.com; three-night minimum stay; ⑤–⑧). A couple of miles down a quiet side road that leads off the highway at mile marker 14, this lovely property perches above long, narrow 'Aliomanu Beach. Originally marketed as being exclusively gay, it nowadays welcomes all visitors. Its well-kept gardens boast a ruined *heiau*. In addition to two tasteful suites and a smaller guest room, the main house offers living and meeting rooms for "executive retreats"; a separate cottage, with kitchen, sleeps up to four. There's a pool and hot tub, and mountain bikes and snorkeling equipment are provided for guests.

Moloa'a Bay and Larsen's Beach

Ko'olau Road, a minor but passable road that cuts off a large bend in the highway from the fruit stand half a mile south of mile marker 17 until shortly before mile marker 20, provides access to a couple of little-known beaches.

First comes the beach at **Moloa'a Bay**, accessible via Moloa'a Road, a right turn roughly a mile along. This road winds through verdant scenery to the unromantic remains of a long-abandoned sugar town. The deeply indented bay here is aligned so directly towards the trade winds that for most of the year it might as well not be sheltered at all. It's a pretty and very sandy spot, though, and in quiet periods the swimming and snorkeling can be excellent.

Larsen's Beach, further along, is most quickly reached from the north end of Ko'olau Road. Slightly over a mile down from there, a dirt road leads *makai* for a mile, leaving you with a five-minute walk at the end; access has been made delib-erately difficult to spare the beach from overuse. Named after a former manager of Kīlauea Plantation who had a beachfront home here, Larsen's Beach is a stretch of perfect sand that runs for over a mile, interrupted in the middle by Pākala Point. Once again swimming is not recommended, this time because it's so shallow and rocky this side of the reef. The snorkeling can be good when the water's calm, provided you stay well away from the strong currents around the stream channel. At low tide, local families wade out to the edge of the reef to gather the edible red seaweed known as *limu kohu*.

Na 'Āina Kai Botanical Gardens

Begun in the early 1980s as a labor of love by the former wife of *Peanuts* creator Charles Schultz, and open to the public since 2000, the **Na 'Āina Kai Botanical Gardens** stand half a mile down Wailapa Road, which heads oceanward from the Kūhiō Highway halfway between mile markers 21 and 22 (Tues–Thurs only; tours, to no fixed schedule, $25–70; ℡808/828-0525; ⓦwww.naainakai.com). The plural is appropriate; the 240-acre site holds thirteen separately themed gardens, including a desert garden, a palm garden, a Japanese garden, a hardwood plantation, and a bog. It's all very exquisite, though you may feel it's less of a thrill to see these beautiful plants in such a manicured setting, scattered with slightly twee bronze sculptures. The "Under the Rainbow" section, intended for children and the focus of the cheapest, $25 tours, holds slides and tunnels, and there's also an intricate, very green maze composed of mock-orange plants.

The North Shore

Kauai's **North Shore** may be the most astonishingly beautiful place you will ever see. If photographs of stunning Pacific landscapes – sheer green cliffs rippling with subtle variations of shade and light, and pristine valleys bursting with tropical vegetation – are what enticed you to come to Hawaii, this is where to find the real thing. On all the Hawaiian islands, the north and northeastern shores, being the most exposed to the ocean winds and rain, offer spectacular eroded scenery. As the oldest island, Kauai's coastline has had that much longer to be sculpted into fabulous formations, surpassing anything else in the state.

The **Nā Pali coast**, at the western end of the North Shore, is the most dramatic stretch. Its name literally means "the cliffs," but it's often spoken of in quasi-religious awe as "the Cathedral." Though inaccessible by car, it can be seen from offshore boats, up close along a superb hiking trail, from high above in Kōke'e Park (see p.517), or from helicopter sightseeing flights.

Thanks to high rainfall and local resistance to the expansion of tourism, Kauai's northern coast is far less developed than its east and south shores, though **Princeville** has grown to become a faceless clifftop resort, albeit redeemed by the sublime views from its most expensive hotels. Beyond Princeville you reach sea level by crossing the first of a succession of single-lane bridges, which serve to slow down not merely the traffic but the whole pace of life. **Hanalei Bay** is a ravishing mountain-framed crescent, home to the funky town of **Hanalei**, while the ten verdant miles to the end of the road are lined by beach after gorgeous beach.

For the sake of clarity, this book follows the highway from east to west. In reality, however, almost every visitor presses on nonstop to Hanalei, and you're more likely to explore the area around Kīlauea and Kalihiwai as you head back.

Kīlauea

The North Shore is commonly reckoned to start at Kauai's northernmost point, **KĪLAUEA**, which is more of a name on a map than a community in any real sense. Nine miles out of Anahola, a *makai* turn at a gas station leads from Kūhiō Highway past the small Kong Lung mall and two miles on to **Kīlauea Point**. This lonely promontory shares its name, which means "much spewing," with the active volcano on the Big Island, but here the reference is to crashing waves, not erupting lava. When it was built, in 1913, the 52-foot **lighthouse** at its tip boasted the largest clamshell lens in the world. The red-capped white shaft still stands proud, but it's no longer in use, having been supplanted by the otherwise inconspicuous fourteen-foot tower just beyond.

The lighthouse is now the focus of the **Kīlauea Point National Wildlife Refuge** (daily 10am–4pm; $3 per person; National Parks passes accepted), which protects such soaring Pacific seabirds as albatrosses, wedge-tailed shearwaters, red-footed boobies, frigatebirds, and red- and white-tailed tropicbirds. Thanks to a vigorous anti-development campaign, the refuge has since 1988 extended four miles east to Mokolea Point, while Moku'ae'ae Island just offshore is set aside for nesting. Displays in the visitor center near the lighthouse explain the natural history in great detail, and include a relief model of the whole island chain. Visitors can then walk out to the end of the promontory, where free binoculars

THE NORTH SHORE

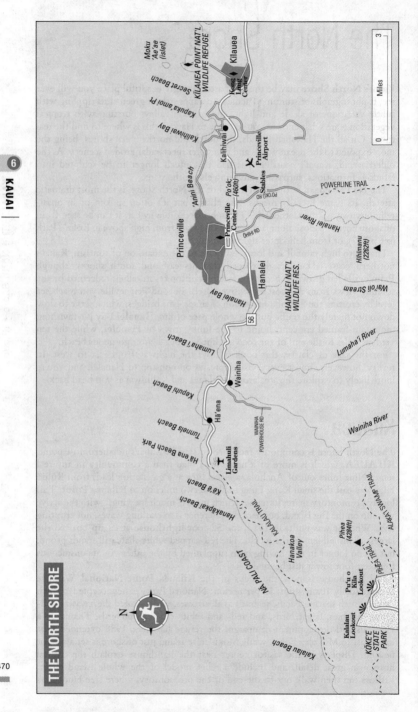

N

Moku
'Ae'ae (islet)

KĪLAUEA POINT NAT'L
WILDLIFE REFUGE

Kīlauea

Secret Beach

Kong Lung
Center

Kapuka'amoi Pt.

Kalihiwai Bay

Kalihiwai

Princeville
Airport

'Anini Beach

Princeville
Center

Po'okū
(460ft)

Stables

POWERLINE TRAIL

PO'OKŪ RD

'ŌHIHI RD

Princeville

Hanalei River

Hīhīmanu
(2262ft)

Hanalei Bay

Hanalei

56

HANALEI NAT'L
WILDLIFE RES.

Wai'oli Stream

Lumaha'i Beach

Lumaha'i River

Wainiha

Kēpuhi Beach

Hā'ena

Tunnels Beach

WAINIHA
POWERHOUSE RD

Wainiha River

Hā'ena Beach Park

Limahuli
Gardens

Kē'ē Beach

Hanakāpī'ai Beach

KALALAU TRAIL

NĀ PALI COAST

Hanakoa
Valley

Pihea
(4284ft)

PIHEA TRAIL

ALAKA'I SWAMP TRAIL

Pu'u o
Kila Lookout

Kalalau Lookout

KŌKE'E
STATE PARK

Kalalau Beach

0   3

Miles

enable you to get close-up views of all those birds, and also cast your eyes along the length of the North Shore. During the winter, this exposed spot becomes a prime venue for **whale-watching**.

In addition, every morning, rangers lead guided one-hour hikes to the summit of nearby Crater Hill for an overview of the whole area; reservations are essential (daily 10am; no additional charge; ☎808/828-0383).

Practicalities

Kīlauea abounds in freshly grown tropical fruit, with the orchards of the Guava Kai farm rising *mauka* of the highway. If you fancy something more than fruit, the **Kong Lung Center**, half a mile off the highway, is your best bet. Tucked into the center's garden courtyard is the *Kīlauea Bakery & Pau Hana Pizza* (Mon–Sat 6.30am–9pm; ☎808/828-2020), a friendly café-cum-bakery. It serves fresh breads and pastries to early risers, and then from 11am on, pizza (spiced up with smoked *ono* or tiger prawns) by the $5 slice. Its closest neighbor, the *Lighthouse Bistro* (daily 11am–2pm & 5.30–9.30pm; ☎808/828-0480), is a bit more formal, offering Italian-influenced food with an island twist, in a nice breezy setting. Lunchtime sandwiches and wraps cost around $12, while evening entrees like mango cherry chicken are $20–40.

Kalihiwai

As you drive along the highway, it's easy to pass through **KALIHIWAI**, a couple of miles west of Kīlauea, without noticing anything more than a high bridge spanning a valley. Glancing to either side at this curve is a bit of a risk, but reveals glimpses of a pretty bay to the north, and a tumbling waterfall off to the south.
Until a tsunami whisked away another bridge, lower down near the sea, it was possible to loop off the highway, look at the beach, and climb back up on the far side. **Kalihiwai Road** still exists, but with the bridge gone it now consists of two entirely separate segments, on either side of the river. Its eastern end is no longer marked; look out for the *makai* turning just short of milepost 24. The people who venture down here nowadays tend to know exactly where they're going and prefer to keep it to themselves.

Secret Beach

Long, golden **Secret Beach** – officially, Kauapea Beach – is one of Kauai's finest-looking strands of sand. It's "secret" partly because it's not visible from any road – in fact you barely see it before you step onto it – and partly because, despite the opposition of local landowners, it has a reputation for attracting campers and nudists.

To reach it, turn first onto the eastern half of Kalihiwai Road, as described above. Very soon after leaving the highway, Kalihiwai Road curves sharply to the left; turn right immediately beyond the bend to follow a reasonably well-surfaced dirt road, at first through a deep cutting. From a simple parking lot a few hundred yards down, a footpath skirts the edge of the hilltop, with fine homes to one side and a barbed-wire fence to the other, then drops down a steep but safe gully to the beach. You'll hear the crashing surf well before you see the sea.

The path emerges at an inlet set slightly back from the ocean. From rocky Kapuka'amoi Point, immediately to your left, the beach runs east for just over half a mile towards Kīlauea Point, with the lighthouse at its tip. Depending on the season, it's either a magnificent expanse of coarse-grained yellow sand or, as winter progresses, a narrow, shelving ribbon battered by immense surf.

△ Secret Beach

Even in its more placid moods, Secret Beach is not a particularly safe place to take a swim, but a long stroll is irresistible. Spinner dolphins can often be seen just offshore, while at the far end a waterfall cascades down the cliffs. You'll probably pass a handful of meditating nudists and would-be yogis scattered among the palms and fallen coconuts (though you should bear in mind that Kauai's police can and do arrest nude sunbathers here).

On the grassy slopes above the beach is *Secret Beach Hideaway*, whose umbrella name covers three lavishly equipped one-bedroom cottages sharing spacious gardens, and two full-sized houses (T 1-800/820-2862, W www.secretbeachkauai.com; ⑨).

Kalihiwai Beach

Kalihiwai Beach is at the point where Kalihiwai Road is cut in two, a mile or so down from the highway. It spreads beneath you as the road rounds its final sweeping curve, an exquisite little crescent that manages to hang on to its sand year-round. Residential properties line the *mauka* side of the road, but you can park in the shade of the high ironwoods rooted in the sand itself.

Surfers congregate below the cliffs to the east, while boogie-boarders and body-surfers ride into the heart of the beach, where the waves break across a broad sandbar. Rinse off the salt at the mouth of the Kalihiwai River, the put-in point for kayakers heading upstream (see opposite). There's hardly any sand on the far side of the river, at the end of the other half of the severed road.

Kalihiwai Falls

Whether or not you succeed in reaching **Kalihiwai Falls**, the broad waterfall visible from the highway bridge, it's worth making your way down to the meadows that fringe the riverbanks. Finding anywhere to park nearby is a problem, but if you can manage it you should be able to pick up a muddy trail that plummets down the hillside from the *mauka*, inland, side of the east end of the bridge.

The short drop into the valley involves clambering over fallen trees and hacking through giant spiders' webs. Once out on the flood plain, you join a dirt road that meanders through bucolic fields before curving back to meet the river. If you want to go any further than this tranquil little dell filled with songbirds, make sure you're not wearing or carrying anything you wouldn't want to get wet. The only way forward is to wade into the river and head upstream. The rocks underfoot are green and slimy, amorphous amphibians scuttle in and out of the water as you approach, and the undergrowth on either bank seems impenetrable, but it's a lovely place. With luck, you'll spot the often-overgrown trail that climbs the far bank. That soon leads to the falls, which consist of two separate cascades bubbling over a broad slope of exposed rock. If you haven't found the trail within a few hundred yards, you'll probably be forced to turn back, as the river grows progressively deeper.

Other ways to reach the falls include **kayaking** up the river from the beach, or **riding** down on horseback, through the woods up top (Princeville Ranch Stables offers tours; see p.474).

'Anini Beach

Superb beaches come thick and fast as you continue along the North Shore. Turn right on the other branch of Kalihiwai Road, as the highway climbs west of the bridge, and fork left after a couple of hundred yards to find yourself back down at sea level skirting a gorgeous long strip of yellow sand known as **'Anini Beach**. (It was originally called Wanini Beach, but the "W" broke off a sign many years ago, and the new name stuck.) No signs give the faintest inkling that the beach is here, but the road winds on for a full three miles, before reaching a dead end below Princeville.

All the way along, the beach is paralleled a couple of hundred yards out to sea by one of the longest reefs in the state. Coral reefs take millions of years to form, so it's not surprising that Hawaii's largest are in the oldest region of its oldest island. This one shields an expanse of shallow, clear turquoise water that offers some of the safest swimming on the North Shore. Snorkelers and scuba divers explore the reef; if it's calm enough, you can peek at the huge drop-off beyond its outer edge. Other than during winter surf, the only area to avoid is around the outlet of the 'Anini Stream at the western end, which is plagued by treacherous currents that sweep out through a gap in the reef. The inshore area is a good place to learn to **windsurf**, but surfing and boogie-boarding are largely precluded by the jagged coral where the waves break.

'Anini was once reserved as a fishing ground of the kings of Kauai, and it's still one of Kauai's most exclusive residential areas. That explains the **polo field** on the *mauka* side of the road; ponies graze nearby all week, and you might see a game of a Sunday afternoon. The almond trees on the beach side, however, shelter one of Kauai's best **campgrounds**, fully equipped with showers, rest rooms and picnic pavilions. Reservations can be made through the county parks office in Līhu'e (see p.448).

Po'okū

Roughly halfway between Princeville Airport and the Princeville resort itself, small, paved Po'okū Road runs off from the highway and into the hills. This area, officially known as Po'okū, was once the site of an important *heiau*, but now there's barely a building to be seen. Princeville Ranch Stables (☎808/826-6777, ⓦwww.princevilleranch.com) operates **horseback** riding tours from its headquarters just up from the turnoff. Choices include four-hour picnic trips to the top of Kalihiwai Falls (Mon–Sat 9.30am & 11am; $135 per person), two- or three-hour "private rides" (Mon–Sat; $140 and $185), and a ninety-minute "Paniolo Cattle Drive Ride" (no fixed schedule; $135).

The Powerline Trail

Apart from horseback riding, the main reason to head to Po'okū is to hike the thirteen-mile **Powerline Trail**, the broad dirt track that starts two miles down Po'okū Road. This was built for the local electricity company, whose cables stretch from pylon to pylon through the little-known interior of Kauai, but hikers are free to walk along it. Even if you just go a couple of miles rather than all the way to Keahua Arboretum (see p.465), it offers an easy and painless way to see high waterfalls and glorious flowers, without having to make any steep ascents. Starting with sweeping views of Hanalei Valley, it runs for most of its route along the crest of a ridge that parallels the Hanalei River.

Princeville

Despite being the main center for tourism on the North Shore, **PRINCEVILLE** is not exactly a town; it's too short of shops, public amenities, or even a permanent population. Instead it's a "planned resort community," consisting of neat rows of quasi-suburban vacation homes mixed in with a few larger condo complexes, two golf courses and a couple of luxury hotels. The general sense of placid domesticity is somehow heightened by the fact that the whole place is overlooked by the magnificent mountain wilderness that fills the western horizon.

Princeville stands on a well-watered plateau that abuts Hanalei Bay to the west and the open ocean to the north. Once this was the site of a sprawling grove of *hala* (pandanus) trees. In contrast to the common farming lands of Hanalei Valley below, it served as a residential area for the island's elite.

Soon after Europeans arrived on the island, the Russian-backed German adventurer **George Schäffer** renamed this district "Schäffertal" and constructed the short-lived **Fort Alexander** on the Pu'u Pōā headland now occupied by the *Princeville Resort*. The general outline of the fort is still discernible on the lawn near the main hotel entrance. In its centre, a small pavilion holds explanatory displays and enjoys superb views across the bay to Lumaha'i Beach and beyond. (For more on the bizarre Dr Schäffer, who was also responsible for Waimea's Fort Elizabeth, see p.510).

In the 1830s, the British consul **Richard Charlton** leased most of the land between Kīlauea and Hanalei to pasture a herd of one hundred cattle. He failed to pay his rent, however, and after the Great Mahele (see p.536), **Robert Crichton Wyllie**, Hawaii's Foreign Minister for twenty years, acquired the land. Wyllie built an overambitious sugar mill beside the Hanalei River, equipped with machinery imported from his native Scotland. He was visited in 1860 by King Kamehameha IV, Queen Emma and the young Prince Albert. The name "Princeville," adopted in Albert's honor, has stuck ever since, although Albert died two years later at the age of four. Just four months after Wyllie died in 1865, his nephew and heir committed suicide upon realizing that he had inherited a mountain of debt.

Sheep farming subsequently proved no more profitable than sugar, and Princeville was, until 1969, a cattle ranch. The entire area was then bought by an American

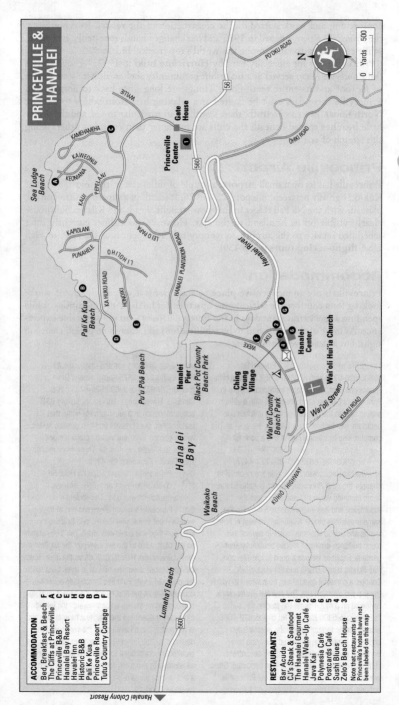

PRINCEVILLE & HANALEI

▲ Hanalei Colony Resort

ACCOMMODATION

Bed, Breakfast & Beach	F
The Cliffs at Princeville	C
Princeville B&B	E
Hanalei Bay Resort	H
Havalei Inn	G
Historic B&B	B
Pali Ke Kua	D
Princeville Resort	F
Tutu's Country Cottage	

RESTAURANTS

Bar Acuda	6
CJ's Steak & Seafood	1
The Hanalei Gourmet	6
Hanalei Wake-Up Café	2
Java Kai	6
Polynesia Café	6
Postcards Café	5
Sushi Blues	4
Zelo's Beach House	3

Note that restaurants in
Princeville's hotels have not
been labeled on this map

Sea Lodge Beach

Pali Ke Kua Beach

Pu'u Pōā Beach

KAMEHAMEHA

KAWEONUI
KEONIANA
KAUI
PEPELANI
KAPIOLANI
PUNAHELE
LEI O PAPA
LI HOLIHO
HONO'IKI
KA HUKU ROAD
HANALEI PLANTATION ROAD

Gate
House

Princeville Center

WAI'ILE

560

56

PO'OKU ROAD

ŌHIKI ROAD

Hanalei River

Hanalei Bay

Waikoko Beach

Lumaha'i Beach

560

Hanalei
Pier

Black Pot County
Beach Park

Wai'oli County Beach Park

Ching Young Village

Hanalei Center

Wai'oli Hui'ia Church

Wai'oli Stream

KUMU ROAD

KŪHIŌ HIGHWAY

WEKE

AKU

N

0   Yards   500

consortium, and work started on the construction of the **resort**. Its centerpiece, the *Princeville Resort*, opened in 1985 and has changed hands repeatedly ever since, while continuing to rank among the world's top tropical hideaways.

Princeville was hit especially hard by **Hurricane Iniki** in 1992; for several days the *Princeville Resort* served as a makeshift community shelter, despite losing most of its roof and its entire tenth floor. Things are long since back to normal, and Princeville these days can't be faulted as a relaxing base from which to explore North Kauai. Even so, in truth, there's nothing in particular to see, and the pretty little **beaches** tucked beneath the cliffs are no better than countless others along this stretch of coast.

Princeville Airport

Princeville has its own small **airport**, a couple of miles east of the resort, *mauka* of Kūhiō Highway between mileposts 25 and 26. It stands in a superb position on the plateau, with the Nā Pali ridges in full view straight ahead, and Kīlauea lighthouse clearly visible on its headland to the east. However, no airlines currently offer scheduled service to the airport, so its only role at present is as the base for Heli USA **flight-seeing tours** (see p.439).

Accommodation

Princeville is not an inexpensive **place to stay**, nor is it very lively. But if you're looking for a comfortable self-catering apartment it holds plenty of options, while spending a few extravagant days in the *Princeville Resort* is an unforgettable experience. As most of the resort had to be rebuilt after Iniki, there's no period charm in sight, but at least everything works.

The Cliffs at Princeville 3811 Edward Rd ☎808/826-6219 or 1-800/367-7052, ⓦwww.cliffs -princeville.com. Comfortable individual houses in Princeville's biggest condo complex, with a clifftop setting next to the golf course. Each unit has one bedroom, two bathrooms, a kitchen, and a *lānai*. The complex also has tennis courts and a pool. ❺–❻

Hanalei Bay Resort 5380 Honoiki Rd ☎808/826-6522 or 1-800/827-4427, ⓦwww.hanaleibayresort.com. This luxury resort is cheaper than the *Princeville Resort*, but shares the same stunning views of Hanalei Bay and the mountains, and has a short footpath down to the same irresistible beach. A wide assortment of hotel rooms and condo apartments are in several low-slung buildings arranged around beautifully kept gardens. Facilities include a good jungle-like pool, free floodlit tennis courts and the *Happy Talk Lounge*, a convivial cocktail bar from which to watch the sun set over Bali Hai. The *Bali Hai Restaurant* is reviewed on p.478. Rooms ❻, studios ❼, suites ❽

Pali Ke Kua 5300 Ka Huku Rd ☎808/826-9066; also available through the rental agents listed opposite. Roughly one hundred one- and two-bedroom condos, arrayed along the oceanfront cliffs above Pali Ke Kua Beach (see opposite). Often works out slightly cheaper than most Princeville options, but still offering pool, spa and full maid service, as well as a bar and restaurant. ❺–❻

Princeville B&B 3875 Kamehameha Drive ☎808/826-6733 or 1-800/826-6733 (US & Canada), ⓦwww.pixi.com/~kauai. Luxury B&B accommodation in a plush private home that features two guest rooms and two upscale suites, with a garden *lānai* and views across the golf course to Kīlauea Lighthouse. Three-night minimum stay. Rooms ❹, suites ❻–❽

Princeville Resort 5520 Ka Huku Rd ☎808/826-9644 or 1-866/, ⓦwww .princevillehotelhawaii.com. The opulent resort hotel that is Princeville's *raison d'être* has one of the world's most scenic panoramas, and facilities more luxurious than you could ever need. The lobby stands on the bluff, open to the full sweep of the Nā Pali mountains across Hanalei Bay. It's on the ninth floor; the hotel drops down the hillside in three tiers, with the pool and lovely Puʻu Pōā Beach (see opposite) accessible from the first floor of the lowest building. Some guest rooms are angled towards the inland mountains rather than the bay; few have *lānais*, and in the rest you can't even open the windows. From down below, the Princeville is far from attractive; its architects were obliged to keep it as inconspicuous as possible to avoid environmental offense. Even as a last-minute bargain, you're unlikely to find a room for under $500. ❾

Rental agencies

Shopping around for a **vacation apartment to rent** in Princeville is an unpredictable business. As a rule, the owner of each individual house or apartment is free to let the property through whichever agent they wish, so you may find identical lodgings at widely differing rates. Reckon on spending anything upwards of $125 per day for a one- or two-bedroom place, at least $200 for three bedrooms. You can expect discounts for longer stays amounting to roughly one "free" day per week. Most condos charge around $50 for (obligatory) once-weekly cleaning, and considerably more for daily service. Note that some of these agents also rent properties in the Hanalei area (particularly Hanalei North Shore Properties), as well as further along the North Shore.

Hanalei North Shore Properties ☎808/826-9622 or 1-800/488-3336, ⓦwww .rentalsonkauai.com.

Marc Resorts Hawaii ☎808/922-9700 or 1-800/535-0085, ⓦwww.marcresorts.com.

Remax Kauai ☎808/826-9675 or 1-877/838-8149, ⓦwww.remaxkauai.com.

The resort and its beaches

Not far west of milepost 27, just beyond the marked approach road to Princeville proper, the **Princeville Center** mall stands *makai* of Kūhiō Highway. Shielded from the road by orange *lehua* trees, it's a small cluster of low buildings arranged around separate courtyards and ringed by shady *lānais*. Apart from the Foodland supermarket, and the snack bars and restaurants described overleaf, the main business of the mall is **real estate**. Incidentally, the Princeville Center's Chevron gas station is the last before the end of the road.

The quietest and most secluded **beaches** in Princeville face north from the foot of the headland. That exposed position ensures that in winter the surf is too high for swimming and can obliterate the beaches altogether. At other times, however, stay within the reef and you can swim and snorkel safely. The three main alternatives are similar, each five to ten minutes' walk from the town along cliffside footpaths and stairways that can be slippery after rain.

Working from east to west, the first is **SeaLodge Beach**, which despite its rich thick sand and fine summer snorkeling is often deserted. One route down starts at the western edge of the ugly *SeaLodge* condo complex, but access is easier if you continue along the driveway at the end of Keoniana Road, then drop through some of Princeville's few surviving *hala* trees. Next comes the **Queen's Bath**, where there's little sand, but you can bathe in natural lava pools; it's reached by a meandering path off Kapiolani Road. **Pali Ke Kua Beach**, also known (especially by surfers) as **Hideaways**, lies down a steep staircase at the end of a path from the tennis courts of the *Pali Ke Kua* condos, not far from the *Princeville Resort*. Two distinct patches of sand nestle in the rocks, and the snorkeling here is great in summer, when you stand a good chance of spotting turtles, dolphins, and even monk seals.

Larger, sandier **Pu'u Pōā Beach**, below the *Princeville Resort*, is around the corner within Hanalei Bay. Set at the edge of a marsh that still holds vestiges of an ancient fishpond, it commands lovely views of the rising Nā Pali ridges. The inshore swimming and snorkeling is good; further out the waves get much higher. This is a perfect spot to watch surfers swirling and plummeting at the mouth of the bay. Access – as ever – is open to all, though the only facilities, back from the sea, are reserved for hotel guests (who can rent surfboards, kayaks, and other equipment). Walk a short way south to reach the Hanalei River, which should be shallow enough for you to wade across to Black Pot Beach County Park (see p.482). Hanalei itself is not far beyond.

Restaurants

All the hotel **restaurants** listed below are happy to welcome nonguests, but the only place where you can browse menus looking for a bite to eat is in the Princeville Center, next to the highway.

Bali Hai Restaurant *Hanalei Bay Resort*, 5380 Honoiki Rd ☎808/826-6522. Roomy, cool restaurant under an enormous *hala*-thatched roof, with superb views across a lagoon-style pool to Hanalei Bay and within earshot of the live jazz performed most evenings in the adjoining *Happy Talk Lounge*. Breakfast tends to be unexciting hotel food, but the dinner menu has a definite Pacific Rim tinge, with sashimi and blackened *ahi* on the list of appetizers ($12–15), and an assortment of Asian-influenced fresh fish entrees, as well as traditional steak preparations, for $30–35. Daily 7–11am & 5.30–9.30pm.

Café Hanalei *Princeville Resort* 5520 Ka Huku Rd ☎808/826-9644. The (slightly) less formal option at the *Princeville Resort*, with a great view and open daily for all meals. The overpriced buffet breakfasts ($19 continental, $26 full) and light salad lunches are nothing special, but the Pacific Rim-style dinners are consistently good, and Japanese alternatives, including sushi, are always available. Typical entrees such as steamed snapper or Kauai coffee rack of lamb, cost $30–40, or you can opt for a $58 three-course set menu.

There's also a magnificent $50 seafood buffet on Friday, and a $42 champagne brunch on Sunday. Daily 6.30am–2.30pm & 5.30–9.30pm.

CJ's Steak & Seafood Princeville Center ☎808/826-6211. The largest and most conventional of the Princeville Center places. It's open for $8–12 burger and sandwich lunches, and full dinners, when entrees of steak, chicken, ribs or fish cost $25 and upwards. Cocktails are available all day, and there's live Hawaiian music on Fri and Sat evenings. Mon–Fri 11.30am–2.30pm & 6–9.30pm, Sat & Sun 6–9.30pm.

La Cascata *Princeville Resort* 5520 Ka Huku Rd ☎808/826-9644. Smart, romantic resort restaurant, serving fine Italian cooking with Pacific ingredients. The menu features inexpensive soups and salads, even a cheeseburger, but a full meal will cost around $56 a head for the food alone – in fact there's a $65 three-course set menu. Among à la carte appetizers are pan-seared scallops for $18, while entrees (about $30–40) include grilled beef tenderloin and crispy-skin *onaga* (snapper). Go early for a view of the sun setting over Bali Hai. Daily 6–10pm.

Hanalei

With its perfect semicircular curve, fronted by tumbling white surf, fringed with coconut palms and yellow sand, and backed by jagged green peaks, **Hanalei Bay** is a strong candidate for the most beautiful bay in Hawaii. An easy thirty-mile drive from Līhu'e, it's not exactly inaccessible, but other than the *Princeville Resort*, peeking down from the east, it has so far been spared major development.

The local will to resist change is greatly aided by the fact that the Hanalei River, which meanders its way into the eastern side of the bay, can only be crossed by means of a flimsy single-lane bridge. What's more, this is just the first of seven similar bridges before the end of the road: so long as attempts to widen or replace them can be thwarted, the North Shore should remain unspoiled. Even its largest community, **Hanalei** itself, is a relatively tiny affair, surviving partly on traditional agriculture and partly on tourism.

Until the Hanalei was bridged in 1912, all travelers, along with their horses and baggage, were hauled across the river on a raft, guided by ropes suspended between a mango tree on one side and a plum tree on the other. The flood plain to the west still constitutes one of the largest surviving **wetland** areas in the state. Ancient Hawaiians waded knee-deep in gooey *lo'i* in order to grow taro to make into *poi*. Later attempts to cultivate sugar or coffee were unsuccessful, but for almost a century most of the valley was given over to the paddy fields of generations of Chinese and Japanese immigrants. Now, however, it has reverted to taro production, and the landscape and its fauna are returning to their original state.

△ Hanalei Valley

Keep in mind that when driving on the North Shore, if an oncoming vehicle is crossing a narrow bridge towards you, you're expected to allow up to three or four cars behind it to cross as well.

Accommodation

To the casual visitor, Hanalei seems to hold very little **accommodation**; the nearest sizeable lodging options are back in Princeville, or the *Hanalei Colony Resort* further down the coast (see p.485). However, for short-term stays, there's a handful of **B&Bs**, while a high proportion of the homes in Hanalei can be **rented** by the week through agencies such as those listed on p.477.

Bed, Breakfast & Beach PO Box 748, Hanalei HI 96714 ☏ 808/826-6111, ⊛ www.bestofhawaii.com /hanalei. Well-furnished private home, just back from the center of the beach near the foot of Aku Road, where each of the three separate B&B rooms has its own en-suite bath. No credit cards. ④–⑤

Hanalei Surf Board House 5459 Weke Rd ☏ 808/826-9825, ⊛ www.hanaleisurfboardhouse .com. English-owned B&B, just back from the beach, that offers two en-suite studio units; one is bursting with Elvis memorabilia, the other has a "cowgirl" theme, and there's a three-night minimum stay. No credit cards. ⑤

Tutu's Country Cottage PO Box 748, Hanalei HI 96714 ☏ 808/826-6111, ⊛ www.bestofhawaii .com/hanalei. Carolyn Barnes, owner of Bed, Breakfast & Beach (see left), also rents out this central detached two-bedroom cottage, available by the week only. No credit cards. Equivalent daily rate ⑤

⑥ Hanalei National Wildlife Refuge

Immediately west of Princeville, just before Kūhiō Highway drops towards the river, an overlook on its *mauka* side offers the best view you can get of the full expanse of Hanalei Valley. The flat valley floor stretches west to the bay and south into the hills, crisscrossed by channels that create a green and brown patchwork of fields. As it curves its way around Hīhīmanu ("Beautiful") Mountain, the Hanalei River nestles between gentle grass slopes.

Most of what you can see belongs to the **Hanalei National Wildlife Refuge**. Hawaii's natural wetlands have dwindled to cover just five percent of their former area, and the population of waterbirds has declined in step. By helping farmers to reintroduce taro, the refuge provides an ideal habitat for waterbirds. The birds feed in the young taro patches, find shelter in the plants as they grow, and eventually breed on the mud flats and islands that appear during the annual cycle of planting, irrigation and harvesting. Among the indigenous species here are the *'alae 'ula,* the Hawaiian gallinule or mud hen, with its yellow-tipped red beak, seen March through August; the *'alae ke'o ke'o,* or Hawaiian coot, seen March through September; the *koloa maoli,* Hawaiian duck, seen December through May; and the *ae'o,* or Hawaiian black-necked stilt, with its long red legs, which nests between March and July. The river itself holds introduced and native fishes, such as the *o'opu* or native goby, and shrimp.

You'll get a close-up look at the valley as you cross the bridge down below. Turn left as soon as you're over and you can drive for a couple of miles along Ohiki Road, but venturing into the refuge is forbidden. The easiest way to go exploring is to rent a **kayak** (rental outlets are listed on p.443) and paddle your way upstream. It's a lovely ride, though if you start from the ocean you're in for a long haul before you reach the taro farms.

It is also possible to **hike** up into the hills, for further stupendous views of the valley, by taking the **'Okolehau Trail**, which starts at a footbridge near the Chinese cemetery on the right of Ohiki Road, 0.6 miles from the bridge. The first section of this literally breathtaking climb follows a red-dirt road immediately to the left of the cemetery that's way too rutted to be passable in any vehicle. Two thirds of a mile up, at a massive utility-company pole, you double back sharply to the left onto a much narrower and even steeper foot trail. The path rapidly mounts a slick ridge that overlooks not only the valley and Hanalei Bay, but also more verdant valleys in the opposite direction towards distant Anahola. The trail ultimately dead-ends two miles up from the road, though you can turn back well before then and still be satisfied you've seen some of the best scenery Kauai has to offer, in a round-trip hike of around ninety strenuous minutes.

Hanalei town

The town of **HANALEI** stretches for several hundred yards along the highway, around half a mile on from the bridge and a couple of hundred yards in from the beach. Little more than a village – you can almost be out the far end before you realize you've even arrived – it's home to an ever-changing mixture of laid-back old-timers, spaced-out New Age newcomers, and hyperactive yuppies and Gen-Xers. Sadly, year on year, it feels less like Kauai and more like a colony of California.

The main center of activity lies at the point where two low-slung, somewhat ramshackle shopping malls face each other across the street. On the *mauka* side, the assorted buildings of the **Hanalei Center** include a converted school, and hold several restaurants and snack bars as well as a handful of upmarket clothing and gift stores. The Yellowfish Trading Co, tucked away in the back (☎808/826-1227), is highly recommended as a source of hard-to-find Hawaiiana, including some great 1950s souvenirs. The **Ching Young Village** opposite is a bit larger than it first looks, as it stretches a little way back from the road. In addition to a couple of outdoor-adventure and equipment-rental companies, it offers some grocery stores, and some cheaper eating options.

Hanalei was the location of Kauai's second Christian **mission** (the first was in Waimea), established in 1834 by Rev William Alexander. The mission buildings, gathered in a large meadow at the western end of town, are now Hanalei's only historic sites. The most photogenic is the clapboard **Wai'oli Hui'ia Church**, with its stained-glass windows and neat belfry. Painted bright green to blend in with the hills, and shaded by tall palms, it's a quintessential little Hawaiian church. It's a lot newer than its neighbors, however, having been built in 1912. Set back to the right is its predecessor, the original **Wai'oli Church**, which was erected in 1841. This long, low building, surrounded by a broad *lānai* and topped with a high slanted roof, now serves as the Wai'oli Social Hall.

Behind the two churches is the **Wai'oli Mission House** (tours Tues, Thurs & Sat 9am–3pm; donations welcome; ☎808/245-3202). Although it began life as the New England-style home of the Alexanders, it's better known now for having housed Abner and Lucy **Wilcox**, who ran the mission from 1846 until 1869. Members of the Wilcox dynasty became some of Kauai's leading landowners; you'll see the family name all over the island. (For example, Grove Farm in Līhu'e was founded by George Wilcox, see p.451). Family descendants lived in this house until the late 1970s, but it's now open for tours. The place is outfitted with nineteenth-century artifacts (though few belonged to the Wilcoxes themselves) and provides a real sense of long-ago life in Hanalei. Out back you'll find the restored kitchen garden and family taro patch.

Hanalei Bay and its beaches

Hanalei means a *lei-* or crescent-shaped bay, and **Hanalei Bay** is lined for its entire sweeping two-mile curve with a wide shelf of yellow sand. Though it constitutes one of Kauai's very best **beaches**, each of its named segments has different characteristics, and not all are safe for swimming. **Weke Road**, which runs along the edge of the bay in Hanalei, is exclusively residential.

The underwater map of the bay is a lot more complex than what you see on the surface. The headlands to either side are ringed by coral reefs, but the channel through the middle is barely protected from the force of the ocean. While the resultant high surf places Hanalei among Kauai's favorite **surfing** destinations, it makes it a less than ideal **harbor**.

In May of 1824, the royal yacht of King Liholiho, the son and heir of Kamehameha the Great, foundered in the bay. No lives were lost, but teams of locals failed to haul the *Pride of Hawaii* ashore, and it swiftly broke up. Marine archeologists finally located the wreckage in the mid-1990s, and have retrieved a treasure trove of historical artifacts. At the time of the sinking, Kauaians saw a certain justice in the fact that the yacht had been used three years before to kidnap their own ruler, Kaumuali'i (see p.436), and that the loss occurred at the exact moment that Kaumuali'i died in exile.

For the next century, Hanalei was a significant port, with the valley's rice crop being shipped out and cattle and other supplies being shipped in. The jetty at the mouth of Hanalei River reached its present length in 1912 (obviously a busy year in Hanalei), but Hawaii has long since ceased to be a net exporter of rice or taro, and these days the bay is used only by pleasure craft. During the summer it welcomes private yachts from around Hawaii, as well as a surprising number of trans-Pacific sailors; in winter it falls quiet.

The beach from which the pier juts out is officially **Black Pot Beach County Park**. Long a local hangout – the "black pot" was a large communal cooking pot – this site was bought up by developers in the late 1960s. After years of failing to obtain the necessary permits, the would-be builders sold the land back to the county, and it was set aside as a public park. Strong currents render it unsafe for swimming in winter, but it's busy the rest of the year. Until a few years ago, this was also the main launching point for Nā Pali boat trips. However, as a result of environmental damage to the river's mouth caused by the daily crowds, the trips have now been greatly curtailed (see p.490).

Hanalei Pavilion Beach County Park, a short distance west, is similar to Black Pot Beach. When the surf isn't too ferocious, the lack of inshore rocks makes it a suitable spot to develop your surfing or boogie-boarding skills; otherwise, settle for enjoying a picnic in the open-fronted pavilion. With permission from the county parks office in Līhu'e (see p.448), you can **camp** here on Fridays, Saturdays and holidays only.

The next beach along, **Wai'oli Beach County Park**, is marked by the fine stand of ironwood trees responsible for its nickname, "Pinetrees Park." Currents that swirl over the offshore sandbar, partly caused by Wai'oli Stream as it flows into the bay just to the west, lend it the more prosaic name of "Toilet Bowls." This is the most popular launching point for the champion surfers who swim right out to the colossal waves in the mouth of the bay.

On the far side of Wai'oli Stream, right beside the highway towards the western end of the bay – and further than you'd choose to walk from central Hanalei – **Waikoko Beach** is the safest of the beaches for year-round family swimming. Thanks to the broad stretch of reef that shield them, the waters just offshore remain placid even in winter. The sea floor is sandy underfoot, and snorkelers can approach the coral with relative ease.

Restaurants

The **restaurants** of Hanalei rank among the most enjoyable on Kauai, though most aim for a family or alternative feel rather than a romantic atmosphere. None has sea views, but the mountains and gardens compensate for that. Several breakfast places open at, or even before, dawn to enable early-bird hikers, surfers and boaters to stock up. **Fast-food** options in the Hanalei Center include *Bubba Burgers* and the *Wishing Well*, which serves anything from shave ice, smoothies and *saimin* to BBQ chicken and ribs. In the Ching Young Village, try *Pizza Hanalei* or the *Village Snack and Bakery Shop*.

While several Hanalei restaurants put on **live music** in the evenings, perhaps the most enjoyable place to hang out and listen to gentle Hawaiian sounds is *Tahiti Nui* (☏808/826-6277), a former eatery at Aku Road in the center of town that now functions primarily as a bar. There's no fixed music schedule, but if you're around for a few days there's likely to be something going on.

Bar Acuda Hanalei Center ☎808/826-7081. This high-class, dinner-only restaurant, geared towards Spanish-style tapas, creates a bit of a conundrum. Its setting and decor, partly indoors and partly on a mountain-view terrace, across from the Ching Young Village in central Hanalei, are unarguably attractive. And the food is very good, ranging from sub-$10 dishes like house-cured chorizo sausage, by way of roasted scallops for $12 or braised short ribs for $14, up to whole baked fish or grilled steak for almost $30. However, it seems to attract a braying, Californian crowd, totally at odds with the traditional laidback ambience of Hanalei. Daily except Mon 5–10pm.

The Hanalei Gourmet Hanalei Center ☎808/826-2524. Mountain breezes blow through Hanalei's former schoolhouse to cool the open deck at the front. There you can enjoy tasty deli sandwiches ($7–10), salads, fish dips, or boiled shrimp, as well as $20–27 dinner specials, such as pan-fried crab cakes or mac-nut fried chicken, until 9.30pm. The same menu is available from the takeout counter alongside, at the same prices. The bar is a busy center of local life, with live music every night except Mon & Thurs: jazz, Hawaiian (especially for the Sun jam, 6–9pm), R&B, reggae, and rock 'n' roll. Daily 8am–10pm.

Hanalei Wake-Up Café 148 Aku Rd ☎808/826-5551. Next to *Tahiti Nui* as you come into Hanalei from the east. Big breakfasts, such as omelets and "custard French toast," at low prices, are served from the crack of dawn. Daily 6–11am.

🏃 Java Kai Hanalei Center ☎808/826-6717. Small, friendly espresso bar across from the Ching Young Village. Hanalei's best bet for an early pick-me-up breakfast, with a nice *lānai* for specialty coffees and creamy waffles. Hours vary slightly seasonally, but typically it's open daily 6.30am–7pm.

Polynesia Café Ching Young Village ☎808/826-1999. Large deli/café where the eat-in seating is in a sort of open-sided bandstand a few yards away.

They claim to serve "gourmet food on paper plates"; in fact the $16 daily dinner special, such as *mahimahi* green curry, is well below gourmet standards, and given the lack of service is a little overpriced, but the regular menu holds some real bargains, including a $7 Hawaiian Variety Plate of *kālua* pork, *ahi poke* and *lomi lomi* salmon, *char siu* chicken for $7, and similarly cheap sandwiches and Chinese and Mexican offerings. Daily 8am–9pm.

Postcards Café Kūhiō Hwy ☎808/826-1191. Seafood and vegetarian restaurant housed in a former museum, *mauka* of the highway from Princeville as it comes into Hanalei. Appetizers include homegrown taro fritters or summer rolls, both $9. Vegetarian entrees – some featuring tofu, others simply a mixture of sautéed or roasted vegetables – cost around $18, while fresh fish specials, cooked in a variety of styles, are more like $20–30. Daily 6–9pm.

Sushi Blues Ching Young Village ☎808/826-9701. Bustling second-floor dining room above the Ching Young shops, with table seating and a sushi counter. An enthusiastic crowd is drawn by the top-notch Japanese food as well as the live music (Wed, Thurs, Sat & Sun), which includes jazz, reggae, Hawaiian and blues, and usually keeps going long after the food service has ended. Sushi is sold by the piece ($4–10) and in a full range of combos, including good-value options at $17 and $22, and is available flash-fried. You can also get fresh fish entrees for $20. Daily except Mon 6–10pm.

Zelo's Beach House Restaurant & Grill Kūhiō Hwy at Aku Rd ☎808/826-9700. This funky roadhouse is not in fact by the beach, but in the heart of Hanalei. Nevertheless, it's a great place for a meal or cocktail. Salads, burgers, sandwiches, tacos and wraps are served during the day; in the evening there are pasta dinner entrees for $16–20, as well as pork, ribs, or tasty fresh fish specials for around $25. Mon–Thurs & Sun 11am–3.30pm & 5.30–10pm, Fri & Sat 11am–3.30pm & 5.30–11pm.

To the end of the road

As it continues westward along the coast beyond Hanalei Bay, Hwy-56 becomes Hwy-560, and acquires the feel of a rural lane. For the half-dozen miles until the sheer Nā Pali cliffs definitively bar any further progress, it's lined by a succession of ravishing beaches. Some, like famous **Lumaha'i Beach**, are photogenic but treacherous; others are perfectly suited for surfing, snorkeling, diving or swimming. Small private homes nestle in the undergrowth to either side, but there are no real towns or even villages, and only at **Hā'ena** has there been any commercial development.

Lumaha'i Beach

At the western edge of Hanalei Bay, just where a sharp hairpin bend in the highway finally takes you out of sight of Princeville, a makeshift roadside parking lot well before milepost 5 serves as both overlook and trailhead for **LUMAHA'I BEACH**. With its broad yellow sands, crashing white surf and green mountain backdrop, Lumaha'i has starred in countless movies and TV dramas such as *South Pacific* and *The Thorn Birds*, but always seems to have enough space to accommodate another couple of wistful tourists. Romantic daydreams are a much safer way to spend time here than venturing into the water: currents are consistently ferocious, and there's no reef to stop unwary bathers from being swept far out to sea.

From beside the "Danger" sign at the head of the overlook, an easy trail drops down to the east end of the beach. Most of Lumaha'i's sand migrates here in winter; at other times the stark outcrops of black lava emerge more fully from the sea, making it clearer why this area is sometimes regarded as a separate beach in its own right, named Kahalahala.

In summer the sand piles in opulent drifts at the far end, two miles west near the mouth of the Lumaha'i River, occasionally blocking it altogether. That can make swimming in the river a possibility – it's one of the least spoiled in all Hawaii, bursting with native fish. For most of the year, however, it's extremely dangerous, with flash floods raging down from the mountains and the seabed shelving away very steeply immediately offshore. Access to the beach's western end is straightforward, with a sea-level parking lot amid the ironwoods alongside the river.

Wainiha and Kepuhi

At a sweeping turn in the road shortly before milepost 7, Hwy-560 crosses two branches of the **Wainiha River** in quick succession, over a two-part wooden bridge. Sinuous Wainiha Valley winds several miles inland from this point, though unless you take a helicopter ride, you can only see its full extent by walking the full length of the mind-boggling Alaka'i Swamp Trail (see p.522). Now all but uninhabited, the valley once held a sizeable agricultural community. Historians

△ Lumaha'i Beach

wrestling over the existence of the *menehune*, said to have been the first settlers of Hawaii (see p.531), have been intrigued to note that during the first census of Kauai, early in the nineteenth century, 65 people in Wainiha actually characterized themselves as *menehune*.

What the Hawaiians referred to as the "unfriendly waters" of Wainiha were harnessed in 1906 by the construction of a hydroelectric generating station a couple of miles upstream. It's still in use, with a chain of pylons carrying electricity around eastern Kauai (along the Powerline Trail; see p.474) to the south coast. The wharf, warehouses and light railroad built along the shoreline at the same time were, however, destroyed by the tsunami of April 1946.

Neither **Wainiha Beach**, immediately west of the bridges, nor **Kepuhi Beach** just beyond that, is recommended for swimming. Silt churned up by the river keeps the sea almost permanently cloudy at Wainiha, precluding the growth of a protective reef, so the currents are capable of dragging swimmers way out into the ocean. There is a reef at Kepuhi, much frequented by local fishermen, but it is punctuated by so many gaps that it's equally unsafe.

Palm-fringed Kepuhi Beach nonetheless makes a superb setting for the North Shore's westernmost **hotel**, a delightful tropical retreat just two miles from the start of the Nā Pali coast. The highly recommended oceanfront ☆ *Hanalei Colony Resort* (☏808/826-6235 or 1-800/628-3004, ⓦwww.hcr.com; garden view ⑥, ocean view ⑦) consists of a small cluster of two-story buildings following the curve of an exposed headland, affording magnificent beach and ocean views, and arrayed around a central lawn. Each of the units has two bedrooms and at least one bathroom, plus a kitchen, living room and *lānai*, though no phones or TVs; there's also a pool and hot tub, as well as a day spa that offers therapeutic massage treatments and even yoga classes. Between June and mid-September, and at Christmas, rates rise by around ten percent, and there's a five-night minimum stay at those times.

Housed in a seafront building that shares its parking lot with the *Hanalei Colony Resort*, and enjoying great views at lunchtime, the *Mediterranean Gourmet* **restaurant** (Mon–Sat 11am–9pm; ☏808/826-9875) serves pretty good meat and fish entrees, costing around $20 for dinner. Virtually every dish seems to come with copious quantities of the owner's delicious home-made hummus. A separate room beside the doorway holds a small espresso-and-sandwiches café, the *Nā Pali Art Gallery & Coffee Shop* (daily 7am–7pm; ☏808/826-1844).

Shortly before the *Hanalei Colony Resort*, three tenths of a mile past the 7-mile marker, *Hale Hoʻo Maha*, 7083 Alamihi Rd (☏808/826-7083 or 1-800/851-0291, ⓦwww.aloha.net/~hoomaha; ⑤) is a four-bedroom **B&B** a short walk from Tunnels Beach, where guests share use of a kitchen, living room and whirlpool spa.

A short distance beyond the *Hanalei Colony Resort*, the *YMCA of Kauai Camp Naue* (reservations PO Box 1786, Līhuʻe, HI 96766; ☏808/246-9090; ①) is a real bargain for budget travelers. **Dorm beds** in either of its two simple oceanfront bunkhouses cost $12 per night (bring your own linen), and you can also set up a tent on the four-acre grounds for $10.

Tunnels Beach and Hāʻena Beach County Park

From the first headland beyond Kepuhi Beach, just beyond milepost 8 and barely visible from the highway, a huge reef curves like a fishhook out to sea. In the calmer summer months, the lagoon it encloses is a safe anchorage for light sailing boats, as well as a great family snorkeling spot. Together with its fringe of golden sand, this popular area is known as **Tunnels Beach**, though divers and surfers dispute whether the name comes from its underwater lava tubes or its curling winter waves.

Taylor Camp

A dense grove of trees at the mouth of Limahuli Stream – roughly a mile east of Kē'ē Beach, and only accessible by walking along the shore – was the site of the once-notorious **Taylor Camp**.

Elizabeth Taylor's brother Howard bought this seven-acre seafront plot in 1969. Having cleared the land and constructed a dirt road, however, he found that it was due to become a state park. Unable to sell the property or build there himself, he invited a group of hippies then camping on the beach to take it over. They survived for seven years, occupying tents and free-form "structures" without electricity or basic sanitation. Most lived on welfare, while some made money on the side by growing marijuana.

Following publicity given to a "tree house" built by a former Berkeley architecture student, hordes of would-be back-to-the-landers – and surfers above all – were lured to Kauai. More tree houses were built, in a style one journalist called "Jimi Hendrix meets the Swiss Family Robinson." Before long there was simply no more room, and a waiting list for tree houses was set up. Further media attention came when Liz Taylor was photographed wearing "jewelry" produced at the camp by stringing together the *puka* shells scattered along the beach. For the next year or two, anklets, bracelets and necklaces of these tiny shells commanded high prices, and beaches across the entire state were all but stripped bare.

Howard Taylor himself almost never went to the camp, and simply let the matter lie, building another house near Tunnels Beach. Sanitary regulations and general moral outrage motivated the authorities to instigate eviction proceedings, but by the time Taylor succumbed to pressure and handed the land over to the state in 1974, some campers had been there long enough to be entitled to claim squatters' rights. It took three more years, and guarantees of resettlement, before the camp was finally bulldozed.

Tunnels can be accessed via a dirt road at the headland or by walking back to its western end from roadside **Hā'ena Beach County Park**. Manoa Stream ensures that the latter beach lacks a reef of its own, so it's no place to swim; but palms aplenty, broad lawns and crisp white sands make it ideal for picnicking or lazing. It also offers a well-maintained **campground** (get permission from the county authorities in Līhu'e; ℡808/241-6660; see p.448). While convenient to the Kalalau Trail, it's slightly too public for most campers to feel comfortable about leaving their gear unattended during the day. Across the highway from the beach, **Maniniholo Dry Cave** is a lava tube that once lay below sea level. Beyond its wave-widened entrance, it penetrates a considerable distance into the mountains, without being particularly interesting or rewarding to explore.

Limahuli Gardens

Not far beyond Hā'ena Beach, and halfway between mileposts 9 and 10, **Limahuli Gardens** (Tues–Fri & Sun 9.30am–4pm) are part of the private nonprofit National Tropical Botanical Garden, which has another branch close to Po'ipū on the South Shore (see p.503). The grounds can be seen either on self-guided tours (adults $15, under-13s free), or, by reservation, on 2hr 30min guided tours ($25; ℡808/826-1053; ⊛www.ntbg.org). The gardens are set in a narrow, steep-sided valley reminiscent of Maui's 'Iao Valley (see p.321); the fifteen acres nearest the highway can be explored via a half-mile walking trail, while a thousand more inaccessible acres further back are a natural preserve. Centuries-old terraces along the Limahuli Stream have been restored to cultivate taro in the ancient style, in small pond-like enclosures known as *lo'i*. Colorful native trees nearby include plumeria, with its white *lei*-making flowers; the *pāpala kepau*, whose sticky sap was used to trap birds; and several varieties of *'ōhi'a lehua*. From higher up the slopes, as the path skirts the cool mountain forest, you get superb views of the ocean, and there's a strong possibility of seeing whales in winter.

Hā'ena State Park and Kē'ē Beach

The western boundary of Hā'ena Beach County Park abuts the eastern edge of **Hā'ena State Park**, where the aim is to protect natural and archeological features from development rather than to display them to tourists. For most of its length, private residences stand between the road and the ocean, and only experienced surfers bother to make their way along the rocky seashore.

Few visitors see more of the park than lovely **Kē'ē Beach**, right where the highway ends alongside milepost 10. Swarms of vehicles are usually parked here, in the roadside mud or under the thick trees that back the beach, but the beach itself remains glorious. Swimming and snorkeling from its steep shelf of yellow sand is almost irresistible, but despite the usual crowds it's only safe when the sea is at its calmest. At this time, the waters inshore of the reef are ideal for fish-watching; at other times the surf that surges over the reef rushes out with even stronger force through gaps in it, especially at the western (left) end. Kē'ē Beach is a lovely spot for a sunset stroll; the further east you walk, away from the road, the further west it's possible to see along the majestic coastline.

The Tale of Hi'iaka and Lohi'au

Several sites around Kē'ē Beach are renowned as the setting for the best-known legend of ancient Hawaii. However, no two sources agree exactly on what took place between its three central figures – **Pele** the volcano goddess, her sister **Hi'iaka**, and the Kauaian chief **Lohi'au**.

One version begins with Pele lying asleep in her home at Kīlauea Crater on the island of Hawaii, and finding her dreams filled with sweet, mysterious music. In search of its source, her spirit left her body and set off from island to island, until she finally came to this remote spot. The principal performer in the *hula* celebration that was taking place was the young chief Lohi'au, to whom Pele was uncontrollably drawn. After three days of blissful (though unconsummated) love, their idyll was shattered when Pele's slumbering body back at Kīlauea was awoken by her sister, Hi'iaka.

Pele despatched Hi'iaka to fetch Lohi'au. Her perilous voyage to Kauai involved countless obstacles on all the other islands, which Hi'iaka only survived thanks to the magical aid of her companion *wahine 'ōma'o*, or "green woman." Arriving on Kauai she found that Lohi'au had hanged himself in grief and lay buried nearby. She captured his free-floating spirit and managed to force it back into the corpse through a slit in the big toe, whereupon he rushed off to purify himself by surfing from Kē'ē Beach.

As they returned to Kīlauea, however, Hi'iaka and Lohi'au fell in love with each other. Lohi'au was repelled when he finally saw Pele's true bodily form (she was an elderly witch), and the jealous goddess retaliated by engulfing him in lava. This time it took two of Pele's brothers to restore him to life. They carried him back to Kauai, where he was reunited with Hi'iaka at Kapa'a.

According to local lore, the rudimentary walls of Lohi'au's house now poke from the undergrowth immediately opposite the foot of the Kalalau Trail, while the *hula* platform above the beach was the site of his first meeting with Pele, and his grave is just above Waikapala'e wet cave. It's also said that other houses nearby belonged to friends and relatives of Lohi'au who figured in the drama, and rock formations on the nearby cliffs are all that remain of *mo'o* (giant lizards) and other creatures killed by Hi'iaka.

△ Kē'ē Beach

Two **wet caves** – filled with water, unlike Maniniholo (see p.486) – are located
a short distance back from the end of the road, and marked by road signs. One,
Waikanaloa, is alongside the highway, while Waikapala'e is just up the hillside.
Why divers would choose to explore these dismal caverns rather than the nearby
ocean is anyone's guess.

Ke Ahu A Laka

A small trail heads west from Kē'ē Beach, along the black seafront rocks just below the state-owned Allerton House, which is not open to visitors. It leads within a hundred yards to the ancient site of **Ke Ahu A Laka**. The island of Molokai has stronger claims to being "the birthplace of *hula*" (see p.430), but this was once the most celebrated *hālau hula* in all Hawaii, the highest academy where students were taught the intricacies of the form by teachers known as *kumu hula*. (For more on the art of *hula*, see p.562).

In the hope of deterring casual tourists, there are no directional or explanatory signs in the area. Finding the assortment of low-lying ruins is easy enough, however, so with no guidance to direct them, people end up wandering aimlessly around and across the site, creating new trails and damaging the stone walls. No one knows whether the various structures were built simultaneously as parts of a single complex or should be thought of as a group of unrelated buildings. Archeologists identify the site's lower level as the Ka Ulu A Pā'oa *heiau*, but it doesn't correspond to any of the usual kinds of *heiau*, and may have served some specific function for *hula* practitioners. Performances took place on the large flat terrace higher up, a few hundred yards back against the base of the *pali*. An altar, probably located within a thatched enclosure, was dedicated to Laka, the patroness of *hula*. Local *hālau hula* come to the site in pilgrimage, but there are no public performances.

When a member of the *ali'i* graduated from the *hālau hula*, or on other great occasions, the Hawaiians would celebrate by flinging flaming firebrands at night from the towering cliffs above Kē'ē. Burning branches of *hau*, *pāpala*, and other light-wooded trees, dried and then soaked in *kukui* oil, were sent spinning out into the darkness, to be caught and held aloft by the trade winds as they curled up the cliff faces. Spectators would gather below in offshore canoes as the sky rained fire about them.

The Nā Pali coast

Beyond Kē'ē Beach, and beyond the reach of any vehicle, lie the green, inviolate valleys of the **Nā Pali coast**. Separated one from the next by knife-edge ridges of rock that thrust down to the ocean from heights of up to four thousand feet, these are among the last great Hawaiian wildernesses, playing host to a magnificent daily spectacle of ever-changing colors. Intruders enter this world only on sufferance, clinging to the contours on perilous hiking trails or buffeted in small boats out at sea.

Nā Pali simply means "the cliffs." It comes from the same root as the name of the country, Nepal: the word *pali* is thought to be of Himalayan origin, having entered the Polynesian language long before recorded history, and is here applied to a landscape of truly Himalayan proportions. Although for the ancient Hawaiians, Kē'ē was proverbially the remotest spot on the islands, Nā Pali valleys such as Kalalau and Nu'alolo Kai once held substantial populations of taro farmers. After the last Hawaiians left Kalalau in 1919, the region remained uninhabited until a sudden influx of hippies in the late 1960s. Official attempts to get rid of them led to the creation of the **Nā Pali Coast State Park**, and all access is now tightly controlled.

The Kalalau Trail

The eleven-mile **Kalalau Trail** passes through first **Hanakāpī'ai** and then **Hanakoa** valleys en route to **Kalalau Valley**, where it's defeated by a mighty buttress of stone.

Taking an **ocean-going tour** enables visitors to see the cliffs, valleys, beaches and waterfalls of the Nā Pali coastline, looking even more dramatic than they do from the fly-on-the-wall perspective of the Kalalau Trail.

Nā Pali boat tours start from either **Hanalei** on the North Shore, or from either **Kīkīaola Harbor**, 1.6 miles west of Waimea, or **Port Allen** on the **West Shore**. Although tours from either side of the island tend to end up at the same places – most half-day trips include a view of Kalalau Valley and a snorkeling stop at the reef just off Nu'alolo Kai – it has to be said that starting from Hanalei is the better alternative. That way you get to see Lumaha'i and Kē'ē beaches, as well as the full length of the Kalalau Trail; and since the distance from Kē'ē to Kalalau is only six miles by water, as opposed to eleven strenuous miles on foot, you can explore the full length in a half-day trip. Boats that depart from the West Shore, on the other hand, cruise for much of the way alongside featureless sand dunes, though at least both Kīkīaola and Port Allen are significantly more convenient to reach for visitors based in the Po'ipū resorts.

The whole issue of Nā Pali boat tours has been embroiled in political controversy for years. During the 1990s, so many trips were setting off from Hanalei each day that both Hanalei Bay and River became seriously polluted. As a result, Hawaii's state government issued a series of decrees forbidding Nā Pali cruise operators from using Hanalei as their departure point. Almost all the operators therefore transferred their base of activities to the West Shore instead. In 2002, court challenges on behalf of the three defiant companies who remained in Hanalei won them – and only them – the right to resume trips from there. All that boils down to the confusing situation that even though Hanalei is the best place from which to take a tour, and three companies do indeed offer tours from there, the majority of Nā Pali boats leave from the West Shore, and official sources often still deny that it's even possible to take a boat from Hanalei. Just to complicate matters further, operators on both sides of the island give the impression in their printed brochures, on their websites and on the phone, that their trips depart to a regular schedule every day of the year, whereas in fact, especially in winter (October to April), and especially from Hanalei, weather conditions can prevent them from sailing for days at a time.

Tour operators use either inflatable **Zodiac rafts** – highly maneuverable in calm waters, when they can dart into sea caves along the coast, but bumpy and slow in rougher conditions – or **catamarans**, which offer a smoother and faster ride but fewer close-up views and less of an adrenalin rush. Between December and April, when cruises can only cover shorter distances, the main compensation is the

---

Honopū, Awa'awapuhi, Nu'alolo Kai, and Miloli'i valleys, further west, are only accessible by sea, though they can be surveyed from Kōke'e State Park far above (see p.517). Along the trail, there are **beaches** at Hanakāpī'ai (in summer) and Kalalau (all year) and **campgrounds** in all three valleys, though only one-night stopovers are permitted at Hanakāpī'ai and Hanakoa. Arduous at all times, the trail also gets progressively more dangerous; indeed, the final five-mile stretch from Hanakoa to Kalalau, which involves scrambling along a precipitous, shadeless wall of crumbling red rock, has occasionally to **close** for up to six months to allow repairs, so it's worth checking with the state parks office before you make any travel plans.

Any Kalalau Trail hike requires careful **preparation**. Most obviously, the 22-mile trek to Kalalau and back is too far to attempt in a single day. Hanakoa Valley itself being a grueling twelve-mile return trip (and one that requires a permit), the most realistic target for a day-hike is Hanakāpī'ai Beach, with a possible side-trip to the falls at the head of the valley. Allow a minimum of 4hr 30min for the trek from Kē'ē Beach to Hanakāpī'ai Falls and back. Neither food nor water is available at

likelihood of seeing humpback whales. Passengers scour the horizon for water spouts or a glint of tail flukes, and the catamarans venture a couple of miles out to sea in the hope of sightings. From that distance, the entire Nā Pali coast appears as a single rounded monolith.

The three operators that sail **from Hanalei** are: Nā Pali Catamaran (T1-866/255-6853 or 808/826-6853, Wwww.napalicatamaran.com), which offers a four-hour snorkeling cruise every morning and afternoon between May and September, costing $140, and when weather permits between October and April provides a three-hour cruise devoted solely to sightseeing; Captain Sundown (T808/826-5585, Wwww.captainsundown.com), which between May and December offers a six-hour morning cruise that includes snorkeling and fishing (adults $162, ages 7–12 $138, under-7s not permitted), and a three-hour afternoon cruise devoted solely to sightseeing ($138/$120); and Hanalei Sport Fishing (T808/826-6114), which operates to a less regular schedule.

Operators **from the West Shore** include Captain Andy (T1-800/535-0830 or 808/335-6833, Wwww.napali.com), and Kauai Sea Tours (T1-800/733-7997 or 808/826-7254, Wwww.kauaiseatours.com), both of which offer both catamaran and raft trips; Catamaran Kahanu (T1-888/213-7111 or 808/335-3577, Wwww.catamarankahanu.com) and Liko Kauai Cruises (T1-888/732-5456 or 808/338-0333, Wwww.liko-kauai.com), which use catamarans; and Nā Pali Explorer (T1-877/335-9909 or 808/338-9999, Wwww.napali-explorer.com), which uses hard-hulled rafts. Expect to pay $90–120 per adult for a 4hr snorkel trip and $125–150 for a 5hr 30min tour that includes a beach picnic.

In addition to their regular Nā Pali tours, two more West-Shore operators, both based at Port Allen – Blue Dolphin (T1-877/511-1311 or 808/335-5553, Wwww.kauaiboats.com) and Holoholo Charters (T808/335-0815 or 1-800/848-6130, Wwww.holoholocharters.com) – offer extended tours that combine a Nā Pali trip with a cruise to the "Forbidden Island" of **Niihau**; see p.512.

It's also possible to join a guided **kayak** expedition from Hanalei. As detailed on p.443, Kayak Kauai (T808/826-9844, Wwww.kayakkauai.com) charges $185 for an escorted tour, available between May and September; only the most experienced of ocean kayakers should set off unaccompanied.

All Kauai's **helicopter** companies fly over the Nā Pali coast, but only Heli USA (T1-866/966-1234 or 808/826-6591, Wwww.heliusa.com) is based on the North Shore, at Princeville Airport; a 30min tour costs $130.

Kē'ē, let alone anywhere along the trail. However far you go, the path is rugged and uneven throughout, varying from slippery clay to shifting sand, so solid footwear is essential. And choose your hiking clothes carefully – thanks to the Kalalau Trail's notorious red dirt, chances are you won't ever be able to wear them again.

The trail rises and falls constantly, with several vertigo-inducing moments; it crosses, and can be blocked by, mountain streams; and emergency help is only available if fellow hikers manage to summon a helicopter. Bear in mind, too, that the sea undercuts the trail in many places, so that dropped or dislodged objects can hit passengers in boats below. Leaving a car parked overnight at the trailhead is not recommended; Hā'ena Beach County Park is preferable for this purpose.

The trail to Hanakāpī'ai

The Kalalau Trail climbs sharply away from its trailhead opposite milepost 10 at Kē'ē Beach, a few yards back from the ocean. Although much of its first half-mile was cobbled during the 1930s, the initial ascent is one of the most demanding

Nā Pali permits

To hike any further than Hanakāpī'ai, even for the day; to **camp** at any of the Kalalau Trail campgrounds (for a maximum of five nights); or to land by **boat** at Kalalau, Nu'alolo Kai or Miloli'i, you must have a **permit** from the **state parks office** at 3060 Eiwa St in Līhu'e (☎808/274-3444; see p.448; call ☎808/245-6001 for the latest weather information). With so many accidents and drownings along the way – and the possibility of a repetition of Hurricane Iniki, when hundred-foot waves necessitated the evacuation of all campers – a record of who may be missing is vital.

Permits cost $10 per person per day and are issued for groups of up to five named individuals. All must supply ID, and specify exactly who is camping where each night. Hikers along the Kalalau Trail are forbidden to spend two consecutive nights at either Hanakāpī'ai or Hanakoa, while boaters can stay no more than three nights at Miloli'i. To minimize environmental damage, up to sixty people are permitted to camp in the park each day between mid-May and mid-September; for the rest of the year, that number drops to just thirty. As the park is frequently fully booked, it's essential to make reservations in advance. Most tour operators obtain permits for their clients, and block-book them several months ahead; as a result, last-minute applicants often leave empty-handed.

sections of the whole trail. It's also among the most beautiful: conditions are much wetter here than further along, and the vegetation is correspondingly thicker. You soon find yourself clambering across the gnarled roots of the splay-footed *hala* (pandanus) tree and sloshing through mini-waterfalls as they gush over the path.

Shortly after the trail rounds the first promontory, still during the first climb and still in sight of Kē'ē Beach, you should be able to make out the ruined walls of the Ka Ulu A Pā'oa *heiau* on a small grassy oceanfront plateau below (see p.489). Views of the successive headlands that lie ahead, and of the islands of Niihau and Lehua further towards the horizon, start to open up half a mile along.

Ancient Hawaiians supposedly took just twenty minutes to reach Hanakāpī'ai Beach, but few modern hikers manage to cover the two-mile distance within an hour. The obvious place to catch your breath en route is at the halfway point, where the trail tops out at 400 feet before starting to drop back down again. A couple of small streams remain to be crossed, and the trail swings well away from the shoreline into a sheltered mini-valley, before Hanakāpī'ai spreads out at your feet. As you make the final descent, but still far above the valley, a warning sign marks the height to which you should climb if a tidal wave threatens.

Hanakāpī'ai Valley and Falls

Hanakāpī'ai Valley is the only spot between Kē'ē Beach and Kalalau Valley where the trail returns to sea level. Crossing Hanakāpī'ai Stream to reach the valley proper is normally straightforward; even if the stepping stones are submerged, there should be a strategically placed rope or branch to help you wade across. If the stream rises any higher than your thighs, turn back – it's not safe here, and it'll be worse still further along.

In summer Hanakāpī'ai boasts a broad white-sand **beach** which, though crowded with sunbathers, is still one of Kauai's most notorious sites for **drownings**. Even if local body-surfers seem to be having the time of their lives, anyone unfamiliar with Hawaiian waters should stay well clear of the ocean. Deaths occur at an average rate of more than one per year, with most of the victims simply wading at the shoreline. The dangerous currents are due to the lack of a reef, and that's what allows the sand to be swept away in winter, leaving a bare gray wall of small boulders.

△ Nā Pali coast, as seen from Princeville

Hanakāpī'ai's overnight **campground** is a little way uphill, beyond both beach and stream. You can't camp any further *mauka* than this, but you can detour away from the main trail to explore the valley. An energetic hour's hike, which requires several stream crossings and a lot of climbing up little rock faces and over fallen trees, brings you to the natural amphitheater of **Hanakāpī'ai Falls**. In addition to long-abandoned taro terraces, you'll pass the remains of a nineteenth-century coffee mill. Descendants of the 20,000 coffee trees planted at that time still grow wild throughout the valley.

Hanakāpī'ai to Hanakoa

For the nine miles between Hanakāpī'ai and Kalalau, the coastline is indented by successive "**hanging valleys,**" cut by streams that end in cliff-top waterfalls. The trail out of Hanakāpī'ai switchbacks steeply up the *pali*, rising 840 feet in little more than a mile. A false step here could be your last, and the concentration and effort of the climb allow little chance for enjoying the views. At the highest point a giant boulder *makai* of the trail – known to some as **Space Rock** – provides some welcome shade. Creep around behind it to confront the sheer drop down to the ocean, as well as a prospect that stretches from Kē'ē in the east to Kalalau in the west.

The nature reserve of **Ho'olulu Valley** comes next, swiftly followed by **Waiahuakua Valley**; the trail winds deep into both of them, forcing its way through the rampant undergrowth. Rounding each headland tends to involve a struggle against the swirling wind, but each brings a new view. Pristine green slopes soar skywards, their every fold covered with the intense blues, purples and yellows of tiny flowers, and white tropicbirds, with their distinctive long tails, glide across the cavernous spaces in between.

Roughly an hour out of Hanakāpī'ai, immediately beyond a truly hair-raising section of the trail, you reach the first overlook into Hanakoa Valley, with multitiered waterfalls tumbling far inland. This is also the first point where you're confronted by the full fluted majesty of the Nā Pali "cathedral," and the rounded Honopū headland in the distance.

Hanakoa Valley and Falls

Soon after entering **Hanakoa Valley**, you pass a cluster of campgrounds in a clearing on your right. This may seem a long way up from the sea, but it's as close as you'll get in the valley. Shortly afterwards, just beyond a burned-out wooden shelter on the left, you cross **Hanakoa Stream** twice in very quick succession. Once again, don't attempt to get through if the water is high, but with several boulders scattered around the streambed you shouldn't have any problem. There are usually plenty of people around, bathing in the stream and picnicking beneath the trees. More campgrounds lie on the far side, set amid the stone walls of former taro terraces a little way up the hillside, and many campers stay longer than their one allotted night. The only drawback is the large population of **mosquitoes**.

Another side trail leads off inland from the terraces, this time to the 2000-foot **Hanakoa Falls**, which you may have glimpsed as you came into the valley. Follow the sign: the route may appear to be blocked by fallen trees, but that's just what the trail is like. Look out for ribbons tied to the trees, and be aware that if you don't recross the western channel of the stream within 100 yards of setting off, you've gone in the wrong direction. For steepness and mud this trail is even worse than the one to Hanakāpī'ai Falls (see p.493), but only a third of a mile of spongy rotting trees has to be negotiated before you come to the sheer-walled waterfall, where you can cool off in the pool. However tempted you may be, don't drink the water; there are people, and goats, up top.

Hanakoa to Kalalau

As mentioned on p.490, the Kalalau Trail may be closed beyond Hanakoa; check with the state parks office. Assuming that it *is* open, the last five miles of the Kalalau Trail, from **Hanakoa to Kalalau**, include its most dangerous and exposed stretches. Each of the Nā Pali valleys receives less rainfall than its neighbors to the east, so they grow progressively less indented and more precipitous. To the casual eye the vegetation still seems dense, but plants find it harder to grow. They therefore recover more slowly from the onslaught of wild goats, and the denuded slopes become prone to landslides. By this stage the trail cuts repeatedly across raw patches of red sandy gravel, where every footfall sends a shower of small stones tumbling down to the sea. With the path set at a slight angle to the hillside, open to the sun, and only in as good a condition as the last rains left it, such sections can be most unnerving.

However, the rewards at the end make it all worthwhile. Having skirted several small valleys, the trail emerges to access a full panorama of Kalalau Valley. Unfortunately, the final descent, while spectacular, is the worst of all. From the saddle that connects the pinnacle of **Pu'ukula**, or "Red Hill," with the main bulk of the island, the trail skitters down the crumbling hillside in a tangle of alternative strands, none safer than the rest, before pulling itself together to cross one last stretch of grassland down to Kalalau Stream.

Kalalau Valley

Kalalau Valley, the largest of the Nā Pali valleys at almost a mile wide and two miles deep, was the last to lose its native population. Its broad, gently sloping floor, cradled between mighty walls, nurtured many generations of Hawaiians before the arrival of the Europeans, and there were enough left in the nineteenth century for missionaries to consider it necessary to build a school and church here. Until 1919, when those Hawaiians who hadn't been wiped out by disease finally left, they were still living in thatched *hales*, cultivating taro and fishing with *hukilau* nets. They traded by canoe with their coastal neighbors, but were largely self-sufficient. For the next fifty years the valley was devoted to cattle ranching, especially by the

Robinson family of Niihau fame (see p.512). State authorities felt that cattle were damaging the valley's ecology and, when squatters began to move in as well, they set aside this whole section of coastline as a state park.

Before reaching the valley floor, hikers have first to wade the **Kalalau Stream**, where a rope serves as a handrail. The stream comes shortly after the 10-mile marker; take the right fork on the far side, and the final mile of the trail takes you down to, and along, the low bluffs above Kalalau's lovely white-sand **beach**. The only beach along the trail to retain its sand year-round, this nonetheless varies greatly with the seasons. In winter it's a narrow shelf little more than 100 yards long, while in summer enough sand piles up for you to round the tumbled boulders and continue west for half a mile. Swimming during the winter or spring high surf is obviously dangerous, but even the calm summer seas are ripped through by powerful currents, and casual dips are never advisable.

Individual campgrounds line the trail above the beach, but the prime spot is considered to be around Ho'ole'a Falls at the far western end. When the sea caves here dry out in summer, campers pitch their tents inside, despite the risk of rock slides. The falls are the valley's best source of fresh water, though it should still be purified before use.

Though camping is only permitted near the beach, the spur trail that forks left immediately after the stream crossing provides an easy and enjoyable two-mile walk back into the valley. Alternating between short climbs up to valley views, and jungle hikes through wild fruit groves (with guavas and mangoes for the picking), this ends after several hundred feet at a bathing hole known simply as **Big Pool**. Vegetation has reclaimed most signs of habitation in the valley, but you might glimpse the ruins of a *heiau* near the trail junction, or the stone walls of the mission church further inland.

See p.519 for details of the Kalalau, Pu'u O Kila and Pihea lookouts in Kōke'e State Park, which look down on Kalalau Valley.

Beyond Kalalau

The cliffs west of Kalalau are too fragile to hold a trail, so the magnificent valleys beyond can only be seen on the boat tours listed on p.490. The first of them, **Honopū**, is just half a mile from Kalalau; strong swimmers sometimes swim there, though heavy currents make the return leg all but impossible. Two beaches beautify the waterfront, but the valley itself stands atop a 150-foot bluff.

Koolau the Leper

The "flower-throttled gorge" of Kalalau Valley was the setting of Jack London's famous short story *Koolau the Leper*, a flamboyant retelling of a true-life incident. The real Koolau, a *paniolo* from Waimea, was diagnosed as a leper in 1889 and duly condemned to permanent exile, far from family and friends, on the island of Molokai (see p.420). He fled instead with his wife and young child to the mountain fastness of Kalalau, to join a band of fellow sufferers. Sheriff Louis Stolz came in search of Koolau in June 1893, only to be shot dead, whereupon a large posse was sent to round up the fugitives. All except Koolau and his family were captured; Koolau, however, retreated to a cave only accessible via a knife-edge ridge, and picked off two of his pursuers as they inched their way after him. No one was ever to claim the $1000 reward for his arrest; his wife Pi'ilani emerged from Kalalau in 1896, to tell the world that both Koolau and their son had died.

The tale of Koolau also provided the central theme for W. S. Merwin's epic book-length poem, *The Folding Cliffs* (see p.577).

Stunning **Awaʻawapuhi**, a few hundred yards along, slithers out of sight behind the cliffs like the *puhi* (eel) after which it is named. It, too, is a hanging valley, so from water level there's little to see; only the Awaʻawapuhi Trail in Kōkeʻe Park (described on p.524) offers complete views.

Next come **Nuʻalolo ʻĀina** and **Nuʻalolo Kai**, respectively the inland and oceanfront portions of Nuʻalolo Valley. Separated by a 75-foot cliff, they were in ancient times connected by a perilous man-made ladder. Together they constitute one of the richest archeological sites in Hawaii, continuously occupied since the twelfth century. The overhanging cliff sheltered a row of stone-built house terraces, which have yielded layer upon layer of fishhooks, gourds and the like. The valley floor above, though narrow and shaded, was extensively irrigated for taro. Most Nā Pali tour boats aim to spend an hour or two anchored at the coral reef that embraces Nuʻalolo Kai, enabling passengers to snorkel among its plentiful fish; some also allow brief excursions ashore.

Miloliʻi, a mile on, is the last of the Nā Pali valleys, just four miles from the rolling dunes of Polihale State Park on the West Shore (see p.514). It, too, is protected by a reef, and was once home to a seafront fishing community. Boat landings on its pretty beach are permitted, but few operators do so.

The South and West shores

Thanks to its guaranteed sun and safe, sandy beaches, the **South Shore** ranks as the center of Kauai's tourist industry. Its only resort, **Poʻipū**, holds the island's largest concentration of upmarket hotels, condo developments, golf courses and gourmet restaurants. On the other hand, Poʻipū has never been a town in any real sense; it's very much a family destination, fine if watersports are your main priority, but it holds next to nothing of interest otherwise. None of the area's other towns is especially worth visiting, either. The plantation villages of **Kōloa**, nearby, and **Hanapēpē** ten miles on, boast some appealing early-twentieth-century storefronts but have definitely seen better days, while **Lāwaʻi** and **Kalāheo** are just blink-and-you-miss-them highway intersections.

Waimea, the only sizable town on the **West Shore**, has a dramatic past as the site of Captain Cook's first Hawaiian landing. Although it offers one of Kauai's most characterful hotels, it too suffers from an undistinguished present.

Few visitors would see the highway towns were they not on the way to the wonderful state parks of **Waimea Canyon** and **Kōkeʻe**, covered in a separate section from p.514 onwards. As it is, however, all the settlements earn extra income catering to passing day-trippers, and there are a few interesting stores and galleries where you can while away the odd spare half-hour.

The Knudsen Gap

All traffic **west of Līhuʻe** is obliged after six miles to squeeze between Hāʻupu Ridge and the interior massif, through the **Knudsen Gap**. In the nineteenth century this narrow pass, named after Valdemar Knudsen, a Norwegian immigrant who managed

Grove Farm during the 1850s, was a renowned haunt of thieves and outlaws. These days it serves simply as the gateway to Kauai's South and West shores.

Kōloa

Immediately west of the Knudsen Gap, Maluhia Road heads *makai* from Hwy-50. Its first straight stretch passes through an avenue of mighty eucalyptus trees long known as the **Tree Tunnel**, where the trees meet and intermingle overhead. Three miles down, where the road ends, vehicles shuffle right to cross Waikomo Stream before turning left to continue on to Po'ipū. The small group of stores at this busy intersection constitutes **KŌLOA**, a nineteenth-century plantation town that was also the site of Kauai's first mission school. Its first teacher, in 1855, was Rev Daniel Dole; pupils included his son Sanford, the only President of the short-lived Republic of Hawaii (see p.539).

Other snippets of local and island lore are recounted on the walls of the **Kōloa History Center**, set slightly back from the road just west of the stream. This open-sided structure doesn't even have a door, so naturally there are no opening hours or admission fees. Kōloa's raised wooden boardwalks hold assorted clothes and souvenir stores, including the Progressive Expressions Surf Shop, Kahn Galleries, and a Crazy Shirts outlet.

Practicalities

There's no **accommodation** in Kōloa, but the town's best-known **restaurant** is *Pizzetta* (daily 11am–9.30pm; ☎808/742-8881), set in a former *poi* factory along the boardwalk, with an open-air *lānai* out back. Huge, tasty lunchtime *panini* cost $8, a calzone is $10, pasta specials are around $10, and full-size pizzas range $15–25. They also serve fine smoothies, and you can spend an interesting evening working your way through a long list of cocktails.

Both the food and the atmosphere in the garden courtyard of the nearby *Tom Kats Grille* (daily 7am–10pm; ☎808/742-8887) are similar. In addition to lunchtime burgers and sandwiches, they feature evening specials such as steak ($22) and seafood linguine ($18). Also on the boardwalk, *Lapperts* (Mon–Thurs & Sun 6am–9pm, Fri & Sat 6am–10pm), serves ice cream and coffees to take out or to enjoy on the shady *lānai*. Just across the stream, part of the *Kōloa Country Store* (Mon–Sat 8am–8.30pm, Sun 9am–5pm) is set aside as an espresso bar and **Internet café**.

Po'ipū

PO'IPŪ, the southernmost point on Kauai, is also its principal vacation resort. Though *po'ipū* means "completely overcast," its **white-sand beaches** receive more sunshine than anywhere else on the island and are filled with tourists year-round. For surfing, windsurfing, scuba diving, snorkeling or general family fun, it's a great place. However, beaches are about all there is here; there's no town to wander through and virtually nothing else to see or do. What's more, most of the beaches are not visible from the confusing network of roads, so on first impression you might not even realize they were there.

Matters were not helped in 1992, when **Hurricane Iniki** left Po'ipū in a terrible state. The roofs of its hotels were ripped off, plush rooms buried in sand, and rental cars flipped and stacked like matchwood. It took several years for things to get back

Though Kōloa has never been more than a small village, it played a crucial role in the development of modern Hawaii, as the birthplace of the islands' first **sugar plantation**. From its origins in the highlands of New Guinea, the sweet grass we know as sugar cane was carried throughout the Pacific by Polynesian voyagers. Ancient Hawaiians cultivated around forty separate varieties of *ko*, which they chewed as medicine, an aphrodisiac, baby food, emergency rations, and simply for pleasure.

Wild sugar grew rampant in Kōloa, whose name meant "long cane," so it made an ideal testing ground for commercial sugar production. In 1835, Ladd & Co secured permission from Kamehameha III to farm almost a thousand acres east of the Waihohonu Stream – the first such lease ever granted to outsiders – and sent 26-year-old William Hooper to establish a plantation. He set 25 *kanakas* (native Hawaiians) to clear the grass on September 13, with the deliberate intention not only of making a profit but also of transforming the Hawaiian way of life.

Until that time ordinary Hawaiians were regarded as owing unlimited labor to the ruling *ali'i*, a form of serfdom that had been grotesquely abused in the sandalwood trade (see p.535). For Hooper, the plantation was an "entering wedge . . . to upset the whole miserable system of 'chief labor.'" To his workers, uprooted from seaside villages and brought to the new plantation settlement, however, this new system must have seemed little different from the old. They dragged the ploughs themselves, drilled the soil by hand using traditional *'o'o* digging sticks, and crushed the raw cane using heavy *koa*-wood logs as rollers. By paying them in coupons that could only be redeemed at the company store, Hooper introduced them to consumerism. Each month, as the *kanakas* tired of the previous consignment of cheap goods and textiles shipped over from Honolulu, there'd be a frantic search for new items to import.

By March 1838, the plantation employed one hundred laborers. An ever-increasing proportion of the sugar boilers were women, who at just six cents per day were paid less than half the men's wage. Hooper saw the Hawaiians as intelligent shirkers – "they display so little interest for their employment that it makes my heart ache" – who worked only when they were being watched and even learned to forge counterfeit coupons and avoid working altogether. As a result, he began to recruit Chinese laborers from a group who had been grinding wild cane at Waimea until the new plantation drove them out of business. These were housed in separate quarters at Kōloa, as were the white overseers, and patterns of race and class division emerged that became standard for all subsequent plantations.

Soon after Hooper left in 1839, Ladd & Co managed to go bankrupt, despite being offered exclusive rights to all sugar production in Hawaii for a century. However, the plantation at Kōloa prospered, with the construction of a dam and a more sophisticated mill. The great boom came during the US Civil War, when the farms of the South stopped feeding the sweet tooth of the North. A leap in the price of Hawaiian sugar stimulated the opening of dozens of plantations on the Kōloa model, starting on the Big Island in 1863, and then on Oahu and Maui in 1864. When prices dropped at the end of the war, sugar dominated the Hawaiian economy; the US annexation of the islands was largely the result of campaigns by sugar producers to guarantee access to the American market.

Sugar production in Kōloa finally came to an end in 2000; the former sugar fields are progressively being replanted with coffee. All that remains of the original 1841 mill, located just north of the town center, is a ruined chimney marked with a commemorative plaque.

to normal, but the damage is now entirely repaired. Although most individual properties have been rebuilt to an even higher standard than before, Po'ipū still feels more like a random assortment of buildings than a cohesive community.

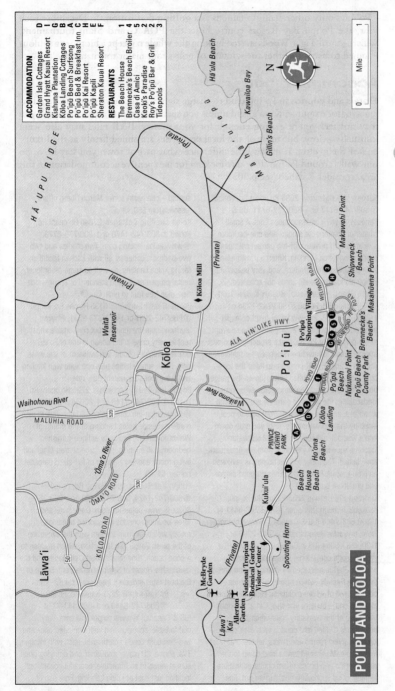

PO'IPŪ AND KŌLOA

ACCOMMODATION
Garden Isle Cottages   D
Grand Hyatt Kauai Resort   I
Kiahuna Plantation   G
Kōloa Landing Cottages   B
Po'ipū Beach Surfsong   A
Po'ipū Bed & Breakfast Inn C
Po'ipū Kai Resort   H
Po'ipū Kapili   E
Sheraton Kauai Resort   F

RESTAURANTS
The Beach House   1
Brennecke's Beach Broiler   4
Casa di Amici   5
Keoki's Paradise   2
Roy's Po'ipū Bar & Grill   2
Tidepools   3

N

0   Mile   1

Poʻipūʻs only other claim to fame is as a **golfing** destination. In December each year, the Poʻipū Bay Resort course hosts the **PGA Grand Slam** tournament, which – until Tiger Woods started making the whole concept a bit more nebulous – aimed to bring together the winners of golf's four major tournaments.

Accommodation

Hotels and **condos** in Poʻipū tend to charge significantly more than their equivalents in, for example, Kapaʻa, and unless you spend all your time on the beach you may not feel you're getting enough for your money. **B&B** rates may also seem unusually pricey, but most of the local properties are aimed firmly at the luxury end of the market. It makes little difference what part of town you stay in, as no one walks around Poʻipū. If you're looking for inexpensive accommodation in this area, consider Kalāheo (see p.505).

Garden Isle Cottages 2658 Puʻuholo Rd, Poʻipū ☎808/742-6717 or 1-800/742-6711 (US & Canada), ⓦwww.oceancottages.com. A small cluster of comfortable studio- and one-bedroom apartments, in private cliff-top garden cottages overlooking Kōloa Landing. Kitted out with island-style paintings and furniture, and very peaceful by Poʻipū standards. Credit cards not accepted. ⑥

🏃 **Grand Hyatt Kauai Resort & Spa** 1571 Poʻipū Rd, Poʻipū ☎808/742-1234 or 1-800/554-9288, ⓦwww.kauai-hyatt.com. Six-hundred-room giant, sprawling along the seafront at the east end of Poʻipū, that's arguably the nicest tropical resort in Hawaii – especially for families, with its "Camp Hyatt" program to keep the kids busy. Formal antique-filled lobby, top-of-the-range bedrooms and great sea views, plus some amazing landscaping; the terraced gardens are filled with waterfalls, and you can swim from pool to pool, aided by the odd waterslide, until you drop down into a luscious network of artificial saltwater lagoons, squeezed in just back from the (unremarkable) beach. The *Tidepools* restaurant is reviewed on p.504, while *Ilima Terrace* serves good dinner and breakfast buffets. ⑨

Kiahuna Plantation 2253 Poʻipū Rd, Poʻipū; bookable through Outrigger, ☎808/742-6411 or 1-800/688-7444 (US & Canada), ⓦwww.outrigger .com, or Castle Resorts, ☎808/742-2200 or 1-800/367-5004 (US & Canada), ⓦwww .castleresorts.com. Huge, sprawling oceanfront property. Part is managed by Outrigger and part by Castle Resorts (which offers its best rates online), each of whom maintains separate offices at either end – be sure you check in at the right one. Each of the two-story "plantation-style" buildings is divided into condos with their own kitchens, living rooms and *lānais*; all sleep at least four people. Manicured lawns lead down to the sea, where a fine beach offers sheltered inshore bathing, good snorkeling and, further out, fine

surfing – champion surfer Margo Oberg offers lessons from $60. ⑥–⑨

Kōloa Landing Cottages 2704b Hoʻonani Rd, Poʻipū ☎808/742-1470 or 1-800/779-8773, ⓦwww.koloa-landing.com. Two studios and two two-bedroom cottages, all with kitchen facilities, facing Kōloa Landing, as well as some other local rental properties. A good standard of accommodation, plus free fruit to pick. ④–⑥

Poʻipū Beach Surfsong 5135 Hoʻona Rd, Poʻipū ☎808/742-2231 or 1-877/373-2331, ⓦwww .surfsong.com. Inexpensive but comfortable vacation rentals, very close to the ocean in one of Poʻipūʻs quietest neighborhoods, and available by the week only. Three small studios plus one suite with kitchen and living room. Equivalent daily rate ④

Poʻipū Inn Bed & Breakfast 2720 Hoʻonani Rd, Poʻipū ☎808/742-1146 or 1-800/808-2330, ⓦwww.poipu-inn.com. Pink B&B bungalow in nice gardens, beside Kōloa Landing at the mouth of Waikomo Stream. Exquisite antique-furnished bedrooms, all en suite, plus large shared *lānai* and living room, and any number of full-sized carousel horses. ④–⑤

Poʻipū Kai Resort 1941 Poʻipū Rd, Poʻipū ☎808/742-7424, 808/742-7400 or 1-800/367-8020, ⓦwww.poipu-kai.com. One-, two- and three-bedroom condos in assorted buildings, mostly well back from the sea with the exception of the plush Poʻipū Sands section, which is close to a good beach. Nine tennis courts, six pools, and the reasonable *House of Seafood* restaurant. Some of the best rates include a free rental car. ④–⑧

🏃 **Poʻipū Kapili** 2221 Kapili Rd, Poʻipū ☎808/742-6449 or 1-800/443-7714 (US & Canada), ⓦwww.poipukapili.com. Very comfortable, spacious and well-equipped one- and two-bedroom condo apartments, each with kitchen, TVs, phone, CD player and *lānai*, and enjoying great sunset views in an attractive, peaceful oceanfront location just east of Kōloa Landing. Free use of central pool and floodlit tennis courts; five-day minimum stay. ⑥

Sheraton Kauai Resort 2440 Ho'onani Rd, Po'ipū ☎808/742-1661 or 1-866/716-8109, ⊛www .sheraton-kauai.com. Despite its superb oceanfront location, this luxury resort is clearly second best to the *Grand Hyatt*. Rooms in the Ocean and Beach wings enjoy spectacular views, but the Garden wing is a bit disappointing. The pool is a little small, and the restaurants are unexceptional, but with such a good beach at hand you may feel it doesn't matter. Shop online for the best rates. Garden view ⑥, ocean view ⑧

The Po'ipū shoreline: east of Kōloa Landing

Po'ipū has two distinct sections of oceanfront, to either side of Waikomo Stream. When Kōloa Plantation first opened, **Kōloa Landing**, on the eastern bank of the river mouth, was briefly Kauai's major port, and as such Hawaii's third whaling port after Lahaina and Honolulu. Only a basic boat ramp now survives, though the area is popular with divers and snorkelers.

East of Kōloa Landing, a rocky headland marks the beginning of the long narrow shelf of **Po'ipū Beach**, interrupted by two smaller headlands. The sea areas are separated by parallel reefs; the inshore segment makes a perfect swimming spot for young children, while windsurfers glide along the waters beyond when the wind picks up, and an expert **surfing** site known as First Break lies half a mile out to sea. Different parts of the beach are known by the names of the adjacent hotels; apart from Sheraton Beach at the end of Ho'onani Road, most of Po'ipū Beach can only be reached by walking along the sand. Oceanfront kiosks throughout Po'ipū, many attached to hotels, rent snorkels, kayaks and other beach equipment.

Nukumoi Point, the craggy easternmost point of Po'ipū Beach, is one of only three *tombolos* in Hawaii, all on Kauai. A *tombolo* is a cross between an island and a headland, joined to the mainland by a slender sand bar that all but disappears at high tide. **Po'ipū Beach County Park** beyond has the only public facilities along the Po'ipū coast, with a children's playground and a lifeguard station, and is thus the beach of choice for local families. Swimming in the lee of Nukumoi Point is generally safe, while snorkeling at its base is excellent.

A little way further along, boogie-boarders and body-surfers jostle for position among the fierce waves that break over the offshore sand bar at **Brennecke's Beach**. The crowds are such that surfers are banned. Brennecke's was named after a doctor whose house stood here until 1982, when it was wrenched from its foundations by Hurricane Iwa. That hurricane took most of the sand from the beach too, and Iniki removed a lot more ten years later.

East of Brennecke's, the beaches are interrupted by conical **Po'ipū Crater**, a vestige of Kauai's final burst of volcanic activity. It's now ringed by small condos, with high bluffs along the seafront. On the far side, the *Grand Hyatt* dominates the crescent of **Shipwreck Beach**. Most of the sand scooped up by the hurricanes landed here, where it buried not only the eponymous shipwreck, but also a field of ancient petroglyphs. Even with all that sand, it's not much fun getting into the water across the shoreline rocks, so Shipwreck is largely the preserve of boogie-boarders and windsurfers.

Māhā'ulepū

Makawehi Point, at the eastern end of Shipwreck Beach, marks the start of the **Makawehi Dunes**, crisp-topped mounds of lithified sandstone filled with the bones of extinct flightless birds. Po'ipū Road ends alongside the golf course east of the *Hyatt*, but it's possible to keep going along the dirt road beyond. A couple of miles along, shortly after a closed gate forces you to turn right, you'll come to a gatehouse. In daylight hours, you can sign a waiver here and proceed into the region known as **Māhā'ulepū**, which has three unspoiled, secluded beaches along its two-mile ocean frontage. The entire area belongs to the Grove Farm company, and thus now to Steve Case of AOL fame, but he is said to have no plans to develop it in any way.

The road reaches the sea in the middle of **Gillin's Beach**, typical of the Māhā'ulepū beaches in being too exposed for safe swimming. Windsurfers prepared to carry their equipment this far take advantage of the strong waves, and naturalists set off into the dunes in search of rare native plants. Hikers head east, first to **Kawailoa Bay**, and then, across a stretch of lava indented with spectacular caves, to **Ha'ula Beach** half a mile further along. CJM Stables runs **horseback trips** in the Māhā'ulepū area ($90–115; reservation required; ☎808/742-6096, ⓦ www.cjmstables.com).

Note that it's against the law to come within 100 feet of the endangered monk seals that sun themselves on the beaches of Po'ipū – let alone touch or harass them.

The Po'ipū shoreline: west to Spouting Horn

The coast **west of Waikomo Stream** can offer few beaches to compete with the luxuriant expanses to the east. Only for the first mile or so is there much sign of sand, and that tends to get stripped to almost nothing by each high tide. At **Ho'ona Beach**, the first possibility, the merest pocket of sand is tucked in among the rocks, and is appropriately nicknamed "Baby Beach."

Even less sand clings to the shoreline of Ho'ai Bay, just beyond. Across from the sea, the lawns of **Prince Kūhiō Park** commemorate the birthplace of Prince Jonah Kūhiō Kalaniana'ole (1871–1922), Hawaii's delegate to Congress from 1902 until 1922. A bronze bust of the prince stands on an imposing plinth, with a flagpole to either side. Behind it, in front of a fine spread of bougainvillea, is a black lava platform that once held the Ho'ai *heiau*, looking considerably sturdier than many of the new condos nearby.

Just past the next small headland is **Beach House Beach**, named after a nearby restaurant that continues to battle on, despite hammerings from the two hurricanes. This narrow roadside strip makes for a good quick snorkel stop, and there are some expert-only surf breaks further out.

Coach tours galore continue beyond the bobbing yachts of tiny Kukui'ula Harbor to **Spouting Horn County Park**, a natural freak a mile or so on at the end of the road. From the viewing area at the edge of the parking lot, you look down onto a flat ledge of black lava, just above sea level. As each wave breaks against it, clouds of spume and spray jet into the air through the "spouting horn," a hole in the lava. Obviously enough, the highest fountains coincide with the biggest waves, while rainbows hang in the spray when the eruptions come in quick succession. The rhythmic suction of air in and out of the hole creates a loud "breathing" sound, once attributed by Hawaiians to a giant *mo'o* or lizard. A larger hole alongside the existing one was dynamited by plantation owners at the start of the twentieth century, in order to stop salt spray from damaging crops in the nearby fields.

If disappointment with what is often a less than enthralling spectacle tempts you to scramble down onto the rocks below, don't. The view isn't any better, and there's a risk of severe injury.

Allerton and McBryde gardens

Across the street from Spouting Horn, a restored plantation home serves as the visitor center for the **National Tropical Botanical Garden** (Mon–Sat 8.30am–5pm; ☎808/742-2623, ⑩www.ntbg.org). Although it sells assorted crafts and plant-related products, its main function is as the starting point for tours of **Allerton** and **McBryde gardens**, which fill over two hundred acres of the otherwise inaccessible **Lāwa'i Valley**, a little further west. Originally created by a Chicago banking family, these beautiful gardens are now maintained as sanctuaries and research centers devoted to rare plant species, but Allerton in particular also makes an absolutely ravishing spectacle for casual tourists.

Allerton Garden occupies the seaward half of the valley, stretching several hundred yards from the former Allerton home, which is not currently open to visitors, up to exquisite little **Lāwa'i Kai** Beach. Walking tours of the garden set off at 9am, 10am, 1pm and 2pm, daily except Sunday (adults $35, ages 10–12 $20, under-10s not permitted). All tours last two and a half hours, and it's essential to make reservations as far in advance as possible.

The Allertons laid the garden out as a succession of "rooms," each with its own character, but despite the abundance of classical statuary, formal fountains and gazebos, the overall impression is of a glorious profusion of tropical color. The plants here are drawn from all over the world. Flaming torch gingers, lobster-claw heliconia and birds of paradise erupt on all sides, and nature feels barely tamed. Appropriately enough, it was amid the roots of one especially enormous banyan tree that the dinosaur's egg was discovered in the movie *Jurassic Park*.

McBryde Garden, by contrast – but like the NTBG's other Kauai property, at Limahuli on the North Shore (see p.486) – focuses exclusively on Hawaiian species. In fact, it holds the most extensive collection of Hawaiian plants to be found anywhere on earth. Trams down to the garden leave the visitor center hourly on the half-hour, from 9.30am until 2.30pm daily; no reservations are necessary. Once at the bottom, you can take a self-guided walking tour before catching the tram back up (adults $20, ages 6–12 $10, under-6s free).

Restaurants

Po'ipū has a fine selection of **restaurants**, with *Roy's* in particular attracting diners from all over the island. However, surprisingly few are located along the seafront, and it's also notably short of budget choices, although one or two cheaper alternatives, such as *Pattaya's Asian Café* with its tasty Thai food, can be found in the Po'ipū Shopping Village. Most of the larger hotels have their own dining rooms, which serve reasonably good food, but only the *Hyatt* is especially worth visiting for a meal.

The Beach House 5022 Lāwa'i Rd ☎808/742-1424. An irresistible oceanfront setting ensures this fashionable Pacific Rim restaurant is crammed to the brim early each evening; as the sunset gets under way, diners abandon their meals to take endless photos on the adjoining lawns. The food is almost as spectacular as the sunsets, making this Kauai's premier venue for romantic couples, and the prices are at premium levels. Appetizers such as shiitake-crusted mussels cost around $10, or you can get a great "*ahi* taster" for $18; entrees like the mint coriander rack of lamb or the rich seafood "Kauai Paella" are typically $25–32. Daily: May–Sept 6–10pm; Oct–April 5.30–10pm.

Brennecke's Beach Broiler 2100 Ho'one Rd ☎808/742-7588. Little expense may have been lavished on the no-frills interior and *lānai* of this family seafood restaurant, but with the waving palms of Po'ipū Beach Park in sight, Brennecke's always manages to be full. Most of the menu is devoted to inexpensive sandwiches and burgers, though at dinner interesting appetizers include ceviche ($12) and sashimi ($14), while among the fancier seafood entrees are *cioppino* for $28 and lobster at $35 plus. Standard steaks, ribs, and combos are also available, and they serve sunset cocktails, too. Daily 11am–10pm.

🏃 **Casa di Amici** 2360 Nalo Rd ☎808/742-1555. Breezy, open-sided restaurant, tucked away in an obscure but central side street a hundred yards back from the ocean. A true hidden gem, it serves Po'ipū's finest food at less than exorbitant prices. The bulk of the menu is Italian, with plenty of pastas and some delicious risottos, plus veal and chicken served in marsala, piccatta and gorgonzola sauces, all available in light ($18–20) and regular ($23–25) sizes. There are also a handful of adventurous Pacific Rim options, such as "Japanese mahogany glazed salmon and grilled black tiger prawns sprinkled with bonito *furikake* and served with black *frijoles chonitos* and jalapeño-tequila *aioli*" ($25), which may sound over the top but has a strong claim to be the single best dish sold on Kauai. Everything is beautifully presented; entrees come with a superb assortment of local-flavored side dishes, such as spinach creamed with coconut and corn with orange cilantro; and the staff are extremely friendly. Save room for the Bananas Foster dessert, at $12 for two. Daily 6–10pm.

Keoki's Paradise Po'ipū Shopping Village ☎808/742-7534. Mall cocktail lounge that's been given an appealing Polynesian make-over, with a thatched bar, a waterfall and a meandering lagoon; ersatz it may be, but it still turns dining here into an atmospheric experience. The food isn't bad, despite the mix'n'match approach to world cuisines. Lunchtime sandwiches and local plates are mostly under $10. For dinner, appetizers such as sashimi, *mushu* pork ($7), and Thai shrimp sticks ($10) are followed by fresh fish ($22–29), steaks (from $20), or Kōloa pork ribs ($19). Daily 11am–11.30pm.

🏃 **Roy's Po'ipū Bar & Grill** Po'ipū Shopping Village, 2360 Kiahuna Plantation Drive ☎808/742-5000. Busy "Euro-Asian" joint, whose kitchens are visible at the back, and whose tables spread through this upscale mall. Appetizers range from pasta, satay and snails ($7–15), to potstickers, crab cakes and a Granny Smith Apple Salad. Entrees range $27–35, with standard menu items like honey-mustard short ribs and hibachi salmon complemented by a lengthy list of daily specials, including fish selections such as a crispy whole *moi* in black bean sauce. Desserts include a legendary dark chocolate soufflé at $9.50, and there's a great wine list. Everything tastes as good as it sounds, and reservations are essential. Daily 5.30–9.30pm.

Tidepools *Grand Hyatt Kauai Resort*, 1571 Po'ipū Rd ☎808/742-6260. Very romantic dinner-only restaurant, consisting of semi-private open-air thatched huts arrayed around the resort's waterfalls and lagoon; the lights can be so low that you can hardly see your food. The relatively short menu features some interesting appetizers such as Thai spiced crab cake with fiddlehead ferns and *ahi poke* with *kukui* nuts and taro chips (both $15), while the entrees, at $32–38, include contemporary Hawaiian classic like seared *opah* alongside garlic-rubbed prime rib. Reservations are advisable. Daily 6–10pm.

Kāhili Mountain Park

Less then a mile beyond the Knudsen Gap on Hwy-50, a dirt road climbs for a mile inland to reach **Kāhili Mountain Park**. An idyllic spot, this little-known private enclave holds a number of very inexpensive rental **cabins**, but they're only available to guests with a connection to its owners, the Seventh Day Adventist Church (☎808/742-9921, ⓦwww.kahilipark.org; ❷–❸).

The park is of more significance to visitors as the starting point of the **Kāhili Ridge Trail**, the finest hike on the southern side of Kauai, and one that makes an easy half-day outing for visitors based in Po'ipū. To find the trailhead, look for a water tower to the right of the dirt road, shortly beyond the final, highest cabin. Park nearby and follow a dirt track for a hundred yards past the tower until you come to a small clearing. Chances are the track will be barred at this point; in any case, continue instead, in much the same direction, through an obvious "tunnel" of overhanging low flowering shrubs.

As it climbs a slender spur towards the main mountain ridge, the trail swiftly degenerates to no more than a muddy rut. It's barely two feet wide in places, and bursts of steep climbing are interspersed with precarious ridge walking. Colorful flowers and orchids grow to either side, while the vegetation occasionally thins out to offer views down past Hā'upu Ridge to Līhu'e.

Just how far you get will depend on your head for heights and the rain conditions. It's not possible, however, to climb all the way to the 3089-foot summit of Kāhili, which is itself just a pimple on the island's central spine, running north to Kawaikini. The trail ends instead at a radio mast less than two miles up from the park. Bear in mind that coming down is harder than going up, especially if the path is wet and slippery.

Lāwa'i

LĀWA'I, the first village that Kaumuali'i Highway (Hwy-50) passes through west of Līhu'e, after ten miles, is connected directly with Kōloa via the three-mile rural Kōloa Road. This is primarily a residential area, and with the tiny shopping complex at the highway intersection apparently defunct, there's no reason whatsoever to stop here. A few minutes' drive south, however, just north of Kōloa Road, the *Kauai Banyan Inn* is a pleasant country **B&B**, with five self-contained suites, each with private bathroom and *lānai* offering long-range views down towards the ocean (3528-B Mana Hema Place, Lāwa'i; ☎1-888/786-3855, ⓦwww.kauaibanyan.com; ❸–❹).

Kalāheo

Two miles on from Lāwa'i, the larger town of **KALĀHEO** consists of a cluster of shops, restaurants and gas stations kept busy by its predominantly Portuguese community. Half a mile south of the center, **Kukui O Lono** public park (daily 6.30am–6.30pm; free) is an invaluable local resource, with a nine-hole golf course and attractively landscaped avenues, but it's unlikely to detain any tourist for long.

Heading off the highway into the network of small roads *makai* of Kalāheo makes for some picturesque country driving, but you can't get as far as the sea. Much of this former sugar land is now given over to cultivating coffee instead, and extensive groves cover the sunny, south-facing slopes. At **NUMILA**, just over two miles southwest of Kalāheo down Halewili Road, the **Kauai Coffee Company Visitor Center** explains the intricacies of coffee production and sells simple gifts (daily 9am–5pm; free; ☎808/335-0813, ⓦwww.kauaicoffee.com). Staff members offer free samples of local-grown java, while a coffee bar sells espressos, hot dogs, sodas and pastries.

Practicalities

Surprisingly enough, Kalāheo boasts an old-fashioned **motel**, the *Kalāheo Inn*, a few yards south of the main road, but tucked out of sight at 4444 Papalina Rd (☎808/332-6023 or 1-888/332-6023, ⓦwww.kalaheoinn.com; ❸). Recently upgraded, it's a real bargain, with each of its fifteen suites offering its own kitchen, and beach equipment available for free loan. There's also inexpensive but good-quality **B&B** accommodation just up from Kalāheo at *Classic Vacation Cottages*, 2687 Onu Place (☎808/332-9201, ⓦwww.classiccottages.com; ❷–❸). They offer two houses, four garden cottages, and three studio apartments; all have private bathrooms and some form of kitchen.

If you're looking to pick up a snack as you pass through on the main highway – and especially useful if you're en route to or from Waimea Canyon – the ✈ *Kalāheo Café & Coffee Co*, 2-2560 Kaumualiʻi (Sun–Tues 6.30am–2.30pm, Wed–Sat 6.30am–2.30pm & 5.30–9.30pm; ☎808/332-5858), offers a vast selection of coffees from Kauai and beyond, plus cooked breakfasts and a wide assortment of burgers and salads later on. More serious **restaurants** include the *Brick Oven Pizza*, immediately opposite (Tues–Sun 11am–10pm; ☎808/322-8561), which is renowned for serving the best pizzas on Kauai, and the self-explanatory *Kalāheo Steak House*, alongside the *Kalāheo Inn* on Papalina Road (daily 6–10pm; ☎808/332-9780), where a full steak dinner costs under $20.

Hanapēpē Valley

Shortly after Kalāheo, the fields to the right of the highway drop away, and a roadside pull-out overlooks a colorful and deeply-worn gorge beneath a high mountain ridge. Many visitors imagine they're getting their first sight of Waimea Canyon, but this is in fact **Hanapēpē Valley**, a miniature version of the real thing. Watered by the broad Hanapēpē River, this fertile valley was once a major taro-growing center. As at the similar valley of Hanalei (see p.478), the land was turned over to rice by Chinese and Japanese immigrants at the end of the nineteenth century, but is now reverting to taro. The overlook was the scene of a bloody battle in August 1824, when forces led by Governor Hoapili of Maui defeated a band of insurgent Kauaians under Prince George, the son of the recently deceased chief Kaumualiʻi (see p.436).

ʻEleʻele and Port Allen

As it starts to drop towards sea level, the highway reaches **ʻELEʻELE**, making a sweeping rightward curve in front of the small ʻEleʻele Shopping Village complex. Following a minor road down behind the mall swiftly brings you to a dead end at **PORT ALLEN**, a small commercial harbor that's the base for several Nā Pali-tour boat companies (see p.490). Until the 1920s, when it was supplanted by the newly dredged Nāwiliwili Harbor, Port Allen was Kauai's main port; at the same time, the adjacent airport of Burns Field was replaced by Līhuʻe.

The only reason you might pause in ʻEleʻele itself is for a bite to **eat** in the Shopping Village. Right on the highway, *Grinds* (daily 6am–9pm; ☎808/335-6027) serves coffees and pastries to fishermen, boat trippers and other early risers, full cooked breakfasts for around $8, and later, sandwiches, plate lunches and pizzas for $8–10.

Hanapēpē

HANAPĒPĒ, at the foot of the hill beyond ʻEleʻele, is often lauded as one of Kauai's quaintest little villages. Driving straight through on the highway you'd barely notice it was there, and there's not all that much more to see if you take the half-mile detour down its old main street, just inland. Captioned photos tell you what each of the gently fading wooden stores of this former plantation town used to be, and it's worth pausing to take a look at those which have reinvented themselves as art galleries and specialty stores. Kauai Fine Arts (☎808/335-3778) has some interesting old maps and *aloha* shirts, while Vintage Aloha (☎808/332-7405) sells funky postcards, prints and gifts, and the café is a welcoming place to stop. The whole town stays open late on Friday evenings, which is much the liveliest time to visit.

The Hanapēpē River is not quite visible from the main street, but for more views you can either walk across the swinging rope bridge roughly opposite the café, which provides access to a riverbank footpath on the far side, or drive for a mile or two up Awawa Road just past the bridge at the west end of town.

Hanapēpē is also the only place where Hawaiian "**rock salt**" or *pa'a kai* is still manufactured by the traditional method of evaporation – a far from picturesque process, unfortunately. Turn *makai* of the highway just past town and you'll pass the "pans," expanses of red mud where sea water is collected and then allowed to dry away. Judging by the air of dilapidation, the pans are easily mistaken for refuse dumps. Souvenir shops on Kauai sell what they call Hawaiian salt, but it's unlikely to be the genuine article.

The road continues as far as **Salt Pond Park**, a little further on at the flat, windswept southwestern corner of the island. Windsurfers come here in droves, and the sheltered inshore bathing is good for children, but Iniki scoured away what little beauty the crescent beach possessed. There's plenty of room to **camp**, however (with a county permit; see p.448), so some budget travelers make it their base for exploring south and west Kauai.

Practicalities

Though Hanapēpē is devoid of accommodation, it does have a small selection of **restaurants**. On the old main street, the ⚘ *Hanapēpē Café & Espresso*, a former service station and drug store at 3830 Hanapēpē Rd (Mon–Thurs 11am–3pm, Fri 6–9pm; ☎808/335-5011), is a friendly, largely **vegetarian** establishment with a blue-tiled, horseshoe-shaped espresso bar. As well as smoothies and coffees it serves fine $7–9 sandwiches, like a roasted vegetable focaccia, as well as salads, *frittatas*, and specials like a $10 *bouillabaisse*. On Friday evenings it reopens for dinner, accompanied by slack-key guitar music; the menu changes every week, but the $18–25 entrees usually include international-themed dishes such as the baked eggplant Imam Biyaldi ($20) or a Russian *coulibac* of *mahi mahi*, baked in a brioche ($24).

Out on the highway, the *Green Garden* (Mon & Wed–Sat 10.30am–2pm & 5–9pm, Sun 7.30am–2pm & 5–9pm; ☎808/335-5422) offers a much less interesting menu of meats and sandwiches in a pleasant but often crowded garden setting.

Kaumakani

Kaumuali'i Highway turns northwest after Hanapēpē, heading towards Waimea through the extensive landholdings of the **Gay and Robinson family**. Though best known for owning the entire island of Niihau (see p.512), the family also owns what has become Kauai's last **sugar plantation**. This corner of the island is a patchwork quilt of cane fields (largely screened from view behind roadside trees and great swathes of bougainvillea) and open ranch land, used to pasture over three thousand head of cattle.

The plantation centers on the tiny community of **KAUMAKANI**, just over two miles out of Hanapēpē, where a picturesque Methodist church stands *mauka* of the highway. Across the road, an imposing avenue of trees leads down between twin rows of plantation houses. One of these is now the headquarters for two-hour **bus and walking tours** of the plantation (Mon–Sat 8.45am & 12.45pm; adults $34, ages 8–12 $25, under-8s not allowed; ☎808/335-2824 or 1-888/335-8687, Ⓦwww.robinsonadventures.com), for which advance reservations are required. In season, between April and October, you may well get to don a hard hat and see the mill in full operation; in winter, you'll still see the actual fields, but will have to content yourself with a video depicting what becomes of the cane. More adventurous visitors can explore backcountry areas of the plantation on what they call the **Jungle Pool ATV Adventure** (Mon–Sat 7.45am, 4hr 30min, $145; Mon–Sat 12.30pm, 3hr, $100).

Waimea

Six miles beyond Hanapēpē, the circle-island highway drops once more to sea level, crossing Waimea River to enter the town of **WAIMEA**. Sadly, despite being the spot where ancient Hawaiians first came into contact with European sailors, and despite its location at the portals of the magnificent Waimea Canyon, modern Waimea is a somewhat run-down, even seedy place.

The coming of Captain Cook

Captain James Cook sailed north from the Society Islands in December 1777, hoping to fulfill the aim of his third Pacific voyage – the discovery of the Northwest Passage back to the Atlantic. Instead he came upon an uncharted group of islands, north of the equator, in such a strategic location that he immediately recognized this as the crowning moment of his career.

Cook's two ships, the *Resolution* and the *Discovery*, had sailed from London in July 1776. On January 18, 1778, having passed far to the west of Hawaii and Maui, lookouts sighted first Oahu, and then Kauai. The following day, off the southeast corner of Kauai, two canoes came alongside, each carrying three or four men: "We were agreeably surprised to find them of the same Nation as the people of Otaheite [Tahiti] and the other islands we had lately visited," Cook wrote in his journal.

The ships sailed along the island's south coast looking for a place to land. With those canoes that dared to approach, they exchanged nails and small pieces of iron for "roasting pigs and some very fine Potatoes." When they finally found what seemed to be a safe anchorage, Cook allowed the natives of the nearest village, which he understood to be Wymoa, to come aboard:

"I never saw Indians so much astonished at the entering a ship before, their eyes were continually flying from object to object . . . However the first man that came on board did not with all his surprise, forget his own interest, the first moveable thing that came in his way was the lead and line, which he without asking any questions took to put into his Canoe and when we stopped him said 'I am only going to put it into my boat.'"

On the next day, January 20, Third Lieutenant Williamson was sent ashore in a small boat. Before he could set foot on dry land, he found himself besieged by curious Hawaiians. Despite feeling in no physical danger, and with the "greatest reluctance," he shot and killed "a tall handsome man about 40 years of age [who] seemed to be a chief." Williamson didn't even mention the incident to Cook until some weeks later, but wrote in his journal that "These barbarians must be [initially] quelled by force, as they afterwards readily believe that whatever kindness is then shown them proceeds from love, whereas otherwise they attribute it to weakness, or cowardice."

When Captain Cook arrived in 1778, Waimea Valley was a major population center, with taro farmers exploiting the rich soil inland, and fishermen plundering both river and ocean. *Waimea* literally means "reddish water," but the red earth scoured by the river from the mountains is deposited along the shoreline as a fine gray silt, leaving the beaches looking dirty and unappealing.

The town and the beaches

Waimea today amounts to little more than a short street, off the far end of which leads the lesser of the two poorly marked roads up to the canyon. There are no shops to speak of, apart from a Big Save supermarket, Da Booze Shop and the Wishy Washy Laundry.

A statue of Captain Cook stands on the small green in town – it's an exact replica of one in Cook's home port of Whitby, England – but the navigator's memory is not greatly honored in Waimea. The beach where he landed, west of the river mouth, is pointedly named **Lucy Wright Beach Park**, after the first native Hawaiian teacher at the local school. There is, at least, a very inconspicuous and much graffitied National Park Service plaque commemorating the exact spot; stuck atop a lava boulder, it offers no detail whatsoever, not even a date.

Cook himself landed near the mouth of the Waimea River later that day. "Several hundreds... were assembled on a sandy beach before the Village. The very instant I leaped ashore, they all fell flat on their faces, and remained in that humble posture till I made signs to them to rise. They then brought a great many small pigs and gave us without regarding whether they got any thing in return." Together with a small party of sailors and a "tolerable train" of Hawaiians, Cook walked up the valley, which was extensively planted with taro, sugar, plantains, and paper mulberry trees. He was led to a nearby *heiau* and told it had recently been used for human sacrifice.

Above all else, the Hawaiians were eager to trade for **iron**. The fact that they already owned tiny quantities of the metal might point to previous, unrecorded contact with Spanish explorers. Cook's men, however, noticed a worm-eaten piece of fir, washed up as driftwood, and speculated that the iron might have arrived in the same way. Local women found it easy to obtain scraps of metal from the sailors, and venereal diseases along with it, which despite all Cook's hand-wringing were established throughout the islands within a year.

The English ships stayed at Waimea for just three days. They were repeatedly blown from their moorings in the high winter seas, and having weighed anchor on January 23, were unable to get back in. Instead they spent a few days on Niihau, before continuing north. Cook's rendition of the name of Kauai as **Atoui** was not such a bad mistake, for it came from a mishearing of "and Kauai"; as the most leeward of the islands, Kauai tends to come at the end of the list. He named the archipelago the **Sandwich Islands**, in honor of the Earl of Sandwich (the same one for whom the sandwich had been named in 1762).

For an account of Cook's return to Hawaii in 1779, and his death at Kealekekua Bay, see p.186. Waimea was thereafter a principal port of call for Western ships, with the first fur-traders arriving in 1786. Captain John Kendrick of the *Lady Washington*, who picked up firewood here in 1791, sailed straight back again when he realized that his load included precious sandalwood. In doing so, he sparked the first boom in the Hawaiian economy, and fatally undermined the old political order (see p.539).

You're still likely to see locals surfing at the river mouth – it's a popular learning site for kids in summer – but this is one of the grubbiest and most polluted beaches in the state, and not suitable for swimming. You can, however, **camp** if you choose, with a county permit (see p.448).

Head upriver on either Menehune Road or Ala Wai Road, and shortly after they join, a mile or so along, you may spot traces of the **Menehune Ditch** at the foot of the bluff on the left. Whether or not this ancient irrigation channel was built by the legendary *menehune*, the care with which its stones were shaped makes it unique in Hawaii. However, little of it has survived. The road narrows and peters out not far beyond. For more about the *menehune*, see p.451.

Russian Fort Elizabeth State Historical Park

On the headland on the eastern side of Waimea River, the ruins of **Russian Fort Elizabeth** bear witness to a strange interlude in Kauaian history. When a Russian-American Company ship was wrecked off Waimea in 1815, the Kauaian chief Kaumuali'i seized both the vessel and its cargo of Alaskan furs. The company sent a German surgeon, **George Schäffer**, disguised as a botanist, to persuade Kamehameha the Great to talk Kaumuali'i into returning its property. That circuitous plan failed, so Schäffer decided to negotiate directly with Kaumuali'i instead. Soon Kaumuali'i had agreed to a secret treaty under which Schäffer would supply arms and ships for Kauai to invade Oahu, Maui, Molokai and Lanai, in return for Russian control over half of Oahu and various other concessions. To strengthen Kauai's defences, Schäffer started construction of a star-shaped fortress at Waimea in 1816. However, American merchantmen got wind of his plans, were told by other Russians that Schäffer was not acting on orders, and hatched their own plot to get rid of him. They managed to convince the whole population of Kauai, including Schäffer, that Russia and the United States were at war. In May 1817, Schäffer fled, as he thought, for his life.

Nonetheless, the fort was completed and used by the Hawaiian government until 1864. Though it has now been minimally reconstructed, with rudimentary walls laid out according to a ground plan decided more by guesswork than by excavation, it would take a lot of imagination to derive any interest from this tumble-down relic, overgrown with dandelions. Official statistics show that it's the most visited attraction on Kauai, with 300,000 tourists per year, though footnotes in the HVB report reveal that the vast majority are tour-bus passengers using the rest rooms en route to Waimea Canyon.

Practicalities

The **West Kauai Technology & Visitor Center**, at the north end of town at the foot of Waimea Canyon Drive, and so named because it's intended to promote business opportunities in this otherwise depressed corner of the island, provides informative displays on local history and attractions (Mon–Fri 9.30am–5pm; ☎808/338-1332, ⓦwww.wkbpa.org/visitorcenter.html). Free, two-hour walking tours of Waimea leave from here at 9.30am on Mondays.

Western Kauai's only **accommodation** possibility is one of the most appealing and characterful properties on the island. *ResortQuest Waimea Plantation Cottages*, just west of Waimea at 9400 Kaumuali'i (☎808/338-1625 or 1-866/774-2924; ⓦwww.resortquesthawaii.com; ⑤–⑧), are the former homes of Waimea Sugar Mill Company employees, gathered in a coconut grove and fully renovated. Ordinary plantation workers may not have lived this close to the sea, or have had such luxurious bathrooms, but the atmosphere feels authentic, and the wooden floors, linen draperies and breezy *lānais* make the one-, two- and three-bedroom cottages a delight. The sea isn't safe for swimming and the beach is gray, but there's a pool, and the garden hammocks have good views of Niihau.

Alongside the plantation headquarters, just off the highway amid the coconut palms, the *Waimea Brewing Company* calls itself the "world's westernmost **brewpub**" (daily 7–10am & 11am–9pm; ☎808/338-2300). It's a pleasant spot, with plenty of shaded seating out on the terrace, wild chickens on the prowl, and a faded turquoise wooden bar inside. There's a reasonable food menu, with a seared *poke* wrap or *kālua* pork sandwich for $10–12, while entrees such as mango stout barbecue ribs or crusted *ono* range up to $26, but sadly the beer itself – a 16oz glass of the wittily named Wai'ale'ale Ale costs $5 – is nothing special.

Waimea proper also holds a handful of inexpensive restaurants, including the central *Wranglers Steakhouse* (Mon–Thurs 11am–8.30pm, Fri 11am–9pm, Sat 5–9pm; ☎808/338-1218), and the good *Pacific Pizza & Deli* (daily 11am–9pm; ☎808/338-1020) next door.

West of Waimea

Virtually all the tourists who make it as far west as Waimea are traveling en route to Waimea Canyon and Kōke'e State Park, described on p.514 onwards. If you ignore both the roads that head off up the canyon, however, it's possible to continue further **west from Waimea** as far as one of the longest, largest beaches in all Hawaii.

Kekaha

Just over a mile beyond *Waimea Plantation Cottages*, the highway passes the approach road to the small-boat harbor at **Kīkīaola**, the point of departure for many Nā Pali boat tours (see p.490). A mile or so on, it briefly runs along the shoreline at **KEKAHA**. The beach here starts to consist of sand, rather than the muddy dirt of Waimea, but thanks to Iniki very little of it is left. As a rule, only expert surfers enter the water; the waves are usually too powerful for swimming.

Away from the sea, Kekaha boasts a few minor **churches** and a gigantic, rusting sugar mill. A little mall at the foot of Kōke'e Road, the second and more important canyon approach road holds a *Lapperts* ice-cream store and the *Menehune Food Mart* supermarket.

Pacific Missile Range Facility

The long straight section of Kaumuali'i Highway immediately past Kekaha, much loved by island motorcycle freaks, ends ten miles out of Waimea, where a sharp left turn leads to the US Navy's **Pacific Missile Range Facility (PMRF)**. This installation is part of a network of naval early warning systems developed after World War II in an attempt to prevent any repetition of the attack on Pearl Harbor.

In the last few years, against a backdrop of military cutbacks elsewhere, the base has become a linchpin of US defense strategy. The Navy's only research site that can test missiles, aircraft, surface warships and submarines, it benefits from having over forty thousand square miles of open ocean to the northwest that are entirely unused by commercial aircraft. Lying, supposedly, within range of North Korea's nuclear capability, the facility has played a crucial role in developing and testing the so-called "Son of Star Wars" missile shield. As well as increasingly successful intercepts of incoming dummy missiles by the Navy's SM-3 missiles, it's also the headquarters for work on the Army's equivalent program, known as Theater High Altitude Area Defense (THAAD).

Very few outsiders see anything more of the island of **Niihau** than a misty silhouette on the horizon, eighteen miles off the west coast of Kauai. The "Forbidden Island" remains the private property of the Scottish **Gay and Robinson family**, who bought it during the nineteenth century. Paradoxically, by turning the whole island into a cattle ranch, they also effectively froze it in time, and Niihau is widely seen as a sanctuary of traditional Hawaiian culture. Under the Robinsons' quasi-feudal patronage, the islanders are reasonably free to come and go, but unauthorized visitors are arrested and expelled.

The smallest of the seven inhabited Hawaiian islands, Niihau measures eighteen miles long by six miles wide. It receives just twelve inches of rain a year, so almost all of its 73 square miles are desert, and there are no permanent forests. While the bulk of the island consists of low, arid dunes, its northeast coast – the part most easily seen from Kauai – is lined by sheer sea cliffs. These are thought to have formed the west rim of the volcano that created Niihau (the rest is long since submerged); the highest point is **Pāni'au**, at 1281 feet. Off the north coast is the islet of **Lehua**, an eroded crescent-shaped tuff cone like Molokini off Maui (and equally good for divers). The southern plains hold two lakes, the 182-acre **Halulu** and the 860-acre **Halali'i**, Hawaii's largest lake.

Little is known of Niihau's ancient history; only one archeologist has ever been allowed on to the island, to make a brief survey in 1912. It's thought, however, that as many as ten thousand Hawaiians lived here, fishing and growing yams and sugar cane – enough people for two rival chiefs to fight a war before the island could be united.

Captain Cook called at Niihau in 1778, having been driven away from Kauai by adverse winds (see p.509). Niihau was the recipient of his first gifts: goats, pigs, pumpkin and melon seeds, and onions. On Kauai, he had been relatively successful in preventing his crew from spreading venereal diseases to the Hawaiians. Here, however, they proved uncontrollable, and the infections had spread throughout the entire island chain by the time he returned a year later.

The population of Niihau had slumped by 1864, when **Elizabeth Sinclair** arrived with her extended family. She had previously farmed for twenty years in Scotland, and another twenty in New Zealand. A widow with five children (two of whom had married men called **Gay** and **Robinson**), she was en route to a new life in California when she decided to live in Hawaii instead. Negotiating with King Kamehameha IV for a $10,000 tract of farming land, she was offered a stretch of the Oahu coastline that took in all of Waikīkī and most of what's now downtown Honolulu. Instead, she opted for the island of Niihau; family tradition has it that the Sinclair party arrived to inspect the island shortly after one of its very rare rain showers, and were deceived by the greenness.

The people of Niihau were appalled at the idea of their homeland being sold. They petitioned the king to be allowed to buy it themselves, and many emigrated when the sale went through. One family had already purchased their own lands, but the Sinclairs soon bought them out, stacking $1000 in dollar coins, one by one, until they could resist no longer. Barely a hundred islanders were left when **Niihau Ranch** was set up.

Well before she died in 1892 at the age of 93, Mrs Sinclair had realized Niihau was of only marginal use for agriculture and started to buy land on western Kauai. Her descendants have continued to do so ever since, and Gay and Robinson (as the family business is known) now holds almost as many acres on Kauai as on Niihau.

In addition, as part of NASA's "Helios" project, the PMRF is the base for ongoing experiments with unmanned, solar-powered, propeller-driven aircraft, including one model intended to fly in the skies of **Mars**. Finally, with all that sonar scanning equipment, the facility has a sideline recording the songs of humpback whales.

The Robinson family imposed a strict way of life on the island, obliging every inhabitant to attend church services and banning the ownership of dogs. The policy of isolation from the outside world, however, only developed after Hawaii was annexed by the US in 1898, when the Robinsons became convinced it was their mission to preserve Niihau from the changes taking place elsewhere in the islands.

Around 160 people now live on Niihau, almost all of them in its one village, **Pu'uwai** ("heart"), a tangle of red-dirt roads on the west coast. The island has no airport and no cars and lacks modern plumbing. In the last few years, raising sheep and cattle on the Niihau Ranch has proved increasingly unprofitable, so there are no real jobs beyond maintaining the ranch infrastructure at a minimal level. Instead, almost all island families are on welfare, supplementing their income perhaps by fishing, raising mullet, making charcoal and collecting honey. Niihau is also renowned for necklaces made from the tiny shells that wash up on its beaches. Most households run small electric generators, and have radios but not TVs. The favorite game of local children is said to be reciting Bible verses to each other and trying to identify them.

What makes Niihau truly unique, however, is that it's the only place where everyone still speaks **Hawaiian** as a first language. As the island never fell prey to the missionary attempts to standardize and simplify the language (see p.581), the version spoken on Niihau is believed to be the purest, and most authentically pronounced, that survives.

The people of Niihau were alone among Hawaiians in voting against statehood in 1959, and the state government has repeatedly tried to buy back the island. Particularly controversial is the fact that the Robinsons refuse to recognize the state law that guarantees free access to all Hawaiian beaches. The Hawaiian media has a tradition of running exposés that "reveal" the true state of affairs on Niihau – one TV documentary, for example, alleged that its inhabitants were kept in conditions not far removed from slavery – and its public image in the rest of the state is not good.

In the late 1990s, partly to strengthen the island's ailing economy and partly to placate state legislators, the Robinsons invited the US Navy to expand its Pacific Missile Range Facility (see p.511) onto Niihau. The plan was to install missile launchers, tracking equipment, and even an airfield. It seems to have fallen through, however, because the state demanded a thorough archeological survey of the island first. The family are said to fear that were ancient artifacts to be discovered, Niihau would become a *cause célèbre* with Hawaiian activists, much like Kahoolawe (see p.332).

The only legal way to set foot on Niihau is as a passenger in the **helicopter** that serves as an air ambulance for island medical emergencies. To defray costs, this runs three-hour trips from western Kauai to Niihau whenever four passengers are prepared to pay $325 each for the privilege. It lands twice, at the northernmost and southernmost beaches on the island, Kamakalepo Point and Keanahaki, and does not go anywhere near Pu'uwai. For full details, contact Niihau Helicopters, PO Box 690370, Makaweli HI 96769 (☏1-877/441-3500 or 808/335-3500; ✉niihauisland@hawaiian.net).

To get a close-up view of the island, you can also join a **snorkeling cruise** from Port Allen. Both Holoholo Charters (☏808/335-0815 or 1-800/848-6130, ⊛www.holoholo charters.com; $160 if booked online), and Blue Dolphin (☏1-877/511-1311 or 808/335-5553, ⊛www.kauaiboats.com; $175), run seven-hour trips that combine a Nā Pali cruise with crossing the Kaulakahi Channel to Niihau. There they sail just offshore and stop either in the lee of South Point, where the lack of run-off and scant visitation creates some of the very best snorkeling conditions in all of Hawaii, or at Lehua.

Depending on current activities, the sentries may permit you to drive to one of the exposed on-site beaches, of interest mainly to surfers. Keep your eyes peeled – who knows what you might see?

Polihale State Park

So long as you don't mind driving on unsurfaced roads, you can skirt around the test facility and continue up the coast. Keep going straight past the entrance, and the main road veers sharply inland, where a sign soon directs you left onto a straight dirt road. Bumpy and dusty it may be, running for much of the year through head-high cane fields, but it's perfectly manageable. Slowly the hills to the right climb upwards and turn into cliffs, until progress is barred after just over five miles by the start of the Nā Pali coast.

This spot, **Polihale State Park**, protects a segment of a fifteen-mile-long beach that stretches to Kekaha. The main parking lot is half a mile short of the boulders that mark the first Nā Pali headland; trudge to the end and you'll be able to make out another three or so headlands beyond that. While the endless sands and crashing surf make a compelling spectacle, drownings in the mighty waves are all too common; even beachcombers have been swept away. Park facilities remain minimal to say the least, but with a $5-per-night permit from the state parks office (see p.448) you're welcome to **camp**.

Walking back south along the coast from Polihale, you soon come to the undulating dunes known as the **Barking Sands**. Rising up to a hundred feet high at the Nohili Point headland, they owe their name to an ability to produce strange sounds, variously described as growling or hooting as well as barking. Each grain of sand is said to be hollow, so they reverberate when rubbed together. Suggested methods of making the sands perform include grinding handfuls together, sliding down the dunes, and dragging a companion as fast as possible across them.

Waimea Canyon and Kōke'e State Park

Two of the major scenic attractions in all Hawaii – the gorge of **Waimea Canyon** and **Kōke'e State Park** (with its views of the Nā Pali coast to one side and the sodden Alaka'i Swamp to the other) – can only be reached from the west coast of Kauai. Waimea Canyon is always seen from above, from the viewpoints along the eighteen-mile **Waimea Canyon Drive**, which climbs its western flank. That starts just beyond Waimea, is joined eight miles up by the easier **Kōke'e Road** from further along the coast, and then carries on for another ten miles, entering Kōke'e State Park beyond the canyon proper and ending at the vertiginous cliffs above Kalalau Valley. The ancient Hawaiians continued on foot from there, scrambling down to the North Shore, but now neither road nor trail attempts the descent.

Although you can rent a cabin or camp overnight in Kōke'e, the great majority of visitors see both canyon and park on a single day-trip. While you can enjoy superb and widely differing views without having to **hike**, trails lead off to further unforgettable spots.

Waimea Canyon

It was supposedly Mark Twain who first called **Waimea Canyon** the "Grand Canyon of the Pacific." In fact, Twain never visited the island, but the comparison is not unreasonable. At something over three thousand feet, it may not be quite as deep as its Arizona rival, but the colors – all shades of green against the red earth – and the way it is squeezed into such a tiny island, are absolutely breathtaking.

Like all the Hawaiian islands, Kauai was once a vast volcano, of whose original contours little trace remains. Torrential rains have eroded Waimea Canyon into its present form, but that process began when a massive geological fault cracked the island down the middle. Eventually, the canyon will wear its way back to meet Kalalau Valley, and possibly split the island in two; for the moment, the two are separated by the eerie basin of the Alaka'i Swamp.

Waimea Canyon Drive

The most dramatic route up to Waimea Canyon is along **Waimea Canyon Drive** (Hwy-550), which turns right off the highway as you leave Waimea, soon after the *Shrimp Station* restaurant and just after a sign indicating that you should *not* turn right. The other route, **Kōke'e Road** (Hwy-55), sets off from Kekaha (see p.511), roughly three miles on. Because of its greater width and shallower gradient, all the tour buses go that way, so it's likely to be a much slower drive.

This is not to say, however, that you should race up Waimea Canyon Drive. Speeding around the curves is far too dangerous, and even if you don't stop, it takes almost an hour to drive the eighteen miles to the top. Following Waimea Canyon Drive from the start enables you to watch the canyon grow alongside you, turning from a gentle tree-covered valley to an ever-deeper gash.

By the time Kōke'e Road comes in from the left, after eight miles, the canyon has reached a mile wide. It's worth stopping at each of the roadside lookouts from here

△ Waimea Canyon

onwards. The first, 10.5 miles up from Waimea, is **Waimea Canyon Lookout**. It's also the lowest, of course, but 3400 feet straight down from the edge still seems a very long way. Located at the junction of several distinct fissures in the rock, it tends to be very misty in the morning. The bare red earth slips away beneath your feet into the vagueness, while the weathered cliffs immediately below resemble the pinnacles of the Nā Pali coast. In the late afternoon the view is utterly different, glowing orange and red in the setting sun.

Next comes the **Pu'u Ka Pele Lookout**, shortly before milepost 13. From opposite the start of Polihale Ridge Road – which runs a short distance towards the cliffs above Polihale – this surveys a side chasm as it drops down towards the main canyon. On the far wall, you may be able to make out Waipo'o Falls (see below).

Less than a mile further on comes the large **Pu'u Hinahina Lookout**. The viewing area, perched above crumbling jagged slopes, looks straight down the head of another gorge. Far below, Waiahulu Stream plunges towards the main valley, echoing with the distant bleating of goats. A thousand shades of two main colors fill the canyon walls, mixed in different proportions as the shadows lengthen: by the evening, one side radiates warm russet highlights, the other luxuriates in dark green, and gray mists spill over both edges. The Canyon Trail (see below) runs along the promontory almost directly in front of you, slightly below and off to the left.

Best visited early in the day, the **Niihau Lookout**, to the right of the same parking lot, offers views out to the cloud-shrouded island of Niihau (see p.512), floating on the Pacific, way beyond the trees. Its profile is three-dimensional, with flat leaves of land jutting from below a central plateau; to its right is tiny pyramid-shaped **Lehua**.

Waimea Canyon hikes

The best way to take a **day-hike** in the Waimea Canyon area is to pick your own combination of the Cliff, Canyon and Black Pipe trails, which lead off **Halemanu Valley Road**. This dirt road heads right shortly after milepost 14 on Waimea Canyon Drive, but is seldom fit to drive in an ordinary vehicle; park at one of the pull-outs around the intersection, and set off on foot.

All the above trails start on the same path, which cuts away to the right after half a mile once the road has dipped to cross Halemanu Stream and then risen again. Ignore the turnoff for the Canyon and Black Pipe trails not far along, and keep going towards the end of the **Cliff Trail**, a walk of barely five minutes.

The narrow footpath soon emerges from the woods to run along a railed bluff, with the green, sharp planes of the canyon to your right and wooded hills to your left; from here you can look all the way down the canyon. Though the trail appears to continue, first on to a ridge immediately below you, and then across to a worn red-earth track above the steep drop ahead, there's no direct connection, and the promontory in front of the railing is not recommended.

However, you can reach the trail visible in the distance – the **Canyon Trail** – by retracing your steps as far as the intersection mentioned above and turning right. As this path dips into the gullies between the exposed headlands, the terrain constantly changes, from dry brush in semi-desert to lush green. The Canyon Trail proper starts a third of a mile along, with a sharp descent through thick woodlands. It then comes out on the rounded red ridge you've already seen from the Cliff Trail, which gently curves away towards an abysmal drop. Pick your way along that, and the path soon doubles back on itself towards two small waterfalls, reached by clambering through thick vegetation and across boulders. The pool at the upper end of the **Waipo'o Falls**, where the stream springs out of the rock, is ideal for cooling off after the hike; lower down, you can let the main flow tumble over you. Don't try to go any lower, however; the huge main falls soon bar your way.

From this point you can head back to join the **Black Pipe Trail**, which loops through the forest to rejoin Halemanu Valley Road after some steep but spectacular climbing. That makes a total hike of between two and three hours. Alternatively, the Canyon Trail heads onwards around the lip of the canyon to meet up with Kumuwela Ridge, from which it's possible to make a larger loop, via two other trails, back to your starting point. At least two of the day-hikes in Kōke'e park are more rewarding, however (see p.520), so that option only makes sense if you have several days to spare.

Kōke'e State Park

The boundaries that separate Waimea Canyon State Park from Kōke'e State Park – and, for that matter, from the Pu'u Ka Pele Forest Reserve and the Nā Pali-Kona Forest Reserve – are imperceptible, and in places not even defined. Broadly speaking, **Kōke'e State Park** starts beyond the Pu'u Hinahina Lookout, as the highway veers away from the canyon rim. To the south and east, the park abuts the high valleys that lead into Waimea Canyon; to the north and west, it drops to the sheer cliffs of the Nā Pali coast. Waimea Canyon Drive follows the crest of Kaunuohua Ridge as it climbs and narrows through the woods until it finally peters out.

Although much of Kōke'e consists of alpine forest, its most remarkable feature is the all-but-impenetrable **Alaka'i Swamp**. In this natural volcanic bowl, cupped between the mountaintops, the heaviest rainfall on earth collects to form a strange, primordial quagmire. More of a very wet rainforest than a conventional swamp, it remains home to a unique range of flora and fauna. The few humans who manage to penetrate the mists are assailed on all sides by the shrills, whistles and buzzes of a jungle without any mammals (save the odd tiny mouse) or snakes. The word "Alaka'i" means "leader" or "to lead" in Hawaiian; the name reflects the fact that anyone venturing into the swamp alone before the modern trail was built was very likely to get lost.

The park headquarters: Kanaloahuluhulu

Kōke'e State Park has its headquarters in a grassy clearing to the left of the road, just after milepost 15. While much of the forest of Kōke'e has been cut down and replanted in the last two centuries, this meadow has been here since ancient times. The Hawaiians who paused here on the trek to Kalalau called it **Kanaloahuluhulu**, claiming it had been cleared by the god Kanaloa to get rid of an evil spirit who had been attacking travelers.

A small hut at the entrance to the parking lot calls itself the park visitor center, but is rarely open. You can pick up information at either *Kōke'e Lodge*, beyond it on the left, or a few yards further on at **Kōke'e Natural History Museum** (daily 10am–4pm; $1 donation). The museum consists of a couple of large rooms in a wooden cabin, where the staff sell a wide range of books and maps and provide up-to-the-minute hiking tips. All the major trails are shown on a relief model of the island; wall displays cover meteorology and, especially, Hurricane Iniki, and there are several cases of stuffed birds and other exhibits.

The larger *Kōke'e Lodge* building holds a souvenir store, public rest rooms and a reasonable and inexpensive cafeteria open daily for breakfast (served 9–11am) and lunch (9am–3.30pm). Takeout sandwiches are available from 9.30am onwards, while lunch specials include local dishes such as the $6.25 Portuguese bean soup.

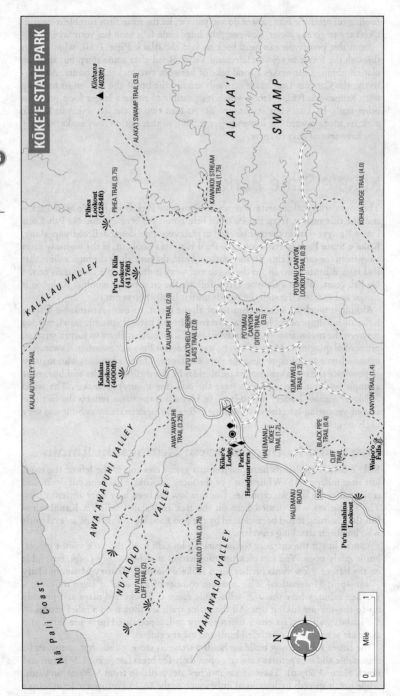

KŌKE'E STATE PARK

Nā Pali Coast

KALALAU VALLEY

AWA'AWAPUHI VALLEY

NU'ALOLO VALLEY

MAHANALOA VALLEY

ALAKA'I SWAMP

▲ Kilohana
(4030ft)

Pihea Lookout
(4284ft)

PIHEA TRAIL (3.75)

ALAKA'I SWAMP TRAIL (3.5)

KAWAIKOI STREAM
TRAIL (1.75)

KOHUA RIDGE TRAIL (4.0)

Pu'u O Kila
Lookout
(4176ft)

KALALAU VALLEY TRAIL

KALUAPUHI TRAIL (2.0)

PU'U KA'OHELO-BERRY
FLATS TRAIL (2.0)

PO'OMAU CANYON
LOOKOUT TRAIL (0.3)

PO'OMAU
CANYON
DITCH TRAIL (3.5)

Kalalau
Lookout
(4000ft)

AWA'AWAPUHI
TRAIL (3.25)

KUMUWELA
TRAIL (1.2)

NU'ALOLO
CLIFF TRAIL (2)

NU'ALOLO TRAIL (3.75)

Kōke'e
Lodge

Park
Headquarters

HALEMANU-
KŌKE'E
TRAIL (1.2)

BLACK PIPE
TRAIL (0.4)

CANYON
TRAIL (1.4)

CLIFF
TRAIL

HALEMANU ROAD

550

Waipo'o
Falls

Pu'u Hinahina Lookout

N

Mile

0   1

Footpaths lead up behind the lodge to the ⅍ *Kōke'e Lodge Housekeeping Cabins* (PO Box 367, Waimea HI 96796; ℡808/335-6061; ❸). Each of these **rental cabins** sleeps from three to seven persons, and is available for a maximum of five days (Fri & Sat can only be rented together). They have bed linen, hot water, fridges and wood stoves – bring your own food for evening meals and buy firewood from the store, as it gets cold up here at night. Ideally you should reserve in advance, but if you haven't, it's worth enquiring at the *Lodge* to see if a cabin is available.

You can also **camp** just north of the meadow, so long as you have a $5 permit from the state parks office in Līhu'e (see p.448), which can also provide details of other campgrounds tucked away on the dirt roads to either side of Waimea Canyon Drive. *YWCA Camp Sloggett* (℡808/335-6060; ❶), across the highway from the Kanaloahuluhulu meadow, offers **hostel** accommodation in its bunkhouse for $20 per bed (bring your own linen). There's also a ten-person lodge, rented out to one group of five or more visitors at a time, again for $20 each, and a campground that charges tent campers $10 per person.

The highway lookouts

Waimea Canyon Drive continues three miles beyond *Kōke'e Lodge* before squeezing to a halt above Kalalau Valley. There's little to see in this final stretch – you pass a couple of trailheads and glimpse the white "golf ball" belonging to Kauai's missile defense system – before the **Kalalau Lookout** at milepost 18.

As you leave your car to walk towards the viewing area, it looks as though nothing lies beyond the railings. Then, framed by scattered *lehua* trees and arching ferns, comes the vast, magnificent panorama of Kalalau Valley, seen here from the head of its slightly shorter west branch. To either side of the broad valley floor, rich with trees, soar sheer green walls, pleated into deep clefts through which plunge slender white waterfalls. Occasional red slashes in the hillsides show where landslides have sheared the razorback ridges. Reaching up from immediately below you, and hard to distinguish from the background, are several separate stand-alone pinnacles.

The views are at their best early in the morning; later on, the valley repeatedly fills with mist, and there's a risk you may see nothing. Clouds appear from nowhere; you won't see them approach across the ocean, as this is the spot where they are born, when Pacific winds are forced to climb 4000 feet. For an account of Kalalau Valley at ground level, see p.494.

Tear your gaze away to trace the brief ridge that curves east from where you're standing towards the end of the road. This is the last tiny remnant of the caldera rim of the volcano that built Kauai.

Depending on the current state of the road beyond the Kalalau Lookout, which is frequently closed for long periods while awaiting repair, you can either walk or drive another half-mile to reach the **Pu'u O Kila Lookout**, which commands another stunning prospect, looking directly down the main body of Kalalau Valley. Only one wall is revealed in all its majesty, but the bonus here is that you can look inland as well, across the wilderness of the Alaka'i Swamp to the summit of Mount Wai'ale'ale. One second the entire valley basin can be brimming with mist; the next second the swirling clouds may unveil a staggering prospect of the Nā Pali coastline. Even when nothing is visible to the north, the swamplands to the south can remain clear, and you can watch the flight-seeing helicopters cross Alaka'i and drop down into Kalalau.

Kōke'e hikes

Kōke'e is fortunate in boasting several excellent **hiking trails**, many of which were upgraded using federal funds in the wake of Hurricane Iniki. They're easy to follow and equipped with small, yellow-on-brown wayside signs marking each quarter-mile. Some trails marked on older maps, however, no longer exist, while others are not maintained and tend to involve much hopeful but potentially dangerous wandering through the forests; call at Kōke'e Museum (see p.517) for information before you set off. Whichever route you choose, get going **early**, before the clouds set in. Note also that **hunting** for feral goats and pigs is allowed on weekends and holidays, so casual hikers should wear bright clothing.

While you should certainly stick to the named trails, don't feel obliged to follow just one trail from start to finish; most of the best hikes involve **combinations** of different trails. If you have just one day, an ideal route would be to follow the **Pihea Trail** down from Pu'u O Kila Lookout as far as its intersection with the **Alaka'i Swamp Trail**, walk the last two miles of that to Kilohana, and then retrace your steps. The round-trip takes six hours, allowing for an hour's stop at the end. You can walk the other half of both trails – less exciting but, at two hours, much quicker – by taking the Alaka'i Swamp Trail from its trailhead to the same intersection, then following the Pihea Trail down as far as the **Kawaikoi Stream Trail**, and looping back to the Alaka'i trailhead along that.

For the best views of the Nā Pali cliffs, another good combination – though not recommended for anyone with vertigo – is to hike down the **Awa'awapuhi Trail**, follow the **Nu'alolo Cliff Trail** along the ridge, and return to the road via the **Nu'alolo Trail**. If you set off early enough, the six-hour hike will have you back at *Kōke'e Lodge* in time for lunch.

The Pihea Trail

Waimea Canyon Drive was originally intended to run on beyond the Pu'u O Kila Lookout, and to connect somehow with the North Shore. Mountain mud swallowed several earth-moving vehicles before that project was abandoned, but its planned route remains obvious. This broad, undulating groove continues straight ahead from the lookout, cutting through the red clay of the ridge, and now forms the start of the **Pihea Trail**. Hikers can choose between a short out-and-back stroll offering views of both Kalalau Valley and the Alaka'i Swamp, or a more demanding trek down into the swamp itself.

The first mile of the Pihea Trail follows the high crest of Kalalau Valley. At the far end, the **Pihea Lookout** is (at 4284 feet) the highest peak of all. If you can see it below the clouds from Pu'u O Kila, it makes for a great hour's hike. For over half the way, the trail is wide and even; then you have to pick your way over tree roots and scramble up hills. It's safe and manageable, but narrows at times to a few feet, with precipitous drops on either side, while visibility regularly drops to nothing as clouds siphon across the ridge.

Just before the final climb up to the Pihea Lookout – which is almost vertical, and usually extremely muddy – the Pihea Trail proper makes a sharp right turn to descend into the swamp. After a hundred yards of slithering down the clay slope, a plank boardwalk makes an appearance. It soon becomes a smooth, gradual staircase down the hillside, which reaches the obvious **four-way intersection** of boardwalks with the Alaka'i Swamp Trail 1.75 miles from the parking lot.

As suggested above, turning left at this point enables you to combine the best of both trails; see p.522 for an account of how the trail continues if you choose to do so. If you continue down the Pihea Trail, however, the boardwalk ends within a minute or two and the path drops ever more steeply. In dry weather, this is a green and lovely walk. The ground is so spongy underfoot, with its thick carpeting of moss, and the trees and shrubs to either side are so small and stunted, that it can feel almost surreal, as though you've blundered into Lilliput. Lizards scuttle into the undergrowth as you approach, and bright birds call melodiously from the branches.

The trail zigzags down the thickly vegetated *pali* to reach babbling Kawaikoi Stream, then heads right, following the bank through pleasant woodlands, and once or twice crossing small side-streams. Shortly after a basic picnic shelter at the 3-mile marker, you ford the wide main stream via rocks in the riverbed, then join the **Kawaikoi Stream Trail** on the far side. Away to the left, this makes a mile-long loop around some luscious mountain streams; turning right brings you (in about fifteen minutes) to a plank footbridge, two miles from Alaka'i junction, that marks the end of the trail.

The Birds of Kōke'e

Thanks to its remoteness, Kōke'e State Park is one of the last great sanctuaries for native Hawaiian **birds**, safe here from their two main predators. When the **mongoose** was imported into Hawaii (see p.551), it lived off the eggs of defenseless ground-nesting birds. Kauai, however, was the only island spared the mongoose invasion, so many native species of bird that were wiped out on the other islands survived here; a reported sighting of a mongoose on Kauai in 2004 might augur the worst. **Mosquitoes** first came to Hawaii when a whaling ship taking on fresh water on Maui discharged its stagnant casks into a handy stream; the insects have been infecting native birds with avian malaria ever since. In theory, they can't live more than 3500 feet above sea level, so the Alaka'i Swamp has remained protected, though there are alarming reports that Hawaiian mosquitoes may be evolving to cope with higher altitudes.

Those birds that established themselves in Hawaii before the arrival of the Polynesians did so by chance. Thus a single blown-astray finch evolved into over fifty separate species of honey-creeper, each adapted to some specific habitat or diet. In Kōke'e these included the bright scarlet **'i'iwi**, with its black wings, orange legs and salmon-colored sickle-shaped bill, perfect for sipping nectar; the **'apapane**, which also has a red body and black wings but has a short, slightly curved black bill; the tiny greenish-yellow **'anianiau**; and the predominantly black **mamo**. In addition there was the **pueo**, or Hawaiian owl, which flies by day, not night, and the rust-colored **'elepaio** flycatcher. Meanwhile, majestic **tropicbirds** soar above the Nā Pali coast and Waimea Canyon. The white-tailed variety, the *koa'e kea*, cruises the wind-currents high above the valleys, then plummets into the ocean in pursuit of fish and squid.

Ancient Hawaiians never lived in Kōke'e, but they climbed this high to collect feathers. The *mamo* would be trapped on a sticky branch, its long yellow tail plumage plucked for use in ceremonial cloaks and *leis*, and then released; the *'i'iwi* was stripped bare and kept for food. The Hawaiians also came looking for the tall, straight *koa* trees, thrusting from the steepest valleys, that made the best canoes. They were guided by the *'elepaio*; if it settled for too long on a *koa*, that meant the tree was riddled with insects and thus unsuitable for use.

All the native birds found on Kauai at the time of Captain Cook are thought to have survived until 1964, when the last *akialoa* died. After that, the rarest was another honey-creeper, the **'ō'ō 'ā'ā**, whose yellow "garter" feathers were prized by the Hawaiians. Before Hurricane Iwa hit Kōke'e in 1982, there were thought to be fewer than ten birds left, living deep in the Alaka'i Swamp. Only one was ever subsequently spotted, tending its treetop nest and calling for a mate that never answered.

By far the most conspicuous bird in Kōke'e today is the **moa**, or **red jungle fowl**. Hawaii's only surviving descendants of the chickens brought by the Polynesians, these raucous creatures strut around outside the museum and restaurant at Kanaloa-huluhulu, or scurry down the trails. For all their haughty demeanor, they're not exactly intelligent; they peck away indiscriminately, and will no doubt try to eat your license plate or rearview mirror.

For more about Hawaiian birds, see the "Environment" section in Contexts, starting on p.549.

The **Kawaikoi Picnic Area** here is a broad meadow with two more shelters and a restroom. If you turn right onto the dirt road at the far end, a fifteen-minute climb brings you to the Alaka'i picnic area and the trailhead of the **Alaka'i Swamp Trail**. If you've parked up at Pu'u O Kila, you could walk to the Pihea/Alaka'i intersection, then back up the Pihea Trail, and be back at your car within about five hours. By road, following the dirt road to the park headquarters and then climbing Waimea Canyon Drive, it's much further.

Another four miles or so of dirt road lie beyond the Kawaikoi Picnic Area, but you'd need a 4WD vehicle, and a lot of time, to take advantage of the remote trails that lead along and down the far side of Waimea Canyon.

The Alaka'i Swamp Trail

For many years the **Alaka'i Swamp Trail** had the reputation of being not only the most arduous hike on Kauai, but also the dirtiest, a protracted wade through thigh-deep mud guaranteed to ruin your clothes. Since the Kōke'e trails were upgraded, however, a boardwalk has covered almost its entire 3.5-mile length, and it is nowhere near as fearsome as legend suggests.

Nonetheless, hikers still have to wage a constant battle of wits against the cloying black swamp, as thrusting tree roots and subsiding mud holes ensure that the boardwalk can never fully be relied upon. Apart from the magnificent **view** at the far end, the main reward for hikers is the swamp's rare and resplendent **vegetation**. Giant ferns dangle above the trail, and orchids gleam from the undergrowth, while the trees – especially in June – erupt into brilliant flowering displays.

As outlined on p.520, the second and more interesting half of the trail can be combined with walking the Pihea Trail from the Pu'u O Kila Lookout. If you want to hike the whole thing, however, start by driving as close as possible to the trailhead along the dirt road (marked *YWCA Camp Sloggett*) that leads right from Waimea Canyon Drive just beyond the entrance to the Kōke'e State Park headquarters. Keep going beyond the YWCA camp until you reach a sign, 1.7 miles from the highway, warning that only 4WD vehicles can proceed; there should be room to park here.

Now walk about a mile further along the road, first sharply down to cross the Kauaikanana Stream and then back up again, until you come to a sign announcing the Nā Pali-Kona Forest Reserve, and another pointing to the various trails nearby. This spot is the **Alaka'i Picnic Area**; ahead of you spreads your first large-scale overview of the swamp itself, while on the horizon to the left is the ridge that holds the highway and the Kalalau lookouts.

Before continuing, take the short spur trail to your right. After a few yards it stops at the end of a high promontory pointing straight towards **Po'omau Canyon**, one of the narrow gorges that feed into the top end of Waimea Canyon. A sheltered picnic table at the edge of the abyss commands superb views of the chasm below.

The Alaka'i Swamp trailhead is a five-minute walk down the rutted ridge-top track that leads left off the road. The narrow path starts by dropping abruptly, shored up against the precipices to either side; it then climbs and widens again to become a pleasant, grassy path. Half a mile along, the boardwalk – two parallel planks overlaid with rusty wire mesh – begins. Despite the mud, and the regularity with which the planks sink into it, the trail is high and exposed, and for a while the trees thin out altogether. Another half-mile on, just as the ground starts to feel really soggy, you meet the Pihea Trail at the **four-way intersection** (see p.520).

Continuing on the Alaka'i Swamp Trail from here, the boardwalk turns into a playful, willful companion. For most of the time one plank meets the next, but

△ Kilohana Viewpoint

at some point, as they grow tauntingly further apart, you're bound to slip into the mud. For the first half-mile, the trail drops toward a gentle tributary of the Kawaikoi Stream, most (but not quite all) of the descent on a wooden stairway. As you cross the stream, by stepping stones, you're still a full hour short of the end. Soon afterwards, the boardwalk stops as the trail climbs a high and relatively dry ridge through the forest, with thick green moss to either side. While the last significant climb is now behind you, the highest part of the swamp turns out to be the wettest, little more than one large pool of gloopy mud. Only the red blossoms of tiny, stunted *'ohi'a lehua* plants relieve the monotony. The boardwalk then returns to guide you across first a bog, then a rainforest, and finally a bleak, marshy plain.

523

The trail eventually comes to a dead end at a small wooden platform high on a hillside, which for most of the time is engulfed in swirling mists. Waiting for the clouds to clear, in the wettest place in the world, can feel like a loser's game, but the wind forever rustling the trees around you is a guarantee that they will. You'll then see that you've walked the length of the Nā Pali coast. This viewpoint – officially named **Kilohana** – stands on top of the towering western wall of Wainiha Valley; far below, Wainiha Stream runs through its center towards the ocean. Down the coast beyond the mouth of the valley curves the crescent of Hanalei Bay, with Princeville visible at the tip of the far headland. Away to the right, inland, the high *pali* opposite stretches as far as the eye can see.

A constant succession of clouds race in to stream up the slopes, feeding the dense rainforest that somehow clings to their sides. In the intervals when you seem entirely cut off, you can reflect that in January 1871, Queen Emma (see p.107) somehow reached this lonely eminence with a retinue of over one hundred companions. They camped out along the way, with the Queen singing songs to keep their spirits up in the swamp, but were disappointed at the last. According to the official commemorative chant, *"ē huli hoʻiʻo ka lani, ua kū ka ʻohu i nā pali"* – "the queen turned to go back, for the fog rested on the mountain."

A ground-level description of Wainiha Valley appears on p.484.

The Awaʻawapuhi Trail

The **Awaʻawapuhi Trail** starts on the left of Waimea Canyon Drive, halfway between the Kōkeʻe headquarters and Kalalau Lookout, and drops steeply through three miles of forest to the **Awaʻawapuhi Valley**, tucked between the Nā Pali cliffs. Walking to the end takes little more than an hour, though climbing back up again is a different matter. The only views come right at the end, but they're stupendous enough to make this one of Kauai's finest hikes. Before you set off, pick up the Awaʻawapuhi Botanical Trail Guide from the museum for a description (albeit rather out of date since Iniki) of the plants indicated by the 57 numbered markers along the trail. Also be aware that the Awaʻawapuhi trailhead is notorious for vehicle break-ins, so leave nothing valuable in your car.

The trail begins its inexorable descent from the left side of the lot. It's easy underfoot, and there's none of the sense of battling against encroaching vegetation that you get on the Kalalau Trail (see p.489). At first the forest is largely *ʻohiʻa,* but as the path drops into hotter, drier territory, *koa* starts to predominate. Though most of the route remains in shade, after 1.5 miles the tree cover begins to thin out, and you get your first glimpses of the high parallel ridges to either side. At the 2.75-mile marker, a magnificent *hala pepe* tree has individual palm-like fronds growing from its branches. Shortly after that, keep going past the junction with the Nuʻalolo Cliff Trail.

The end of the trail comes at mile marker 3, when suddenly, 2400 feet above sea level, it runs out of ridge. The railing straight ahead marks the overlook at the head of the Awaʻawapuhi Valley. Far below, the Awaʻawapuhi River twists its way between two equally sinuous red ridges. Ancient Hawaiians said the valley was shaped by an eel slithering into the sea; its final thrashings mean that its ocean outlet is not visible. You can, however, see a huge expanse of ocean, and hear the distant roar of the surf. Most visitors venture a few steps beyond the railing, in search of the perfect photo; some fall and die.

Back to your left, another viewpoint looks out across Nuʻalolo Valley to the bare red top of the higher Nuʻalolo Ridge. Unlike in the Awaʻawapuhi Valley, which is in perpetual shade, trees can be seen on the valley floor. If the sight of the exposed ridge makes you reluctant to attempt the Nuʻalolo Trail, you won't be comforted to know that where you're standing looks just as bad from over there.

The Nuʻalolo Cliff Trail

In order to combine the Awaʻawapuhi and Nuʻalolo trails you have to edge your way along the gulf between the two, by means of the two-mile **Nuʻalolo Cliff Trail**. This is the one Kōkeʻe trail that you really *must* avoid if you have problems with vertigo.

From the intersection near the end of the Awaʻawapuhi Trail, described opposite, the Nuʻalolo Cliff Trail dips down into a small patch of rainforest. There it crosses a gentle stream, slowly gathering pace as it approaches the plummet ahead; don't be tempted by any of the side trails. The path goes on to traverse some attractive meadows, one of which holds a picnic shelter. Near the 1.75-mile marker, however, it rounds a fearsome bend above a colossal drop. The ground is just loose red gravel, the trail a narrow slanting groove scuffed against the hillside. Dislodged pebbles tumble thousands of feet into the abyss, and the wayside rock, clutched for support, crumbles to dust in your hand.

Just after that you join the Nuʻalolo Trail, here 3.25 miles from its starting point, with the Lolo Vista Point another three-quarters of a mile away to your right.

The Nuʻalolo Trail

Like the parallel but slightly shorter Awaʻawapuhi Trail, the **Nuʻalolo Trail** is a footpath down a long ridge that culminates with sweeping Nā Pali views. If you're making the loop trip with the Awaʻawapuhi Trail, as outlined on p.520, it's best to walk the Nuʻalolo Trail from bottom to top, as it's marginally the easier climb of the two. The description that follows, however, starts from the road and works down.

From its trailhead just below *Kōkeʻe Lodge*, the Nuʻalolo Trail starts with a surprise, switchbacking up and over Kaunuohua Ridge. Thereafter it drops progressively downhill, at times winding gently through the thick grass of the pretty upland meadows. After two straightforward miles, it begins to descend ever more steeply through a channel that in places is worn deep into the mud. While seldom dangerous, the last half-mile is precipitous in the extreme, straight down the slippery crest of the ridge. The fifteen-minute totter beyond the junction with the Nuʻalolo Cliff Trail, along the exposed ridge towards **Lolo Vista Point**, is regarded as a separate trail, and one best left to the brave.

Contexts

Contexts

A history of Hawaii

If a big wave comes in, large fishes will come from the dark Ocean which you never saw before, and when they see the small fishes they will eat them up. The ships of the white men have come, and smart people have arrived from the great countries which you have never seen before, they know our people are few in number and living in a small country; they will eat us up, such has always been the case with large countries, the small ones have been gobbled up.

David Malo, to the future King Kamehameha IV, 1837

The human history of Hawaii divides into three very distinct chapters. First came the era when the islands developed their own unique culture, as Polynesian settlers adapted their traditional way of life to this remote and pristine archipelago. Then came the islands' encounter with the rest of the world, and a hundred years of increasingly doomed resistance to the inevitable takeover by stronger foreign powers. The third stage began when Hawaii was incorporated into the United States, in 1898. Ever since then, the islands have been at the mercy of economic and political events in the rest of the world.

The age of migrations

The fiery origins of the Hawaiian islands have decisively shaped their destiny. They are the remotest islands on earth; as they have never been attached to a larger continent, humans have only ever been able to get here by crossing at least two thousand miles of treacherous ocean. Furthermore, being composed entirely of lava, they are devoid of metals and workable clays, the raw materials used to build civilizations elsewhere.

Until less than two thousand years ago, the islands remained unknown specks in the vast Pacific, populated by the mutated descendants of what few organisms had been carried here by wind or wave (see p.549). Carbon dating of fishhooks and artifacts found at sites such as Bellows Beach on Oahu and Ka Lae (South Point) on the Big Island suggests that Hawaii's earliest human settlers arrived during the second or third centuries AD. Except perhaps for their first chance landfall, they came equipped to colonize, carrying goats, dogs, pigs, coconut palms, bananas, and sugarcane, among other essentials.

These first inhabitants were **Polynesians**, and probably arrived from the Marquesas Islands, northeast of Tahiti in the South Seas. Their ancestors had originally spread from the shores of Asia to inhabit Indonesia and the Solomon Islands around 30,000 years ago. Such migrations, across coastal waters shallower than they are today, would for the most part have involved hopping from island to island without having to cross open ocean. Twenty-five thousand years later they acquired the techniques to venture further afield. For more on how such migrations were carried out, see p.546.

The ancient Hawaiians

For a full account of the daily life, traditions, and culture of the **ancient Hawaiians**, see p.542; for more about the **voyaging techniques** they employed in reaching Hawaii in the first place, see p.546.

Just over three thousand years ago, during the period when the "Little Climatic Optimum" made wind and sea conditions milder, the voyagers reached Fiji. They then spread via Tahiti to populate the entire "Polynesian Triangle," extending from Easter Island in the east to Hawaii in the north and finally down to New Zealand (which they called Aotea Roa) in the south.

Recent archeological and scientific investigations have shed more light on the ancient history of Hawaii, while throwing a number of long-cherished beliefs into doubt. Thanks to DNA testing, for example, it is now certain that the Polynesians entered the Pacific from southeast Asia. Thor Heyerdahl's argument for an American origin, as also promulgated by the Mormon church in Oahu's Polynesian Cultural Center, has been finally disproved. On the other hand, Polynesians do seem to have reached the Americas. Evidence of Polynesian-style religious structures, dating to around 600 AD, has been found on the Channel Islands, off the coast of California. Some voyagers must have returned to Polynesia via South America, too, as that's the only way the sweet potato could have reached the islands.

The traditional historical account of the settling of Hawaii describes the arrival of successive waves of migrants at widely spaced intervals. Marquesas Islanders are said to have continued to arrive until the eighth century, after which there was a gap before they were followed by Tahitians between the eleventh and fourteenth centuries. It's said that the warrior-priest Pa'ao was forced to flee Tahiti for some transgression, chanced upon the peaceful islands of Hawaii, and returned to Tahiti to report that these wonderful new lands were ripe for the picking. Certainly, as described on p.545, the elaborate, restrictive *kapu* system, along

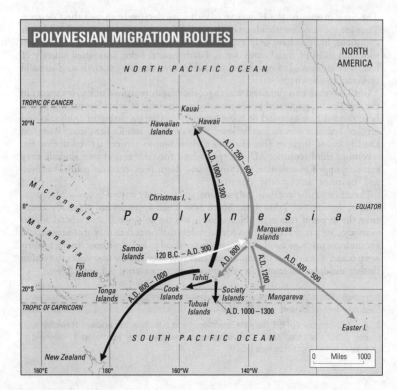

with the cult of human sacrifice, seems to have reached Hawaii around the twelfth century, and it seems clear that a new hierarchical order was imposed by force, with each island being violently invaded and conquered in turn. The very name "**Hawaii**" is known previously to have been an alternative, "poetic" name for the largest of the leeward Tahitian islands, Raiatea, the site of the voyaging temple of Taputapuatea.

It may be that this was not the first time the Marquesans had been overrun. In legend, the earliest Hawaiians frequently figure as the **menehune**, often described these days as having been hairy elves or leprechauns who worked at night and hid by day. It seems likely that the word is, in fact, a corruption of the Tahitian *manhune*, which means "lacking in lineage," and was the name of the original

Was Captain Cook the first?

Although Captain Cook always gets the credit for "discovering" Hawaii, there is considerable circumstantial evidence of pre-Cook contact between Hawaiians and outsiders. **Spanish** vessels disappeared in the northern Pacific in the 1520s onwards, while during the two centuries, starting in 1565, that the "Manila Galleons" made annual voyages across the Pacific between Mexico and the Philippines, at least nine such ships were lost. Cook observed that the first Hawaiians he encountered were familiar with iron, and even suggested that some bore European features.

Hawaiian legends collected during the nineteenth century speak of several plausible encounters. Thanks to the many detailed genealogies of Hawaiian families, it's possible to work out roughly when they took place. The earliest known was in the middle of the thirteenth century, when a vessel remembered as *Mamala* arrived at Wailuku on Maui. The crew of five, men and women, were pale, and became the ancestors of a light-skinned family. As no Europeans were in the Pacific at that time, it's possible they had drifted astray from Japan. On the Big Island, during the reign of Keali'iokaloa, the son of Umi, a ship called *Konaliloha* was wrecked on the reef in or near Kealakekua Bay. The only survivors were a brother or sister who swam ashore, where they remained and had children. That can be dated to November 1527, when two small Spanish ships, the *Santiago* and the *Espiritu Santo*, went missing in the north Pacific. Distorted versions of the same story are told on Maui and Kauai, and it's also said that more Spanish mariners were shipwrecked on the north coast of Lanai later in the sixteenth century.

Written evidence from Western sources includes the log of the Dutch ship *Lefda* in 1599, which spoke of eight seamen deserting to an unknown island at this latitude. Most compelling of all, in 1555, the Spanish navigator **Juan Gaetano** named and charted a group of islands that he called the Islas da Mesa, or "The Table Islands." They subsequently appeared on Spanish naval maps, at the correct latitude but roughly ten degrees too far east. Longitude at the time was estimated by dead reckoning, so such mistakes were easily made, especially in the face of unfamiliar ocean currents. British sailors captured such a map in 1742, showing "La Mesa," "Los Monges," and "La Desgraciada," and Cook's crew debated whether these were the same islands that they had found.

Spanish influence might explain the similarity of the red and yellow feather headdresses of Hawaiian warriors to the helmets of Spanish soldiers, and account for what seemed the phenomenal speed with which syphilis spread through the islands after it was supposedly introduced by the Cook expedition. The skeleton of a young woman was recently unearthed on Oahu who appears to have died of syphilis in the mid-seventeenth century; other contemporary burials have been shown to contain small scraps of sailcloth. Finally, there are also much earlier legends of inter-island wars for the possession of a mighty Excalibur-style iron sword, which may have been washed ashore accidentally from medieval Japan.

Polynesian people of Tahiti. These could well have been displaced by warriors from Raiatea first from their homeland to the Marquesas, then forced to escape from there to Hawaii, before the Tahitians finally followed them to Hawaii itself. Rather than literally being dwarfs, they were probably treated as social inferiors by their conquerors, and became the lowest caste in Hawaiian society.

It's not known for certain whether large-scale migration from Tahiti actually took place, or whether a small warrior elite simply arrived and took over. It's still possible to meet Hawaiians, however, who proudly trace their ancestry back to the Marquesans rather than the Tahitians. Whether or not Tahitians did reach Hawaii in significant numbers, by the time the Europeans appeared, no two-way voyaging between Hawaii and the South Pacific had taken place for perhaps as long as five hundred years.

The coming of the foreigners

No Western ship is known for certain to have chanced upon Hawaii before that of **Captain Cook**, in January 1778; the first European to sail across the Pacific, the Portuguese Ferdinand Magellan, did so without seeing a single island. When Cook first encountered Hawaii, he failed to spot both Maui and the Big Island before stumbling upon the western shores of Kauai. He was en route to the north Pacific, in search of the Northwest Passage (which at the time did not exist, though reportedly it's about to be created as a result of global warming). When he returned a year later, his two ships, the *Discovery* and the *Resolution*, skirted Maui and then, to the fury of their crews, cruised the coast of the Big Island for almost seven weeks, before anchoring in Kealakekua Bay. There Cook met with the chief of the island, Kalaniopu'u, and was greeted in ceremonies at the Hikiau *heiau*; there, too, within

More Hawaiian history

Detailed histories of each individual Hawaiian island appear in the relevant chapter introductions throughout this book. Additional features on specific historical themes, events, and personalities include the following, listed in rough chronological order:

a few weeks, he was killed. See p.186 for an account of the events leading to his death, and the legends that grew up around it.

Cook named the **"Sandwich Islands"** after Lord Sandwich. News of their existence reached the rest of the world after his death by way of the **Russians**, as his ships later halted for provisions on the Siberian coast. Hawaii swiftly became a port of call for all traders crossing the ocean, and especially for ships carrying furs from the Pacific Northwest to China.

Kamehameha the Great

For a few brief years the Hawaiians remained masters of their own destiny, with the major beneficiary of the change in circumstances being the astute young warrior **Kamehameha** on the Big Island.

Although he remains the greatest Hawaiian hero, to some extent Kamehameha played into the hands of the newcomers who flocked to the islands from all over the world. Most governmental representatives were under orders not to trade **guns** with the Hawaiians, but Russian fur traders, in particular, had no such scruples, and surprise Hawaiian attacks on merchant vessels also enabled Kamehameha to build up his own arsenal of foreign weapons. His subsequent conquest of the entire archipelago, and his creation of a single Hawaiian kingdom, greatly simplified the maneuvers that enabled outsiders to achieve first economic, and eventually political, domination over the islands.

The future Kamehameha the Great was born in northern Kohala on the Big Island, in 1758. Both his mother, Kekuiapoiwa, and father, Keōuau, were of royal blood, though it's not clear whether they were niece and nephew of the then ruler of the Big Island, Alapaʻi, or of Kahekili, the ruler of Maui. It has even been suggested that Kahekili himself was Kamehameha's true father. The infant Kamehameha was raised in seclusion in Waipiʻo Valley.

By the time Kamehameha grew to adulthood, Kalaniopuʻu had become high chief of the Big Island. Kamehameha proved a valuable warrior for the king and was present on the waterfront at the death of Captain Cook. When Kalaniopuʻu died in 1782, he designated his son Kīwalaʻo to be his heir, but civil war broke out almost immediately. By defeating Kīwalaʻo in battle, Kamehameha took control of the Kona, Kohala, and Hāmākua regions; however, Kīwalaʻo's brother **Keōua** survived to establish his own power base in Kaʻū.

For more than a decade a three-way struggle for domination raged back and forth between Kamehameha, Keōua, and Kahekili, who at this point was ruler of both Maui and Oahu. It looked for a while as though Kahekili might be the man to unite all the islands, but his hopes of capturing the Big Island were dashed by the **Battle of the Red-Mouthed Gun** off Waipiʻo Valley in 1791, when for the first time Hawaiian fleets were equipped with cannons, operated by foreign gunners. The long campaign against Keōua (many of whose warriors were wiped out by an eruption of Kīlauea; see p.267) finally came to an end that same year. At the dedication of the great *heiau* at Puʻukoholā, the last of the *luakinis*, Keōua himself was the chief sacrifice.

Kamehameha had previously conquered **Maui** through a bloody victory at ʻĪao Valley in 1790, only to lose it again when he was forced to turn his attention back to Keōua. As sole ruler of the Big Island, he went on to reconquer first Maui and Lanai, then to capture **Molokai** in 1794, and to take **Oahu** after one last battle at Nuʻuanu Valley, in 1795. Finally, after two unsuccessful attempts to invade **Kauai**, he settled for accepting tribute from its ruler, Kaumualiʻi. So eager was Kamehameha to obtain military assistance from the Europeans at this time that he briefly ceded the Big Island to Great Britain, though this was never made formal (hence the British "Union Jack" that's still incorporated into the Hawaiian flag). Kamehameha even considered the possibility of launching expeditions against the islands of the South Pacific.

By now, many Europeans had settled permanently on the islands. Kamehameha's most important foreign advisers were John Young and Isaac Davis (see p.301), who, in return for royal patronage, led his armies into battle, personally gunning down enemy warriors in droves. In addition, practical skills of all kinds were introduced to the islands by European artisans such as blacksmiths, carpenters, and stonemasons.

For some time Kamehameha had his capital in the fledgling port of Lahaina on Maui. By the time he died in 1819, however, he had returned to live in a palace on the Kona coast of the Big Island.

The end of the old order

Kamehameha's successor, his son Liholiho – also known as **Kamehameha II** – was a weak figure who was dominated by the regent **Queen Ka'ahumanu** (see p.368). As a woman, she was excluded from the *luakini heiaus* that were the real center of political power, so she set out to bring down the priesthood. Liholiho was plied with drink and cajoled into dining with women at a public banquet; that simple act brought about the end of the *kapu* system (see p.545) and precipitated a civil war in which the upholders of the ancient religion were defeated in a battle near Hōnaunau on the Big Island. Altars and idols at *heiaus* throughout Hawaii were overthrown and destroyed.

Hawaii found itself thrown into moral anarchy at the very moment when the first Puritan **missionaries** arrived. The creation of the Sandwich Islands Mission stemmed from a visit to New England by **Henry 'Opukaha'ia**. A *kahuna* priest from Hikiau *heiau* on the Big Island, he converted to Christianity, but died in his early twenties while a student at the Foreign Mission School in Cornwall, Connecticut. As he breathed his last, he lamented his failure to return to Hawaii to convert his brethren.

The heartfelt prayer and hard cash of New England worthies, deeply moved by the young man's tragic end, enabled the mission's first two ministers, **Rev Hiram Bingham** and **Rev Asa Thurston**, to sail from Boston in the brig *Thaddeus* on October 23, 1819. According to their instructions, they were sent for "no private end, for no earthly object," but "wholly for the good of others and for the glory of God our Savior. You are to aim at nothing short of covering those islands with fruitful fields and pleasant dwellings, and schools and churches."

After a five-month, eighteen-thousand-mile journey, they reached Kailua Bay on April 4, 1820. If Asa Thurston did not immediately take to Hawaii – he described Kailua as "a filthy village of thatched huts . . . on which the fervent sun poured its furnace heat every day of the year" – neither did the Hawaiians take to him. Ka'ahumanu didn't exactly jump at the chance to replace the old priests with a new bunch of interfering moralizers, and there was considerable debate as to whether the missionaries should be allowed to land at all. In the end, the counsel of the aging John Young played a decisive role, but only Thurston was allowed to remain in Kailua. Bingham was obliged to settle in Honolulu, where, scurrilously known as "King Bingham," he denounced his flock as the "stupid and polluted worshippers of demons."

The missionaries' wholehearted capitalism, and their harsh strictures on the easygoing Hawaiian lifestyle, might have been calculated to compound the chaos. They set about obliging Hawaiian women to cover unseemly flesh in billowing *mu'umu'u* "Mother Hubbard" dresses, condemning the *hula* as lascivious and obscene, and discouraging surfing as a waste of time, liable to promote gambling and lewdness.

Meanwhile, Liholiho, who never did quite take to the imposition of the new faith, had been seized with an urge to visit England. He died of measles in London in 1824, without ever meeting King George IV (who referred to him as a "damned cannibal"). When the news reached Hawaii, he was succeeded by his brother Kauikeaouli, who reigned as **Kamehameha III**, although Queen Kaʻahumanu remained very much in control. She had become an enthusiastic promoter of Christianity after being nursed through a grave illness by Bingham's wife, Sybil (whom he had known for two weeks and been married to for one week when they left Boston).

In general, the missionaries concentrated their attentions on the ruling class, the *aliʻi*, believing that they would then bring the commoners into the fold. They also devised Hawaii's first alphabet and founded countless schools; one on Kauai famously started out using surfboards for desks. On Maui in particular, the support of the ardently Christian Governor Hoapili facilitated a hugely successful program of education, to the extent that Hawaii achieved the highest literacy rate on earth.

At first, great tensions manifested themselves between the missionaries and the new breed of foreign entrepreneurs. These were to disappear as their offspring intermarried, acquired land and formed the backbone of the emerging middle class.

The foreigners take control

For ordinary Hawaiians, the sudden advent of capitalism was devastating. Any notion of Hawaiian self-sufficiency was abandoned in favor of selling the islands' resources for cash returns. The most extreme example of this was perhaps the earliest: the **sandalwood** trade.

Even greater than the economic impact of the foreigners was the sheer physical impact of the **diseases** they brought with them. Epidemic after epidemic swept the islands, reducing the native Hawaiian population from something between 300,000 and 500,000 at the time of Cook's arrival to little over fifty thousand a century later. As agricultural laborers were imported from the rest of the world, the Hawaiians came to be outnumbered in their own islands.

Sandalwood: the first sell-out

Sandalwood logs were first picked up from Hawaii in 1791, when the crew of the *Lady Washington* spotted them in a consignment of fuel collected at Waimea on Kauai. Traders had been searching for years for a commodity they could sell to the Chinese in return for tea to meet English demand. Once it was realized that the Chinese would pay enormous prices for the fragrant wood (the scent of a bowl of sandalwood chips lasts for up to fifty years), the race was on.

Kamehameha had a monopoly on the trade until his death, but thereafter individual chiefs out for their own profit forced all the commoners under their sway to abandon taro farming and fishing and become wage slaves. The wood was sold in units known as *piculs*, which weighed just over 133 pounds. "*Picul* pits," the exact size and shape of a ship's hold, were dug in the hills and filled with logs; one can still be seen in the rainforest above east Molokai (see p.414). Men, women, and children then carried the wood down to the sea on their naked backs. As the trees became rarer, the burden of the laborers, forced to search ever higher in the mountains, grew worse; it's said that they deliberately uprooted saplings to drive the tree to extinction and ensure that their children would not have to do the same cruel work.

Each *picul* of sandalwood sold for one cent in Hawaii and 34 cents in China; most of the profits went to New England merchants. By the end of the 1820s, the forests were almost entirely denuded, the traditional Hawaiian agricultural system had collapsed, and many chiefs found themselves greatly in debt to foreign merchants, with no obvious way to pay.

In a bizarre footnote, the young *ali'i* **Boki** – a former governor of Oahu, who had traveled to London with Liholiho and later attempted to organize an armed rebellion against Ka'ahumanu – equipped a military expedition to search for a new source of sandalwood in the South Seas. His ship, the *Kamehameha*, sailed from Honolulu in 1829 with 250 men on board. Neither he nor they were ever seen again.

Whaling

The first **whaling ships** arrived in Hawaii in 1820, the same year as the missionaries. They had an equally dramatic impact. With the ports of Japan closed to outsiders, Hawaii swiftly became the center of the industry. Not that any whales were actually hunted in Hawaii; although visitors often assume that it was the humpback whales seen in Hawaiian waters today that attracted the whaling fleet to the islands, humpbacks were not in fact hunted during the nineteenth century. When caught with the technology of the time, they sank uselessly to the bottom of the sea. Instead, the whalers would chase other species in the waters around Japan in winter and in the Arctic in summer, and then call at Hawaii each spring and fall to unload oil and baleen to be shipped home in other vessels, to stock up, and to change crew.

Any Pacific port would have seemed a godsend to the whalers, who were away from New England for three years at a time and paid so badly that most were either fugitives or plain mad. Hawaii was such a paradise that up to fifty percent of each crew would desert, to be replaced by Hawaiian *sailamokus*, born seafarers eager to see the world.

From the very first, Westerners recognized **Honolulu** as possessing the finest deep-water harbor in the Pacific (in reference to the current city, not Pearl Harbor, which did not become usable until it was dredged much later). Hawaiians had never required such anchorages, and Honolulu in ancient times had been the smallest of villages. It swiftly became the whalemen's favorite port, a status it retained until the capital, and the missionary presence that went with it, moved to Honolulu from **Lahaina** on Maui in 1845. The whalers swapped the other way, and both ports became notorious for such diseases as syphilis, influenza, measles, typhoid, and smallpox.

Provisioning the whaling ships became the main focus of the Hawaiian economy. The uplands of Maui were irrigated for the first time, to grow temperate crops such as white potatoes, while cattle ranches were established on both Maui and the Big Island. The Hispanic cowboys imported to work there, known as **paniolos** (a corruption of *españoles*), were among the first of the many overseas ethnic groups to make their homes in Hawaii.

The Great Mahele

By 1844, foreign-born fortune-seekers dominated the Hawaiian government. Fourteen of King Kamehameha III's closest advisers were white, including his three most important ministers. The various foreign powers jostled for position; it is easy to forget now that it was not inevitable that the islands would become American. After all, it was not until the 1840s that New Zealand was snapped up by the English, and Tahiti by the French, and both those European powers retained ambitions in Hawaii. In 1843, a British commander captured Honolulu, claiming all Hawaii for Queen Victoria, and it was six months before word arrived from London that it had all been a mistake. (It was at the restoration celebration, in Honolulu on July 31, 1843, that King Kamehameha III delivered the short speech that remains the official motto of Hawaii to this day – "*ua mau ke ea o ka 'āina i ka pono*," "the life of the land is perpetuated in righteousness"). In 1849, a French admiral did much the same thing, but this time everyone simply waited until he got bored and sailed away again.

The most important obstacle to the advance of the foreigners was that they could not legally own land. In the old Hawaii there was no private land; all was held in trust by the chief, who apportioned it to individuals at his continued pleasure only. The king was requested to "clarify" the situation. A land commission was set up, under the direction of a missionary, and its deliberations resulted in the **Great Mahele** ("Division of Lands") in 1848. In theory all the land was parceled out to native Hawaiians only, with sixty percent going to the crown and the government, thirty-nine percent to just over two hundred chiefs, and less than one percent to eleven thousand commoners. Claiming and keeping the land involved complex legal procedures and required expenditures that few Hawaiians, paid in kind not cash, were able to meet. In any case, within two years the *haoles* (non-Hawaiians) were also permitted to buy and sell land. The often-heard jibe that the missionaries "came to Hawaii to do good – and they done good" stems from the speed with which they amassed vast acreages; their children became Hawaii's wealthiest and most powerful class.

Many Hawaiians were denied access to the lands they had traditionally worked, arrested for vagrancy, and used as forced labor on the construction of roads and ports for the new landowners. Meanwhile, a simultaneous **water grab** took place, with new white-owned plantations diverting water for their thirsty foreign crops from the Hawaiian farmers downstream.

The sugar industry and the US Civil War

At the height of the whaling boom, many newly rich entrepreneurs began to put their money into **sugar**. Hawaii's first sugar plantation started in 1835 in Kōloa on Kauai (for a full history, see p.498), and it swiftly became clear that this was an industry where large-scale operators were much the most efficient and profitable. By 1847 the field had narrowed to five main players, four of whom had started out by provisioning whaling ships. These **Big Five** were Hackfield & Co (later to become Amfac), C Brewer & Co, Theo Davies Co, Castle & Cooke (later Dole), and Alexander & Baldwin. Thereafter, they worked in close cooperation with each other, united by common interests and, often, family ties.

When **Civil War** hit the United States, and the markets of the North began to cast about for an alternative source of sugar to the Confederate South, Hawaii was poised to take advantage. The consequent boom in the Hawaiian sugar industry, and the ever-increasing integration of Hawaii into the American economic mainstream, was the most important factor in the eventual loss of Hawaiian sovereignty.

The Civil War also coincided with the decline of the whaling industry. Several ships were bought and deliberately sunk to blockade Confederate ports, while the discovery of petroleum had diminished the demand for whale oil. The final disaster came in 1871, when 31 vessels lingered in the Arctic too long at the end of the season, became frozen in, and had to be abandoned.

By the 1870s, cane fields were spreading across all the islands. The ethnic mixture of modern Hawaii is largely the product of the search for laborers prepared to submit to the draconian conditions on the plantations. Once the Hawaiians had demonstrated their unwillingness to knuckle under, agents of the Hawaiian Sugar Planters Association scoured the world in search of peasants eager to find new lives.

As members of each ethnic group in turn got their start on the plantations, and then left to find more congenial employment or establish their own businesses, a new source of labor had to be found. It soon became clear that few single men chose to stay on the plantations when their contracts expired – many left for California to join the Gold Rush – so the planters began to try to lure families to Hawaii, which meant providing better housing than the original basic dormitories.

First came the **Chinese** (see p.96), recruited with a $10 inducement in Hong Kong, shipped over for free, and then signed to five-year contracts at $6 or less per month. The **Portuguese** followed, brought from Madeira and the Azores from 1878 onwards by planters who thought they might adjust more readily than their Asian counterparts to the dominant *haole*-Hawaiian culture. **Koreans** arrived during the brief period between 1902, when they were first allowed to leave their country, and 1905, when it was invaded by the **Japanese**, who themselves came in great numbers until 1907, when the so-called Gentleman's Agreement banned further immigration. **Filipinos**, whose country had been annexed by the US in 1898, began to arrive in their stead, to find the climate, soil, and crops were all similar to their homelands.

Smaller-scale plantations were also established to grow other crops, such as **pineapples** (discovered in Paraguay early in the sixteenth century), which spread to cover much of Oahu, Maui, and Lanai, and **coffee**, which was brought to Hawaii by chief Boki in 1825 and grew most successfully on the Kona slopes of the Big Island (see p.183).

The end of the Kingdom of Hawaii

Hawaii is ours. As I look back upon the first steps in this miserable business, and as I contemplate the means used to complete the outrage, I am ashamed of the whole affair.

US President Grover Cleveland, 1893

After sugar prices dropped at the end of the Civil War, the machinations of the sugar industry to get favorable prices on the mainland moved Hawaii inexorably toward **annexation** by the US. In 1876 the Treaty of Reciprocity abolished all trade barriers and tariffs between the US and the Kingdom of Hawaii; within fifteen years sugar exports to the US had increased tenfold.

By now, the Kamehameha dynasty had come to an end, and the heir to the Hawaiian throne was chosen by the national legislature. The first such king, William Lunalilo, died in 1874, after barely a year in office. In the ensuing elections, **Queen Emma**, the Anglophile widow of Kamehameha IV (see p.107), lost to **King David Kalākaua**. The "Merrie Monarch" is affectionately remembered today for his role in reviving traditional Hawaiian pursuits such as *hula* and surfing, but he was widely seen as being pro-American, and a riot protesting his election in 1874 virtually destroyed Honolulu's Old Court House. King Kalākaua was to a significant extent the tool of the plantation owners. In 1887 an all-white (and armed) group of "concerned businessmen" forced through the "Bayonet Constitution," in which he surrendered power to an assembly elected by property owners (of any nationality) rather than citizens. The US government was swiftly granted exclusive rights to what became Pearl Harbor.

Kalākaua died in San Francisco in 1891, shortly after recording a farewell address to his people on a newly invented Edison recording machine. In his absence, he had appointed his sister **Lili'uokalani** to serve as his regent, and she now became queen. When she proclaimed her desire for a new constitution, the same group of

The Hawaiian monarchy

Kamehameha I	1791–1819
Kamehameha II (Liholiho)	1819–1824
Kamehameha III (Kauikeaouli)	1825–1854
Kamehameha IV (Alexander Liholiho)	1854–1863
Kamehameha V (Lot Kamehameha)	1863–1872
William C. Lunalilo	1873–1874
David Kalākaua	1874–1891
Liliʻuokalani	1891–1893

businessmen, who had now convened themselves into an "**Annexation Club**," called in the US warship *Boston*, then in Honolulu, and declared a provisional government. President Grover Cleveland (a Democrat) responded that "Hawaii was taken possession of by the United States forces without the consent or wish of the government of the islands. . . . [It] was wholly without justification . . . not merely a wrong but a disgrace." With phenomenal cheek, the provisional government rejected his demand for the restoration of the monarchy, saying the US should not "interfere in the internal affairs of their sovereign nation." They found defenders in the Republican US Congress and declared themselves a **republic** on July 4, 1894, with **Sanford Dole** as their first President.

Following an abortive coup attempt in 1895, Queen Liliʻuokalani was charged with **treason**. She was placed under house arrest, first in ʻIolani Palace and later at her Honolulu home of Washington Place (see p.91). Though she lived until 1917, all hopes of a restoration of Hawaiian independence were dashed in 1897, when a Republican president, McKinley, came to office claiming "annexation is not a change. It is a consummation." The strategic value of Pearl Harbor was emphasized by the Spanish-American War in the Philippines, and on August 12, 1898, Hawaii was formally **annexed** as a territory of the United States.

△ ʻIolani Palace

A territory and a state

At the moment of annexation there was no question of Hawaii becoming a state; the whites were outnumbered ten to one and had no desire to afford the rest of the islanders the protection of US labor laws, let alone to give them the vote. (Sanford Dole said that natives couldn't expect to vote "simply because they were grown up.") Furthermore, as the proportion of Hawaiians of Japanese descent (*nisei*) increased (to 25 percent by 1936), Congress feared the prospect of a state whose inhabitants might consider their primary allegiance to be to Japan. Consequently, Hawaii remained for the first half of the twentieth century the virtual fiefdom of the Big Five, who, through their control of agriculture (they owned 96 percent of the sugar crop), dominated transport, banks, utilities, insurance, and government.

The endemic racism of Hawaii's ruling elite was notoriously exposed during the 1930s by the ongoing saga of the so-called **Massie Case**. After Thalia Massie, the (white) wife of a naval officer, alleged that she'd been gang-raped in 1931, a group of five young men, of assorted ancestry, were arrested on flimsy evidence. When a jury failed to reach a guilty verdict, Thalia's mother and husband abducted and murdered one of the supposed suspects. Several elements in the case – including threats by a senior US naval official at Pearl Harbor to promote a coup if the verdict was not to his liking; the astonishing anti-Hawaiian racism of the US media; and the release of the murderers after an hour's detention – all unexpectedly conspired to create a new solidarity among ordinary Hawaiian residents. For the first time, Hawaii's many immigrant groups found common cause with each other and with the native Hawaiians, and a new identity started to emerge that was to reshape the islands.

That change truly began to take place during World War II. The Japanese offensive on Pearl Harbor (see p.112) meant that Hawaii was the only part of the United States to be attacked in the war, and it demonstrated just how crucial the islands were to the rest of America. Military bases and training camps were established throughout Hawaii, many of which remain operational to this day. In addition, Hawaiian troops played an active role in the war. Veterans of the much-decorated 442nd Regimental Combat Team – composed of Japanese Hawaiians who, for obvious reasons, were sent to fight in Europe – have been a leading force in Hawaiian politics ever since.

The main trend in Hawaiian history since the war has been the slow decline of agriculture and the rise of **tourism**. Strikes organized along ethnic lines in the sugar plantations had consistently failed in the past, but from 1937 on, labor leaders such as Jack Hill and Harry Bridges of the International Longshoremen's and Warehousemen's Union began to organize workers of all races and all crafts, in solidarity with mainland unions. In September 1946, the plantation workers won their first victory. Thanks to the campaigns that followed, the long-term Republican domination of state politics ended, and Hawaii's agricultural workers became the highest paid in the world. Arguably, this led to the eventual disappearance of all their jobs in the face of Third World competition. Sixty years later, almost all the sugar plantations have closed; one remains on Kauai, and one on Maui.

Hawaii finally became the fiftieth of the United States in 1959, after a plebiscite showed a seventeen-to-one majority in favor, with the only significant opposition coming from the few remaining native Hawaiians. **Statehood** coincided with the first jet flight to Hawaii, which halved the previous nine-hour flight time from California. These two factors triggered a boom in tourism – many visitors had had their first sight of Hawaii as GIs in the war – and also in migration from the mainland to Hawaii.

Official figures showing the growth of the Hawaiian economy since statehood conceal a decline in living standards for many Hawaiians, with rises in consumer prices far outstripping rises in wages. Real estate prices in particular have rocketed, so that many islanders are obliged to work at two jobs, others end up sleeping on the beaches, and young Hawaiians emigrate in droves with no prospect of being able to afford to return.

The sovereignty movement

During the late 1980s, broad-based support mushroomed for the concept of **Hawaiian sovereignty**, meaning some form of restoration of the rights of native Hawaiians. Pride in the Polynesian past was rekindled by such means as the voyages of the *Hōkūleʻa* canoe (see p.546) and the successful campaign to claim back the island of **Kahoolawe**, which had been used since the war as a Navy bombing range (see p.332).

In retrospect, the movement can be seen to have culminated in 1993, when massive demonstrations outside ʻIolani Palace commemorated the centenary of the coup against Queen Liliʻuokalani. Later that year, President Clinton signed an official **Apology to Native Hawaiians**, in which the US government formally acknowledged the illegality of the US overthrow of the Hawaiian monarchy. At that point, everyone in Hawaii seemed to expect that some form of sovereignty lay just over the horizon.

In the decade since then, however, the sovereignty movement has fragmented. A state-sponsored political debate as to the form sovereignty might take revealed deep divisions. Many Hawaiian activists advocated the re-emergence of Hawaii as an independent nation once again, recognized by the international community, with full citizenship perhaps restricted either to those born in Hawaii or prepared to pledge sole allegiance to Hawaii. Others were prepared to settle for the granting to native Hawaiians of nation-within-a-nation status, as with Native American groups on the mainland, while perhaps the majority of state residents argued that it would be more realistic to preserve the existing political framework within the context of full economic reparations to native Hawaiians. While the transition of the governorship from a Democrat to a Republican, Linda Lingle, has done little to diminish the state government's long-established sympathy with native Hawaiians, the advent of a Republican president in Washington in 2001 effectively put an end to any federal interest in addressing Hawaiian sovereignty.

There has also been a considerable backlash within Hawaii among elements of the state's non-native (and, in particular, Caucasian) population. High-profile court cases have seen successful challenges to various state programs designed to benefit native Hawaiians, and any meaningful recognition of Hawaiian sovereignty seems as far away as ever.

Ancient culture and society

No written record exists of the centuries between the arrival of the Polynesians and the first contact with Europeans. Sacred chants, passed down through the generations, show a history packed with feuds and forays between the islands and the rise and fall of dynasties, but they didn't concern themselves with the requirements of modern historians, and specific dates are conspicuous by their absence. However, oral traditions do provide us with a detailed picture of the day-to-day life of ordinary Hawaiians in years gone by.

Developing a civilization on such isolated islands, without metals and workable clays, presented the settlers with many challenges. Nevertheless, by the late eighteenth century, when Europeans arrived, the Hawaiian islands were home to around a million people. Two hundred years later, the population has climbed back to a similar level. Now, however, virtually no pure-blooded Hawaiians remain, and the islands are no longer even close to being self-sufficient in terms of food. The population distribution has changed, too; it's striking how often the accounts of the early explorers describe being greeted by vast numbers of canoes in areas which are now all but uninhabited. The Big Island's population would have been far larger than the 145,000 it is today, and Oahu's population smaller, but no precise figures are known.

Daily life

In a sense, ancient Hawaii had no economy, not even barter. Although then, as now, most people lived close to the coast, each island was organized into wedge-shaped land divisions called **ahupua'a**, which stretched from the ocean to the mountains. *Ahupua'a* literally means a place where hogs were stored or gathered, and the boundaries between one and the next were marked by an altar bearing a carved image of a pig's head. The abundant fruits of the earth and sea were simply shared among the inhabitants within each *ahupua'a*.

There's some truth in the idea of pre-contact Hawaii as a leisured paradise, but it had taken a lot of work to make it that way. Coconut palms were planted along the seashore to provide food, clothing, and shade for coastal villages, and bananas and other food plants distributed inland. Crops such as sugarcane were cultivated with the aid of complex systems of terraces and irrigation channels. Taro, whose leaves were eaten as "greens" and whose roots were mashed to produce the staple *poi*, was grown in *lo'i*, which (like rice paddies) are kept constantly submerged, in the lush windward valleys such as Hanalei on Kauai, Waimea on Oahu, Hālawa on Molokai, and Waipi'o on the Big Island.

Most **fishing** took place in shallow inshore waters. Fishhooks made from human bone were believed to be especially effective; the most prized hooks were made from the bones of chiefs who had no body hair, so those unfortunate individuals were renowned for their low life expectancy. Nets were never cast from boats, but shallow bays were dragged by communal groups of wading men drawing in *hukilau* nets. (Elvis did it in *Blue Hawaii*, and you occasionally see people doing it today.) There was also a certain amount of freshwater fishing in the mountain streams, especially for shrimp, catfish, and goby. Fish were caught by placing basket-like nets at a narrow point, then dislodging stones upstream.

In addition, the art of **aquaculture** – fish-farming – was more highly developed in Hawaii than anywhere in Polynesia. It reached its most refined form in the extensive networks of fishponds that ringed much of Hawaii's shoreline; the best surviving examples are along the southeast coast of Molokai (see p.408) and near Līhu'e on Kauai. Such fishponds were usually constructed to demonstrate the power of a particular chief and increase his wealth; the fish would be reserved for his personal consumption.

Few people lived in the higher forested slopes, but these served as the source of vital raw materials such as *koa* wood for canoes and weapons. The ancients even ventured to the summit of Mauna Kea on the Big Island; as the only point in the Pacific to be glaciated during the last Ice Age, it has the hardest basalt on the islands. Stone from the **adze quarry**, 12,400 feet up, was used for all basic tools.

Ordinary commoners – the **maka'āinana** – lived in simple windowless huts known as *hales*. Most of these were thatched with *pili* grass, though in the driest areas ordinary people didn't bother with roofs. Buildings of all kinds were usually raised on platforms of stone; rounded boulders were taken from riverbeds and hauled long distances for that purpose, and were also used to make roads. Matting would have covered the floor, while the pounded tree bark called *kapa* (known as *tapa* elsewhere in the Pacific, and decorated with patterns) served as clothing and bedding. Lacking pottery, households made abundant use of gourds, wooden dishes, and woven baskets; chiefs would sometimes decorate bowls and calabashes with the teeth of their slain enemies, as a deliberate desecration of their remains.

The most popular pastime was **surfing**. Petroglyphs depicting surfers have been found, and there were even surfing *heiaus*. Ordinary people surfed on five- to seven-foot boards known as *alaia*, and also had *paipus*, the equivalent of the modern boogie board; only the *ali'i* used the thick sixteen-foot *olo* boards, made of dark oiled *wiliwili* or *koa* wood. On land the *ali'i* raced narrow sleds on purpose-built, grass-covered *hōlua* slides and staged boxing tournaments.

The ali'i

The ruling class, the **ali'i**, stood at the apex of Hawaiian society. In theory, heredity counted for everything, and great chiefs demonstrated their fitness to rule by the length of their genealogies. In fact the *ali'i* were educated as equals, and chiefs won the very highest rank largely through physical prowess and force of personality. To hang on to power, the king had to be seen as devoutly religious and to treat his people fairly.

For most of Hawaiian history, each island was divided into a varying number of chiefdoms, with major potential for intrigue, faction, and warfare. Canoes being the basic means of transportation, it was also feasible for chiefs to launch inter-island campaigns. Kauai managed to remain consistently independent, thanks to the wide, dangerous channel separating it from the Windward Islands, but as the centuries went by large-scale expeditions between Oahu, Maui, and the Big Island became ever more frequent. As a rule, Lanai and Molokai fell under the sway of whoever happened to be ruling Maui at the time.

Complex genealogies of the great *ali'i* still survive, but little is recorded other than their names. Summaries of the major figures on each island appear in the relevant chapter introductions in this book. Among the most important of these was **'Umi-a-Liloa**; sometime between the twelfth and sixteenth centuries, he became the first ruler to unite the Big Island, from his base amid the taro fields of Waipi'o Valley. 'Umi is said to have inherited the throne by defeating his brother in a *hōlua* sledding contest. Listed as representing the sixtieth generation after the sky god Wākea, he was responsible for Hawaii's first legal code – the *kanawai*, which concerned itself with the equal sharing of water from Waipi'o's irrigation ditches – and was among the first to make human sacrifice an instrument of state policy. Other important figures include the sixteenth-century **Pi'ilani**, who was the first chief to control all Maui and built the first paved road around any island, and the ferocious tattooed **Kahekili**, also from Maui, who almost conquered the entire archipelago shortly before Kamehameha the Great finally did so.

Perhaps the most enigmatic figure was **Lono**, who may have been 'Umi's grandson. Legends suggest that he lost his throne after quarreling with, or even murdering, his wife and left the Big Island in a half-crazed fit of self-loathing. Some say that he regained his sanity, returned to unite the island, and was subsquently deified as Lonoikamakahiki, patron of the annual *makahiki* festival. Others claim that the Hawaiians predicted his return for centuries and believed these prophecies to be fulfilled by the arrival of Captain Cook (see p.508).

Religion

It's all but impossible now to grasp the subtleties of ancient Hawaiian **religion**. So much depends on how the chants and texts are translated; if the word *akua* is interpreted as meaning "god," for example, historians can draw analogies with Greek or Hindu legends by speaking of a pantheon of battling, squabbling "gods" and "goddesses" with magic powers. Some scholars, however, prefer to translate *akua* as "spirit consciousness" – which might correspond to the soul of an ancestor or even the motivational force present in a modern wristwatch – and argue that the antics of such figures are peripheral to a more fundamental set of attitudes regarding the relationship of humans to the natural world.

The **Kumulipo**, Hawaii's principal creation myth, has been preserved in full as a chant, passed down from generation to generation. It tells how, after the emergence of the earth "from the source in the slime . . . [in] the depths of the darkness," more complicated life forms developed, from coral to pigs, until finally men, women, and "gods" appeared. Not only was there no Creator god, but the gods were much of a kind with humans. It took a hundred generations for the divine ancestors of the people of Hawaii to be born: Wākea, the god of the sky, and Papa, an earth goddess.

It may well be misleading to imagine that all Hawaiians shared the same beliefs; different groups sought differing ways of augmenting their *mana*, or spiritual power. Quite possibly only the elite *ali'i* paid much attention to the bloodthirsty warrior god **Kū**, while the primary allegiance of ordinary families and, by extension, villages and regions, may have lain toward their personal *'aumākua* – a sort of clan symbol, which might be a totem animal such as a shark or an owl, or a more abstract force, such as that embodied by **Pele**, the volcano goddess.

Spiritual and temporal power did not necessarily lie in the same hands, let alone in the same places. Hawaiian "priests" were known as **kahunas** (literally, "men who know the secrets") and were the masters of ceremonies at temples called **heiaus**. The design of a *heiau* was not always consistent, but as a rule it consisted of a number of separate structures standing on a rock platform (*paepae*). These might include the *hale mana* ("house of spiritual power"), the *hale pahu* ("house of the drum"), and the *anu'u* ("oracle tower"), from the top of which the *kahunas* would converse with the gods. Assorted *ki'i akua*, symbolic wooden images of different gods, would stand on all sides, and the whole enclosure was fenced or walled off. In addition to the two main types of *heiau* – the **luakinis**, which were dedicated to the war god Kū and held *leles* or altars used for human sacrifice, and **māpeles**, peaceful temples to Lono – there were also *heiaus* to such entities as Laka, goddess of the *hula*. Devotees of Pele, on the other hand, did not give their protectress formal worship at a *heiau*.

Most *heiaus* were built for some specific occasion and did not remain in constant use. Among the best-preserved examples are the *luakinis* at Puʻukoholā on the Big Island, at Puʻu O Mahuka on Oahu, and at ʻIliʻiliʻōpae on Molokai; the *hula heiau* above Kēʻē Beach on Kauai; and the healing *heiau* at Keaīwa, outside Honolulu.

Hawaiian religion in the form encountered by Cook was brought to the Big Island, and subsequently to the rest of the archipelago, by the Tahitian warrior-priest Paʻao, who led the last great migration to Hawaii. The war god Kū received his first human sacrifices on the Big Island, at *luakini* temples such as Wahaʻula *Heiau* near Kīlauea, which was destroyed by lava flows during the 1990s.

Paʻao is also credited with introducing and refining the complex system of **kapu**, which circumscribed the daily lives of all Hawaiians. *Kapu* is the Hawaiian version of the Polynesian *tabu*, often written in English as "taboo." Like all such systems, it served many purposes. Some of its restrictions were designed to augment the power of the kings and priests, while others regulated domestic routine or attempted to conserve scarce natural resources.

Many had to do with **food**. Women were forbidden to prepare food or to eat with men; each husband was obliged to cook for himself and his wife in two separate ovens and to pound the *poi* in two distinct calabashes. The couple had to maintain separate houses, as well as a *Hale Noa*, where a husband and wife slept together. Women could not eat pork, bananas, or coconuts, or several kinds of fish. Certain fish could only be caught in specified seasons, and a *koa* tree could only be cut down provided two more were planted in its place.

No one could tread on the shadow of a chief; the highest chiefs were so surrounded by *kapus* that some only went out at night. Although bloodlines defined one's place in the *kapu* hierarchy, might dominated over right, so the ruling chiefs did not necessarily possess the highest spiritual status. One of Kamehameha's wives, Kapiʻolani, was so much his superior that he could only approach her naked, backwards, and on all fours.

The only crime in ancient Hawaii was to break a *kapu*, and the only punishment was death. It was possible for an entire *ahupuaʻa* to break a *kapu* and incur death, but the penalty was not always exacted. One way for guilty parties to avoid execution was by hotfooting it to a *puʻuhonua*, or "place of refuge." Each island is thought to have had several of these; the one in Hōnaunau on the Big Island remains among the best-preserved ancient sites in all Hawaii (see p.187). In addition, the monarch was considered to be a *puʻuhonua*.

The return of the voyagers

Although archeological and linguistic evidence had long made it clear that the Polynesians deliberately colonized the Pacific, how they did so remained a mystery until about thirty years ago. In 1973, a group of Hawaiians set out to rediscover the skills and techniques of their ancestors. Ben Finney, an anthropologist from Honolulu's Bishop Museum; Tommy Holmes, a racing canoe paddler; and the artist Herb Kane founded the **Polynesian Voyaging Society** to build replicas of the ancient ocean-going vessels and use them to reproduce the early voyages. In particular, they were determined to prove that it was possible to make sustained, long-distance return trips across the Pacific without modern instruments or charts, despite the trade winds that consistently blow from the northeast.

The great Polynesian sailing canoes, or *wa'a*, were developed to their ultimate level of sophistication in Hawaii itself. This followed the discovery of the native Hawaiian *koa*, a gigantic hardwood tree whose wood was the perfect material for canoe construction. Each canoe was scooped from a single *koa* trunk, six feet in diameter and at least fifty feet long, using stone adzes and knives made of bone, shell, or coral. Surfaces were sanded with the skin of manta rays, and the hulls waterproofed with gum from the breadfruit tree. When lashed together, two such vessels formed a double-hulled long-distance sailing canoe. Using the word "canoe" to describe the *wa'a* is somewhat misleading to modern ears; each was up to 150 feet long and capable of holding five or six hundred people. For comparison, they were three times the size of the largest Viking longboat and faster than nineteenth-century clipper ships, traveling an average of 120 nautical miles per day.

Voyaging canoes were equipped with sails made from plaited pandanus leaves (*lau hala*), while a *lei hulu*, made from bright feathers, was the attractive equivalent of a windsock. The crew would be unlikely to catch many fish on the long voyage between Tahiti and Hawaii, but they could cook on a hearth lined with stone and coral and lived mainly on fermented breadfruit.

The Polynesian Voyaging Society's first vessel was the *Hōkūle'a*, named after the "Star of Gladness" that passes over Hawaii. Though constructed of plywood and fiberglass rather than *koa*, it was designed to duplicate the performance of a traditional double-hulled canoe. Petroglyph images served as blueprints for the shape of the sails, and extensive sea trials were required before the crew felt confident in handling the unfamiliar craft.

Perhaps the biggest problem was finding a **navigator**. In ancient times, the children of master navigators were apprenticed from the age of 5 to learn the secrets of their trade. Eventually the student would have, as a nineteenth-century canoe captain explained, "his head all same as compass." Navigators prepared intricate "stick charts," using twigs and shells to depict ocean currents, swells, and islands. Memorized rather than carried on board, these were used to guide canoes across the Pacific. Once settled in Hawaii, however, the Polynesians had no need of such skills, and as the older generations died, the knowledge was lost. Only the barest details of the migrations could be gleaned from Hawaiian lore.

When the *Hōkūle'a* embarked on its maiden long-distance voyage in 1976, it was navigated by **Mau Piailug**, from the Central Caroline islands of Micronesia, who was able to chart his course owing to years of experience on the Pacific and the relative familiarity of the night sky. In personal terms, thanks in part to the presence of a team from *National Geographic*, the voyage was fraught with tensions; by reaching Tahiti in just thirty days, however, it triumphantly achieved its purpose.

Western scientists, unwilling to credit **Polynesian culture** with any degree of sophistication, struggled for two hundred years to account for the very existence of the Hawaiians. When Captain Cook reached the Hawaiian islands, he was amazed to find a civilization that shared a culture and language with the people of the South Pacific.

Europeans had only just developed the technology to make expeditions such as Cook's possible. The recent development of a pendulum-free clock that remained accurate at sea – which earned its inventor a prize of £20,000 – had finally enabled sailors to calculate their longitude. As a result, they found it hard to believe that the Polynesians were already able to plot and sail a precise course across a three-thousand-mile expanse of ocean. The Hawaiians in turn were unable to explain how their ancestors had achieved this feat; although their chants and legends were explicit about their Tahitian origin, they no longer undertook long-distance sea trips, so the specific **navigational skills** had been forgotten.

At first it was proposed that the Hawaiians came from an as-yet-undiscovered continent; when that proved not to exist, it was suggested that they had survived its submergence. Some argued that the islanders had simply been deposited by God. The consensus came to be that the Polynesians had drifted accidentally from island to island, with groups of storm-tossed unfortunates making lucky landfalls on unoccupied islands. One hypothesis, "demonstrated" by Thor Heyerdahl's *Kon Tiki* expedition in 1947, was that the Polynesians came originally from South America, having been swept out to sea on balsa wood rafts as they fished off the coast.

There are strong reasons to reject the theory of accidental drift. The islands of the Pacific are so tiny and so far apart that vast quantities of drifting rafts would be required to populate every one. Moreover, the fact that migratory groups clearly brought the plants and animals necessary for survival indicates that the colonization was planned, and almost certainly involved return trips to the home base. But the most crucial evidence, in the case of Hawaii, is that neither wind nor wave alone will carry a vessel across the Equator; travel between Hawaii and Tahiti is only possible on a craft that uses some form of power, be it oar or maneuverable sail. Modern authorities believe the most likely explanation for the discovery of Hawaii was as part of a deliberate program of exploration for new lands. The most likely strategy for that would have been for Polynesian seafarers to wait until a moment the wind was blowing in the opposite direction to usual, then to sail before it as far as possible until supplies began to run short and/or the wind reversed direction once again.

One of the linchpins of Heyerdahl's argument was the presence in Polynesia of the sweet potato, which is unquestionably of South American origin. His claims that Polynesian languages showed South American roots have, however, been disproved by modern analysis, which shows a linguistic spread from Asia, as well as by conclusive DNA evidence. At some point, quite possibly deliberately, Polynesians must have reached South America and succeeded in returning.

In subsequent years, the *Hōkūleʻa* sailed all over the Pacific. By using a nor wind to sail east from Samoa to Tahiti, it refuted Heyerdahl's statement that it impossible for canoes from Asia to sail into the trade winds of the Pacific. Betw 1985 and 1987 it went to New Zealand and back, a 12,000-mile round. Meanwhile, a young Hawaiian crew member of the *Hōkūleʻa*, **Nainoa Thom** became fascinated with the lost art of navigation and set out to rediscov specific techniques that the ancient Hawaiians themselves would have used

The navigator's task consists of two main elements: way-finding ar finding. **Way-finding** is the ability to plot and keep track of a long course as accurately as possible. Although way-finding involves c monitoring the state of the ocean, the winds, and the currents (except i catnaps, the navigator has to remain awake for the entire voyage), it is rooted in close astronomical observation. In a fascinating partnership with modern science, Thompson gleaned a lifetime's worth of experience of the motions of the night sky through spending long hours in the planetarium at Honolulu's Bishop Museum. The precise techniques he developed, which involved finding "matching pairs" of stars that set or rise at the same time, may not be identical to those used by the original Polynesians. They have, however, conclusively demonstrated that long voyages without navigational aids are possible.

The other essential component to navigation is **land-finding**, the art of detecting land when you know it must be close. From the deck of a sailing canoe on the open Pacific, the horizon is just four miles away; to avoid sailing right past your objective, you have to watch for the many signs that land is nearby. The most obvious of these is the behavior and color of cloud formations; the Big Island, for example, is usually "visible" from about a hundred miles away, thanks to the stationary clouds over its giant volcanoes. The nightly homeward flight of birds to their island nests is another indication, while much can also be read into the swells and currents of the sea itself.

The **Hawai'iloa**, a canoe made of wood at the Bishop Museum and launched in 1993, went another step toward reproducing past glories. Unfortunately, no *koa* tree large enough to build such a canoe was found; instead the Tlingit of Alaska donated two four-hundred-year-old Sitka spruces. Soon afterwards, the **Mauloa**, a 26-foot-long, single-hulled *koa*-wood canoe, was constructed at the Pu'uhonua O Hōnaunau on the Big Island, under the supervision of Mau Piailug.

According to legend, during the heyday of Polynesian voyaging, regular gatherings of canoes from throughout the Pacific took place at the *Marae Taputapuatea* (temple of Lono) at Raiatea, not far from Tahiti in what are now called the Society Islands. The last such occasion, in 1350 AD, broke up after a Maori navigator was murdered. As a result, the Maori placed a *kapu* on the temple, and the era of ocean voyaging came to an end. After that date, no further expeditions sailed to or from Hawaii, although the last known long-distance voyage in Polynesia was as recent as 1812, from the Marquesas Islands.

In March 1995, the canoes gathered again, for the first time in more than six centuries. Both the *Hōkūle'a* and *Hawai'iloa* sailed from Hawaii to Tahiti, taking a mere three weeks, and then continued on to Raiatea. Maori elders conducted ceremonies at the *marae* to lift the ancient *kapu*, and canoes from Tahiti, New Zealand, and the Cook Islands joined their Hawaiian counterparts in proclaiming a new era of pan-Polynesian solidarity. Five years later, the *Hōkūle'a* traveled safely to and from Rapa Nui, or Easter Island. By venturing to this remote spot in the southeast Pacific, it formally completed the final leg of the "Polynesian Triangle," demonstrating that the ancient Polynesians did indeed deliberately colonize the entire ocean.

The canoes have become perhaps the most potent symbol of a Polynesian Renaissance. Their every movement is eagerly followed by children throughout the Pacific, and a new generation of navigators is being trained to assume the mantle of Nainoa Thompson and Mau Piailug. For the latest information, access the Polynesian Voyaging Society's website, ⊛pvs.kcc.hawaii.edu.

The Hawaiian environment

Of all the places in the world, I should like to see a good flora of the Sandwich Islands.

Charles Darwin, 1850

Much of the landscape in Hawaii seems so unspoiled and free from pollution that many visitors remain unaware of how fragile the environmental balance really is. Native life forms have had less than two millennia to adapt to the arrival of humans, while the avalanche of species introduced in the last two centuries threatens to overwhelm the delicate ecosystems altogether.

Hawaii is a unique ecological laboratory. Not only are the islands isolated by a "moat" at least two thousand miles wide in every direction, but, having emerged from the sea as lifeless lumps of lava, they were never populated by the diversity of species that spread across the rest of the planet.

Those plants and animals that found a foothold evolved into specialized forms unknown elsewhere. Of the more than ten thousand species of insect catalogued in the islands, for example, 98 percent are unique to Hawaii, while at least five thousand further species are thought to remain unidentified. Recent discoveries include the tiny "happy-face spiders" of the rainforests, whose markings are now familiar from postcards sold all over the state.

Such species are particularly vulnerable to external threats; half of Hawaii's indigenous plants and three-quarters of its birds are already extinct, while 73 percent of all the species in the US classified as threatened or endangered are unique to the islands. More than one hundred species of Hawaiian plants now have fewer than twenty remaining individuals in the wild.

The arrival of life

During the first seventy million years after the Hawaiian islands started to arise from the ocean, new plants and animals arrived only by sheer happenstance, via a few unlikely routes. Such were the obstacles that a new species only established itself once every 100,000 years. That's a total of seven hundred altogether, of which the great majority are thought to have come from the west, from Asia, and the Pacific.

Some drifted, clinging to flotsam washed up on the beaches; others were borne on the wind as seeds or spores; and the odd migratory bird found its way here, perhaps bringing seeds or seeds. The larvae of shallow-water fish from Indonesia and the Philippines floated across thousands of miles of ocean to hatch in the Hawaiian coral reefs.

Of **birds**, only the strongest fliers made it here; the *nēnē*, Hawaii's state bird, is thought to have evolved from a Canadian goose injured during its annual migration and forced to remain on the islands. Its descendants adapted to walking on raw lava by losing the webbing from their feet. No land-based amphibians or reptiles reached Hawaii, let alone large land mammals. At some point a hoary bat and an intrepid monk seal must have gotten here, as these were the only two mammals whose arrival pre-dated that of humans.

Each species mutated from a single fertilized female to fill numerous ecological niches with extraordinary speed. Hundreds of variations might develop from a single fruit fly or land snail, and many species adapted themselves to conditions in specific areas of individual islands.

Although the Hawaiian environment was not entirely free of competition, many plants prospered without bothering to keep up their natural defenses. Thus there are nettles with no stings, and mints with no scent. Conversely, normally placid creatures turned savage; caterpillars content to munch leaves elsewhere catch and eat flies in Hawaii. These evolutionary changes have taken place so fast that five species of banana moth have evolved in the 1500 years since the Polynesians brought the banana to the islands.

As each new island emerged, it was populated by species from its neighbors as well as stragglers from further afield. This process can still be seen on the Big Island – the youngest and least densely populated island – where Hawaii's last remaining stand of pristine rainforest still attempts to spread onto the new land created by Kīlauea. Although lava flows destroy existing life, fresh lava is incredibly rich in nutrients. Water collects in cavities in the rock, and seeds or spores soon gather. The basic building block of the rainforest is the *hapu'u* tree fern. Patches of these grow and decay, and in the mulch the *'ohi'a lehua* gains a foothold as a gnarled shrub; in time it grows to become a gigantic tree, forcing its roots through the rock. After several hundred years, the lava crumbles to become soil that will support a full range of rainforest species. In addition, lava flows swirl around higher ground, or even random spots, to create isolated "pockets" of growth that quickly develop their own specialized ecosystems.

The Polynesian world

The first humans to arrive on the Hawaiian scene swiftly realized that the islands lacked the familiar comforts of their South Seas homelands. Many of what might seem quintessentially Hawaiian species, such as coconut palms, bananas, taro, and sugarcane, were in fact brought from Tahiti by the Polynesians, who also introduced the islands' first significant mammals – goats, dogs, and pigs.

The settlers set about changing the island's physical environment to suit their own needs. They constructed terraces and irrigation channels in the great wetland valleys, such as Hālawa on Molokai and Waipi'o on the Big Island, planted coconuts along the shoreline, and built fishponds out into the ocean (see p.408). While their animals wrought destruction on the native flora, the settlers also had a significant impact on the bird population. Around twenty species of flightless birds, for example, swiftly became extinct. Forest birds were snared so their feathers could be used to make cloaks, helmets, and *leis*; bright red feathers came from the *i'iwi* bird, while yellow became the most prized color of all, so yellow birds such as the *mamo* and *'ō'ō* grew progressively rare. The *nēnē* was hunted for food, and the *auku'u* heron, the curse of the fishponds, was driven from its native habitat.

On the whole, however, the Hawaiians lived in relative harmony with nature, with the *kapu* system helping to conserve resources. It was the arrival of foreigners, and the deluge of new species that they introduced, that really strained the ecological balance of Hawaii. Among the first victims were the Hawaiians themselves, decimated by the onslaught of foreign diseases.

Foreign invaders

The ships of early European explorers of the Pacific were explicitly intended to play the role of Noah's Arks. They carried food plants and domestic animals around the world in order to adapt newly discovered lands to the European image and present their benighted natives with the accoutrements deemed necessary for civilization. Hawaii's first **cattle**, for example, were presented to Kamehameha the Great by Captain George Vancouver of the *Discovery* in February 1793. Allowed to run wild on the Big Island, they ate through grasslands and forests, as well as through the crops of the Hawaiians. When they were eventually rounded up and domesticated, it formalized the change in land usage they had already effected. **Horses** had a similar initial impact, and wild goats remain a problem to this day.

Foreign **plants**, too, were imported, ranging from the scrubby mesquite trees of the lowlands (now known as *kiawe*) to the Mexican cacti that dot the mountainsides of Maui and the strawberry guava that runs riot along forest trails.

Along with such deliberate introductions came the stowaways, such as rats and forest-choking weeds. An especially unwelcome arrival was the **mosquito**. Scientists have pinpointed the exact moment it turned up, in 1826, when the whaling vessel *Wellington* emptied its rancid water casks into a stream near Lahaina prior to filling up with fresh water; they've even decided from which Peruvian river the water, and the mosquito larvae it contained, was originally drawn.

Another spectacular disaster was the importation to Hawaii of the **mongoose** by sugar plantation owners in the hope that it would keep down the rat population. Unfortunately, this plan failed to take into consideration the fact that while rats are nocturnal, mongooses are not. The rodents continued to thrive while the mongooses slept, having gorged themselves on birds' eggs during the day. Only Kauai, where the mongoose never became established – myth has it that an infuriated docker threw the island's consignment into the sea after he was bitten – now retains significant populations of the many Hawaiian birds who, in the absence of predators, had decided it was safe to build their nests on the ground. Even here, there have been alarming recent reports of mongoose sightings.

Wild pigs have also had a ravaging effect. It is said that for every twenty humans in Hawaii, there lurks a feral pig. Though tourists are unlikely to spot one, their impact on Hawaiian rainforests has been devastating. For the ancient Hawaiians, the pig god Kama'pua'a was the embodiment of lusty fertility, plowing deep furrows across the islands with his mighty tusks. His modern counterparts combine the strongest characteristics of the Polynesian pigs brought by early settlers with those of later European imports. Rooting through the earth, eating tree ferns, eliminating native lobelias and greenswords, and spreading the seeds of foreign fruits, the pigs have in most places destroyed the canopy that should prevent direct sunlight and heavy raindrops from hitting the forest floor. In addition, they have created muddy wallows and stagnant pools where mosquitoes thrive – the resultant avian malaria is thought to be the major single cause of the extinction of bird species.

Eradicating the wild pig population has become a priority for conservationists. In principle their goal gels with the desire of amateur hunters for sport, though bitter "Pig Wars" have arisen between hunters who want to leave enough wild pigs for their hunting to continue and scientists who want to eliminate them altogether.

Unwanted alien species continue to arrive. Among those reported recently are the **coqui frog** from Puerto Rico, which has already achieved population densities in excess of ten thousand individuals per acre in over a hundred spots on the Big

△ Silversword plant

Island (including Lava Tree State Monument; see p.248) as well as on three other islands, and the Madagascar **giant day gecko**, a foot-long orange-spotted lizard now established on Oahu. Environmentalists fear that Hawaii's next likely arrival will be the **brown tree snake**. Originally found in the Solomon Islands, it has been hitchhiking its way across the Pacific since World War II, sneaking into the holds of ships and planes, then emerging to colonize new worlds that have never seen a single snake. In Guam it has already established itself in concentrations of up to thirty thousand individuals per square mile, happy to eat virtually anything, and wiping out the local bird populations.

Issues and prospects

The state of Hawaii has a short and not very impressive history of legislating to conserve its environment, and what little has been achieved so far appears to be jeopardized by Republican moves to rein in the powers of the Endangered Species Act. One positive development is that the whole state has been officially declared a **humpback whale** sanctuary, though the Navy is dragging its heels about certain areas just offshore from its installations, and there has been much opposition from local fishermen.

Throughout Hawaii, a resurgence of interest in what are seen as native Hawaiian values has dovetailed with the influx of New Age *haoles* to create an active environmental movement, which has had plenty of issues to occupy its attention. In particular, the cyclical depressions to which the Hawaiian economy is prone have made the islands vulnerable to grandiose schemes designed to attract outside funding.

Specific controversies have included the attempt to harness the geothermal power of the Kīlauea volcano, the plan to build a commercial spaceport for the Space Shuttle nearby, and a scheme to get rid of surplus carbon dioxide by pumping it into the deep ocean off Honokōhau, all on the **Big Island**; the US Army's ever-expanding missile program on **Kauai** (see p.511); the proposed construction of an underwater casino three miles off **Maui**; and the long-standing wrangle over the future of the island of **Kahoolawe**, described on p.332. For up-to-date information about these and similar issues, the **Environment Hawaii** website, at ⊕ www.environment-hawaii.org, is highly recommended.

There has also been much discussion over what is to become of the islands' **irrigation channels**. Developed long before European contact, and later adapted and expanded to meet the needs of the plantations, their infrastructure is now rapidly falling into disrepair. As the ancient Hawaiians knew all too well, maintenance is extremely labor-intensive; without swift action, however, the opportunity to revive small-scale agriculture may soon pass.

Conservationists are struggling to combat the disappearance of Hawaii's indigenous **wildlife**. There have been some high-profile successes, such as the preservation of the extraordinary silversword plants of Haleakalā on Maui (see p.354) and the breeding of *nēnē* geese in the national parks on both Maui and the Big Island. However, the rarest bird species survive only in isolated mountain-top sanctuaries like Kōke'e State Park on Kauai (see p.517), the Kamakou Preserve on Molokai (see p.413), and Maui's Kīpahulu Valley (see p.372). So long as they stay at least 3500 feet above sea level, the mosquitoes can't reach them; nonetheless, birds such as the 'ō ō a'a honey-creeper are becoming extinct at an alarming rate. Activists concerned about the destruction of Hawaiian plants by casually imported newcomers point out that all passengers leaving Hawaii for the US are subjected to stringent inspections, to prevent Hawaiian species from reaching the mainland, but there are no equivalent checks on arriving passengers.

The greatest debates of all, however, have revolved around **tourism**. The power of the development lobby has for the last few decades been great enough to override environmental objections to the growth of resorts across all the islands. Anyone who believes that conserving the earth's resources is inherently a good thing is liable to have trouble accepting the kind of conspicuous consumption reflected in the ability of a single hotel to devour seven percent of the Big Island's energy each year. There are also concerns that the resorts are damaging their immediate environment; the combination of golf courses and coral reefs may be ideal for vacationers, but that won't last if fertilizer and silt washed down from the greens and fairways end up choking the reef to death. However, it now looks as though the era of resort building is drawing to a close, albeit due more to economic factors than environmental pressure.

Mark Twain's Hawaii

M ark Twain visited the islands of Oahu, Maui, and Hawaii in 1866, at the age of 31, on assignment for the *Sacramento Union*. The letters he wrote for that newspaper have been published as *Letters from Hawaii* by the University of Hawaii Press; he later reworked his material for inclusion in the more celebrated *Roughing It* (Penguin, 1872).

Though Twain described Hawaii as the "loveliest fleet of islands that lies anchored in any ocean," he never set foot on the islands again. In 1895, he was on board a ship that docked in Honolulu, but owing to a cholera epidemic in the city, passengers were forbidden to disembark.

Mark Twain's account of Kīlauea, parts of which are reprinted below, has to be the most vivid description of an erupting volcano ever written. Kīlauea today is a very different mountain from the one seen by Twain, but if his words inspire you to see it for yourself, you won't be disappointed.

Kīlauea Caldera

After a hearty supper we waited until it was thoroughly dark and then started to the crater. The first glance in that direction revealed a scene of wild beauty. There was a heavy fog over the crater and it was splendidly illuminated by the glare from the fires below. The illumination was two miles wide and a mile high, perhaps; and if you ever, on a dark night and at a distance beheld the light from thirty or forty blocks of distant buildings all on fire at once, reflected strongly against overhanging clouds, you can form a fair idea of what this looked like. A colossal column of cloud towered to a great height in the air immediately above the crater, and the outer swell of every one of its vast folds was dyed with a rich crimson luster, which was subdued to a pale rose tint in the depressions between. It glowed like a muffled torch and stretched upward to a dizzy height toward the zenith. I thought it just possible that its like had not been seen since the children of Israel wandered on their long march through the desert so many centuries ago over a path illuminated by the mysterious "pillar of fire." And I was sure that I now had a vivid conception of what the majestic "pillar of fire" was like, which almost amounted to a revelation.

Arrived at the little thatched lookout house, we rested our elbows on the railing in front and looked abroad over the wide crater and down over the sheer precipice at the seething fires beneath us. The view was a startling improvement on my daylight experience. I turned to see the effect on the balance of the company and found the reddest-faced set of men I almost ever saw. In the strong light every countenance glowed like red-hot iron, every shoulder was suffused with crimson and shaded rearward into dingy, shapeless obscurity! The place below looked like the infernal regions and these men like half-cooled devils just come up on a furlough.

I turned my eyes upon the volcano again. The "cellar" was tolerably well lighted up. For a mile and a half in front of us and half a mile on either side, the floor of the abyss was magnificently illuminated; beyond these limits the mists hung down their gauzy curtains and cast a deceptive gloom over all that made the twinkling fires in the remote corners of the crater seem countless leagues removed – made them seem like the camp-fires of a great army far away. Here was room for the imagination to work! You could imagine those lights the width of a continent away – and that hidden under the intervening darkness were hills, and winding rivers, and weary wastes of plain and desert – and even then the tremendous vista stretched on, and on, and on! – to the fires and far beyond! You could not compass it – it was the idea of eternity made tangible – and the longest end of it made visible to the naked eye!

The greater part of the vast floor of the desert under us was as black as ink, and apparently smooth and level; but over a mile square of it was ringed and streaked and striped with a thousand branching streams of liquid and gorgeously brilliant fire! It looked like a colossal railroad map of the State of Massachusetts done in chain lightning on a midnight sky. Imagine it – imagine a coal black sky shivered into a tangled net-work of angry fire!

Here and there were gleaming holes a hundred feet in diameter, broken in the dark crust, and in them the melted lava – the color a dazzling white just tinged with yellow – was boiling and surging furiously; and from these holes branched number-less bright torrents in many directions, like the spokes of a wheel, and kept a tolerably straight course for a while and then swept round in huge rainbow curves, or made a long succession of sharp worm-fence angles, which looked precisely like the fiercest jagged lightning. These streams met other streams, and they mingled with and crossed and recrossed each other in every conceivable direction, like skate tracks on a popular skating ground. Sometimes streams twenty or thirty feet wide flowed from the holes to some distance without dividing – and through the opera-glasses we could see that they ran down small, steep hills and were genuine cataracts of fire, white at their source, but soon cooling and turning to the richest red, grained with alternate lines of black and gold. Every now and then masses of the dark crust broke away and floated slowly down these streams like rafts down a river. Occasionally the molten lava flowing under the superincumbent crust broke through – split a dazzling streak, from five hundred to a thousand feet long, like a sudden flash of lightning, and then acre after acre of the cold lava parted into fragments, turned up edgewise like cakes of ice when a great river breaks up, plunged downward and were swallowed in the crimson cauldron. Then the wide expanse of the "thaw" maintained a ruddy glow for a while, but shortly cooled and became black and level again. During a "thaw" every dismembered cake was marked by a glittering white border which was superbly shaded inward by aurora borealis rays, which were a flaming yellow where they joined the white border, and from thence toward their points tapered into glowing crimson, then into a rich, pale carmine, and finally into a faint blush that held its own a moment and then dimmed and turned black. Some of the streams preferred to mingle together in a tangle of fantastic circles, and then they looked something like the confusion of ropes one sees on a ship's deck when she has just taken in sail and dropped anchor – provided one can imagine those ropes on fire.

Through the glasses, the little fountains scattered about looked very beautiful. They boiled, and coughed, and spluttered, and discharged sprays of stringy red fire – of about the consistency of mush, for instance – from ten to fifteen feet into the air, along with a shower of brilliant white sparks – a quaint and unnatural mingling of gouts of blood and snow-flakes!

We had circles and serpents and streaks of lightning all twined and wreathed and tied together, without a break throughout an area more than a mile square (that amount of ground was covered, though it was not strictly "square"), and it was with a feeling of placid exultation that we reflected that many years had elapsed since any visitor had seen such a splendid display – since any visitor had seen anything more than the now snubbed and insignificant "North" and "South" lakes in action. We had been reading old files of Hawaiian newspapers and the "Record Book" at the Volcano House, and were posted.

I could see the North Lake lying out on the black floor away off in the outer edge of our panorama, and knitted to it by a web-work of lava streams. In its individual capacity it looked very little more respectable than a schoolhouse on fire. True, it was about nine hundred feet long and two or three hundred wide, but then, under the present circumstances, it necessarily appeared rather insignificant, and besides it was so distant from us.

I forgot to say that the noise made by the bubbling lava is not great, heard as we heard it from our lofty perch. It makes three distinct sounds – a rushing, a hissing, and a coughing or puffing sound; and if you stand on the brink and close your eyes it is no trick at all to imagine that you are sweeping down a river on a large low-pressure steamer, and that you hear the hissing of the steam about her boilers, the puffing from her escape-pipes and the churning rush of the water abaft her wheels. The smell of sulphur is strong, but not unpleasant to a sinner.

We left the lookout house at ten o'clock in a half cooked condition, because of the heat from Pele's furnaces, and wrapping up in blankets, for the night was cold, we returned to our Hotel.

* * * * * * *

The next night was appointed for a visit to the bottom of the crater, for we desired to traverse its floor and see the "North Lake" (of fire) which lay two miles away, toward the further wall. After dark half a dozen of us set out, with lanterns and native guides, and climbed down a crazy, thousand-foot pathway in a crevice fractured in the crater wall, and reached the bottom in safety.

The irruption of the previous evening had spent its force and the floor looked black and cold; but when we ran out upon it we found it hot yet, to the feet, and it was likewise riven with crevices which revealed the underlying fires gleaming vindictively. A neighboring cauldron was threatening to overflow, and this added to the dubiousness of the situation. So the native guides refused to continue the venture, and then every body deserted except a stranger named Marlette. He said he had been in the crater a dozen times in daylight and believed he could find his way through it at night. He thought that a run of three hundred yards would carry us over the hottest part of the floor and leave us our shoe-soles. His pluck gave me back-bone. We took one lantern and instructed the guides to hang the other to the roof of the lookout house to serve as a beacon for us in case we got lost, and then the party started back up the precipice and Marlette and I made our run. We skipped over the hot floor and over the red crevices with brisk dispatch and reached the cold lava safe but with pretty warm feet. Then we took things leisurely and comfortably, jumping tolerably wide and probably bottomless chasms, and threading our way through picturesque lava upheavals with considerable confidence. When we got fairly away from the cauldrons of boiling fire, we seemed to be in a gloomy desert, and a suffocatingly dark one, surrounded by dim walls that seemed to tower to the sky. The only cheerful objects were the glinting stars high overhead.

By and by Marlette shouted "Stop!" I never stopped quicker in my life. I asked what the matter was. He said we were out of the path. He said we must not try to go on till we found it again, for we were surrounded with beds of rotten lava through which we could easily break and plunge down a thousand feet. I thought eight hundred would answer for me, and was about to say so when Marlette partly proved his statement by accidentally crushing through and disappearing to his arm-pits. He got out and we hunted for the path with the lantern. He said there was only one path and that it was but vaguely defined. We could not find it. The lava surface was all alike in the lantern light. But he was an ingenious man. He said it was not the lantern that had informed him that we were out of the path, but his feet. He had noticed a crisp grinding of fine lava-needles under his feet, and some instinct reminded him that in the path these were all worn away. So he put the lantern behind him, and began to search with his boots instead of his eyes. It was good sagacity. The first time his foot touched a surface that did not grind under it he announced that the trail was found again; and after that we kept up a sharp listening for the rasping sound and it always warned us in time.

It was a long tramp, but an exciting one. We reached the North Lake between ten and eleven o'clock, and sat down on a huge overhanging lava-shelf, tired but satisfied. The spectacle presented was worth coming double the distance to see. Under us, and stretching away before us, was a heaving sea of molten fire of seemingly limitless extent. The glare from it was so blinding that it was some time before we could bear to look upon it steadily. It was like gazing at the sun at noonday, except that the glare was not quite so white. At unequal distances all around the shores of the lake were nearly white-hot chimneys or hollow drums of lava, four or five feet high, and up through them were bursting gorgeous sprays of lava-gouts and gem spangles, some white, some red and some golden – a ceaseless bombardment, and one that fascinated the eye with its unapproachable splendor. The more distant jets, sparkling up through an intervening gossamer veil of vapor, seemed miles away; and the further the curving ranks of fiery fountains receded, the more fairy-like and beautiful they appeared.

Now and then the surging bosom of the lake under our noses would calm down ominously and seem to be gathering strength for an enterprise; and then all of a sudden a red dome of lava of the bulk of an ordinary dwelling would heave itself aloft like an escaping balloon, then burst asunder, and out of its heart would flit a pale-green film of vapor, and float upward and vanish in the darkness – a released soul soaring homeward from captivity with the damned, no doubt. The crashing plunge of the ruined dome into the lake again would send a world of seething billows lashing against the shores and shaking the foundations of our perch. By and by, a loosened mass of the hanging shelf we sat on tumbled into the lake, jarring the surroundings like an earthquake and delivering a suggestion that may have been intended for a hint, and may not. We did not wait to see.

We got lost again on our way back, and were more than an hour hunting for the path. We were where we could see the beacon lantern at the lookout house at the time, but thought it was a star and paid no attention to it. We reached the hotel at two o'clock in the morning pretty well fagged out.

Mark Twain, *Roughing It*, 1872

Hawaii in the movies

Moviegoers may not always have known what they were seeing, but the spectacular scenery of Hawaii has featured prominently on the silver screen since the earliest days of the cinema. Kauai, for example, has not only appeared as a tourist paradise in its own right in movies such as *Blue Hawaii* (1961), *Throw Momma from the Train* (1987), and *Honeymoon in Vegas* (1992), but has also doubled as a Caribbean island in *Jurassic Park* (1993), as South America in *Raiders of the Lost Ark* (1981), as Vietnam in *Uncommon Valor* (1983), as Africa in *Outbreak* (1995), and even as Neverland in *Hook* (1992).

The very first footage shot in Hawaii was a travelogue, made by Thomas Edison's company in 1898; free showings of excerpts take place daily in Lahaina's Wo Hing Temple on Maui (see p.296). By 1913, Universal Studios had made a silent feature on Oahu, *The Shark God*, which established a tradition of Hawaii as an all-purpose exotic backdrop for tales of **terror**, mysterious rites, and unbridled passion. Later examples include Boris Karloff's 1957 *Voodoo Island*; Roger Corman's *She God of Shark Reef*, from the following year; the 1976 remake of *King Kong*; and *Aloha Donny and Marie*, featuring the Osmonds, in 1978.

A separate genre, the Hawaii-based **musical comedy**, was instigated by *Waikiki Wedding* in 1937, in which **Bing Crosby** crooned *Blue Hawaii* and *Sweet Leilani*. Hawaii provided a glamorous setting for star vehicles featuring Hollywood's biggest names. Thus Shirley Temple and Betty Grable donned grass skirts and *leis*, while those home-grown actors who managed to appear on camera, such as the singer Hilo Hattie (whose name lives on in her chain of aloha-wear stores) and legendary surfer Duke Kahanamoku, simply played bit parts to add a little local color.

With the invention of Technicolor, film-makers began fully to appreciate the potential of Hawaii. In *Pagan Love Song* (1950), Esther Williams performed one of her trademark aquatic ballets in Kauai's Hanalei Bay – supposedly Tahiti – while

△ Blue Hawaii starring Elvis Presley

CONTEXTS | Hawaii in the movies

559

the smash-hit Rodgers and Hammerstein musical *South Pacific* (1958) turned Kauai into a South Seas Eden. However, it was **Elvis Presley**, his Cherokee ancestry making him at least semi-plausible as a Polynesian, who became most closely identified with Hawaii. As tour guide Chad Gates in his greatest box-office success, *Blue Hawaii* (1961) – promoted with the lame but accurate slogan "You'll Want to Visit Hawaii, After You See *Blue Hawaii*" – Elvis preened at countless Honolulu and Waikīkī locations before finally tying the knot with Joan Blackman in a gloriously kitsch wedding ceremony at Kauai's now-defunct *Coco Palms Resort*. He returned to Hawaii in 1962, for *Girls, Girls, Girls*, but as his adventures as a charter-boat skipper were allegedly taking place off Louisiana, not a single sequence shows a recognizable Hawaiian landmark. By contrast, during his *Paradise, Hawaiian Style* (1966), the camera seizes every opportunity to drift away from the flimsy plot line and linger lovingly on the North Shore cliffs of Kauai.

After World War II, Hawaii also became the ideal location to film stories of the War in the Pacific, whether the producers needed an accessible stand-in for some other, more remote, Pacific island, or wanted to depict actual events on Hawaii. Until it was trumped by Disney's spectacular but ultimately sterile **Pearl Harbor** in 2001, the most famous re-enactment of the attack on Pearl Harbor, for example, came as the climax of **From Here to Eternity**, which won the Academy Award for Best Picture in 1953 (and tends to be best remembered for the scene in which Burt Lancaster and Deborah Kerr frolic in the surf at Oahu's Hālona Cove). **Frank Sinatra**, who received an Oscar for his portrayal of Private Maggio in that movie – having won the role with the behind-the-scenes maneuvering on which the horse's head incident in *The Godfather* is allegedly based – directed his own war epic on Kauai a dozen years later. The war-torn Pacific beach in *None but the Brave* was Pīlaʻa Beach, east of Kīlauea. During filming, Sinatra had to be rescued from drowning when he found himself in difficulties swimming off Wailua Beach. Big **John Wayne** made a number of war movies in Hawaii, including *The Sea Chase*, filmed on the Big Island in 1955, and Otto Preminger's *In Harm's Way* (1965), which featured another depiction of the Pearl Harbor attack. He had a rather happier time touring Kauai's coastline with Dorothy Lamour in the John Ford-directed comedy *Donovan's Reef* (1963).

Visitors with an interest in seeing specific **movie locations** should head straight for **Kauai**. The landscape of **South Pacific**'s fictional Bali Haʻi was created by melding the peak of Makana, near Kēʻē Beach, with assorted Fijian scenes, but the movie's showstopping songs were filmed at genuine North Shore locations. These included a waterfall on Kīlauea River, for *Happy Talk*; Hanalei Bay, for *Some Enchanted Evening*; and Lumahaʻi Beach, under the name of Nurses' Beach, where Mitzi Gaynor sang *I'm Gonna Wash that Man Right Out of My Hair*. The opening sequence of **Raiders of the Lost Ark**, in which Harrison Ford escapes by seaplane from a posse of Amazonian headhunters – as portrayed by Kauai locals with pudding-basin haircuts – was shot on the Hulēʻia Stream just outside Lihuʻe. The first attempt to film on the inaccessible Nā Pali coast came in 1976, when remote Honopū Beach stood in as Skull Island in that year's remake of **King Kong**. Helicopters were again deployed to ferry the crew of **Jurassic Park** into the island's interior, and a helicopter tour is the only way tourists can hope to see the waterfalls in and around Hanapēpē Valley where much of the action takes place. The movie's heroes, however, were disturbed by a sneezing dinosaur as they slept in the branches of a Moreton Bay fig at Allerton Garden on the South Shore, while the gates to the park itself were erected on a cane road above Wailua that leads toward Mount Waiʻaleʻale. Filming on *Jurassic Park* was brought to an abrupt end by Hurricane Iniki in September 1991 – which may explain why the sequel was shot elsewhere – and the movie includes a brief sequence of the hurricane's onslaught on Nawiliwili Harbor. Many Kauai landmarks are even recognizable in Disney's 2002 animation, *Lilo and Stitch*.

Finally, Hawaii may be even more familiar from **television**. Between 1968 and 1980, 262 episodes of **Hawaii Five-O** were filmed on Oahu. Jack Lord starred as Steve McGarrett and James MacArthur as Dano; their arch-enemy, Wo Fat, took his name from a real-life Honolulu restaurant. According to one survey, 25 percent of visitors to Hawaii during the 1970s cited the program as a factor in their decision to come. Upon its demise, *Hawaii Five-0* was immediately replaced by Tom Selleck's **Magnum P.I.**, which ran in turn until 1988. Both *Fantasy Island* (1978–84) and *Gilligan's Island* (1964–67) were also filmed at least partially in Hawaii. Most recently, the hit series **Lost** has been filmed almost entirely on Oahu. Location-spotting fans have pointed out that the crash site of Oceanic Flight 815 is Mokulēʻia Beach; the survivors' initial explorations take place in Kaʻaʻawa Valley, home to the Kualoa Ranch; many rainforest scenes were shot near the *Turtle Bay Resort*; an engagement party in Kora is in fact at the Byōdō-In Temple; and the Hawaii Convention Center doubles as Sydney Airport.

Hula and Hawaiian music

From the moment Europeans first reached the Hawaiian islands, in 1778, **Hawaiian music** has been world music, constantly adapting and changing as new waves of immigrants and visitors have introduced their own traditions and instruments. Appropriately enough, Hawaii provided perhaps the earliest world music craze of all, around a hundred years ago, when its distinctive slide-guitar sound and *hula* dances were taken up first across the US and subsequently all over the world. But despite the islands' lengthy entanglement with tourism, their music has continued to follow its own highly individual path.

Roots

Although the ancient Hawaiians were devotees of the poetic chants they called **meles**, they had no specific word for "song." Meles were composed for various purposes, ranging from lengthy genealogies of the chiefs, put together over days of debate, through temple prayers, to lullabies and love songs. Unaccompanied chanting was known as *mele oli*; when the chant was accompanied by music and dance, the combined performance was known as *mele hula*. The invention of the *hula* was generally credited to the goddess Laka, who is said to have danced for the first time either in the *ʻōhiʻa lehua* groves near Maunaloa on Molokai (see p.430) or above Kēʻē Beach on Kauai (see p.489).

Music was created using instruments such as gourds, rattles and small hand or knee drums made from coconuts. A larger kind of drum, the *pahu*, which was made by stretching shark skin over hollow logs, was said to have been introduced by Hawaii's final wave of settlers from Tahiti, around the thirteenth century; legend tells of the voyagers booming out this menacing new sound as they pulled towards shore.

As a rule the tonal range was minimal and the music monotonous, though occasionally bamboo pipes may also have been played. Complexity was introduced by the fact that the dance, the chant and the music were all likely to follow distinct rhythmic patterns.

The telling of the story or legend was of primary importance; the music was subordinate to the chant, while the feet and lower body of the dancers served mainly to keep the rhythm, and their hand movements supplemented the meaning of the words. Dancers underwent training in a *halau hula* – part school, part temple – and performances were hedged around by sacred ritual and *kapu*.

Missionaries and immigrants, kings and queens

When the first Christian **missionaries** reached Hawaii in the 1820s, immediately after the collapse of the *kapu* system, they saw *hula* as a lascivious manifestation of the islands' general lack of morality. It's clearly true, for example, that the religious subtleties of the so-called "genital *hula*" dances, celebrating the genitals of leading members of the *aliʻi*, were lost on visiting whalemen. Their own church music, however, served to introduce western instruments, concepts of harmony, and vocal styles. Inspired by the *hīmeni* they learned from the first Hawaiian hymn book, local musicians were soon creating their own songs in the Western tradition.

The population of Hawaii changed rapidly, as a massive influx of settlers and sailors, whalemen and laborers was matched by a precipitous decline in its indigenous peoples, exacerbated by new diseases and epidemics. Specific immigrant groups exposed the islands to a wide range of musical influences; thus the Mexican cowboys (known as *paniolos*) who came to work the cattle ranches of the Big Island introduced guitars, while Portuguese sugar farmers arrived from the Azores with the *braguinha*, an early form of *ukelele*.

Towards the close of the nineteenth century, and championed especially by the Hawaiian royal family, a new and distinctive kind of Hawaiian music emerged. The coronation in 1883 of **King David Kalākaua** – the so-called 'Merrie Monarch,' who had his own *'ukulele* group, and co-wrote Hawaii's national anthem, *Hawaii Ponoi* – was marked by the first public *hula* performance in two generations. Kalākaua also recruited bandleader **Henry Berger** from the Prussian army to establish the Royal Hawaiian Band, a brass band that performed arrangements of Hawaiian songs as well as marches and ragtime compositions. For good measure, Berger also taught **yodeling**, which helped to add an idiosyncratic twist to Hawaii's already developing tradition of falsetto singing, in which the *hai*, or break in the voice between falsetto and 'normal' singing, is emphasized rather than hidden. As part of the process of adapting music and dance to suit foreign tastes, incidentally, the **grass skirt** was imported to Hawaii from the Gilbert Islands in the 1870s, as somehow looking more Polynesian.

King David was succeeded in 1891 by his sister, **Queen Lili'uokalani**, who remains perhaps the most celebrated of all Hawaiian composers. She was deposed by a US-inspired coup in 1894, and subsequently imprisoned in her own palace on charges of treason; small wonder she's remembered for such haunting songs as the much-covered *Aloha Oe*.

Thanks in part to their strong association with the much-mourned royal family, and despite the fact that they're already a self-evident mixture of Polynesian forms

△ Hula dancers

The 'ukulele – a Portuguese gift to the Pacific

The 'ukulele – one of the most ubiquitous instruments in Hawaiian (and Polynesian) popular music – is essentially the *braguinha*, a small four-stringed instrument that originated in the **Portuguese** island of Madeira (and a variant of the more common *cavaquinho* of the Portuguese mainland).

In September 1878, 120 Madeira islanders arrived in Honolulu as Hawaii's first Portuguese immigrants, ready to work on the sugar plantations. They were joined a year later by another 400 settlers, including one **João Fernandes**, who had borrowed a *braguinha* from a fellow passenger and learned to play it during the voyage of almost five months. When the boat finally arrived in Honolulu the passengers celebrated their safe arrival with a dance, and Fernandes played the instrument, to the delight of both settlers and Hawaiians. He soon became a fixture at balls and parties and eventually formed a group, which played on occasion for the Hawaiian royalty.

A fellow passenger on that same boat, Manuel Nunes, opened a shop where he made and sold *braguinhas* – by now renamed *'ukuleles*. He and other craftsmen began to use local *kou* and *koa* wood and before long the *braguinha* became a national instrument. The Hawaiian word *'ukulele* literally means 'jumping flea', and is said to originate from the nickname of a small Englishman, Edward Purvis, who played the instrument with quick, jerky movements.

with musical influences from all over the world, it's the songs from this era that are now thought of as typifying traditional Hawaiian music.

Slack key and steel guitar, and hapa haole

In conventional guitar tuning, strumming the open strings produces a dischord. In the late nineteenth century, however, Hawaiians started to retune the strings to create a harmonious chord, and from there developed a whole range of open tunings – a new style that they called *kī hō'alu* or **slack key**. A further innovation soon followed, with the development of the Hawaiian **steel guitar** (*kika kila*): a new guitar sound and a new guitar posture, with the instrument played on the lap or on a stand. Previously, the violin or flute would often figure as the lead instrument in Hawaiian music; now the steel guitar took over as lead, while slack key strumming maintained the rhythm.

After the islands were annexed by the US in 1898, the **hapa haole** (half white) style of song began to emerge, as Hawaiian musicians strove to please visiting Americans and win audiences on the mainland. Though *hapa haole* is often characterized as a form in which English or nonsense lyrics were set to traditional Hawaiian melodies, in truth the music too was heavily influenced by whatever was currently popular in the US. For that matter, at the peak of its popularity much of it was actually written on Tin Pan Alley, by songsmiths who had never visited the islands. Thus while the earliest *hapa haole* songs owed much to ragtime, they shifted towards jazz and blues by the 1920s, big band sounds in the 1930s, and even rock'n'roll by the late 1950s. Often there was a comedy or novelty element, in which the real or supposed sounds of the Hawaiian language were exaggerated for comic event, as with the *Hawaiian War Chant*.

At San Francisco's Panama-Pacific Exposition in 1915 – which celebrated the opening of the Panama Canal – the new Territory of Hawaii invested heavily in its pavilion. America fell in love with the sounds of Hawaii, and by 1916 more Hawaiian records were being sold in the US than any other type of music. Groups such as the **Kalama Quartet** introduced four-part falsetto harmony singing with two steel guitars playing counterpoint, while other recordings featured virtuoso Hawaiian steel-guitarists.

Another cultural collision occurred as these musicians discovered jazz. **Bennie Nawahi** was a key figure in this early fusion – a steel-guitar wizard who performed with equal dexterity on mandolin and *'ukulele*. He started out as a busker, then worked a cruise ship with his brothers, developing along the way an extraordinary showmanship, playing the steel guitar with his feet and the *'ukulele* behind his head with one hand. With America in the grip of *'ukulele* madness, Nawahi played the vaudeville circuit with huge success in the 1920s, being dubbed "King of the *Ukulele*," and launching a recording career that was to stretch nearly fifty years.

During his early busking days Nawahi also worked with steel guitarist **Sol Ho'opii**, who played a technically brilliant synthesis of American jazz and traditional Hawaiian music. Early in his career, Ho'opii developed the tuning that led to the development of the pedal steel guitar and the Nashville country music sound. He too recorded extensively, from 1925 up until the 1950s, and his

Slack key and steel guitar

Slack-key guitar, as its name suggests, involves slackening or loosening the strings in order to retune the guitar to achieve an open chord. Thus if you take the standard guitar tuning (from high to low – EBGDAE) and slacken the first string from E to D, the fifth from A to G and the sixth from E to D, you get a tuning of DBGDGD. This produces an open chord of G when strummed, while placing a finger (or steel bar) across the strings at the fifth and seventh frets will give you the other two chords you'll need for any three-chord song, like a blues.

This is one of the simplest tunings. During the pre-war craze for the music, Hawaiian guitarists made an art out of different tunings, some of which were closely guarded secrets. They also developed two ways of playing with open tunings – slack-key and steel guitar. Slack key involved picking the strings, with the thumb providing a constant bass while the other fingers play a melody (often a slightly altered version of the sung melody) on the upper strings.

The fact that Portuguese guitars often used steel rather than gut strings, and the creation of the National Steel guitar in the 1920s, to aid Hawaiian musicians in the days immediately before electric amplification, have obscured the reality that the "steel" in **steel guitar** is simply another word for "slide." And although many people think that slide guitar originated with blues musicians, it's a Hawaiian invention. **Joseph Kekuku**, an 11-year-old Oahu schoolboy, realized in 1885 that if he slid a solid object up or down the strings after plucking or strumming them, the chord would slide up and down in a glissando. He tried all kinds of objects before settling on the hand-tooled steel rod that gave the style its name; further experiments led him to play seated, with the guitar placed horizontally across his lap, and also to raise his strings so the steel would not touch the frets.

The first electric guitar – a Rickenbacher nicknamed the 'frying pan' – was actually a Hawaiian lap steel guitar made in 1931. In the US this developed into the pedal steel guitar, with its mechanical devices to change tunings and volume. This became the characteristic sound of country music, though it is less favored by Hawaiian musicians.

advanced use of chords, harmony, and phrasing had a profound and lasting effect on a whole generation of island musicians

Inspired by figures like these, musicians the world over explored the Hawaiian sound. From the 1930s, Hawaiian-style bands and steel-guitar players started to appear as far afield as Britain and Germany, Japan, India and Indonesia. In London, for example, the Felix Mendelssohn Hawaiian Serenaders were a hugely popular radio and dancehall act, performing a mix of traditional Hawaiian, *hapa haole*, jazz and popular songs.

Back in Hawaii, a magazine article was complaining as early as 1923 that "the truth of the matter is that the real Hawaiian *hula* has little in common with the coarse imitations served up to sight-seers, magazine readers, and the general public."

Tourism and the Sons of Hawaii

As tourism to Hawaii increased, "Hawaiian music" became an ever more important part of the experience. Visitors were lured to the islands by such means as the *Hawaii Calls* radio program, broadcast around the world from 1935 onwards from the Moana Hotel on Waikīkī Beach, and entertained once they arrived by grass-skirt revues with an emphasis on entertainment rather than education.

An even greater boom in tourism followed after Hawaii became the fiftieth US state in 1959, and the simultaneous arrival of quick jet travel from the US. By the time Elvis Presley filmed *Blue Hawaii* in the islands in 1961, young Hawaiians were turning away from steel guitar towards rock'n'roll. And yet the seeds of a revival of the old-style music were already being sown.

The major figure in the resurgence was slack-key guitarist **Gabby Pahinui**. By the late 1950s, his virtuosity, honed through twenty years of playing in Waikīkī's clubs and revues, meant he was ready to step to the forefront and play slack key as a lead rather than simply a rhythm instrument. He joined with 'ukulele virtuoso **Eddie Kamae** to form the **Sons of Hawaii**, and together they championed the traditional music of Hawaii. Kamae traveled the remote backwaters of the islands in search of old songs and performers, seeking out Hawaii's heritage before it was lost for ever. So few people speak fluent Hawaiian that only elders and experts could tell him the true meaning and pronunciation of many lyrics. Hawaiian is an intensely poetic language, and traditional songs often work on several levels, perhaps celebrating some beautiful place while also hymning the beauty of a loved one, all overlaid with sexual innuendo.

A significant change came into Hawaiian music during the 1970s, when many of the bands that sprang up in the wake of the Sons of Hawaii began to write new songs about contemporary island issues as well as performing older Hawaiian-language material. This new generation was hugely inspired by a wave of pan-Polynesian feeling, triggered especially by the success of the *Hōkūle'a* canoe in emulating the achievements of ancient Polynesian voyagers. (One side effect of that has been that even the *hula* now considered most authentic has come to incorporate elements from elsewhere in Polynesia, especially Tahiti and Samoa.) Among groups who came to prominence during this Hawaiian Renaissance were the **Sunday Manoa**, consisting of Peter Moon alongside brothers **Robert** and **Roland Cazimero**, and **Hui Ohana**, another trio comprising Ledward and Nedward Ka'apana and Dennis Pavao. By now, the *hapa haole* label had become an embarrassment to younger musicians, and ceased to be applied to newly made music, although arguably Hawaiian music

Iz: May 20, 1959 – June 26, 1997

In 1997, the Hawaiian music scene lost the man who was in every sense its biggest star. **Israel Kamakawiwoʻole**, who started out singing in the Makaha Sons of Niʻihau and then went solo in 1990, died of respiratory difficulties in a Honolulu hospital. During his twenty-year career, "Iz" came to epitomize the pride and the power of Hawaiian music. His extraordinary voice adapted equally well to rousing political anthems, delicate love songs, pop standards and "Jawaiian" reggae rhythms, while his personality and his love for Hawaii always shone through both in concert and on record. Like his brother Skippy before him – also a founder member of the Makaha Sons – Iz eventually succumbed to the health problems caused by his immense size. At one point, his weight reached a colossal 757 pounds; he needed a fork-lift truck to get on stage, and could only breathe through tubes. His strength in adversity did much to ensure that he was repeatedly voted Hawaii's most popular entertainer, and after his death he was granted a state funeral, with his body lying in state in the Capitol. His enduring legacy will be the music on the four solo albums released during his lifetime – *Ka Anoi* (1990), *Facing Future* (1993), *Ē Ala E* (1995), and *'n Dis Life* (1996). His medley of *Somewhere over the Rainbow/What a Wonderful World* has become a staple of movie and TV soundtracks, while his haunting rendition of *Hawaiʻi 78* (on *Facing Future*) became the anthem of campaigners seeking to restore native Hawaiian sovereignty.

remained as susceptible as ever to outside influences, including the 'soft rock' then sweeping California.

Meanwhile, Gabby Pahinui had left the Sons of Hawaii for a solo career which saw him team up with other slack-key legends like Atta Isaacs and Sonny Chillingworth; with his four sons, Martin, Bla, Cyril and Philip; and, famously, with Ry Cooder. Gabby's recordings with Cooder, who came in search of him after happening to buy one of his records in Honolulu, crossed slack key over into the US mainstream for the first time. Worn out by a life of hard labor and hard liquor, however, Gabby died aged 59 in 1980.

Hawaiian music today

The typical sound of the Pahinui-inspired revival of Hawaiian groups has settled into a regular, unplugged format of guitars, *'ukulele*, steel guitar, bass and vocals, but no drums. Most play a mix of traditional music, country, rock covers, pop, pan-Pacific styles and reggae – all of them in a typically inclusive Hawaiian way. The musicians don't tour outside of the islands too often, and most discs are local releases, so you really have to go there to hear Hawaiian music at its best.

Hula remains an integral part of performance; Gabby himself was an expert dancer, for example, and musicians will often appeal to the audience: "Does anyone know the *hula* to this one?" Two main forms of *hula* co-exist. The first, *kahiko*, is closer to the old style, consisting of chanting to the beat of drums; the dancers wear knee-length skirts of flat *ti* leaves, and anklets and bracelets of ferns. *'Auana* is the modern style of *hula*, featuring bands of musicians playing Western-style instruments

Among the best currently active performers are the amazing octogenarian falsetto singer **"Auntie" Genoa Keawe**; **Hapa**, consisting of sweet-voiced singer-guitarists Barry Flanagan and Nathan Aweau, plus chanter Charles Kaʻupu; the

Hawaii Live

The best way to experience Hawaiian music is to hear it on its home ground, though it can be hard to track down the finest practitioners amid the countless tourist revues. A handful of hotels and restaurants, especially in Honolulu and Waikīkī – as detailed on p.122 – feature authentic performers; the *Ritz Carlton* on Maui hosts wonderful weekly slack-key concerts (see p.288); and there's a rich year-round program of festivals. There's also always the **radio**: KINE (105 FM; ⓦhawaiian105.com) and KCCN (110.3 FM; ⓦwww.kccnfm100.com) are both full-time Hawaiian music stations with online streaming, while Hawaiian Rainbow (ⓦwww.hawaiianrainbow.com) and Mountain Apple (ⓦwww.mountainapplecompany.com) are online only.

Festivals

April/Big Island: Hilo's wonderful Merrie Monarch Hula Festival draws major *halau* (*hula* troupes) from all the islands, the US and Japan. Book well in advance.

May/Oahu: The Brothers Cazimero host a May Day event at the Waikīkī Shell with a mix of traditional and contemporary acts.

May/Molokai: Molokai Ka Hula Piko; *hula* festival, to celebrate the birth of *hula* on the island, held on the 3rd Sat in May at Pāpōhaku Beach Park.

June/Maui: Kihoalu, slack-key guitar festival, Maui Arts and Cultural Center, Kahului.

July/Big Island: Big Island Hawaiian Music and Slack Key Festival is held at Hilo on the 3rd Sun in July.

Sept–Oct/all islands: Held successively on each island in turn, Aloha Week features genuine grassroots performances with free concerts, parades and parties.

Maui-based *kumu hula* (*hula* teacher) **Keali'i Reichel**, equally acclaimed for a succession of fine albums and his charismatic performing style; slack-key maestros **Dennis Kamakahi** and **Ledward Ka'apana**; and **Amy Gilliom**, whose crystal-clear voice brings out all the beauty of her classic Hawaiian-language material, backed by quick-fire guitarist Willie K. Eddie Kamae still performs regularly as well, though most of his energies in recent years have gone into making compelling documentary movies about Hawaiian music and musicians.

Newer names to look out for include **Raiatea Helm**, a young female falsetto singer from Molokai; **Kaumakaiwa Kanaka'ole**, a chanter, dancer and singer from the Big Island who's keeping up a great family tradition; and **Jake Shimabukuro**, now a mature version of the teenage *'ukulele* whiz-kid who fronted the group Pure Heart.

Discography

Among the few US record companies to feature Hawaiian music are **Rounder**, the Boston-based American roots music label, and **Dancing Cat Records**, based in Santa Cruz, California, who have done sterling work to raise the profile of slack-key guitar music. Their series of Slack Key Master CDs has grown to include pretty much every player of note. Also in California, **Cord International** is steadily re-releasing some of the classic Hawaiian recordings of yesteryear. For Hawaiian music on the web, see ⓦwww.mele.com.

Compilations

Hana Hou! Do it Again! Hawaiian hula chants and songs (Pan, Netherlands). Traditional chants and contemporary dance songs performed in their basic form. Only one or two singers with minimal accompaniment of *ipu heke* (gourd drum), *'ukulele* or guitar.

Hawaiian Drum Dance Chants: Sounds of Power in Time (Smithsonian/Folkways, US). A record of the earliest known forms of Hawaiian music, some of it from old cylinder recordings. As close as you can get to the stuff Captain Cook would have heard.

Hawaiian Slack Key Masters (Dancing Cat, US). If you want to know what slack key is and who is playing it, start here with this 1995 sampler of artists on the Dancing Cat label. Tracks include a duo between Keola Beamer and the label's founder, George "Keoki" Winston, and outstanding cuts from Cyril Pahinui, Sonny Chillingworth, Ray Kane and half a dozen other old and young masters.

Steeling Round the World (Harlequin, England). This utterly delightful, if bizarre, chronicle of how the world went mad for Hawaii features Hawaiian-esque performances recorded in the 1930s and 1940s by soloists and groups from as far afield as Sweden, Indonesia, Greece, Hungary, India, South Africa and New Zealand, plus home-grown Hawaiian acts like the great Kanui and Lula, recorded in Paris in 1934.

Vintage Hawaiian Music: The Great Singers 1928–1934 (Rounder, US). A hugely seductive collection of Slack Key classics compiled by Bob Brozman, featuring Mme Riviere's Hawaiians, the all-male Kalama's Quartet and Sol Ho'opii Trio, and lots more besides. Plenty of falsetto vocals and steel guitar.

Vintage Hawaiian Music: Steel Guitar Masters 1928–1934 (Rounder, US). A companion volume highlighting the golden age of acoustic steel guitar. Tracks from Tau Moe, Sol Ho'opii, King Benny Nawahi and Jim & Bob the Genial Hawaiians.

Vintage Hawaiian Treasures Vol 7 (Cord International, US). A reissue of the first commercial releases of slack key from the 1940s, including seminal Gabby Pahinui cuts. Other standout tracks include Tommy Blaisdell pieces that stomp along like barrelhouse blues.

Individual artists

Edith Kanaka'ole Born in 1913 in Honomu, Edith Kanaka'ole trained as a child in the art of *oli* (poetic chant) and *hula*. In 1946 she started to compose her own *oli* and songs, and she became a professional performer in 1954. She epitomized the synthesis of ancient and modern traditions and values in Hawaiian culture.

Ha'aku'i Pele I Hawaii (Hula Records, Hawaii). The strongest available commercial recording of traditional chant. A major factor in Edith Kanaka'ole's art was her fluency in the Hawaiian language – and her comprehension (*kaona*) of the *oli*'s hidden meanings. Like others she believeds the *oli* to be the foundation of all aspects of Hawaiian cultural history, and the key for Hawaiians to maintain a relationship with the past and future.

Sol Ho'opii

Sol Ho'opii (1902–53) made his fame in the US after stowing away on a liner to San Francisco. Most famous for his classic acoustic recordings, he switched to electric guitar in 1934, then in 1938 became an evangelist and gave up his career in secular music.

Sol Ho'opii – Vols 1: 1926–1929 and Vol 2: 1927–1934 (Rounder, US). Classic tracks from probably the most influential of all Hawaiian steel guitarists. Either album is recommended.

Tau Moe Family

Born in Samoa in 1908, steel guitarist and singer Tau Moe embarked on an astonishing fifty-year world tour in the 1920s. His wife Rose joined Mme Riviere's Hawaiians (Tau and his three uncles) in 1927, for a tour of Asia that lasted from 1928 until 1934; they then toured India and the Middle East until the late 1940s when they moved to Europe, performing there through the 1950s and 1960s, and finally retired back to La'ie on Oahu in the late 1970s. In the mid-1980s, American steel-guitarist Bob Brozman received a letter from Moe ordering a couple of his records, and recognized Moe's name from his legendary 1929 recordings. Brozman called up and discovered to his amazement that it was the self-same man. After Brozman met Moe and Rose, he suggested that they re-record the songs from those old 78s.

Tau Moe Family with Bob Brozman: Remembering the Songs of Our Youth (Rounder, US). Although this disc dates from 1989, it reprises the songs, style and instrumentation of the 1920s and 1930s, with Rose Moe, then in her eighties, handling the lead vocals, backed up by Tau and their two kids Lani and Dorien (in their sixties), vocals from the family and the hugely talented Bob Brozman on steel guitar parts learnt from Tau. It kicks off with the beautiful *Mai Kai No Kauai*, the 1929 version of which opens the Steel Guitar Masters compilation on p.569. An amazing CD.

Bennie Nawahi

Bennie Nawahi (1899-1985) was one of the key figures in the acoustic era of Hawaiian guitar. He played the cruise ship and vaudeville circuits with his brother before pursuing his own career as singer and "King of the *'Ukulele*". He lost his sight, inexplicably, while driving home from a performance in 1935.

Hot Hawaiian Guitar 1928–1949 (Shanachie/Yazoo, US). A lovely disc of Nawahi performing jazz-inflected Hawaiian numbers with fellow master Sol Ho'opii.

Mahi Beamer

All-round musician Mahi Beamer comes from one of Hawaii's great musical dynasties, and has spent much of his fifty-year career playing piano and guitar, as well as dancing *hula*, but he's most renowned for his stunning falsetto voice.

The Remarkable Voice of Hawaii's Mahi Beamer in Authentic Island Songs (Hula Records/EMI Music). Seldom can an album have been more accurately named. Originally released in 1959, it showcases the extraordinary male falsetto of Mahi Beamer, performing songs exclusively in Hawaiian and mostly written by his grandmother. The hauntingly minimal backing includes traditional *hula* implements.

Lena Machado

As she grew up in Honolulu a century ago, Lena Machado's adoptive parents disapproved of her singing. She practiced in secret, was overheard by a producer as she sang high in a mango tree, cut her first record in 1927, and went on to enjoy a fifty-year career. Her *'ukulele* playing, her jazzy songwriting, and above all her unique falsetto style still hold an elevated place in Hawaiian hearts.

Hawaiian Song Bird (Cord International). Most of this lovely CD dates from 1962, but it also includes a few earlier numbers, including Lena's 1927 debut and a version of her trademark *Keyhole Hula* backed by Sol Ho'opii in 1935. Her falsetto is a constant joy, especially on her own sassy, jazz-tinged material like *E Kuu Baby Hot Cha Cha*.

Gabby Pahinui

Gabby Pahinui (1921–80) is without doubt the biggest influence on modern Hawaiian music. A slack-key guitar-player and singer, he released the first commercial recording ever of slack key, *Hi'ilawe*, in 1946, and in the 1960s was responsible for launching not only a revival of interest in slack key but Hawaiian culture in general.

Gabby Pahinui Hawaiian Band Volume 1 and Volume 2 (Edsel, UK). Breathtaking discs of slack guitar, steel guitar and bass from a band of legends – Sonny Chillingworth, Atta Isaacs and the Pahinui Brothers, Cyril, Bla, Phillip and Martin – as well as Gabby himself and a little fairy-dust from Ry Cooder. Along with the Rabbit Island Music Festival (Panini, Hawaii), recorded by the same band but without Cooder, these three albums of Hawaiian string band music are unequalled.

The Sons of Hawaii

Conceived in the late 1950s by Gabby Pahinui and Eddie Kamae, who were subsequently joined for the band's classic line-up by bassist Joe Marshall and steel guitarist extraordinaire David "Feet" Rogers, the Sons of Hawaii spearheaded a revolution in Hawaiian music. Although Pahinui left in the early 1970s, and the other original members have now all passed away, Kamae has continued to use the name on and off, and a roster of greats has passed through the ranks, including slack-key maestro Dennis Kamakahi.

The Folk Music of Hawaii (Panini Records, Hawaii). This classic was the fruit of a reunion of the Sons' original quartet in 1971, joined by Moe Keale on 'ukulele and vocals. Everything about it is just perfect, from Gabby's singing and playing to the long-lost songs rediscovered and burnished by Eddie Kamae, but if one element makes it truly transcendent, it's the staggeringly understated yet precise fills provided by "Feet" Rogers on steel guitar.

Hapa

As singer, songwriter, and slack-key guitarist, New Jersey transplant Barry Flanagan has so deeply immersed himself in Hawaiian musical traditions that his group Hapa, which has been through various line-ups, has for the last decade provided the islands' definitive soundtrack.

Hapa (Coconut Grove, Hawaii). No album by a Hawaiian group has sold more copies than Hapa's eponymous 1995 debut, packed with infernally catchy melodies, Hawaiian lyricism, and beautiful singing and guitar work.

Israel Kamakawiwo'ole

As described on p.567, the solo career of Hawaii's much-loved megastar Iz was cut short by his tragically early death, but his mid-1990s' success raised the profile of Hawaiian music around the world.

Facing Future (Mountain Apple Company, Hawaii). Iz's 1993 master-piece is an unqualified delight, showcasing the extraordinary power and resonance of his voice on *Hawaii 78*, his spritely 'ukulele work on island favourites like *Amaama* and *Henehene Kou Aka*, and his delicacy on *Somewhere over the Rainbow*.

Books

A n extraordinary number of books have been written about Hawaii and all matters Hawaiian, though you're only likely to come across most of them in bookstores on the islands themselves. All the publishers below are based in the US unless otherwise stated. Titles marked with a book symbol (📖) are particularly recommended.

History

Gail Bartholomew *Maui Remembers* (Mutual Publishing). Large-format paperback history of Maui, with lots of early photographs and entertaining stories.

📖 **Emmett Cahill** *The Life and Times of John Young* (Island Heritage Publishing). Lively biography of one of the most fascinating figures of the immediate post-contact era: the Welsh seaman who became Kamehameha's most trusted military adviser.

Gavan Daws *Shoal of Time* (University of Hawaii Press). Definitive if dry single-volume history of the Hawaiian islands, tracing their fate from European contact to statehood.

📖 **Greg Dening** *The Death of William Gooch* (University of Hawaii Press). Elaborate anthropological and metaphysical speculations spun around the 1792 murder of three European sailors in Oahu's Waimea Valley (see p.152).

Michael Dougherty *To Steal a Kingdom: Probing Hawaiian History* (Island Style Press). An eccentric and entertaining look at Hawaiian history, which focuses on the famous names of

the nineteenth century and pulls no punches.

Edward Joesting *Kauai, the Separate Kingdom* (University of Hawaii Press). Dramatic and very readable account of Kauai's early history and how the island resisted incorporation into the Hawaiian mainstream.

Noel J. Kent *Hawaii: Islands Under the Influence* (University of Hawaii Press). Rigorous Marxist account of Hawaiian history, concentrating on the islands' perennial "dependency" on distant economic forces.

Lili'uokalani *Hawaii's Story by Hawaii's Queen* (Mutual Publishing). Autobiographical account by the last monarch of Hawaii of how her kingdom was taken away, written in 1897 when she still cherished hopes of a restoration.

Gananath Obeyesekere *The Apotheosis of Captain Cook* (Princeton University Press/Bishop Museum Press). An iconoclastic Sri Lankan anthropologist reassesses Captain Cook from an anti-imperialist – but, according to most authorities, historically inaccurate – perspective.

Bookstores

The largest bookstores in the Hawaiian islands are all Borders, which has outlets on Oahu in Honolulu's Ward Center, Kauai in the Kukui Grove Shopping Center in Līhu'e, Maui in the Maui Marketplace in Kahului, and the Big Island in both Hilo and Kailua. The best secondhand bookstore is also on the Big Island, in Kapa'au – the Kohala Book Shop (☏808/889-6400, ⓦkohalabooks.big808.com).

Gordon W. Prange *At Dawn We Slept* and *The Verdict of History* (Penguin). Definitive best-selling analysis of the attack on Pearl Harbor. Over two volumes, Prange exhaustively rebuts revisionist conspiracy theories.

A. Grenfell Price (ed) *The Explorations of Captain James Cook in the Pacific* (Dover). Selections from Cook's own journals, including entries about his first landfall on Kauai and his ill-fated return to the Big Island. The story of his death is taken up by his successor as captain.

Luis I. Reyes *Made in Paradise* (Mutual Publishing). Lovingly prepared coffee-table history of how Hollywood has depicted Hawaii, with some great illustrations.

Marshall Sahlins *How Natives Think . . . about Captain Cook, for example* (University of Chicago Press). An impassioned and closely argued response to the Obeyesekere book reviewed opposite. Sahlins is currently considered to be ahead on points.

David A. Stannard *Honor Killing* (Penguin). A riveting account of the Thalia Massie rape-and-murder case on Oahu in the 1930s (see p.540), which brilliantly dissects the racist attitudes towards "natives" that permeated both Hawaii and the US mainland.

Ronald Takaki *Pau Hana* (University of Hawaii Press). Moving history of life on the sugar plantations and the trials experienced by generations of immigrant laborers.

Rerioterai Tava and Moses K. Keale Sr *Niihau, The Traditions of an Hawaiian Island* (Mutual Publishing). Comprehensive collection of fact and legend surrounding Hawaii's least-known island, so detailed that it names each of the island's five breadfruit trees.

Ancient Hawaii

Ross Cordy *Exalted Sits The Chief: The Ancient History of Hawai'i Island* (Mutual Publishing). Cordy has assembled a great deal of valuable raw material about the early history of the Big Island, but the book's poor organization and dry style make it a disappointingly heavy read.

Stephen L. Desha *Kamehameha and His Warrior Kekūhaupi'o* (Kamehameha Schools Press). An invaluable narrative drawn from oral traditions of Kamehameha the Great, originally published in Hawaiian, as newspaper articles, during the 1860s and 1870s.

Abraham Fornander *Ancient History of the Hawaiian People* (Mutual Publishing). While a circuit judge on Maui in the 1870s, the Swedish-born Abraham Fornander assiduously gathered oral histories, to fill in the gaps in Hawaii's unwritten history. The result can be heavy going, with its endless genealogies, but wonderful nuggets are scattered throughout.

Samuel M. Kamakau *The People of Old* (Bishop Museum Press, 3 vols). Anecdotal essays, originally written in Hawaiian and published as newspaper articles in the 1860s. Packed with fascinating nuggets of information, they provide a compendium of Hawaiian oral traditions. Kamakau's longer *Ruling Chiefs of Hawaii* (Bishop Museum Press) details all that is known of the deeds of the kings.

Patrick Kirch *Feathered God and Fishhooks* and *Legacy of the Past* (both University of Hawaii Press). The former is the best one-volume account of ancient Hawaii, though nonspecialists may find the minutiae of specific archeological digs hard going. The latter is an excellent guide to specific Hawaiian sites.

David Malo *Hawaiian Antiquities* (Bishop Museum Press). Nineteenth-century survey of culture and society, written by a native Hawaiian brought up at the court of Kamehameha the Great. As with Kamakau, Malo's conversion to Christianity colors his account, but this is the closest we have to a contemporary view of ancient Hawaii.

Valerio Valeri *Kingship and Sacrifice: Ritual and Society in Ancient Hawaii* (University of Chicago Press). Detailed academic analysis of the role of human sacrifice in establishing the

power of the king – an aspect of Hawaiian religion that many other commentators gloss over.

Koko Willis and Pali Jae Lee *Tales from The Night Rainbow* (Night Rainbow Publishing Co). A fascinating curiosity; an oral history of nineteenth-century Molokai, as told by the matriarchal Kailiʻohe Kameʻekua, who lived from 1816 to 1931. It's hard to sift a coherent narrative from her tales, but they offer glimpses of the world-view of a Hawaiian who witnessed astonishing changes.

Music and hula

Dorothy B. Barrère, Mary K. Pukui, and Marion Kelly *Hula: Historical Perspectives* (Bishop Museum Press). Fascinating essays on ancient Hawaii's most important art form, packed with early eyewitness accounts, and with a special emphasis on Kauai.

Ronna Bolante and Michael Keany *The Fifty Greatest Hawaiʻi Albums* (Watermark Publishing). If you're a newcomer to Hawaiian music, this authoritative list, assembled by *Honolulu Magazine*, will point you to some wonderful discoveries.

Rick Carroll *Iz – Voice of the People* (Bess Press). A lavishly illustrated celebration of the great Israel Kamakawiwoʻole (see p.567).

Samuel H. Elbert and Noelani Mahoe *Nā Mele O Hawaiʻi Nei* (University of Hawaii Press). A definitive short introduction to Hawaiian songs and songwriting, describing how 101 of Hawaii's favorite songs came to be written, and exploring the themes in Hawaiian music.

Jerry Hopkins *Elvis in Hawaii* (Bess Press). An irresistibly obsessive

blow-by-blow account of the King's love affair with Hawaii, from the Arizona Memorial concert of 1961 to *Aloha from Hawaii*.

James D. Houston with Eddie Kamae *Hawaiian Son: The Life and Music of Eddie Kamae* ('Ai Pōhaku Press). Still proselytizing for the islands and their music, the much-loved Eddie Kamae serves up the fascinating inside story of the Sons of Hawaii.

George S. Kanahele (ed) *Hawaiian Music and Musicians: An Illustrated History* (University of Hawaii Press). Put together by a team of experts, this fabulous five-hundred-page encyclopedia was published in 1979, and is now only available secondhand, for almost $200 – but for authoritative details on long-neglected performers and styles, it's the only source there is.

Elizabeth Tatar *Strains of Change: The Impact of Tourism on Hawaiian Music* (Bishop Museum Press). A very readable little booklet that shows how Hawaiian music is really world music.

Contemporary Hawaii

Michael Kioni Dudley and Keoni Kealoha Agard *A Call for Hawaiian Sovereignty* (Na Kane O Ka Malo, 2 vols). Two short books, indispensable for anyone interested in Hawaiian sovereignty. The first attempts to reconstruct the world-view and philosophies of the ancient Hawaiians; the second is the clearest imaginable account of their dispossession.

Randall W. Roth (ed) *The Price of Paradise* (Mutual Publishing, 2 vols). Assorted experts answer questions about life and society in Hawaii in short essays that focus on economic and governmental issues. Of most interest to local residents or prospective migrants, but a useful introduction to ongoing island debates, which sadly has now become somewhat dated.

Haunani Kay Trask *From a Native Daughter: Colonialism and Sovereignty in Hawaii* (University of Hawaii Press). A stimulating and impressive contribution to the sovereignty debate, from one of Hawaii's best-known activists.

Travelers' tales

Isabella Bird *Six Months in the Sandwich Islands* (University of Hawaii Press). The enthralling adventures of an Englishwoman in the 1870s, including sojourns on all the major islands and a cold expedition up Mauna Loa on the Big Island.

A. Grove Day and Carl Stroven (eds) *A Hawaiian Reader and The Spell of Hawaii* (Mutual Publishing, 2 vols). Lively paperback anthologies of writings on Hawaii, including pieces by Mark Twain, Jack London, Isabella Bird, and Robert Louis Stevenson.

William Ellis *A Narrative of an 1823 Tour Through Hawai'i* (Mutual Publishing). On his exhausting tour around the Big Island, early missionary Ellis proved to be a surprisingly sympathetic observer of the traditional Hawaiian way of life he and his fellows were about to destroy.

James Macrae *With Lord Byron at the Sandwich Islands in 1825* (Petroglyph Press). Short pamphlet of extracts from the diary of a Scottish botanist, including descriptions of Honolulu as a small village and the first-known ascent of Mauna Kea.

Andy Martin *Walking on Water* (Minerva, UK). An English journalist attempts to immerse himself in the surfing culture of Oahu's North Shore.

Robert Louis Stevenson *Travels in Hawaii* (University of Hawaii Press). The Scottish novelist spent several months in Hawaii in the late nineteenth century; the highlight of this collection is a moving account of his visit to Kalaupapa on Molokai, and it also includes his famous "Open Letter" in defense of Father Damien (see p.421).

Hunter S. Thompson *The Curse of Lono* (Bantam Books). Inimitably overwrought account of a winter fishing vacation on the Big Island, involving such escapades as abandoning a demented Doberman in Kailua's *King Kamehameha* hotel.

Mark Twain *Letters from Hawaii* (University of Hawaii Press). Colorful and entertaining accounts of nineteenth-century Hawaii, with rapturous descriptions of the volcanoes of Maui and the Big Island, written as a cub reporter. Twain reworked much of the best material for inclusion in *Roughing It* (Penguin), an excerpt from which appears on pp.555–558.

Navigation

Ben Finney *Hōkūle'a: The Way to Tahiti* (Dodd, Mead & Co). Gripping story of the sailing canoe's first eventful voyage to Tahiti, by a founder of the Polynesian Voyaging Society.

Tommy Holmes *The Hawaiian Canoe* (Editions Ltd). Compendious, beautifully illustrated coffee-table presentation of traditions and techniques involved in building and navigating sailing canoes, from the ancient Polynesians to the present day. Also written by a founder of the Polynesian Voyaging Society.

Will Kyselka *An Ocean in Mind* (University of Hawaii Press). Detailed account of the rediscovery of traditional Polynesian navigational techniques and the voyages of the *Hōkūle'a*, by a lecturer at the Bishop Planetarium.

Natural sciences

Peter S. Adler *Beyond Paradise* (Ox Bow Press). Personal essays about life in Hawaii, illuminating if occasionally self-indulgent, with an interesting account of the "Wounded Island" of Kahoolawe.

John R.K. Clark *Beaches of Oahu/the Big Island/Maui County/Kauai and Niihau* (University of Hawaii Press). Clark is a former lifeguard who has visited every beach in the state and researched its history and traditions. His four separate volumes form an invaluable resource for safety issues and make fascinating reading, though the construction boom of the last two decades has rendered them somewhat out of date.

Peter Crawford *Nomads of the Wind* (BBC Books, UK). Enjoyable, well-illustrated overview of the human and natural history of Polynesia, written to accompany the TV series.

Pamela Frierson *The Burning Island* (Sierra Club Books). The most exciting and original volume written about the Big Island; a history and cultural anthropology of the region around Mauna Loa and Kīlauea, combined with a personal account of living with the volcanoes.

Garrett Hongo *Volcano* (Vintage Books). The "Volcano" of the title is the Big Island village where Hongo was born; the book itself is a lyrical evocation of its physical and emotional landscape.

Gordon A. Macdonald and Agatin A. Abbott *Volcanoes in the Sea* (University of Hawaii Press). Thorough technical examination – sadly not illustrated in color – of how fire and water have shaped the unique landscapes of Hawaii.

Frank Stewart (ed) *A World Between Waves* (Island Press). Stimulating collection of essays by authors such as Peter Matthiessen and Maxine Hong Kingston, covering all aspects of Hawaiian natural history.

Food

Roy Yamaguchi *Pacific Bounty* (KQED). Well-illustrated cookbook of delicious recipes, written by one of the prime movers of "East-West cuisine," and based on his TV series *Hawaii Cooks with Roy Yamaguchi*.

Hawaii in fiction

David Lodge *Paradise News* (Penguin). The enjoyable tale of a dry English academic succumbing despite himself to the charms of Hawaii.

Herman Melville *Typee* (Penguin). Largely set in the Marquesas Islands, but with echoes of his time in Hawaii, Melville's wildly romanticized version of the South Seas – originally published as non-fiction – makes a perfect escapist read.

W. S. Merwin *The Folding Cliffs* (Alfred Knopf). A compelling, visually evocative blank-verse retelling – in over three hundred pages – of the story of Koolau the Leper (see p.495), by one of America's leading contemporary poets.

James Michener *Hawaii* (Random House). Another romanticized romp, whose success was a major factor in the growth of Hawaiian tourism.

Paul Theroux *Hotel Honolulu* (Houghton Mifflin US, Hamish Hamilton UK). This funny and very entertaining slice of reportage brilliantly captures the flavor of life in Oahu, packed with tourists passing through as well as local characters; there's even a cameo appearance from Hawaiian music star Iz (see p.567).

Richard Tregaskis *The Warrior King* (Falmouth Press). This fictionalized biography of Kamehameha the Great serves as a readable introduction to a crucial period in Hawaiian history.

Kathleen Tyau *A Little Too Much Is Enough* (Farrar, Straus & Giroux US, The Women's Press UK). Atmospheric and amusing account of growing up as a Chinese-Hawaiian, with an appetizing emphasis on food.

Sylvia Watanabe *Talking to the Dead* (Doubleday US, The Women's Press UK). Short, haunting evocation of village life in West Maui, in the days before the resorts.

Language

Language

Hawaiian

The Hawaiian language is an offshoot of languages spoken elsewhere in Polynesia, with slight variations that arose during the centuries when Hawaii had no contact with the islands of the south Pacific. Among its most unusual features is the fact that there are no verbs "to be" or "to have," and that, although it lacks a word for "weather," it distinguishes between 130 types of rain and 160 types of wind.

Although barely two thousand people speak Hawaiian as their native tongue, it remains a living language, and has experienced a revival in recent years. While visitors to Hawaii are almost certain to hear Hawaiian-language songs, it's rarely spoken in public, and there should be no need to communicate in any language other than English. However, everyday conversations tend to be sprinkled with some of the more common Hawaiian words below, and you'll also spot them in many local place names.

The Hawaiian alphabet

Hawaiian only became a written language when a committee of missionaries gave it an alphabet. The shortest in the world, it consists of just twelve letters – a, e, h, i, k, l, m, n, o, p, u, and w – plus two punctuation marks. When the missionaries were unable to agree on the precise sounds of the language, they simply voted on which letter to include – thus k beat t, and l beat r. As a result, the language has been oversimplified, and scholars argue that no one really knows how it used to sound.

Hawaiian may look hard to **pronounce**, but in fact with just 162 possible syllables – as compared to 23,638 in Thai – it's the least complicated on earth. The letters h, l, m, and n are pronounced exactly as in English; k and p are pronounced approximately as in English but with less aspiration; w is like the English v after an i or an e, and the English w after a u or an o. At the start of a word, or after an a, w may be pronounced like a v or a w.

The **glottal stop** (') has the effect of creating the audible pause heard in the English "oh-oh." Words without macrons (‾) to indicate stress are in theory pronounced by stressing alternate syllables working back from the penultimate syllable. Thanks to the frequent repetition of syllables, this is usually easier than it may sound. "Kamehameha," for example, breaks down into the repeated pattern Ka–meha–meha, pronounced Ka–mayha–mayha.

Pronunciation			
a	*a* as in above	ā	*a* as in car
e	*e* as in bet	ō	*ay* as in day
i	*y* as in pity	ī	*ee* as in bee
o	*o* as in hole	ō	*o* as in hole (but slightly longer)
u	*u* as in full	ū	*oo* as in moon

Glossary of Hawaiian terms

'A'ā rough lava

Ahupua'a basic land division, a "slice of cake" from ocean to mountain

Aikāne friend, friendly

'Āina land, earth

Akua god, goddess, spirit, idol

Ali'i chief, chiefess, noble

Aloha love; hello; goodbye

'Aumākua personal god or spirit; totem animal

'Elepaio bird

Hala tree (pandanus, screw pine)

Halāu longhouse used for *hula* instruction; also a *hula* group

Hale house, building

Hana work

Haole (white) non-native Hawaiian, whether foreign or American resident

Hapa half, as in *hapa haole*, or half-foreign

Hāpu'u tree fern

Heiau ancient place of worship

Honua land, earth

Hui group, club

Hula dance/music form (*hula 'auana* is a modern form; *hula kahiko* is traditional)

Imu pit oven

Ka'a car

Kahuna priest(ess) or someone particularly skilled in any field; *kahuna nui* is chief priest

Kai sea

Kālua to bake in an *imu* (underground oven)

Kama'aina Hawaiian from another island; state resident

Kāne man

Kapa the "cloth" made from pounded bark, known elsewhere as *tapa*

Kapu forbidden, taboo, sacred

Kapu moe prostration

Kaukau food

Keiki child

Kiawe thorny tree, mesquite

Ki'i temple image or petroglyph

Kīpuka natural "island" of vegetation surrounded by lava flows

Koa dark hardwood tree

Kōkua help

Kona leeward (especially wind)

Kukui candlenut tree, whose oil was used for lamps

Lānai balcony, terrace, patio

Lau leaf

Lehua or 'Ōhi'a lehua native red-blossomed shrub/tree

Lei garland of flowers, feathers, shells, or other material

Liliko'i passionfruit

Limu seaweed

Lomi lomi massage or raw salmon dish

Luakini temple of human sacrifice, used by ruling chiefs

Lū'au traditional Hawaiian feast

Mahalo thank you

Mahimahi white fish or dolphin fish (not the mammal)

Makai direction: away from the mountain, toward the sea

Malihini newcomer, visitor

Mana spiritual power

Mauka direction: away from the sea, toward the mountain

Mele ancient chant

Menehune in legend, the most ancient Hawaiian people, supposedly dwarfs

Mo'o lizard, dragon

Mu'umu'u long loose dress

Naupaka a shrub with small white flowers

Nei this here, as in *Hawaii nei*, "this [beloved] Hawaii"

Nēnē Hawaiian goose – the state bird

Nui big, important

O of; or

'Ohana family

'Ōhelo sacred red berry

'Ōhi'a lehua see *lehua*
'Ono delicious
'Ō'ō yellow-feathered bird
'Ōpae shrimp
'Opihi limpet
Pāhoehoe smooth lava
Pali sheer-sided cliff
Paniolo Hawaiian cowboy
Pau finished
Pili grass, used for thatch
Poi staple food made of taro root
Poke raw fish dish
Pua flower, garden
Pua'a pig

Pueo owl
Puka hole; door
Pūpū snack
Pu'u hill, lump
Saimin noodle soup
Taro Hawaiian food plant
Tūtū grandparent; general term of respect
Wa'a sailing canoe
Wahine woman
Wai water
Wikiwiki hurry, fast
Wiliwili native tree

Small print and

Index

A Rough Guide to Rough Guides

Published in 1982, the first Rough Guide – to Greece – was a student scheme that became a publishing phenomenon. Mark Ellingham, a recent graduate in English from Bristol University, had been traveling in Greece the previous summer and couldn't find the right guidebook. With a small group of friends he wrote his own guide, combining a highly contemporary, journalistic style with a thoroughly practical approach to travelers' needs.

The immediate success of the book spawned a series that rapidly covered dozens of destinations. And, in addition to impecunious backpackers, Rough Guides soon acquired a much broader and older readership that relished the guides' wit and inquisitiveness as much as their enthusiastic, critical approach and value-for-money ethos.

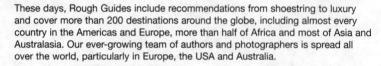

These days, Rough Guides include recommendations from shoestring to luxury and cover more than 200 destinations around the globe, including almost every country in the Americas and Europe, more than half of Africa and most of Asia and Australasia. Our ever-growing team of authors and photographers is spread all over the world, particularly in Europe, the USA and Australia.

In the early 1990s, Rough Guides branched out of travel, with the publication of Rough Guides to World Music, Classical Music and the Internet. All three have become benchmark titles in their fields, spearheading the publication of a wide range of books under the Rough Guide name.

Including the travel series, Rough Guides now number more than 350 titles, covering: phrasebooks, waterproof maps, music guides from Opera to Heavy Metal, reference works as diverse as Conspiracy Theories and Shakespeare, and popular culture books from iPods to Poker. Rough Guides also produce a series of more than 120 World Music CDs in partnership with World Music Network.

Visit www.roughguides.com to see our latest publications.

Rough Guide travel images are available for commercial licensing at www.roughguidespictures.com

Rough Guide credits

Text editor: Stephen Timblin
Layout: Jessica Subramanian
Cartography: Jai Prakash Mishra
Picture editor: Roland Smithies
Production: Vicky Baldwin
Proofreader: Wendy Smith
Cover design: Chloë Roberts
Photographer: Greg Ward
Editorial: London Kate Berens, Claire Saunders, Ruth Blackmore, Polly Thomas, Alison Murchie, Karoline Densley, Andy Turner, Keith Drew, Edward Aves, Nikki Birrell, Alice Park, Sarah Eno, Lucy White, Jo Kirby, Samantha Cook, James Smart, Natasha Foges, Roísín Cameron, Emma Traynor, Emma Gibbs, James Rice, Joe Staines, Duncan Clark, Peter Buckley, Matthew Milton, Tracy Hopkins, Ruth Tidball; **New York** Andrew Rosenberg, Steven Horak, AnneLise Sorensen, Amy Hegarty, April Isaacs, Ella Steim, Anna Owens, Joseph Petta, Sean Mahoney; **Delhi** Madhavi Singh, Karen D'Souza
Design & Pictures: London Scott Stickland, Dan May, Diana Jarvis, Mark Thomas, Jj Luck, Nicole Newman, Sarah Cummins; **Delhi** Umesh Aggarwal, Ajay Verma, Ankur Guha, Pradeep Thapliyal, Sachin Tanwar, Anita Singh, Nikhil Agarwal
Production: Aimee Hampson
Cartography: London Maxine Repath, Ed Wright, Katie Lloyd-Jones; **Delhi** Rajesh Chhibber, Ashutosh Bharti, Rajesh Mishra, Animesh Pathak, Jasbir Sandhu, Karobi Gogoi, Amod Singh, Alakananda Bhattacharya, Swati Handoo
Online: New York Jennifer Gold, Kristin Mingrone; **Delhi** Manik Chauhan, Narender Kumar, Rakesh Kumar, Amit Verma, Rahul Kumar, Ganesh Sharma, Debojit Borah
Marketing & Publicity: London Liz Statham, Niki Hanmer, Louise Maher, Jess Carter, Vanessa Godden, Vivienne Watton, Anna Paynton, Rachel Sprackett; **New York** Geoff Colquitt, Megan Kennedy, Katy Ball; **Delhi** Reem Khokhar
Manager India: Punita Singh
Series Editor: Mark Ellingham
Reference Director: Andrew Lockett
Publishing Coordinator: Helen Phillips
Publishing Director: Martin Dunford
Commercial Manager: Gino Magnotta
Managing Director: John Duhigg

Publishing information

This 5th edition published October 2007 by
Rough Guides Ltd,
80 Strand, London WC2R 0RL
345 Hudson St, 4th Floor,
New York, NY 10014, USA
14 Local Shopping Centre, Panchsheel Park,
New Delhi 110017, India
Distributed by the Penguin Group
Penguin Books Ltd,
80 Strand, London WC2R 0RL
Penguin Group (USA)
375 Hudson Street, NY 10014, USA
Penguin Group (Australia)
250 Camberwell Road, Camberwell,
Victoria 3124, Australia
Penguin Books Canada Ltd,
10 Alcorn Avenue, Toronto, Ontario,
Canada M4V 1E4
Penguin Group (NZ)
67 Apollo Drive, Mairangi Bay, Auckland 1310,
New Zealand

Cover concept by Peter Dyer.
Typeset in Bembo and Helvetica to an original design by Henry Iles.
Printed in Italy by Legoprint S.p.A
© Greg Ward 2007

1   3   5   7   9   8   6   4   2

Help us update

We've gone to a lot of effort to ensure that the fifth edition of **The Rough Guide to Hawaii** is accurate and up to date. However, things change – places get "discovered", opening hours are notoriously fickle, restaurants and rooms raise prices or lower standards. If you feel we've got it wrong or left something out, we'd like to know, and if you can remember the address, the price, the time, the phone number, so much the better.

We'll credit all contributions, and send a copy of the next edition (or any other Rough Guide if you prefer) for the best letters. Please mark letters: "**Rough Guide Hawaii Update**" and send to: Rough Guides, 80 Strand, London WC2R 0RL, or Rough Guides, 345 Hudson St, 4th Floor, New York, New York 10014. Or send an email to **mail@roughguides.com**

Have your questions answered and tell others about your trip at
www.roughguides.atinfopop.com

Acknowledgments

Thanks so much to the many people who made researching this book such a pleasure, including Lawrence Aki, John Alexander, Candy Aluli, Julie Bicoy, Gina Baurile, Nancy Daniels, Mervin Dudoit, Barry Flanagan, Emele Freiberg, Kathy Hansberry, Maria Holmes, Stephanie Jucutan, Eddie Kamae, Paul Konwiser, Yvette Mackler, Preston Myers, Diane Nichols, Denise Park, Maria Quidez, Michael Tuttle, Michael Waddell, and Teri Waros. And heartfelt appreciation above all to my wife Sam Cook, for her hard work on Oahu and the good times on Kauai.

Thanks also to the great team at Rough Guides, and especially my stimulating and supportive editor Stephen Timblin; AnneLise Sorensen and Steven Horak; Katie Lloyd-Jones and the team in Delhi, particularly Jessica Subramanian; and JJ Luck and the new picture editor Roland Smithies.

SMALL PRINT

Readers' letters

Thanks to all the readers who have taken the time to write in with comments and suggestions (and apologies if we've inadvertently omitted or misspelt anyone's name):

Roger Allen, Christian Blaas, Andy Cording, Dick Edwards, Rhona Gardiner, Nette Griggs, Cathy Larson, Michelle Mottley, Ahti Niilisk, Walter Rask, James Sears, Stacey Sebastian, Rick Stankiewicz, Tammy Steinert, Stephen Theobald, Louise Vallières

Photo credits

All photos © Rough Guides except the following:

SMALL PRINT

Index

Map entries are in color.

I

INDEX

591

INDEX

I | **INDEX**

Map symbols

maps are listed in the full index using colored text

[H1]	Freeway	ⵏ	Lighthouse
[50]	Highway	⚓	Shipwreck
———	Road	▬	Boat
══════	Pedestrianized road	⛺	Campsite
∷∷∷∷∷	Track	⛪	Park headquarters
- - - -	Trail	◉	Hotel/Restaurant
━━━━	Railway	✈	Airport
———	River	Ⓗ	Helipad
←	One-way street	🅿	Parking
▲	Peak	⛽	Gas station
⚱	Waterfall	ⓘ	Tourist office
⸺	Marshland	✉	Post office
⛰	Viewpoint	⸸	Church (regional)
🌳	Tree	⛩	Buddhist temple
⸶	Public gardens	🏯	Chinese temple
♦	General point of interest	☐	Market
∴	Ancient site	▮	Building
♣	Museum	⊞	Church (town)
⚔	Battleground	▦	Park/National park
🍇	Winery	▨	Lava flow